Early Editions of the Works of Frédéric Chopin

Frédéric Chopin (1810–1849)

Ingo Kirchner (1930–1983), etching 1964

A Descriptive Catalogue of

EARLY EDITIONS OF THE WORKS OF

FRÉDÉRIC CHOPIN

IN THE UNIVERSITY OF CHICAGO LIBRARY

Second Edition

Revised and Enlarged

&

George W. Platzman

THE UNIVERSITY OF CHICAGO LIBRARY

2003

Published in United States of America by
The University of Chicago Library
1100 East 57th Street, Chicago IL 60637.

For information contact
Special Collections Research Center
http://www.lib.uchicago.edu/e/spcl

Distributed by
The University of Chicago Press
http://www.press.uchicago.edu

ISBN 0-943056-31-4

Printed in the USA by
McNaughton & Gunn, Inc.
Saline, Michigan.

First edition published in 1997.

Cover illustration Title page of *Berceuse*, Opus 57 published by Meissonnier in 1845 (78% of original size)

Cover design Michael Brehm

CONTENTS

FOREWORD

Two notable developments have taken place since the first edition of this catalogue appeared in 1997. These changes made a second edition necessary and also shaped the form it ultimately took. Although the Library's collection of first and early printed editions of works by Frédéric Chopin has grown steadily since 1965, when it numbered approximately 50 scores, the pace of recent growth has been unusual. The 1997 publication included descriptions of some 285 items; the current catalogue describes about 420. And, in the past six years, the capacity to present high-quality scanned images on the World Wide Web, in conjunction with searching of associated metadata within and across collections, has developed to the point where an author must carefully consider the format that will best meet the needs of the intended audience.

George Platzman's decision to produce a second print edition of this catalogue reflects the fact that the detailed descriptions and ancillary materials that it contains are most conveniently used in book form. It also takes into account a project undertaken by the University of Chicago Library to digitize its entire collection of early Chopin scores. The Chopin Web site will make available page images of the complete scores along with bibliographic records extracted from the Library's catalog. This digital collection will serve the needs of musicologists, historians of music printing and publishing, and performers, who also will be able to consult this print catalogue for in-depth information. Conversely the electronic resource makes it possible for users of this catalogue to view the publications described in it and search the Library's holdings by opus number, imprint information, publisher's plate number, and a variety of other data elements. The University of Chicago Library's Chopin Web site *Chopin Early Editions* is available at http://chopin.lib.uchicago.edu.

The Chopin collection described in this catalogue and maintained in the Special Collections Research Center is a highlight of the primary sources in music available to scholars at the University of Chicago Library. Materials housed in Special Collections and in the Music and Recordings Collection (approximately 110,000 volumes and 16,000 recordings) support the teaching programs of the faculty of the Department of Music in music theory and history, ethnomusicology, and composition. Manuscripts, archives, and rare printed editions have come to the collections through gifts and purchases, many supported by the Olga Menn and Paul Menn Foundation. Significant holdings from the eighteenth and nineteenth centuries include an important manuscript source for Händel's *Chandos Anthems* and other compositions, Italian opera libretti, and the corrected publisher's proof copy of the vocal score for Mendelssohn's *Elijah*. Archival collections include the Chicago Jazz Archive and the papers of Easley Blackwood and Ralph Shapey.

Among the Special Collections staff members who provided assistance in the author's work on this second edition are: Valarie Brocato, Barbara Gilbert, Valerie Harris, Debra Levine, Daniel Meyer, Kerri Sancomb, Jay Satterfield, Theresa Smith, Catherine Uecker, and Jessica Westphal. A number of other University of Chicago Library staff members are also involved in work on the Chopin collection. Scott Landvatter, Monographic Cataloger, cataloged the newly acquired scores and reviewed records for the entire collection. Victor Cardell (former Bibliographer for Music), Standley Howell (former Special Services Assistant for Music) and Deborah G. Davis (present Bibliographer for Music) provided important bibliographic assistance. Charles Blair and Elisabeth Long, Co-Directors of the Library's Digital Library Development Center, are leading the effort to produce the Chopin Web site. Kathleen Arthur, Head, Replacement and Reformatting Section, coordinated scanning the scores for *Chopin Early Editions.*

George Platzman conceived this catalogue as a means to distinguish among variant printings in the Chopin collection not revealed in standard library catalog records. Although many collectors have compiled catalogs of works in their personal possession, it is rare indeed for the catalog of an institutional collection to be produced by a private collector. The University of Chicago Library is delighted that this second edition will increase knowledge and use of the substantially augmented Chopin collection and extends sincere gratitude to the author. The catalogue also illustrates that the partnerships between print and digital publications, and between libraries and private collectors, are essential elements in preserving research materials and presenting them to the broadest possible audiences in the twenty-first century.

Alice Schreyer, Director
Special Collections Research Center
University of Chicago Library
January 2003

PREFACE

This descriptive catalogue of the University of Chicago Library's Chopin collection is the second edition, the first having been published in 1997. It includes descriptions of approximately 130 additional scores acquired by the Library in the years 1998 through 2002.

Since it deals with a specific collection, the catalogue is more narrowly focused than, for example, the bibliographical description of an author's complete works. In its general style and arrangement the catalogue is similar to those of the various Hoboken collections. It will succeed in its broad purpose to the extent that it provides a useful description of the principal features of individual scores in the collection, and thereby enables the reader to compare what is in hand with what is in the collection. It can also be used to anticipate what will be found by visiting the Library, or simply to study the varieties of editions in the collection.

Most of Chopin's works were published in distinct first editions nearly simultaneously in several countries, usually France, Germany or Austria, and England. Since his oeuvre consists of 74 opus-numbered works, including nine published posthumously, the total number of first editions in a hypothetical complete collection is relatively small, compared with that of some of his more prolific contemporaries. This remains true if one also includes works published without opus numbers.

By "early editions" is meant publications that followed the first edition during the composer's lifetime (1810–1849) or soon after his death, but in this collection not later than about 1880, approximately 20 years after expiration of the French-edition copyrights. Some of these publications are reissues or re-impressions of the first edition, printed from the same engraved plates, possibly with slight editing. Others, perhaps most, were lithographed, often from the original plates. These secondary editions are useful in filling gaps where the collection lacks first editions. They may also provide a context in which various states of the first edition can be assessed.

This second edition of the catalogue has several new features, while maintaining the first edition's general arrangement and order of presentation. In the Introduction there is an enlarged treatment of the template for descriptions of the scores, with more explicit separation and identification of print-specific and copy-specific elements; there is also an added glossary section. In the descriptions of scores there are the new acquisitions noted above. There are four new Appendices: one compares various title pages of the songs Op. 74; one describes the contents of a volume with the sonatas Opp. 35 and 58; another describes the contents of a volume with the Mazurka, Brown 134; and one describes the collection's title-page stamps. The final new feature of this edition is an index of the score descriptions. With one line of data for each score, including the catalogue page number of the description, the Index presents a consolidated view of the collection for quick reference. A bulleted entry identifies a score added to the collection after publication of the first edition.

Closely related to this second edition is the Library's production of a digital Chopin collection, to be accessible through the World Wide Web. This online site, called *Chopin Early Editions,* will consist of scanned images of every page of each score in the collection and bibliographic records from the Library's catalog. Since the site is scheduled to become available online at about the same time as the expected publication of this catalogue, I decided to omit reproductions of selected title pages, such as appeared in the first edition. The interdependence of the Web site and the print catalogue has many advantages and is consistent with a developing trend in scholarly publishing.

The late Hans Lenneberg (1924–1994), Music Librarian at the University of Chicago, deftly guided me when I developed an interest in early editions of romantic composers and was a source of wisdom and encouragement throughout our thirty-year association. I am also fortunate in having the privilege of ready advice from Chopin scholar Jeffrey L. Kallberg (University of Pennsylvania) and to have been able to benefit from his knowledge and insight for the past twenty or more years.

A memorable source of encouragement was the Library's former Curator of Special Collections, the late Robert Rosenthal (1926–1989), with whom I enjoyed many dialogues on the vagaries and joys of book collecting. Above all, I can say unequivocally that this catalogue could not have come to fruition without the guidance and gracious support of Alice Schreyer, present Director of the Special Collections Research Center. It was she who initiated me into the literature and discipline of descriptive bibliography, which, as one with a background in physical rather than library science, at first seemed to me somewhat occult. With her help I was able to adapt the basic principles to the special problems of cataloging the Chopin collection, and under her direction I was provided with facilities to examine the collection in the most efficient way possible. As this examination had to be repeated more than once, much time and effort was saved by these arrangements. The process of examining and re-examining a large quantity of rare-book material extended over several years. As noted in the Foreword, many staff members in the Special Collections Research Center were at various times engaged in these activities, and all have been consistently supportive and responsive to my needs, which often no doubt were burdensome.

On aspects of an early Wessel edition I was helped by Hanna Wróblewska-Straus of the Fryderyk Chopin Society, Warsaw; and on details of the Fuld collection I was helped by James J. Fuld and by J. Rigbie Turner, Curator at the Pierpont Morgan Library, New York. At the British Library, Robert H. Parker, Curator of Music Services, provided substantial assistance over several years. For translation from Polish of selected parts of the index by Chominski & Turlo, I am indebted to Barbara Mirecki; and in other languages I was helped by my late sister-in-law Eva M. Platzman.

Throughout this work I received spirited and well-aimed advice from Donald W. Krummel (University of Illinois), and I benefited especially notably from numerous discussions about music cataloging with Richard Macnutt, with whom I have enjoyed a rewarding association for over 30 years. Another source of both encouragement and advice has been John Rink (University of London), and I have received valuable advice also from his co-worker Christophe Grabowski (Paris). A further faithful source of comment over several decades is Christel Wallbaum (of H. Baron, London).

The gallery of title-page stamps, new to this edition of the catalogue, was a challenging task. I could not have completed it without advice and help from many quarters. Here too, Alice Schreyer and Donald Krummel were vital, as well as Richard Macnutt, Jeffery Kallberg, and Christel Wallbaum. Lynn Martin assisted in designing the gallery and photographer Ted Lacey produced digital images of the stamps. Kenneth R. Platzman contributed technical support.

George W. Platzman
University of Chicago
January 2003

Introduction

DESCRIPTION DESIGN

DATING METHODS

GLOSSARY AND REFERENCES

DESCRIPTION DESIGN

Take care not to understand editions and title pages too well.
It always smells of pedantry, and not always of learning.

Lord Chesterfield (1694–1773)
in a letter to his son, 1737

GENERAL

The purpose of this catalogue is twofold: to serve as a general guide to the collection of early Chopin editions in the University of Chicago Library, and to provide bibliographic information about characteristics of the large variety of editions in the collection. The catalogue is not intended to fulfill any other library function, or to conform to particular library protocols.

The design of the catalogue's descriptions was formulated with the above objects in view. It attempts to follow norms of descriptive cataloguing in a general way, but deviates in many details to better accommodate the particular features of the material described, and also to simplify the process of description. Departures from *Anglo-American Cataloguing Rules* (see References, AACR2) and from *Descriptive Cataloging of Rare Books* (Library of Congress, 1991) have no significance beyond this catalogue; they are not University of Chicago Library interpretations.

Chopin's works

Chopin was born in 1810 in Zelazowa Wola, Poland. He lived in Warsaw until 1830, then in Paris until his death in 1849. During his lifetime he published 64 works with opus number. Ten more works with opus number were published posthumously (Op. 4 and Opp. 66–74). Of these 74 works, the collection presently has examples of all except the Rondo, Op. 14.

In addition to the opus-numbered works, Chominski & Turlo (1990, pp. 413–14) list 32 works published without opus number (eight in Chopin's lifetime). Of these the present catalogue includes only works that are represented in the collection. At present there are eleven, one of which — the Mazurka in C major, Brown 82 — is a considered by some to be of doubtful authenticity (*op. cit.*, p. 246).

Table 1A (and equivalently, Table 1B) lists the catalogue's 85 works. All of the catalogued works were originally published before 1860 except the Polonaise, Brown 6 (1864); the Polonaise, Brown 36 (1870); the Waltz, Brown 56 (1868); and the Mazurka, Brown 82 (1870).

Description groups and fields

In the Descriptions part of the catalogue, Chopin's works are presented in order of work number. For each work in the collection there are one or more scores issued by one or more publishers at various times. Each work's description begins with a 'work area' consisting of two groups of fields of information: one identifies the work by title and number, the other gives first-edition imprint data and additional work-identifying information. Following the work area, each score for that work is described in a 'score area' consisting of four groups of fields: a score-identification group, a print-specific group, a copy-specific group, and a notes group.

The template on page 11 shows the way the various groups and fields in the two areas are presented in the descriptions. None of the six groups is explicitly identified in the descriptions, but all are indicated in the template, and their identities are more or less evident from their contents. Long dashes (—) separate the four groups of fields in the score area. Single lines across the page separate individual score areas, and double lines mark the beginning and end of the ensemble of score areas for a particular work. Other notation used in the descriptions is shown on page 12.

Field names enclosed in square brackets in the template are not stated explicitly in the descriptions; in these cases the field's content suffices for its identification. Fields with names enclosed in parentheses are optional in the descriptions: these fields are used only when needed for a particular score. All other fields appear in every description. Thus, of the ten fields provided in the print-specific group, four appear for every score, namely title-page transcription, pagination, caption title, and footline; all others are optional. Of the six fields in the copy-specific group, only one — STAMPS — appears for every score; the others are optional.

Terminology

In a work of this kind, clarity is promoted by adopting explicit meanings for the various terms needed, and by using the terms consistently. This is especially important for terms whose meanings in the catalogue may differ from what the reader expects. Such words, and a selection of others with standard meanings, are listed in the Glossary (p. 18). For a few of the most important terms, the following comments enlarge on the brief definitions in the Glossary.

• *Score and copy.* Perhaps the catalogue's principal deviation in terminology is to attach to the word 'score' the function of serving for printed music as the analogue of 'book', in the sense of representing the physical object to be described. (This is consistent with one of the meanings given, for example, in the *New Grove* (Sadie, 1995).) That function is evident in the description template, and it is in this sense that the word is used throughout the catalogue. The point is worth emphasizing, because a common meaning of 'score' is in reference to a form of music notation in which the notes for separate instrumental parts are presented on separate staffs arranged in vertical alignment to indicate simultaneity of performance.

Cataloguers and bibliographers have used a variety of other terms for this purpose. There appear to be two broad categories of such terms, one that represents the item as a physical object, such as 'copy', the other as a bibliographical object, such as 'edition' or 'issue'. Although catalogue designers naturally attempt to make logical decisions about such matters, based on the nature of the material to be described, in the final analysis most decisions about terminology involve personal subjectivity. My own preference is for a non-bibliographical term. Of the possibilities available in addition to score, I will mention three: exemplar, printing, and copy. Taking them in that order, the problem with 'exemplar' is that it could be construed to mean 'ideal copy', an abstract concept of "the most perfect copy of the work as originally completed by the printer and first put on sale by the publisher." (Gaskell, p. 315). (With this interpretation 'exemplar' has the qualities of a bibliographical term.) A recent use of the second term, 'printing', is in a thematic catalogue of works by Sterndale Bennett (Williamson, 1996, pp. xxx–xxxi).

In my view, for this catalogue the most eligible of the three terms is 'copy', although that word has been used with different shades of meaning, often not explicitly stated. Here its use would be based on the first of two meanings given by Carter (1995, p. 73): "A single, therefore unique, example of the complete edition of a book". With that interpretation it could well serve as an alternative to score, although it has the drawback of not being explicitly related to music. I do in fact use it in some contexts.

• *Print-specific and copy-specific elements.* There are two complementary aspects to the description of a score. They are separated in time by the score's transfer, figuratively speaking, from printer to publisher. By 'print-specific' elements is meant those attributes that the score acquired from the printer before that transfer, and by 'copy-specific' those it acquired from other sources subsequently. The distinction can be seen directly from the corresponding two groups of fields in the description template. Regrettably, the two terms do not have a symmetric relation, because copy specific is not a proper antonym to print specific. Nevertheless, copy specific is used here because it is a standard term for this purpose in descriptive cataloguing, and is widely understood to have that meaning.

• *Edition, impression, issue, Titelauflage.* In preparing the descriptions I did not attempt to make systematic music collations of the scores (that is, textual analysis). Doubtless that would have enhanced the usefulness of the catalogue, and in some instances might have improved chronology. However, to have done so would have made the enterprise too formidable for me. Instead, I adopted the more limited aim of providing raw material for a user's more refined investigation of the collection. Partly for this reason, the catalogue makes little reference to edition, impression, issue, and state (except in citing other authors), which often involve difficult matters of bibliographical analysis. Several recent music catalogues and bibliographies, including those by Hopkinson (1980), Hoboken (1986), and Williamson (1996), follow somewhat similar approaches.

As part of the strategy of avoiding bibliographical technicalities, I resisted the convenience of "Titelauflage". As defined by Krummel & Sadie (1990, p. 541), this term is used for an issue "in which the only or principal difference from a previous one is the presence of a newly prepared title." Thus, proper use of the term requires access to other scores as a basis for comparison, and collation of the scores in question. These procedures are outside the scope of the protocols I adopted, and would be practical for me in only a few cases.

• *Printing method.* There is rarely doubt as to whether the music is printed from an engraved or lithographic surface. Moreover, if the music is lithographed, the title page invariably is too. However, Chopin scores with engraved music often have title pages with no visible plate-mark indentations, and in some of these I found it difficult to be certain what printing method was used. In all such cases I arbitrarily assert that the title page is lithographed ('lith').

I have not attempted to distinguish between the various methods of creating lithographic images. All are designated 'lith' in the descriptive part of pagination. As defined by Twyman (1996, chapter 9), the principal methods are (1) direct lithography (music written directly on the lithographic printing surface — stone or metal), (2) transfer of writing (music written directly on transfer paper, then transferred to the printing surface), and (3) transfer of prints (music engraved, then printed on transfer paper, then transferred to the printing surface). In the early to mid-19th century all three methods were in use, but direct lithography probably was dominant (Twyman, p. 113). The word 'transfer' (German, Umschlag) without qualification is often used in music bibliography in reference only to method (3). Twyman (p. 119), however, advocates the separate terms "transfer of writing" and "transfer of prints" respectively for methods (2) and (3).

Another method of transfer lithography in music printing is by photography, or in other words, photolithography. According to Gaskell (p. 271), "... photolithography by the zinc-plate transfer process was firmly established in the early 1860s for the printing of maps and music."

WORK AREA

By 'work' is meant one or more musical compositions identified by a single work number. In works with more than one composition, individual compositions are identified by means of suffixes #1, #2, ... attached to the work number (for example, Op. 9#1). The work area has five fields arranged in two groups, as follows.

Work-identification group

• *Work title.* The work's title here is a name designed for use in this catalogue. It is constructed from conventional elements, including the work's key, but refers to instruments only when the work is not for piano solo. Table 1A lists the adopted work titles in order of work number; Table 1B is an alphabetical rearrangement of the same entries. As explained in Table 1B, the work title differs slightly from the Library's "uniform title" (see Glossary); however, it is not intended as a replacement for the uniform title.

• *Work number.* The work number, on the line after the title field, is simply the opus number or, for works without opus number, the Brown number.

Work-imprint, composed-date, thematic-index group

• *Work imprint.* The first of the three fields in this group presents imprint data for first editions that were issued by Chopin's primary publishers, namely the publishers to whom copyright was assigned at the time of original publication of the work. Most of Chopin's works were published originally almost concurrently in several places, typically Paris, Leipzig (or Berlin or Vienna), and London. In the work imprint field for each of these first editions the place of publication is given, then the publisher's name, then in parentheses the work's plate number. Alphabetical characters and punctuation in the plate number are omitted here; they are included in the footline field. (The only exceptions are for infrequent cases where the plate number belongs to a publisher not the same as the one in the imprint.)

The plate number in the work imprint field is followed by the year of publication of the first edition. The specific dates are those given by Chominski & Turlo (1990, pp. 42–44), derived from Kallberg (1983, pp. 537–538) for France and England. Most of these dates are based on copyright registration. (For a more rigorous assessment, see Grabowski & Rink, forthcoming 2004.) The use of copyright registration is consistent with rules of the Library of Congress (1991, p. 37), as well as with those of the International Association of Music Libraries (Krummel, 1974, p. 51).

• *Work composed date.* The 'composed' field gives the year of the work's composition, as stated by Chominski & Turlo.

• *Thematic index numbers.* The last field in the work area contains the Brown and the Chominski & Turlo index numbers assigned by these authors to individual entries in their thematic indices. The arrangement in Brown's index is chronological by date of composition. If two or more compositions are included in the same work, all have the same Brown number if they were composed at about the same time; otherwise, some have different numbers. For example, the four Mazurkas Op. 41 have Brown numbers 122 (for Op. 41#2) and 126 (for the other three). In such cases, I selected only one number, namely the one where Brown gives publication data (*e.g.*, 122 for Op. 41). Chominski & Turlo's index is alphabetical by title. Since each composition is indexed, works that include more than one composition have more than one index number; for example, the four Mazurkas Op. 41 have Chominski & Turlo numbers 76 through 79. In all such cases, I selected only the first number (76 for Op. 41), because it suffices for locating the publication data.

For publication data, in addition to Brown and Chominski & Turlo I also consulted the catalogue by Hoboken (1986). However, I gave preference to Chominski & Turlo where there are differences. I did not consult the (Hettrich–)Kobylanska (1979) thematic index, because as noted by Kallberg (1981), its publication data are virtually the same as those of Brown.

The dedicatee is not given in the work area. It is included in the score area's title-page transcription. For a list of dedicatees for all of Chopin's works, see Brown (1972, pp. 190–192).

SCORE AREA

The score areas for a particular work describe all of the collection's various scores for that work. The work's scores are arranged first in the order of French, German, English, and other editions, then chronologically within each of these categories. Each score area consists of four groups of fields, as follows.

Score-identification group

The description of an individual score begins with a one-line group containing three fields with different types of identification of the score.

• *Score imprint.* The group starts on the left with the score imprint, in the same arrangement as shown above for the work imprint field. Place of publication and publisher name are taken from the score's title page, and plate number from the footline. However, with rare exceptions the score's date is conjectural and to indicate this, it is enclosed in square brackets. The general principles used in this catalogue for dating scores are discussed in "Dating methods" (p. 13).

• *Score number.* The next field in this group is designed to provide a simple, mnemonic means of identifying the score uniquely. The score number is used throughout the catalogue for cross-reference. It has relevance only to the catalogue, and is not a Library construct. It is a character sequence that consists of three parts separated by hyphens: first the work number, then the publisher name in the code given in Table 2B, and finally an ordinal number for chronology of acquisition to the collection. Thus, 18-W-2 identifies Op. 18, Wessel edition, second such score (of Op. 18, Wessel) acquired for the collection. In most cases, multiple scores of the same work for a particular publisher are not bibliographically identical: they seldom include exact duplicates. For this and other reasons a unique score number is assigned to every score in the collection.

• *Call number.* At the end of the identification line is the University of Chicago Library call number, which is assigned by the Library and is analogous to a shelf list number. It identifies the score for purposes of Library reference and for retrieval from the book stacks (see Glossary for more detail). In some cases two similar scores are marked c.1 and c.2 (copy 1, copy 2) in the call number, but it should not be assumed that they are bibliographically identical.

Print-specific group

By print-specific is meant those attributes that describe the state of the score at the time it left the printer. Ten fields are provided for this group, of which six are optional and are used only if needed for the particular score described. (Additional optional fields, such as for a half title or collective title, are occasionally used.)

Except for title-page transcription and pagination, the identity of which is obvious, the score descriptions explicitly identify each of the fields in this group by its name (see template, p. 11).

The fields in the print-specific group correspond loosely to the "contents" part of descriptive book bibliography. A common feature of these fields is the use of quasi-facsimile transcription embedded in ordinary text, typically indications of page numbers, or sometimes editorial comments. Following convention, the transcription in these cases is enclosed in single quotation marks (' ') to distinguish it from the other text. Double quotation marks (" ") are used in all other contexts in these fields. (In the title-page transcription field, quotation marks are not needed because the entire field consists of quasi-facsimile transcription.)

• *Title-page transcription.* Descriptive book bibliographers continue to debate the merits of 'quasi-facsimile' transcription of title pages versus strict reproduction such as by photography or digital scanning. David Hunter (1989) reviewed the history of this debate, with particular reference to music title pages. For eighteenth-century English opera and songbooks, he used a simplified form of transcription to supplement photo-reproduction. The index of Mozart first editions by Haberkamp (1986) is an example of greater reliance on photo-reproduction.

As it is not primarily concerned with the bibliographically 'ideal' copy, a catalogue of a collection such as the present one is perhaps the most eligible for title-page reproduction. Thirty such reproductions are included in the first edition of the catalogue. However, as mentioned in the Preface to the present edition, in the intervening years the Library began a project to establish a Web site that will contain scanned images of every page of every score in the Chopin collection, including of course the title page. For this second edition of the catalogue, I therefore chose to exclude title-page reproduction. However, I also chose to retain quasi-facsimile transcription, because this feature of the print catalogue is useful for quick reference to a particular score and for comparison of two or more scores. For title-page facsimiles I refer the reader to the online images (The University of Chicago Library, 2003).

In this catalogue quasi-facsimile transcription consists of the complete text of the title page. Since layout and exact wording are often important clues to the score's issue date, they are transcribed as faithfully as possible within a selected set of protocols. In a general way, the transcription is based on methods of descriptive book bibliography, as stated for example by Gaskell (1972). However, I made several simplifications in order to avoid a fruitless attempt to mimic the art of the engraver (or lithographer). Among these are replacing small caps by all caps, and generally omitting both underlines and rules. Further, a single font-type family is used (Adobe Garamond was chosen) and, except for superscripts, a single font size (11-point was chosen, with 13-point line spacing). In agreement with the usual procedure, italics are used when clearly indicated in the original. (In at least one instance in the collection they are needed to distinguish between two slightly different title pages that would otherwise have identical transcriptions.) It would, of course, be possible to apply the full range of font types and styles available in word-processing software. However, the purpose of the transcription is not to seek to create a close visual approximation; rather, it is to provide the bare essentials that enable the reader to distinguish between the texts of similar but not identical title pages.

Following customary notation, the vertical stroke ' | ' is used to indicate line endings, and square brackets '[ ]' are used to enclose editorial insertions. Often two or three unrelated and separated blocks of text appear on the same line of the title page. This is indicated in the transcription by means of left-pointing and right-pointing 'chevrons', symbolically 'L « C » R' where block L is on the left, R is on the right, and C (which may not be present) is centered. (Holoman (1989, p. XIV) uses explicit prefixes "[L.:]" and "[R.:]" for this purpose.) Unless otherwise indicated (as in 'L «' or '» R'), a single block of text shown without a pointer (as in 'C') is tacitly centered. The symbols « » are not enclosed in brackets, since they are clearly editorial insertions.

Occasionally, there are several short, related lines of text within a single block. In the transcription, such lines are separated by the divisor symbol ' ÷ '. (Holoman (*loc. cit.*) uses a different but equivalent device.) Thus, 'L1 ÷ L2 « C » R1 ÷ R2' consists of a central block C accompanied by left-hand and right-hand blocks, each with two short lines. As an example, see the transcription for the Leipzig Hofmeister score 1-Ho-1.

Engravers of scores make frequent use of superscript abbreviations such as C° and N° (respectively for Company and Number). These are more or less faithfully reproduced in the transcription, except for a few complicated situations. For a summary of notation and abbreviations used in the title-page transcription see "Description notation" (p. 12).

Many works in the collection have more than one score from the same publisher. This gives rise to the possibility that the title-page transcriptions of two or more scores may be identical, or almost identical. In such cases the catalogue gives the full transcription for the score that is chronologically first, and replaces subsequent identical transcriptions with the sentence "The transcription of this title page is the same as that of ... [score number].". (The sentence may be qualified by "except here ...".) This simplifies the description of the score and spares the reader from much tedium. However, it is important to emphasize that identical transcriptions do not imply identical title pages. To assert that two title pages are identical, one must look beyond the protocols adopted for quasi-facsimile transcription, and compare their overall designs, including artwork and elements such as font characteristics, curved lines of text, rules, and many other features that express the title-page engraver's or lithographer's style. This can be done only by careful visual comparison of either the scores themselves of their digital images.

• *Pagination.* In the pagination field, first the number of leaves is given and, in parentheses, the paper size (height x width in millimeters). Following this is the complete sequence of page numbers (not, however, the number of pages). Unnumbered pages are assigned inferred numbers shown in square brackets. French and English engravers of Chopin's works generally excluded the title-page leaf from the main sequence of page numbers; in these cases the inferred numbers [i] and [ii] are used here for the recto and verso of that leaf. German engravers usually included the title-page leaf implicitly in the main sequence; then [1] and [2] are used. The following examples of pagination for French, German and English editions are taken from the collection's scores of Op. 1. They are respectively from the M. Schlesinger, Hofmeister, and Wessel editions.

1-mS-1: 8 leaves (350 x 272 mm): pp. [i] engr title page, [ii, 1] blank, 2–13 engr music, [14] blank.
1-Ho-1: 6 leaves (323 x 257 mm): pp. [1] engr title page, 2–11 engr music, [12] blank.
1-W-1: 8 leaves (335 x 250 mm): pp. [i] engr title page, [ii] blank, [1] advt, 2–13 engr music, [14] blank.

In the first case the title-page leaf has a blank verso [ii], and its conjugate has a recto 13 with the last page of music followed by a blank unnumbered verso [14]. Interpretations of the others are similar.

In the descriptive part of the pagination, 'music' means simply printed notes and other signs of music notation, and 'advt' means advertisement. The printing method is indicated by 'engr' for printing from an engraved surface, or 'lith' for printing from a lithographic surface.

• CAPTION TITLE. This field consists of the text above the first system on the first page of music, which may contain information not found in the title-page title (the 'title proper'). The caption title is transcribed in the same manner as described above for title-page transcription. In addition to the opening caption title, there are some cases of internal caption titles, typically in works with more than one composition (such as several mazurkas). These are also noted in the caption-title field. However, indications of tempo, which often appear in the space above the first system, are not included.

• SUB-CAPTION. This optional field is used for supplementary title information that often appears in front of (rather than above) the first system of music. As with the caption title, such information can be on other music pages as well as the first. The sub-caption field is not included if it contains only an indication of tempo, the name of a movement, or the name of an instrument.

• HEADLINE. This optional field is seldom needed, because a headline (or running head) normally is not used for piano solo works, which comprise the bulk of Chopin's oeuvre. A typical use of the headline is in a piano duet, where, for example, the verso pages are headlined 'piano secondo' and the recto pages 'piano primo'.

• FOOTLINE. This field is included in every description, because the footline (or running foot) almost always contains important information, notably about the plate number and also often about the publisher. It is transcribed according to the same conventions as used for title-page transcription.

• SCORE ADVT. The score advertisement field is used only if there is an advertisement by the score's publisher. It is placed next after the footline field if it describes an advertisement printed on what would otherwise be a blank page of the score. Where an advertisement appears on the wrapper, it is described in a separate 'wrapper advt' field after the wrapper field.

• IMPOSITION. Except for a few of the longest compositions, printers of Chopin's works normally imposed the plates to produce a single section of nested bifolia (see *bifolium* in the Glossary). This makes a full collation superfluous. The only cases that may call for notice are those with multiple sections, or with indications of a missing final blank leaf. An example of the former is the M. Schlesinger edition of the Etudes Op. 10 (the collection's 10-mS-1), which was imposed as 14 sections of single bifolia. A good example of the latter is the M. Schlesinger edition of the Rondo Op. 16. The collection's first score (16-mS-1) has 10 leaves including a 'singleton' (a single leaf — a leaf with no conjugate), namely pp. 9 and 10, here tipped to p. 11. In this score a conjugate to the title leaf is not present (the title leaf is tipped to leaf 2), and the verso of the last leaf is the last page of music (p. 18).

These features indicate that in 16-mS-1 the conjugate of the title-page leaf — intended to be a final blank leaf — is missing. Richard Macnutt, to whom I am indebted for this example, reported in his possession a score corresponding to 16-mS-1 with the final blank leaf present. Subsequently, a similar complete score was acquired for the collection (16-mS-3). The impositions of 16-mS-1 and 16-mS-3 are the same as that of the Pleyel edition (16-Pl-1), which preceded them. However, in the collection's second score of the Schlesinger edition, namely 16-mS-2, the printer avoided a singleton by omitting a final blank leaf, even though that caused the last page of music to fall on the verso of the last leaf of the score. It is worth noting that, except for title-page leaves that lack a conjugate, all singletons in the collection are located exactly in the middle of the section, and thus are statistically unlikely to be cancels.

• WRAPPER. The wrapper field is used only if there is a separate bifolium with title information printed on the recto of its first leaf. The format of this field is similar to that of the pagination field. The wrapper title page is usually identical to the full title page of the score, or it may be an abbreviated title similar to a half title, or a series title. The other three pages are typically blank, but often have a publisher advertisement, usually on the verso of the second leaf and sometimes also on the recto. Colored paper frequently is used, typically lighter in weight than the paper used for the score itself.

A print-specific field is not provided for paper, as I have not attempted to make a systematic study of paper or watermarks. Watermarks rarely appear in Chopin scores. In the Hoboken catalogue only seven of the approximately 350 scores are noted as having a watermark (namely Hob-184, 190, 198, 214, 220, 256, and 287), but I was not able to detect a watermark in any of the corresponding scores in the Chicago collection.

Copy-specific group

Six fields are provided for the description of copy-specific elements — that is, typical alterations to a score after it left the printer. All fields in this group are optional except the first.

• STAMPS. The publisher's (or successor's) stamp, if present, is noted. Dealer (and agent) stamps (as defined in the Glossary) are also noted. If none of these types of stamp is present, "none" is entered in this field. For further comments see Appendix 8, "Title-page stamps".

• INSCRIPTIONS. Inscriptions typically consist of a presentation from one person to another (alas, in this collection not from the composer!), or of a date of acquisition by the original owner. Unless otherwise noted, inscriptions are on the title page.

• ANNOTATIONS. Annotations usually involve handwritten or stamped marks, such as pagination related to a collection. Unless otherwise noted, annotations are on the title page.

• CONDITION. Condition is not given much attention, except for scores in unusually poor or in uncommonly good condition. Foxing, for example, is almost always present to some degree, but is generally not noted.

• BOUND WITH. This field is seldom needed, because the majority of scores in the collection are separates with individual enclosures. It is used only when the score being described is bound with other Chopin scores, or in rare cases, with music of other composers.

• BINDING. If there are noteworthy features of the binding, they are briefly described.

Notes group

The notes group is reserved first for the *Date* field, then for optional comments that do not find a convenient place in the other fields of the score's description.

1. *Date*
(2., 3., ... [other notes])

• *Date.* Every score description includes a brief summary of the evidence available for the date of issue. The conjectural date inferred from this evidence is entered in the score imprint field discussed above. Methods used for dating are set out in "Dating methods" (p. 13). Notation used in the *Date* field is given in "Date notation" (p. 17).

• *Other notes.* The remainder of the notes group is used for comments that may not be convenient to include in any of the other groups of fields. Typically such comments could have information about printing or publishing history, or comparison of the score with others in the collection. Occasionally the notes include print-specific aspects of the score, such as comments on the bibliographical state of the music.

DESCRIPTION TEMPLATE

[work-identification group:]

[WORK TITLE]
[work number]

[work imprint: *place:* publisher (plate number) year]	[composed date:]	*Composed* [year]
[and other work imprints as needed]	[thematic index:]	Brown [number]
	[thematic index:]	Chominski & Turlo [number]

[score-identification group:]

[score imprint: ***place:*** **publisher (plate number) year**] **[score number]** **[call number]**

[print-specific group:]

[title-page transcription]

[pagination]

CAPTION TITLE:

(SUB-CAPTION:)

(HEADLINE:)

FOOTLINE:

(SCORE ADVT:)

(IMPOSITION:)

(WRAPPER:)

(WRAPPER ADVT:)

[copy-specific group:]

STAMPS:

(INSCRIPTIONS:)

(ANNOTATIONS:)

(CONDITION:)

(BOUND WITH:)

(BINDING:)

[notes group:]

1. *Date:*

(2., 3., … [other notes])

[next score area for this work]

[• • •]

[last score area for this work]

[next work area]

DESCRIPTION NOTATION

The following list explains notation and abbreviations used in the main fields of the bibliographic descriptions. Many of the terms here are defined in the Glossary.

Imprint

( )	parentheses enclosure for plate number
[ ]	square bracket enclosure for a score's inferred date

Score number

w-p-a	'w' is the work number of the score (Table 1A) 'p' is the coded name of the score's publisher (Table 2B) 'a' is the score's chronological acquisition number (1, 2, 3, ...) for scores that have the same work number and publisher

Quasi-facsimile transcription

|	end of line
÷	end of a short line within a block of text
«	pointer to a left-hand block of text
»	pointer to a right-hand block
ß	Reichsthaler
[ ]	square bracket enclosure for an editorial comment

Pagination

pp.	pages, or pagination
engr	engraved
lith	lithographed (by any method)
music	pages with printed notes and other musical notation
advt	advertisement
[ ]	square bracket enclosure for an inferred page number

Stamps

p/d	stamp style for publisher p (Table 2B) and design d (= A, B, C, ...)

Notes

B-*n*	index number *n* in Brown's thematic index
C&T-*n*	index number *n* in Chominski & Turlo's thematic index
Hob-*n*	catalogue number *n* in the Hoboken Chopin collection

Group separator

———	long dash to separate two successive groups of fields in the score area (as in the template on the preceding page)

DATING METHODS

O! sir, I must not tell you my age.
They say women and music should never be dated.

Oliver Goldsmith (1728–1774)
in *She Stoops to Conquer*, 1773

GENERAL

In the score imprint field, square brackets enclose the inferred date of the score. The brackets are intended to imply that the estimate has a range of uncertainty that depends on the evidence and methods applied. The estimate is of course subject to revision if additional evidence becomes available, for it is rarely possible to be certain an inferred date is correct. The only exceptions to this cautionary statement are the rare cases, probably not more than 10 in this collection, where an explicit date is found in the score. In those cases the enclosing brackets are not used.

For a summary of notation used in the dating aspects of the score descriptions see "Date notation" (p. 17).

SOURCES OF EVIDENCE

Several types of evidence make it possible to assign a conjectural date to a particular score. An invaluable survey of the subject is the *Guide for Dating Early Published Music* compiled by D. W. Krummel (1974). Here it suffices to say that in the present catalogue, the date estimated is intended to be the date of issue of the score in hand, by which is meant, in theory, the earliest date on which the score could have been publicly for sale. In practice, the date is more directly the result of applying certain simple rules derived from the available sources of evidence. The evidence available consists primarily of the contents of the title page, and in principle, of virtually the entire printed content of the score. The procedure is best explained by means of illustrations taken from the collection.

Title page

• *Title proper.* The title-page title occasionally has clues to the chronology of issue. Two scores from the collection provide illustrations. One is the M. Schlesinger edition (1833) of the Etudes Op. 10, score number 10-mS-1. In Schlesinger's first issue (not at present in the collection) the dedication is to "J." instead of 'F.' Liszt. The collection's score has "F.", a correction perhaps made within a short time (weeks, months?). It also has, *"1er Livre"* in a separate line after the composer's name, a line not present in the first issue. This probably was inserted in or after 1837, the year of publication of the Etudes Op. 25, the title page of which is marked "Deuxième livre d'Etudes". For this reason the collection's 10-mS-1 was assigned the date '[after 1836]'. (If it could be established that the music of 10-mS-1 is identical to that of the first issue, one could properly refer to 10-mS-1 as a Titelauflage, but I have not attempted to make that comparison.)

A similar, but more complex case is the French edition of the Concerto Op. 11, also originally published in 1833. The collection's 11-mS-1 has "1ER " as the first line of the title, whereas the first issue (11-mS-2) does not have this designation, which presumably was added at or after publication of the second concerto in 1836. On that basis alone, 11-mS-1 would be dated '[after 1835]'. However, there is also a change of price of the orchestral edition between the two issues, from 24f to 20f. According to Grabowski (1994, p. 32) the change was made between 1844, when 24f was still advertised in *Gazette Musicale*, and 1847, when 20f was advertised in a Brandus catalogue. This suggests it was Brandus who changed the price, after acquiring Schlesinger's firm. Although he had effective control from July 1845, the date of sale was in January 1846 (Devriès & Lesure, p. 72). The date adopted for 11-mS-1 is therefore '[after 1845]', which is consistent with Grabowski's evidence.

Some title pages have publication lists, such as those of many Wessel editions that list all Chopin works published by Wessel up to — and often beyond — the work in question. An example is the collection's 18-W-1 for the Waltz Op. 18, published by Wessel in 1834. The title page lists works through Op. 42, published in 1840. If the score had been issued after that date, presumably the list would have included later works. Consequently, the date assigned is '[*ca* 1840]'. A publication list on the title page serves the function of an advertisement, a source of evidence discussed separately below.

• *Publisher name and address.* Continuing by example, I mention the collection's 65-BD-1, which on the title page names "G. Brandus et S. Dufour" as the publisher. From Table 5A we see that the firm adopted this name in February 1858. On that basis 65-BD-1 is dated '[after 1857]'. In the footline of this score the name and address are those appropriate to the first edition, 65-Bra-1, which indicates that the original music plates probably were used for the later issue. An additional piece of evidence should be mentioned: the collective format of the title. According to Chominski & Turlo (1990, pp. 255–256), Brandus published "Oeuvres complètes pour le piano de Frédéric Chopin" in 1859–78. On this basis one could say '[after 1858]', but that is included in '[after 1857]'.

As an example involving both name and address, 7-mS-1 is dated '[1846–48]'. Although on the title page this score names only Schlesinger as the Paris publisher, the footline has "Brandus et Cie", which is the basis for the earliest year 1846 (in accordance with Table 5A). In both places the address is 97 rue de Richelieu, which is valid only until January 1849, when the firm moved to 87 rue de Richelieu.

Chronologies of names and addresses for Chopin's principal publishers are given in the tables numbered with prefix 5.

• *Cited publishers.* In addition to the publisher of the score in hand, the title page usually cites names and sometimes addresses of other primary publishers of the work. This information should be used with caution. For example, the Leipzig editions of the Rondos Op. 1 and Op. 5 were published by Hofmeister, respectively in 1838 and 1836 (see 1-Ho-1 and 5-Ho-1). Both cite Sennewald as the Warsaw publisher. In fact, Brzezina was the Warsaw publisher, respectively in 1825 and 1828. This firm was acquired by Sennewald *ca* 1830, before the later Hofmeister publications, which doubtless accounts for Hofmeister citing Sennewald. The only inference that can be made here is that the Hofmeister editions must be after *ca* 1830, but that is not useful because independently we know those editions were published much later.

Similarly, the collection's Leipzig edition of the Ballade Op. 23 (score 23-BH-1) cites Brandus as the Paris publisher. When the Leipzig edition was first published, in 1836, Schlesinger was the Paris publisher, but this firm was acquired by Brandus in 1846. We can therefore infer that 23-BH-1 did not appear before 1846. In this case the only other evidence available for dating is the currency, Neugroschen, introduced in 1841, but that evidence is superseded by the cited-publisher information. A slightly different situation is presented by one of the collection's scores of the Leipzig edition of the Polonaise Op. 22, namely 22-BH-2. Here the Paris publisher is cited as "Brandus, Dufour & Co." (strictly, it was G. Brandus, Dufour et Cie), a name the firm adopted in late 1854 (Table 5A).

Two other examples are pertinent. The Paris edition of the Polonaise Op. 22 cites Mori & Lavenu as the London publisher, but in fact Wessel performed that function. According to Brown (1972, p. 63), the citation of Mori & Lavenu "probably represents an unsuccessful bid for the publication of the work." Likewise, one of the collection's Vienna editions of the Polonaise Op. 44 (specifically 44-Mec-3, published in 1841) cites Troupenas, rather than the actual Paris publisher, Schlesinger. That perhaps was simply a reasonable but erroneous assumption by Mechetti from the fact that Troupenas had published Op. 43 in the same year and Opp. 35–41 in the preceding year. It was soon corrected, as in 44-Mec-2. It is an interesting error because it permits the inference that the score with Troupenas precedes the one with Schlesinger.

• *Price and currency.* There are few cases in which a change in price (without change in currency) can serve as the sole basis for dating. Some of these cases are implicit in a table of price changes given by Grabowski (1994, p. 33) for the Paris editions of Opp. 2, 11, 13, 14, 21, and 22.

More frequent evidence is provided by currency units, especially in northern Germany, including Leipzig and Berlin. In this connection an important date for Chopin editions is January 1841, when the Groschen was replaced by the Neugroschen (Fuld, 1988, p. 12), as sub-unit of the Thaler (originally called Reichsthaler). Another useful currency date, although somewhat less important for a collection of early Chopin editions, is

January 1874, when the Mark replaced the Thaler. This followed a transition period of about two years, when both were used. Further details are given in "Date notation" (p. 17).

A good illustration of the 1841 transition is the Leipzig edition of the Mazurkas Op. 6, which appeared originally in 1832 with a price of 10 Groschen (see 6-Ki-1), and was reissued after the change of currency with a price of 12½ Neugroschen (6-Ki-2). The latter score is accordingly dated '[after 1840]' (date code c1, p. 17). Such Leipzig reissues are quite common in the collection. In principle, the range 1841–71 could be used here, because the Mark appeared in the transition years 1872–73. However, for ranges of uncertainty greater than 10 years, I have preferred to give only the earliest year. An illustration of the 1872–73 transition is the Leipzig edition 21-BH-2 of the piano part of the Concerto Op. 21, which has a price 1 Thlr. 20 Ngr. and its equivalent 5 Mk. Since both thaler and mark were used in the transition period, this score is dated '[1872–73]' (date code c3, p. 17).

A further example is Breitkopf's publication of the full score of Op. 21, the collection's 21-BH-4, with price 5.40 Mk. and no equivalent price in thalers, an indication of a date after 1873. This score is unusual in having an explicit date in the footline, "Ausgegeben 1879"; it is one of the few cases in the collection where the date entered in the score imprint field need not be enclosed in brackets.

Two of Chopin's primary publishers were located in Vienna: Haslinger (Opp. 2, 4, and Brown 14, 113) and Mechetti (Opp. 3, 44, 45, 50). The unit of currency in Austria at that time was the Florin, related to other currencies through the "Conventions-Münze", abbreviated "C. M." (Fuld, 1988, p. 13). The price of 2-Ha-1, for example, is *"f4. — C. M."*, and an equivalent is given in North German currency, denoted by the symbol 'ß' for Reichsthaler. For further details see note 3 in 2-Ha-2. Mechetti sometimes used, instead of "C. M." the equivalent designation "A. de C.", for "Argent de Convention". The price of 3-Mec-1, for example, is stated as *"fl 1.15 A. de C."* I am indebted to Richard Macnutt for clarifying these matters, and for pointing out the correct values 24 Groschen and 30 Neugroschen to the Thaler (rather than the 30 Groschen sometimes cited).

• *Plate number.* The tables with prefix 5 give information about the chronology of plate numbers for Chopin's principal publishers. For example, the collection has a late Leipzig edition of the Concerto Op. 11 (originally published in 1833), score number 11-Ki-3. The first edition has plate number 1020.1021.1022, and the later edition prefixes to this the additional number 2340, doubtless because the music was reformatted with a different layout for that edition. From Table 5C we find 2340 to have been used *ca* 1858, which is the date designated for this score.

Similarly, the collection's score 35-BH-3 of the Leipzig edition of the Marche Funèbre extract from the Sonata Op. 35 has plate number 8728, for which Table 5C indicates a date *ca* 1858. This date is assumed to take precedence over citation of the Paris publisher as Troupenas, acquired by Brandus in 1850. Here I ignored the evidence of the cited-publisher name, on the basis that the change probably was known by the Leipzig publisher (Breitkopf & Härtel), but was ignored. A different situation is that of 22-BH-2, which cites Brandus, Dufour & Co. The original publication by Breitkopf & Härtel was in 1836, with plate number 5709. In this case (22-BH-2) the cited-publisher name must take precedence over the plate number, because it could not have been cited in the way it is without Breitkopf & Härtel knowing of the change (from Brandus et Cie) that was made in 1854.

• *Publisher stamp.* All of the information described in the preceding paragraphs is print-specific — that is, it comes to us through the printer. In contrast, a publisher stamp is copy-specific, having been added after the printer's work was done. It provides evidence not for the date of printing, but rather probably for the date of sale. In this collection the most frequent cases of stamps that are ignored as date-of-issue evidence are Brandus stamps on Schlesinger editions, for example 1-mS-1, 6-mS-1, 8-mS-1. Appendix 8 has images of the main publisher stamps found in this collection.

Other sources

• *Advertisement.* The simplest way to use an advertisement is to note known publication dates of the works listed. Most advertisements attached to a Chopin work include other composers as well. Ideally, the object is to find the latest publication date for all items listed, which can then be used as the earliest issue date of the score in hand. In practice, that can be a formidable task. Although in many cases a later date might be found by taking account of other composers, nevertheless for this catalogue I limited the search to Chopin's works.

The advertisement at the beginning of Book 1 of the Etudes Op. 10, in the collection's 10-W-2, lists Chopin works through Op. 27, which establishes 1836 as the earliest year for this score. Wessel's original publication of the work was in 1833. An unusual case is the explicit date that appears in the advertisement included with 18-W-2, one of the collection's scores of the Waltz Op. 18. Chopin's Trio Op. 8 is listed there, with an appended note that reads, in part, "Performed at Mr. Wessel's Soirée, June 1837 … .". This sets an unambiguous earliest date, but such cases are rare.

A title-page publication list is a form of advertisement. The case mentioned above at the end of the discussion of title-page evidence, namely 18-W-1, is interesting because this score also has a separate advertisement that agrees with the title page in listing Chopin works through Op. 42.

• *Wrapper.* Wrappers are generally ignored as a basis for dating in this catalogue, since there is no certain way to establish that a score's wrapper was present when the score first came from the printer. The Paris edition of the Variations Op. 12, for example, was originally published in 1834. The collection's 12-mS-1 has a wrapper with an advertisement by Brandus & Cie at Rue Richelieu 103, an address valid only after 1850 (Table 5A). Nevertheless, there is no other evidence this score is not a first issue, so the date '[= 1834]' is assigned. If the reader prefers a different interpretation, the score's description has the evidence needed for independent judgment.

DATE INFERENCE

After examining sources of evidence in the manner indicated in the foregoing discussion and comparing the score in hand with published descriptions of first editions, such as those in Chominski & Turlo and in Hoboken, a date usually can be estimated. In almost all cases the date has a range of uncertainty that depends on the nature of the evidence. Notational conventions for expressing this range can be found in AACR2 rules (AACR2, 1988). In this catalogue three general forms of notation suffice, as shown under "General date notation" on the next page. These forms are equivalent to three of the 12 rules adopted from AACR2 by the Library of Congress (1991, p. 38), in particular "[ca. 1580]", "[between 1711 and 1749]", and "[not before 1479]". (Specific years are used only for illustration.)

In addition to these three generic forms of date notation, the catalogue includes notation designed for five specific types of date inference that occur frequently in Chopin scores. For convenience of reference each of these recurring types is given a "date code", as indicated on the next page. Foremost among these codes is "fe", for the inference of a first edition. In almost all instances this inference is based on negative rather than positive evidence, which is to say that no evidence was found that conflicts with the hypothesis that the score is a first edition. In these "fe" cases I set the score's date equal to the work's first-edition date for the publisher in question, given in the work imprint field. To indicate this inference, I insert an equal sign in front of the date. An example is '[= 1836]' for 1-mS-1. In assessing such "fe" inferences the reader should keep in mind that, as previously noted, music collation was not systematically attempted in this catalogue, and this introduces an element of uncertainty in cases where there are multiple impressions of the first edition.

DATE NOTATION

Application of the methods indicated in the preceding sections leads to an inferred date of the score. This date, enclosed in square brackets, is placed in the score imprint field. The evidence used for a particular score is indicated in the *Date* field of the notes group, in many cases by means of date codes defined as follows.

Date code fe: first-edition inference

The bibliographic term 'edition' is used sparingly in this catalogue, but many scores in the collection are in fact first editions in the conventional sense. The basis for making this assertion for a particular score is simply a lack of evidence to the contrary. In such cases the score's date is entered as '[= y]', where 'y' is the publication year given in the work imprint field for the publisher in question.

Date codes c1, c2, c3: currency inferences

c1: [after 1840] The dating basis is the change of North German currency in January 1841 from Thaler and Groschen to Thaler and Neugroschen. The assignment is used for works originally published with price in Thaler and/or Groschen, and reissued with price in Thaler and/or Neugroschen. Before the change, one Thaler was equal to 24 Groschen; after the change it was 30 Neugroschen. Both the Groschen and Neugroschen were divided into 10 Pfennig.

c2: [1841–45?] This range is based on the same evidence as in c1 above and in addition, on title-page citation of the Paris publisher as Schlesinger, whose firm was acquired by Brandus in 1846 (Table 5A). It affects only editions by Kistner and by Breitkopf & Härtel. It is a weaker assertion than c1, however, because the Leipzig publishers might neglect to update their citations of the Paris publisher (hence the question mark).

c3: [1872–73] The dating basis is the change of German currency in January 1874 from the Thaler to the Mark. The assignment is used only for scores priced in both Thaler (and/or Neugroschen) and Marks, a transitional form used in 1872–73. One Thaler was equal to 3 Marks, and one Mark was equal to 100 Pfennig.

Date codes W1, W2: Wessel inferences

W1: [1848–56] This refers to Wessel editions with a collective title that lists Op. 64 as the last entry and 229 Regent Street as Wessel's address. The earliest year is inferred from the publication date of Op. 64 (1848). The latest year is inferred from the fact that Wessel moved from 229 Regent Street in 1856 (Table 5D). The range of years is inclusive.

W2: [1856–60] The Hanover Square address of Wessel & Co. dates from 1856 (Table 5D), and the firm was acquired by Ashdown & Parry in 1860. The range of years is inclusive.

General date notation

There are many date inferences in the catalogue that do not conform to any of the above five cases. The most frequent notations are '[after y]' (as in c1 above), where 'y' stands for an appropriate year; and '[y1–y2]'

[*ca* y] approximate year. The nature of the uncertainty is stated in the *Date* field.

[y1–y2] closed range, including starting year "y1" and ending year "y2". In this catalogue when the range is greater than about 10 years, '[after y]' is used instead of [y1–y2].

[after y] open range, starting with the year after "y".

(as in W1 and W2 above) for an inclusive range of appropriate years. Instead of '[after y]' — or '[*post*y]' suggested by Krummel (*loc. cit.*) — one could use the equivalent '[not before y+1]', used by the Library of Congress. Another equivalent is '[y+1 or later]', suggested to me by Richard Macnutt. Rules in AACR2 include date notation not used in this catalogue, such as a decade range '[184-]'. (For these and other notation, see AACR2, 1988; Krummel, 1974, p. 51; Library of Congress, 1991, p. 38.).

GLOSSARY AND REFERENCES

GLOSSARY

The purpose of the following glossary is to be explicit about terms used with particular reference to this catalogue and to Chopin's works. A selection of standard bibliographic terms is also included. Italics are used for occasional cross-reference within the Glossary. For glossary information I consulted Randel (1986), AACR2 (1988, Appendix D), Boorman (Krummel & Sadie, 1990), Library of Congress (1991), Sadie (1995), Carter (1995), Gaskell (1995), and Glaister (1996). I also referred to the glossary in the proposed "Sheet Music Cataloging Guidelines" developed for the Music Library Association (1996).

An asterisk identifies a term for which the meaning adopted in this catalogue may not be conventional.

* **advt:** abbreviation for advertisement.

agent: a vendor of the score who is not the score's publisher but whose name is printed on the title page (see *dealer*). An agent may be a publisher of other works.

area: in this catalogue, one of two parts into which the description template is divided, namely the work area (p. 5) and the score area (p. 6). Each area consists of one or more groups of fields (see *group* and *field*).

bar: a unit of musical time usually consisting of a fixed number of beats in all bars within each movement. Bars are separated by 'bar lines'; they are also called 'measures'.

barcarolle (as in Chopin's Op. 60): Italian gondolier song.

berceuse (as in Chopin's Op. 57): lullaby.

bifolium: a sheet folded once to make two leaves (see *leaf*), thus four *pages;* plural, bifolia; see Boorman in Stanley & Sadie (1990, p. 493).

bolero (as in Chopin's Op. 19): Spanish dance.

Brown number: index number in the *thematic index* of Chopin's works by M.J.E. Brown (1972).

call number: a reference number assigned by the University of Chicago Library to identify an item in the Library's catalog and to shelve and retrieve the item in the book stacks; analogous to 'shelf list'. For music scores and some other monographic publications, the call number consists of three parts. To illustrate, consider the Chopin Sonata Op. 4, in particular score 4-Ha-1 with call number M23.C54 S67. The first part M23 identifies the subject as music (M) and as a piano sonata (23). The second part C54 identifies the composer as Chopin. In the third part, S is taken from the first word of the *uniform title*, which in this case is "Sonatas"; following this the number 67 gives the score a shelf location consistent with locations of other scores of the same work.

caption title: text above the first *system* of music in a *score*.

* **catalogue:** a bibliography of a collection (AACR2, Appendix D). Its concern is with particular physical objects (such as scores), rather than with the more abstract ('ideal copy') entities of a *thematic index.*

Chominski & Turlo number: index number in the *thematic index* of Chopin's works by Chominski & Turlo (1990).

* **collective:** used in reference to a publisher's series of Chopin's works, such as were issued by Brandus, Breitkopf & Härtel, and Wessel, usually with a collective title page. The series may consist of one genre (such as mazurkas), or may be intended to include the composer's complete works.

composition: the basic unit of musical form; thus, a *work* with six mazurkas has six compositions.

conjugate leaf: one *leaf* of a *bifolium* is said to be the conjugate of the other.

contemporary: at or near the time of publication. "In its application to bindings [...] the term is by general agreement interpreted fairly broadly: anything in the style of the decade [...] being accepted as contemporary." (Carter, 1995, p. 73).

* **copy:** In this catalogue, the meaning of 'copy' is analogous to the first of two given by Carter (1995, p. 73): "A single, therefore unique, example of the complete edition of a book." In reference to the physical object to be described, *score* is used here, rather than copy. For further comment, see "Score and copy", p. 4.

copy-specific elements: modifications to a particular *score* after it left the printer (Library of Congress, 1991, p. 64). For a list of the copy-specific elements used in this catalogue, see the description template, p. 9.

dealer: a vendor of the score who is not the score's publisher and whose name is not printed on the title page (see *agent*). A dealer may be a publisher of other works.

* **dealer stamp:** a *title-page stamp* made by a score's *dealer.*

* **description:** detailed information about an individual score, based on the description template, p. 11.

écossaise (as in Chopin's Op. 72#3): Scottish dance.

edition: all copies of a work that are printed in one or more *impressions* based on one writing of the music on a printing surface, including impressions with modifications of the original writing, provided the changes are not extensive; German: Ausgabe; French: édition. (The AACR2 definition includes "and issued by the same entity". Thus, a Brandus printing from Schlesinger plates would be considered a new edition.)

* **engr** (as used in the description's pagination field): abbreviation for 'engraved'.

* **field:** in this catalogue, the base level of organization in a score's *description;* see *group.*

folio format: A score is said to have folio format when each *section* consists only of one or more bifolia (see *bifolium*). Most Chopin scores are imposed to form a single section of nested bifolia. They sometimes include a *singleton* in the middle of the section. Depending on the paper used, there is a practical limit to the number of bifolia that can be accommodated in one section. In the Chopin collection the 23 leaves of score 11-mS-1 were imposed to form one section with 11 nested bifolia and a singleton, while the 28 leaves of 10-mS-1 were imposed in 14 successive sections, each with one bifolium.

* **footline::** in this catalogue, the line of *text* below the last *system* of music on each printed page, usually containing at least the *plate number.*

full score: a form of music notation in which the notes for separate instrumental parts are presented on separate staffs arranged in vertical alignment to indicate simultaneity of performance.

gathering: bibliographically equivalent to *section.*

* **group:** in this catalogue, a set of *fields* having common properties in the organization of a score's *description.* There are two groups in the work area (p. 5) and four in the score area (p. 6); see *area.*

half-title: a shortened form of the full title, printed on the leaf that precedes the title-page leaf, sometimes without imprint information.

headline: the line of *text* — other than the *caption title* — above the first *system* of music on each printed page; typically used in compositions with more than one instrumental part; equivalent to 'running head'.

imposition: printer's arrangement of *plates* for printing one or more pages on one side of a *sheet.*

impression: all copies of an *edition* that are printed at virtually the same time, often to meet demand, but also typically to make small changes in the *music* or *text;* German: Abdruck, Abzug; French: tirage.

imprint: here used in reference to the publisher (not the printer). A score's imprint appears on the title page and includes the name of the publisher and normally the place of publication.

incipit: The first few *bars* of *music,* usually not more than about five and usually for each movement of a *composition,* used as a graphic form of identification.

issue: all copies of a *work* that are printed and identified as one publishing event; German: Auflage; French: tirage.

* **layout:** the music-writer's arrangement of notes into *bars, systems,* and pages of *music.*

leaf: "The basic bibliographical unit: the piece of paper comprising one page on its front side (recto, obverse) and another on its back (verso, reverse)." (Carter, pp. 133–134).

letterpress: "... printing done from raised types or blocks as distinct from intaglio or lithographic plates." (Glaister, p. 280).

* **lith** (as used in the description's pagination field): abbreviation for *lithographed.*

lithographed: in this catalogue, applied to lithographic printing using any of the three main media for writing music: (1) writing directly on stone or other planographic printing surface, (2) writing on transfer paper for transfer to the printing surface, and (3) writing by engraving for transfer to the printing surface. For further comment see "Printing method", p. 5.

mazurka (variant: "mazourka"): Polish dance.

* **music** (as used in the description's pagination field): printed notes and other signs of music notation.

nocturne: a genre of 'night' music with vocal origins, adapted for the piano by Field and Chopin.

opus number: in this catalogue, one of 74 numbers (Op. 1 to Op. 74) assigned to his works by Chopin or his editors or publishers.

page: one side of a *leaf.*

plate: a printing surface of metal or stone, on which a *page* of the *score* is written.

plate number: the publisher's identification number for the plates that make up a *work,* usually placed on the title page and almost always in the *footline* of each of the music pages. Most of Chopin's works have only one plate number, but in some cases there are two or more. For example, the two books of Kistner's edition of the Etudes Op. 10 have separate plate numbers, presumably because they have separate title pages and were sold separately. The same is true of the Wessel edition of this work, but Schlesinger sold both books under one title page, for which there is only one plate number.

polonaise (variant: "polonoise"): Polish dance.

* **primary publisher:** in this catalogue, typically a French, a German, and an English publisher who purchased rights either directly or indirectly from Chopin.

* **print-specific elements:** everything printed on the pages of a *score,* including *music, text* and artwork. For a list of the print-specific elements used in this catalogue, see p. 4.

* **publication date:** in this catalogue, the date of the first *edition* as compiled by Kallberg (1983) and by Chominski & Turlo (1990).

* **publisher stamp:** in this catalogue, a *title-page stamp* made by the score's publisher.

publisher's number: the publisher's identification number for the *work* as a whole. Chopin's publishers used the *plate number,* so there is no reference to publisher's numbers in this catalogue.

* **score:** commonly used in reference to music notation in which separate instrumental parts are presented as separate *systems* in vertical alignment. In this catalogue it has a different meaning: here a 'score' is the physical entity that is the result of printing a particular musical work. It is thus the object whose description is the purpose of the catalogue. For further comment see "Score and copy", p. 4.

* **score number:** in this catalogue, a three-part code for unique identification of a specific *score,* designed mainly for cross-reference within the catalogue. It consists of the *work number* followed by a code for the name of the publisher, then an ordinal acquisition number. For more detail see "Score number", p. 6.

section: a group of printed sheets assembled by the binder before sewing with other sections. Most Chopin scores consist of a single section of two or more nested *bifolium* sheets (see *folio format*).

sheet: a single piece of paper on which one or more pages are printed.

singleton: a *leaf* imposed without a *conjugate.*

staff: a set of five horizontal lines across the page, used as a template for entering notes in music notation.

* **stamp:** in this catalogue, an inked or embossed impression on a title page. The term is restricted here to publisher and dealer stamps.

state: two *scores* are said to be in different states if their *print-specific elements* differ in any way; German: Variant.

* **sub-caption:** *text* in front of (and on the same line as) the first *system* of music of each of the *work's* compositions.

system: Strictly "Two or more staves [staffs] connected by means of braces or bar lines ..." (Randel, 1986, p. 828).

tarantelle (as in Chopin's Op. 43): Italian dance.

* **text:** in this catalogue, any printed material other than *music* and artwork.

* **thematic index:** in this catalogue, a bibliography of a composer's complete works, traditionally including *incipits*, and thus a 'thematic' index; German: Verzeichnis, Werkverzeichnis; French: catalogue thématique.

Titelauflage: an *issue* that differs from previous issues mainly in having a different title page. The term is not used in this catalogue, except in citing its use by others.

* **title-page stamp:** a *copy-specific element* of a title page, consisting of an impression usually made by hand with an inking or embossing tool (see *stamp*).

transfer: a *lithograph* made by transfer of an engraved image. The term is not used in this catalogue.

uniform title: The title by which a work is identified by the Library for cataloguing purposes. For most music scores the first word of the uniform title corresponds to the work's genre (concerto, sonata, ...).

waltz: German dance.

* **work:** in this catalogue, one or more *compositions* identified by a single *work number*.

* **work number:** in this catalogue, the *opus number* or — for works without opus number — the *Brown number*.

* **work title:** a work's title designed for use only in this catalogue; see Table 1A. For further information refer to "Work title", p. 5.

* **wrapper:** a separate *bifolium,* often on tinted paper of slightly lighter stock than the main part of the score. Normally, on the first page it has a duplication of the title-page title, or (rarely) a shortened form of the title, similar to a half title. Frequently, one or more of the other pages have advertisements.

An asterisk indicates a work consulted but not cited.

CHOPIN REFERENCES

BELOTTI Gastone. *Saggi sull'arte e sull'opera de F. Chopin.* Bologna: Antiquae Musicae Italicae Studiosi, 458 pp., 1977.

BORY Robert. *La Vie de Frédéric Chopin par l'Image.* Paris: Horizons de France, 218 pp., n.d. [1951].

British Library. *The Catalogue of Printed Music in the British Library to 1980.* Laureen BAILLIE, main editor. Volume 12. London: Sauer, 380 pp., 1982.

BRONARSKI Ludwik. *Etudes sur Chopin,* 2 vols. Lausanne: La Concorde, 181 pp., 1944; 175 pp., 1946.

* BROWN Maurice J. E. "Chopin and his English publisher.". *Music and Letters,* **39**, 363–371, 1958.

——— . *Chopin. An index of his works in chronological order.* Second, revised edition. London: Macmillan, 214 pp., 1972.

BURGER Ernst. *Frédéric Chopin. Eine Lebenschronik in Bildern und Dokumenten.* München: Hirmer, 358 pp., 1990.

CHOMIŃSKI Jósef Michal & Teresa Dalila TURLO. *Katalog Dziel Fryderyka Chopina. A Catalogue of the Works of Frederick Chopin.* Kraków: Polskie Wydawnictwo Muzyczne, 518 pp., 1990.

* CHOPIN Frédéric. *Selected Correspondence of Fryderyk Chopin.* Abridged from Fryderyk Chopin's correspondence, collected and annotated by Bronislaw Edward SYDOW. Translated and edited, with additional material and a commentary, by Arthur HEDLEY. London: McGraw Hill, 400 pp., 1963.

* ——— . *Chopin's Letters.* Collected by Henryk OPIEŃSKI. Translated, with a preface and editorial notes, by E. L. VOYNICH. New York: Dover, 424 pp., 1988.

DULEBA Wladyslaw. *Chopin.* Kraków: Polskie Wydawnictwo Muzyczne, 307 pp., 1975.

* EIGELDINGER Jean-Jacques. *Chopin: pianist and teacher as seen by his pupils.* Translated by Naomi Shohet, edited by Roy Howat. Cambridge: University Press, 324 pp., 1986.

——— . "Chopin and 'La Note Bleue': An interpretation of the Prelude Op. 45". *Music and Letters,* **78**, 233–253, 1997.

GRABOWSKI Christophe. *L'Ouevre de Frédéric Chopin dans l'édition française,* 3 vols. Thése de doctorat en musicologie, L'Université de Paris IV, Sorbonne, 1992.

——— . *The Original French Editions of Fryderyk Chopin's Music.* Translated from the French by Katharine TYLKO-HILL. Supplement to *Chopin Studies,* vol. 4. Warsaw: Towarzystwo im. Fryderyka Chopina, 42 pp., 1994. This is a summary of the doctoral thesis cited above.

——— . "Les éditions originales françaises des œuvres de Frédéric Chopin". *Revue de Musicologie,* **88**, 213–243, 1996.

——— . "Wessel's *Complete Collection of the Compositions of Frederic Chopin:* the history of a title page". *Early Music,* **29**, 425–433, 2001.

GRABOWSKI Christophe & John RINK. *Annotated Catalogue of Chopin's First Editions.* Cambridge: University Press, (forthcoming 2004).

* HIGGINS Thomas (editor). *Chopin. Preludes, Opus 28.* New York: Norton, 101 pp., 1973.

[HOBOKEN Anthony]. *Katalog der Sammlung Anthony van Hoboken in der Musiksammlung der Österreichischen Nationalbibliothek. Band 4: Johannes Brahms, Frédéric Chopin.* Karin BREITNER & Thomas LEIBNITZ, editors. Tutzing: Hans Schneider, 226 pp., 1986.

HORDYNSKI Wladyslaw (editor). *Fryderyk Chopin. Krakowiak. Grand Rondeau de Concert.* Krakow: Polskie Wydanwnictwo Muzyczne, vii + 75 pp., 1953.

KALLBERG Jeffrey. Review of: Krystyna Kobylanska, *Frédéric Chopin: Thematisch-bibliographisches Werkverzeichnis,* edited by Ernst Hettrich, translated by Helmut Stolze. *Journal of the American Musicological Society,* **34**, 357–365, 1981.

* ——— . *The Chopin Sources: Variants and Versions in Later Manuscripts and Printed Editions.* University of Chicago, doctoral dissertation, 399 pp., 1982.

——— . "Chopin in the marketplace: Aspects of the international publishing industry in the first half of the nineteenth century. Part I: France and England. Part II: The German-speaking states.". *Music Library Association Notes,* **39**, 535–569, 795–824, 1983.

——— . *Chopin at the Boundaries. Sex, History, and Musical Genre.* Cambridge: Harvard University Press, 301 pp., 1996.

* ——— . ' "Voice" and the nocturne'. In *Pianist, Scholar, Connoisseur. Essays in Honor of Jacob Lateiner,* edited by Bruce BRUBAKER & Jane GOTTLIEB. Stuyvesant, NY: Pendragon Press, Festschrift Series No. 15, pp. 1–46, 2000.

——— . "Chopin's March, Chopin's Death". *19th Century Music,* **25**, 3–26, 2001.

* KOBYLANSKA Krystyna. *Frédéric Chopin: Thematisch-bibliographisches Werkverzeichnis,* edited by Ernst HETTRICH, translated by Helmut STOLZE. Munich: Henle, 362 pp. 1979.

NIECKS Frederick. *Frederick Chopin. As a man and musician.* Two volumes. London: Novello, Ewer & Co., 340 pp., 375 pp., 1888. (Reprinted by Paganiniana Publications, Neptune City, N. J., n.d.)

PAUL Oscar. "Thematisches Verzeichnis der in Deutschland im Druck erscheinen Instrumental-Compositionen von Friedr. Chopin, mit Beiflügung der Textanfänge seiner Lieder.". *Musikalisches Wochenblatt,* 4 January 1870, 16 pp., 1870.

PLATZMAN George W. *A Catalogue of Early Printed Editions of the Works of Frédéric Chopin in the University of Chicago Library.* Chicago: University of Chicago Library, 293 pp. 1997.

* RINK John. *Chopin: The Piano Concertos.* Cambridge: University Press, 139 pp., 1997.

* SAMSON Jim. *The Music of Chopin.* Oxford: Clarendon Press, 243 pp., 1994 (paperback reprint of Routledge 1985 edition).

——— . *Chopin: The Four Ballades.* Cambridge: University Press, 104 pp., 1992.

* ——— (editor). *The Cambridge Companion to Chopin.* Cambridge: University Press, 341 pp., 1992.

* ——— . *Chopin.* New York: Schirmer, 322 pp., 1996.

* SMIALEK William. *Frédérick Chopin. A Guide to Research.* New York: Garland Publishing, 190 pp., 2000.

The University of Chicago Library. *Chopin Early Editions,* http://chopin.lib.uchicago.edu, last viewed 5 February 2003.

WEINSTOCK Herbert. *Chopin. The man and his music.* New York: Knopf, 336+xxii pp., 1965.

GENERAL REFERENCES

[AACR2] American Library Association, the Australian Committee on Cataloguing, the British Library, the Canadian Committee on Cataloguing, the Library Association, the Library of Congress. *Anglo-American Cataloguing Rules.* Second edition, 1988 revision. Edited by Michael GORMAN and Paul W. WINKLER. Ottawa: Canadian Library Association; London: Library Association Publishing Limited; Chicago: American Library Association; 677 pp., 1988.

CARTER John. *ABC for Book Collectors.* Seventh edition, with corrections, additions and an introduction by Nicolas Barker. New Castle, Delaware: Oak Knoll Press, 223 pp., 1995.

DEAVILLE James. "Publishing paraphrases and creating collectors: Friedrich Hofmeister, Franz Liszt, and the technology of popularity". Preprint, 10 pp., 1999.

DEUTSCH Otto Erich. *Musikverlags Nummern. Eine Auswahl von 40 datierten Listen 1710–1900.* Second edition. Berlin: Merseburger, 32 pp., 1961.

* ——— . "Music Bibliography and Catalogues". *The Library,* **23**, 151–170, 1943.

DEVRIÈS Anik & François LESURE. *Dictionnaire des éditeurs de musique français.* Volume II. *De 1820 à 1914.* Geneva: Éditions Minkoff, 509 pp., 1988.

DICHTER Harry & Elliott SHAPIRO. *Early American Sheet Music. Its Lure and Its Lore 1768–1889.* New York: Bowker, 287 pp., 1941.

FULD James J. *The Book of World-Famous Music. Classical, popular and folk.* Third edition. New York: Dover, 714 pp., 1988.

GASKELL Philip. *A new Introduction to Bibliography.* (Reprint of the 1974 edition). New Castle, Delaware: Oak Knoll Press (and Winchester: St. Paul's Bibliographies), 438 pp., 1995.

GLAISTER Geoffrey Ashall. *Encyclopedia of the Book.* Second edition, with a new introduction by Donald Farren. New Castle, Delaware: Oak Knoll Press (and London: British Library), 551 pp., 1996.

HABERKAMP Gertraut. *Die Erstdrucke der Werke von Wolfgang Amadeus Mozart,* 2 vols. Tutzing: Hans Schneider, 495 pp., 388 pp., 1986.

HOLOMAN D. Kern. *Catalogue of the Works of Hector Berlioz.* Kassel: Bärenreiter, 527 pp., 1987.

* HOPKINSON Cecil. "The fundamentals of music bibliography". *Journal of Documentation,* **11**, 119–129, 1955.

——— . *A Bibliography of the Musical and Literary Works of Hector Berlioz (1803–1869). With histories of the French music publishers concerned.* Second edition, edited by Richard MACNUTT. Tunbridge Wells: Richard Macnutt, 230 pp., 1980.

HUMPHRIES Charles & William C. SMITH. *Music Publishing in the British Isles from the beginning until the middle of the nineteenth century. A dictionary of engravers, printers, publishers, and music sellers, with a historical introduction.* Second edition, with supplement. Oxford: Blackwell, 392 pp., 1970.

HUNTER David. "Bibliographical Description of Opera and Song Books Issued in England 1703–1726." *Papers of the Bibliographical Society of America,* **83**, 311–335, 1989.

* JENSEN Luke. *Giuseppe Verdi & Giovanni Ricordi with Notes on Francesco Lucca. From* Oberto *to* La Traviata. New York: Garland, 456 pp., 1989.

* JOHNS Adrian. *The Nature of the Book. Print and Knowledge in the Making.* Chicago: University of Chicago Press, 753 pp., 1998.

KRUMMEL D. W. (compiler). *Guide for Dating Early Published Music. A Manual of Bibliographical Practices.* Hackensack: Boonin (and Kassel: Bärenreiter), 268 pp., 1974.

* ——— . "Supplement to the Guide for Dating Early Published Music.". *Fontes Artis Musicae,* **24**, 175–184, 1977.

* ——— . Review of: *Catalogue of the Works of Hector Berlioz,* by D. Kern Holoman. *Journal of the American Musicological Society,* **43**, 367–375, 1990.

* ——— . *The Literature of Music Bibliography.* Berkeley: Fallen Leaf, 447 pp., 1992.

KRUMMEL D.W. & Stanley SADIE (editors). *Music Printing and Publishing.* New Grove Handbooks in Music. New York: Norton, 615 pp., 1990.

* LENNEBERG Hans. "Dating engraved music: The present state of the art.". *Library Quarterly,* **41**, 128–140, 1971.

* ——— . "The haunted bibliographer.". *Music Library Association Notes,* **41**, 239–248, 1984.

* ——— . *Breitkopf und Härtel in Paris. The Letters of their Agent Heinrich Probst between 1833 and 1840.* Stuyvesant NY: Pendragon Press, 130 pp., 1990.

Library of Congress. *Descriptive Cataloging of Rare Books.* Second edition. Washington: Library of Congress, 113 pp., 1991.

* MCMILLAN Barclay. "Tune-book imprints in Canada to 1867: A descriptive bibliography.". *Papers of the Bibliographic Society of Canada,* **16**, 31–57, 1977.

Music Library Association, Bibliographic Control Committee. *Sheet Music Cataloging Guidelines* (proposed). World Wide Web, "http://www.lib.duke.edu/music/sheetmusic/sheetmusic.html", 1996

NEIGHBOUR O. W. & Alan TYSON. *English Music Publishers' Plate Numbers in the first Half of the Nineteenth Century.* London: Faber & Faber, 43 pp., 1991.

RANDEL Don Michael. *The New Harvard Dictionary of Music.* Cambridge: Harvard University Press, 942 pp., 1986.

ROSEN Charles. *The Romantic Generation.* Cambridge: Harvard University Press, 723 pp., 1995.

* ROSS Ted. *The Art of Music Engraving and Processing.* London: Hansen, 278 pp., 1970.

SADIE Stanley (Editor). *The New Grove Dictionary of Music and Musicians.* London: Macmillan, 20 vols., 1995.

SMIRAGLIA Richard P. *Music Cataloging. The Bibliographic Control of Printed and Recorded Music in Libraries.* Englewood, Colorado: Libraries Unlimited, 222 pp., 1989.

TWYMAN Michael. *Early Lithographed Music, a study based on the H. Baron collection.* London: Farrand Press, 578 pp., 1996.

* TYSON Alan. *The Authentic English Editions of Beethoven.* London: Faber & Faber, 152 pp., 1963.

WILLIAMSON Rosemary. *William Sterndale Bennett. A Descriptive Thematic Catalogue.* Oxford: Clarendon Press, 567 pp., 1996.

Descriptions

An index of scores is at the end of the catalogue.

RONDO IN C MINOR
Opus 1

Warsaw: Brzezina (—) 1825
Paris: M. Schlesinger (1986) 1836
Leipzig: Hofmeister (1977) 1834; (2375) 1838
Berlin: A. Schlesinger (2019) 1835
London: Wessel (1423) 1836

Composed 1825
Brown 10
Chominski & Turlo 192

***Paris:* M. Schlesinger (1986) [= 1836]** **94-4** **1-mS-1** **M25.C54 R19**

RONDO | Pour LE Piano | *dedié à* | Madame de Linde | PAR | F. CHOPIN |
Op. 1. « » Pr. 6 .f | Paris, chez Maurice Schlesinger, Rue Richelieu, 97.

8 leaves (350 x 272 mm): pp. [i] engr title page, [ii, 1] blank, 2–13 engr music, [14] blank.

CAPTION TITLE: p. 2, 'F. CHOPIN. Op. 1. «'.

SUB-CAPTION: p. 2, 'RONDO.'.

FOOTLINE: pp. 2–13, 'M.S. 1986.'. On p. 9 the plate number is "1989".

WRAPPER (pale green): pp. [1] same as title page, [2–4] blank.

STAMPS: successor, style Bra/A (see Appendix 8).

1. *Date:* first-edition inference (date code fe, p. 17).
2. Chominski & Turlo (p. 188) refer to an edition by Schlesinger of the four-hand version, probably issued simultaneously.

***Leipzig:* Hofmeister (2375) [= 1838]** **1-Ho-2** **M25.C54 R202**

Premier | RONDEAU | *POUR LE* | Piano-Forte | *Composé et Dédié* | à M$^{\underline{me}}$ de Linde |
PAR | FRÉDERIC CHOPIN. | Œuv. 1. « Propriété des Editeurs. » Prix 12 Gr. |
à Varsovie, ÷ *chez Gust. Sennewald.* « » à Leipzig, ÷ *chez Fred. Hofmeister.* |
Ce Rondeau est arrangé aussi p. Pfte. à 4 mains. | *2375*

6 leaves (322 x 257 mm): pp. [1] engr title page, 2–11 engr music, [12] blank.

CAPTION TITLE: p. 2, '» *F. Chopin. Op.* 1.'.

SUB-CAPTION: p. 2, 'RONDO.'.

FOOTLINE: pp. 2–11, '2375'.

STAMPS: none.

INSCRIPTION: owner's signature "Zofia Hryszkiewicz".

1. *Date:* first-edition inference (date code fe, p. 17).
2. Hofmeister's earlier edition (plate number 1977) is for piano four hands (Hob-179), probably arranged by the composer (Brown, p. 9; Chominski & Turlo, p. 188).

1-Ho-2 *(continued)*

1-Ho-2 *(concluded)*

3. Using a newly-available Hofmeister archive, Deaville (1999) compiled print-run data that provide insights into the reception of a selection of works by Liszt and by a few contemporaries including Chopin. (I am indebted to James Deaville for permission to quote these data.) For the four-hand edition of the Rondo Op. 1, which preceded 1-Ho-2 by about four years, the first print run was 100 copies, in July 1834. Through 1869 a total of 1,300 copies of this edition was printed, on average about 37 annually. For the two-hand edition (1-Ho-2) the first run was 100 copies, in May 1939. Through 1879 a total of 2,825 copies was printed, on average about 70 annually. Evidently the two-hand edition was in greater demand.

***Leipzig:* Hofmeister (2375) [after 1840]** **1-Ho-1** **M25.C54 R2**

The transcription of this title page is the same as that of 1-Ho-2, except here the price is "20 Ngr." and instead of the plate number, the last line is "Pr. 20 Ngr." (for the four-hand edition).

6 leaves (323 x 257 mm): pp. [1] engr title page, 2–11 engr music, [12] blank.

CAPTION TITLE: p. 2, '» *F. Chopin. Op.* 1.'.

SUB-CAPTION: p. 2, 'RONDO.'.

FOOTLINE: pp. 2–11, '2375'.

STAMPS: none.

1. *Date:* currency inference (date code C1, p. 17).

***London:* Wessel (1423) [*ca* 1840]** **1-W-1** **M25.C54 R21**

Nº [blank] OF | WESSEL & Cº.'s COMPLETE COLLECTION | OF | *the Compositions* | OF | FREDERIC CHOPIN | FOR THE | Piano Forte. | Solo & Duet | [Wessel number]
1 "ADIEU *à* VARSOVIE" *Rondeau, (Edited by I.* [*sic*] *Fontana) in C min. Op. 1. 4/– [Duet] 4/6* |
[list of works, Wessel 2–45] | *Ent. Sta. Hall. « Copyrights. » Price. Solo* [blank] ÷ " *Duet* [blank] |
LONDON, | WESSEL & Cº *Importers and Publishers of,* FOREIGN MUSIC, |
(by special Appointment) to, H.R.H. the Duchess of Kent. | Nº 67, Frith Street, Corner of Soho Square.

8 leaves (335 x 250 mm): pp. [i] engr title page, [ii] blank, [1] advt, 2–13 engr music, [14] blank.

CAPTION TITLE: p. 2, '*ADIEU à VARSOVIE.* | *RONDEAU Composé par FREDERIC CHOPIN.* | *Nouvelle Edition Corrigée.*'.

FOOTLINE: p. 2, '(W & Cº Nº 1423.)'; pp. 3–12, 'ADIEU à VARSOVIE. « (W & Cº Nº 1423.)'; p. 13, 'ADIEU à VARSOVIE. (Nº 1423.) WESSEL & Cº Nº 6, Frith Street, Soho Square.'.

ADVT: p. [1], '*MODERN PIANO-FORTE MUSIC.* | PUBLISHED AT WESSEL & Cºs FOREIGN MUSIC WAREHOUSE Nº 6 FRITH STREET SOHO SQUARE.'. The lists have no works by Chopin.

STAMPS: none.

1. *Date:* based on the last work listed on the title page, Op. 42, published by Wessel in 1840. In 1839 the firm's address changed from 6 Frith Street (in the footline and advertisement) to 67 Frith Street, the title-page address (Table 5D).
2. Wessel's first edition (1836) was issued as the first in his series "L'Amateur Pianiste" (Chominski & Turlo, p. 446. Their title-page transcription on p. 188 is a composite from later sources.).

VARIATIONS IN B FLAT MAJOR FOR PIANO AND ORCHESTRA
('Là ci darem la mano')
Opus 2

Composed 1827

Vienna: Haslinger (5489) 1830 — Brown 22

London: Wessel (820) 1833 — Chominski & Turlo 225

***Paris:* M. Schlesinger (1312) [= 1833]** — **2-mS-1** — **M37.C54 V2**

"La ci darem la mano" | Varié | POUR | *LE* | Piano Forte | *DÉDIÉ* | *à M.r Titus Woyciechowski* | *PAR* | Frédéric Chopin. | de Varsovie. | *Op: 2.* « » *Pr:* {*Pour le Piano 7.f50 c.* ÷ *avec Orch.tre 15 . „* ÷ *avec Quatuor 12 . „* | *PARIS, Chez Maurice* SCHLESINGER, *M.d de Musique, Editeur des Œuvres de Mozart, Rossini, Hummel, &c.* | *Rue de Richelieu, 97.* | M.S. 1312

14 leaves (327 x 232 mm): pp. [i] engr title page, [ii] blank, 1–25 engr music, [26] blank.

CAPTION TITLE: p. 1, 'Frederic CHOPIN op: 2. ÷ La ci darem la mano. «'.

FOOTLINE: p. 1, 'Chopin op: 2. « M.S. 1312. » Maurice Schlesinger Rue de Richelieu N.o 97.'; pp. 2–24, 'M.S. 1312.'; p. 25, same as p. 1.

STAMPS: publisher, style mS/B (see Appendix 8).

ANNOTATIONS: Odd numbers 187 through 211 are handwritten on each recto starting with the title page (but p. 23 was overlooked).

1. *Date:* first-edition inference (date code fe, p. 17).
2. Brown (p. 23), states "The French edition was based on a printed copy of the Viennese edition, corrected by Chopin himself."

***Paris:* Brandus & Dufour (M.S. 1312) [after 1857]** — **2-BD-1** — **M37.C54 V21**

ÉDITION ORIGINALE | OEUVRES COMPLÈTES POUR LE PIANO | DE | FRÉDÉRIC CHOPIN | SEULE ÉDITION AUTHENTIQUE | SANS CHANGEMENTS NI ADDITIONS, PUBLIÉE D'APRÈS LES ÉPREUVES CORRIGÉES PAR L'AUTEUR LUI-MÊME. | [list of works, Op. 1] | Op. 2. La ci darem la mano, de DON JUAN, varié, en *si* bémol. 9 " [f] | L'orchestre .... 15 " — Le quatuor .... 9 " | [list of works, Opp. 3–65 and three works without opus number] | Paris, G. BRANDUS ET S. DUFOUR, Éditeurs | 103, rue de Richelieu, 103. | [below the decorated border:] IMPRIMERIE CENTRALE DES CHEMINS DE FER. « » A. CHAIX ET C.o, RUE BERGÈRE, 20, A PARIS. | 10304

14 leaves (350 x 269 mm): pp. [i] lith title page, [ii] blank, 1–25 engr music, [26] blank.

CAPTION TITLE: p. 1, 'Frederic CHOPIN op: 2. ÷ La ci darem la mano. «'.

FOOTLINE: p.1, 'Chopin op: 2. « M.S. 1312. » Maurice Schlesinger Rue de Richelieu N.o 97'; pp. 2–24, 'M.S. 1312.'; p. 25, same as p. 1.

STAMPS: publisher, style BD/D (see Appendix 8).

2-BD-1 *(continued)*

2-BD-1 *(concluded)*

1. *Date:* based on the publisher name (Table 5A). Chominski & Turlo (p. 255) give 1859–78 for the Brandus collected edition.
2. The title page lists works Opp. 1–65, followed by the mazurkas B134 and B140, the etudes B130, and the Duo Concertant B70, the latter in a four-hand arrangement as well as for piano and cello.

Vienna: **Haslinger (5489) [= 1830]** **2-Ha-2** **M1010.C54 V21**

"La ci darem la mano" | VARIÉ | *pour le* | PIANO-FORTE | *avec accompagnement d'Orchestre* | *dedié* | à Mr Titus Woyciechowski | *par* | *Frédéric Chopin.* | *Oeuvre 2.* | *N° 5489.* « *Propriété de l'Editeur.* » *Prix f 4. – C.M.* ÷ ß [Rthlr.] *2.16 gr.* | *Vienne, chez Tobie Haslinger,* | *Editeur de Musique,* | *dans la maison de la caisse d'épargne,* | *sur le Graben N° 572.*

Piano-forte: 14 leaves (343 x 262 mm): pp. [i] engr title page, [ii] blank, 1–25 engr music, [26] blank.

CAPTION TITLE: none.

FOOTLINE: p. 1, '(5489.) | Eigenthum u. Verlag von Tobias Haslinger in Wien.'; pp. 2–25, 'T.H. 5489.'.

Violino Primo: 2 leaves (339 x 267 mm): pp. 1–3 engr music, [4] blank.

HEADLINE: pp. 1–3, 'VIOLINO PRIMO.'.

FOOTLINE: pp. 1–3, 'T.H. 5489.'.

Violino Secondo: 2 leaves (338 x 267 mm): pp. 1–3 engr music, [4] blank.

Viola: 2 leaves (338 x 267 mm): pp. 1–3 engr music, [4] blank.

Violoncello e Basso (338 x 266 mm): 2 leaves: pp. 1–4 engr music.

Flauto Primo: 1 leaf (341 x 260 mm): pp. 1–2 engr music.

Flauto Secondo: 1 leaf (341 x 260 mm) conjugate to Flauto Primo: pp. 1–2 engr music.

Clarinetto Primo in B: 1 leaf (341 x 262 mm): pp. 1–2 engr music.

Clarinetto Secondo in B: 1 leaf (341 x 262 mm) conjugate to Clarinetto Primo: pp. 1–2 engr music.

Oboa Prima: 1 leaf (339 x 261 mm): pp. 1–2 engr music (see Imposition).

Oboa Seconda: 1 leaf (339 x 261 mm) conjugate to Corno Primo: p. 1 engr music (see Imposition).

Fagotto Primo: 1 leaf (341 x 262 mm): pp. 1–2 engr music.

Fagotto Secondo: 1 leaf (341 x 262 mm) conjugate to Fagotto Primo: pp. 1–2 engr music.

Corno Primo: 1 leaf (339 x 261 mm) conjugate to Oboa Seconda: pp. 1–2 engr music (see Imposition).

Corno Secondo: not present (see Imposition).

Timpani in B. F.: 1 leaf (338 x 260 mm): pp. [1] engr music, [2] blank.

IMPOSITION: This copy is defective as a result of the following imposition errors: (a) The recto of the Corno Primo leaf repeats the verso, causing this part to lack the Introduzione through variation 3; (b) The leaf conjugate to Corno Primo has Oboa Seconda (complete in one page) on both recto and verso; thus, Corno Secondo is absent. Doubtless the proper imposition would have placed the Oboa Seconda leaf (with blank verso) conjugate to Oboa Prima, and the Corno Secondo leaf (with blank verso) conjugate to Corno Primo.

STAMPS: none.

---

1. *Date:* first-edition inference (date code fe, p. 17).

2-Ha-2 *(continued)*

2-Ha-2 *(concluded)*

2. All orchestral parts have headlines analogous to that of Violino Primo, and footlines the same as that of Violino Primo. In the headlines of the clarinet parts, "in B." is added on p. 1.
3. On the title page, the price "2.16", preceded by the symbol ß for Rthlr. and followed by "gr.", means 2 Rthlr. 16 gr. The stated equivalent 4 florins implies a ratio of 1.5 fl. per Rthlr, in agreement with the ratio implied by the prices of B113-Ha-1.
4. This copy lacks the series title page (see Hoboken, p. 81).

Vienna: **Haslinger (5489)** [= 1830] **2-Ha-1** **M37.C54 V19 c.1**

The transcription of this title page is the same as that of 2-Ha-2.

14 leaves (313 x 253 mm): pp. [i] engr title page, [ii] blank, 1–25 engr music, [26] blank.

CAPTION TITLE: none.

FOOTLINE: p. 1, '(5489.) | Eigenthum u. Verlag von Tobias Haslinger in Wien.'; pp. 2–25, 'T.H. 5489.'.

STAMPS: none.

BOUND WITH: 22-BH-1.

BINDING: contemporary marbled boards, with handwritten label on front "La ci darem la mano. | Air variée p: le P:F: | Op: 2. | Grande Polonaise brillante Op: 22. | avec accompagnement | d'Orchestre. | Brunswick". "Brunswick" may be (Maria) Therese Brunswick (1775–1861), friend and pupil of Beethoven.

1. *Date:* first-edition inference (date code fe, p. 17).
2. The title page does not show a separate price for the piano part. See 2-Ha-2, note 3 for another comment about price.

Vienna: **Haslinger (5489)** [= 1830] **2-Ha-3** **M37.C54 V19 c.2**

The transcription of this title page is the same as that of 2-Ha-2.

14 leaves (340 x 265 mm): pp. [i] engr title page, [ii] blank, 1–25 engr music, [26] blank.

CAPTION TITLE: none.

FOOTLINE: p. 1, '(5489.) | Eigenthum u. Verlag von Tobias Haslinger in Wien.'; pp. 2–25, 'T.H. 5489.'.

STAMPS: none.

CONDITION: This copy is in original condition — a clear impression and untrimmed, unblemished leaves.

1. *Date:* first-edition inference (date code fe, p. 17).
2. See 2-Ha-1, note 2, which also applies to 2-Ha-3.

London: Wessel (820) [= 1833] 2-W-1 M37.C54 V192

LIV. XVII. | ALBUM DES PIANISTES DE PREMIÈRE FORCE. | HOMAGE À MOZART, | *Introduction,* | et | Grandes Variations Brillantes, | *sur le Duo favorit de Don Giovanni,* | "LA CI DAREM LA MANO", | *pour le* | Piano Forte, | Dediées à | *Monsieur Charles Czerny,* | par | FREDERIC CHOPIN. | *OP.* 2. « *Ent. Sta. Hall.* » *Price 6/6* | *LONDON,* | WESSEL & C°. Importers and Publishers of FOREIGN MUSIC, | (by special Appointment) to H.R.H. the Duchess of Kent, | N°. 6, Frith Street, Soho Square. | *Where are Published by the same Author.* | *First Grand Trio for Piano, Violin, & Violoncello. Pr. 10/6 "Les Murmures de la Seine". 3 Nocturnos, 2 Books, ea 2/6* | *"Souvenir de Pologne". 8, Mazurkas, in 2 Books, ea. 2/6*

14 leaves (340 x 253 mm): pp. [i] engr title page, [ii] blank, 1–25 engr music, [26] advt.

CAPTION TITLE: p. 1, '*HOMAGE à MOZART.* | *ALBUM des PIANISTES de PREMIÈRE FORCE.* | (*LIV. XVII.*) | *INTRODUCTION et GRANDES VARIATIONS BRILLANTES, sur le DUO CÉLÈBRE* | *DE DON GIOVANNI, dediées à MONS. CHARLES CZERNY, PAR* | *FREDERIC CHOPIN.* | (OP: 2.)'.

HEADLINE: pp. 2–25, 'PIANO-FORTE.'.

FOOTLINE: p. 1, '(W & C°. N°. 820.)'; pp. 2–24, 'ALBUM des PIANISTES, N°. 17. « (W & C°. N°. 820.)'; p. 25, 'The Orchestral Accomp^ts. Pr: 10.^s 6.^d | 'ALBUM des PIANISTES, N°. 17. (N°. 820.) WESSEL & C°. N°. 6 Frith Street, Soho Square.'. On pp. 3, 11, 12 the footline is "ALBUM des PIANISTES, N°. 18. [*sic*] « (W & C°. N°. 821. [*sic*])", except on p. 12, where the "1" in "821" is corrected to "0" in the plate.

ADVT: p. [26], 'WESSEL and C°.'s | NEW PUBLICATIONS OF, | *FLUTE AND CLARINET MUSIC,* | to be had at their Foreign Music Warehouse, N°. 6, Frith S^t. Soho Sq: London.'.

STAMPS: publisher, style W/A (see Appendix 8).

1. *Date:* first-edition inference (date code fe, p. 17).
2. The footline indicates that Wessel also published the orchestral parts.

POLONAISE IN C MAJOR FOR PIANO AND CELLO
Opus 3

Paris: Richault (3301) 1835	*Composed* 1829–30
Vienna: Mechetti (2178) 1831	Brown 41
London: Wessel (1662) (1663) 1836	Chominski & Turlo 148

Paris: **Richault (4360) [*ca* 1860]** **3-Rich-1** **M233.C54 I59**

à Mr Joseph Merk | POLONAISE | *BRILLANTE* | *précédée d'une Introduction* | *POUR* | Piano et Violoncelle | PAR | F. CHOPIN | *Œuv: 3* « » *Prix: 10 f* | *N^ta La Partie de Violoncelle est arrangée par Mr Franchomme* | *PARIS,* S. RICHAULT, *EDIT^r*, | *Boulev^t Poissonniére, 26 au 1er* | *4360 R* | Æ

Piano: 11 leaves (350 x 270 mm): pp. [i] engr title page, [ii, 53] blank, 54–71 engr music, [72] blank.

CAPTION TITLE: p. 54, 'à Monsieur Joseph MERK. | POLONAISE BRILLANTE. | Pour PIANO et VIOLONCELLE ÷ F. CHOPIN. Oeuv: 3. « » La partie de Violoncelle est ÷ arrangée par A. FRANCHOMME.'.

FOOTLINE: pp. 54–71, '4360. R.'.

Violoncelle: 3 leaves 345 x 268 mm): [1] blank, 2–5 engr music, [6] blank.

CAPTION TITLE: p. 2, 'à Monsieur Joseph MERK. | POLONAISE BRILLANTE. | Pour PIANO et VIOLONCELLE ÷ F. CHOPIN Op: 3. « » *La partie de Violoncelle est ÷ arrangée par A. FRANCHOMME.*'.

HEADLINE: pp. 2–5, 'VIOLONCELLE.'.

FOOTLINE: pp. 2–5, '4360. R.(2)'.

WRAPPER (pale yellow): pp. [1] same as title page, [2–4] blank.

STAMPS: publisher, style Rich/A (see Appendix 8); dealer, Flaxland, Paris.

1. *Date:* This score is from volume 10 of the 12 volumes of Chopin's collected works edited by Tellefsen and published by Richault *ca* 1860, with plate numbers 4351 to 4362 (Chominski & Turlo, p. 279; Brown, p. 185). The title-page address, 26 Boulevard Poissonniére, was occupied from 1841 until the firm moved to 4 Boulevard des Italiens in October 1862 (Devriès & Lesure, p. 365).
2. The piano part includes the cello staff.
3. Included with this copy is a manuscript of an arrangement of the cello part for violin.
4. According to Brown (p. 44), "The French edition was bought from Richault by M. Schlesinger, Paris, *c.* 1841 …". Chominski & Turlo (p. 163) give an earlier date, 1837. However, Grabowski (1994, p. 11) argues that such a transaction never took place, and instead points to the earlier 'foreign' publication (in 1831) by Mechetti, which according to French copyright law, made the work public property in France, thus allowing Richault to reprint it without publication rights.
5. Brown (*loc. cit.*) refers to an arrangement for piano solo published by Schlesinger (plate number 3729) in 1842, and Chominski & Turlo (*loc. cit.*) say that Schlesinger simultaneously issued a new edition for piano and cello (plate number 2447). (The edition with plate number 2447 is confirmed in a curious way by Hob-186, which describes the edition that corresponds to 3-Mec-1. The Hoboken score has two copies of the cello part, one for the Mechetti edition, the other with plate number M.S. 2447.)

Vienna: Mechetti (2178.2723) [*ca* 1836] 3-Mec-1 M233.C54 I61

INTRODUCTION | et | POLONAISE BRILLANTE | *pour le* | Pianoforte et Violoncelle | ou Violon | *Dédiée à* | MONSIEUR JOSEPH MERK | *par* | FRÉDÉRIC CHOPIN. | *Propriété de l'Editeur.* | *Enregistré dans l'Archive de l'Union.* | *Oeuvre 3.* « VIENNE, » *Prix fl 1.15 „ A. de C.* | chez Pietro Mechetti qm Carlo, | *Place St-Michel. No. 1153.*

Piano: 8 leaves (342 x 263 mm): pp. [1] engr title page, [2] blank, 3–15 engr music, [16] blank.

CAPTION TITLE: p. 3, '» Fr. Chopin Oeuvre 3.'.

FOOTLINE: p. 3, 'Pietro Mechetti No 2178.2723.'; pp. 4–15, 'P. M. No 2178.2723.'.

Violoncello: 2 leaves (340 x 263 mm): pp. 1–3 engr music, [4] blank.

CAPTION TITLE: p. 1, 'VIOLONCELLO. » Fr. Chopin Oeuvre 3.'.

FOOTLINE: p. 1, 'Pietro Mechetti No 2178.'; pp. 2–3, 'P. M. No 2178.'.

STAMPS: dealer, Schirmer, New York.

1. *Date:* Deutsch (p. 17) gives 1836 for Mechetti plate number 2723.
2. The piano part of 3-Mec-1 does not have the cello (or violin) staff.
3. Plate number 2723 is for the violin part (arranged), and 2178.2723 for the piano part of the "ou Violon" edition; see Hob-185.
4. This score corresponds to Hob-186 (with title page in plate 13, p. 84).

London: Wessel (1860) [*ca* 1840] 3-W-2 M38.C54 I618

No. [handwritten "3"] OF | WESSEL & Co.'s COMPLETE COLLECTION | OF | *the Compositions* | OF | FREDERIC CHOPIN | FOR THE | Piano Forte. | Solo & Duet | [list of works, Wessel 1–2] | 3 "LA GAITÉ" *Intr. et Polonoise brillante in C. Op. 3. 4/– [Duet] 6/–* | [list of works, Wessel 4–45] | *Ent. Sta. Hall.* « *Copyrights.* » *Price. Solo* [handwritten "4/–"] ÷ " *Duet* [blank] | *LONDON,* | WESSEL & Co. *Importers and Publishers of,* FOREIGN MUSIC, | *(by special Appointment) to, H.R.H. the Duchess of Kent.* | No. 67, Frith Street, Corner of Soho Square.

8 leaves (335 x 250 mm): pp. [i] engr title page, [ii] blank, 1–13 engr music, [14] advt.

CAPTION TITLE: p. 1, '*LE PIANISTE MODERNE, N. 50.* | LA GAITÉ, POLONOISE BRILLANTE composée par FREDERIC CHOPIN. | Edited by his pupel [*sic*] | *I.* [*sic*] *FONTANA.*'.

FOOTLINE: p. 1, '» W & Co. No. 1860)'; pp. 2–12, 'LE PIANISTE MODERNE, No. 50. « » (W & Co. No. 1860)'; p. 13, 'LE PIANISTE MODERNE, No. 50. « | (No. 1860) WESSEL & Co. No. 6, FRITH STREET, SOHO SQUARE.'.

ADVT: p. [14], 'PAGE A. | CATALOGUE OF WESSEL & CO.'S CHOICE PUBLICATIONS OF MODERN PIANO-FORTE MUSIC, | No 6, FRITH STREET, SOHO SQUARE, LONDON.'. The latest Chopin work in the lists is Op. 27.

STAMPS: publisher, style W/C (see Appendix 8).

3-W-2 *(continued)*

3-W-2 *(concluded)*

1. *Date:* Brown (p. 44) states that Wessel's "... arrangement for PF. Solo, published in October 1837 (publisher's number 1860), was republished *c.* 1845 as no. 50 in his series 'Le Pianiste Moderne'.". However, the last work listed on the title page of 3-W-2 is Op. 42, published by Wessel in 1840, which is title-page evidence for the earlier date of this score. Moreover, the firm moved from 6 to 67 Frith Street in 1839 (Table 5D). While the latter address appears on the title page, the former is still used in the colophon and advertisement.
2. This edition is an arrangement for piano solo. Wessel also published arrangements for piano and violin (see 18-W-2, note 3), piano and viola, and piano and flute (Brown, p. 44).

London: Wessel (1662) [1856–60] 3-W-1 M233.C54 I62

LA GÂITÉ. | Introduction, | et | POLONOISE BRILLANTE, | *pour le* | Piano Forte et Violoncello, | DEDIÉE À | MONSIEUR JOSEPH MERK, | Par | FRÉDÉRIC CHOPIN, | *New Edition, revised and fingered by his Pupil* | I. [*sic*] FONTANA. | *Copyright of the Publishers.* | *Op. 3.* « *Ent. Sta. Hall.* » *Price 6/–* | *Paris, Schlesinger, — Vienna, Mechetti.* | *LONDON,* | WESSEL & C° *Importers of Foreign Music & Publishers of the Works* | of CHOPIN, MAYSEDER, KUHLAU, ROMBERG, DOTZAUER, KRAFT, &c | 18. HANOVER SQUARE.

Piano: 8 leaves (326 x 252 mm): pp. [i] engr title page, [ii] blank, 1–13 engr music, [14] advt.

CAPTION TITLE: p. 1, ' "LA GAÎTÉ" | INTRODUCTION et POLONOISE BRILLANTE, Composée par F. CHOPIN.'.

FOOTLINE: p. 1, '(W & C° N° 1662)'; p. 2–12, 'CHOPIN. La Gaîté. « » (W & C° N° 1662)'; p. 13, 'CHOPIN. La Gaîté. « WESSEL & C° 18. Hanover Square. » (N° 1662)', followed by a list of Chopin works: [Duo concertant], Opp. 1, 16, 6, 7, 9, 15, 11, 21, "4 Concerto pieces", Opp. 10, 25.

ADVT: p. [14], 'WESSEL & Co.'s SERIES OF GERMAN SONGS, (THIRD LIST. No. 274 to 500.)'.

Violoncello: The cello part (plate number 1663) is not present in this copy.

STAMPS: none.

1. *Date:* Wessel inference (date code W2, p. 17).
2. The piano part does not include the cello staff.
3. This score (3-W-1) is the only one in the collection that was issued after 1840 without the collective title.

SONATA IN C MINOR
Opus 4

Paris: Richault (10868) 1851 — *Composed* 1827–28
Vienna: Haslinger (8147) 1851 — Brown 23
London: Cocks (9727) 1852 — Chominski & Turlo 201

***Vienna:* Haslinger (8147) [= 1851]** **4-Ha-1** **M23.C54 S67**

GRANDE SONATE | pour le | Pianoforte | *composée* | par | FRÉDÉRIC CHOPIN. | Oeuvre 4. | *Propriété des Editeurs.* | *Nº 8147.* « *Enrégistré dans l'Archive de l'Union.* » *Prix f 2 — C.M.* | Vienne, | *chez Charles Haslinger quondam Tobie,* | *Marchand de Musique etc. de la Cour Imp. et Royale.* | *Leipsic, chez B. Hermann.* | Londres, chez R. Cocks & Cº « Milan, chez Jean Ricordi. » Paris, chez Simon Richault.

16 leaves (342 x 266 mm): pp. [i] engr title page, [ii, 1] blank, 2–29 engr music, [30] blank.

CAPTION TITLE: p. 2, 'SONATE | *par* | FR. CHOPIN. | Oeuvre 4.'.

FOOTLINE: p. 2, '(8147.) | Eigenthum und Verlag der K.K. Hof-Kunst-und Musikalienhandlung des Tobias Haslinger in Wien.'; pp. 3–29, '(T.H. 8147.)'.

STAMPS: dealers, Ringt, New York; Schmidt, Philadelphia.

1. *Date:* first-edition inference (date code fe, p. 17).
2. According to Brown (p. 25), Tobias Haslinger "... had engraved the Sonata as early as the summer of 1839, which accounts for the publisher's number.".

***Leipzig:* Breitkopf & Härtel (C.XIII.32) 1880** **4-BH-1** **M23.C54 S675**

Friedr. Chopin's | Werke. | Band XIII. | Nachgelassene Pianofortewerke | [list of works, items 1–31 | 32. Sonate. C moll. (Op. 4) « » 2 [M] — [Pf] | [list of works, items 33–35] | Band XIII in zwei broch. Bänden. Bd. I. Nr. 1–26. Pr. *M* 5.70. n. Eleg. geb. Pr. *M* 7.70. n. | Bd. II. Nr. 27–35. Pr. *M* 4.80. n. Eleg. geb. Pr. *M* 6.80. n. | Verlag von Breitkopf & Härtel in Leipzig.

13 leaves (332 x 266 mm): pp. [1] lith title page [series title in red], 2–25 lith music, [26] advt.

CAPTION TITLE: p. 2, 'Chopin's Werke « SONATE ÷ für das Pianoforte ÷ von ÷ FRIEDRICH CHOPIN. ÷ Nachgelassenes Werk. (Op. 4.) » Band XIII. Nº 32.'.

FOOTLINE: p. 2, 'Stich und Druck von Breitkopf & Härtel in Leipzig. « C.XIII.32. » Ausgegeben 1880.'; pp. 3–25, 'C.XIII.32.'.

ADVT: p. [26], 'FRIEDRICH CHOPIN'S WERKE. | Erste kritisch durchgesehene Gesamtausgabe. | Verlag von BREITKOPF & HÄRTEL in Leipzig.'. Fourteen volumes are listed, the first with the four ballades, the last with the 17 songs of Op. 74.

WRAPPER (pale blue): pp. [1–4] advt.

ADVT: wrapper p. [1], 'Friedrich Chopin | Sämtliche Kompositionen für Pianoforte zu 2 Händen | [list of works Op. 1–33] | Berlin ÷ Brüssel « Breitkopf & Härtel, Leipzig » London ÷ New York'; pp. [2–3], piano works by Philipp Scharwenka; p. [4], piano works by Xaver Scharwenka.

4-BH-1 *(continued)*

4-BH-1 *(concluded)*

STAMPS: publisher, style BH/M (see Appendix 8).

---

1. *Date:* Note the explicit publication date in the footline.
2. This score is from the penultimate volume in Breitkopf & Härtel's collected edition of 1878–80, edited by Bargiel, Brahms, Franchomme, Liszt, Reinecke, and Rudorff (Chominski & Turlo, pp. 257–58).

RONDO IN F MAJOR
Opus 5

Warsaw: Brzezina (—) 1828	
Paris: M. Schonenberger (608.606.602) 1840	*Composed* 1826
Leipzig: Hofmeister (2121) 1836	Brown 15
London: Wessel (1552) 1837	Chominski & Turlo 193

***Leipzig:* Hofmeister (2121) [= 1836]** **5-Ho-1** **M25.C54 R214**

RONDEAU | à la Mazur | pour le | Pianoforte | Dedié à Mademoiselle la Comtesse | Alexandrine de Moriolles | et composé par | FREDERIC CHOPIN. | Op. 5. « Propriété de l'Editeur. » Pr. 14 Gr. | *à Varsovie, chez G. Sennewald.* | à Leipzig, chez Fréd. Hofmeister. | *2121.*

7 leaves (323 x 257 mm): pp. [1] lith title page, 2–13 engr music, [14] blank.

CAPTION TITLE: p. 2, '» F. Chopin. Op. 5.'.

SUB-CAPTION: p. 2, 'RONDO.'.

FOOTLINE: pp. 2–13, '2121'.

STAMPS: dealer, Dunst, Frankfort.

1. *Date:* first-edition inference (date code fe, p. 17).
2. Brzezina (the first publisher) was acquired by Sennewald *ca* 1830 (Brown, p. 8), which accounts for Hofmeister's citation of Sennewald on the title page. Brown also quotes a letter written by Chopin's sister, which implies that Hofmeister acquired all of Sennewald's Chopin works in 1831. Presumably, this included Opp. 1 and 5. However, there is no evidence in Brown, Chominski & Turlo, Hoboken or the *CPM* that Sennewald issued either of these works under his own imprint.

***London:* Wessel (1552) [1837–39]** **5-W-1** **M25.C54 R213**

LE PIANISTE MODERNE. Nº XI. | LE POSIANA. | RONDEAU À LA MAZUR. | *pour le* | Piano Forte, | *Dédié à* | *Mademoiselle la Comtesse* | Alexandrina de Moriolles, | *et Composé par* | FREDERIC CHOPIN. | *(de Varsovie)* | *Edited by his Pupil. I. [sic] Fontana.* | *Ent. Sta. Hall.* | OP. *5* « COPYRIGHT. » *Price 4/–* | *Leipzig. F. Hoffmeister [sic]. Paris. Schlesinger.* | *LONDON,* | WESSEL & Cº *Importers of Foreign Music & Publishers of the Works of* | CHOPIN. CZERNY. THALBERG. HUMMEL. PIXIS. WEBER. &c. | Nº 6, Frith Street, Soho Square.

9 leaves (335 x 252 mm): pp. [i] engr title page, [ii] blank, [1] advt, 2–15 engr music, [16] blank.

CAPTION TITLE: p. 2, '*LE PIANISTE MODERNE, Nº 11.* | *RONDEAU à la MAZUR, Composé par FRED. CHOPIN.* | Edited by his Pupil, | *I. [sic] FONTANA.*'.

FOOTLINE: p. 2, 'OP: 5. « (W & Cº Nº 1552.)'; pp. 3–14, '*PIANISTE MODERNE, Nº 11.* « (W & Cº Nº 1552.)'; p. 15, '*PIANISTE MODERNE, Nº 11.* « | (Nº 1552.) WESSEL & Cº Nº 6, FRITH STREET, SOHO SQUARE.'.

ADVT: p. [1], 'PAGE A. | CATALOGUE OF WESSEL & CO.'S CHOICE PUBLICATIONS OF

5-W-1 *(continued)*

5-W-1 *(concluded)*

MODERN PIANO-FORTE MUSIC, | Nº 6, FRITH STREET, SOHO SQUARE, LONDON.'. The latest Chopin work in the lists is Op. 27.

STAMPS: publisher, styles W/B and W/C (see Appendix 8).

---

1. *Date:* According to Brown (p. 16), Wessel "... reissued the Rondo *c.* 1846 as no. 11 of the series called 'Le Pianiste Moderne ...". However, the address, 6 Frith Street in the footline and advertisement as well as on the title page, indicates this score was issued before 1840 (Table 5D).

MAZURKAS IN F SHARP MINOR, C SHARP MINOR, E MAJOR, E FLAT MINOR
Opus 6

Paris: M. Schlesinger (1341) 1833	*Composed* 1830–32
Leipzig: Kistner (996) 1832	Brown 60
London: Wessel (958) 1833	Chominski & Turlo 51

***Paris:* M. Schlesinger (1341) [= 1833]** **6-mS-1** **M32.C54 M43**

Cinq Mazurkas | POUR | *LE* | Piano Forte | *DEDIÉS À* | *Mademoiselle la Comtesse Pauline* | PLATER | par | Fréd. Chopin. | *P.é de l Ed.r « » Prix: 5.f* | Op: 6. | *PARIS, Chez Maurice* SCHLESINGER, *Md de Musique, Ed.r des Œuvres de Mozart, Rossini, &c. &c.* | *Rue de Richelieu, 97* | *LEIPZIG, Chez KISTNER*

6 leaves (329 x 258 mm): pp. [i] engr title page, [ii, 1] blank, 2–10 engr music.

CAPTION TITLE: p. 2, 'F. CHOPIN Op: 6. ÷ 5. Mazourkas. «'.

SUB-CAPTION: p. 2, 'Mazourka. | N.o 1.'; and so on through p. 10, 'Mazourka. | N.o 5.'.

FOOTLINE: p. 2, 'Chopin 5 Mazourkas Op: 6. « M.S. 1341. » Maurice Schlesinger rue de Richelieu N.o 97.'; pp. 3–9, 'M.S. 1341.'; p. 10, same as p. 2.

IMPOSITION: An even number of leaves and an imposed singleton (leaf 4) indicate that a final blank leaf is missing. Hob-198 has this leaf, as does 6-Bra-1.

STAMPS: successor, style Bra/B (see Appendix 8).

1. *Date:* first-edition inference (date code fe, p. 17).
2. The first edition of Op. 6 was published at the same time as that of Op. 7 by each of the three publishers, Kistner first (1832), and Schlesinger and Wessel in the following year. However, the three pairs of editions differ in the placement of the C-major mazurka, which appears as the fifth mazurka in Schlesinger's Op. 6 (as in 6-mS-1) and in Kistner's Op. 7 (as in 7-Ki-1). Regarding Wessel's editions, see 6-W-1, note 4.
3. The situation is complicated by the fact that there is an earlier "Quatre Mazurkas" edition of Schlesinger's Op. 6, without the C-major mazurka (Chominski & Turlo, p. 110 and plate 4; see also Grabowski, p. 18). The same is true of Kistner's Op. 7; see 7-Ki-1, note 4.
4. Most authors and bibliographers — except Chominski & Turlo — follow the second Kistner edition in assigning five mazurkas to Op. 7 and four to Op. 6, as is done here.

***Paris:* Brandus (M.S. 1341) [after 1850]** **6-Bra-1** **M32.C54 M439**

Cinq Mazurkas | POUR | *LE* | Piano Forte | *DEDIÉS À* | *Mademoiselle la Comtesse Pauline* | PLATER | par | Fréd. Chopin. | *P.é de l Ed.r « » Prix: 6.f* | Op: 6. | *PARIS, BRANDUS et C.ie Editeurs, 103. Rue Richelieu.* | *S.t Petersbourg Maison Brandus* | *LEIPZIG, Chez KISTNER*

7 leaves (352 x 271 mm): pp. [i] engr title page, [ii, 1] blank, 2–10 engr music, [11, 12] blank.

CAPTION TITLE: p. 2, 'F. CHOPIN Op: 6. ÷ 5. Mazourkas. «'.

SUB-CAPTION: p. 2, 'MAZOURKA. | N.o 1.'; and so on through p. 10, 'Mazourka. | N.o 5.'.

6-Bra-1 *(continued)*

6-Bra-1 *(concluded)*

FOOTLINE: p. 2, 'Chopin 5 Mazourkas Op: 6. [almost illegible] « M.S. 1341. » Maurice Schlesinger rue de Richelieu Nº 97. [almost illegible]'; pp. 3–9, 'M.S. 1341.'; p. 10, same as p. 2.

WRAPPER (yellow): pp. [1] same as title page, [2–4] blank.

STAMPS: publisher, style Bra/A (see Appendix 8).

---

1. *Date:* based on the address (Table 5A).
2. Brandus included the C-major mazurka in Op. 6, following Schlesinger (see 6-mS-1, note 3).

***Leipzig:* Kistner (996) [= 1832]** **6-Ki-1** **M32.C54 M435**

Quatre | MAZURKAS | pour le | PIANOFORTE | composées et dédiées | à Mademoiselle la Comtesse | *PAULINE PLATER* | par | FRÉD. CHOPIN. | *Liv. 1.* « Oeuvre 6. » *Pr. 10 Gr.* | Propriété des Editeurs. | Enregistré aux Archives de l'Union. | *Leipzig, chez Fr. Kistner.* | *Paris, chez M. Schlesinger.* | *996.*

5 leaves (321 x 253 mm): pp. [1] lith title page, 2–9 engr music, [10] blank.

CAPTION TITLE: p. 2, '» F. Chopin. Op. *6.*'.

SUB-CAPTION: p. 2, 'Nº 1.'; and so on through p. 9, 'Nº 4.'.

FOOTLINE: pp. 2–9, '*996*'.

STAMPS: dealer, Tschurtschenthaler, Innsbruck.

---

1. *Date:* first-edition inference (date code fe, p. 17).
2. The text and lettering of this title page correspond to Hob-194 and Chominski & Turlo, p. 111. However, Hob-194 is a variant state with an erroneous imposition that has two leaves of Op. 7 (pp. 9, 10), perhaps reflecting the initial uncertainty about placement of the C-major mazurka; see 6-mS-1, note 4.
3. The title page is printed in sepia.

***Leipzig:* Kistner (996) [1833–40]** **6-Ki-3** **M32.C54 M438**

The transcription of this title page is the same as that of 6-Ki-1, except here there is an additional line "Nouvelle Edition." at the end.

5 leaves (322 x 260 mm): pp. [1] lith title page, 2–9 engr music, [10] blank.

CAPTION TITLE: p. 2, '» F. Chopin. Op. 6.'.

SUB-CAPTION: p. 2, '*Nº* 1.'; and so on through p. 9, '*Nº* 4.'.

FOOTLINE: pp. 2–9, '*996*'.

STAMPS: none.

---

1. *Date:* based on "Nouvelle Edition" and currency (see date code c1, p. 17).
2. The title page is printed in sepia.
3. This score is an early impression of the "Nouvelle Edition", with price 10 Gr.

Leipzig: Kistner (996) [1841–45?] 6-Ki-2 M32.C54 M436

QUATRE | MAZURKAS | pour le | Pianoforte | composées et dédiées | à Mademoiselle la Comtesse | PAULINE PLATER | par | FRÉD. CHOPIN. | Liv. I. « Oeuvre 6. » Pr. 12 1/2 Ngr. | Propriété des Editeurs. | Enregistré aux Archives de l'Union. | *Leipzig, chez Fr. Kistner* | *Paris, chez M. Schlesinger.* | *996.* | Nouvelle Edition.

5 leaves (324 x 261 mm): [1] lith title page, 2–9 engr music, [10] blank.

CAPTION TITLE: p. 2, '» F. Chopin Op. 6.' (slanted backwards).

SUB-CAPTION: p. 2, 'N° 1.'; and so on through p. 9, 'N° 4.'.

FOOTLINE: pp. 2–9, '*996*'.

PLATES: The music plates are not the same as those of 6-Ki-3.

STAMPS: dealer, Scharfenberg, New York.

1. *Date:* currency inference (date code c2, p. 17), but see note 2.
2. Since Brandus acquired Schlesinger in 1846, citation of Schlesinger on the title page suggests a date earlier than this. However, Hob-197 also cites Schlesinger and has a price only in Marks, which implies a date later than 1873. Apparently, in these re-issues, Kistner ignored the acquisition of Schlesinger by Brandus.
3. This score is the second issue of the "Nouvelle Edition"; see 6-Ki-3, note 3. It corresponds to Hob-196.

London: Wessel (958) [1836–39] 6-W-1 M32.C54 M437

L'AMATEUR PIANISTE, N° 8 et 9. | SOUVENIR DE LA POLOGNE. | EIGHT MAZURKAS, | for the | PIANO FORTE, | BOOK 8, OP. 6. | *Dedicated to* | MAD^LLE^ LA COMTESSE PAULINE PLATER. | BOOK 9, OP. 7. | *Dedicated to* | MONS^R^ JOHNS DE LA NOUVELLE ORLEANS | par | FRED. CHOPIN. | *Ent. Sta. Hall.* « BOOK. [handwritten "1"] » *Price 2/6 each.* | *LONDON,* | WESSEL & C° Importers & Publishers of FOREIGN MUSIC, | *(by special Appointment) to H.R.H. the Duchess of Kent,* | N° 6, Frith Street, Soho Square.

6 leaves (335 x 253 mm): pp. [i] engr title page, [ii, 1] blank, 2–9 engr music, [10] blank.

CAPTION TITLE: p. 2, '*SOUVENIR de la POLOGNE.* | *EIGHT MAZURKAS, Composed by FRED. CHOPIN.* | *(N° I. Op: 6.)* | *Dedicated to MADEMOISELLE la COMTESSE PAULINE PLATER.*'.

SUB-CAPTION: p. 2, '*N° I.*'; and so on through p. 9, '*N° 4.*'.

HEADLINE: pp. 2–9, 'Piano-Forte.'.

FOOTLINE: p. 2, '(W & C° N° 958.)'; pp. 3–8, 'CHOPIN, Souvenir de la Pologne. N° 1. « (W & C° N° 958.)'; p. 9, 'CHOPIN, Souvenir de la Pologne. N° 1. (N° 958.) | Sets 1, 2, 3 & 4 are also published as DUETS, by | WESSEL & C° N° 6, Frith Street, Soho Square. | Publishers of all the Compositions of FR. CHOPIN, CZERNY, KUHLAU, MAYSEDER, &c.'.

STAMPS: publisher, styles W/B and W/C (see Appendix 8).

6-W-1 *(continued)*

6-W-1 *(concluded)*

1. *Date:* The lower limit on the date is based on title-page reference to the series "L'Amateur Pianiste", which began with Chopin's Op. 1, published by Wessel in 1836. This date is consistent with footline reference on p. 9 to "Sets 1, 2, 3 & 4" of the mazurkas, respectively Opp. 6, 7, 17, 24, the last of which was published in 1836. The upper limit on the date is from the address (Table 5D).
2. For this series issue, Wessel modified the original title page by adding the top line "L'Amateur Pianiste, N° 8 et 9.", removing a line "OP. 6 and 7." under "PIANO FORTE,", changing "Book 1" to "Book 8", and changing "Book 2" to "Book 9".
3. The first (1833) Wessel editions of Opp. 6 and 7 were issued without the series designation.
4. Wessel did not at first include the C-major mazurka in either Opp. 6 or 7, but eventually inserted it in a late edition of Op. 7; see 7-W-3, note 3.
5. Hob-199 is the same as 6-W-1; it should not be designated the "Englischer Erstdruck". Hoboken shows the title page in plate 15 (p. 91).

London: Wessel (958) [1856–60] 6-W-2 M32.C54 M4372

N° [handwritten "5"] OF | WESSEL & C°.'s COMPLETE COLLECTION | OF | *the Compositions* | OF | FREDERIC CHOPIN | FOR THE | Piano Forte. | [list of works, Wessel 1–4] | 5 "SOUVENIR *de* LA POLOGNE" *1st Set of Mazurkas* } *as played by* ÷ *M.* LISZT *at* ÷ *his Concerts* { *Op. 6. 3/–* | [list of works, Wessel 6–71] | *Ent. Sta. Hall.* « *Copyrights.* » *Price* , [handwritten "3/–"] | *LONDON,* | WESSEL & C° *Importers and Publishers of* FOREIGN MUSIC, | *(by special Appointment) to H.R.H. the Duchess of Kent.* | 18, HANOVER SQUARE.

6 leaves (332 x 250 mm): [i] engr (or letterpress) title page, [ii] blank, [1] advt, 2–9 engr music, [10] blank.

CAPTION TITLE: p. 2, '*SOUVENIR de la POLOGNE.* | *FIRST SET OF MAZURKAS, Composed by FRED. CHOPIN.* | *(N° I. Op: 6.)* | *Dedicated to MADEMOISELLE la COMTESSE PAULINE PLATER.*'.

SUB-CAPTION: p. 2, '*N° 1*'; and so on through p. 9, '*N°* 4.'.

HEADLINE: pp. 2–9, 'Piano-Forte.'.

FOOTLINE: p. 2, '(W & C° N° 958)' [almost illegible]; pp. 3–8, 'CHOPIN, Souvenir de la Pologne. N° 1. « (W & C° N° 958.)'; p. 9, 'CHOPIN, Souvenir de la Pologne. N° 1. (N° 958.) « | Sets 1, 2, 3, & 4 are also published as DUETS, by | WESSEL & C° | Publishers of all the Compositions of FR. CHOPIN, CZERNY, KUHLAU, MAYSEDER, &c.'. The address was removed on p. 9.

ADVT: p. [1], 'PIANOFORTE COMPOSITIONS | BY | ROBERT GOLDBECK, | *(OF BERLIN).*' | [at the foot:] 'LONDON: — WESSEL & Co., 18, HANOVER SQUARE.'.

PLATES: The music plates are the same as those of 6-W-1, except in the footline on p. 9.

STAMPS: publisher, style W/E (see Appendix 8); dealer, Scheurmann, London.

1. *Date:* Wessel inference (date code W2, p. 17).
2. For additional comments on Wessel's editions of Opp. 6 and 7, see the notes in 6-W-1.

MAZURKAS IN B FLAT MAJOR, A MINOR, F MINOR, A FLAT MAJOR, C MAJOR
Opus 7

Paris: M. Schlesinger (1342) 1833	*Composed* 1824–32
Leipzig: Kistner (997) 1832	Brown 61
London: Wessel (959) 1833	Chominski & Turlo 56

***Paris:* M. Schlesinger (1342) [= 1833]** **7-mS-2** **M32.C54 M441**

4 Mazurkas | *POUR LE* « PIANO FORTE » *DÉDIÉS À* | Monsieur Johns | *de la Nouvelle Orléans* | PAR | FRÉD. CHOPIN. | *Œuv: 7.* « » *Prix: 5.f* | *Propriété des Editeurs.* | *PARIS, Chez Maurice* SCHLESINGER, *M.d de Musique, Ed.r des Œuvres de Beethoven, Weber, &c.* | *Rue de Richelieu, 97* | *LEIPZIG, Chez KISTNER.*

6 leaves (335 x 257 mm): pp. [i] engr title page, [ii, 1] blank, 2–9 engr music, [10] blank.

CAPTION TITLE: p. 2, 'F. CHOPIN Op: 7. ÷ 4 Mazourkas. «'.

SUB-CAPTION: p. 2, 'Mazourka. | N.o 1.'; and so on through p. 8 system 5, 'Mazourka. | N.o 4.'.

FOOTLINE: p. 2, 'Chopin 4 Mazourka [*sic*] Op: 7. « M.S. 1342. » Maurice Schlesinger rue de Richelieu N.o 97.'; pp. 3–8, 'M.S. 1342.'; p. 9, same as p. 2.

STAMPS: publisher, style mS/B (see Appendix 8).

1. *Date:* first-edition inference (date code fe, p. 17).
2. Regarding the C-major mazurka, see 6-mS-1, notes 3 and 4.

***Paris:* M. Schlesinger (1342) [1846–48]** **7-mS-3** **M32.C54 M442 c.2**

The transcription of this title page is the same as that of 7-mS-2, except here the price is "*6.f*".

6 leaves (333 x 263 mm): pp. [i] engr title page, [ii, 1] blank, 2–9 engr music, [10] blank.

CAPTION TITLE: p. 2, 'F. CHOPIN. Op: 7. ÷ 4 Mazourkas. «'.

SUB-CAPTION: p. 2, 'N.o 1. | MAZOURKA.'; and so on through p. 8 system 5, 'N.o 4. | MAZOURKA.'.

FOOTLINE: p. 2, 'Chopin Op: 7. 4 Mazourkas. « B et Cie 1342. » Brandus et Cie Rue Richelieu 97.'; pp. 3–8, 'B et Cie 1342.'; p. 9, same as p. 2.

STAMPS: successor, style BD/B (see Appendix 8); dealer, Beauvais, Tours.

1. *Date:* The lower limit on the date is based on the Brandus acquisition of Schlesinger in January 1846, and the upper limit is from the address in the footline; see Table 5A.
2. It is strange that the Brandus imprint is in the footline but not on the title page.
3. Regarding the C-major mazurka, see 6-mS-1, notes 3 and 4.

***Paris:* M. Schlesinger (1342) [1846–48]** **7-mS-1** **M32.C54 M442 c.1**

The transcription of this title page is the same as that of 7-mS-3.

7-mS-1 *(continued)*

7-mS-1 *(concluded)*

6 leaves (323 x 247 mm): pp. [i] engr title page, [ii, 1] blank, 2–9 engr music, [10] blank.

CAPTION TITLE: p. 2, 'F. CHOPIN. Op: 7. ÷ 4 Mazourkas. «'.

SUB-CAPTION: p. 2, 'N° 1. | MAZOURKA.'; and so on through p. 8 system 5, 'N° 4. | MAZOURKA.'.

FOOTLINE: p. 2, 'Chopin Op: 7. 4 Mazourkas. « B et Cie 1342. » Brandus et Cie Rue Richelieu 97.'; pp. 3–8, 'B et Cie 1342.'; p. 9, same as p. 2.

STAMPS: successor, style BD/C (see Appendix 8); dealer, Retté, Paris.

---

1. *Date:* The lower limit on the date is based on the Brandus acquisition of Schlesinger in January 1846, and the upper limit is from the address in the footline; see Table 5A.
2. It is strange that the Brandus imprint is in the footline but not on the title page.
3. Regarding the C-major mazurka, see 6-mS-1, notes 3 and 4.
4. Except for the stamp, this copy appears to be the same as 7-mS-3.

***Leipzig:* Kistner (997) [= 1832]** **7-Ki-1** **M32.C54 M44**

CINQ | MAZURKAS | pour le | Pianoforte | composées et dédiées | À MONSIEUR JOHNS | de la Nouvelle Orléans | par | FRÉD. CHOPIN. | Liv. II. « Oeuvre 7. » Pr. 10 Gr. | Propriété des Editeurs. | Enregistré aux Archives de l'Union. | *Leipzig, chez Fr. Kistner.* | *Paris, chez M. Schlesinger.* | *997.*

5 leaves (321 x 254 mm): pp. [1] lith title page, 2–10 engr music.

CAPTION TITLE: p. 2, '» F. Chopin. Op. *7.*'.

SUB-CAPTION: p. 2, 'N° 1.'; and so on through p. 10, 'N° 5.'.

FOOTLINE: pp. 2–10, '*997*'.

IMPOSITION: An odd number of leaves and a central singleton (leaf 3) indicate that this copy is complete; thus a final blank leaf probably was not intended. Hob-200 also lacks this leaf, while Hob-201, a "Titelauflage" with six leaves and a final blank, probably has no singleton (as in 7-Ki-2).

STAMPS: dealer, Tschurtschenthaler, Innsbruck.

---

1. *Date:* first-edition inference (date code fe, p. 17).
2. The title page is printed in sepia.
3. There is an earlier "QUATRE | MAZURKAS" issue of Kistner's Op. 7 without the C-major mazurka (Chominski & Turlo, p. 113 and plate 12); for additional comments, see 6-mS-1, note 3.

***Leipzig:* Kistner (997) [*ca* 1840]** **7-Ki-2** **M32.C54 M4401**

The transcription of this title page is the same as that of 7-Ki-1, except here the price is "12 1/2 Ngr. ÷ 10 g Gr. " and there is an additional line "Nouvelle Edition." at the end.

6 leaves (326 x 258 mm): pp. [1] lith title page, 2–10 engr music, [11–12] blank.

CAPTION TITLE: p. 2, '» F. Chopin Op. 7.'.

SUB-CAPTION: p. 2, '*N°* 1.'; and so on through p. 10, '*N°* 5.'.

7-Ki-2 *(continued)*

7-Ki-2 *(concluded)*

FOOTLINE: pp. 2–10, '997'.

PLATES: The music plates are not identical to those of 7-Ki-1, but the differences appear to be limited to performance marks.

STAMPS: dealer, Eck & Buke (?), Amsterdam.

---

1. *Date*: currency inference (date code c1, p. 17). The price is given in both Ngr. and Gr., which indicates a transition year, probably 1840.
2. The title page is printed in sepia.
3. This "Nouvelle Edition" is one of several variants noted by Chominski & Turlo (p. 113).
4. Kistner issued an earlier "QUATRE | MAZURKAS" edition without the C-major mazurka (Chominski & Turlo, p. 113 and plate 12); for additional comments see 6-mS-1, note 4.

Leipzig: **Kistner (997) [1841–45?]** 7-Ki-3 M32.C54 M4402

The transcription of this title page is the same as that of 7-Ki-1, except here the price is "12 ½ Ngr." and there is an additional line "Nouvelle Edition." at the end.

5 leaves (333 x 261 mm): pp. [1] lith title page, 2–10 engr music.

CAPTION TITLE: p. 2, '» F. Chopin. Op. 7.' [slanted backward].

SUB-CAPTION: p. 2, '*N*º 1.'; and so on through p. 10, '*N*º 5.'.

FOOTLINE: p. 2, 'Stich & Druck von Fr. Kistner in Leipzig. « 997'; pp. 3–10, '997'.

PLATES: The music plates differ from those of 7-Ki-1 and from those of 7-Ki-2.

STAMPS: dealer, Lose, Copenhagen.

---

1. *Date:* currency inference (date code c2, p. 17), but see 6-K-2, note 2.
2. The title leaf lacks its original blank conjugate, and consequently was tipped to leaf 2. However, in rebinding, it was detached and joined to a new blank conjugate.
3. See 7-Ki-2, notes 3 and 4.

London: **Wessel (959) [1836–39]** 7-W-2 M32.C54 M443

L'AMATEUR PIANISTE, Nº 8 et 9. | SOUVENIR DE LA POLOGNE. | EIGHT MAZURKAS, | for the | PIANO FORTE, | BOOK 8, OP. 6. | *Dedicated to* | MADLLE LA COMTESSE PAULINE PLATER. | BOOK 9, OP. 7. | *Dedicated to* | MONSR JOHNS DE LA NOUVELLE ORLEANS | par | FRED. CHOPIN. | *Ent. Sta. Hall* « BOOK. [handwritten "2"] » *Price 2/6 each.* | *LONDON,* | WESSEL & Cº Importers & Publishers of FOREIGN MUSIC, | *(by special Appointment) to H.R.H. the Duchess of Kent,* | Nº 6, Frith Street, Soho Square.

5 leaves (335 x 253 mm): pp. [1] engr title page, 2–9 engr music, [10] blank.

CAPTION TITLE: p. 2, '*SOUVENIR de la POLOGNE.* | *EIGHT MAZURKAS, Composed by FRED. CHOPIN.* | *2d Set, Op: 7.)* | *Dedicated to MONSIEUR JOHNS, de la Nouvelle Orleans.*'.

SUB-CAPTION: p. 2, '*Nº 5.*'; and so on through p. 8 system 5, '*Nº 8.*'.

7-W-2 *(continued)*

7-W-2 *(concluded)*

HEADLINE: pp. 2–9, 'Piano–Forte.'.

FOOTLINE: p. 2, '(W & Co N° 959.)'; pp. 3–8, 'CHOPIN, Souvenir de la Pologne. N° 2. « (W & Co N° 959.)'; p. 9, 'CHOPIN, Souvenir de la Pologne. N° 2. (N° 959.) « | WESSEL & Co N° 6, Frith Street, Soho Square.

IMPOSITION: obscured by rebinding.

STAMPS: publisher, styles W/B and W/C (see Appendix 8).

---

1. *Date:* See 6-W-1, note 1; also Chominski & Turlo pp. 113–114 and 445.
2. A copy of the first Wessel edition of Op. 7 is in the New York Public Library (shelfmark *MYD).
3. For additional comments on Wessel's editions of Opp. 6 and 7, see the notes in 6-W-1.

London: **Wessel (959) [*ca* 1843]** **7-W-1** **M32.C54 M445**

N^{o} [handwritten "6"] OF | WESSEL & Co.'s COMPLETE COLLECTION | OF | *the Compositions* | OF | FREDERIC CHOPIN | FOR THE | Piano Forte. | Solo & Duet | [list of works, Wessel 1–5] | 6 ___ *2nd Set of do.* { *as played by* ÷ *M.* LISZT *at* ÷ *his Concerts.* } *Op. 7.* *3/–* [*Duet*] *4/–* | [list of works, Wessel 7–55] | *Ent. Sta. Hall.* « *Copyrights.* » *Price, Solo* [handwritten "3/–"] ÷ " *Duet* [blank] | *LONDON,* | WESSEL & Co *Importers and Publishers of* FOREIGN MUSIC, | *(by special Appointment) to H.R.H. the Duchess of Kent.* | N° 67, Frith Street, Corner of Soho Square.

6 leaves (337 x 252 mm): [i] engr title page, [ii] blank, [1] advt, 2–9 engr music, [10] blank.

CAPTION TITLE: p. 2, '*SOUVENIR de la POLOGNE.* | *SECOND SET OF MAZURKAS, Composed by FRED. CHOPIN.* | *Dedicated to MONSIEUR JOHNS, de la Nouvelle Orleans.*'.

SUB-CAPTION: p. 2, '*N° 5.*'; and so on through p. 8 system 5, '*N° 8.*'.

HEADLINE: pp. 2–9, 'Piano-Forte.'.

FOOTLINE: p. 2, '(W & Co N° 959.)'; pp. 3–8, 'CHOPIN, Souvenir de la Pologne. N° 2. « (W & Co N° 959.)'; p. 9, 'CHOPIN, Souvenir de la Pologne. N° 2. (N° 959.) | WESSEL & Co N° 6, Frith Street, Soho Square.'.

ADVT: p. [1], '[first line probably clipped] CONTINUATION OF WESSEL & STAPLETON'S CATALOGUE OF THEIR PIANOFORTE PUBLICATIONS, | COMPRISING THE SOLO WORKS OF BEETHOVEN, CHOPIN, LISZT, HENSELT, &c. ORGAN MUSIC, | PIANOFORTE STUDIES, TRIOS, QUARTETTS, QUINTETTS, &c. &c. &c. | No. 67, FRITH STREET, CORNER OF SOHO SQUARE, LONDON. | SEE CATALOGUES A, B, C, D, &c. FOR MUSIC, PIANO SOLO, AND FOR TWO PERFORMERS ON THE PIANO.'. This is Wessel's "Page E". Chopin works for piano solo are listed through Op. 42; also listed is the trio Op. 8. Under pianoforte studies, where Op. 28 is listed again, the comment is made that Liszt "has latterly introduced some of them to the British Public.".

STAMPS: publisher, style W/C (see Appendix 8).

---

1. *Date:* Wessel published Op. 51 in 1843, which is title-page evidence for the date of this issue.
2. For additional comments on Wessel's editions of Opp. 6 and 7, see the notes in 6-W-1.

London: Wessel (959) [1856–60] 7-W-3 M32.C54 M4452

N° [handwritten "6"] OF | WESSEL & C°.'s COMPLETE COLLECTION | OF | *the Compositions* | OF | FREDERIC CHOPIN | FOR THE | Piano Forte. | [list of works, Wessel 1–5] | 6 ___ *2nd Set of do.* } *as played by ÷ M.* LISZT *at ÷ his Concerts* { *Op. 7* *3/–* | [list of works, Wessel 7–71] | *Ent. Sta. Hall.* « *Copyrights.* » *Price*, [handwritten "3/–"] | *LONDON,* | WESSEL & C° *Importers and Publishers of* FOREIGN MUSIC, | *(by special Appointment) to H.R.H. the Duchess of Kent.* | 18, HANOVER SQUARE.

6 leaves (332 x 250 mm): [1] engr (or letterpress) title page, 2–10 engr music, [11–12] blank.

CAPTION TITLE: p. 2, '*SOUVENIR de la POLOGNE.* | *SECOND SET OF MAZURKAS, Composed by FRED. CHOPIN.* | *Dedicated to MONSIEUR JOHNS, de la Nouvelle Orleans.*'.

SUB-CAPTION: p. 2, '*N° 5.*'; and so on through p. 10, '*N° 9.*'.

HEADLINE: pp. 2–10, 'Piano-Forte.'.

FOOTLINE: p. 2, '(W & C° N° 959)' [almost illegible]; pp. 3–8, 'CHOPIN, Souvenir de la Pologne. N° 2. « (W & C° N° 959.)'; p. 9, 'CHOPIN, Souvenir de la Pologne. N° 2. (N° 959.) « | » (W & C° N° 956.) [*sic*]'; p. 10, CHOPIN, Souvenir de la Pologne. N° 2. « (N° 959) WESSEL & C° '.

PLATES: Up to p. 10, the plates are the same as those of 7-W-1.

STAMPS: publisher, style W/E (see Appendix 8); dealer, Scheurmann, London (see Appendix 8). The publisher stamp is on the recto page of every leaf.

1. *Date:* Wessel inference (date code W2, p. 17).
2. The collective title page of this score lacks the line "Solo & Duet" after "Piano Forte", and does not have the columns of prices of duets. In this respect it corresponds to 6-W-2.
3. Previous Wessel editions of Op. 7 do not include the fifth mazurka, in C major, which here appears on p. 10. See notes in 6-W-1 for further comments about Wessel's editions of Opp. 6 and 7.
4. Pagination with [1] (rather than [i]) for the title page is unusual in Wessel's Chopin editions.
5. This edition was apparently unknown to Chominski & Turlo (p. 36).

TRIO IN G MINOR FOR PIANO, VIOLIN, AND CELLO
Opus 8

Paris: M. Schlesinger (1344) 1833	*Composed* 1828–29
Leipzig: Kistner (999) 1832	Brown 25
London: Wessel (924) 1833	Chominski & Turlo 206

Paris: **M. Schlesinger (1344) [= 1833]** **8-mS-1** **M312.C54 T82**

Premier Trio | pour Piano, Violon et Violoncelle | DÉDIÉ | *à son Altesse Monsieur le Prince* | Antoine Radziwill | PAR | FRÉD. CHOPIN. | *Œuv: 8 « » Prix: 12 f.* | *Propriété des Editeurs.* | *PARIS, Chez Maurice* SCHLESINGER, *Md de Musique, Edr des Œuvres de Mozart, Rossini, &c.* | *Rue de Richelieu, 97* | *LEIPZIG, Chez KISTNER.*

Piano: 16 leaves (353 x 270 mm): pp. [i] engr title page, [ii, 1] blank, 2–28 engr music, [29, 30] blank.

CAPTION TITLE: p. 2, 'CHOPIN Op: 8. ÷ 1er Trio. «'.

SUB-CAPTION: p. 2, 'TRIO.'.

FOOTLINE: p. 2, 'Chopin 1r Trio Op: 8. « M.S. 1344. » Maurice Schlesinger Rue de Richelieu No 97.'; pp. 3–28, 'M.S. 1344.'.

Violino: 3 leaves (353 x 270 mm): pp. 1–5 engr music, [6] blank.

CAPTION TITLE: p. 1, same as Piano.

SUB-CAPTION: p. 1, same as Piano.

HEADLINE: pp. 1–5, 'VIOLINO.'.

FOOTLINE: p. 1, 'CHOPIN op: 8. 1er Trio « M.S. 1344. » Maurice Schlesinger rue de Richelieu No 97.'; pp. 2–5, 'M.S. 1344.'.

Violoncello: 3 leaves (353 x 270 mm): pp. 1–5 engr music, [6] blank.

CAPTION TITLE: p. 1, same as Piano.

SUB-CAPTION: p. 1, same as Piano.

HEADLINE: pp. 1–5, 'VIOLONCELLO.'.

FOOTLINE: p. 1, same as Violino.

WRAPPER (blue): pp. [1] same as title page, [2, 3] blank, [4] advt.

ADVT: wrapper p. [4], 'BRANDUS ET Ce, EDITEURS, 103, RUE RICHELIEU. | MUSIQUE DE VIOLON | OEuvres de CH. DE BÉRIOT.'.

STAMPS: successor, style BD/C (see Appendix 8).

---

1. *Date:* first-edition inference (date code fe, p. 17); also see note 3.
2. The piano part has only the piano staves.
3. The Brandus wrapper dates from after 1850, and the publisher's stamp from after 1857. However, this score appears to be printed from Schlesinger's original, unaltered plates, and there is no evidence it is not a first edition.

Leipzig: **Kistner (999) [= 1832]** **8-Ki-1** **M312.C54 T81**

Premier | TRIO | pour | Pianoforte, Violon et Violoncelle | composé et dédié | à son Altesse Monsieur le Prince | ANTOINE RADZIWILL | par | FRÉD. CHOPIN. | Oeuv: 8. « » Pr. 1 Rthlr. 20 Gr. | Propriété des Editeurs. | Enregistré aux Archives de l'Union. | *Leipzig, chez Fr. Kistner,* | *Paris, chez M. Schlesinger.* | *999.*

Pianoforte: 14 leaves (343 x 267 mm): pp. [1] lith title page, 2–28 engr music.

CAPTION TITLE: p. 2, '» F. Chopin. Op. 8.'.

SUB-CAPTION: p. 2, '1er | TRIO.'.

FOOTLINE: pp. 2–28, '999'.

IMPOSITION: one section of seven nested bifolia.

Violino: 3 leaves (341 x 266 mm): pp. 1–5 engr music, [6] blank.

CAPTION TITLE: p. 1, same as piano.

SUB-CAPTION: p. 1, same as piano.

HEADLINE: pp. 1–5, 'VIOLINO.'.

FOOTLINE: pp. 1–5, same as piano.

Violoncello: 3 leaves (342 x 266 mm): pp. 1–5 engr music, [6] blank.

CAPTION TITLE: p. 1, same as piano.

SUB-CAPTION: p. 1, same as piano.

HEADLINE: pp. 1–5, 'VIOLONCELLO.'.

FOOTLINE: pp. 1–5, same as piano.

STAMPS: none.

INSCRIPTIONS: owner's signature "O. Goldschmidt" in the upper-right corner of the title page and on the first page of each part. Otto Goldschmidt (1829–1907) was a pianist, composer and conductor, whose wife was Jenny Lind (1820–1887). He met Chopin in Paris a year before the latter's death.

ANNOTATIONS: In the Adagio movement of the piano part, the violin and cello staves are interlineated by hand, presumably by Goldschmidt.

1. *Date:* first-edition inference (date code fe, p. 17).
2. The piano part has only the piano staves.

NOCTURNES IN B FLAT MINOR, E FLAT MAJOR, B MAJOR
Opus 9

Paris: M. Schlesinger (1287) 1833 — *Composed* 1832
Leipzig: Kistner (995) 1832 — Brown 54
London: Wessel (916) (917) 1833 — Chominski & Turlo 108

Paris: M. Schlesinger (1287) [= 1833] — **9-mS-1** — **M25.C54 N58**

TROIS NOCTURNES | Pour Le Piano | *DÉDIÉS A* | *Madame Camille Pleyel* | *PAR* | Frédéric Chopin | *A.L.* | *Opéra 9.* « » *Prix: 6 f* | *Propriété des Editeurs.* | *PARIS, chez* Maurice Schlesinger, *Md. de Musique, Editeur des Œuvres de Mozart, Rossini, Hummel &c. Rue Richelieu, 79* [*sic*]. | *Leipzig, Chez Kistner* | *M.S. 1287.*

8 leaves (335 x 256 mm): [i] engr title page, [ii, 1] blank, 2–13 engr music, [14] blank.

CAPTION TITLE: p. 2, 'F. CHOPIN Op: 9. ÷ Trois Nocturnes. « 1er. NOCTURNE.'; p. 6, '2d. NOCTURNE.'; p. 8, '3me. NOCTURNE.'.

FOOTLINE: pp. 2–13, 'M.S. 1287'.

STAMPS: publisher, style mS/A (see Appendix 8); dealer, Filliette, Boulogne.

ANNOTATIONS: handwritten "2" on each recto page.

1. *Date:* first-edition inference (date code fe, p. 17).
2. The number "79" in the address on the title page is an engraver's error for 97.

Paris: Brandus (M.S. 1287) [1851–58] — **9-Bra-1** — **M25.C54 N5902**

3 | NOCTURNES | POUR | LE PIANO | *Dédiés à* | Madame Camille Pleyel | PAR | F. CHOPIN | *A. Lafont.* | *Op: 9.* « » *Prix: 7 f. 50 c.* | *À PARIS,* | *BRANDUS et Cie. Editeurs,* | *103. Rue Richelieu* | *St. Petersbourg, Maison Brandus.* « » *Leipzig, Kistner.*

8 leaves (329 x 256 mm): [i] engr title page, [ii, 1] blank, 2–13 engr music, [14] blank.

CAPTION TITLE: p. 2, 'F. CHOPIN Op: 9. ÷ Trois Nocturnes. « 1re. NOCTURNE.'; p. [6], '2d. NOCTURNE.'; p. 8, '3me. NOCTURNE.'.

FOOTLINE: pp. 2–13, 'M.S. 1287.'.

STAMPS: successor, style BD/B (see Appendix 8).

1. *Date:* The lower limit for the date is implied by the address (Table 5A), the upper limit by the publisher stamp.
2. The page number is "2" on p. [6]; it is missing on p. [7].
3. The music plates appear to be the same as those of 9-mS-1.

Leipzig: **Kistner (995) [= 1832]** | **9-Ki-3** | **M25.C54 N5908**

TROIS | NOCTURNES | pour le | Pianoforte | composés et dédiés à Madame | CAMILLE PLEYEL | par | FRÉD. CHOPIN. | *Oeuvre 9.* « » *Pr. 14 Gr.* | Propriété des Editeurs. | Enregistré aux Archives de l'Union. | *Leipzig, chez Fr. Kistner.* | *Paris, chez M. Schlesinger.* | *995.*

7 leaves (321 x 255 mm): pp. [1] lith title page, 2–13 engr music, [14] blank.

CAPTION TITLE: p. 2, '» F. Chopin. Op. *9.*'.

SUB-CAPTION: p. 2, '1$^{\underline{er}}$ | NOCTURNE.'; p. 6, '2$^{\underline{d}}$ | NOCTURNE.'; p. 8, '3$^{\underline{me}}$ | NOCTURNE.'.

FOOTLINE: pp. 2–13, '*995*'.

STAMPS: dealer, Tschertschenthaler, Innsbruck.

1. *Date:* first-edition inference (date code fe, p. 17).
2. This score corresponds to Hob-207.

Leipzig: **Kistner (995) [1841–45?]** | **9-Ki-1** | **M25.C54 N6 c.1**

The transcription of this title page is the same as that of 9-Ki-3, except here the price is *"Pr. 17 1/2 Ngr."* and there is an additional line "*N$^{\underline{o}}$ 2 séparément – 5 Ngr.*" at the end.

7 leaves (323 x 257 mm): pp. [1] lith title page, 2–13 engr music, [14] blank.

CAPTION TITLE: p. 2, '» F. Chopin. Op. *9.*'.

SUB-CAPTION: p. 2, '1$^{\underline{er}}$ | NOCTURNE.'; p. 6, '2$^{\underline{d}}$ | NOCTURNE.'; p. 8, '3$^{\underline{me}}$ | NOCTURNE.'.

FOOTLINE: pp. 2–13, '*995*'.

STAMPS: none.

1. *Date:* currency inference (date code c2, p. 17), but see 6-Ki-2, note 2.
2. This score corresponds to Hob-208. It is from the same plates as 9-Ki-3, except for the last line of the title page, which is not present in 9-Ki-3.
3. See Chominski & Turlo p. 139 for a discussion of various Kistner re-issues.

Leipzig: **Kistner (995) [1841–45?]** | **9-Ki-2** | **M25.C54 N6 c.2**

The transcription of this title page is the same as that of 9-Ki-1.

7 leaves (321 x 250 mm): pp. [1] lith title page, 2–13 engr music, [14] blank.

CAPTION TITLE: p. 2, '» F. Chopin Op. 9.' (slanted backward).

SUB-CAPTION: p. 2, '1$^{\underline{er}}$ | NOCTURNE.'; p. 6, '2$^{\underline{de}}$ | NOCTURNE.'; p. 8, '3$^{\underline{me}}$ | NOCTURNE.'.

FOOTLINE: pp. 2–13, '*995*'.

STAMPS: dealer, Krompholz, Berne.

9-Ki-2 *(continued)*

9-Ki-2 *(concluded)*

1. *Date:* currency inference (date code c2, p. 17), but see 6-Ki-2, note 2.
2. The layout of this score is the same as that of 9-Ki-1, but the engravings are different. Since the music plates of 9-Ki-1 are the same as those of the first edition 9-Ki-3, it is likely that 9-Ki-2 is later than 9-Ki-1.

***Leipzig:* Kistner (995) [1841–45?]** | **9#2-Ki-1** | **M25.C54 N6102**

The transcription of this title page is the same as that of 9-Ki-1.

2 leaves (323 x 252 mm): pp. [i] lith title page, 6–7 engr music, [8] blank.

CAPTION TITLE: none.

SUB-CAPTION: p. 6, '2de | NOCTURNE.'.

FOOTLINE: pp. 6–7, '*995*'.

STAMPS: none.

1. *Date:* currency inference (date code c2, p. 17), but see 6-Ki-2, note 2.
2. This score's music plates appear to be identical to those of 9-Ki-2, except that they consist of only one folio, having only the second nocturne, with p. 6 on the verso of the title page.

***Leipzig:* Kistner (3616) [*ca* 1869]** | **9-Ki-4** | **M25.C54 N62**

TROIS | NOCTURNES | pour le | Pianoforte | composés et dédiés | à Madame Camille Pleyel |
PAR | FRÉD. CHOPIN. | OP. 9. « » (2ME EDITION) PR. 10 Ngr. NETTO |
Propriété de l'Editeur. | Enregistré aux Archives de l'Union. | LEIPZIG, FR. KISTNER. |
(MEDAILLE D'OR DE L'EMPEREUR D'AUTRICHE.) | 3616.

6 leaves (260 x 167 mm): pp. [i] lith title page, 2–13 lith music, [14] blank.

CAPTION TITLE: p. 2, '» F. CHOPIN Op. 9.'.

SUB-CAPTION: p. 2, '1er | NOCTURNE.'; p. 6, '2me | NOCTURNE.'; p. 8, '3me | NOCTURNE.'.

FOOTLINE: p. 2, 'Stich & Druck von Fr. Kistner in Leipzig. « 3616'; pp. 3–13, '3616'.

STAMPS: none.

1. *Date:* based on the plate number (Table 5C).
2. According to Chominski & Turlo (p. 139), the "2ME EDITION" is Kistner's final form of Op. 9.
3. This octavo edition is in a small format (26 x 17 cm), perhaps designed for reading rather than playing.

London: Wessel (916) [*ca* 1840] 9#1,2-W-1 M25.C54 N613

N° [handwritten "7"] OF | WESSEL & C°.'s COMPLETE COLLECTION | OF | *the Compositions* | OF | FREDERIC CHOPIN | FOR THE | Piano Forte. | Solo & Duet | [list of works, Wessel 1–6] | 7 "MURMURES DE LA SEINE" *1st Set of Notturnos,* } *as played by* ÷ *M.* LISZT *at* ÷ *his Concerts.* { *Op. 9. 2/6* [*Duet*] *3/–* | [list of works, Wessel 8 [2nd set] –45] | *Ent. Sta. Hall.* « *Copyrights.* » *Price, Solo* [handwritten "2/6"] ÷ " *Duet* [blank] | *LONDON,* | WESSEL & C° *Importers and Publishers of,* FOREIGN MUSIC, | *(by special Appointment) to, H.R.H. the Duchess of Kent.* | N° 67, Frith Street, Corner of Soho Square.

6 leaves (335 x 253 mm): pp. [i] engr title page, [ii] blank, [1] advt, 2–7 engr music, [8] blank.

CAPTION TITLE: p. 1, '*LES MURMURES de la SEINE.* | N° 1 de | *TROIS NOCTURNES* Composés par *FRED: CHOPIN.*'; p. 6, the same except with "N° 2".

FOOTLINE: p. 2, '(W & C° N° 916.)'; pp. 3–5, 'Chopin, Murmures de la Seine. N° *1.* « (W & C° N° 916.)'; p. 6, 'Book. 1. « (W & C° N° 916.)'; p. 7, 'Chopin, Murmures de la Seine. N° *1.* (N° 916.) Wessel & C° N° 67, Frith Street, Soho Square.'.

ADVT: p. [1], '[clipped to] THE WORKS OF BEETHOVEN, CHOPIN, LISZT, &c. PIANO SOLO AND ORGAN MUSIC. | No. 67, FRITH STREET, CORNER OF SOHO SQUARE.'. The list of Chopin works for piano solo ends with Op. 42. It includes the present work, Op. 9 (1st set), but with 8 as the opus number. This conflicts with a separate list — the "Series of Modern Trios" — the first entry of which is Chopin's Op. 8. See 9#3-W-1, note 3.

STAMPS: publisher, style W/C? (see Appendix 8).

1. *Date:* The date of this issue is inferred from the last work listed on the title page, Op. 42, published by Wessel in 1840. It is consistent with the address and advertisement.

London: Wessel (917) [= 1833] 9#3-W-1 M25.C54 N612

LES MURMURES DE LA SEINE | TROIS NOCTURNES, | pour le | Piano Forte, | LIV. 1, Contenant, | *N° 1, en D Majeur, N° 2, E Majeur,* | LIV. II, | *N° 3 en B Majeur,* | Dediés à | Madame Camille Pleyel, | par | FREDERIC CHOPIN. | *Ent. Sta. Hall.* | OP. 9. « Book [handwritten "2"] » Price 2/6 ea. | *By the same Author:* | *Grand Var. "La ci darem", "Album des Pianistes N° 17", Grand Trio, Piano,* | *Violin & Violoncello, Op. 8. "Souvenir de la Pologne", Four Mazurkas,* | *LONDON,* | WESSEL & C° Importers and Publishers of FOREIGN MUSIC, | *(by special Appointment) to H.R.H. the Duchess of Kent,* | N° 6, Frith Street, Soho Square.

5 leaves (335 x 253 mm): pp. [i] engr title page, [ii] blank, [1] advt, 2–7 engr music, [8] blank.

CAPTION TITLE: p. 2, '*LES MURMURES de la SEINE.* | N° 3 de | *TROIS NOCTURNES* Composés par *FRED: CHOPIN.*'.

FOOTLINE: p. 2, '(W & C° N° 917.)'; pp. 3–6, 'Chopin, Murmures de la Seine. N° 3. « (W & C° N° 917.)'; p. 7, 'Chopin, Murmures de la Seine. N° 3. (N° 917.) Wessel & C° N° 6, Frith Street, Soho Square.'.

ADVT: p. [1], 'WESSEL and C°.'s | NEW PUBLICATIONS OF | *FLUTE AND CLARINET MUSIC,* | to be had at their Foreign Music Warehouse, N° 6, Frith St Soho Sq: London.'.

9#3-W-1 *(continued)*

9#3-W-1 *(concluded)*

STAMPS: publisher, styles W/A and W/B (see Appendix 8).

1. *Date:* first-edition inference (date code fe, p. 17). Brown (p. 59) asserts that Wessel first issued Op. 9 without opus number. This Book 2 has the opus number, but there is no evidence it is not the first issue.
2. The title page gives incorrect keys for the two nocturnes of Book 1.
3. Op. 9 is the second of Chopin's works issued by Wessel, preceded only by Op. 2.
4. Only Wessel issued Op. 9 in two books.
5. According to Brown (p. 27), "Occasionally Wessel (e.g. in 1841) advertised the first two nocturnes of Op. 9 as 'Op. 8', calling the third nocturne 'Op. 9'.".

London: **Wessel (917) [1848–56]** **9#3-W-2** **M25.C54 N6132**

Nº [handwritten "8"] OF | WESSEL & Cº.'s COMPLETE COLLECTION | OF | *the Compositions* | OF | FREDERIC CHOPIN | FOR THE | Piano Forte. | [list of works, Wessel 1–7 Book 1] | 8 ___ *2nd Set of do.* ___ *Op. 9 2/6* | [list of works, Wessel 9–71] | *Ent. Sta. Hall. « Copyrights. »* *Price ,* [handwritten "2/6"] | *LONDON,* | WESSEL & Cº *Importers and Publishers of* FOREIGN MUSIC, | *(by special Appointment) to H.R.H. the Duchess of Kent.* | Nº 229, Regent Street, Corner of Hanover Street.

5 leaves (333 x 250 mm): pp. [i] engr title page, [ii] blank, [1] advt, 2–7 engr music, [8] blank.

CAPTION TITLE: p. 2, '*LES MURMURES de la SEINE,* | Nº 3 de | *TROIS NOCTURNES* Composés par *FRED: CHOPIN.*'.

FOOTLINE: p. 2, '(W & Cº Nº 917.)'; pp. 3–6, 'Chopin, Murmures de la Seine, Nº 3. « (W & Cº Nº 917.)'; p. 7, 'Chopin, Murmures de la Seine, Nº 3. (Nº 917.) Wessel & Cº '.

ADVT: p. [1], '[cut down to] WESSEL & CO.S CATALOGUE OF MODERN PIANOFORTE WORKS, CONTINUED FROM PAGES A. B. C. E. & S.'. There are no Chopin works.

STAMPS: publisher, style W/D? (see Appendix 8).

1. *Date:* Wessel inference (date code W1, p. 17).
2. This collective title page lacks the line "Solo & Duet" after "Piano Forte", and does not have the columns of prices of duets. In this respect it corresponds to 6-W-2 and 7-W-3.

Milan: **Lucca (1557) [*ca* 1836]** **9-Lu-1** **M25.C54 N5906**

TROIS | Nocturnes | POUR | PIANO | *dediés a Madame* | CAMILLE PLEYEL | PAR | FR. CHOPIN | *1557 « » Fr. 3* | *Op. 9* | *Propriete de l'Editeur* | MILAN F. LUCCA | *Florence, Dacci « Turin, Blanchi » Naples Girard et C.*

8 leaves (332 x 254 mm): p. [i] engr title page, [ii] blank, 1–13 engr music, [14] blank.

CAPTION TITLE: p. 1, 'TROIS NOCTURNES ÷ Nº 1. » CHOPIN. Op. 9.'; p. 6, '2me NOCTURNE'; p. 8, '3me NOCTURNE'.

FOOTLINE: p. 1, '*Milan chez F. Lucca* « c 1557 c'; pp. 2–13, 'c 1557 c'.

STAMPS: none.

1. *Date:* Chominski & Turlo, p. 272.

ETUDES
Opus 10

Paris: M. Schlesinger (1399) 1833
Leipzig: Kistner (1018) (1019) 1833
London: Wessel (960) (961) 1833

Composed 1829–33
Brown 42
Chominski & Turlo 14

Paris: **M. Schlesinger (1399) [*ca* 1837]** **10-mS-1** **M25.C54 E71**

ETUDES | Pour le Piano | *Dediées à son Ami* | F. LISZT | *PAR* | Fred. Chopin | *1er Livre.* | *Propriété des Editeurs* | *Op. 10* « » *Prix: 18 f* | *PARIS, chez* MAURICE SCHLESINGER, *Md de Musique, Editeur des Œuvres de Mozart Rossini &c., Rue Richelieu 97* | *Leipzick, chez Kistner* | » *A. L.*

28 leaves (350 x 270 mm): pp. [i] engr title page, [ii] blank, 1–54 engr music.

CAPTION TITLE: p. 1, 'F. CHOPIN. Op. 10. ÷ Etudes. «'.

SUB-CAPTION: p. 1, 'No 1.'; and so on through p. 49, 'No 12.'.

FOOTLINE: pp. 1–54, 'M.S. 1399.'.

PLATES: The title-page impression is weak and in some places barely legible.

IMPOSITION: The imposition of 10-mS-1 is unusual: it consists of 14 sections, each with one bifolium. A final blank section may have been included originally. (It is absent also in Hob-214.)

STAMPS: publisher, style mS/B (see Appendix 8).

1. *Date:* based on *"1er Livre"* on the title page (see notes 2 and 3).
2. The first impression of the Schlesinger edition has "J." instead of "F." Liszt on the title page, as in Livre I of 10-Ki-2. This impression corresponds to Hob-214 (shown in plate 16, p. 97), and is noted by Grabowski (1994, p. 18). Grabowski also notes a second impression, with "J." corrected to "F." Liszt. This can be seen in the British Library copy with shelflist h.471.j.(14.). The "J." Liszt error also affected the title pages of the other two publishers (Livre I of 10-Ki-2, and 10-W-2), but there appears to be no clear evidence as to when the correction was first made.
3. Unlike 10-mS-1, neither of the impressions identified in note 2 has *"1er Livre"* on the title page. The insertion of this line probably was made in about 1837, the time of publication of the Etudes Op. 25, the title page of which is marked "Deuxieme livre d'Etudes". Grabowski (*loc. cit.*) refers to the issue that corresponds to 10-mS-1 as the third impression.
4. Only Schlesinger issued Op. 10 in one volume.

Paris: **H. Lemoine (2775) [*ca* 1842]** **10-hL-1** **M25.C54 E683**

ETUDES | Pour le Piano | *Dediées à son Ami* | F. LISZT | *PAR* | Fred. Chopin | *1er Livre.* | *Propriété des Editeurs* | *Op. 10* « » *Prix: 18 f* | *PARIS, chez Henry LEMOINE, Professeur de Piano, et Editeur de Musique,* | *Rue de l'Echelle. No 9.* | *2775. HL.*

28 leaves (340 x 260 mm): pp. [i] engr title page, [ii] blank, 1–54 engr music.

CAPTION TITLE: p. 1, 'F. CHOPIN. Op. 10. ÷ Etudes. «'.

10-hL-1 *(continued)*

10-hL-1 *(concluded)*

SUB-CAPTION: p. 1, 'Nº 1.'; and so on through p. 49, 'Nº 12.'.

FOOTLINE: p. 1, 'Paris chez Henry Lemoine, « 2775. HL. » Rue de l'Echelle Nº 9.'; pp. 2–54, '2775. HL.'. The plate number is off-center on many pages.

PLATES: The title-page impression is weak and in some places barely legible. However, the music-plate impressions are excellent. The plates are those of M. Schlesinger (see note 2).

STAMPS: successor, style aL/A (see Appendix 8). See note 3.

BOUND WITH: 25-hL-1 (plate number 2776).

BINDING: contemporary, red quarter calf; on the backstrip: 'CHOPIN | ÉTUDES | POUR | LE PIANO'.

---

1. *Date:* based on the plate number (Devriès & Lesure, p. 280); also see note 2.
2. "In 1842 Lemoine bought the copyright to the *Études* Op. 10 and Op. 25 and to the *Waltz* Op. 18 from Maurice Schlesinger. He used the original plates in his impressions of these compositions and inserted his firm's name and address on the title pages, also changing the publisher's numbers of Op. 10 (HL 2775), Op. 25 (HL 2776), Op. 18 (HL 2777). The musical text is identical to Schlesinger's version." (Grabowski, 1954, p. 28). Note the similarity of the title-page transcriptions of 10-mS-1 and 10-hL-1.
3. In the center of the dealer stamp is 'B 77745'. This is a stamp of Achille Lemoine, son of Henry Lemoine, at '256 Rue Sᵗ Honoré', address of the firm after the death of Henry in 1854 (Devriès & Lesure, p. 278).

Leipzig: **Kistner (1018) (1019) [= 1833]** 10-Ki-2 **M25.C54 E7 c.2**

Livre I (etudes 1–6)

Douze | GRANDES ÉTUDES | pour le | Pianoforte | composées et dédiées | À SON AMI J. [*sic*] LISZT | par | FRÉD. CHOPIN. | Oeuvre 10. « Liv. I. » Pr. 1 1/6 Rthlr. | Propriété des Editeurs. | Enregistré aux Archives de l'Union. | *Leipzig, chez Fr. Kistner.* | *Paris, chez M. Schlesinger.* | *1018. 1019.*

14 leaves (324 x 258 mm): pp. [1] lith title page, 2–27 engr music, [28] blank.

CAPTION TITLE: p. 2, '» F. Chopin. Op. *10.* Liv. *1.*'.

SUB-CAPTION: p. 2, 'Nº 1.'; and so on through p. 25, 'Nº 6.'.

FOOTLINE: pp. 2–27, '*1018*'.

Livre II (etudes 7–12)

The title page is identical to that of Livre I, except with "Liv. II." instead of "Liv. I.", and "F. LISZT" instead of "J. LISZT".

14 leaves (325 x 259 mm): pp. [1] lith title page, 2–27 engr music, [28] blank.

CAPTION TITLE: p. 2, '» F. Chopin. Op. *10.* Liv. *2.*'.

SUB-CAPTION: p. 2, 'Nº 7.'; and so on through p. 23, 'Nº 12.'.

FOOTLINE: pp. 2–27, '*1019*'.

STAMPS: none.

BOUND WITH: The two books are bound together, but Livre II precedes Livre I in the binding.

---

1. *Date:* first-edition inference (date code fe, p. 17); also see note 2.

10-Ki-2 *(continued)*

10-Ki-2 *(concluded)*

2. In this score, Livre II, with the correction "F." Liszt, is slightly later than Livre I, with "J." Liszt, but it is not known when the correction was made. (The copies described by Chominski & Turlo, p. 85, and by Fuld, p. 219, have "F." in both books, as do 10-Ki-1 and Hob-212.)
3. In Livre I, etude 1, p. 4, bar 5, the third from last note is G. (It should be F, as in 10-mS-1.)

Leipzig: **Kistner (1018) (1019) [*ca* 1833]** **10-Ki-1** **M25.C54 E7 c.1**

Livre I (etudes 1–6)

The transcription of this title page is the same as that of 10-Ki-2 Livre I, except here Liszt's initial is "F." instead of "J".

14 leaves (312 x 257 mm): pp. [1] lith title page, 2–27 engr music, [28] blank.

CAPTION TITLE: p. 2, '» F. Chopin. Op. *10.* Liv. *1.*'.

SUB-CAPTION: p. 2, 'Nº 1.'; and so on through p. 25, 'Nº 6.'.

FOOTLINE: pp. 2–27, '*1018*'.

Livre II (etudes 7–12)

The title page is identical to that of Livre I, except with "Liv. II." instead of "Liv. I.".

14 leaves (312 x 257 mm): pp. [1] lith title page, 2–27 engr music, [28] blank.

CAPTION TITLE: p. 2, '» F. Chopin. Op. *10.* Liv. *2.*'.

SUB-CAPTION: p. 2, 'Nº 7.'; and so on through p. 23, 'Nº 12.'.

FOOTLINE: pp. 2–27, '*1019*'.

STAMPS: "Plaidy" (in a 14 x 19 mm oval).

BOUND WITH: The two books are bound together.

BINDING: library cloth.

1. *Date:* first-edition inference (date code fe, p. 17). However, the date is somewhat uncertain, because it is not known when "J." Liszt was corrected to "F." Liszt (see 10-Ki-2, note 2).
2. See 10-Ki-2, note 3.

Leipzig: **Kistner (1018) (1019) [1841–45?]** **10-Ki-3** **M25.C54 E713 c.1**

Livre I (etudes 1–6)

DOUZE | GRANDES ÉTUDES | POUR LE | PIANOFORTE | composées et dédiées |
À SON AMI | *F. LISZT* | PAR | FRÉD. CHOPIN. | Ouevre 10. « Liv. I » Pr. 1 Thlr. 5 Ngr. |
Propriété des Editeurs. | Enregistré aux Archives de l'Union. | LEIPSIC, CHEZ FR. KISTNER. |
PARIS, CHEZ M. SCHLESINGER. | *1018. 1019.* | Nouvelle Edition. |
Fr. Krätzschmer [slanted backward, under the decorative frame]

14 leaves (331 x 255 mm): pp. [1] lith title page, 2–27 engr music, [28] blank

CAPTION TITLE: p. 2, '» F. Chopin Op. 10. [slanted backward] Liv. 1.'.

SUB-CAPTION: p. 2, 'Nº 1.'; and so on, through p. 25, 'Nº 6.'.

FOOTLINE: pp. 2–27, '*1018*'.

10-Ki-3 *(continued)*

10-Ki-3 *(concluded)*

Livre II (etudes 7–12)

The title page is identical to that of Livre I, and the "I" in "Liv. I" has been changed by hand to "II".

14 leaves (331 x 255 mm): pp. [1] lith title page, 2–27 engr music, [28] blank.

CAPTION TITLE: p. 2, '» F. Chopin Op. 10. [slanted backward] Liv. 2.'.

SUB-CAPTION: p. 2, 'N° 7.'; and so on, through p. 23, 'N° 12.'.

FOOTLINE: pp. 2–27, '*1019*'.

STAMPS: none.

ANNOTATIONS: owner's signature; handwritten "46." on title page of Livre I, and "47." on Livre II.

BOUND WITH: The two books are bound together.

BINDING: old blue boards, quarter calf; gold-stamped "Otto Bacher." on the front cover.

---

1. *Date:* currency inference (date code c2, p. 17), but see 6-Ki-2, note 2.
2. According to Chominski & Turlo (p. 445), there are at least three different issues of the "Nouvelle Edition", all engraved.

Leipzig: **Kistner (1018) (1019) [1841–45?]** 10-Ki-4 **M25.C54 E713 c.2**

Livre I (etudes 1–6)

DOUZE | GRANDES ÉTUDES | POUR LE | PIANOFORTE | composées et dédiées | À SON AMI | *F. LISZT* | PAR | FRÉD. CHOPIN. | Ouevre 10. « Liv. I » Pr. 1 Thlr. 5 Ngr. | Propriété des Editeurs. | Enregistré aux Archives de l'Union. | LEIPZIG, FR. KISTNER. | PARIS, M. SCHLESINGER. | 1018. 1019. | Nouvelle Edition.

14 leaves (330 x 263 mm): pp. [1] lith title page, 2–27 engr music, [28] blank

CAPTION TITLE: p. 2, '» F. Chopin Op. 10. Liv. 1. [all slanted backward]'.

SUB-CAPTION: p. 2, 'N° 1.'; and so on, through p. 25, 'N° 6.'.

FOOTLINE: pp. 2–27, '1018'.

Livre II (etudes 7–12)

The title page is identical to that of Livre I, and the "I" in "Liv. I" has been changed by hand to "II".

14 leaves (330 x 263 mm): pp. [1] lith title page, 2–27 engr music, [28] blank.

CAPTION TITLE: p. 2, '» F. Chopin Op. 10. Liv. 2. [all slanted backward]'.

SUB-CAPTION: p. 2, 'N° 7.'; and so on, through p. 23, 'N° 12.'.

FOOTLINE: pp. 2–27, '1019'.

STAMPS: dealer, illegible.

BOUND WITH: The two books are in separate enclosures.

---

1. *Date:* currency inference (date code c2, p. 17), but see 6-Ki-2, note 2.
2. This score differs slightly from 10-Ki-3. For example, the title page lacks "CHEZ" in the imprint line, and the plate numbers are not in italics.

10-Ki-4 *(continued)*

10-Ki-4 *(concluded)*

3. According to Chominski & Turlo (p. 445), there are at least three different issues of the "Nouvelle Edition", all engraved.

London: Wessel (960) (961) [1836–39] 10-W-2 M25.C54 E68

Book 1 (etudes 1–6)

WESSEL & C^{os} | NEW & REVISED EDITION. | Douze | GRANDES ETUDES. | (en Deux Livraisons.) | *pour le* | Piano Forte, | *dediées à ses amis* | *J.* [*sic*] *LISZT, ET FERD. HILLER,* | Par | FREDERIC CHOPIN. | (de Varsovie.) | *Edited with additional fingering by his Pupil,* | I. [*sic*] FONTANA. | *Ent. Sta. Hall.* « Op. 10, Book. [handwritten "1"] » *Price 6/- each.* | *LONDON,* | WESSEL & Co *Importers of Foreign Music & Publishers of the Works of* | CZERNY, KUHLAU, HUMMEL, MAYSEDER, PIXIS, &c. | N° 6, Frith Street, Soho Square.

13 leaves (334 x 253 mm): pp. [i] engr title page, [ii] blank, [1] advt, 2–23 engr music, [24] blank.

CAPTION TITLE: p. 2, 'DOUZE GRANDES ETUDES dediées à J. [*sic*] LISZT et F. HILLER. | par | FRED. CHOPIN. | Edited with additional fingering by his Pupil | J. FONTANA.'.

SUB-CAPTION: p. 2, 'N^o I.'; and so on through p. 22, 'N° VI.'.

FOOTLINE: p. 2, '(W & Co N° 960)'; pp. 3–22, 'CHOPIN, Op: 10, N° 1. « » (W & Co N° 960)'; p. 23, 'CHOPIN, Op: 10, N° 1. « | (N° 960) WESSEL & Co N° 6, FRITH STREET, SOHO SQUARE.'.

ADVT: p. [1], 'PAGE A. | CATALOGUE OF WESSEL AND CO.'S CHOICE PUBLICATIONS OF MODERN PIANO-FORTE MUSIC. | N° 6, FRITH STREET, SOHO SQUARE, LONDON.' The lists include Chopin works through op. 27 (entry 84 in the series "L'Amateur Pianiste").

Book 2 (etudes 7–12)

The title page is identical to that of Book 1, but with handwritten "2" after "Book".

14 leaves (334 x 254 mm): pp. [i] engr title page, [ii] blank, [1] advt, 2–25 engr music, [26] blank.

CAPTION TITLE: p. 2, 'DOUZE GRANDES ÉTUDES dediées à J. [*sic*] LISZT et F. HILLER. | par | FRED. CHOPIN. | Edited with additional fingering by his Pupil | J. FONTANA. | Book 2. «'.

SUB-CAPTION: p. 2, 'N° VII.'; and so on through p. 21, 'N° XII.'.

FOOTLINE: p. 2, '(W & Co N° 961)'; pp. 3–24, 'CHOPIN, Op: 10, N° 2. « » (W & Co N° 961)'; p. 25, 'CHOPIN, Op: 10, N° 2. « | (N° 961) WESSEL & Co N° 6, FRITH STREET, SOHO SQUARE.'.

ADVT: p. [1], heading clipped; the lists include Chopin through Op. 20.

STAMPS: publisher, style W/C (see Appendix 8) on each title page.

BOUND WITH: The two books are in separate enclosures.

---

1. *Date:* The lower limit on the date is based on the advertisement in Book 1, which includes Op. 27, published by Wessel in 1836. The upper limit is based on the address (Table 5D).
2. Fontana's initial is "I" on the title page and "J" in the caption title. Liszt's initial is "J" in both places.

London: Wessel (960) (961) [1849–56] 10-W-1 M25.C54 E681

Book 1 (etudes 1–6)

Nº [handwritten "9"] OF | WESSEL & Cº.'s COMPLETE COLLECTION | OF | *the Compositions* | OF | FREDERIC CHOPIN | FOR THE | Piano Forte. | Solo & Duet | [list of works, Wessel 1–8] | 9 "DOUZE GRANDES ETUDES" *ded. to* LISZT *and* HILLER *with* | *add!. fingering by* I. [*sic*] FONTANA. *Bk 1 Op. 10. 6/–* | 10 " [*Bk*] *2 Op. 10. 6/–* | [list of works, Wessel 11–71] | *Ent. Sta. Hall. « Copyrights. » Price. Solo* [handwritten "6/"] ÷ " *Duet* [blank] | *LONDON,* | WESSEL & Cº *Importers and Publishers of* FOREIGN MUSIC, | *(by special Appointment) to H.R.H. the Duchess of Kent.* | Nº 229, Regent Street, Corner of Hanover Street.

12 leaves (344 x 253 mm): pp. [1] engr title page, 2–23 engr music, [24] advt. An extra blank leaf is tipped to the recto of the title page.

CAPTION TITLE: p. 2, 'DOUZE GRANDES ETUDES dediées à J. [*sic*] LISZT et F. HILLER. | par | FRED. CHOPIN. | Edited with additional fingering by his Pupil | J. FONTANA.'.

SUB-CAPTION: p. 2, 'Nº I.'; and so on through p. 22, 'Nº VI.'.

FOOTLINE: p. 2, '(W. & Cº Nº 960)'; pp. 3–22, 'CHOPIN, Op: 10, Nº 1. « » (W. & Cº Nº 960)'; p. 23, 'CHOPIN, Op: 10, Nº 1. « | (Nº 960) WESSEL & Cº '. The address on p. 23 appears to have been removed from the plate.

ADVT: p. [24], 'PAGE S. | WESSEL & Co.'s EDITIONS OF THE PIANOFORTE WORKS (SOLO) BY CHOPIN | HELLER, SCHULHOFF, KULLAK, AND AGUILAR.'. The list for Chopin consists of the 71 entries in Wessel's collection, and in addition, the Marche Funèbre extracted from Op. 35, which was issued by Wessel in 1849 (Brown, p. 119). In a footnore is the comment "An essay on the works of Frederic Chopin may be had on application to Wessel & Co.".

Book 2 (etudes 7–12)

The title page is identical to that of Book 1, but with handwritten "10" in the first line, instead of "9".

14 leaves (344 x 255 mm): pp. [i] engr title page, [ii] blank, [1] advt, 2–25 engr music, [26] blank.

CAPTION TITLE: p. 2, 'DOUZE GRANDES ETUDES dediées à J. [*sic*] LISZT et F. HILLER. | par | FRED. CHOPIN. | Edited with additional fingering by his Pupil | J. FONTANA.'.

SUB-CAPTION: p. 2, 'Nº VII.'; and so on through p. 21, 'Nº XII.'.

FOOTLINE: p. 2, '(W. & Cº Nº 961)'; pp. 3–24, 'CHOPIN, Op: 10, Nº 2. « » (W. & Cº Nº 961)'; p. 25, 'CHOPIN, Op: 10, Nº 2. « | (Nº 961) WESSEL & Cº '. The address on p. 25 appears to have been removed from the plate.

ADVT: p. [1], 'PAGE A. | CATALOGUE OF WESSEL & CO.'S CHOICE PUBLICATIONS OF MODERN PIANO-FORTE MUSIC.'. The lists include Chopin works through Op. 27 (entry 84 in the series "L'Amateur Pianiste").

STAMPS: publisher, style W/D (see Appendix 8) on each title page.

INSCRIPTIONS: book 1: "S R Sutherland | 30th Aug. 51. – 8th Feb. 55. | 2nd Feb. 56. | 9th May 1851.".

BOUND WITH: The two books are in the same enclosure but are not bound together.

1. *Date:* The lower limit on the date is based on the publication list in the advertisement of Book 1. The upper limit is based on the address (Table 5D).

Milan: **Lucca (1378) (1379) [*ca* 1836]** **10-Lu-1** **M22.C54 P93**

Livre I (etudes 1–6)

Douze | GRANDES ETUDES | pour le | Pianoforte | composées et dediées | A SON AMI F. LISZT | par | FRÉD. CHOPIN. | Op. 10. « Liv. I. » Fr 5.50 | 1378 = 79 « | MILAN | Chez F. LUCCA vis à vis la grand théâtre a la Scala

15 leaves (340 x 255 mm): pp. [i] lith title page, [ii, 1] blank, 2–27 engr music, [28] advt.

CAPTION TITLE: p. 2, ' » F. Chopin. Op: 10. Liv. 1.'.

SUB-CAPTION: p. 2, 'Nº 1.'; and so on through p. 25, 'Nº 6.'.

FOOTLINE: pp. 2–4, 'B 1378'; pp. 5–24, 'F 1378'; pp. 25–27, 'B 1378'.

ADVT: p. [28], 'ELENCO DELLA OPERA | DI CHOPIN, DÖHLER, DE MEYER, LISZT, PRUDENT, THALBERG, WILMERS. | *PUBLICATE DA FRANC. LUCCA*'. The Chopin list has Opp. 9, 10, 12, 14, 16, 18, 19, 20, 22, 23, 25, 27, 28, 30.

IMPOSITION: Leaf 8 is a singleton.

Livre II (etudes 7–12)

The title page is identical to that of Livre I (including "Liv. I" instead of Liv. II).

15 leaves (340 x 255 mm): pp. [i] lith title page, [ii] blank, [1] advt, 2–27 engr music, [28] advt.

CAPTION TITLE: none.

SUB-CAPTION: p. 2, 'Nº 7.'; and so on through p. 23, 'Nº 12.'.

FOOTLINE: pp. 2–18, 'F 1379'; p. 19, 'F 1378'; pp. 20–27, 'F 1379'.

ADVT: p. [1], 'OPERA TEORICHE, METODI, STUDJ E PRINCIPJ' (continued on p. [28]). The Chopin list has Opp. 10, 25, 28.

IMPOSITION: Leaf 8 is a singleton.

STAMPS: dealer, Ferrara, Nice (blind stamp on each title page).

BOUND WITH: 25-Lu-1 and 28-Ca-1.

BINDING: contemporary (?) quarter calf.

1. *Date:* Belotti (pp. 428–430) argues that the price Fr 5.50 corresponds to the first edition, which he dates 1836. In 1862 Lucca re-issued Op. 10 in a collection, at which time the price was Fr 5.00.
2. The title page was probably designed to apply to both books, but the engraver entered "I" after "Liv.", presumably intending a blank. The design strongly resembles that of the Kistner edition.
3. The two books of Op. 10 are the second and third of Lucca's publication of Chopin's works; the first is the waltz Op. 18 (18-Lu-1) (see Chominski & Turlo, p. 272).

CONCERTO IN E MINOR FOR PIANO AND ORCHESTRA
Opus 11

Paris: M. Schlesinger (1409) 1833
Leipzig: Kistner (1020–1022) 1833
London: Wessel (1086) 1834

Composed 1830
Brown 53
Chominski & Turlo 47

***Paris:* M. Schlesinger (1409) [= 1833]** | **11-mS-3** | **M37.C54 C694 c.2**

CONCERTO | Pour Le Piano | *avec accompagnement* | D'ORCHESTRE | *Dédié à Monsieur* | F. KALKBRENNER | *PAR* | Fréd. Chopin. | *Op: 11 ÷ Propriété des Editeurs.* « » *PRIX:* { *Avec Orchestre: 24* $\dot{.}^{f}$ *÷ Piano seul: 12* $\dot{.}^{f}$ | *PARIS, chez* MAURICE SCHLESINGER, *M^d de Musique Editeur des Œuvres de Mozart Rossini &c. Rue Richelieu N°. 97* | *Leipsick, chez Kistner.*

23 leaves (321 x 257 mm): pp. [i] engr title page, [ii, 1] blank, 2–44 engr music.

CAPTION TITLE: p. 2, 'F. CHOPIN Op: 11. ÷ Concerto. «'.

FOOTLINE: pp. 2–44, 'M.S. 1409.'.

IMPOSITION: The original final blank leaf is missing; a replacement has been supplied by a conservator.

STAMPS: publisher, style mS/B (see Appendix 8).

CONDITION: excellent.

1. *Date:* first-edition inference (date code fe, p. 17).
2. This score corresponds to the piano part of Hob-220 (which is the orchestral edition).

***Paris:* M. Schlesinger (1409) [= 1833]** | **11-mS-2** | **M37.C54 C694 c.1**

The transcription of this title page is the same as that of 11-mS-3.

24 leaves (320 x 250 mm): pp. [i] engr title page, [ii, 1] blank, 2–44 engr music, [45, 46] blank.

CAPTION TITLE: p. 2, 'F. CHOPIN Op: 11. ÷ Concerto. «'.

FOOTLINE: pp. 2–44, 'M.S. 1409.'.

STAMPS: publisher, style mS?/B? (see Appendix 8).

CONDITION: The title page is damaged, but the music pages are good, clear impressions. This copy was received in poor condition, having been badly mutilated by excessive use of paper tape in most margins, but except for the title page, it has been largely restored. Parts of the text of the title page are illegible, however.

1. *Date:* first-edition inference (date code fe, p. 17).
2. This score is identical to 11-mS-3.

Paris: M. Schlesinger (1409) [after 1845] 11-mS-1 M37.C54 C6942

The transcription of this title page is the same as that of 11-mS-3, except here there is an additional line "1ER" at the beginning, and the orchestral price is *"l'Orchestre: 20 f"* (instead of *"Avec Orchestre: 24 f"*).

23 leaves (318 x 249 mm): pp. [i] engr title page, [ii, 1] blank, 2–44 engr music.

CAPTION TITLE: p. 2, 'F. CHOPIN Op: 11. ÷ Concerto. «'.

FOOTLINE: pp. 2–44, 'M.S. 1409.'.

IMPOSITION: An odd number of leaves and a central singleton (leaf 12) imply that a final blank leaf was not intended. (Note that 11-mS-2 and 11-mS-3 are imposed without the singleton.) The gathering consists of one section of 11 nested bifolia and one singleton section.

STAMPS: successor, style Bra/B (see Appendix 8).

1. *Date:* based on "1ER" on the title page (see note 2).
2. The title of the first edition (11-mS-3) does not have "1ER" and has a higher price 24 f for the orchestral edition. Presumably "1ER" was added at or after publication of the second concerto in 1836, and on this basis 11-mS-1 must have been issued after 1835. However, Grabowski (1994, table on p. 33) cites an advertisement of 24 f in *Gazette Musicale* in 1844, and a price of 20 f in a Brandus catalogue in 1847. From this evidence he suggests (p. 32) *ca* 1847 for an issue such as 11-mS-1. He also states that "1ER" was added at the same time the price was changed. Here I assume only that it was Brandus who made these changes, and therefore that 11-mS-1 could have been issued any time after 1845 (Table 5A).

Leipzig: Kistner (1020. 1021. 1022) [= 1833] 11-Ki-1 M37.C54 C695

GRAND | CONCERTO | pour le | PIANOFORTE | avec Accompagnement d'Orchestre | ou de Quintuor ad libitum | composé et dédié à Monsieur | FRÉD. KALKBRENNER | par | FRÉD. CHOPIN. | *Oeuvre 11.* « » *Pr.* { *avec Orchestre 4 Rthlr. 12 Gr.* ÷ *avec Quintuor 3 Rthlr. 8 Gr.* ÷ *sans Accomp. 2 Rthlr.* | Propriété des Editeur*s*. | Enregistré aux Archives de l'Union. | *Leipzig, chez Fr. Kistner.* | *Paris, chez M. Schlesinger.* | *1020. 1021. 1022.* | *Exécuté par l'Auteur dans ses Concerts à Paris.*

23 leaves (322 x 251 mm): pp. [1] colored lith title page, 2–44 engr music, [45–46] blank.

CAPTION TITLE: p. 2, '» F. Chopin. Op. *11.*'.

SUB-CAPTION: p. 2, 'CONCERTO.'.

FOOTLINE: pp. 2–44, '*1020.1021.1022.*'.

STAMPS: none.

BINDING: contemporary boards, with handwritten label on front "G. Concerto | von Chopin | avec Accompagnement d'Orchestre | Brunswick". The owner may be (Maria) Therese Brunswick (1775–1861), friend and pupil of Beethoven.

1. *Date:* first-edition inference (date code fe, p. 17).
2. The title page has a 'sunburst' pattern in the background.
3. This score corresponds to Hob-.

Leipzig: Kistner (1020. 1021. 1022) [after 1833] 11-Ki-4 M37.C54 C6951

The transcription of this title page is the same as that of 11-Ki-1, except here the orchestral and quintet prices are stated respectively "*4 1/2 Thlr.*" and "*3 1/3 Thlr.*".

23 leaves (320 x 260 mm): pp. [1] lith title page, 2–44 engr music, [45–46] blank.

CAPTION TITLE: p. 2, '» F. Chopin. Op. *11.*'.

SUB-CAPTION: p. 2, 'CONCERTO.'.

FOOTLINE: pp. 2–44, '*1020.1021.1022.*'.

IMPOSITION: Leaf 12 is a singleton.

STAMPS: dealer, Sennewald, Warsaw (see Appendix 8).

1. *Date:* The date is based on the price, in which equivalent fractions of a Thaler replace the Groschen of 11-Ki-1. It is possible this change occurred at about the time Groschen were replaced by Neugroschen (1841), but before Neugroschen were in full circulation (see date code c1, p. 17).
2. The design of the title page is identical to that of 11-Ki-1 except that it lacks the sunburst background.
3. This edition is noted by Chominski & Turlo (p. 103). It is not in Hoboken.

Leipzig: Kistner (2340, 1020.1021.1022) [*ca* 1858] 11-Ki-3 M37.C54 C6954

The transcription of this title page is the same as that of 11-Ki-4.

24 leaves (338 x 270 mm): pp. [1] lith title page, 2–47 lith music, [48] blank.

CAPTION TITLE: p. 2, '» F. Chopin Op. 11.' (slanted backward).

SUB-CAPTION: p. 2, 'CONCERTO.'.

FOOTLINE: pp. 2–47, '2340 | 1020.1021.1022.'.

PLATES: The layout of the music in 46 pages (as in Hob-219) differs from that of the first edition (11-Ki-1), which has 43 pages of music.

STAMPS: dealer, Heuser, New York.

1. *Date:* based on the added plate number 2340 in the footline (Table 5C).
2. This score corresponds to Hob-219, stated there to be a lithographic transfer. An engraved version is noted by Chominski & Turlo (p. 103).

Leipzig: Kistner (4528) [*ca* 1875] 11-Ki-5 M1010.C54 C67

GRAND | CONCERTO | (MI-MINEUR) | pour | Pianoforte | AVEC | Accompagnement d'Orchestre | PAR | FRÉD. CHOPIN. | OP. 11. « » PR. M. 12, __ . netto. | PARTITION. | PROPRIÉTÉ DE L'EDITEUR. | ENREGISTRÉ AUX ARCHIVES DE L'UNION. | LEIPZIG, FR. KISTNER. | (Médaille d'or de l'Empereur d'Autriche.) | 4528.

79 leaves (270 x 192 mm): pp. [1] lith title page, [2] blank, 3–158 lith music (full score).

11-Ki-5 *(continued)*

11-Ki-5 *(concluded)*

CAPTION TITLE: p. 3, 'CONCERTO, | » F. Chopin Op. 11.'; p. 82, 'ROMANZE.'; p. 102, 'RONDO.'.

SUB-CAPTION: p. 3, eight staves for winds: 'Flauti. | Oboi. | Clarinetti ÷ in C. | Fagotti. | Corni I & II ÷ in E. | Corni III & IV ÷ in C. | Clarini ÷ in C. | Trombone. |'; one stave for 'Timpani in H.C.E. |'; two staves for 'Pianoforte. |'; five staves for strings: 'Violino I. | Violino II. | Viola. | Violoncello. | Basso. |'; p. 82 (second movement), four staves for winds: 'Flauti. | Clarinetti ÷ in C. | Fagotti. | Corni I & II ÷ in E. |', pianoforte and strings the same as on p. 3; p. 102 (third movement), seven staves for winds: 'Flauti. | Oboi. | Clarinetti ÷ in A. | Fagotti. | Corni I & II ÷ in E. | Clarini ÷ in E. | Trombone. |'; one stave for 'Timpani in H.E. |', pianoforte and strings the same as p. 3.

FOOTLINE: p. 3, 'Stich von E. Aaron. « 4528 » Druck von C.G. Röder.'; pp. 4–158, '4528'.

IMPOSITION: octavo.

WRAPPER (pink): pp. [1] same as title page, [2, 3, 4] blank.

STAMPS: none.

---

1. *Date:* based on the plate number (Table 5C).
2. This "octavo" full score corresponds to Hob-222.

Leipzig: **Kistner** (4870) [*ca* 1877] 11-Ki-2 M554.C54 C696

GRAND | CONCERTO | pour le | PIANOFORTE | avec Accompagnement d'Orchestre |
ou de Quintuor ad libitum | composé et dédié à Monsieur | FRÉD. KALKBRENNER |
par | FRÉD. CHOPIN. | *Oeuvre 11.* « » *Pr.* { *avec Orchestre* M. 13. 50. ÷ *avec Quintuor* M. 12. 75. ÷
sans Accomp M. 6. – | Propriété des Editeurs | Enregistré aux Archives de l'Union |
Leipzig, chez Fr. Kistner. | *Paris, chez M. Schlesinger.* | *1020. 1021. 1022.* |
Les parties de Qintuor sont arrangées par Rich. Hofmann. | *4870.*

Violino I: 7 leaves (339 x 270 mm): pp. [1] lith title page, 2–13 lith music, [14] blank.

CAPTION TITLE: p. 2, '» Fr. Chopin Op. 11. ÷ Quintett–Stimme.'.

SUB-CAPTION: p. 2, 'CONCERTO.'.

HEADLINE: pp. 2–13, '*Violino I.*'.

FOOTLINE: p. 2, '*Stich von E. Aaron.* « 4870 » *Druck von C. G. Röder.*'; pp. 3–13, '4870', except no plate number on pp. 3, 5, 10.

Violino II: 6 leaves (339 x 270 mm): pp. 1–11 lith music, [12] blank.

Viola: 5 leaves (339 x 270 mm): pp. 1–10 lith music.

Violoncello: 5 leaves (339 x 270 mm): pp. 1–10 lith music.

Basso: 4 leaves (339 x 270 mm): pp. 1–8 lith music.

STAMPS: none.

---

1. *Date:* based on the plate number (Table 5C).
2. All parts have caption title and sub-caption identical to those of Violino I. The Violino II, Viola, Violoncello, and Basso parts have headlines analogous to that of Violino I, and footlines with only "4870" on each page of music.
3. This edition is not in Hoboken.

VARIATIONS IN B FLAT MAJOR
('Hérold')
Opus 12

Paris: M. Schlesinger (1499) 1834 — *Composed* 1833
Leipzig: Breitkopf & Härtel (5495) 1833 — Brown 80
Chominski & Turlo 226

Paris: M. Schlesinger (1499) [= 1834] — **12-mS-1** — **M27.C54 V21 c.1**

Variations Brillantes | *POUR LE* | Piano – Forte | *sur la Ronde favorite* | «Je vends des Scapulaires» | de | LUDOVIC | *dédiées à Mlle Emma Horsford* | par | CHOPIN | *M.V.* | *Op: 12.* « » *Prix: 6.^{f}* | *Propriété des Editeurs.* | *A PARIS, Chez* MAURICE SCHLESINGER *Rue Richelieu, 97* | *Londres, chez Cramer Adisson* [*sic*] *et Beale* | *Leipzick chez Breitkopf et Haertel*

7 leaves (352 x 268 mm): pp. [i] engr title page, [ii, 1] blank, 2–11 engr music, [12] blank.

CAPTION TITLE: p. 2, 'CHOPIN. Op 12. ÷ Variations sur LUDOVIC. « RONDE de LUDOVIC.'.

FOOTLINE: p. 2, 'M.S. 1499. » Paris Chez Maurice Schlesinger rue de Richelieu N° 97.'; pp. 3–10, 'M.S. 1499.'; p. 11, 'CHOPIN Op. 12. « M.S. 1499. » Paris chez Maurice Schlesinger rue de Richelieu 97.'.

WRAPPER (green): pp. [1] same as title page, [2, 3] blank, [4] advt.

ADVT: wrapper p. [4], 'PUBLIÉ PAR | BRANDUS & CIE, | EDITEURS DE MUSIQUE, | *Rue Richelieu, n^{o}* 103. | 1re SÉRIE DES | SUCCÈS UNIVERSELS | MORCEAUX DE PIANO DIFFICILES.'. Selected Chopin works are listed through Op. 64.

STAMPS: successor, style Bra/A (see Appendix 8).

1. *Date:* first-edition inference (date code fe, p. 17). The wrapper dates from after 1850, but there is no evidence this score is not the first issue.
2. Grabowski (1994, p. 7) prefers a first-edition publication date of 1833.

Paris: M. Schlesinger (1499) [= 1834] — **12-mS-2** — **M27.C54 V21 c.2**

The transcription of this title page is the same as that of 12-mS-1.

7 leaves (337 x 265 mm): pp. [i] engr title page, [ii, 1] blank, 2–11 engr music, [12] blank.

CAPTION TITLE: p. 2, 'CHOPIN. Op 12. ÷ Variations sur LUDOVIC. « RONDE de LUDOVIC.'.

FOOTLINE: p. 2, 'M.S. 1499. » Paris Chez Maurice Schlesinger rue de Richelieu N° 97.'; pp. 3–10, 'M.S. 1499.'; p. 11, 'CHOPIN Op. 12. « M.S. 1499. » Paris chez Maurice Schlesinger rue de Richelieu 97.'.

STAMPS: publisher, style mS/A (see Appendix 8).

INSCRIPTIONS: owner's signature.

1. *Date:* first-edition inference (date code fe, p. 17).

Leipzig: **Breitkopf & Härtel (5495) [= 1833]** **12-BH-1** **M27.C54 V2**

VARIATIONS | *brillantes* | Pour Le Pianoforte | *sur le Rondeau favori: „Le vends des Scapulaires"* | de Ludovic | de | HEROLD et HALEVY | *dédiées* | *à Mademoiselle Emma Horsford* | par | Fréd. Chopin. | Propriété des Editeurs. | *Oeuv. 12.* « » *Pr. 16 Gr.* | Leipsic, | *Chez Breitkopf & Härtel.* | *London, chez Cramer, Addison & Beale. Paris, chez M. Schlesinger.* | *Enregistré dans les Archives de l'Union.*

7 leaves (306 x 236 mm): pp. [1] lith title page, [2, 3] blank, 4–13 engr music, [14] blank.

CAPTION TITLE: p. 4, '» Chopin Op. 12.'.

FOOTLINE: pp. 4–13, '5495'.

STAMPS: publisher, style BH/D (see Appendix 8).

1. *Date:* first-edition inference (date code fe, p. 17).
2. This score corresponds to Hob-223.

Leipzig: **Breitkopf & Härtel (5495) [1841–45]** **12-BH-2** **M27.C54 V212**

The transcription of this title page is the same as that of 12-BH-1, except here the price is "*20 Ngr.*".

7 leaves (340 x 268 mm): pp. [1] lith title page, [2, 3] blank, 4–13 engr music, [14] blank.

CAPTION TITLE: p. 4, '» Chopin Op. 12.'.

FOOTLINE: pp. 4–13, '5495'.

WRAPPER: pp. [1] same as title page, [2] blank; lacks original conjugate leaf.

STAMPS: publisher, style BH/J? (see Appendix 8).

1. *Date:* currency inference (date code c2, p. 17).
2. This score corresponds to Hob-224.

Leipzig: **Breitkopf & Härtel (C.X.1) 1879** **12-BH-3** **M27.C54 V214**

Friedr. Chopin's | Werke. | Band X. | Verschiedene Werke für das Pianoforte. | 1. Brillante Variationen. Op. 12. B dur « » Pr. — [M] 90 [Pf] n. | [list of works, items 2–10] | Verlag von Breitkopf & Härtel in Leipzig.

6 leaves (340 x 270 mm): pp. [1] lith title page [series title in red], 2–11 lith music, [12] advt.

CAPTION TITLE: p. 2, 'Chopin's Werke « Brillante Variationen ÷ für das Pianoforte ÷ von ÷ FRIEDRICH CHOPIN. ÷ Op. 12. ÷ Fräulein Emma Horsford gewidmet. » Band X. N° 1.'.

FOOTLINE: p. 2, 'Stich und Druck von Breitkopf & Härtel in Leipzig. « C.X.1. » Ausgegeben 1879.'; pp. 3–11, 'C.X.1.'.

ADVT: p. [12], 'Verlag von Breitkopf & Härtel in Leipzig. | FRIEDRICH CHOPIN'S WERKE.'. Fourteen volumes are listed, the first with the four ballades, the last with the 17 songs of Op. 74. Prices are shown for the first 12 volumes, but not for the last two.

12-BH-3 *(continued)*

12-BH-3 *(concluded)*

STAMPS: publisher, styles BH/L and BH/M (see Appendix 8).

---

1. *Date:* Note the explicit publication date in the footline.
2. This score is from the 10th volume in Breitkopf & Härtel's collected edition of 1878–80, edited by Bargiel, Brahms, Franchomme, Liszt, Reinecke, and Rudorff (Chominski & Turlo, pp. 257–58).
3. The title page is printed in red and black.

FANTAISIE IN A MAJOR FOR PIANO AND ORCHESTRA
Opus 13

Paris: M. Schlesinger (1574) 1834	*Composed* 1828
Leipzig: Kistner (1033.1034) 1834	Brown 28
London: Wessel (1083) 1834	Chominski & Turlo 41

Leipzig: **Kistner (1033.1034) [= 1834]** 13-Ki-2 M37.C54 G79

GRANDE | FANTAISIE | sur des Airs polonais | pour Le Pianoforté | avec Accompagnement d'Orchestre | composée et dédiée | À SON AMI J. P. PIXIS | par | FRÉD. CHOPIN. | Oeuvre 13. « »
Pr. { avec Accomp. 1 Rthlr. 20 Gr. ÷ sans Accomp. _ 20 Gr. | Propriété des Editeurs. |
Enregistré aux Archives de l'Union. | *Leipsic, chez Fr. Kistner.* | Moscóu, chez C. L. Lehnhold. |
Paris, ÷ chez M. Schlesinger. « *1033. 1034.* » Londres, ÷ chez Wessel & C°.

10 leaves (317 x 248 mm): pp. [1] lith title page, 2–19 engr music, [20] blank.

CAPTION TITLE: p. 2, ' » F. Chopin. Op. 13.'.

FOOTLINE: pp. 2–19, '*1033. 1034.*'.

STAMPS: none.

1. *Date:* first-edition inference (date code fe, p. 17).
2. This score corresponds to the piano part of Hob-227.

Leipzig: **Kistner (1033.1034) [1841–45]** 13-Ki-1 M37.C54 G792

The transcription of this title page is the same as that of 13-Ki-2, except here the price with accompaniment is "1 Rthlr. 25 Ngr.", and the price without accompaniment is "1 Rthlr.".

10 leaves (323 x 256 mm): pp. [1] lith title page, 2–19 engr music, [20] blank.

CAPTION TITLE: p. 2, '» F. Chopin. Op. 13.'.

FOOTLINE: pp. 2–19, '*1033. 1034.*'.

STAMPS: none.

1. *Date:* currency inference (date code c2, p. 17).
2. This score is probably somewhat earlier than Hob-228, which is lithographed and has "Stich & Druck von Fr. Kistner in Leipzig" in the footline.

RONDO IN F MAJOR FOR PIANO AND ORCHESTRA
('Krakowiak')
Opus 14

Paris: M. Schlesinger (1586) 1834
Leipzig: Kistner (1038, 1039) 1834
London: Wessel (1084) 1834

Composed 1828
Brown 29
Chominski & Turlo 194

There is no score of Opus 14 among the collection's printed editions. However, the collection includes a facsimile publication of the manuscript of the full score (Hordynski, 1953).

NOCTURNES IN F MAJOR, F SHARP MAJOR, G MINOR
Opus 15

Paris: M. Schlesinger (1529) 1833	*Composed* 1833
Leipzig: Breitkopf & Härtel (5502) 1833	Brown 55
London: Wessel (1093) 1834	Chominski & Turlo 111

Paris: M. Schlesinger (1529) [= 1833] 15-mS-1 M25.C54 N71

Trois Nocturnes | *POUR* | *LE PIANO* | *dédiés à son ami* | Ferdinand Hiller | *PAR* | Frédéric Chopin. | *Op. 15.* « » *Prix. 6*^{f} | *Propriété des Editeurs.* | *A PARIS, Chez* MAURICE SCHLESINGER *Rue Richelieu 97.* | *Leipzig, chez Breitkopf et Hartel* « » *Londres, chez Wessel et C*^{o} | *M.S. 1529.*

7 leaves (327 x 257 mm): pp. [i] engr title page, [ii, 1] blank, 2–11 engr music, [12] blank.

CAPTION TITLE: p. 2, 'F. CHOPIN. Op: 15. « | TROIS NOCTURNES.'.

SUB-CAPTION: p. 2, '1er NOCTURNE.'; p. 6, '2me NOCTURNE.'; p. 9, '3me NOCTURNE.'.

FOOTLINE: p. 2, 'F. Chopin. Op: 15. « M.S. 1529. » Maurice Schlesinger rue de Richelieu N° 97.'; pp. 3–10, 'M.S. 1529.'; p. 11, 'Maurice Schlesinger rue de Richelieu N° 97. « M.S. 1529.'.

STAMPS: successor, style Bra/B (see Appendix 8).

1. *Date:* first-edition inference (date code fe, p. 17), but also see note 2.
2. The registration date is in December 1833 (Kallberg, 1983, p. 537, adopted by Chominski & Turlo, p. 140). As pointed out by Brown (1972, p. 60), the actual first publication by Schlesinger was in January 1834 in *Album des Pianistes.* The present score is the independent issue, which appeared somewhat later. Grabowski (1994, p. 18) refers to this issue as the second impression
3. This score corresponds to Hob-237. (Note that Hob-236, with price omitted, is a presentation copy from the composer. It is shown in Hoboken's plate 18, p. 111.)

Leipzig: Breitkopf & Härtel (5502) [1841–45] 15-BH-1 M25.C54 N7

Trois | NOCTURNES | Pour Le Pianoforte | *composés et dédiés* | *A son ami Ferdinand Hiller* | par | FR. CHOPIN. | *Propriété des Editeurs.* | *Oeuv. 15.* « à Leipsic, ÷ *Chez Breitkopf & Härtel.* » *Pr. 20 Ngr.* | à Paris, ÷ *Chez Maur. Schlesinger.* « » à Londres, ÷ *Chez Wessel & C*^{o}. | *Enregistré dans les Archives de l'Union.*

7 leaves (325 x 256 mm): pp. [1] lith title page, [2] blank, 3–13 engr music, [14] blank.

CAPTION TITLE: p. 3, 'NOCTURNE I. | » F. Chopin. Op. 15.'; p. 7, 'NOCTURNE II.'; p. 11, 'NOCTURNE III.'.

FOOTLINE: p. 3, 'Stich und Druck von Breitkopf & Härtel in Leipzig. « 5502'; pp. 4–13, '5502'.

STAMPS: publisher, style BH/G (see Appendix 8).

INSCRIPTIONS: owner's signature dated 1859.

1. *Date:* currency inference (date code c2, p. 17).

15-BH-1 *(continued)*

15-BH-1 *(concluded)*

2. This score appears to be chronologically intermediate between Hob-234 (the first edition) and Hob-235. Like Hob-234 it does not have a plate number on the title page, and the music is engraved. Like Hob-235 it is priced in Ngr. but the latter is lithographed and has a different title page.

Leipzig: **Breitkopf & Härtel (5502) [1841–45]** **15-BH-2** **M25.C54 N712**

TROIS | NOCTURNES | pour le | PIANOFORTE | composés et dédiés | à son ami Ferdinand Hiller | par | FR. CHOPIN. | OP. 15. | Propriété des Editeurs. | *Leipzig, Breitkopf & Härtel.* | *Paris, M. Schlesinger. Londres, Wessel & Cº* | Pr. 20 Ngr. | *Enrégistré aux Archives de l'Union.* | *5502.*

7 leaves (340 x 267 mm): pp. [1] lith title page, [2] blank, 3–13 lith music, [14] blank.

CAPTION TITLE: p. 3, 'NOCTURNE I. | » F. Chopin. Op. 15.'; p. 7, 'NOCTURNE II. | » F. Chopin. Op. 15.'; p. 11, 'NOCTURNE III. | » F. Chopin. Op. 15.'.

FOOTLINE: p. 3, 'Stich und Druck von Breitkopf & Härtel in Leipzig. « 5502'; pp. 4–13, '5502'.

WRAPPER (buff): pp. [1] lith collective title page, [2, 3] blank, [4] advt.

COLLECTIVE TITLE: wrapper p. [1], 'OEUVRES DE PIANO | DE | FRÉD. CHOPIN.' The list of works is classified in eleven genres: Valses, Notturnos, Ballades, Sonates, Etudes, Mazurkas, Polonaises, Scherzos, Impromptus, Preludes, and Concertos, Variations etc. The last opus number listed is 65.

ADVT: wrapper p. [4], 'SIGISMUND THALBERG'S WERKE | im Verlage von | Breitkopf und Härtel in Leipzig.'.

STAMPS: publisher, styles BH/I and BH/J (see Appendix 8); dealer, Schirmer, New York.

1. *Date:* currency inference (date code c2, p. 17).
2. This lithographed edition is from the "Notturnos" volume of the Breitkopf & Härtel collected edition of 1852–67 (Chominski & Turlo, p. 256), but with the original plates. There are eleven volumes in the collected edition, of which the "Notturnos" is the second.

London: **Wessel (1093) [= 1834]** **15-W-1** **M25.C54 N713**

[handwritten "Nº 3"] | LES ZEPHYRS. | 7me 8me et 9me | NOCTURNES. | pour le | Piano Forte, | Dediées à son ami | Ferdinand Hiller, | par | FRED. CHOPIN. | (de Varsovie.) | COPYRIGHT. | *Op. 15. « Ent. Sta. Hall » Price 3/–* | *Paris, M. Schlesinger. Leipzig, Breitkopff* [*sic*] *& Härtel.* | *LONDON,* | WESSEL & Cº Importers & Publishers of FOREIGN MUSIC, | *(by special Appointment) to H.R.H. the Duchess of Kent.* | Nº 6, Frith Street, Soho Square. | *Where are Published all CHOPIN'S Works.*

6 leaves (335 x 254 mm): pp. [1] engr title page, 2–11 engr music, [12] blank.

CAPTION TITLE: p. 2, '*LES ZEPHYRS.* | *7me 8me et 9me NOCTURNES, Composées par FRED. CHOPIN.*'.

SUB-CAPTION: p. 2, '*7me* | *NOCTURNE.*'; p. 6, '*8me* | *NOCTURNE.*'; p. 9, '*9me* | *NOCTURNE.*'.

FOOTLINE: p. 2, '(W & Cº Nº 1093.)'; pp. 3–10, 'CHOPIN, Op: 15. « (W & Cº Nº 1093.)'; p. 11, 'CHOPIN, Op: 15. (Nº 1093.) WESSEL & Cº Nº 6, Frith Street, Soho Square.'.

STAMPS: publisher, styles W/A and W/B (see Appendix 8).

15-W-1 *(continued)*

15-W-1 *(concluded)*

1. *Date:* first-edition inference (date code fe, p. 17).
2. The title page has "7me 8me et 9me" for Wessel's numbering of these nocturnes, but the numbers should be 4, 5, 6, having been preceded only by the three nocturnes of Op. 9. The correction was made in the caption title of 15-W-2.

London: **Wessel (1093) [1856–60]** **15-W-2** **M25.C54 N7132**

N^{o} [handwritten "14"] OF | WESSEL & Co.'s COMPLETE COLLECTION | OF | *the Compositions* | OF | FREDERIC CHOPIN | FOR THE | Piano Forte. | [list of works, Wessel 1–13] | 14 "LES ZEPHIRS" 3rd *Set of Notturnos. Op. 15. 3/6* | [list of works, Wessel 15–71] | *Ent. Sta. Hall.* « *Copyrights.* » *Price,* [handwritten "3/6"] | *LONDON,* | WESSEL & Co *Importers and Publishers of* FOREIGN MUSIC, | *(by special Appointment) to H.R.H. the Duchess of Kent.* | 18, HANOVER SQUARE.

7 leaves (333 x 249 mm): pp. [i] engr (or letterpress) title page, [ii] blank, [1] advt, 2–11 engr music, [12] blank.

CAPTION TITLE: p. 2, '*LES ZEPHYRS.* | *4me 5me et 6me NOCTURNES, Composées par FRED. CHOPIN.*'.

SUB-CAPTION: p. 2, '*4me* | *NOCTURNE.*'; p. 6, '*5me* | *NOCTURNE.*'; p. 9, '*6me* | *NOCTURNE.*'.

FOOTLINE: p. 2, '(W & Co N° 1093.)'; pp. 3–10, 'CHOPIN, Op: 15. "Les Zephyrs" « (W & Co N° 1093.)'; p. 11, 'CHOPIN, Op: 15. (N° 1093.) WESSEL & Co [address crudely deleted from plate]'.

ADVT: p. [1], 'PIANOFORTE COMPOSITIONS | BY | ROBERT GOLDBECK, | *(OF BERLIN).*' | [at the foot:] LONDON: — WESSEL & Co., 18, HANOVER SQUARE.'.

STAMPS: publisher, style W/E (see Appendix 8); dealer, Scheurmann, London.

---

1. *Date:* based on the address (Table 5D).

Mendrisio: **Pozzi (315) [after 1833]** **15-Po-1** **M25.C54 N72**

Trois | NOCTURNES | Pour le Pianoforte | *composés et dediés* | *A son ami Ferdinand Hiller* | par | FR. CHOPIN | *N. 315.* « *Op: 15.* « *Fr 2.50.* | *Mendrisio, chez C. Pozzi*

6 leaves (323 x 249 mm): pp. [1] engr title page, 2–11 engr music, [12] blank.

CAPTION TITLE: p. 2, '» F. Chopin. Op. 15.'.

SUB-CAPTION: p. 2, '1er | NOCTURNE.'; p. 6, '2me | NOCTURNE.'; p. 9, '3me | NOCTURNE.'.

FOOTLINE: pp. 2–11, '315'.

STAMPS: dealer (agent?), Ricordi, [Milan]. The stamp is embossed with text "T. R. | 58 | 7".

---

1. *Date:* No evidence was found, but it is likely the Italian edition was derived from the German.

RONDO IN E FLAT MAJOR
Opus 16

Paris: Pleyel (16) 1834	*Composed* 1833
Leipzig: Breitkopf & Härtel (5525) 1834	Brown 76
London: Wessel (1143) 1834	Chominski & Turlo 195

***Paris:* Pleyel (16) [= 1834]** **16-Pl-1** **M25.C54 R23**

RONDO | *POUR* | Piano - Forte | *dédié à son Elève* | *Mademoiselle* | Caroline Hartmann, | *PAR* | FRÉD. CHOPIN. | *Op: 16.* « » *Prix: 7 ^{f} 50.* | *Propriété des Editeurs.* | *A PARIS, Chez Ignace* PLEYEL *et Cie, Boulev^{t} Montmartre.* | *Leipzig, chez Breitkopf et Härtel.* « *(I.P. 16.)* » *Londres, chez Wessel et Co*

11 leaves (342 x 263 mm): pp. [i] engr title page, [ii, 1] blank, 2–18 engr music, [19, 20] blank.

CAPTION TITLE: p. 2, '» F. Chopin. Op: 16.'.

FOOTLINE: pp. 2–18, 'I.P. 16.'.

WRAPPER: pp. [1] same as title page, [2] blank, [3, 4] advt.

ADVT: wrapper p. [3], 'Catalogue | *Des Ouvrages composés par* | FRÉDÉRIC KALKBRENNER. | A Paris, chez IGN. PLEYEL et CIE, | BOULEVART MONTMARTRE.'; p. [4], 'CHOIX | *D'ouvrages intéressans pour le Piano.* | CHEZ IGN. PLEYEL ET C^{o}, A PARIS.'. Chopin Opp. 16 and 17 are listed on p. [4].

IMPOSITION: Leaf 6 is a singleton

STAMPS: publisher, style Pl/A (see Appendix 8); dealer, Denizot, Tours.

CONDITION: superb!

1. *Date:* first-edition inference (date code fe, p. 17). The first-edition date follows Grabowski (1994, p. 7).

***Paris:* M. Schlesinger (1703) [= 1834]** **16-mS-2** **M25.C54 R22 c.2**

RONDO | *POUR* | Piano – Forte | *dédié à son Elève* | *Mademoiselle* | Caroline Hartmann, | *PAR* | FRÉD. CHOPIN. | *Op: 16.* « » *Prix: 7 ^{f} 50.* | *Propriété de l'Editeur.* | *PARIS, Chez MAURICE SCHLESINGER, Ed^{r} de Musique, R. Richelieu, 97.* | *M.S. 1703.*

10 leaves (351 x 269 mm): pp. [i] engr title page, [ii, 1] blank, 2–18 engr music.

CAPTION TITLE: p. 2, '» F: Chopin. Op: 16.'.

FOOTLINE: pp. 2–18, 'M.S. 1703.'.

WRAPPER (faded pink): pp. [1] same as title page, [2, 3] blank, [4] advt.

ADVT: wrapper p. [4], 'Musique nouvelle publiée en 1844 par MAURICE SCHLESINGER, 97, rue Richelieu.'. The list includes Chopin Opp. 50–54.

IMPOSITION: In contrast to 16-mS-1 and 16-mS-3, this score was imposed with no singleton. As a result, the last page of music is on the verso of the final leaf.

STAMPS: publisher, style mS/A (see Appendix 8).

CONDITION: All plates have excellent, clear impressions.

16-mS-2 *(continued)*

16-mS-2 *(concluded)*

1. *Date:* first-edition inference (date code fe, p. 17). Schlesinger acquired Opp. 16 and 17 from Pleyel in 1834 and published them several weeks later (Brown, p. 80; Chominski & Turlo, p. 192; Grabowski, 1994, p. 18). The wrapper refers to Schlesinger publications in 1844, but there is no evidence this score is not the first issue.
2. The plates are those of Pleyel, modified with Schlesinger's imprint and plate number.

Paris: **M. Schlesinger (1703) [= 1834]** **16-mS-1** **M25.C54 R22 c.1**

The transcription of this title page is the same as that of 16-mS-2.

RONDO | *POUR* | Piano – Forte | *dédié à son Elève* | *Mademoiselle* | Caroline Hartmann, | *PAR* | FRÉD. CHOPIN. | *Op: 16.* « » *Prix: 7.f 50.* | *Propriété de l'Editeur.* | *PARIS, Chez MAURICE SCHLESINGER, Edr. de Musique, R. Richelieu, 97.* | *M.S. 1703.*

10 leaves (332 x 263 mm): pp. [i] engr title page, [ii, 1] blank, 2–18 engr music.

CAPTION TITLE: p. 2, '» F. Chopin. Op: 16.'.

FOOTLINE: pp. 2–18, 'M.S. 1703.'.

IMPOSITION: Leaf 6 (pp. 9, 10) is a singleton. A final blank leaf is missing (as in Hob-244). The title leaf is tipped to leaf 2.

STAMPS: successor, style BD/D (see Appendix 8); dealer, Retté, Paris (see Appendix 8).

ANNOTATIONS: stamped page numbers 59–78 (see 20-mS-1).

1. *Date:* as in 16-mS-2.
2. For further comments see "Pagination" in the "Descriptions design" section of the Introduction.

Paris: **M. Schlesinger (1703) [= 1834]** **16-mS-3** **M25.C54 R22 c.3**

The transcription of this title page is the same as that of 16-mS-2.

11 leaves (342–350 x 268 mm): pp. [i] engr title page, [ii, 1] blank, 2–18 engr music, 19–20 blank.

CAPTION TITLE: p. 2, '» F: Chopin. Op: 16.'.

FOOTLINE: pp. 2–18, 'M.S. 1703.'.

WRAPPER (faded pink): pp. [1] same as title page, [2, 3] blank, [4] advt.

ADVT: wrapper p. [4], 'CHEZ G. BRANDUS ET S. DUFOUR, ÉDITEURS, 103, RUE RICHELIEU, AU 1ER, | NOUVELLE MUSIQUE DE PIANO'. The list does not have works by Chopin.

STAMPS: successor, style BD/D (see Appendix 8).

CONDITION: The plate of the title page is quite worn.

1. *Date:* as in 16-mS-2.
2. This score is identical to 16-mS-1 (above), except that it has the final blank leaf conjugate to the title leaf. It also has a wrapper.

Leipzig: **Breitkopf & Härtel (5525) [= 1834]** **16-BH-1** **M25.C54 R5**

RONDEAU | pour le | Piano – Forte | composé et dédié | à son Elève | *Mademoiselle Caroline Hartmann* | par | FRÉD. CHOPIN. | Propriété des Editeurs. | Oeuv. 16. « » Pr. 1 Rthlr. | à Leipsic, | *Chez Breitkopf & Härtel.* | à Londres, *chez Wessel & C.º* _ à Paris, *chez Pleyel & C.º* | *Enrégistré dans les Archives de l'Union.*

10 leaves (319 x 256 mm): pp. [1] lith title page, [2, 3] blank, 4–20 engr music.

CAPTION TITLE: p. 4, '» F. Chopin. Op. 16.'.

FOOTLINE: pp. 4–20, '5525'.

IMPOSITION: Leaf 6 is a singleton. A final bank leaf is shown in Hob-240 but is missing here. The title leaf is tipped to leaf 2.

STAMPS: publisher, style BH/J (see Appendix 8).

BINDING: library cloth.

1. *Date:* first-edition inference (date code fe, p. 17).

London: Wessel (1094) [*ca* 1840] **16-W-1** **M25.C54 R49**

Nº [handwritten "15"] OF | WESSEL & C°.'s COMPLETE COLLECTION | OF | *the Compositions* | OF | FREDERIC CHOPIN | FOR THE | Piano Forte. | Solo & Duet | [list of works, Wessel 1–14] | 15 RONDO ELEGANT *ded, à Mlle Hartmann, in E* [flat] *Op. 16. 4/– [Duet] 5/–* | [list of works, Wessel 16–45] | *Ent. Sta. Hall. « Copyrights. » Price, Solo* [handwritten "4/–"] ÷ " *Duet* [blank] | *LONDON,* | WESSEL & C° *Importers and Publishers of,* FOREIGN MUSIC, | *(by special Appointment) to, H.R.H. the Duchess of Kent.* | Nº 67, Frith Street, Corner of Soho Square.

10 leaves (335 x 252 mm): pp. [1] title page, 2–18 engr music, [19] advt, [20] blank.

CAPTION TITLE: p. 2, '*RONDO ELEGANT.* | *(OP: 16.)* | *Composé par* | *FREDERIC CHOPIN.*'.

FOOTLINE: p. 2, '(W & C° Nº 1094.)'; pp. 3–17, 'CHOPIN, Op: 16. « (W & C° Nº 1094.)'; p. 18, 'CHOPIN, Op: 16. (Nº 1094.) WESSEL & C° Nº 6, Frith Street, Soho Square.'.

ADVT: p. [19], '[clipped: Page E. | CATALOGUE OF WESSEL & Co.'s PUBLICATIONS OF PIANOFORTE TRIOS, QUARTETTS, QUINTETTS,] | THE WORKS OF BEETHOVEN, CHOPIN, LISZT, &c. PIANO SOLO AND ORGAN MUSIC. | No. 67, FRITH STREET, CORNER OF SOHO SQUARE.'. Chopin works are listed through Op. 42.

STAMPS: publisher, styles W/B and W/C (see Appendix 8).

1. *Date:* based on the publication list on the title page, which ends with Op. 42, published by Wessel in 1840.
2. The street number "67" on the title page has the appearance of having been edited from "6", while "6" in the footline on p. 18 was not changed.

Milan: Lucca (1564) [ca 1836] **16-Lu-1** **M25.C54 R492**

RONDO | *POUR* | Piano–Forte | *dédié à son Elève* | *Mademoiselle* | Caroline Hartmann | PAR | FRÈD. [*sic*] CHOPIN | *Op. 16* « » 1564 Prix 4^{f} | *Milan chez François Lucca*

11 leaves (345 x 252 mm): pp. [i] engr title page, [ii, 1] blank, 2–18 engr music, [19, 20] blank.

CAPTION TITLE: p. 2, '» F. Chopin Op. 16.'.

FOOTLINE: pp. 2–18, '1564'.

STAMPS: none.

1. *Date:* Belotti (p. 430) gives 1836 for Op. 16.
2. This is the eighth of Lucca's publications of Chopin's works (the first is the waltz Op. 18; see Chominski & Turlo, p. 272).

MAZURKAS IN B FLAT MAJOR, E MINOR, A FLAT MAJOR, A MINOR
Opus 17

Paris: Pleyel (2912) 1833	*Composed* 1833
Leipzig: Breitkopf & Härtel (5527) 1834	Brown 77
London: Wessel (1144) 1834	Chominski & Turlo 60

***Paris:* M. Schlesinger (1704) [*ca* 1834]** — **17-mS-1** — **M32.C54 M452**

Quatre | MAZURKAS | *POUR LE* | Piano Forte | dédiées | *à Madame Lina Freppa* | par | *FRÉD. CHOPIN.* | *Op: 17.* « » *Prix: 6* ^{f} | *Propriété des Editeurs.* | *PARIS, Chez MAURICE SCHLESINGER, R. Richelieu, 97.* | *Leipzig, chez Breitkopf et Härtel* « » *Londres, chez Wessel et Co* | *M.S. 1704.*

7 leaves (347 x 268 mm): pp. [i] engr title page, [ii, 1] blank, 2–11 engr music, [12] blank.

CAPTION TITLE: p. 2, '» Fréd. Chopin. Op: 17. Mazourkas.'.

SUB-CAPTION: p. 2, 'N° 1. | MAZOURKA.'; and so on through p. 8, 'N° 4. | MAZOURKA.'.

FOOTLINE: pp. 2–11, 'M.S. 1704.'.

WRAPPER (yellow): pp. [1] same as title page, [2–4] blank.

PLATES: The plates are those of Pleyel, edited with Schlesinger's imprint and plate number. The title-page impression is weak and partly illegible.

STAMPS: successor, style Bra/A (see Appendix 8); dealer, Massieu, Havre.

1. *Date:* Schlesinger acquired Opp. 16 and 17 from Pleyel in 1834 and published them several weeks later (Brown, p. 80; Chominski & Turlo, p. 192; Grabowski, 1994, p. 18).

***Leipzig:* Breitkopf & Härtel (5527) [= 1834]** — **17-BH-3** — **M32.C54 M4528 c.1**

Quatre | MAZURKAS | pour le | Piano-Forte | composées et dédiées | *à Madame Lina Freppa* | par | FRÉD. CHOPIN. | Propriété des Editeurs. | *Oeuv.* 17. « À LEIPSIC, » *Pr. 16 Gr.* | *Chez Breitkopf & Härtel.* | à Paris, | *Chez J. Pleyel & Cie* | *Enrégistré dans les Archives de l'Union.*

7 leaves (316 x 256 mm): pp. [1] lith title page, 2–3 blank, 4–13 engr music, [14] blank.

CAPTION TITLE: p. 4, '» di Chopin.'.

SUB-CAPTION: p. 4, 'N° 1. | MAZOURKA.'; p. 6, 'N° 2. | MAZOURKA.'; p. 8, 'N° 3. | MAZOURKA.'; p. 10, 'N° 4. | MAZOURKA.'.

FOOTLINE: pp. 4–13, '5527'.

STAMPS: none.

1. *Date:* first-edition inference (date code fe, p. 17).
2. This edition has no plate number on the title page. It corresponds to Hob-246.

Leipzig: **Breitkopf & Härtel** (5527) [= 1834] **17-BH-4** **M32.C54 M4528 c.2**

The transcription of this title page is the same as that of 17-BH-3.

7 leaves (340 x 265 mm): pp. [1] lith title page, 2–3 blank, 4–13 engr music, [14] blank.

CAPTION TITLE: p. 4, '» di Chopin.'.

SUB-CAPTION: p. 4, 'Nº 1. | MAZOURKA.'; p. 6, 'Nº 2. | MAZOURKA.'; p. 8, 'Nº 3. | MAZOURKA.'; p. 10, 'Nº 4. | MAZOURKA.'.

FOOTLINE: pp. 4–13, '5527'.

STAMPS: publisher, style BH/A (see Appendix 8). This is the collection's only example of a BH blind stamp.

CONDITION: This copy is in original condition — a clear impression and untrimmed, unblemished leaves.

1. *Date:* first-edition inference (date code fe, p. 17).
2. This edition has no plate number on the title page.

Leipzig: **Breitkopf & Härtel** (5527) [after 1840] **17-BH-5** **M32.C54 M4531**

The transcription of this title page is the same as that of 17-BH-3, except here the price is *"20 Ngr."*.

7 leaves (340 x 265 mm): pp. [1] lith title page, 2–3 blank, 4–13 engr music, [14] blank.

CAPTION TITLE: p. 4, '» di Chopin.'.

SUB-CAPTION: p. 4, 'Nº 1. | MAZOURKA.'; p. 6, 'Nº 2. | MAZOURKA.'; p. 8, 'Nº 3. | MAZOURKA.'; p. 10, 'Nº 4. | MAZOURKA.'.

FOOTLINE: pp. 4–13, '5527'.

IMPOSITION: Leaf 4 is a singleton.

STAMPS: none.

1. *Date:* currency inference (date code c1, p. 17); see also note 2.
2. This edition appears to be identical to the first edition 17-BH-3, except for the price, which is in Neugroschen. Chronologically it follows 17-BH-3 and precedes 17-BH-2.
3. Although Op. 17 was acquired from Pleyel by Schlesinger in 1834, and Pleyel's firm was acquired by Prilipp in the same year, the title page of 17-BH-5 still cites Pleyel as the publisher. The same is true of the somewhat later issues, 17-BH-2 and 17-BH-1.

Leipzig: **Breitkopf & Härtel** (5527) [after 1840] **17-BH-2** **M32.C54 M453 c.2**

The transcription of this title page is the same as that of 17-BH-3, except here the price is *"20 Ngr."*.

6 leaves (322 x 255 mm): pp. [1] lith title page, 2–11 engr music, [12] advt.

17-BH-2 *(continued)*

17-BH-2 *(concluded)*

CAPTION TITLE: p. 2, 'MAZURKA I. | » F. Chopin, Op. 17.'; p. 4, 'MAZURKA II.'; p. 6, 'MAZURKA III.'; p. 8, 'MAZURKA IV.'.

FOOTLINE: p. 2, 'Stich und Druck von Breitkopf & Härtel in Leipzig. « | 5527'; pp. 3–11, '5527'.

ADVT: p. [12], 'Publications Nouvelles pour le Pianoforte | de | BREITKOPF & HÆRTEL à LEIPZIG.'. There are no Chopin works in the list.

STAMPS: publisher, style BH/E (see Appendix 8).

---

1. *Date:* currency inference (date code c1, p. 17); see also notes 2 and 3.
2. The imposition in six leaves differs from that of the first edition 17-BH-3, which is in 7 leaves, and there are textual differences as well, such as in the caption title and footline.
3. Since the title page of 17-BH-2 is the same as that of the first edition 17-BH-3, this score is doubtless an earlier issue than 17-BH-1, which has the same music plates but a different title page.

Leipzig: **Breitkopf & Härtel (5527) [after 1840]** 17-BH-1 M32.C54 M453 c.1

Quatre | MAZURKAS | pour le | PIANO-FORTE | composées et dédiées | à Madame Lina Freppa | PAR | FRÉD. CHOPIN. | Ouev. 17. « » Pr. 20 Ngr. | Propriété des Editeurs. | Leipzig, Breitkopf & Härtel. | Paris, I. Pleyel & C? | *Enrégistré aux Archives de l'Union.* | *5527.*

6 leaves (332 x 262 mm): pp. [1] lith title page, 2–11 engr music, [12] blank.

CAPTION TITLE: p. 2, 'MAZURKA I. | » F. Chopin, Op. 17.'; p. 4, 'MAZURKA II.'; p. 6, 'MAZURKA III.'; p. 8, 'MAZURKA IV.'.

FOOTLINE: p. 2, 'Stich und Druck von Breitkopf & Härtel in Leipzig. « | 5527'; pp. 3–11, '5527'.

STAMPS: publisher, style BH/G (see Appendix 8).

---

1. *Date:* currency inference (date code c1, p. 17); see also 17-BH-2, note 3.
2. In contrast to the first edition 17-BH-3 and 4, and to 17-BH-5 and 2, the title page of this score has the plate number.

London: **Wessel (1144) [1835–39]** 17-W-1 M32.C54 M454

SOUVENIR DE LA POLOGNE. | *TROISIÈME RECUEIL,* | DE | MAZURKAS, | pour le | *PIANO FORTE,* | dédiées à | Madame Lina Treppa [*sic*], | PAR | FRED. CHOPIN. | (de Varsovie.) | *Ent. Sta. Hall.* | *OP. 17.* « COPYRIGHT. » *Price 3/–* | *Paris, M. Schlesinger — Leipzig, Breitkopff* [*sic*] *& Härtel.* | *LONDON,* | WESSEL & C? Importers & Publishers of FOREIGN MUSIC, | *(by special Appointment) to H.R.H. the Duchess of Kent,* | N? 6, Frith Street, Soho Square.

7 leaves (335 x 254 mm): pp. [i] engr title page, [ii, 1] blank, 2–11 engr music, [12] advt.

CAPTION TITLE: p. 2, ' "SOUVENIR de POLOGNE." | Troisième Recueil de | *QUATRE MAZURKAS* Composée par *FRED. CHOPIN.*'.

SUB-CAPTION: p. 2, 'N? *9.*'; and so on through p. 8, 'N? *12.*'.

17-W-1 *(continued)*

17-W-1 *(concluded)*

FOOTLINE: p. 2, 'COPYRIGHT. « (W & Co N° 1144.)'; pp. 3–10, 'CHOPIN, Op: 17. Mazurkas. « » (W & Co N° 1144.)'; p. 11, 'CHOPIN, Op: 17. Mazurkas. « | (N° 1144) WESSEL & Co N° 6, FRITH STREET, SOHO SQUARE. | CHOPIN, Souvenir de la Pologne Mazurkas 1 to [blank] 2 Books each 2/6. | Murmures de la Seine Nocturnos 1 to 6 2 Books each 2/6 | Les Zephirs [*sic*] 7. 8 & 9me Nocturnes 3/- | Rondo Elegant Op: 6 [*sic*] in A 4/- | Invitation pour la Danse Grand Valse Brillante 3/-'.

ADVT: p. [12], heading clipped. The last Chopin work listed is Op. 20.

STAMPS: publisher, style W/C (see Appendix 8). The text of the stamp is illegible.

---

1. *Date:* The lower limit on the date is based on the listing of Op. 20 in the advertisement. The upper limit is based on the address (Table 5D).

WALTZ IN E FLAT MAJOR
Opus 18

Paris: M. Schlesinger (1599) 1834	*Composed* 1833
Leipzig: Breitkopf & Härtel (5545) 1834	Brown 62
London: Wessel (1157) 1834	Chominski & Turlo 207

Paris: **M. Schlesinger (1599) [= 1834]** **18-mS-1** **M32.C54 W391**

Grande Valse | Brillante | pour *LE* Piano | *dédiéé à* | *Mademoiselle Laura Horsford* | *PAR* | Frédéric Chopin | *Opera: 18.* « » *Prix: 6 f.* | Paris | MAURICE SCHLESINGER | *R. Richelieu, 97.* | *LONDRES, Chez WESSEL, et Cie* « » *LEIPZICK, Chez BREITKOPF et HAERTEL* | *Prop.é des Ed.rs* | *M.S. 1599*

6 leaves (318 x 257 mm): pp. [i] engr title page, [ii, 1] blank, 2–9 engr music, [10] blank.

CAPTION TITLE: p. 2, 'F. CHOPIN Op: 18. ÷ Grande Valse brillante. «'.

SUB-CAPTION: p. 2, 'VALSE.'.

FOOTLINE: pp. 2–9, 'M.S. 1599'.

WRAPPER (buff): pp. [1] half-title page, [2, 3] blank, [4] advt.

HALF TITLE: wrapper p. [1], 'GRANDE | VALSE BRILLANTE | pour le | PIANO, | par | F. CHOPIN. | OP. 18.'.

ADVT: wrapper p. [4], 'OUVRAGES POUR LE PIANO, PAR FRÉDÉRIC CHOPIN. | Publiés par Maurice Schlesinger, rue Richelieu, 97.'. The list has Chopin Opp. 2, 6–12, 15, and the Duo Concertant (B70), all published before Op. 18.

STAMPS: publisher, style mS/B (see Appendix 8).

INSCRIPTIONS: on wrapper p. [1], inscription cut down at margin.

ANNOTATIONS: on wrapper p. [1]: below the half-title, "Consolation!".

1. *Date:* first-edition inference (date code fe, p. 17).
2. This score appears to differ slightly from Hob-251, which does not have "Grande Valse brillante" in the caption title, and has slight differences in capitalization in the half-title on the wrapper.

Paris: **Brandus & Dufour (10,192) [*ca* 1859]** **18-BD-1** **M32.C54 W395**

GRANDE | VALSE | *BRILLANTE* | POUR | Piano, | PAR | F. CHOPIN. | *Op: 18.* « » *Prix: 6 f.* | *A.V.* | *PARIS, G. BRANDUS et S. DUFOUR, editeurs,* | *103, rue Richelieu, au 1er*

6 leaves (331 x 259 mm): pp. [i] engr title page, [ii, 1] blank, 2–9 engr music, [10] blank.

CAPTION TITLE: p. 2, 'GRANDE VALSE BRILLANTE | par | F. CHOPIN. | Op: 18.'.

FOOTLINE: p. 2, 'B. D. 10.192. » G. Brandus et Dufour 103 r. Richelieu.'; pp. 3–8, 'B. D. 10.192.'; p. 9, 'Imp: Thierry F.S 1. Cité Bergère. « B. D. 10.192.'.

STAMPS: publisher, style BD/C (see Appendix 8).

1. *Date:* based on the plate number (Table 5A).

Paris: **H. Lemoine (2777) [*ca* 1842]** **18-hL-2** **M32.C54 W39**

Grande Valse | Brillante. | pour *LE* Piano | *dédiée à* | *Mademoiselle Laura Horsford* | *PAR* | Frédéric Chopin | *Opera 18* « » *Prix 6* ^{f}. | Paris | *chez Henry LEMOINE, Professeur de Piano, et Editeur de Musique* | *Rue de l'Echelle. N.º 9.* | *2777. HL.*

6 leaves (326 x 253 mm): pp. [i] engr title page, [ii, 1] blank, 2–9 engr music, [10] blank.

CAPTION TITLE: p. 2, 'F. CHOPIN Op: 18. ÷ Grande Valse Brillante. «'.

SUB-CAPTION: p. 2, 'VALSE.'.

FOOTLINE: pp. 2–8, '2777. HL.'; p. 9, 'Paris chez Henry LEMOINE. « 2777. HL. » Rue de l'Echelle N.º 9.'.

STAMPS: publisher, style hL/A (see Appendix 8).

CONDITION: The title-page plate impression is weak, and some of the diacriticals and punctuation indicated in the above transcription are uncertain.

1. *Date:* based on the plate number (Devriès & Lesure, p. 280); see note 2.
2. "In 1842 Lemoine bought the copyright to the *Études* Op. 10 and Op. 25 and to the *Waltz* Op. 18 from Maurice Schlesinger. He used the original plates in his impressions of these compositions and inserted his firm's name and address on the title pages, also changing the publisher's numbers of Op. 10 (HL 2775), Op. 25 (HL 2776), Op. 18 (HL 2777). The musical text is identical to Schlesinger's version." (Grabowski, 1954, p. 28). Note the similarity of the title-page transcriptions of 18-mS-1 and 18-hL-2.

Paris: **H. Lemoine (5344) [*ca* 1859]** **18-hL-1** **M32.C54 W396**

à Mademoiselle | LAURA HORSFORD. | GRANDE | VALSE | *BRILLANTE,* | POUR | Piano, | PAR | FRÉD. CHOPIN. | *(OP: 18.)* | *Prix : 6 francs.* | *A.V.* | *PARIS* | *HENRY LEMOINE, éditeur,* | *256, rue Saint Honoré* | *COMMISSION (HL. 5344) EXPORTATION*

6 leaves (332 x 255 mm): pp. [1] lith title page, 2–11 lith music, [12] blank.

CAPTION TITLE: p. 2, 'GRANDE VALSE | BRILLANTE. | FRÉD. CHOPIN Op. 18. « » *à M*^{elle} *Laura HORSFORD.*'.

FOOTLINE: p. 2, '14e Degré des Tablettes du Pianiste de Hry LEMOINE. « 5344 : HL.'; pp. 3–11, '5344 HL.', except p. 5, '5344'.

STAMPS: successor, style aL/B (see Appendix 8); dealer, Flaxland, Paris.

1. *Date:* based on the plate number (Devriès & Lesure, p. 280).
2. This publication is the first volume of the Lemoine collected edition of 1859–94 (Chominski & Turlo, p. 270).

Leipzig: **Breitkopf & Härtel (5545) [= 1834]** **18-BH-2** **M32.C54 W398**

GRANDE VALSE | brillante | Pour Le Pianoforte | *composée et dédiée* | *A Mademoiselle Laura Harsford* [*sic*] | par | FRÉD. CHOPIN. | Propriété des Editeurs. | *Oeuvre 18.* « » *Pr. 16 Gr.* | à Leipsic, | *Chez Breitkopf & Härtel.* | *London, chez Wessel & Co* « » *Paris, chez M. Schlesinger.* | *Enrégistré dans les Achives de l'Union.*

6 leaves (319 x 252 mm): pp. [1] lith title page, [2, 3] blank, 4–11 engr music, [12] blank.

CAPTION TITLE: p. 4, '» F. CHOPIN. Op. 18. | GRANDE VALSE BRILLANTE.'.

SUB-CAPTION: p. 4, '*VALSE.*'.

FOOTLINE: pp. 4–10, '5545.'; p. 11, 'Gravé par Adam. « 5545.'.

STAMPS: publisher, style BH/D (see Appendix 8).

1. *Date:* first-edition inference (date code fe, p. 17).
2. The misspelling of Horsford (in the dedication) is mentioned by Brown (p. 68).

Leipzig: **Breitkopf & Härtel (5545) [1841–45]** **18-BH-1** **M32.C54 W4**

GRANDE VALSE | BRILLANTE | Pour le Pianoforte | *composée et dédiée* | *A Mademoiselle Laura Harsford* [*sic*] | par | FRÉD. CHOPIN. | *Op. 18.* « Propriété des Editeurs. » *Pr. 20 Ngr.* | *Leipzig, chez Breitkopf & Härtel.* | *Londres, chez Wessel & Co.* « » *Paris, chez M. Schlesinger.* | *5545.* | *Enrégistré aux Archives de l'Union.*

6 leaves (299 x 244 mm): pp. [1] lith title page, [2, 3] blank, 4–11 engr music, [12] blank.

CAPTION TITLE: p. 4 'GRANDE VALSE BRILLANTE. | » F. CHOPIN. op. 18.'.

SUB-CAPTION: p. 4, 'VALSE.'.

FOOTLINE: pp. 4–11, '5545.'.

STAMPS: publisher, style BH/F (see Appendix 8).

BINDING: library boards.

1. *Date:* currency inference (date code c2, p. 17).

Leipzig: **Breitkopf & Härtel (9618) [*ca* 1858]** **18-BH-3** **M32.C54 W399**

GRANDE VALSE | BRILLANTE | pour le Pianoforte | composée et dédiée | *A Mademoiselle Laura Harsford* [*sic*] | par | FRÉD. CHOPIN. | *Op. 18.* « Propriété des Editeurs. » *Pr. 20 Ngr.* | Leipzig chez Breitkopf & Härtel. | Londres, chez Wessel & Co « » Paris, chez M. Schlesinger. | *9618.* | *Enrégistré aux Archives de l'Union.*

6 leaves (329 x 256 mm): pp. [1] lith title page, [2] blank, 3–11 lith music, [12] blank.

CAPTION TITLE: p. 3 'GRANDE VALSE BRILLANTE. | pour le | PIANO | PAR | FRÉD. CHOPIN. | OP. 18.'.

FOOTLINE: p. 3, 'Stich und Druck von Breitkopf & Härtel in Leipzig. | 9618'; pp. 4–11, '9618'.

18-BH-3 *(continued)*

18-BH-3 *(concluded)*

STAMPS: publisher, style BH/J (see Appendix 8).

1. *Date:* based on the plate number (Table 5C).

London: **Wessel (1157) [1837–39]** **18-W-2** **M32.C54 W412**

L'AMATEUR PIANISTE, Nº 28. | INVITATION POUR LA DANSE. | *GRANDE VALSE BRILLANTE,* | pour le | Piano Forte, | *Composée et dediée à* | MADEMOISELLE LAURA HORSFORD, | par | FREDERIC CHOPIN. | (de Varsovie.) | COPYRIGHT OF THE EDITORS. | *Op. 18,* « *Ent. Sta. Hall* » *Price 3/– ÷ as Duets 4/6* | *Paris, M. Schlesinger, — Leipzig, Breitkopff* [*sic*] *& Härtel.* | *LONDON,* | WESSEL & Cº Importers & Publishers of FOREIGN MUSIC, | *(by special Appointment) to H.R.H. the Duchess of Kent.* | Nº 6, Frith Street, Soho Square.

6 leaves (335 x 254 mm): pp. [i] engr title page, [ii] blank, [1] advt, 2–9 engr music, [10] blank.

CAPTION TITLE: p. 2, 'INVITATION pour la DANSE. | GRANDE VALSE BRILLANTE. | Composée par | FREDERIC CHOPIN.'.

FOOTLINE: p. 2, '(W & Cº Nº 1157)'; pp. 3–8, 'CHOPIN, Invitation pour la Danse. « » (W & Cº Nº 1157)'; p. 9, 'CHOPIN, Invitation pour la Danse. « | (Nº 1157) Wessel & Cº Nº 6, Frith St: Soho Square. Publishers of all Chopin's Works: Notturnos, | Mazurkas, Fantasias, Studies, Concertos, &c:'.

ADVT: p. [1], '[top lines clipped] Nº 6, FRITH STREET, SOHO SQUARE, LONDON.' | [...] | 'GRAND VIOLIN SCHOOL BY LOUIS SPOHR, | [...] |'. The list includes the Chopin trio Op. 8, as #1 under 'WESSEL & Cº.'s SERIES OF MODERN TRIOS [...]'. An appended note reads, in part, "Performed at Mr. Wessel's Soirée, June 1837 [...].". In addition to Op. 8, the advt lists arrangements of Op. 3 and "Op. 12" (actually B70), both under the heading "Piano and violin concertante".

STAMPS: publisher, styles W/B and W/C? (see Appendix 8).

1. *Date:* The lower limit on the date is based on the date in the advertisement noted above (unusual, because explicit dates rarely appear in Chopin editions). The upper limit is based on the address (Table 5D).
2. This series edition is a re-issue. A copy of the first impression — which does not have "L'AMATEUR PIANISTE, Nº 28" as the first line of the title — is in the British Library (shelfmark h.104.(4.)). Its title page is reproduced in Duleba (1975, p. 158).

London: **Wessel (1157) [*ca* 1840]** **18-W-1** **M32.C54 W41**

Nº [handwritten "17"] OF | WESSEL & Cº.'s COMPLETE COLLECTION | OF | *the Compositions* | OF | FREDERIC CHOPIN | FOR THE | Piano Forte. | Solo & Duet | [list of works, Wessel 1–16] | 17 "INVITATION *pour* LA DANSE" *Grande* VALSE, *in E* [flat] *Op. 18. 3/-* [*Duet.*] *4/-* | [list of works, Wessel 18–45] | *Ent. Sta. Hall.* « *Copyrights.* » *Price . Solo* [handwritten "3/–"] ÷ " *Duet* [blank] | *LONDON,* | WESSEL & Cº *Importers and Publishers of* FOREIGN MUSIC, | *(by special Appointment) to H.R.H. the Duchess of Kent.* | Nº 67, Frith Street, Corner of Soho Square.

6 leaves (340 x 251 mm): pp. [i] engr title page, [ii] blank, [1] advt, 2–9 engr music, [10] blank.

CAPTION TITLE: p. 2, 'INVITATION pour la DANSE. | GRAND VALSE BRILLANTE. | Composée par | FREDERIC CHOPIN.'.

18-W-1 *(continued)*

18-W-1 *(concluded)*

FOOTLINE: p. 2, '(W & C° N° 1157)'; pp. 3–8, 'CHOPIN, Invitation pour la Danse. « » (W & C° N° 1157)'; p. 9, 'CHOPIN, Invitation pour la Danse. « | (N° 1157) Wessel & C° N° 6, Frith St: Soho Square. Publishers of all Chopin's Works: Notturnos, | Mazurkas, Fantasias, Studies, Concertos, &c:'.

ADVT: p. [1], 'Page E. | CATALOGUE OF WESSEL & Co.'s PUBLICATIONS OF PIANOFORTE TRIOS, QUARTETTS, QUINTETTS, | THE WORKS OF BEETHOVEN, CHOPIN, LISZT, &c. PIANO SOLO AND ORGAN MUSIC. | No. 67, FRITH STREET, CORNER OF SOHO SQUARE.'. Chopin works are listed through Op. 42.

STAMPS: publisher, style W/C (see Appendix 8).

---

1. *Date:* based on the publication list on the title page (and advertisement), which ends with Op. 42 (Wessel 45), published by Wessel in 1840.

London: **Brewer (—) [*ca* 1870]** **18-Bre-1** **M32.C54 W413**

Invitation pour la Danse, | Grande Valse Brillante | COMPOSÉE | PAR | FREDERIC CHOPIN. | *Ent. Sta. Hall.* « OP. 18. » *Price 3 s/-* | London, | BREWER & C° 23, BISHOPSGATE STREET WITHIN.

5 leaves (335 x 254 mm): pp. [1] lith title page, 2–9 lith music, [10] blank.

CAPTION TITLE: p. 2, 'INVITATION POUR LA DANSE. | GRANDE VALSE. | » F. CHOPIN.'.

SUB-CAPTION: p. 2, 'VALSE.'.

FOOTLINE: p. 2, none; pp. 3–9, 'Invitation pour la Danse. CHOPIN. «'.

STAMPS: dealer, Corbet, Limerick.

---

1. *Date:* based on the *CPM,* p. 58, shelflist h.471.s.(8.).
2. This edition is not in Brown, Chominski & Turlo, or Hoboken.

Milan: **Lucca (1377) [*ca* 1836]** **18-Lu-1** **M32.C54 W414**

GRAND | Valse Brillante | *Pour le Piano* | Par | F. CHOPIN. | Op. 18 N. 1377. « » L. 2. It | *Milan chez F. Lucca*

6 leaves (322 x 242 mm): pp. [i] engr title page, [ii, 1] blank, 2–9 engr music, [10] blank.

CAPTION TITLE: none.

SUB-CAPTION: p. 2, 'VALSE.'.

FOOTLINE: pp. 2–9, '1377'.

STAMPS: none.

---

1. *Date:* based on Belotti (p. 430).
2. This is the first of Lucca's publications of Chopin's works (Chominski & Turlo, p. 272).

BOLERO IN C MAJOR
Opus 19

Paris: Prilipp (237) 1834	*Composed* 1833
Leipzig: Peters (2505) 1834	Brown 81
London: Wessel (1491) 1835	Chominski & Turlo 8

***Paris:* Prilipp (237) [= 1834]** **19-Pr-1** **M32.C54 B64**

BOLERO | POUR LE | Piano-Forte | DÉDIÉ | *à Mademoiselle la Comtesse* | Emilie de Flahault | PAR | FRÉDÉRIC CHOPIN. | *OP: 19 « » PRIX: 7.f 50.c* | *Propriété des Editeurs.* | *à PARIS, au Magasin de Musique de PRILIPP et Cie* | *Acquéreurs d'une Partie du Fonds* D : IGN. PLEYEL & Cie *Boulevard Montmartre, No 18.* | *Continuation de l'Abonnomte Musical.* | *à Londres chez WESSEL et Compie à Leipsig chez C. F. PETERS*

8 leaves (348 x 269 mm): pp. [i] engr title page, [ii] blank, 1–12 engr music, [13, 14] blank.

CAPTION TITLE: p. 1, '» Frédéric Chopin. Op: 19.'.

FOOTLINE: pp. 1–12, 'C.237.P.'.

WRAPPER (pale pink): pp. [1] same as title page, [2–4] blank.

TEXT: Page number 12 is erroneously in the recto position.

STAMPS: publisher, style Pr/A (see Appendix 8).

1. *Date:* first-edition inference (date code fe, p. 17); also see note 2.
2. According to Brown (p. 87) "Prillip's [*i.e.*, Prilipp's] first edition has no publisher's number; it was added to later editions." Grabowski (1994, p. 21) makes a similar statement, "The copy of the Bolero Op. 19 registered in October 1834 is the first impression of the work. In the next impression the missing publisher's number 237 which corresponds to the period of publication has been added." Neither author specifies whether this comment refers to the title page or the footline, or to both. In 19-Pr-1 the publisher number does not appear on the title page, but it is in the footline. (The same is true for Hob-255.) However, the British Library copy h.471.j.(3.) has no plate number in either place (Robert Parker, personal communication), so is presumably the first impression, while 19-Pr-1 is the second.
3. The title page of the copy described by Chominski & Turlo (p. 78) corresponds to that of 19-Pr-1. They do mention the plate number, but it is given after the pagination, which implies that it came from some source other than the title page, possibly from the footline.
4. The title page of the Hoboken copy differs from that of 19-Pr-1 in the way the imprint is stated. Which of these impressions is the first is unknown to this writer.
5. Page number 12 is in the recto position.

***Paris:* Richault (4356) [*ca* 1860]** **19-Rich-1** **M32.C54 B63**

dédié à Madelle la Comtesse | Emilie de Flahault | BOLERO | POUR | le Piano | PAR | F. CHOPIN | *Op: 19 « » Pr: 7.f 50* | *PARIS,* S. RICHAULT, *EDITr,* | *Boulevart Poissoniére, 26 au 1er.* | Æ | *4356 R*

8 leaves (346 x 267 mm): pp. [i] engr title page, [ii] blank, 51–62 engr music, [63] advt, [64] blank.

19-Rich-1 *(continued)*

19-Rich-1 *(concluded)*

CAPTION TITLE: p. 51, 'F. CHOPIN. ÷ Op: 19. « BOLERO. | » a Mademoiselle la Comtesse Emilie de FLAHAULT.'.

FOOTLINE: pp. 51–62, '4356.R.'.

ADVT: p. [63], 'COLLECTION DES ŒUVRES | POUR LE PIANO | DE FRÉDERIC CHOPIN. | PUBLIÉS PAR | T.D.A. TELLEFSEN.', and followed by a general description of the Tellefsen edition, "(NOTE DE L'ÉDITEUR.)".

STAMPS: publisher, style Rich/B (see Appendix 8).

---

1. *Date:* This score is from volume 6 of the 12 volumes of Chopin's collected works edited by Tellefsen and published by Richault *ca* 1860, with plate numbers 4351 to 4362 (Chominski & Turlo, p. 279; Brown, p. 185). The title-page address, 26 Boulevard Poissonniére, was occupied from 1841 until the firm moved to 4 Boulevard des Italiens in October 1862 (Devriès & Lesure, p. 365).

Leipzig: **Peters (2505) [after 1840]** **19-Pe-1** **M32.C54 B62**

BOLERO | pour le | Pianoforte | *composé et dédié* | *à Mademoiselle la Comtesse* | EMILIE DE FLAHAULT | par | FRÉD. CHOPIN. | Oeuv. 19. « Propriété de l'Editeur. » Pr. 25 Ngr. | *Leipzig,* | *au Bureau de Musique de C. F. Peters.* | *Paris, chez Prilipp & C°* ÷ *Londres, chez Wessel & C°* « » *St Petersbourg, chez J. C. Paez.* ÷ *Mosco, chez C. L. Lehnhold.* | *Enregistré aux archives de l'union.* | *2505.*

8 leaves (329 x 250 mm): pp. [1] lith title page, [2] blank, 3–14 engr music, [15, 16] blank.

CAPTION TITLE: p. 3, '» Frédéric Chopin. Op. 19.'.

FOOTLINE: pp. 3–14, '2505'.

WRAPPER (green): pp. [1] same as title page, [2–4] blank.

PLATES: The title page has a sunburst pattern in the background. It is shown by Hoboken (plate 19, p. 115).

STAMPS: publisher, style Pe/A (see Appendix 8).

---

1. *Date:* currency inference (date code c1, p. 17).

Leipzig: **Breitkopf & Härtel (C.X.2) 1879** **19-BH-1** **M32.C54 B66**

Friedr. Chopin's | Werke. | Band X. | Verschiedene Werke für das Pianoforte. | [list of works, item 1] | 2. Bolero. Op. 19. C dur « » " [Pr.] — [M] 90 [Pf] n. | [list of works, items 3–10 | Verlag von Breitkopf & Härtel in Leipzig.

6 leaves (338 x 270 mm): pp. [1] lith title page [series title in red], 2–11 lith music, [12] advt.

CAPTION TITLE: p. 2, 'Chopin's Werke « Bolero ÷ für das Pianoforte ÷ von ÷ FRIEDRICH CHOPIN. ÷ Op. 19. ÷ Frau Gräfin E. von Flahault gewidmet. » Band X. N° 2.'.

FOOTLINE: p. 2, '» Originalverleger C.F. Peters in Leipzig. | Stich und Druck von Breitkopf & Härtel in Leipzig. « C.X.2. » Ausgegeben 1879.'; pp. 3–11, 'C.X.2.'.

19-BH-1 *(continued)*

19-BH-1 *(concluded)*

ADVT: p. [12], 'Verlag von Breitkopf & Härtel in Leipzig. | FRIEDRICH CHOPIN'S WERKE.'. Fourteen volumes are listed, the first with the four ballades, the last with the 17 songs of Op. 74. Prices are shown for the first 12 volumes, but not for the last two.

STAMPS: publisher, styles BH/L and BH/M (see Appendix 8).

---

1. *Date:* Note the explicit publication date in the footline.
2. This score is from the 10th volume in Breitkopf & Härtel's collected edition of 1878–80, edited by Bargiel, Brahms, Franchomme, Liszt, Reinecke, and Rudorff (Chominski & Turlo, pp. 257–58).
4. The title page is printed in red and black.

London: **Wessel (1491) [= 1835]** **19-W-1** **M32.C54 B61**

L'AMATEUR PIANISTE, N°. 54. | *SOUVENIR D'ANDALOUSIE.* | BOLERO, | *pour le* | Piano Forte, | *DEDIÉ À* | *Mademoiselle la Comtesse* | Emilie de Flahault, | PAR | FREDERIC CHOPIN. | (de Varsovie.) | Copyright of the Publishers. | *Op. 19. « Ent. Sta. Hall. » Price 4/–* | *Paris, at Phillip* [*sic*] *& C°. — Leipzig, C.F. Peters.* | *LONDON,* | WESSEL & C°. *Importers of Foreign Music and Publishers of* ALL *the* | Works of CHOPIN, CZERNY, MAYSEDER, BLAHETKA, SPOHR, &c. | N°. 6, Frith Street, Soho Square.

7 leaves (335 x 254 mm): pp. [i] engr title page, [ii] blank, 1–12 engr music.

CAPTION TITLE: p. 1, '*"L'AMATEUR PIANISTE."* | *N°. 54.* | *SOUVENIR d'ANDALOUSIE.* | *BOLERO, Composé par FREDERIC CHOPIN.*'.

FOOTLINE: p. 1, 'Souvenir d'Andalousie, as a Piano Duet $4^{s}.6^{d}$. « (W & C°. N°. 1491.)'; pp. 2–11, 'CHOPIN, Souvenir d'Andalousie. « (W & C°. N°. 1491.)'; p. 12, 'CHOPIN, Souvenir d'Andalousie. « | (N°. 1491.) WESSEL & C°. N°. 6, Frith Street, Soho Square.'.

IMPOSITION: Binding and rebinding have obscured the imposition, but the last leaf may be a singleton.

STAMPS: publisher, styles W/B and W/C (see Appendix 8).

---

1. *Date:* first-edition inference (date code fe, p. 17).
2. It is possible this work was first issued without the series title, but I have not located such an example.

SCHERZO IN B MINOR
Opus 20

Paris: M. Schlesinger (1832) 1835 | *Composed* 1833
Leipzig: Breitkopf & Härtel (5599) 1835 | Brown 65
London: Wessel (1492) 1835 | Chominski & Turlo 197

***Paris:* M. Schlesinger (1832) [= 1835]** **20-mS-1** **M25.C54 S41 c.1**

Scherzo | Pour Le Piano | *Dédié* | *à Monsieur T. Albrecht* | Sécretaire de Légation de S.M. le Roi de Saxe | PAR | F. CHOPIN. | *Opera: 20.* « » *Prix: 7 f 50 c* | *PARIS, chez* MAURICE SCHLESINGER, *Rue Richelieu, 97.* | *Londres, chez Wessel et Cie* « » *Leipsick, chez Breitkopf et Härtel* | *Propté des Edrs*

10 leaves (332 x 264 mm): pp. [i] engr title page, [ii, 1] blank, 2–17 engr music, [18] blank.

CAPTION TITLE: p. 2, 'F. CHOPIN Op: 20. «'.

FOOTLINE: p. 2, 'Paris chez Maurice Schlesinger. « M.S. 1832. » rue de Richelieu N° 97.'; pp. 3–16, 'M.S. 1832.'; p. 17, same as p. 2.

STAMPS: successor, style Bra/A (see Appendix 8).

ANNOTATIONS: stamped page numbers 35–54 (see 16-mS-1).

1. *Date:* first-edition inference (date code fe, p. 17); also see note 2.
2. About two months before this separate issue, Schlesinger published the Scherzo in the *Gazette Musicale* (Brown, p. 72).

***Paris:* M. Schlesinger (1832) [= 1835]** **20-mS-2** **M25.C54 S41 c.2**

Scherzo | Pour Le Piano | *Dédié* | *à Monsieur T. Albrecht* | Sécretaire de Légation de S.M. le Roi de Saxe | PAR | F. CHOPIN. | *Opera: 20.* « » *Prix: 7 f 50 c* | *PARIS, chez* MAURICE SCHLESINGER, *Rue Richelieu, 97.* | *Londres, chez Wessel et Cie* « » *Leipsick, chez Breitkopf et Härtel* | *Propté des Edrs*

10 leaves (350 x 270 mm): pp. [i] engr title page, [ii, 1] blank, 2–17 engr music, [18] blank.

CAPTION TITLE: p. 2, 'F. CHOPIN Op: 20. «'.

FOOTLINE: p. 2, 'Paris chez Maurice Schlesinger. « M.S. 1832. » rue de Richelieu N° 97.'; pp. 3–16, 'M.S. 1832.'; p. 17, same as p. 2.

PLATES: This copy has excellent plate impressions.

STAMPS: publisher, style mS/B (see Appendix 8).

1. *Date:* first-edition inference (date code fe, p. 17).
2. About two months before this separate issue, Schlesinger published the Scherzo in the *Gazette Musicale* (Brown, p. 72).

***Leipzig:* Breitkopf & Härtel (5599) [= 1835]** **20-BH-3** **M25.C54 S4 c.2**

SCHERZO | Pour Pianoforte | composé et dédié | À MONSIEUR T. ALBRECHT | *Sécretaire de Legation de Sa M. le Roi de Saxe* | par | F. CHOPIN. | Propriété des Editeurs. | Oeuv. 20. « » Pr. 1 Rthlr. | à Leipsic, | *Chez Breitkopf & Härtel.* | *Londres, chez Wessel & C°. Paris, chez M. Schlesinger.* | *St Petersbourg, chez M. Bernard. Varsovie chez G. Sennewald.* | *Enrégistré dans les Archives de l'Union.*

10 leaves (340 x 265 mm): pp. [1] lith title page, [2, 3] blank, 4–19 engr music, [20] blank.

CAPTION TITLE: p. 4, '» F. Chopin. Op. 20.'.

SUB-CAPTION: p. 4, 'SCHERZO.'.

FOOTLINE: pp. 4–19, '5599.'.

STAMPS: publisher, style BH/D (see Appendix 8).

CONDITION: This copy is in original condition, with a clear impression and untrimmed, unblemished leaves.

1. *Date:* first-edition inference (date code fe, p. 17).

***Leipzig:* Breitkopf & Härtel (5599) [= 1835]** **20-BH-1** **M25.C54 S4 c.1**

The transcription of this title page is the same as that of 20-BH-3.

10 leaves (338 x 265 mm): pp. [1] lith title page, [2, 3] blank, 4–19 engr music, [20] blank.

CAPTION TITLE: p. 4, '» F. Chopin. Op. 20.'.

SUB-CAPTION: p. 4, 'SCHERZO.'.

FOOTLINE: pp. 4–19, '5599.'.

STAMPS: publisher, style BH/C (see Appendix 8).

BINDING: library cloth.

1. *Date:* first-edition inference (date code fe, p. 17).

***Leipzig:* Breitkopf & Härtel (5599) [after 1835]** **20-BH-2** **M25.C54 S402**

The transcription of this title page is the same as that of 20-BH-3.

10 leaves (341 x 268 mm): pp. [1] lith title page, [2, 3] blank, 4–19 lith music, [20] blank.

CAPTION TITLE: p. 4, '» F. Chopin. Op. 20.'.

SUB-CAPTION: p. 4, 'SCHERZO.'.

FOOTLINE: pp. 4–19, '5599'.

STAMPS: publisher, styles BH/B and BH/I (see Appendix 8); dealer, Risom, Copenhagen.

1. *Date:* see note 2.
2. This lithographed score probably corresponds to Hob-257, a transfer reprinting of the first edition (1835).

London: Wessel (1492) [1836–39] 20-W-1

L'AMATEUR PIANISTE — Nº 56. | *LE BANQUET INFERNAL.* | SCHERZO, | *pour le* | Piano Forte, | *DEDIÉ À* | *MONSIEUR T. ALBRECHT.* | *Secretaire de Legation de S.M. le Roi de Saxe.* | Par | FRED. CHOPIN. | *(DE VARSOVIE.)* | Copyright of the Publishers. | *Op. 20.* « *Ent. Sta. Hall.* » *Price 4/6* | *Paris, M. Schlesinger, Leipzig, Breitkopff* [*sic*] *& Härtel.* | LONDON, | WESSEL & Cº *Importers & Publishers of* FOREIGN MUSIC, | *(by special Appointment) to H.R.H. the Duchess of Kent.* | Nº 6, Frith Street, Soho Square.

10 leaves (336 x 252 mm): pp. [i] engr title page, [ii, 1] blank, 2–17 engr music, [18] blank.

CAPTION TITLE: p. 2, '*L'AMATEUR PIANISTE.* | *Nº 56.* | *"LE BANQUET INFERNAL."* | *SCHERZO, Composé par FREDERIC CHOPIN.*'.

FOOTLINE: p. 2, ' (W & Cº Nº 1492.)'; pp. 3–16, 'CHOPIN, Le Banquet Infernal. « (W & Cº Nº 1492.)'; p. 17, 'CHOPIN, Le Banquet Infernal. « | (Nº 1492.) WESSEL & Cº Nº 6, Frith Street, Soho Square.'.

STAMPS: publisher, styles W/A and W/B (see Appendix 8).

1. *Date:* The lower limit on the date is based on the series "L'Amateur Pianiste", which began with Chopin's Op. 1, published by Wessel in 1836. The upper limit is from the address (Table 5D).
2. According to Brown (p. 72), Wessel's first issue of this work did not have a serial title.

CONCERTO IN F MINOR FOR PIANO AND ORCHESTRA
Opus 21

Paris: M. Schlesinger (1940) 1836 — *Composed* 1829
Leipzig: Breitkopf & Härtel (5654) 1836 — Brown 43
London: Wessel (1642) 1836 — Chominski & Turlo 48

Paris: **M. Schlesinger (1940) [after 1836]** — **21-mS-1** — M37.C54 C73

Second | CONCERTO | Pour le Piano | Avec Acc^{t} d'Orchestre | DÉDIÉ À MADAME | *la Comtesse Delphine Potocka* | née de Komar | *PAR* | FRÉD. CHOPIN | *Op. 21.* « » *l'Orchestre* 20^{f} ÷ — *Quatuor* 18. ÷ — *Piano seul* 12. | *Propriété des Editeurs* | *PARIS, chez MAURICE SCHLESINGER, Rue Richelieu, N° 97.* | *Leipzig, Breitkopf et Hartel* « » *Londres, chez Wessel et Cie*

19 leaves (318 x 247 mm): pp. [i] engr title page, [ii] blank, 1–35 engr music, [36] blank.

CAPTION TITLE: p. 1, 'F. CHOPIN Op: 21. « '.

SUB-CAPTION: p. 1, 'CONCERTO.'.

FOOTLINE: pp. 1–35, 'M.S. 1940.'.

STAMPS: successor, style Bra/B (see Appendix 8).

1. *Date:* Grabowski (1994, p. 33, table) indicates that the price 20 francs for the orchestral edition first appeared in a Brandus catalogue of 1847, the original price having been 24 francs.

Leipzig: **Breitkopf & Härtel (5654) [= 1836]** — **21-BH-5** — M37.C54 C74

SECOND CONCERTO | Pour le Piano | *Avec Accompagnem^{t} de l'Orchestre* | *ou avec Quintuor* | *dédié* | *A Madame la Comtesse* | Delphine Potocka née de Komar | par | FRÉDERIC CHOPIN. | Oeuv. 21. « *Propriété des Editeurs.* » Pr. *av. Orchestre Rthlr. 4.– – ÷ av. Quintuor „ 3.– – ÷ av. Piano seul „ 1. 16.* – | Leipsic, chez Breitkopf & Härtel. | *Londres, chez Wessel & Co* | *Paris, chez M. Schlesinger* | *St Petersbourg, chez Bernard & Holtz.* « » *Varsovie, chez G. Sennewald.* | *Enregistré dans les Archives de l'Union.*

19 leaves (329 x 261 mm): pp. [1] lith title page, [2] blank, 3–37 engr music, [38] blank.

CAPTION TITLE: p. 3, '» FR. CHOPIN.'.

SUB-CAPTION: p. 3, 'CONCERTO.'.

HEADLINE: pp. 3–37, 'PIANOFORTE.'.

FOOTLINE: pp. 3–37, '5654'.

STAMPS: publisher, style BH/C (see Appendix 8).

BINDING: contemporary (?) blue paper, with label "Chopin | 2^{d} Clavier Concert | f moll | op. 21.".

1. *Date:* first-edition inference (date code fe, p. 17).
2. According to Hoboken, there is an earlier issue without citations of other publishers (see note at the end of Hob-260).

Leipzig: **Breitkopf & Härtel (5654) [1841–45]** **21-BH-7** **M1010.C54 C682**

The transcription of this title page is the same as that of 21-BH-5, except here the price for the piano-only edition is *"1. 20. Ngr."* (that is, Rthlr. 1 and 20 Ngr. instead of Rthlr. 1 and 16 Gr.).

Pianoforte: 19 leaves (340 x 270 mm); pagination, caption title, sub-caption, headline, and footline are the same as those of 21-BH-5.

Violino I: 4 leaves (340 x 271 mm): pp. 1–7 engr music, [8] blank. Caption title, sub-caption, headline, and footline as in Pianoforte except for 'VIOLINO I.' in the headline instead of 'PIANOFORTE'.

Violino II: 4 leaves (343 x 270 mm): pp. 1–7 engr music, [8] blank.

Viola: 4 leaves (345 x 270 mm): pp. 1–7 engr music, [8] blank.

Violoncello E Basso: 5 leaves (346 x 270 mm): pp. 1–10 engr music.

Flauto I: 2 leaves (345 x 272 mm): pp. 1–3 engr music, [4] blank.

Flauto II: 1 leaf (346 x 271 mm): pp. 1–2 engr music, with conjugate **Clarinetto II in B:** 1 leaf (346 x 271 mm): pp. 1–2 engr music.

Oboe I: 1 leaf (348 x 270 mm): pp. 1–2 engr music.

Oboe II: 1 leaf (347 x 267 mm): pp. 1–2 engr music.

Clarinetto I in B: 2 leaves (345 x 270 mm): pp. 1–3 engr music, [4] blank.

Fagotto I: 1 leaf (347 x 270 mm): pp. 1–2 engr music.

Fagotto II: 1 leaf (347 x 268 mm): pp. 1–2 engr music.

Corno I in F: 1 leaf (346 x 270 mm): pp. 1–2 engr music.

Corno II in F: 1 leaf (347 x 268 mm): pp. 1–2 engr music.

Trompa I in B: 1 leaf (343 x 269 mm): pp. 1–2 engr music.

Trompa II in B: 1 leaf (343 x 270 mm): pp. 1–2 engr music.

Trombone Basso: 1 leaf (344 x 267 mm): pp. 1–2 engr music.

Timpani F.C.: 1 leaf (344 x 270 mm): pp. 1–2 engr music.

TEXT: All orchestral parts have caption title, sub-caption, headline, and footline as in Violino I except for the appropriate instrument name in the headline instead of 'VIOLINO I'.

STAMPS: publisher, style BH/C (see Appendix 8); dealer, Roothaan, Amsterdam.

1. *Date:* currency inference (date code c2, p. 17).
2. Also present are manuscript copies of Violino I, Violino II and Viola.

Leipzig: **Breitkopf & Härtel (5654) [1841–45]** **21-BH-6** **M614.C54 C74**

The transcription of this title page is the same as that of 21-BH-5, except here the price for the piano-only edition is *"1. 20. Ngr."* (that is, Rthlr. 1 and 20 Ngr. instead of Rthlr. 1 and 16 Gr.).

Pianoforte: 19 leaves (343 x 268 mm): pp. [1] lith title page, [2] blank, 3–37 engr music, [38] blank.

CAPTION TITLE: p. 3, '» FR. CHOPIN.'.

SUB-CAPTION: p. 3, 'CONCERTO.'.

HEADLINE: pp. 3–37, 'PIANOFORTE.'.

21-BH-6 *(continued)*

21-BH-6 *(concluded)*

FOOTLINE: pp. 3–37, '5654'.

Violino I: 4 leaves (343 x 268 mm): pp. 1–7 engr music, [8] blank.

Violino II: 4 leaves (343 x 268 mm): pp. 1–7 engr music, [8] blank.

Viola: 4 leaves (343 x 268 mm): pp. 1–7 engr music, [8] blank.

Violoncello e basso: 5 leaves (343 x 268 mm): pp. 1–10 engr music.

TEXT: The accompaniment parts have caption title, sub-caption, and footline identical to those of the pianoforte part, and headlines analogous to that of the pianoforte part.

STAMPS: publisher, style BH/G (see Appendix 8).

1. *Date:* currency inference (date code c2, p. 17).

Leipzig: **Breitkopf & Härtel (6485) [*ca* 1841]** **21-BH-1** **M210.C54 C72**

SECOND CONCERTO | arrangé | pour le Piano à quatre mains | composé et dedié | *À Madame la Comtesse Delphine Potocka* | par | FRÉDÉRIC CHOPIN. | *Op. 21.* « Propriété des Editeurs. » *Pr. 2 Thlr.* | *Leipzig, chez Breitkopf & Härtel.* | *Paris, chez M. Schlesinger.* « » *Londres, chez Wessel & Co* | *6485.* | *Enrégistré aux Archives de l'Union.*

24 leaves (250 x 327 mm, oblong): pp. [1] lith title page, 2–47 engr music, [48] blank.

CAPTION TITLE: p. 2, '» Fr. Chopin, Op. 21.'; p. 3, same as p. 2.

SUB-CAPTION: p. 2. 'CONCERTO.'; p. 3, the same.

HEADLINE: pp. 2–47, 'SECONDO.' on verso, 'PRIMO.' on recto.

FOOTLINE: pp. 2–47, '6485'.

STAMPS: publisher, style BH/F (see Appendix 8).

1. *Date:* based on the plate number (Table 5C).
2. This four-hand version is noted by Paul (p. II).

Leipzig: **Breitkopf & Härtel (10721) [*ca* 1865]** **21-BH-8** **M1010.C54 C684**

SECOND | CONCERTO | pour le Pianoforte | avec accompagnement de l'Orchestre | composé | par | FRÉD. CHOPIN. | Op. 21. | PARTTION. | Propriété des Editeurs. | *Leipzig, Breitkopf & Härtel.* | *London, Wessel & Co* « Pr. 5 Thlr. » *Paris, M. Schlesinger.* | *Enrégistré aux Archives de l'Union.* | *10721.*

106 leaves (266 x 170 mm): pp. [i] lith title page, [ii] blank, 1–210 lith music (full score).

CAPTION TITLE: p. 1, '*Concerto II.* | » *Fr. Chopin. Op. 21.*'.

SUB-CAPTION: p. 1, seven staves for winds: '*Flauti.* | *Oboi.* | *Clarinetti in B.* | *Fagotti.* | *Trombone Basso.* | *Corni in F.* | *Trombe in B.* |'; one stave for '*Timpani in F.C.* |' |; two staves for '*Pianoforte.* |'; five staves for strings: '*Violino I.* | *Violino II.* | *Viola.* | *Violoncello.* | *Basso.*'; p. 96 (second movement), same as p. 1; p. 126 (third movement), same as p. 1.

FOOTLINE: p. 1, '10721.'; pp. 2–210, '10,721.'. See note 3, below.

WRAPPER (gray): p. [1] same as title page, [2, 3] blank, [4] advt.

21-BH-8 *(continued)*

21-BH-8 *(concluded)*

ADVT: wrapper p. [4] 'Partituren | im Verlag von Breitkopf & Härtel in Leipzig.', with three groups: 'Symphonien für Orchester.', 'Overturen für Orchester', and 'Diverse.'.

PLATES: The lithography of the music plates is by transfer of writing, and the transfer may be by photolithography. (I am indebted to Michael Twyman for these comments and for comments on imposition (personal communication, September 2001).)

IMPOSITION: Two half sheets of octavo, gathered in fours (Gaskell, Fig. 52). I am indebted to Michael Twyman for his comments.

STAMPS: publisher, style BH/B (see Appendix 8).

INSCRIPTIONS: 'Wilhelm Ganz | 1882.'. In the year of this inscription Wilhelm Ganz (1833–1914) was conductor of "Mr. Ganz's Orchestral Concerts" in London.

ANNOTATIONS: conductor's notes in blue pencil on many pages.

---

1. *Date:* based on the plate number (Table 5C).
2. This "octavo" full score corresponds to Hob-261. Hoboken notes that the plate number is missing on pp. 77, 99, and 119. In this copy it is missing on pp. 77 and 119 but does appear very faintly on p. 99.

***Leipzig:* Breitkopf & Härtel (5654) [1872–73]** **21-BH-2** **M37.C54 C75**

SECOND CONCERTO | POUR LE | PIANO | avec Accompagnement de l'Orchestre | ou avec Quintuor | dédié | *à Madame la Comtesse* | DELPHINE POTOCKA NÉE DE KOMAR | par | Fréd. Chopin. | Op. 21. | Propriété des Editeurs. | Leipzig, Breitkopf & Härtel. | London, Wessel & C.º « » Paris, M. Schlesinger. | Pr. { *avec Orchestre 4 Thlr. — Ngr. = Mk. 12. — ÷ „ Quintuor 3 " " "9. — ÷* *pour Piano seul 1 "20 " " 5. —* | *Enrégistré aux Archives de l'Union.* | *5654.*

19 leaves (341 x 270 mm): pp. [1] lith title page, [2] blank, 3–37 lith music, [38] advt.

CAPTION TITLE: p. 3, '» Fr. Chopin, Op. 21.'.

SUB-CAPTION: p. 3, 'CONCERTO.'.

HEADLINE: pp. 3–37, 'PIANOFORTE.'.

FOOTLINE: p. 3, 'Stich und Druck von Breitkopf & Härtel in Leipzig. « 5654'; pp. 4–37, '5654'.

ADVT: p. [38], 'Klassische und moderne Musikwerke. | Rothe Bände. | Verlag von BREITKOPF & HÄRTEL in Leipzig.'. Under Chopin are listed eight volumes of a Breitkopf & Härtel collected edition.

STAMPS: publisher, style BH/I (see Appendix 8).

1. *Date:* currency inference (date code c3, p. 17).

***Leipzig:* Breitkopf & Härtel (10807) [1872–73]** **21-BH-3** **M1011.C54 C748**

SECOND CONCERTO | POUR LE | PIANO | avec Accompagnement de l'Orchestre | ou avec Quintuor | dédié | *à Madame la Comtesse* | DELPHINE POTOCKA NÉE DE KOMAR | par | Fréd. Chopin. | Op. 21 | Arrangement pour deux Pianos à quatre mains par Aug. Horn. | *La partie du premier piano est identique avec la partie principale de l'original.* | Propriété des Editeurs. | Leipzig, Breitkopf & Härtel. | *Pr. 2 Thlr. 25 Ngr. – Mk. 8.50.* | *Enrégistré aux Archives de l'Union.* | *10,807.*

21-BH-3 *(continued)*

21-BH-3 *(concluded)*

12 leaves (335 x 270 mm): pp. [1] lith title page, [2] blank, 3–23 engr music, [24] blank.

CAPTION TITLE: p. 3, 'CONCERTO II. | » Fr. Chopin, Op. 21.'.

SUB-CAPTION: p. 3, 'PIANOFORTE II.'.

FOOTLINE: pp. 3–23, '10807'.

STAMPS: publisher, style BH/B? (see Appendix 8).

---

1. *Date:* currency inference (date code c3, p. 17).
2. This edition is a second-piano part, based on the reduction that appears in the piano-solo part. It is designed to be paired with 21-BH-2.

Leipzig: **Breitkopf & Härtel (C.XII.5) 1879** **21-BH-4** **M1010.C54 C683**

Friedrich Chopin's | Werke. | Erste kritisch durchgesehene Gesamtausgabe | Band XII. |
CONCERTE UND CONCERTSTÜCKE | für das Pianoforte | mit Begleitung des Orchesters. |
N° 1. Là ci darem la mano. Op. 2. B dur.
N° 2. Grosses Concert. Op. 11. E moll.
N° 3. Grosse Phantasie. Op. 13. A dur.
N° 4. Krakowiak. Grosses Concert-Rondo. Op. 14. F dur.
N° 5. Zweites Concert. Op. 21. F moll.
N° 6. Grosse brillante Polonaise. Op. 22. Es dur.
N° 5. Zweites Concert Op. 21. F moll. | PARTITUR. | Leipzig, Verlag von Breitkopf & Härtel. |
Die Resultate der kritischen Revision dieser Ausgabe sind | Eigenthum der Verleger.

36 leaves (337 x 271 mm): pp. [i] lith title page, [ii] blank, 1–68 engr music, [69, 70] blank.

CAPTION TITLE: p. 1, 'Chopin's Werke. « ZWEITES CONCERT ÷ für das Pianoforte ÷ mit Begleitung des Orchesters ÷ von ÷ FRIEDRICH CHOPIN. ÷ Op. 21. ÷ Frau Gräfin Delphine Potocka geb. Gräfin Komar gewidmet » Band XII N° 5.'.

FOOTLINE: p. 1, 'Stich und Druck von Breitkopf & Härtel in Leipzig. « C.XII.5. » Ausgegeben 1879.'; pp. 2–68, 'C.XII.5.'.

WRAPPER (gray): pp. [1] lith series title page, [2] blank; lacks conjugate leaf.

SERIES TITLE: wrapper p. [1], 'Friedr. Chopin's | Werke. | Band XII. | Concerte und Concertstücke | für das Pianoforte mit Begleitung des Orchesters. | No. 5. Zweites Concert. Op. 21. F moll. | PARTITUR. | Preis Mark 5.40 n. | Verlag von Breitkopf & Härtel in Leipzig.'.

STAMPS: none.

INSCRIPTIONS: wrapper inscribed "J. Albert Jeffery | Leipzig | 1879".

---

1. *Date:* Note the explicit publication date in the footline.
2. This edition is the full score (in folio).

POLONAISE IN E FLAT MAJOR FOR PIANO AND ORCHESTRA
Opus 22

Paris: M. Schlesinger (1926) 1836 — *Composed* 1830–35
Leipzig: Breitkopf & Härtel (5709) 1836 — Brown 58
London: Wessel (1643) 1836 — Chominski & Turlo 149

***Paris:* M. Schlesinger (1926) [= 1836]** **22-mS-1** **M37.C54 P79**

Grande | POLONAISE BRILLANTE | *précédée d'un* | ANDANTE SPIANATO | *pour le* | Piano | *avec accompt d'Orchestre* | dédiée à | Madame d'Est | *Par* | F. CHOPIN | *Op. 22.* « » *Propriété des Editeurs.* | *Prix* | *Avec Orchestre* . 18f. | — *Quatuor* ..... 12. | *Piano Seul* ..... 7. 50c. | *Paris, chez Maurice Schlesinger, Rue Richelieu, 97.* | *Leipzig, Breitkopf et Härtel.* « » *Londres, Mori et Lavenu*

12 leaves (345 x 275 mm): pp. [i] engr title page, [ii, 1] blank, 2–22 engr music.

CAPTION TITLE: p. 2, 'F. CHOPIN. op: 22 ÷ Grande Polonaise. «'.

SUB-CAPTION: p. 2, 'Andante | SPIANATO.'.

FOOTLINE: pp. 2–22, 'M.S. 1926.'.

WRAPPER (green): pp. [1] same as title page, [2, 3] blank, [4] advt.

ADVT: wrapper p. [4], 'PUBLIÉ PAR | BRANDUS & CIE , | EDITEURS DE MUSIQUE, | *Rue Richelieu, no* 103. | 1re SÉRIE DES | SUCCÉS UNIVERSELS | *MORCEAUX DE PIANO DIFFICILES.*'. The Chopin list consists of Opp. 6, 7, 9, 11, 20, 21, 23, 24, 27, 29, 31, 32, 24, 35, "La Marche funèbre seule", 43, 64.

IMPOSITION: There is no singleton: a final blank leaf was not intended.

STAMPS: successor, style Bra/A (see Appendix 8).

1. *Date:* first-edition inference (date code fe, p. 17).
2. The Brandus wrapper is from after 1848. Except for the wrapper, this score corresponds to Hob-263.

***Paris:* Heugel (3137) [after 1867]** **22-Heu-1** **M37.C54 P812**

[at the head:] ÉDITION CLASSIQUE | APPROUVÉE PAR MM. | AUBER, G. ROSSINI, G. MEYERBEER, F. HALÉVY, CARAFA, AD. ADAM, ONSLOW, | A. THOMAS, REBER, H. BERLIOZ, CH. GOUNOD, CLAPISSON ET G. KASTNER, | Membres de l'Institut. | [at the sides: names of composers in the series, but not Chopin] [in the passe-partout center:] *A Madame d'Est* | GRANDE | POLONAISE | *AVEC* | Andante | *PAR* | F. CHOPIN | *A.V.* | *Op: 22.* « » *Pr: 9 f.* | *(Trés difficile)* | [at the foot:] 1RE, 2E, 3E, 4E ET 5E SÉRIES DES CHEFS-D'ŒUVRE CLASSIQUES DU PIANO | ACCOMPAGNÉS D'OBSERVATIONS TRADITIONELLES SUR LA MANIÈRE D'EXÉCUTER CES ŒUVRES | REVUS, DOIGTÉS ÷ ET ÷ ACCENTUÉS PAR « MARMONTEL » PROFESSEUR ÷ AU ÷ CONSERVATOIRE. | HEUGEL et Cie, Éditeurs-Fournisseurs « » du CONSERVATOIRE. | Paris, AU MÉNESTREL, 2 bis, r. Vivienne. | 609 — Typ. Charles de Mourgues frres, « » rue J.-J.Rousseau, 58. – 3994.

14 leaves (337 x 264 mm): pp. [i] lith title page, [ii] blank, [iii] preface, [iv] blank, 1–23 engr music, [24] advt.

22-Heu-1 *(continued)*

22-Heu-1 *(concluded)*

PREFACE: p. [iii], 'FRÉDÉRIC CHOPIN, | NÉ EN POLOGNE LE 1er MARS 1809, MORT A PARIS LE 17 OCTOBRE 1849. | PRÉFACE. | (*Tablettes du Pianiste*, MÉNESTREL du 5 décembre 1859.)'. The Preface is by Marmontel.

CAPTION TITLE: p. 1, 'GRANDE POLONAISE. « F. CHOPIN » OP – 22.', followed by a 10-line paragraph of discussion, presumably by Marmontel.

FOOTLINE: p. 1, 'Paris, AU MÉNESTREL, 2 bis, r. Vivienne. « H. 3137. » Imp: [illegible]'; pp. 2–23, 'H. 3137.'.

ADVT: p. [24], 'MUSIQUE DE CHAMBRE'; the lists do not include works by Chopin. In the bottom line is a reference to the expositions of 1855 and 1867.

STAMPS: publisher, style Heu/A (see Appendix 8); dealer, Rouget, Toulouse.

---

1. *Date:* based on the advertisement.
2. The preface quotes an article by Léon Gatayes published 5 December 1859.

Leipzig: **Breitkopf & Härtel (5709) [= 1836]** **22-BH-1** **M37.C54 V19**

GRANDE | POLONAISE | brillante | précédée d'un Andante spianato | Pour le Piano |
avec accompagnement de l'Orchestre | dédiée | à Madame la Baronne d'Est | par | F. CHOPIN. |
Oeuvre 22. « » *Pr.* { *av. Orch. 2 Rthlr. 12 Gr. ÷ p. P.º seul. 1 „ 8 „* | Propriété des Editeurs. |
à Leipsic, chez Breitkopf & Härtel. | *Londres, chez Wessel & C.º* « » *Paris, chez M. Schlesinger.* |
St. Petersbourg, chez Bernard & Holtz. | *Varsovie, chez G. Sennewald.* | *Enrégistré dans les Archives de l'Union.*

13 leaves (313 x 253 mm): pp. [1] lith title page, [2, 3] blank, 4–24 engr music, [25, 26] blank.

CAPTION TITLE: p. 4, '» F. Chopin, Grande Polonaise. Oe. 22.'.

SUB-CAPTION: p. 4, 'ANDANTE | SPIANATO.'; p. 9, 'POLONAISE.'.

FOOTLINE: pp. 4–24, '5709'.

STAMPS: publisher, style BH/D (see Appendix 8).

BOUND WITH: 2-Ha-1.

---

1. *Date:* first-edition inference (date code fe, p. 17).

Leipzig: **Breitkopf & Härtel (5709) [1841–45]** **22-BH-4** **M37.C54 P816**

GRANDE | POLONAISE | brillante | précédée d'un Andante spianato | Pour le Piano |
avec accompagnement de l'Orchestre | dédiée | à Madame la Baronne d'Est | par | F. CHOPIN. |
Oeuvre 22. « » *Pr.* { *av. Orch. 2 Rthlr. 15 Ngr. ÷ p. P.º seul. 1 „ 10 „* | Propriété des Editeurs. |
à Leipsic, chez Breitkopf & Härtel. | *Londres, chez Wessel & C.º* « » *Paris, chez M. Schlesinger.* |
St. Petersbourg, chez Bernard & Holtz. | *Varsovie, chez G. Sennewald.* | *Enrégistré dans les Archives de l'Union.*

13 leaves (320 x 260 mm): pp. [1] lith title page, [2, 3] blank, 4–24 engr music, [25, 26] blank.

CAPTION TITLE: p. 4, '» F. Chopin, Grande Polonaise. Oe. 22.'.

SUB-CAPTION: p. 4, 'ANDANTE | SPIANATO.'; p. 9, 'POLONAISE.'.

FOOTLINE: pp. 4–24, '5709'.

22-BH-4 *(continued)*

22-BH-4 *(concluded)*

WRAPPER (tan): pp. [1] same as title page, [2, 3] blank, [4] advt. The wrapper is mounted on card stock.

ADVT: wrapper p. [4], 'JOSEPH HAYDN'S WERKE | im Verlage von | BREITKOPF & HÄRTEL IN LEIPZIG.'.

STAMPS: publisher, style BH/E (see Appendix 8).

---

1. *Date:* currency inference (date code c2, p. 17).

***Leipzig:* Breitkopf & Härtel (8805) [*ca* 1854]** **22-BH-3** **M37.5.C54 P815**

ANDANTE SPIANATO | pour le Piano | tiré de la | Grande Polonaise Brillante | Op. 22. | de |
F. CHOPIN. | Propriété des Editeurs. | Leipzig, chez Breitkopf & Härtel. | Londres, chez Wessel & C$^{\underline{o}}$ « »
Paris, chez Brandus & C$^{\underline{o}}$ | *Pr. 10 Ngr.* | *Enrégistré aux Archives de l'Union.* | *8805.*

4 leaves (337 x 266 mm): pp. [1] lith title page, [2] blank, 3–7 engr music, [8] blank.

CAPTION TITLE: p. 3, 'ANDANTE SPIANATO | par | F. CHOPIN.'.

FOOTLINE: pp. 3–7, '8805'.

WRAPPER (blue): pp. [1] collective title page, [2, 3] blank, [4] advt.

COLLECTIVE TITLE: wrapper p. [1], 'OEUVRES DE PIANO | DE FRÉD. CHOPIN.'. The list of works is classified in eleven genres: Valses, Notturnos, Ballades, Sonates, Etudes, Mazurkas, Polonaises, Scherzos, Impromptus, Preludes, and Concertos, Variations etc. The last opus number listed is 65.

ADVT: wrapper p. [4], 'SIGISMUND THALBERG'S WERKE | im Verlage von | Breitkopf und Härtel in Leipzig.'.

STAMPS: publisher, styles BH/I (wrapper) and BH/J (see Appendix 8); dealer, Schirmer, New York.

---

1. *Date:* based on the plate number (Table 5C).
2. This extract edition is from the "Polonaises" volume of the Breitkopf & Härtel collected edition of 1852–67 (Chominski & Turlo, p. 256), but with the original plates. There are eleven volumes in the collected edition, of which the "Polonaises" is the seventh.

***Leipzig:* Breitkopf & Härtel (5709) [after 1854]** **22-BH-2** **M37.C54 P814**

GRANDE | POLONAISE | brillante | précédée d'un Andante spianato | POUR LE PIANO |
avec accompagnement de l'Orchestre | dédiée | à Madame la Baronne d'Est | par | F. CHOPIN. |
Oeuvre 22. « » Pr. { *av. Orch. 2 rf. 15 Ngr. ÷ p. P^{o} seul. 1 „10 „* | Propriété des Editeurs. |
LEIPZIC, chez BREITKOPF & HÄRTEL. | Londres, chez Wessel & C$^{\underline{o}}$ |
Paris, chez Brandus, Dufour & C$^{\underline{o}}$ | *5709.* | *Enrégistre aux Archves* [*sic*] *de l'Union.*

13 leaves (338 x 268 mm): pp. [1] lith title page, [2, 3] blank, 4–24 engr music, [25, 26] blank.

CAPTION TITLE: p. 4, '» F. Chopin, Grande Polonaise. Oe. 22.'.

SUB-CAPTION: p. 4, 'ANDANTE | SPIANATO.'; p. 9, 'POLONAISE.'.

FOOTLINE: pp. 4–24, '5709'.

WRAPPER (blue): pp. [1] series title page, [2] blank; lacks conjugate leaf.

22-BH-2 *(continued)*

22-BH-2 *(concluded)*

SERIES TITLE: wrapper, p. [1], 'POLONAISEN | FÜR DAS PIANOFORTE | VON | FR. CHOPIN. | Op. 22. in Es « » 1 Thlr. 10 Ngr. | [a list of polonaises, Opp. 26, 40, 53, 61] | Eigenthum der Verleger. | LEIPZIG, BREITKOPF & HÄRTEL. | Eingetragen in das Vereins-Archiv. | (Diese Polonaisen sind in demselben Verlage für das Pianoforte zu 4 Händen erscheinen.)'.

STAMPS: publisher, style BH/J (see Appendix 8); dealers, Schuberth, New York; Werneke, New York (blind).

1. *Date:* based on the name of the Paris publisher (Table 5A).

BALLADE IN G MINOR
Opus 23

Paris: M. Schlesinger (1928) 1836 — *Composed* 1833
Leipzig: Breitkopf & Härtel (5706) 1836 — Brown 66
London: Wessel (1644) 1836 — Chominski & Turlo 2

Paris: M. Schlesinger (1928) [= 1836] — **23-mS-1** — **M25.C54 B12**

Ballade | pour Le Piano | dédiée à | *M.r Le Baron de Stockhausen* | PAR | F. CHOPIN | *Op: 23* « » *Pr: 7.f 50 c.* | *Propriété des Editeurs.* | *PARIS, chez MAURICE SCHLESINGER, Rue Richelieu, 97* | *Leipsig, chez Breitkopf et Härtel* « » *Londres, chez Wessel et Comp.ie*

9 leaves (333 x 263 mm): pp. [i] engr title page, [ii, 1] blank, 2–15 engr music, [16] blank.

CAPTION TITLE: p. 2, 'F. CHOPIN Op: 23. ÷ Ballade. «'.

FOOTLINE: pp. 2–15, 'M.S. 1928.'.

TEXT: In agreement with a Chopin manuscript (Brown, p. 73), this edition has E flat (instead of D) in bar 7.

STAMPS: successor, style Bra/B (see Appendix 8).

ANNOTATIONS: stamped page numbers 111–128.

1. *Date:* first-edition inference (date code fe, p. 17).

Paris: H. Lemoine (5416) [*ca* 1863] — **23-hL-1** — **M25.C54 B122**

à Monsieur | Le Baron de Stockhausen. | 1.re | BALLADE | POUR | PIANO | *PAR* | FR. CHOPIN | OP. 23. | *Prix 8.f* | P. | *PARIS.* | *Henry LEMOINE, Editeur,* | *Rue S.t Honoré, 256.* | *COMMISSION* « *HL. 5416.* » *EXPORTATION.* | *Imp. L. Salmé, R. de la Poterie, 20.*

9 leaves (335 x 259 mm): pp. [i] engr title page, [ii, 1] blank, 2–15 engr music, [16] blank.

CAPTION TITLE: p. 2, '1re BALLADE | FR. CHOPIN Op. 23. « » *à Mr le Baron de STOCKHAUSEN.*'.

FOOTLINE: p. 2, '15.e Degré des Tablettes du Pianiste de Hry LEMOINE. « 5416. HL. » *M.me V.e RIS graveur.*'; pp. 3–14, '5416. HL'; p. 15, '5416. HL. » Paris, Imp. L. Salmé, rue de la Poterie, 20.'.

TEXT: In agreement with a Chopin manuscript (Brown, p. 73), this edition has E flat (instead of D) in bar 7.

STAMPS: successor, style aL/C (see Appendix 8), with "373,241"; dealer, Frey, Geneva.

1. *Date:* based on the plate number (Devriès & Lesure, p. 280).
2. This score is part of the Lemoine collected edition of 1859–94 (Chominski & Turlo, p. 270).

Leipzig: **Breitkopf & Härtel (5706) [= 1836]** **23-BH-3** **M25.C54 B124**

BALLADE | Pour le Piano | *composée et dédiée* | *à Mr. Le Baron de Stockhausen* | par | F. CHOPIN. | Propriété des Editeurs. | Oeuv. 23. « » Pr. 20 Gr. | *à Leipsic* | *Chez Breitkopf & Härtel.* | *Paris,* chez *M. Schlesinger.* « » *Londres, chez Wessel & Co.* | *St. Petersbourg, chez Bernard & Holtz.* « » *Varsovie, chez G. Sennewald.* | *Enregistré dans les Archives de l'Union.* | *Lith. de Fr. Krätzschmer à Leipsic.*

9 leaves (343 x 268 mm): pp. [1] lith title page, [2–3] blank, 4–17 engr music, [18] blank.

CAPTION TITLE: p. 4, '» F. Chopin. OP. 23.'.

SUB-CAPTION: p. 4, 'BALLADE.'.

FOOTLINE: pp. 4–17, '5706.'.

STAMPS: publisher, style BH/D (see Appendix 8).

1. *Date:* first-edition inference (date code fe, p. 17).
2. There is no plate number on the title page.

Leipzig: **Breitkopf & Härtel (5706) [1841–45]** **23-BH-2** **M25.C54 B11**

BALLADE | Pour le Piano | *composée et dédiée* | *à Mr. Le Baron de Stockhausen* | par | F. CHOPIN. | Propriété des Editeurs. | Oeuv. 23. « » Pr. 25 Ngr. | *à Leipsic* | *Chez Breitkopf & Härtel.* | *Paris, chez M. Schlesinger.* « » *Londres, chez Wessel & Co.* | *St. Petersbourg, chez Bernard & Holtz.* « » *Varsovie, chez G. Sennewald.* | *Enregistré dans les Archives de l'Union.*

9 leaves (315 x 255 mm): pp. [1] lith title page, [2–3] blank, 4–17 engr music, [18] blank.

CAPTION TITLE: p. 4, '» F. Chopin. OP. 23.'.

SUB-CAPTION: p. 4, 'BALLADE.'.

FOOTLINE: pp. 4–17, '5706.'.

STAMPS: none.

1. *Date:* currency inference (date code c2, p. 17).
2. There is no plate number on the title page.

Leipzig: **Breitkopf & Härtel (5706) [*ca* 1846–54]** **23-BH-1** **M25.C54 B1**

BALLADE | Pour le Piano | composée et dédiée | à Mr. Le Baron de Stockhausen | par | F. CHOPIN. | Propriété des Editeurs. | Oeuv. 23. « » Pr. 25 Ngr. | Leipzig, chez Breitkopf & Härtel. | PARIS, ÷ chez Brandus & Co. « » LONDRES, ÷ chez Wessel & Co. | 5706. | *Enrégistré aux Archives de l'Union.*

9 leaves (317 x 259 mm): pp. [1] lith title page, [2–3] blank, 4–17 engr music, [18] advt.

CAPTION TITLE: p. 4, '» F. Chopin. OP. 23.'.

SUB-CAPTION: p. 4, 'BALLADE.'.

FOOTLINE: pp. 4–17, '5706.'.

23-BH-1 *(continued)*

23-BH-1 *(concluded)*

ADVT: p. [18], 'Publications Nouvelles pour le Pianoforte | de | BREITKOPF & HÆRTEL à LEIPZIG.'. There are no Chopin works in the list.

STAMPS: publisher, style BH/C (see Appendix 8); dealer, Andre, [...?].

1. *Date:* based on the name of the Paris publisher (Table 5A).
2. This title page differs from that of 23-BH-2.

London: Wessel (1644) [1837–39] 23-W-1 M25.C54 B123

L'AMATEUR PIANISTE, | N° 69. | LA FAVORITE, | Ballade, | *pour le* | PIANO = FORTE, | *dédiée à* | M.r Le Baron de Stockhausen, | *par* | FRED. CHOPIN. | (de Varsovie.) | *Ent. Sta. Hall.* | *OP. 23. « Copyright of the Publishers » Price 4/–* | *Paris, M. Schlesinger. — Leipzig, Breitkopff* [*sic*] *& Härtel.* | *LONDON,* | WESSEL & C.° *Importers of Foreign Music, and Publishers of All the Works* | of CHOPIN, CZERNY, KUHLAU, HUMMEL, SOWINSKI, THALBERG, &c. | N° 6, Frith Street, Soho Square.

8 leaves (335 x 244 mm): pp. [i] engr title page, [ii] blank, [1] advt, 2–13 engr music, [14] blank.

CAPTION TITLE: p. 2, ' *"L'AMATEUR PIANISTE." (N° 69.)* | *"LA FAVORITE" BALLADE, Composée par FREDERIC CHOPIN, OP: 23* | *DEDIÉE À MONS. LE BARON DE STOCKHAUSEN.*'.

FOOTLINE: p. 2, '(W & C.° N° 1644.)'; pp. 3– 12, '*CHOPIN, OP: 23.* « (W & C.° N° 1644.)'; p. 13, '*CHOPIN, OP: 23.* (N° 1644.) WESSEL & C.° N° 6, FRITH STREET, SOHO SQUARE.'.

ADVT: p. [1], 'PAGE B [?] | CATALOGUE OF WESSEL & CO,'S CHOICE PUBLICATIONS OF MODERN-PIANO FORTE MUSIC. | N° 6, FRITH STREET, SOHO SQUARE, LONDON.'. The Chopin works listed are Opp. 5, 10, 25.

STAMPS: publisher, styles W/C (?) and W/B (see Appendix 8).

1. *Date:* The lower limit on the date is based on Op. 25 in the advertisement. The upper limit is based on the address (Table 5D).
2. According to Brown (p. 73) this series edition is a re-issue.
3. On the basis of bar 7, Grabowski (personal communication 30 May 2000) considers this score to be a second impression of the first edition.

MAZURKAS IN G MINOR, C MAJOR, A FLAT MAJOR, B FLAT MINOR
Opus 24

Paris: M. Schlesinger (1870) 1835	*Composed* 1833
Leipzig: Breitkopf & Härtel (5647) 1836	Brown 89
London: Wessel (1645) 1836	Chominski & Turlo 64

***Paris:* M. Schlesinger (1870) [= 1835]** **24-mS-1** **M32.C54 M461**

Quatre Mazurkas | *Pour* | Le Piano | dédiés | *à Monsieur le Comte de Perthius* | PAR | FRÉD. CHOPIN |
Op: 24. « » *Pr: 7.f 50 c.* | *PARIS, chez MAURICE SCHLESINGER, Rue de Richelieu, 97.* |
Leipsick, chez Breitkopf et Haertel. | *Propriété des Editeurs.*

9 leaves (325 x 258 mm): pp. [i] engr title page, [ii, 1] blank, 2–15 engr music, [16] blank.

CAPTION TITLE: p. 2, 'Fr. CHOPIN. op: 24. « | Quatre MAZURKAS. «'.

SUB-CAPTION: p. 2, 'No. 1. | MAZURKA.'; and so on through p. 10, 'No. 4. | MAZURKA.'.

FOOTLINE: pp. 2–15, 'M.S. 1070. [*sic*]'; see note 2.

STAMPS: publisher, style mS/B (see Appendix 8).

1. *Date:* first-edition inference (date code fe, p. 17).
2. The footline plate number "1070" is probably an engraver's error for 1870. Brown (p. 93) gives plate number "1870" without comment, while Hoboken (Hob-274) and Chominski & Turlo (p. 117) both give "1070" without comment. Number 1070 is in the range of plate numbers assigned in years 1830–31 (Table 5A), and number 1870 falls in the year 1835, the date of Schlesinger's publication of Op. 24.

***Leipzig:* Breitkopf & Härtel (5647) [= 1836]** **24-BH-1** **M32.C54 M462 c.1**

4 | MAZURKAS | pour Le Pianoforte | dédiées | à Monsieur le Comte de Perthius | *composées* | par |
FRÉDR. CHOPIN. | Propriété des Editeurs. | Oeuv. 24. « » Pr. 20 Gr. | *Leipsic* | *chez Breitkopf & Härtel.* |
Londres, *chez Wessel & Co.* | Paris, *chez M Schlesinger* | *St. Petersbourg, chez Bernard & Holtz.* « »
Varsovie, chez G. Sennewald. | *Enregistré dans les Archives de l'Union.*

9 leaves (315 x 249 mm): pp. [1] lith title page, [2, 3] blank, 4–17 engr music, [18] blank.

CAPTION TITLE: p. 4, '» Chopin Op. 24.'.

SUB-CAPTION: p. 4, 'N. I. | Masurka. [*sic*]'; and so on through p. 12, 'N. IV. | Masurka. [*sic*]'.

FOOTLINE: pp. 4–17, '5647.'.

STAMPS: publisher, style BH/J (see Appendix 8); dealer, Scharfenberg & Luis, New York.

1. *Date:* first-edition inference (date code fe, p. 17).

Leipzig: **Breitkopf & Härtel (5647) [= 1836]** **24-BH-2** **M32.C54 M462 c.2**

The transcription of this title page is the same as that of 24-BH-1.

9 leaves (323 x 249 mm): pp. [1] lith title page, [2, 3] blank, 4–17 engr music, [18] blank.

CAPTION TITLE: p. 4, '» Chopin Op. 24.'.

SUB-CAPTION: p. 4, 'N. I. | Masurka. [*sic*]'; and so on through p. 12, 'N. IV. | Masurka. [*sic*]'.

FOOTLINE: pp. 4–17, '5647.'.

STAMPS: publisher, style BH/C (see Appendix 8).

1. *Date:* first-edition inference (date code fe, p. 17).
2. The plates of 24-BH-2 are the same as those of 24-BH-1.

Leipzig: **Breitkopf & Härtel (5647) [1841–45]** **24-BH-3** **M32.C54 M463**

The transcription of this title page is the same as that of 224-BH-1, except here the price is "25 Ngr.".

9 leaves (319 x 256 mm): pp. [1] lith title page, [2, 3] blank, 4–17 engr music, [18] blank.

CAPTION TITLE: p. 4, '» Chopin Op. 24.'.

SUB-CAPTION: p. 4, 'N. I. | Masurka. [*sic*]'; and so on through p. 12, 'N. IV. | Masurka. [*sic*]'.

FOOTLINE: pp. 4–17, '5647.'.

STAMPS: none.

1. *Date:* currency inference (date code c2, p. 17).
2. The music plates of 24-BH-3 are the same as those of 24-BH-1.

London: Wessel (1645) [1836–39] 24-W-1 M32.C54 M464

L'AMATEUR PIANISTE N° 80. | SOUVENIR DE LA POLOGNE, | 4e Recueil de | QUATRE MAZURKAS, | *pour le* | Piano Forte, | Dédiés à | Monsieur le Comte de Perthuis. | par | FRED. CHOPIN. | (de Varsovie.) | *Copyright of the Publishers.* | *Op. 24.* « *Ent. Sta. Hall.* » *Price 3/6* | *Paris, M. Schlesinger, Leipzig, Breitkopff* [*sic*] *& Härtel.* | *LONDON,* | WESSEL & C° *Importers and Publishers of* FOREIGN MUSIC, | *(by special Appointment) to H.R.H. the Duchess of Kent,* | N° 6, Frith Street, Soho Square.

7 leaves (335 x 254 mm): pp. [i] engr title page, [ii] blank, [1] advt, 2–11 engr music, [12] blank.

CAPTION TITLE: p. 2, '*SOUVENIR de la POLOGNE.* | *4e Recueil de QUATRE MAZURKAS, COMPOSES PAR* | *FREDERIC CHOPIN.*'.

SUB-CAPTION: p. 2, 'N° *1.*'; and so on through p. 8, 'N° *4.*'.

FOOTLINE: p. 2, '(W & C° N° 1645.)'; pp. 3–10, 'CHOPIN. Mazurkas. Set 4. « (W & C° N° 1645.)'; p. 11, 'CHOPIN, Mazurkas. Set 4. (N° 1645.) WESSEL & C° N° 6, FRITH STREET, SOHO SQUARE.

ADVT: p. [1], heading clipped. Chopin works are listed through Op. 20.

24-W-1 *(continued)*

24-W-1 *(concluded)*

STAMPS: publisher, styles W/B and W/C (see Appendix 8).

---

1. *Date:* The lower limit on the date is based on the date of the first edition. The upper limit is based on the address (Table 5D).
2. According to Brown (p. 94) this series edition is a re-issue.

ETUDES
Opus 25

Paris: M. Schlesinger (2427) 1837
Leipzig: Breitkopf & Härtel (5832) (5833) 1837
London: Wessel (1832) (1833) 1837

Composed 1835–37
Brown 78
Chominski & Turlo 26

Paris: M. Schlesinger (2427) [= 1837] **25-mS-1** **M25.C54 E827**

Etudes | POUR *LE* PIANO | Dédiées à | *Madame la Comtesse d'Agoult* | PAR | F. CHOPIN | A. L. | *Op: 25.* « » *Prix: 18.f* | Deuxième livre d'Etudes | *PARIS, chez Maurice SCHLESINGER, Editeur Rue Richelieu, 97.* | *Leipsick, chez Breitkopf & Hartel.* « » *Londres, chez Wessel & Cie*

28 leaves (335 x 256 mm): pp. [i] engr title page, [ii] blank, 1–53 engr music, [54] blank.

CAPTION TITLE: p. 1, 'F. CHOPIN. op: 25 « ÷ 2me *LIVRE D'ÉTUDES.* « 1re ÉTUDE.'; p. 6, 2me ÉTUDE.'; and so on through p. 48, '12me ÉTUDE.'.

FOOTLINE: pp. 1–53, 'M.S. 2427.'.

STAMPS: publisher, style mS/B (see Appendix 8).

1. *Date:* first-edition inference (date code fe, p. 17).
2. Only Schlesinger issued Op. 25 in one volume.
3. Chominski & Turlo's (p. 89) transcription of the title has "2me Livre" instead of the above "Deuxième livre".

Paris: M. Schlesinger (2776) [*ca* 1842] **25-hL-1** **M25.C54 E683**

Etudes | POUR *LE* PIANO | Dédiées à | *Madame la Comtesse d'Agoult* | PAR | F. CHOPIN | A. L. | *Op: 25.* « » *Prix: 18.f* | Deuxième livre d'Etudes | *PARIS, chez Henry LEMOINE, Professeur de Piano, et Editeur de Musique,* | *Rue de l'Echelle. No 9.* | *2776. HL.*

28 leaves (340 x 260 mm): pp. [i] engr title page, [ii] blank, 1–53 engr music, [54] blank.

CAPTION TITLE: p. 1, 'F. CHOPIN. op: 25 ÷ 2me *LIVRE D'ÉTUDES.* « 1re ÉTUDE.'; p. 6, 2me ÉTUDE.'; and so on through p. 48, '12me ÉTUDE.'.

FOOTLINE: pp. 1–52, '2776. HL.'; p. 53, 'Paris chez Henry Lemoine, « 2776. HL. » Rue de l'Echelle No. 9.'. The plate number is off-center on many pages.

PLATES: The title-page impression is weak and in some places barely legible. However, the music-plate impressions are excellent. The plates are those of M. Schlesinger (see note 2 in 10-hL-1).

STAMPS: successor, style aL/A (see Appendix 8). See note 3.

BOUND WITH: 10-hL-1 (plate number 2775).

BINDING: contemporary, red quarter calf; on the backstrip: 'CHOPIN | ÉTUDES | POUR | LE PIANO'.

1. *Date:* based on the plate number (Devriès & Lesure, p. 280); also see note 2 in 10-hL-1.

25-hL-1 *(continued)*

25-hL-1 *(concluded)*

2. "In 1842 Lemoine bought the copyright to the *Études* Op. 10 and Op. 25 and to the *Waltz* Op. 18 from Maurice Schlesinger. He used the original plates in his impressions of these compositions and inserted his firm's name and address on the title pages, also changing the publisher's numbers of Op. 10 (HL 2775), Op. 25 (HL 2776), Op. 18 (HL 2777). The musical text is identical to Schlesinger's version." (Grabowski, 1954, p. 28). Note the similarity of the title-page transcriptions of 25-mS-1 and 25-hL-1.
3. In the center of the dealer stamp is 'A 617999'. This a stamp of Achille Lemoine, son of Henry Lemoine, at '256 Rue St Honoré', address of the firm after the death of Henry in 1854 (Devriès & Lesure, p. 278).

Leipzig: **Breitkopf & Härtel (5832) (5833) [= 1837]** **25-BH-1** **M25.C54 E8**

Livre I (etudes 1–6)

DOUZE | ETUDES | pour Le Piano | *dédiées* | à Madame la Comtesse d'Agoult | par | F. CHOPIN. | Propriété des Editeurs. | *Oeuvre 25. ÷ Liv. I.* « » *Pr. 1 Thlr. 12 Gr.* | *à Leipsic* | *Chez Breitkopf & Härtel* | PARIS, ÷ *CHEZ M. SCHLESINGER.* « » LONDRES, ÷ *CHEZ WESSEL & Co.* |
Enregistré dans les Archives de l'Union | *Fr. Kr.*

15 leaves (315 x 256 mm): pp. [1] lith title page, [2] blank, 3–30 engr music.

CAPTION TITLE: p. 3, '» F. CHOPIN. Oeuv. 25. Liv. 1.'.

SUB-CAPTION: p. 3, '1re | ETUDE.'; and so on through p. 26, '6 | ETUDE.'.

FOOTLINE: pp. 3–30, '5832.'.

IMPOSITION: There is no imposed singleton in this score of Livre I, which has 15 leaves. The blank conjugate of the title leaf is not present; perhaps it was removed in binding. Hob-275 has this leaf.

Livre II (etudes 7–12)

The title page is identical to that of Livre I, except with "Liv. II".

15 leaves (317 x 259 mm): pp. [1] lith title page, [2] blank, 3–30 engr music.

CAPTION TITLE: p. 3, '» F. CHOPIN. Oeuv. 25. Liv. 2.'.

SUB-CAPTION: p. 3, '7me | ETUDE.'; and so on through p. 24, '12me | ETUDE.'.

FOOTLINE: pp. 3–30, '5833.'.

IMPOSITION: There is no imposed singleton in this score of Livre II, which has 15 leaves. The blank conjugate of the title leaf is not present; perhaps it was removed in binding. After p. 30, Hob-275 describes this leaf as "1 LS" (1 blank page); presumably this "1" should be 2.

STAMPS: publisher, style BH/D (see Appendix 8) on each title page; dealer, Holtz, Moscow.

BOUND WITH: The two books of 25-BH-1 are bound separately.

BINDING: Livre I, library cloth.

---

1. *Date:* first-edition inference (date code fe, p. 17).
2. This score corresponds to Hob-275.

Leipzig: **Breitkopf & Härtel (5832) (5833) [after 1845]** **25-BH-2** **M25.C54 E826**

Livre I (etudes 1–6)

DOUZE | ETUDES | pour Le Piano | dédiées | à Madame la Comtesse d'Agoult | par | F. CHOPIN. | Propriété des Editeurs | Oeuvre 25. ÷ Liv. I. « » Pr. 1 Thlr. 15 Ngr. | *Leipzig, chez Breitkopf & Härtel.* | PARIS, ÷ *CHEZ BRANDUS & Co* « » LONDRES, ÷ *CHEZ WESSEL & Co* | 5832 u. 5833. | *Enrégistré aux Archives de l'Union.*

16 leaves (312 x 253 mm): pp. [1] lith title page, [2] blank, 3–31 lith music, [32] blank;

CAPTION TITLE: p. 3, '» F. Chopin, Op. 25, Heft 1.'.

SUB-CAPTION: p. 3, 'ÉTUDE I.'; and so on, through p. 26, 'ÉTUDE VI.'.

FOOTLINE: p. 3, 'Stich und Druck von Breitkopf u. Härtel in Leipzig. « 5832'; pp. 4–31, '5832'.

Livre II (etudes 7–12)

The title page is identical to that of Livre I (including "Liv. I." instead of Liv. II.).

16 leaves (314 x 253 mm): pp. [1] lith title page, [2] blank, 3–31 engr music, [32] blank.

CAPTION TITLE: p. 3, '» F. Chopin, Op. 25. Heft 2.'.

SUB-CAPTION: p. 3, 'ÉTUDE VII.'; and so on, through p. 24, 'ÉTUDE XII.'.

FOOTLINE: p. 3, 'Stich und Druck von Breitkopf & Härtel in Leipzig. « 5833'; pp. 4–31, '5833'.

STAMPS: publisher, style BH/J (see Appendix 8) on each title page.

1. *Date:* based on the name of the Paris publisher (Table 5A).
2. Livre I corresponds to Hob-276, except that in the latter the composer's name is capitalized in the caption title. Livre II corresponds to Hob-278, except that the latter is lithographed.
3. This score differs from 25-BH-1 in various ways, including music layout and performance marks, as well as title-page artwork. For example, etude 6 is laid out in five pages in BH-1 and in six pages in BH-2, while etude 12 is seven pages in BH-1 and in eight pages in BH-2.

London: **Wessel (1832) (1833) [1848–56]** **25-W-1** **M25.C54 E83**

Book 1 (etudes 1–6)

N^{o} [handwritten "24"] OF | WESSEL & Co's COMPLETE COLLECTION | OF | *the Compositions* | OF | FREDERIC CHOPIN | FOR THE | Piano Forte. | Solo & Duet | [list of works, Wessel 1–23] | 24 DOUZE ETUDES *3rd Set of Studies. Op. 25. 6/–* | 25 IDEM *4th Set of Studies. Op. 25. 6/* | [list of works, Wessel 26–71] | *Ent. Sta. Hall. « Copyrights. » Price . Solo* [handwritten "6/"] ÷ " *Duet* [blank] | *LONDON,* | WESSEL & Co *Importers and Publishers of* FOREIGN MUSIC, | *(by special Appointment) to H. R. H. the Duchess of Kent.* | N° 229, Regent Street, Corner of Hanover Street.

14 leaves (346 x 255 mm): pp. [i] engr title page, [ii] blank, [1] advt, 2–25 engr music, [26] blank.

CAPTION TITLE: p. 2, '*DOUZE ETUDES*, OP. 25, de FREDERIC CHOPIN.* | (Third Book of Studies.)'.

SUB-CAPTION: p. 2, '*N° 13.*'; and so on through p. 20, '*N° 18.*'.

25-W-1 *(continued)*

25-W-1 *(concluded)*

FOOTLINE: p. 2, '*Copyright. « (W. & C° N° 1832.)'; pp. 3–24, 'CHOPIN, Op: 25. Studies, Bk: 3. « (W. & C° N° 1832.)'; p. 25, 'CHOPIN, Op: 25. Studies, Bk: 3. « (N° 1832.) | N.B. __ The 2 First Books of Studies by CHOPIN, are Edited by his Pupil Fontana, | & now generally adopted by the Royal Academies of Music at London, Paris, Prague, Munich &c. &c. | WESSEL & C° «'. The address in the imprint appears to have been removed from the plate.

ADVT: p. [1], 'PAGE A. | CATALOGUE OF WESSEL AND CO.'S CHOICE PUBLICATIONS OF MODERN PIANO-FORTE MUSIC.'. The lists include Chopin works through op. 27 (entry 84 in the series "L'Amateur Pianiste").

Book 2 (etudes 7–12)

The title page is identical to that of Book 1, except with handwritten "25" instead of "24" (first line).

15 leaves (346 x 255 mm): pp. [i] engr title page, [ii] blank, 1–27 engr music, [28] advt.

CAPTION TITLE: p. 1, '*DOUZE ETUDES, OP: 25, de FREDERIC CHOPIN.* | (Fourth Book of Studies.)'.

SUB-CAPTION: p. 1, '*N° 19.*'; and so on through p. 22, '*N° 24.*'.

FOOTLINE: p. 1, '*Copyright. « (W. & C° N° 1833.)'; pp. 2–26, 'CHOPIN, Op: 25. Studies, Bk: 4. « (W. & C° N° 1833.)'; p. 27, 'CHOPIN, Op: 25. Studies, Bk: 4. « (N° 1833.) | N.B __ The First 2 Books of Studies by CHOPIN, are Edited by his Pupil FONTANA, | & now generally adopted by the Royal Academies of Music at London, Paris, Prague, Munich &c. | WESSEL & C°.« '. The address in the imprint appears to have been removed from the plate.

ADVT: p. [28], 'PAGE S. | WESSEL & CO.S EDITIONS OF THE PIANOFORTE WORKS (SOLO) BY CHOPIN, | HELLER, SCHULHOFF, KULLAK, AND AGUILAR.'. The list for Chopin consists of the 71 entries in Wessel's collection, and in addition, the Marche Funèbre extracted from Op. 35, which was issued by Wessel in 1849 (Brown, p. 119).

IMPOSITION: Leaf 8 is a singleton.

STAMPS: publisher, style W/D (see Appendix 8) on each title page.

BOUND WITH: The two books are in the same enclosure.

---

1. *Date:* Wessel inference (date code W1, p. 17).
2. Hoboken (plate 20, p. 127) shows the title page of Book 1.

Milan: **Lucca (1721) (1722) [*ca* 1837]** **25-Lu-1** **M22.C54 P93**

Cover

DOUZE | ETUDES | pour Le Piano | *dedieés* | à Madame la Comtesse d'Agoult | par | F. CHOPIN | *Cahier* [blank] « *Op. 25* » *Prix 6.f.50* | MILAN | *Chez F. Lucca Rue S. Marguerite N° 1131* | » 1721–22.

pp. [1] engr title page (as above), [2, 3] blank, [4] advt.

ADVT: cover p. [4], 'ELENCO DELLA OPERA | DI CHOPIN, DÖHLER, DE MEYER, LISZT, PRUDENT, THALBERG E WILMERS. | *PUBLICATE DA FRANC. LUCCA*'. The Chopin list has Opp. 9, 10, 12, 14, 16, 18, 19, 20, 22, 23, 25, 27, 28, 30.

25-Lu-1 *(continued)*

25-Lu-1 *(concluded)*

Cahier 1 (etudes 1–6)

14 leaves (340 x 255 mm): pp. 1–28 engr music.

CAPTION TITLE: p. 1, ' » F. CHOPIN. Oeuv. 25. Liv. 1.'.

SUB-CAPTION: p. 1, '1re | ETUDE.'; and so on through p. 24, '6 me | ETUDE.'.

FOOTLINE: pp. 1–28, '1721'.

PLATES: An "h" (engraver's mark?) appears in the lower right-hand corner of each plate.

Cahier 2 (etudes 7–12)

14 leaves (340 x 255 mm): pp. 1–28 engr music.

CAPTION TITLE: p. 1, '» F. CHOPIN. Oeuv: 25. Liv: 2.'.

SUB-CAPTION: p. 1, '7 me | ETUDE.'; and so on through p. 22, '12 me | ETUDE'.

FOOTLINE: pp. 1–28, '1722'.

PLATES: An "a" (engraver's mark?) appears in the lower right-hand corner of each plate.

STAMPS: dealer, Ferrara, Nice (not blind) on cover.

BOUND WITH: 10-Lu-1 and 28-Ca-1.

BINDING: contemporary (?) quarter calf.

---

1. *Date:* According to Belotti (p. 430), Lucca published Op. 28 (listed in the advertisement) in 1839.
2. The title page is printed only on the cover, but has a blank space for entering the Cahier number. This indicates that what is here used as a cover for both books was designed to be used as an outer bifolium for each book. The paper stock of the cover is slightly heavier than that of the internal leaves.
3. Both the layout and the style of the title-page strongly resemble those of the Breitkopf edition, 25-BH-1, which has two title pages.
4. The two books of Etudes Op. 25 are the 14th and 15th of Lucca's publications of Chopin's works (Chominski & Turlo, p. 272).

POLONAISES IN C SHARP MINOR, E FLAT MINOR
Opus 26

Paris: M. Schlesinger (1929) 1836	*Composed* 1835
Leipzig: Breitkopf & Härtel (5707) 1836	Brown 90
London: Wessel (1647) 1836	Chominski & Turlo 150

Paris: M. Schlesinger (1929) [=1836] **26-mS-1** **M32.C54 P804**

DEUX | POLONAISES | Pour le Piano | *dédiées à son ami* | J. Dessauer | *PAR* | F. CHOPIN | *Op: 26.* « » *Pr: 7.f 50.c* | *Propriété des Editeurs* | *PARIS, chez MAURICE SCHLESINGER, Rue Richelieu, N.o 97.* | *Leipsig, chez Breitkopf et Hartel* « » *Londres, chez Wessel et Comp.ie*

9 leaves (326 x 261 mm): pp. [i] engr title page, [ii] blank, 1–15 engr music, [16] blank.

CAPTION TITLE: p. 1, 'F. CHOPIN Op: 26. ÷ Deux Polonaises. «'.

FOOTLINE: pp. 1–15, 'M.S. 1929.'.

STAMPS: successor, style Bra/B (see Appendix 8).

1. *Date:* first-edition inference (date code fe, p. 17).

Paris: Richault (4354) [_ca_ 1860] **26-Rich-1** **M32.C54 P8054**

dédieés à son Ami | *J. Dessauer.* | DEUX | POLONAISES | pour le Piano | PAR | F. CHOPIN | *Op: 26.* « » *Prix: 9.f* | *3.e* et *4.e Polonaise* | *PARIS,* RICHAULT, *EDIT.r* | *Boulevart Poissonière, 26 au 1.er* | *4354. R.* | AE

9 leaves (334 x 262 mm): pp. [i] lith title page, [ii] blank, 37–51 lith music, [52] advt.

CAPTION TITLE: p. 1, 'F. Chopin ÷ Op: 26. « 3me POLONAISE. » à son Ami J. Dessauer.'; p. 42, '4.me POLONAISE.'.

FOOTLINE: pp. 37–51, '4354. R.'. On p. 39 the 'R.' is missing.

ADVT: p. [52], 'COLLECTION DES ŒUVRES | POUR LE PIANO | DE FRÉDERIC CHOPIN. | PUBLIÉS PAR | T.D.A. TELLEFSEN.', and followed by a general description of the Tellefsen edition, '(NOTE DE L'ÉDITEUR.)'.

IMPOSITION: Leaf 5 is a singleton.

STAMPS: publisher, style Rich/B (see Appendix 8).

1. *Date:* This score is from volume 4 of the 12 volumes of Chopin's collected works edited by Tellefsen and published by Richault *ca* 1860, with plate numbers 4351 to 4362 (Chominski & Turlo, p. 279; Brown, p. 185). The title-page address, 26 Boulevard Poissonniére, was occupied from 1841 until the firm moved to 4 Boulevard des Italiens in October 1862 (Devriès & Lesure, p. 365).

Leipzig: **Breitkopf & Härtel** (5707) [= 1836] **26-BH-2** M32.C54 P8051

DEUX | POLONAISES | Pour Le Piano | *composées et dédiées* | *à son Ami* | *J. DESSAUER* | par | F. CHOPIN. | Op. 26. « » Pr. 20 Gr. | Propriété des Editeurs. | *Leipsic, chez Breitkopf & Härtel.* | *Paris, chez Maurice Schlesinger.* « » *Londres, chez Wessel & C.º.* | *S.t Petersbourg, chez Bernard & Holtz.* « » *Varsovie, chez G. Sennewald.* | *Enregistré dans les Archives de l'Union.* | Lith. de Fr. Krätzschmer.

9 leaves (325 x 258 mm): pp. [1] lith title page, [2] blank, 3–17 engr music, [18] blank.

CAPTION TITLE: p. 3, '» F. Chopin. Op. 26.'; p. 8, none.

SUB-CAPTION: p. 3, 'POLONAISE 1.'; p. 8, 'POLONAISE 2.'.

FOOTLINE: pp. 3–17, '5707'.

STAMPS: none.

1. *Date:* first-edition inference (date code fe, p. 17).
2. The title page does not have a plate number.
3. This score corresponds to Hob-281.

Leipzig: **Breitkopf & Härtel** (5707) [1841–45] **26-BH-1** M32.C54 P805

The transcription of this title page is the same as that of 26-BH-2, except here the price is "25 Ngr." and the last line of 26-BH-2 (about the lithographer) is absent.

9 leaves (338 x 262 mm): pp. [1] lith title page, [2] blank, 3–17 engr music, [18] blank.

CAPTION TITLE: p. 3, '» F. Chopin. Op. 26.'; p. 8, none.

SUB-CAPTION: p. 3, 'POLONAISE 1.'; p. 8, 'POLONAISE 2.'.

FOOTLINE: pp. 3–17, '5707'.

STAMPS: none.

BINDING: library cloth.

1. *Date:* currency inference (date code c2, p. 17).
2. The title page does not have a plate number. Apart from the price, its syntax is identical to that of the first edition (26-BH-2), except that it lacks a final line with the name of the lithographer.
3. Three non-first editions are noted by Chominski & Turlo (p. 167), all with price 25 Ngr.: (a) an issue apparently the same as 26-BH-1 and Hob-282; (b) an issue the same as 26-BH-3 (not in Hoboken), with title page shown in their plate 25; (c) an issue the same as 26-BH-4 and Hob-283, with title page shown in their plate 24. Schlesinger is cited as Paris publisher in (a), but both (b) and (c) cite Brandus.
4. Chominski & Turlo imply that all three variants are engraved. This collection's variants (a) (BH-1) and (b) (BH-3) are engraved; however, variant (c) (BH-4) is not.
5. In terms of chronology, detailed comparison of the syntax and layout of the title pages indicates with near certainty that the variants were published in the order (a), (b), (c) (that is, BH-1, 3, 4).

Leipzig: **Breitkopf & Härtel (5707) [after 1845]** **26-BH-3** **M32.C54 P8052**

DEUX | POLONAISES | Pour le Piano | composées et dédiées | À SON AMI | J. DESSAUER | par | F. CHOPIN. | *Op. 26.* « Propriété des Editeurs. » *Pr 25 Ngr.* | *Leipzig, chez Breitkopf & Härtel.* | *Paris, chez Brandus & Cº* « » *Londres, chez Wessel & Cº* | *Enrégsistré aux Archives de l'Union.* | *5707.*

9 leaves (315 x 259 mm): pp. [1] lith title page, [2] blank, 3–17 engr music, [18] blank.

CAPTION TITLE: p. 3, '» F. Chopin, Op. 26.'.

SUB-CAPTION: p. 3, 'POLONAISE I.'; p. 8, 'POLONAISE II.'.

FOOTLINE: pp. 3–17, '5707'.

PLATES: The layout of the music is the same as that of the first edition (26-BH-2), but the engraving is different.

STAMPS: publisher, style BH/J (see Appendix 8).

1. *Date:* based on the name of the Paris publisher (Table 5A).
2. For comments about variant title pages of Breitkopf & Härtel's Op. 26, see 26-BH-1, notes 3–5. This score corresponds to variant (b).

Leipzig: **Breitkopf & Härtel (5707) [after 1845]** **26-BH-4** **M32.C54 P8053**

DEUX | POLONAISES | pour le Piano | composées et dédiées | À SON AMI J. DESSAUER | par | F. Chopin. | Op. 26. | Propriété des Editeurs. | Leipzig, chez Breitkopf & Härtel. | Londres, chez Wessel & C°. | « » Paris, chez Brandus & C°. | *Pr. 25 Ngr.* | °. *Enrégistré aux Archives de l'Union.* | *5707.*

9 leaves (315 x 258 mm): pp. [1] lith title page, [2] blank, 3–17 lith music, [18] blank.

CAPTION TITLE: p. 3, '» F. Chopin, Op. 26.'.

SUB-CAPTION: p. 3, 'POLONAISE I.'; p. 8, 'POLONAISE II.'.

FOOTLINE: pp. 3–17, '5707'.

STAMPS: publisher, style BH/G? (see Appendix 8).

1. *Date:* based on the name of the Paris publisher (Table 5A).
2. For comments about variant title pages of Breitkopf & Härtel's Op. 26, see 26-BH-1, notes 3–5. This score corresponds to variant (2).

NOCTURNES IN C SHARP MINOR, D FLAT MAJOR
Opus 27

Paris: M. Schlesinger (1935) 1836	*Composed* 1835
Leipzig: Breitkopf & Härtel (5666) 1836	Brown 91
London: Wessel (1648) 1836	Chominski & Turlo 114

***Paris:* M. Schlesinger (1935) [= 1836]** **27-mS-1** **M25.C54 N81**

DEUX | NOCTURNES | *pour le* | Piano | DÉDIÉS | *à Madame la Comtesse d'Appony* | *PAR* | FRÉD. CHOPIN | *Op: 27. « » Pr: 6.f* | *PARIS chez MAURICE SCHLESINGER, Rue Richelieu, 97.* | *Leipsig, Breitkopf et Hartel. « » Londres, chez Wessel et Comp.ie* | *Propriété des Editeurs.*

7 leaves (347 x 269 mm): pp. [i] engr title page, [ii, 1] blank, 2–11 engr music, [12] blank.

CAPTION TITLE: p. 2, 'P F. CHOPIN Op: 27. ÷ Deux nocturnes. «'.

SUB-CAPTION: p. 2, 'NOCTURNE I.'; p. 7, 'NOCTURNE II.'.

FOOTLINE: pp. 2–11, 'M.S. 1935.'.

WRAPPER (blue): pp. [1] same as title page, [2–4] blank.

STAMPS: successor, style Bra/B (see Appendix 8).

1. *Date:* first-edition inference (date code fe, p. 17).

***Leipzig:* Breitkopf & Härtel (5666) [1841–45]** **27-BH-2** **M25.C54 N812**

Deux | NOCTURNES | pour le | Pianoforte | *dédiés* | *à Madame la Comtesse d'Appony* | par | FRÉD. CHOPIN. | Oeuv. 27. | Propriété des Editeurs. | À LEIPSIC | *Chez Breitkopf & Härtel.* | *à LONDRES, chez Wessel & C.o . « » à Paris, chez M. Schlesinger* | *à S.t PETERSBOURG, chez Bernard & Holtz. « » à VARSOVIE, chez G. Sennewald.* | *Pr. 20 Ngr.* | *Enregistré dans les Archives de l'Union.*

7 leaves (310 x 255 mm): pp. [1] lith title page, [2, 3] blank, 4–13 engr music, [14] blank.

CAPTION TITLE: none.

SUB-CAPTION: p. 4, 'NOCTURNE I.'; p. 9, 'NOCTURNE II.'.

FOOTLINE: pp. 4–13, '5666.'.

STAMPS: publisher, style BH/K (see Appendix 8).

1. *Date:* currency inference (date code c2, p. 17).
2. This score, with citation of Schlesinger, is presumably earlier than 27-BH-1, which cites Brandus.

Leipzig: **Breitkopf & Härtel (5666) [after 1845]** 27-BH-1 M25.C54 N8

DEUX | NOCTURNES | pour le | Pianoforte | dédiés | à Madame la Comtesse d'Appony | par | FRÉD. CHOPIN. | Op. 27. | Propriété des Editeurs. | Leipzig, chez Breitkopf & Härtel. | Londres, chez Wessel & C° « » Paris, chez Brandus & C° | *Pr. 20 Ngr.* | 5666. | *Enrégistré aux Archives de l'Union.*

7 leaves (327 x 260 mm): pp. [1] lith title page, [2, 3] blank, 4–13 lith music, [14] blank.

CAPTION TITLE: p. 4, '» F. Chopin, Op. 27.'; p. 9, the same.

SUB-CAPTION: p. 4, 'NOCTURNE I.'; p. 9, 'NOCTURNE II.'.

FOOTLINE: p. 4–13, '5666'.

STAMPS: publisher, style BH/J (see Appendix 8).

1. *Date:* based on the name of the Paris publisher (Table 5A).
2. The title-page design of this score differs in various ways from that of 27-BH-2.
3. This score corresponds to Hob-288.

Milan: **Lucca (1568) [*ca* 1836]** 27-Lu-1 M25.C54 N813

Deux | NOCTURNES | Pour | Piano Forte | *dedies* | *à M^e la Comtesse d'Appony* | PAR | FRED. CHOPIN | N. 1568. « » L. 3. | Op. 27. | *Milan Chez F. Lucca*

7 leaves (323 x 249 mm): p. [i] engr title page, [ii, 1] blank, 2–11 engr music, [12] blank.

CAPTION TITLE: p. 2, '» *F. CHOPIN. Op.* 27.'

SUB-CAPTION: p. 2, 'NOCTURNE. I.'; p. 7, 'NOCTURNE. II.'.

FOOTLINE: pp. 2–11, '*E* 1568'.

STAMPS: none.

INSCRIPTIONS: "N. Benvenuti 27 Novembre 1848 [?]".

1. *Date:* Chominski & Turlo, p. 272.
2. The owner's inscription is that of Nicola Benvenuti (1783–1867), organist and composer.

PRELUDES
Opus 28

Paris: Catelin (560) 1839 | *Composed* 1838–39
Leipzig: Breitkopf & Härtel (6088) 1839 | Brown 107
London: Wessel (3098) (3099) 1839 | Chominski & Turlo 166

***Paris:* Catelin (560) [= 1839]** **28-Ca-1** **M22.C54 P93**

Livre 1 (preludes 1–12)

24 | PRÉLUDES | POUR | le Piano, | *dédiés à son ami* | *CAMILLE PLEYEL,* | *PAR* | FRÉD. CHOPIN | [handwritten "1er"] *Livre.* « » *Prix 7 f 50.* | *Divisés en deux Livres* | *PARIS, chez* AD. CATELIN et CIE *Editeurs des Compositeurs réunis, Rue Grange Batelière, No 26.* | *Londres, chez Wessel et Co* « *Ad. C.* (560) *et CIE* » *Leipzig, chez Breitkopf et Haertel.* | *Gravé par A. Vialon.*

10 leaves (340 x 255 mm): pp. [i] engr title page, [ii, 1] blank, 2–17 engr music, [18] blank.

CAPTION TITLE: p. 2, '*F. CHOPIN.* « » 24 *PRÉLUDES.*'.

SUB-CAPTION: p. 2, 'I.'; and so on through p. 16, 'XII.'.

FOOTLINE: pp. 2–16, '1er Liv: « Ade C. (560) & Cie '; p. 17, '1er Liv: Ade CATELIN & Cie « Ade C. (560) & Cie » 26. Rue Grange Batèliere.'.

Livre 2 (preludes 13–24)

The title page is identical to that of Livre 1, except for the handwritten volume number.

14 leaves (340 x 255 mm): pp. [i] engr title page, [ii, 1] blank, 2–25 engr music, [26] blank.

CAPTION TITLE: none.

SUB-CAPTION: p. 2, 'XIII.'; and so on through p. 23, 'XXIV.'.

FOOTLINE: p. 2, '2d Liv: des 24 études [*sic*] de Chopin. « Ade C. (560) & Cie '; p. 3, '2er Liv: Ade CATELIN & Cie « Ade C. (560) & Cie » 26. Rue Grange Batèliere.'; pp. 4–24, '2d Liv: « Ade C. (560) & Cie '; p. 25, same as p. 3.

STAMPS: publisher, style Ca/A (see Appendix 8) on each title page; dealer, Ferrara, Nice (blind stamp, on each title page).

BOUND WITH: 10-Lu-1 and 25-Lu-1.

BINDING: contemporary (?) quarter calf.

1. *Date:* first-edition inference (date code fe, p. 17).
2. Grabowski (1994, p. 21) found two impressions of the Catelin first edition, of which 28-Ca-1 is the second. The first has "J. CHOPIN" in the caption title and roman numerals for the number of preludes. He does not comment on the price, which presumably is the same in the two impressions.
3. Hob-298 (Livre 2 only), although dated as a first edition, has a price of 9 f, and according to Grabowski (1994, p. 33) is in fact the first of several issues by Brandus, who acquired the copyright in 1846.
4. In the first editions, the opus number appeared only in that of Breitkopf & Härtel (28-BH-1).

Paris: **Brandus (4594) [after 1850]** **28-Bra-1** **M25.C54 P806**

Livre 1 (preludes 1–12)

24 | PRÉLUDES | POUR | Le Piano, | *dédiés à son ami* | *CAMILLE PLEYEL,* | *PAR* | FRÉD. CHOPIN | *Op: 28.* « » *Prix 9 f.* | *Divisés en deux Livres* | *N.º* [blank] | *PARIS,* | *chez BRANDUS et C.ie Editeurs. 103. Rue Richelieu.* | *S.t Petersbourg, Maison Brandus.* | *Londres, chez Wessel et C.º* « *B. et C.ie 4594.* » *Leipzig, chez Breitkoff* [*sic*] *et Haertel.* | *Gravé par A. Vialon.*

10 leaves (333 x 256 mm): pp. [i] engr title page, [ii, 1] blank, 2–17 engr music, [18] blank.

CAPTION TITLE: p. 2, '*F. CHOPIN.* « » *24 PRELUDES.*'.

SUB-CAPTION: p. 2, 'I.'; and so on through p. 16, 'XII.'.

FOOTLINE: p. 2, plate too worn to read, but see Livre 2; pp. 3–16, '1.er Liv: « B. et C.ie 4594.'; p. 17, '1.er Liv: Brandus et C.ie « B. et C.ie 4594. » 97 rue Richelieu.'.

PLATES: The plates are those of the Catelin edition, 28-Ca-1, with changes (on the title page and in the footline) required by the Brandus republication.

Livre 2 (preludes 13–24)

The title page is identical to that of Livre 1.

14 leaves (333 x 256 mm): pp. [i] engr title page, [ii, 1] blank, 2–25 engr music, [26] blank.

CAPTION TITLE: none.

SUB-CAPTION: p. 2, 'XIII.'; and so on through p. 23, 'XXIV.'.

FOOTLINE: p. 2, '2.d Liv: des 24 études [*sic*] de Chopin. « B. et C.ie 4594.'; pp. 3–24, '2.d Liv: « B. et C.ie 4594.'; p. 25, '2.d Liv: « B. et C.ie 4594. » Brandus et C.ie 97 rue Richelieu.'.

PLATES: see Livre I.

STAMPS: publisher, style Bra/A (see Appendix 8) on Livre 1.

ANNOTATIONS: handwritten leaf numbers 152–161 on recto pages of Livre I, and 162–175 on Livre II.

BOUND WITH: The two books are in the same enclosure.

1. *Date:* based on the address on the title page.
2. The title page is consistent with impression "e)" in the list of six described by Grabowski (1994, p. 34), dated by him 1852–54.

Leipzig: **Breitkopf & Härtel (6088) [= 1839]** **28-BH-1** **M25.C54 P8**

Vingt-quatre | PRÉLUDES | pour le Piano | dédiés à son ami | J. C. KESSLER | par | FRÉD. CHOPIN. | Oeuvre 28. « Propriété des Editeurs. » Pr. 2 Rthlr. | *Leipsic, chez Breitkopf & Härtel.* | *Paris, chez Pleyel & C.º* | *6088.* | *Enrégistré dans l'Archive de l'Union.*

20 leaves (317 x 258 mm): pp. [1] lith title page, [2, 3] blank, 4–39 engr music, [40] blank.

CAPTION TITLE: p. 4, '» F. CHOPIN. Op. 28.'.

SUB-CAPTION: p. 4, 'N.º 1.'; and so on through p. 36, 'N.º 24.'.

FOOTLINE: pp. 4–39, '6088.'.

28-BH-1 *(continued)*

28-BH-1 *(concluded)*

IMPOSITION: This score consists of bifolia gathered as (in sequence) one section in 2s (one bifolium), four sections in 4s (each two bifolia), and one section in 2s (one bifolium). The first and last sections are tipped to their adjacent neighbors.

STAMPS: publisher, style BH/D (see Appendix 8); dealer, Holtz, St. Petersburg.

1. *Date:* first-edition inference (date code fe, p. 17).
2. Only Breitkopf & Härtel issued Op. 28 in one volume.
3. This score corresponds to Hob-295 (strictly 296 with no wrapper); there is also a later variant (Hob-297).

***Leipzig:* Breitkopf & Härtel (6088) [1872–73]** **28-BH-2** **M25.C54 P801**

Vingt-quatre | PRÉLUDES | pour le Piano | DÉDIÉS À SON AMI | J. C. KESSLER |
par | FRÉDÉRIC CHOPIN. | Op. 28. | En quatre Cahiers. | Propriété des Editeurs. |
Leipzig, chez Breitkopf & Härtel. | *Paris, chez Pleyel & Co.* | *Cah. I.* [*Pr. 15 Ngr. ÷ Mk. 1.50.*]
Cah. II. [*Pr. 15 Ngr. ÷ Mk. 1.50.*] *Cah. III.* [*Pr. 20 Ngr. ÷ Mk. 2.–*] *Cah. IV.* [*Pr. 15 Ngr. ÷ Mk. 1.50.*] |
Enrégistré aux Archives de l'Union. | *6088. (1 – 4)*

8 leaves (326 x 258 mm): pp. [1] lith title page, [2] blank, 3–15 lith music, [16] blank.

CAPTION TITLE: none.

SUB-CAPTION: p. 3, 'N° 13.'; and so on through p. 15, 'N° 18.'.

FOOTLINE: pp. 3–15, '6088.'.

STAMPS: none.

1. *Date:* currency inference (date code c3, p. 17).
2. This score is Cahier III. Op. 28 was published in four books also by Jurgenson (28-Jur-1).

***London:* Wessel (3098) [= 1839]** **28-W-1** **M25.C54 P805 v. 1**

Book 1 (preludes 1–14)

Book [handwritten "1"] of | *Twenty Four* | GRAND PRELUDES. | *through all Keys.* | *for the* | Piano Forte. |
PERFORMED ÷ BY THE AUTHOR « *Dedicated to his Friend,* » AT THE COURT ÷ OF ST CLOUD. |
Camille Pleyel, | BY | FRED. CHOPIN. | *Copyright of the Publishers.* | OP. [blank] « *Ent. Sta. Hall.* »
Price 6/- ea. | THIS WORK FORMS BOOK 5. & 6. OF CHOPIN'S GRAND STUDIES. |
LONDON, | WESSEL & C° *Importers of Foreign Music & Publishers of all the Works of* |
CHOPIN, KUHLAU, HUMMEL, &c. | N° 67, Frith Street, Corner of Soho Square. |
Paris, Catelin & C° *Leipzig, Breitkopff* [*sic*] *& C°*

11 leaves (340 x 250 mm): pp. [i] engr title page, [ii, 1] blank, 2–20 engr music.

CAPTION TITLE: p. 2, '*TWENTY FOUR GRAND PRELUDES, BY FREDERIC CHOPIN.* | *DEDICATED to CAMILLE PLEYEL.*'.

SUB-CAPTION: p. 2, '*N° 1.*'; and so on through p. 20, '*N° 14.*'.

28-W-1 *(continued)*

28-W-1 *(concluded)*

FOOTLINE: p. 2, 'BOOK 1. « (W & C° N° 3098.)'; pp. 3–19, 'CHOPIN. 24 Grand Preludes. Bk: 1. « (W & C° N° 3098.)'; p. 20, 'CHOPIN. 24 Grand Preludes. Bk: 1. « WESSEL & C° N° 67, FRITH St CORNER OF SOHO SQUARE. » (N° 3098.)'.

IMPOSITION: This copy of Book 1 is disbound, but appears to be gathered in single bifolia. Which leaf is a singleton is not clear, but probably a final blank leaf is missing.

Book 2 (preludes 15–24)
not present in this copy

STAMPS: publisher, style W/C (see Appendix 8).

---

1. *Date:* first-edition inference (date code fe, p. 17).
2. In the first editions of this work, the opus number appeared only in that of Breitkopf & Härtel (see 28-BH-1).
3. It is curious that Wessel put 14 preludes into Book 1, leaving only 10 for Book 2. Perhaps this was done because it gives the two books about the same number of pages.

London: **Wessel (3098) (3099) [1848–56]** **28-W-2** **M25.C54 P804**

Book 1 (preludes 1–14)

N° [handwritten "28"] OF | WESSEL & C°.'s COMPLETE COLLECTION | OF | *the Compositions* | OF | FREDERIC CHOPIN | FOR THE | Piano Forte. | Solo & Duet | [list of works, Wessel 1–27] | 28 TWENTY FOUR GRAND PRELUDES *through all Keys* | *5th Set of Studies. Op. 28. 6 /–* | 29 IDEM *6th Set of Studies. Op. 28. 6 /–* | [list of works, Wessel 30–71] | *Ent. Sta. Hall.* « *Copyrights.* » *Price . Solo* [handwritten "6 /"] ÷ " *Duet* [blank] | *LONDON,* | WESSEL & C° *Importers and Publishers of* FOREIGN MUSIC, | *(by special Appointment) to H.R.H. the Duchess of Kent.* | N° 229, Regent Street, Corner of Hanover Street.

11 leaves (346 x 252 mm): pp. [i] engr title page, [ii] blank, [1] advt, 2–20 engr music.

CAPTION TITLE: p. 2, 'BOOK 1, of | *TWENTY FOUR GRAND PRELUDES, BY FREDERIC CHOPIN.* | *DEDICATED to CAMILLE PLEYEL.*'.

SUB-CAPTION: p. 2, '*N° 1.*'; and so on through p. 20, '*N° 14.*'.

FOOTLINE: p. 2, 'BOOK 1. « (W. & C° N° 3098.)'; pp. 3–19, 'CHOPIN. 24 Grand Preludes. Bk: 1. « (W. & C° N° 3098.)'; p. 20, 'CHOPIN. 24 Grand Preludes. Bk: 1. « WESSEL & C° » (N° 3098.)'. The imprint on p. 20 is worn and is not fully legible (or perhaps the address was removed).

ADVT: p. [1], 'PAGE A. | CATALOGUE OF WESSEL AND CO.'S CHOICE PUBLICATIONS OF MODERN PIANO-FORTE MUSIC.' The lists include Chopin works through op. 27 (entry 84 in the series "L'Amateur Pianiste").

IMPOSITION: The title leaf is tipped to leaf 2. Its blank conjugate was removed, perhaps in binding. There is no singleton.

Book 2 (preludes 15–24)

The title page is identical to that of Book 1, except with handwritten "29" instead of "28" (first line).

14 leaves (346 x 255 mm): pp. [i] engr title page, [ii] blank, [1] advt, 2–24 engr music, [25, 26] blank.

28-W-2 *(continued)*

28-W-2 *(concluded)*

CAPTION TITLE: p. 2, '*TWENTY FOUR GRAND PRELUDES, BY FREDERIC CHOPIN.* | *DEDICATED TO CAMILLE PLEYEL.*'.

SUB-CAPTION: p. 2, '*N.º 15.*'; and so on through p. 21, '*N.º 24.*'.

FOOTLINE: p. 2, 'BOOK 2. « (W. & C.º N.º 3099.)'; p. 3, 'CHOPIN. 24 Grand Preludes. Book: 2. « (W. & C.º N.º 3099.)'; pp. 4–6, 'CHOPIN. 24 Grand Preludes. « (W. & C.º N.º 3099.)'; p. 7, 'CHOPIN. 24 Grand Preludes. Bk: 2. « (W. & C.º N.º 3099.)'; pp. 8–16, same as p. 3; pp. 17–23, same as p. 7; p. 24, 'CHOPIN. 24 Grand Preludes. Bk: 2. « WESSEL & C.º » (N.º 3099.)'. The imprint on p. 24 is worn and is not fully legible (or the address was removed).

ADVT: p. [1], same as in Book 1.

STAMPS: publisher, style W/D (see Appendix 8) on each title page.

BOUND WITH: The two books are in the same enclosure.

---

1. *Date:* Wessel inference (date code W1, p. 17).

Moscow: **Jurgenson (2004a) (2004b) 1875** **28-Jur-1** **M25.C54 P84**

Livres 1, 2 (preludes 1–12)

EDITION JURGENSON. | OEUVRES DE FR. CHOPIN. | REVUES DOIGTÉES ET SOIGNEUSEMENT | CORRIGÉES D'APRÉS LES ÉDITIONS | DE PARIS, LONDRES ET LEIPSIC | PAR CHARLES KLINDWORTH | SEULE ÉDITION AUTHENTIQUE. |
[list of Chopin pianoforte works (see notes 3 and 4 below), including Op. 28 in Tome III, as follows:]

„ [Op.] 28.	Vingt-quatre Préludes		1 [Rs.] 35 [K.]
	Livr. 1.	C dur, A moll, G dur, E moll, D dur, H moll	— 30
	„ 2.	A dur, Fis moll, E dur, Cis moll, H dur, Gis moll	— 35
	„ 3.	Fis dur, Es moll, Des dur, B moll, As dur, F moll	— 50
	„ 4.	Es dur, C moll, B dur, G moll, F dur, D moll	— 45

Prix de six volumes Rb. 15. | Moscou chez P. Jurgenson. | St. Petersbourg J. Jurgenson. | NEW YORK & PHILADELPHIA, EDW. SCHUBERTH & C°. | [ten agents in other locations, including Stanley Lucas, Weber & C.º in London] | [transliteration of bottom line (in Cyrillic):] Dozvokheno tsenzuroyu. Moskva, 15 anvarya 1875 g. « » Typografiya A. I. Mamontova i K°, Leont'evskiy per., N.º 5.]

7 leaves (323 x 255 mm): pp. [1] lith title page, 2–14 lith music.

CAPTION TITLE: p. 2, 'A M.r J. C. Kessler. « | VINGT QUATRE PRÉLUDES. | » Liv. 1. ÷ Fr. Chopin, Op. 28.'.

SUB-CAPTION: p. 2, 'N.º 1.'; and so on through p. 13, 'N.º 12.'.

FOOTLINE: p. 2, 'Gravé et Impr. chez P. Jurgenson à Moscou. « 2004.ª'; pp. 3–7, '2004.ª'; pp. 8–14, '2004.ᵇ'.

IMPOSITION: The original blank leaf at the end is missing; a replacement has been supplied by a conservator.

28-Jur-1 *(continued)*

28-Jur-1 *(concluded)*

Livres 3, 4 (preludes 13–24)
not present in this copy

STAMPS: agent, Stanley Lucas, Weber, London.

---

1. *Date:* The date is given explicitly on the bottom line of the title page.
2. Translation of bottom line on title page: 'Authorized by the censor. Moscow, 15 January 1875 « » Printed by A. I. Mamontov & Co, Leontevsky St., N° 5.'.
3. This collective title page lists six volumes of Chopin works for solo piano or piano and orchestra. (The above transcription shows only the volume for Op. 28.) Included are all such works through Op. 72, followed by Variations in E major (presumably B14), 'Trois Nouvelles Etudes' (B130), two Mazurkas in A minor (B134 and B140), and three works of doubtful authenticity (two mazurkas and a waltz).
4. The title page indicates that Op. 28 was issued in four books, each with a group of six preludes. This score has the first two groups, with two plate numbers, as shown above, but with continuous pagination and no caption title for the second group. As it lacks the original, presumably blank leaf conjugate to the title page, perhaps it is half of an issue of the complete work.

***Milan:* Lucca (2274) [*ca* 1839]** **28-Lu-1** **M25.C54 P803 v.2**

Livre 1 (preludes 1–12)
not present in this copy

Livre II (preludes 13–24)

24 | PRÉLUDES | POUR | le Piano | *dédiés à son ami* | *CAMILLE PLEYEL,* |
PAR | FRÉD. CHOPIN | *Divisés en deux Livres* | *N.º 2273–74* « » *Liv. 1 F.4* ÷ *Liv.2* [*sic*] *F. 6* |
MILAN | *Chez F. Lucca S. Marguerite N. 1131*

14 leaves (332 x 247 mm): pp. [i] engr title page, [ii, 1] blank, 2–25 engr music, [26] blank.

CAPTION TITLE: none.

SUB-CAPTION: p. 2, 'XIII.'; and so on through p. 23, 'XXIV.'.

FOOTLINE: pp. 2–25, '2274'.

STAMPS: none.

---

1. *Date:* Chominski & Turlo, p. 272.

IMPROMPTU IN A FLAT MAJOR
Opus 29

Paris: M. Schlesinger (2467) 1837	*Composed* 1837
Leipzig: Breitkopf & Härtel (5850) 1838	Brown 110
London: Wessel (2166) 1837	Chominski & Turlo 43

***Paris:* M. Schlesinger (2467) [= 1837]** **29-mS-1** **M25.C54 I3**

IMPROMPTU | *Pour le Piano* | Dédié à | *Mademoiselle* | CAROLINE DE LOBAU | Par | F. CHOPIN | *A.L.* | *Opera. 29.* « » *Prix. 6.f* | *Propriété des Editeurs.* | *PARIS, chez Maurice SCHLESINGER, Editeur, Rue Richelieu, 97* | *Londres Wessel & C.o* « » *Leipzig chez Breitkopf & Haertel*

6 leaves (332 x 256 mm): pp. [i] engr title page, [ii, 1] blank, 2–9 engr music, [10] blank.

CAPTION TITLE: p. 2, 'CHOPIN. Op: 29 « | IMPROMPTU.'.

FOOTLINE: pp. 2–9, 'M.S. 2467.'.

STAMPS: publisher, style mS/B (see Appendix 8).

1. *Date:* first-edition inference (date code fe, p. 17).

***Paris:* H. Lemoine (5385) [*ca* 1859]** **29-hL-1** **M25.C54 I312**

à Mademoiselle | Caroline de Lobau. | IMPROMPTU | *POUR* | PIANO | *PAR* | FR. CHOPIN | OP. 29. | *Prix: 6.f* | P. | *PARIS.* | *Henry LEMOINE, Editeur,* | *Rue S.t Honoré, 256.* | *COMMISSION (HL. 5385.) EXPORTATION.* | *Imp. Léon Salme, Rue du Louvre, 18.*

6 leaves (321 x 255 mm): pp. [i] engr title page, [ii, 1] blank, 2–8 engr music, [9, 10] blank.

CAPTION TITLE: p. 2, 'IMPROMPTU | FR. CHOPIN. Op: 29. « » *à M.elle Caroline de LOBAU.*'.

FOOTLINE: p. 2, '13e des Tablettes du Pianiste de Hry LEMOINE. « 5385. HL. » *M.me V.e RIS graveur.*'; pp. 3–8, '5385. HL.'; p. 9, '5385. HL. » Paris Imp: Léon Salme rue du Louvre 18.'.

STAMPS: successor, style aL/C (see Appendix 8). In the center is "894,497".

1. *Date:* based on the plate number (Devriès & Lesure, p. 280).
2. An owner's signature is on p. 2.

***Leipzig:* Breitkopf & Härtel (5850) [1841–45]** **29-BH-1** **M25.C54 I31 c.1**

IMPROMPTU | POUR LE | Pianoforte | dédié | *à Mademoiselle* | *LA COMTESSE DE LOBAU* | par | FRÉD. CHOPIN. | Oeuv. 29. « » Pr. 15 Ngr. | *Propriété des Editeurs.* | *Leipsic, chez Breitkopf & Härtel.* | *Paris, chez M. Schlesinger.* | *Londres, chez Wessel & C.o* | *S.t Petersbourg, chez Bernard & Holtz* « » *Varsovie, chez G. Sennewald.* | *Enregistré aux Archives de l'Union.*

5 leaves (347 x 272 mm): pp. [1] lith title page, [2] blank, 3–8 engr music, [9, 10] blank.

29-BH-1 *(continued)*

29-BH-1 *(concluded)*

CAPTION TITLE: p. 3, '» F. CHOPIN. Op. 29.'.

SUB-CAPTION: p. 3, 'IMPROMPTU.'.

FOOTLINE: pp. 3–8, '5850'.

STAMPS: publisher, style BH/F (see Appendix 8); dealer, Micko, no place.

---

1. *Date:* currency inference (date code c2, p. 17).
2. Except for the price, the syntax of this title page is identical to that of the first edition, as transcribed by Chominski & Turlo (pp. 96–97).
3. Three non-first editions are mentioned by Chominski & Turlo (p. 97), all with price 15 Ngr.: (a) an engraved issue that, like the first edition, does not have the plate number on the title page; (b) a somewhat later engraved issue with title page shown in their plate 22; (c) a still later re-engraved issue with title page shown in their plate 23.
4. This collection's 29-BH-1 corresponds to variant (a); 29-BH-4 and 29-BH-3 correspond to variant (b); and 29-BH-2 corresponds to variant (c), except that it is lithographed.
5. Hoboken has three Breitkopf scores of Op. 29: Hob-301 corresponds to variant (c), while Hob-302 and 303 are described as like 301 but with "Breitkopf & Härtel in Leipzig" in the footline on p. 2. To this extent they appear to qualify as a fourth variant.

Leipzig: **Breitkopf & Härtel (5850) [1841–45]** **29-BH-4** **M25.C54 I31 c.3**

IMPROMPTU | pour le | Pianoforte | dédié | *à Mademoiselle* | LA COMTESSE DE LOBAU |
par | FRÉD. CHOPIN. | Oeuv. 29. « Propriété des Editeurs. » Pr. 15 Ngr. |
Leipzig, chez Breitkopf & Härtel. | Paris, chez M. Schlesinger. Londres, chez Wessel & C$^{o}_{.}$ |
S$^{t}_{.}$ Petersbourg, chez Bernard & Holtz. Varsovie, chez G. Sennewald. | *5850.* |
Enregistré aux Archives de l'Union.

5 leaves (314 x 257 mm): pp. [1] lith title page, [2] blank, 3–8 engr music, [9] blank, [10] advt.

CAPTION TITLE: p. 3, '» F. CHOPIN. Op. 29.'.

SUB-CAPTION: p. 3, 'IMPROMPTU.'.

FOOTLINE: pp. 3–8, '5850.'.

IMPOSITION: Leaf 3 is a singleton.

STAMPS: publisher, style BH/C (see Appendix 8).

---

1. *Date:* currency inference (date code c2, p. 17).
2. This score corresponds to variant (b) identified in 29-BH-1, note 3.

Leipzig: **Breitkopf & Härtel (5850) [1841–45]** **29-BH-3** **M25.C54 I31 c.2**

The transcription of this title page is the same as that of 29-BH-4.

4 leaves (324 x 251 mm): pp. [1] lith title page, [2] blank, 3–8 engr music.

29-BH-3 *(continued)*

29-BH-3 *(concluded)*

CAPTION TITLE: p. 3, '» F. CHOPIN. Op. 29.'.

SUB-CAPTION: p. 3, 'IMPROMPTU.'.

FOOTLINE: pp. 3–8, '5850.'.

IMPOSITION: Leaf 3 is a singleton. The original leaf 5 (presumably blank) is missing; a replacement conjugate to the title leaf has been supplied by a conservator.

STAMPS: publisher, style BH/C (see Appendix 8).

---

1. *Date:* currency inference (date code c2, p. 17).
2. This score corresponds to variant (b) identified in 29-BH-1, note 3.

Leipzig: **Breitkopf & Härtel** (5850) [1841–45] **29-BH-2** M25.C54 I313

IMPROMPTU | pour le | Pianoforte | dédié | à Mademoiselle | LA COMTESSE DE LOBAU | par | FRÉD. CHOPIN. | Op. 29. | Propriété des Editeurs. | Leipzig, chez Breitkopf & Härtel. | Paris, chez M. Schlesinger. Londres, chez Wessel & C$^{\underline{o}}$ | St. Petersbourg, chez Bernard & Holtz. Varsovie, chez G. Sennewald. | *Pr. 15 Ngr.* | *Enrégistré aux Archives de l'Union.* | *5850.*

4 leaves (340 x 270 mm): pp. [1] lith title page, 2–7 lith music, [8] blank.

CAPTION TITLE: p. 2, 'IMPROMPTU. | » F. CHOPIN, Op. 29.'.

FOOTLINE: p. 2, 'Stich und Druck von Breitkopf & Härtel in Leipzig. « 5850'; pp. 3–7, '5850'.

WRAPPER (light brown): pp. [1] same as title page, [2, 3] blank, [4] advt.

ADVT: wrapper p. [4], 'Publications Nouvelles pour le Pianoforte | de | BREITKOPF & HÆRTEL à LEIPZIG.'. The list does not have works by Chopin.

TEXT: The layout of the music differs from that of 29-BH-1 (which corresponds to that of the first edition).

STAMPS: publisher, style BH/G (see Appendix 8).

---

1. *Date:* currency inference (date code c2, p. 17); also see note 2.
2. Chominski & Turlo (p. 97) assign a date *ca* 1860, without explanation. The citation of Schlesinger on the title page indicates a date before 1846 (Table 5A), especially because the page was newly designed for this edition.
3. Except that it is lithographed, this score corresponds to variant (b) identified in 29-BH-1, note 3.

MAZURKAS IN C MINOR, B MINOR, D FLAT MAJOR, C SHARP MINOR
Opus 30

Paris: M. Schlesinger (2489) 1837	*Composed* 1837
Leipzig: Breitkopf & Härtel (5851) 1838	Brown 105
London: Wessel (2170) 1837	Chominski & Turlo 68

***Paris:* M. Schlesinger (2489) [= 1837]** **30-mS-1** **M32.C54 M469**

QUATRE | MAZURKAS | *POUR LE* | PIANO | *dédiées à Madame* | LA | PRINCESSE DE WURTEMBERG née PRINCESSE CZARTORYSKA | PAR | FRED. CHOPIN |
Prix: 7 ^{f} 50 ^{c} [?] | *Op. 30.* | *Paris, chez Maurice Schlesinger, Editeur, Rue de Richelieu, N°. 97.* | *Leipzig, Breitkopf & Härtel* « » *Londres chez Wessel et Cie* | » *Propriété des Editeurs*

8 leaves (348 x 269 mm): pp. [i] engr title page, [ii, 1] blank, 2–13 engr music, [14] blank.

CAPTION TITLE: p. 2, 'F. CHOPIN op: 30 ÷ *QUATRE MAZURKAS.* «'.

SUB-CAPTION: p. 2, 'N°. 1.'; and so on through p. 9, 'N°. 4.'.

FOOTLINE: pp. 2–13, 'M.S. 2489.'.

WRAPPER (yellow): pp. [1] same as title page, [2–4] blank.

STAMPS: successor, style Bra/A (see Appendix 8); dealer, Janin, Paris.

CONDITION: Parts of the title page are barely legible.

1. *Date:* first-edition inference (date code fe, p. 17).

***Leipzig:* Breitkopf & Härtel (5851) [= 1838]** **30-BH-2** **M32.C54 M468 c.1**

QUATRE | MAZURKAS | *POUR LE* | Piano | par | F. CHOPIN. |
Oeuv. 30. « Propriété des Editeurs. » *Pr. 20 Gr.* | *Leipsic, chez Breitkopf & Härtel.* | *Paris,* ÷ *chez M. Schlesinger.* « » *Londres* ÷ *chez Wessel & C°.* | *St Petersbourg, chez Bernard & Holtz.* | *Varsovie, chez G. Sennewald.* | *Enregistré dans les Achives de l'Union.*

8 leaves (306 x 234 mm): pp. [1] lith title page, [2, 3] blank, 4–15 engr music, [16] blank.

CAPTION TITLE: p. 4, '» F. CHOPIN. Op. 30.'.

SUB-CAPTION: p. 4, 'N°. 1. | MAZURKA.'; and so on through p. 11, 'N°. 4. | MAZURKA.'.

FOOTLINE: pp. 4–15, '5851.'.

STAMPS: publisher, style BH/D (see Appendix 8).

1. *Date:* first-edition inference (date code fe, p. 17).

***Leipzig:* Breitkopf & Härtel (5851) [= 1838]** **30-BH-3** **M32.C54 M468 c.2**

The transcription of this title page is the same as that of 30-BH-2.

30-BH-3 *(continued)*

30-BH-3 *(concluded)*

8 leaves (337 x 265 mm): pp. [1] lith title page, [2, 3] blank, 4–15 engr music, [16] blank.

CAPTION TITLE: p. 4, '» F. CHOPIN. Op. 30.'.

SUB-CAPTION: p. 4, 'N° 1. | MAZURKA.'; and so on through p. 11, 'N° 4. | MAZURKA.'.

FOOTLINE: pp. 4–15, '5851.'.

WRAPPER (blue): pp. [1] same as title page, [2–3] blank, [4] advt.

ADVT: wrapper p. [4], 'Publications Nouvelles | DE | Breitkopf & Härtel à Leipzig.'. The following Chopin works are listed: Opp. 12, 15–18, 20–27, 29–31 (including four-hand arrangements for Opp. 16–18, 23, 24, 26, and piano-solo reductions for Opp. 21, 22.).

STAMPS: publisher, style BH/D (see Appendix 8).

CONDITION: This copy is in original condition — a clear impression with untrimmed, unblemished leaves.

---

1. *Date:* first-edition inference (date code fe, p. 17).

***Leipzig:* Breitkopf & Härtel (5851) [1841–45]** — **30-BH-1** — **M32.C54 M47**

The transcription of this title page is the same as that of 30-BH-2, except here the price is "*25 Ngr.*".

8 leaves (340 x 267 mm): pp. [1] lith title page, [2, 3] blank, 4–15 engr music, [16] blank.

CAPTION TITLE: p. 4, '» F. Chopin. Op. 30.'.

SUB-CAPTION: p. 4, 'N° 1. | MAZURKA.'; and so on through p. 11, 'N° 4. | MAZURKA.'.

FOOTLINE: pp. 4–15, '5851.'.

STAMPS: publisher, style BH/J (see Appendix 8).

---

1. *Date:* currency inference (date code c2, p. 17).
2. This score corresponds to Hob-307.

***Mendrisio:* Pozzi (199) [after 1838]** — **30-Po-1** — **M32.C54 M471**

QUATRE | MAZURKAS | *POUR LE* | Piano | par | F. CHOPIN | *Op. 30.* | *N. 199.* « » *Fr. 3.* ___. | *Mendrisio, chez C. Pozzi*

7 leaves (340 x 249 mm): pp. [1] engr title page, 2–13 engr music, [14] blank.

CAPTION TITLE: p. 2, '» F. CHOPIN. Op. 30.'.

SUB-CAPTION: p. 2, 'N° 1. | MAZURKA.'; and so on through p. 9, 'N° 4. | MAZURKA.'.

FOOTLINE: pp. 2–13, '199'.

STAMPS: none.

INSCRIPTIONS: "A. Kraus".

---

1. *Date:* no evidence was found, but it is likely the Italian edition was derived from the German.

SCHERZO IN B FLAT MINOR
Opus 31

Paris: M. Schlesinger (2494) 1837	*Composed* 1837
Leipzig: Breitkopf & Härtel (5852) 1838	Brown 111
London: Wessel (2168) 1837	Chominski & Turlo 198

***Paris:* M. Schlesinger (2494) [= 1837]** **31-mS-1** **M25.C54 S521**

Scherzo | POUR PIANO | *Dédié à Mademoiselle* | Adèle de Furstenstein | *PAR* | F. CHOPIN | *A. L.* | *Opera: 31.* « » *Prix: 7 f. 50 c.* | *Propriété des Editeurs* | *PARIS, chez Maurice SCHLESINGER, Editeur de Musique Rue Richelieu, 97.* | *Leipsic, chez Breitkopf & Hartel.* « » *Londres, chez Wessel.*

11 leaves (349 x 269 mm): pp. [i] engr title page, [ii] blank, 1–19 engr music, [20] blank.

CAPTION TITLE: p. 1, 'F. CHOPIN Op: 31. ÷ SCHERZO. «'.

FOOTLINE: pp. 1–19, 'M.S. 2494.'.

STAMPS: publisher, style mS/A (see Appendix 8).

1. *Date:* first-edition inference (date code fe, p. 17).

***Leipzig:* Breitkopf & Härtel (5852) [= 1838]** **31-BH-2** **M25.C54 S522 c.1**

SCHERZO | pour Le Piano | DÉDIÉ | *à Mademoiselle la Comtesse* | *ADÈLE DE FÜRSTENSTEIN* | par | FR. CHOPIN. | Oeuv. 31. « » Pr. 1 Thlr. 4 Gr. | Propriété des Editeurs. | *Leipsic, chez Breitkopf & Härtel.* | *Paris, chez M. Schlesinger.* « » *Londres, chez Wessel & Co.* | *S.t Petersbourg, chez Bernard & Holtz.* « » *Varsovie, chez G. Sennewald.* | *Enregistré dans les Archives de l'Union.* | *Lith de K. & B.*

12 leaves (314 x 256 mm): pp. [1] lith title page, [2] blank, 3–23 engr music, [24] blank.

CAPTION TITLE: p. 3, '» CHOPIN. Op. 31.'.

SUB-CAPTION: p. 3, 'SCHERZO.'.

FOOTLINE: pp. 3–23, '5852'.

STAMPS: none.

1. *Date:* first-edition inference (date code fe, p. 17).

***Leipzig:* Breitkopf & Härtel (5852) [= 1838]** **31-BH-3** **M25.C54 S522 c.2**

The transcription of this title page is the same as that of 31-BH-2.

12 leaves (345 x 265 mm): pp. [1] lith title page, [2] blank, 3–23 engr music, [24] blank.

CAPTION TITLE: p. 3, '» CHOPIN. Op. 31.'.

SUB-CAPTION: p. 3, 'SCHERZO.'.

FOOTLINE: pp. 3–23, '5852'.

31-BH-3 *(continued)*

31-BH-3 *(concluded)*

WRAPPER (yellow): pp. [1] same as title page, [2–3] blank, [4] advt.

ADVT: wrapper p. [4], 'Publications Nouvelles | DE | Breitkopf & Härtel à Leipzig.'. The following Chopin works are listed: Opp. 12, 15–18, 20–27, 29–31 (including four-hand arrangements for Opp. 16–18, 23, 24, 26, and piano-solo reductions for Opp. 21, 22.).

STAMPS: publisher, style BH/D (see Appendix 8).

CONDITION: This copy is in original condition — a clear impression with untrimmed, unblemished leaves.

---

1. *Date:* first-edition inference (date code fe, p. 17).

***Leipzig:* Breitkopf & Härtel (9671) [*ca* 1858]** **31-BH-1** **M25.C54 S52**

SCHERZO | pour Le Piano | DÉDIÉ | *à Mademoiselle la Comtesse* | *ADÈLE DE FÜRSTENSTEIN* | par | FR. CHOPIN. | Oeuv. 31. « » Pr. 1 Thlr. 5 Ngr. | Propriété des Editeurs. | *Leipzig, chez Breitkopf & Härtel.* | *Paris, chez Brandus & Co. Londres, chez Wessel & Co.* | *S.t Petersbourg, chez Bernard. Varsovie, chez G. Sennewald.* | *9671.* | *Enrégistré aux Archives de l'Union.*

12 leaves (316 x 253 mm): pp. [1] lith title page, [2] blank, 3–23 lith music, [24] blank.

CAPTION TITLE: p. 3, 'SCHERZO. | » F. Chopin, Op. 31.'.

FOOTLINE: p. 3, 'Stich und Druck von Breitkopf & Härtel in Leipzig. « 9671'; pp. 4–23, '9671'.

STAMPS: publisher, style BH/G (see Appendix 8).

---

1. *Date:* based on the plate number (Table 5C).

NOCTURNES IN B MAJOR AND A FLAT MAJOR
Opus 32

Paris: M. Schlesinger (2500) 1837	*Composed* 1837
Berlin: A. Schlesinger (2180) 1837	Brown 106
London: Wessel (2169) 1837	Chominski & Turlo 116

***Paris:* M. Schlesinger (2500) [= 1837]** **32-mS-1** **M25.C54 N83**

DEUX NOCTURNES | Pour Piano | *DÉDIÉS* | *à Madame la Baronne de Billing* | NÉE DE COURBONNE | *PAR* | FRÉD. CHOPIN | *Op. 32.* « » *Pr. 6.^{f}* | *Paris, chez Maurice Schlesinger, Editeur, Rue Richelieu, 97.* | *Berlin, A. M. Schlesinger* « » *Londres, Wessel et Cie.* | » *Propriété des Editeurs.*

6 leaves (328 x 260 mm): pp. [i] engr title page, [ii, 1] blank, 2–9 engr music, [10] blank.

CAPTION TITLE: p. 2, 'F. Chopin. Op: 32. « | DEUX NOCTURNES.'.

SUB-CAPTION: p. 2, '1e Nocturne.'; p. 6, '2e Nocturne.'.

FOOTLINE: pp. 2–9, 'M.S. 2500.'.

STAMPS: successor, style Bra/A (see Appendix 8).

INSCRIPTIONS: inscription dated 1857.

1. *Date:* first-edition inference (date code fe, p. 17).

***Berlin:* A. Schlesinger (2180(1)) [*ca* 1837]** **32#1-aS-1** **M25.C54 N832 c.1**

Deux | NOCTURNES | Pour Piano | *DEDIÉS* | *à Madame la Baronne de Billing* | NÉE DE COURBONNE | *PAR* | FRÉD. CHOPIN | Op. 32. *N^{o}* [blank] | *PROPRIÉTÉ DES EDITEURS* « » *ENREGISTRÉAUX ARCHIVES DE L'UNION.* | » Pr. { N^{o} I. 1/3 Thlr. ÷ — II. 1/2 __ ÷ *compl.* 5/6 __ | *Berlin, chez* A^{d} Mt SCHLESINGER,* *U. d. Linden, N° 34.* | *Paris, chez M. Schlesinger.* « » *Londres, chez* [blank] | *S. 2180* | **Editeur de Chopin et Franchomme, Duo concertant p. Piano et Violon sur Robert le diable Op. 15* [*sic*], *dito pour Piano et V^{celle} — Field, 11^{e} Nocturne, Nocturne pas-* | *torale, Nouv. Fantaisie. — Mendelssohn-Bartholdy, Capriccio, 2 Quatuors, 1e Sinfonie. — Schunke, Gr. Variations di bravura s. l. Juive de Halevy. Op. 32.*

4 leaves (325 x 258 mm): pp. [1] engr title page, [2, 3] blank, 4–7 engr music, [8] blank.

CAPTION TITLE: p. 4, 'DEUX NOCTURNES | *composées par* | FERD. [*sic*] CHOPIN. | Op. 32. | N° 1. «'.

FOOTLINE: p. 4, 'S. 2180(1) » Berlin, Propriété de Ad. Mt. Schlesinger.'; pp. 5–7, 'S. 2180(1)'.

STAMPS: publisher, style aS/B (see Appendix 8).

1. *Date:* first-edition inference (date code fe, p. 17); but also see note 2.
2. This score — with three prices on the title page and the misspelled "FERD." in the caption title — corresponds to Hob-314, dated 1837. However, Chominski & Turlo (p. 143) imply that this edition is a re-engraving of an earlier issue with only a single price on the title page.
3. See also 32#2-aS-1, note 2.

Berlin: A. Schlesinger (2180(1)) [*ca* 1837] 32#1-aS-2 M25.C54 N832 c.2

The transcription of this title page is the same as that of 32#1-aS-1.

4 leaves (314 x 255 mm): pp. [1] engr title page, [2, 3] blank, 4–7 engr music, [8] blank.

CAPTION TITLE: p. 4, 'DEUX NOCTURNES | *composées par* | FRÉD. CHOPIN. | Op. 32. | Berlin, Propriété de Ad. Mt. Schlesinger.'.

SUB-CAPTION: p. 4, 'N° 1. | Nocturne.'.

FOOTLINE: p. 4, 'S. 2180(1) » Berlin, Propriété de Ad. Mt. Schlesinger.'; pp. 5–7, 'S. 2180(1)'.

STAMPS: publisher, style aS/B (see Appendix 8).

CONDITION: The footline is illegible in some places.

---

1. *Date:* first-edition inference (date code fe, p. 17); but probably a later impression than 32#1-aS-1 (see notes that follow).
2. The title page of this score is identical to that of 32#1-aS-1. However, the caption title differs in two ways: the misspelling "FÉRD." is corrected, and an imprint line is added.
3. For related comments, see 32#1-aS-1, note 2.

Berlin: A. Schlesinger (2180(2)) [*ca* 1837] 32#2-aS-1 M25.C54 N833

The transcription of this title page is the same as that of 32#1-aS-1.

4 leaves (328 x 248 mm): pp. [1] engr title page, [2] blank, 3–7 engr music, [8] blank.

CAPTION TITLE: p. 3, 'DEUX NOCTURNES | composées par | FRÉD. CHOPIN. | Op: 32. | Berlin, Propriété de Ad. Mt. Schlesinger.'.

SUB-CAPTION: p. 3, 'N° II | Nocturne.'.

FOOTLINE: pp. 3–7, 'S. 2180(2)'.

STAMPS: publisher, style aS/?; dealer, Paling, Rotterdam.

---

1. *Date:* first-edition inference (date code fe, p. 17); but see 32#1-aS-1, note 2.
2. The title page of this score comes from the same plate as that of 32#1-aS-1, with three prices. However, the misspelling in the caption title of 32#1-aS-1 is corrected here. Hob-315 also has the correct spelling, but unlike 32#2-aS-1, it has only one price on the title page, namely 1/3 Thlr. This is curious, because as can be seen from 32#1-aS-1, the price of the second nocturne should be 1/2 Thlr.

London: **Wessel (2169) [1848–52]** **32-W-1** **M25.C54 N834**

Nº [handwritten "33"] OF | WESSEL & Cº.'s COMPLETE COLLECTION | OF | *the Compositions* | OF | FREDERIC CHOPIN | FOR THE | Piano Forte. | Solo & Duet | [list of works, Wessel 1–32] | 33 "IL LAMENTO *e* LA CONSOLAZIONE" *5th. Set of Notturnos. Op: 32. 3 /* [duet] *4 /* | [list of works, Wessel 34–71] | *Ent. Sta. Hall.* « *Copyrights.* » *Price, Solo* [handwritten "3/"] ÷ " *Duet* [blank] | *LONDON,* | WESSEL & Cº *Importers and Publishers of,* FOREIGN MUSIC, | *(by special Appointment) to, H.R.H. the Duchess of Kent.* | Nº 229, Regent Street, Corner of Hanover Street.

6 leaves (344 x 250 mm): pp. [i] engr title page, [ii] blank, [1] advt, 2–9 engr music, [10] blank.

CAPTION TITLE: p. 2, ' *"IL LAMENTO" e "LA CONSOLAZIONE"* « » *Cinquième Recueil de NOCTURNES. OP. 32.* | *Composées par FREDERIC CHOPIN.*'; p. 6, '*LA CONSOLAZIONE.*'.

SUB-CAPTION: p. 2, '*9 me.* | *NOCTURNE.*'; p. 6, '*10 me.* | *NOCTURNE.*'.

FOOTLINE: p. 2, '*Copyright « (W. & Cº Nº 2169.)'; pp. 3–8, 'CHOPIN, Il Lamento e la Consolazione. « (W. & Cº Nº 2169.)'; p. 9, 'CHOPIN, Il Lamento e la Consolazione. « | WESSEL & Cº « » (Nº 2169.)'. The imprint on p. 9 is worn and is not fully legible.

ADVT: p. [1], 'PAGE A. | CATALOGUE OF WESSEL AND CO.'S CHOICE PUBLICATIONS OF MODERN PIANO-FORTE MUSIC.'. The lists include Chopin works through op. 27 (entry 84 in the series "L'Amateur Pianiste").

STAMPS: publisher, style W/D (see Appendix 8).

INSCRIPTIONS: title page inscribed "Rosa Woodward | from Mama | April / 52.".

1. *Date:* The lower limit on the date is based on the list of works on the title page, which ends with Op. 64, published by Wessel in 1848. The upper limit is based on the inscription on the title page (see above).

MAZURKAS IN G SHARP MINOR, C MAJOR, D MAJOR, B MINOR
Opus 33

Paris: M. Schlesinger (2714) 1838	*Composed* 1838
Leipzig: Breitkopf & Härtel (5985) 1838	Brown 115
London: Wessel (2279) 1838	Chominski & Turlo 72

***Paris:* M. Schlesinger (2714) [= 1838]** **33-mS-1** **M32.C54 M477**

QUATRE | Mazurkas | *pour le* | PIANO | dédiées | *à Mademoiselle la Comtesse Rose Mostowska* | *PAR* | F. CHOPIN | *Œuv. 33.* « » *Pr. 7 f. 50 c.* | *Paris, chez Maurice Schlesinger, Rue de Richelieu, 97.* | *Londres, chez Wessel et Cie.* « » *Leipzig, chez Breitkopf et Hartel.* | M.S. 2714. | » *Propriété des Editeurs.*

10 leaves (345 x 272 mm): pp. [i] engr title page, [ii, 1] blank, 2–16 engr music, [17, 18] blank.

CAPTION TITLE: p. 2, 'F. CHOPIN Op: 33. ÷ 4 MAZOURKAS. « Nº 1.'; p. 4, 'Nº 2.'; p. 5, 'Nº 3.'; p. 10, 'Nº 4.'.

FOOTLINE: p. 2, 'F. Chopin Op: 33 4 Mazourkas. « M.S. 2714. » Paris chez Maurice Schlesinger rue Richelieu 97'; pp. 3–15, 'M.S. 2714.'; p. 16, same as p. 2.

WRAPPER (pale yellow): pp. [1] same as title page, [2, 3] blank, [4] advt.

ADVT: wrapper p. [4], 'Chez BRANDUS et Ce, éditeurs, 103, rue Richelieu. | MUSIQUE FACILE DE PIANO'. No Chopin works are listed.

PLATES: The title-page impression is weak, and in some places almost illegible, but the impressions of the music plates are good.

STAMPS: successor, style BD/B (see Appendix 8); dealer, Janin, Paris (embossed stamp).

1. *Date:* first-edition inference (date code fe, p. 17); also see note 2.
2. The wrapper dates from after 1850, and the publisher's stamp from 1854–58, but there is no evidence this score is not a first edition.
3. The second and third mazurkas in this score are in the order C major, D major, as in the separate publication of Op. 33 by Schlesinger in the *Gazette Musicale* (see Brown, p. 120 and Chominski & Turlo, p. 121). The same order is followed in the Wessel edition.

***Leipzig:* Breitkopf & Härtel (5985) [= 1838]** **33-BH-2** **M32.C54 M4781**

Quatre | MAZURKAS | *pour le Piano* | composées et dediées | à Mademoiselle | la Comtesse Mostowska | par | FRÉD. CHOPIN. | Oeuv. 33. « Propriété des Editeurs. » Pr. 1 Thlr. | LEIPSIC, CHEZ BREITKOPF & HÄRTEL. | Paris, chez Schlesinger. « » Londres, chez Wessel & Comp. | Nº 5985. | *Enrégistré dans l'Archive de l'Union.*

9 leaves (346 x 272 mm): pp. [1] lith title page, [2] blank, 3–16 engr music, [17, 18] blank.

CAPTION TITLE: p. 3, 'MAZURKAS | *composées* | *par* | FRÉDÉRIC CHOPIN. | MAZURKA Nº I.'; p. 5, 'MAZURKA Nº II.'; p. 10, 'MAZURKA Nº III.'; p. 11, 'MAZURKA Nº IV.'.

SUB-CAPTION: p. 3, 'Nº 1.'; and so on through p. 11, 'Nº 4.'.

33-BH-2 *(continued)*

33-BH-2 *(concluded)*

FOOTLINE: p. 3, '5985. | Leipsic chez Breitkopf et Härtel. « Propriété des Éditeurs. » Paris chez M. Schlesinger.'; pp. 4–16, '5985'.

PLATES: The title page has a decorated border, as in Hob-321 (plate 22, p. 141).

IMPOSITION: Leaf 5 is a singleton.

STAMPS: dealer, Mück, Vienna.

---

1. *Date:* first-edition inference (date code fe, p. 17).
2. The second and third mazurkas here (and in 33-BH-1) are in the order D major, C major, the reverse of their order in the Schlesinger and Wessel editions (Chominski & Turlo, p. 121).
3. Concurrently with this separate first edition, Breitkopf & Härtel published the G sharp minor and D major mazurkas in *Album für Pianoforte und Gesang für das Jahr 1839 mit Beiträgen von Fr. Chopin. Ad. Henselt. Fr. Kalkbrenner. Felix Mendelssohn-Bartholdy. Giacomo Meyerbeer. Louis Spohr. S. Thalberg. Clara Wieck.*
4. In the *Album* publication the two Chopin mazurkas are on pp. 24–30. Strangely, the same page numbers appear in the separate publication 33-BH-2 (as well as in the later 33-BH-1), in addition to the proper numbers 3–9 for continuous pagination of the four mazurkas. Moreover, although the same plates were used, the superfluous *Album* page numbers 24–30 in 33-BH-2 (and 33-BH-1) are located at the foot of the plate (and in their original recto/verso positions). Presumably this was done to avoid conflict with the page numbers of the separate edition, which are at the head, but it is baffling that the *Album* page numbers were not simply removed for the separate publication. (I am indebted to Richard Macnutt for providing a photocopy of the *Album* title page and of pp. 24–30.)
5. Brown (p. 120) notes the *Album* publication and adds, "All four were then published as shown above [that is, with D major, C major as the second and third] with the PN as it had occurred in the consecutive numbering of the pieces in the *Album*." Chominski & Turlo (p. 121) also note the *Album* publication, but neither they nor Brown comments on the presence of *Album* page numbers in the separate edition, nor does Hoboken (Hob-321).
6. It is strange that the French publisher is cited in the footline (p. 3), as well as on the title page.

***Leipzig:* Breitkopf & Härtel (5985) [after 1845]** **33-BH-1** **M32.C54 M478**

QUATRE | MAZURKAS | pour le Piano | composées et dediées | à Mademoiselle | la Comtesse Mostowska | par | FRÉD. CHOPIN. | Op. 33. « » Pr. 1 Thlr. | Propriété des Editeurs. | Leipzig, chez Breitkopf & Härtel. | Paris, chez Brandus & Cº « » Londres, chez Wessel & Cº | 5985. | *Enrégistré aux Archives de l'Union.*

9 leaves (332 x 258 mm): pp. [1] lith title page, [2] blank, 3–16 engr music, [17, 18] blank.

CAPTION TITLE: p. 3, 'MAZURKAS | *composées* | *par* | FRÉDÉRIC CHOPIN | MAZURKA Nº I.'; p. 5, 'MAZURKA Nº II.'; p. 10, 'MAZURKA Nº III.'; p. 11, 'MAZURKA Nº IV.'.

SUB-CAPTION: p. 3, 'Nº 1.'; and so on through p. 11, 'Nº 4.'.

FOOTLINE: p. 3, '5985. | Leipsic chez Breitkopf et Härtel. « Propriété des Editeurs. » Paris chez M. Schlesinger.'; pp. 4–16, '5985'.

IMPOSITION: Leaf 5 is a singleton.

33-BH-1 *(continued)*

33-BH-1 *(concluded)*

STAMPS: publisher, style BH/K (see Appendix 8); dealer, Schott, Rotterdam.

---

1. *Date:* based on the Paris publisher's name on the title page (Table 5A), but note that Schlesinger remains in the footline.
2. The title page of this score differs slightly in syntax, and significantly in design, from that of the first edition (33-BH-2); see Hoboken plate 22, p. 141. Chominski & Turlo (p. 121) mention two non-first editions, both with Brandus as the Paris publisher, as in 33-BH-1.
3. For additional comments see 33-BH-2, notes 2, 3, 4.

WALTZES IN A FLAT MAJOR, A MINOR, F MAJOR
Opus 34

Paris: M. Schlesinger (2715.1) (2716.2) (2717.3) 1838
Leipzig: Breitkopf & Härtel (6032) (6033) (6034) 1838
London: Wessel (2280) (2281) (2282) 1838

Composed 1835, 1834, 1838
Brown 94
Chominski & Turlo 208

Opus 34, Waltz 1

***Paris:* M. Schlesinger (2715.1) [= 1838]** **34#1-mS-1** **M32.C54 W5 c.1**

N° 1 | à Mademoiselle de Thun Ljohenstein | TROIS | VALSES | BRILLANTES | pour le Piano | COMPOSÉES PAR | FRÉD. CHOPIN | *Œuv. 34* ÷ N° 1. « » *Pr. 6.^{f}* | *Paris, chez Maurice Schlesinger, Rue de Richelieu, N° 97.* | *Leipsig chez Breitkopf et Hartel.*« » *Londres Wessel et Cie* | M.S. 2715. | » *Propriété des Editeurs.*

6 leaves (331 x 257 mm): pp. [i] engr title page, [ii, 1] blank, 2–4 engr music, 5–6 missing, 7–11 engr music, [12] blank.

CAPTION TITLE: p. 2, 'N° 1 | GRANDE VALSE | BRILLANTE | Pour Le Piano | *PAR* | FRÉD. CHOPIN'.

FOOTLINE: p. 2, 'Chopin 3 Valses Brillantes Op: 34. M.S. 2715.1. Maurice Schlesinger 97 rue Richelieu.'; pp. 3–10, 'M.S. 2715.1.'; p. 11, same as p. 2.

IMPOSITION: The missing leaf 4 is a singleton.

STAMPS: publisher, style mS/B (see Appendix 8).

1. *Date:* first-edition inference (date code fe, p. 17).
2. The title-page designs of Schlesinger's Opp. 34#1, 2, 3 are all different (see Grabowski, 1992, Figures 45, 46, 47). Differences in syntax are evident from the transcriptions in 34#1-mS-1, 34#2-mS-1, 34#3-mS-1.
3. This score corresponds to Hob-331.

***Paris:* M. Schlesinger (2715.1) [= 1838]** **34#1-mS-2** **M32.C54 W5 c.2**

The transcription of this title page is the same as that of 34#1-mS-1.

7 leaves (349 x 271 mm): pp. [i] engr title page, [ii, 1] blank, 2–11 engr music, [12] blank.

CAPTION TITLE: p. 2, 'N° 1 | GRANDE VALSE | BRILLANTE | Pour Le Piano | *PAR* | FRÉD. CHOPIN'.

FOOTLINE: p. 2, 'Chopin 3 Valses Brillantes Op: 34. M.S. 2715.1. Maurice Schlesinger 97 rue Richelieu.'; pp. 3–10, 'M.S. 2715.1.'; p. 11, same as p. 2.

IMPOSITION: Leaf 4 is a singleton.

STAMPS: successor, style BD/D (see Appendix 8).

1. *Date:* first-edition inference (date code fe, p. 17).
2. This score differs from 34#1-mS-1 only in having the singleton leaf.

Paris: **Leduc (2312) [1859–60]** **34#1-Led-1** **M32.C54 W493**

à Mademoiselle | de Thun Ljohenstein | 1ère | GRANDE | VALSES | brillante | *POUR* | *PIANO* | PAR | FRÉD. CHOPIN | *Op: 34* « » *Prix: 6.f* | *Paris, chez ALPHONSE LEDUC, rue de la Bourse, 2* | Æ

6 leaves (336 x 250 mm): pp. [1] lith title page, 2–11 lith music, [12] blank.

CAPTION TITLE: p. 2, 'Nº 1 | GRANDE VALSE | *BRILLANTE* | POUR LE PIANO | PAR | FRÉD. CHOPIN | Op. 34.'.

FOOTLINE: p. 2, 'A.L. 2312 » Imp. MICHELET. Rue Lafitte. 27.'; pp. 3–10, 'A.L. 2312.'.

STAMPS: publisher, style Led/A (see Appendix 8).

1. *Date:* based on the plate number and address (Devriès & Lesure, pp. 268–69).

Leipzig: **Breitkopf & Härtel (6032) [1841–45]** **34#1-BH-1** **M32.C54 W49 v.1**

Trois | VALSES | Brillantes | *POUR LE* | PIANO | *composées* | par | FRÉD. CHOPIN. | *Op. 34. Nº I.* « Propriété des Editeurs. » *Pr. 17 1/2 Ngr.* | *Leipzig, chez Breitkopf & Härtel.* | *Paris, chez M. Schlesinger.* « » *Londres, chez Wessel & Cº* | *6032. 33. 34.* | *Enrégistré aux Archives de l'Union.*

6 leaves (330 x 255 mm): pp. [1] lith title page, 2–11 engr music, [12] blank.

CAPTION TITLE: p. 2, 'Nº 1. | Grande Valse | BRILLANTE | pour le PIANO composée | *par* | FRÉD. CHOPIN.'.

FOOTLINE: pp. 2–11, '6032.'.

STAMPS: publisher, style BH/F? (see Appendix 8).

1. *Date:* currency inference (date code c2, p. 17).
2. The design of this score's title page is D2 (see Appendix 1, also Hob-328).

Leipzig: **Breitkopf & Härtel (9620) [*ca* 1858]** **34#1-BH-3** **M32.C54 W491**

Trois | VALSES | BRILLANTES | pour le Piano | composées | par | FRÉDERIC CHOPIN. | Propriété des Editeurs. | *Op. 34, Nº I.* « » *Pr. 17 1/2 Ngr.* | Leipzig, chez Breitkopf & Härtel. | Paris, chez M. Schlesinger. « » Londres, chez Wessel & Cº | *9620. 6033. 34.* | *Enrégistré aux Archives de l'Union*

6 leaves (315 x 257 mm): pp. [1] lith title page, 2–11 lith music, [12] blank.

CAPTION TITLE: p. 2, 'Trois | VALSES BRILLANTES | par | FRÉD. CHOPIN. | Op. 34. Nº 1.'.

FOOTLINE: p. 2, 'Stich und Druck von Breitkopf & Härtel in Leipzig. « | 9620'; pp. 3–11, '9620'.

STAMPS: publisher, BH/?.

1. *Date:* based on the plate number (Table 5C).
2. The design of this score's title page is D4 (see Appendix 1).

Leipzig: **Breitkopf & Härtel (9620) [1872–73]** **34#1-BH-2** **M32.C54 W492**

The transcription of this title page is the same as that of 34#1-BH-3, except here the price is *"17 1/2 Ngr. – Mk. 1.75"*.

6 leaves (318 x 252 mm): pp. [1] lith title page, 2–11 lith music, [12] blank.

CAPTION TITLE: p. 2, 'Trois | VALSES BRILLANTES | par | FRÉD. CHOPIN. | Op. 34. N° 1.'.

FOOTLINE: p. 2, 'Stich und Druck von Breitkopf & Härtel in Leipzig. « | 9620'; pp. 3–11, '9620'.

STAMPS: publisher, style BH/I (see Appendix 8); dealer, Schirmer, New York.

1. *Date:* currency inference (date code c3, p. 17).
2. The design of this score's title page is D4 (see Appendix 1).

London: **Wessel (2280) [*ca* 1842]** **34#1-W-1** **M32.C54 W512**

N° [handwritten "35"] OF | WESSEL & C°.'s COMPLETE COLLECTION | OF | *the Compositions* | OF | FREDERIC CHOPIN | FOR THE | Piano Forte. | Solo & Duet | [list of works, Wessel 1–34] | N° 35 TROIS GRANDES VALSES *Bk. 1 in A* [flat] *Op. 34. 3/6* | [list of works, Wessel 36–54] | *Ent. Sta. Hall. « Copyrights. » Price, Solo* [handwritten "3/6"] ÷ " *Duet* [blank] | *LONDON,* | WESSEL & C° *Importers and Publishers of* FOREIGN MUSIC, | *(by special Appointment) to H.R.H. the Duchess of Kent.* | N° 67, Frith Street, Corner of Soho Square.

7 leaves (337 x 252 mm): pp. [i] engr title page, [ii] blank, [1] advt, 2–11 engr music, [12] blank.

CAPTION TITLE: p. 2, '*LE PIANISTE MODERNE N° 95.* | *TROIS GRANDES VALSES BRILLANTES.* | (LA PREMIÈRE VALSE, DEDIÉE À MADEMOISELLE DE THUN-HOHENSTEIN.) | PAR | *FREDERIC CHOPIN.* | » OP: 34.'.

FOOTLINE: p. 2, 'Copyright of WESSEL & C° « (W & C° N° 2280.)'; pp. 3–10, 'CHOPIN. Op: 34. 1re. Valse. « (W & C° N° 2280.)'; p. 11, 'CHOPIN. Op: 34. 1re. Valse. « (N° 2280.) | WESSEL & C° N° 6, FRITH STREET, SOHO SQUARE. | CHOPIN'S Invitation pour la Danse, Gr. Valse, Op: 18. for Piano Solo, 3s. Duet, 4s. .'.

ADVT: p. [1], 'PAGE E. | CONTINUATION OF WESSEL & STAPLETON's CATALOGUE OF THEIR PIANOFORTE PUBLICATIONS, | COMPRISING THE SOLO WORKS OF BEETHOVEN, CHOPIN, LISZT, HENSELT, &c. ORGAN MUSIC, | PIANOFORTE STUDIES, TRIOS, QUARTETTS, QUINTETTS, &c. &c. &c. | N° 67, FRITH STREET, CORNER OF SOHO SQUARE, LONDON.'. Chopin's works are listed through Op. 42.

STAMPS: publisher, style W/C (see Appendix 8).

1. *Date:* inferred from the last work listed on the title page, Op. 50, published by Wessel in 1842.

Mendrisio: **Pozzi (398) [after 1838]** **34#1-Po-1** **M32.C54 W494**

TROIS | VALSES BRILLANTES | Pour le Piano | COMPOSÉES | *PAR* | FRÉD. CHOPIN | *Op. 34.* | *N. 398. 399. 400. « » Fr. 2. ___.* | *N.* [blank] | *Mendrisio, chez C. Pozzi*

34#1-Po-1 *(continued)*

34#1-Po-1 *(concluded)*

6 leaves (323 x 249 mm): pp. [1] engr title page, 2–11 engr music, [12] blank.

CAPTION TITLE: p. 2, 'N° 1. | GRANDE VALSE | BRILLANTE | pour le PIANO composée | *PAR* | FRÉD. CHOPIN.'.

FOOTLINE: pp. 2–11, '398'.

STAMPS: none.

1. *Date:* No evidence was found, but it is likely the Italian edition is derived from the German.
2. On the title page, plate numbers 399 and 400 are struck through by hand.

Opus 34, Waltz 2

***Paris:* M. Schlesinger (2716.2) [= 1838]** **34#2-mS-1** **M32.C54 W506**

N° 2. | À MADAM LA BARONNE C. D'IVRY | Trois Valses | *Brillantes* | pour le | PIANO | Composées par | FRÉD. CHOPIN | *Œuv. 34.* ÷ N° 2. « » *Pr. 6.f* | *Paris, chez MAURICE SCHLESINGER, Rue de Richelieu, 97.* | *Leipsig, chez Breitkopf et Hartel.* « » *Londres, Wessel et C.ie* | M.S. 2716. | » *Propriété des Editeurs.*

6 leaves (325 x 259 mm): pp. [i] engr title page, [ii, 1] blank, 2–9 engr music, [10] blank.

CAPTION TITLE: p. 2, 'N° 2 | Grande Valse | BRILLANTE | Pour le PIANO Composée *PAR* | FRÉD _ CHOPIN'.

FOOTLINE: p. 2, 'Chopin: 3 Valses Brillantes Op: 34. M.S. 2716.2. Maurice Schlesinger 97 rue Richelieu.'; pp. 3–8, 'M.S. 2716.2.'; p. 9, same as p. 2.

STAMPS: publisher, style mS/B (see Appendix 8).

1. *Date:* first-edition inference (date code fe, p. 17).
2. For comments about the designs of Schlesinger's Op. 34 title pages, see 34#1-mS-1, note 2.

***Leipzig:* Breitkopf & Härtel (6033) [= 1838]** **34#2-BH-2** **M32.C54 W51**

TROIS | VALSES | Brillantes | *POUR LE* | PIANO | composées | par | FRÉD. CHOPIN. | *Propriété des Editeurs.* | Oeuv. 34. ÷ *N° I.* [altered by hand to "II"] « » Pr. 14 Gr. | *Leipsic, chez Breitkopf & Härtel.* | *Paris, chez M. Schlesinger.* « » *Londres, chez Wessel & C°.* | 6032. 33. 34. | *Enrégistré dans les Archives de l'Union.* | Lithog. v. F. Krätzschmer [almost illegible].

5 leaves (315 x 250 mm): pp. [1] lith title page, [2] blank, 3–9 engr music, [10] blank.

CAPTION TITLE: p. 3, 'N° 2. | Grande Valse. | BRILLANTE | pour le Piano composée | *PAR* | FRÉD. CHOPIN'.

FOOTLINE: pp. 3–9, '6033.'.

STAMPS: publisher, style BH/D (see Appendix 8).

1. *Date:* first-edition inference (date code fe, p. 17).
2. The design of this score's title page is D1 (see Appendix 1, also Hob-326).

Leipzig: **Breitkopf & Härtel (6033) [1841–45]** **34#2-BH-3** **M32.C54 W507 c.1**

The transcription of this title page is the same as that of 34#2-BH-2, except here the price is "17 1/2 Ngr.".

5 leaves (325 x 259 mm): pp. [1] lith title page, [2] blank, 3–9 engr music, [10] blank.

CAPTION TITLE: p. 3, 'N° 2. | Grande Valse | BRILLANTE | pour le Piano composée | *PAR* | FRÉD. CHOPIN'.

FOOTLINE: pp. 3–9, '6033.'.

STAMPS: publisher, style BH/F (see Appendix 8).

1. *Date:* currency inference (date code c2, p. 17).
2. Except for the price and omission of the lithographer line, the title page of this score appears to be identical to that of 34#2-BH-2.
3. The design of this score's title page is D1 (see Appendix 1, also Hob-326).

Leipzig: **Breitkopf & Härtel (6033) [1841–45]** **34#2-BH-4** **M32.C54 W507 c.2**

Trois | VALSES | Brillantes | *POUR LE* | PIANO | *composées* | par | FRÉD. CHOPIN. | *Op. 34. N^{o} I.* [altered by hand to "II"] « Propriété des Editeurs. » *Pr. 17 1/2 Ngr.* | *Leipzig, chez Breitkopf & Härtel.* | *Paris, chez M. Schlesinger.* « » *Londres, chez Wessel & Co 6032. 33. 34.* | *Enrégistré aux Archives de l'Union.*

5 leaves (320 x 255 mm): pp. [1] lith title page, [2] blank, 3–9 engr music, [10] blank.

CAPTION TITLE: p. 2, 'N° 2. | Grande Valse | BRILLANTE | pour le Piano composée | *PAR* | FRÉD. CHOPIN'.

FOOTLINE: pp. 2–11, '6033.'.

STAMPS: publisher, style BH/F (see Appendix 8).

1. *Date:* currency inference (date code c2, p. 17).
2. The design of this score's title page is D2 (see Appendix 1, also Hob-330).

Leipzig: **Breitkopf & Härtel (6033) [1841–45]** **34#2-BH-1** **M32.C54 W49 v.2**

Trois | VALSES | Brillantes | pour le | PIANO | composées | par | FRÉD. CHOPIN. | *Op. 34. N^{o} I.* [*sic*] « Propriété des Editeurs. » *Pr. 17 1/2 Ngr.* | Leipzig, chez Breitkopf & Härtel. | Paris, chez M. Schlesinger. « » Londres, chez Wessel & Co | *6032. 33. 34.* | *Enrégistré aux Archives de l'Union.*

5 leaves (317 x 249 mm): pp. [1] lith title page, [2] blank, 3–9 engr music, [10] blank.

CAPTION TITLE: p. 3, '*N° 2.* | GRANDE VALSE BRILLANTE | pour le PIANO composée | PAR | FRÉD. CHOPIN. | *OP. 34.*'.

FOOTLINE: pp. 3–9, '6033'.

STAMPS: publisher, style BH/C (see Appendix 8).

BINDING: library cloth.

1. *Date:* currency inference (date code c2, p. 17).

34#2-BH-1 *(continued)*

34#2-BH-1 *(concluded)*

2. The caption title differs from those of 34#2-BH-2, 3, 4.
3. The design of this score's title page is D3 (see Appendix 1).

Mendrisio: **Pozzi (399) [after 1838]** **34#2-Po-1** **M32.C54 W495**

TROIS | VALSES BRILLANTES | Pour le Piano | COMPOSÉES | *PAR* | FRÉD. CHOPIN | *Op. 34.* | *N. 398. 399. 400..* « » *Fr. 2. ___.* | *N.* [blank] | *Mendrisio, chez C. Pozzi*

5 leaves (323 x 249 mm): pp. [i] engr title page, [ii] blank, 1–7 engr music, [8] blank.

CAPTION TITLE: p. 1, 'Nº 2. | GRANDE VALSE | BRILLANTE | pour le PIANO composée | *PAR* | FRÉD. CHOPIN.'.

FOOTLINE: pp. 1–7, '399'.

STAMPS: none.

1. *Date:* No evidence was found, but it is likely the Italian edition is derived from the German.
2. On the title page, plate numbers 398 and 400 are struck through by hand.

Opus 34, Waltz 3

Paris: **M. Schlesinger (2717.3) [= 1838]** **34#3-mS-1** **M32.C54 W502**

Nº 3. | *À Mademoiselle A. d'Eichthal* | TROIS | VALSES | Brillantes | *Composées* | Pour *LE* Piano | *PAR* | FRÉD. CHOPIN | *Œuv. 34.* ÷ Nº 3 « » *Pr. 6.f* | *Paris, chez Maurice Schlesinger, Rue de Richelieu, Nº 97.* | *Leipsig, chez Breitkopf et Härtel.*« » *Londres, Wessel et Cie* | M.S. 2717.[3] | » *Propriété des Editeurs.*

6 leaves (331 x 257 mm): pp. [i] engr title page, [ii, 1] blank, 2–9 engr music, [10] blank.

CAPTION TITLE: p. 2, 'Nº 3. | Grande Valse | BRILLANTE | POUR LE Piano *COMPOSEE* | *PAR* | FRÉD. CHOPIN'. "POUR LE" is slanted backwards.

FOOTLINE: p. 2, 'Chopin 3 Valses Brillantes Op: 34. M.S. 2717.3. Maurice Schlesinger 97 rue Richelieu.'; pp. 3–8, 'M.S. 2717.3.'; p. 9, same as p. 2.

STAMPS: publisher, style mS/B (see Appendix 8).

1. *Date:* first-edition inference (date code fe, p. 17).
2. For comments about the designs of Schlesinger's Op. 34 title pages, see 34#1-mS-1, note 2.
3. This score corresponds to Hob-332.

Paris: **H. Lemoine (5366) [*ca* 1861]** **34#3-hL-1** **M32.C54 W52**

à Mademoiselle A. d'Eichthal. | 3 | VALSES | Brillantes | *POUR* | PIANO | *PAR* | FR. CHOPIN | Op. 34. Nº 3. | *Prix net* 55 *Centimes.* | *à Paris, H. LEMOINE, Editeur.* | *Rue St Honore, Nº 256.* | *COMMISSION (HL. 5366.) EXPORTATION.* | *Lith. Boisgontier Bould St Jacques 16.* | P.

4 leaves (301 x 224 mm): pp. [1] lith title page, 2–7 lith music, [8] blank.

34#3-hL-1 *(continued)*

34#3-hL-1 *(concluded)*

CAPTION TITLE: p. 2, 'VALSE BRILLANTE | FR. CHOPIN Op. 34. « » *à M*[elle] *A. D'EICHTHAL.* | N° 3.'.

FOOTLINE: p. 2, '11e Degré des Tablette du Pianiste de Hry LEMOINE. « 5366. HL. » *M*[me] *V*[e] *RIS graveur.*'; pp. 3–7, '5366. HL.'.

STAMPS: successor, style aL/C (with "A 081,253") (see Appendix 8); dealer, Emery, Geneva.

1. *Date:* based on Chominski & Turlo (p. 270); see note 2.
2. Devriès & Lesure (p. 280) indicate 1859 for plate number 5366, but they note unspecified irregularities between 5333 and 5500.
3. This score is part of the Lemoine collected edition of 1859–94 (Chominski & Turlo, p. 270).

Leipzig: **Breitkopf & Härtel (6034) [= 1838]** **34#3-BH-3** **M32.C54 W5218**

TROIS | VALSES | Brillantes | *POUR LE* | PIANO | composées | par | FRÉD. CHOPIN. |
Propriété des Editeurs. | Oeuv. 34. ÷ *N° I.* [*sic*] « » Pr. 14 Gr. | *Leipsic, chez Breitkopf & Härtel.* |
Paris, chez M. Schlesinger. « » *Londres, chez Wessel & C°* | 6032. 33. 34. |
Enrégistré dans les Archives de l'Union. | *Lithog. v. F. Krätzschmer.*

5 leaves (315 x 255 mm): pp. [1] lith title page, [2] blank, 3–9 engr music, [10] blank.

CAPTION TITLE: p. 3, 'N° 3. | GRANDE VALSE | BRILLANTE | *pour le Piano composée* | *PAR* | FRÉD. CHOPIN'.

FOOTLINE: pp. 3–9, '6034'.

STAMPS: none.

1. *Date:* first-edition inference (date code fe, p. 17).
2. The design of this score's title page is D1 (see Appendix 1, also Hob-327).

Leipzig: **Breitkopf & Härtel (6034) [= 1838]** **34#3-BH-4** **M32.C54 W5217**

The transcription of this title page is the same as that of 34#3-BH-3.

5 leaves (349 x 265 mm): pp. [1] lith title page, [2] blank, 3–9 engr music, [10] blank.

CAPTION TITLE: p. 3, 'N° 3. | GRANDE VALSE | BRILLANTE | *pour le Piano composée* | *PAR* | FRÉD. CHOPIN'.

FOOTLINE: pp. 3–9, '6034'.

WRAPPER (blue): pp. [1] same as title page, [2–3] blank, [4] advt.

ADVT: wrapper p. [4], 'Publications Nouvelles | DE | Breitkopf & Härtel à Leipzig.'. The following Chopin works are listed: Opp. 25–27, 29–31, 33, 34 (including a four-hand arrangement for Op. 26).

STAMPS: none.

CONDITION: This copy is in original condition — a clear impression with untrimmed, unblemished leaves.

1. *Date:* first-edition inference (date code fe, p. 17).
2. The design of this score's title page is D1 (see Appendix 1, also Hob-327).

Leipzig: **Breitkopf & Härtel (6034) [1841–45]** **34#3-BH-1** **M32.C54 W49 v.3**

Trois | VALSES | Brillantes | pour le | PIANO | composées | par | FRÉD. CHOPIN. | *Op. 34. N°. I.* [*sic*] « Propriété des Editeurs. » *Pr. 17 1/2 Ngr.* | Leipzig, chez Breitkopf & Härtel. | Paris, chez M. Schlesinger « » Londres, chez Wessel & C°. | *6032. 33. 34.* | *Enrégistré aux Archives de l'Union.*

5 leaves (305 x 249 mm): pp. [1] lith title page, [2] blank, 3–9 engr music, [10] blank.

CAPTION TITLE: p. 3, 'N°. 3. | GRANDE VALSE | BRILLANTE | *pour le Piano composée* | *PAR* | FRÉD. CHOPIN.'.

FOOTLINE: pp. 3–9, '6034'.

STAMPS: publisher, style BH/H (see Appendix 8).

BINDING: library cloth.

1. *Date:* currency inference (date code c2, p. 17).
2. The design of this score's title page is D3 (see Appendix 1).

Leipzig: **Breitkopf & Härtel (6034) [1841–45]** **34#3-BH-2** **M32.C54 W522**

Trois | VALSES | BRILLANTES | pour le Piano | composées | par | FRÉDERIC CHOPIN. | Propriété des Editeurs. | *Op. 34, N°. I.* [changed by hand to 'III'] « » *Pr. 17 1/2 Ngr.* | Leipzig, chez Breitkopf & Härtel. | Paris, chez M. Schlesinger. « » Londres, chez Wessel & C°. | *6032. 33. 34.* | *Enrégistré aux Archives de l'Union.*

4 leaves (325 x 258 mm): pp. [1] lith title page, [2] blank, 3–8 engr music (see note 2 below).

CAPTION TITLE: p. 3, 'N°. 3. | GRANDE VALSE | BRILLANTE | *pour le Piano composée* | *PAR* | FRÉD. CHOPIN.'.

FOOTLINE: pp. 3–8, '6034'.

STAMPS: publisher, style BH/C (see Appendix 8).

1. *Date:* currency inference (date code c2, p. 17).
2. This copy lacks the conjugate to the title leaf, with the final page of music (p. 9) and blank verso.
3. The design of this score's title page is D4 (see Appendix 1).

Mendrisio: **Pozzi (400) [after 1838]** **34#3-Po-1** **M32.C54 W496**

TROIS | VALSES BRILLANTES | Pour le Piano | COMPOSÉES | *PAR* | FRÉD. CHOPIN | *Op. 34.* | *N. 398. 399. 400..* « » *Fr. 2. ___.* | *N.* [blank] | *Mendrisio, chez C. Pozzi*

6 leaves (323 x 249 mm): pp. [i] engr title page, [ii] blank, 1–7 engr music, [8] blank.

CAPTION TITLE: p. 1, 'N°. 3. | GRANDE VALSE | BRILLANTE | pour le PIANO composée | *PAR* | FRÉD. CHOPIN.'.

FOOTLINE: pp. 1–7, '400'.

34#3-Po-1 *(continued)*

34#3-Po-1 *(concluded)*

STAMPS: none.

ANNOTATIONS: On the title page the plate number "(400)" is entered by hand.

---

1. *Date:* No evidence was found, but it is likely the Italian edition is derived from the German.

SONATA IN B FLAT MINOR
Opus 35

Paris: Troupenas (891) 1840 — *Composed* 1837–39
Leipzig: Breitkopf & Härtel (6329) 1840 — Brown 128
London: Wessel (3549) 1840 — Chominski & Turlo 202

Paris: **Troupenas (891) [= 1840]** **35-T-1** **M23.B41 S6992**

SONATA | Pour Le Piano | Composée par | FRED. CHOPIN | *Op: 35. Prix: 9.f* | *A. L.* | *à PARIS, chez E. TROUPENAS & Cie Rue Neuve Vivienne, 40.* | *à Leipsig, chez Breitkopf & Haertel* | *à Londres, chez Wessel & Cie*

11 leaves (328 x 259 mm): pp. [i] engr title page. [ii] blank, 1–19 engr music, [20] blank.

CAPTION TITLE: p. 1, 'SONATE. | » *CHOPIN*. Op: 35.'.

FOOTLINE: p. 1, 'T. 891. » *F. Benoit, Grav.–Impr.*'; pp. 2–19, 'T. 891.'.

STAMPS: publisher, style T/A (see Appendix 8).

BOUND WITH: 58-Mei-2; for details, see Appendix 2.

BINDING: red morocco prize binding; see Appendix 2.

1. *Date:* first-edition inference (date code fe, p. 17).
2. This score corresponds to the O'Meara copy, the final Troupenas impression (Grabowski, 1994, p. 34). For a discussion of four states of the Troupenas edition see Kallberg (2001, pp. 11–12).

Paris: **Brandus (6475) [*ca* 1851]** **35-Bra-1** **M23.C54 S69**

This copy lacks the title leaf (see note 2 below).

9 leaves (325 x 253 mm): pp. 1–18 engr music (see note 2).

CAPTION TITLE: p. 1, 'SONATE. | » *CHOPIN*. Op: 35.'.

FOOTLINE: p. 1, 'T. 891. » B. et Cie 6475. *F. Benoit, Grav. Impr.* [?]'; pp. 2–18, 'T. 891.'.

STAMPS: See note 2.

ANNOTATIONS: handwritten odd numbers 29–45 on recto pages.

CONDITION: water stained and generally worn.

1. *Date:* based on the Brandus plate number in the footline (Table 5A).
2. This copy lacks the title leaf (pp. [i, ii]) and its conjugate (pp. 19, [20]). The missing p. 19 has the last 30 bars of the Presto.
3. The engraver's name appears on p. 1, and E flat on p. 12. According to Fuld (p. 238), this implies the plate is not from the proof impression deposited at the Conservatoire, as is consistent with its status as a re-issue by Brandus.

Paris: **Brandus (6475) [*ca* 1851]** **35-Bra-3** **M23.C54 S6901**

SONATA | Pour Le Piano | Composée par | FRED. CHOPIN | *Op: 35. Prix: 9 f* |
A. L. | *à PARIS, chez E. TROUPENAS & Cie Rue Neuve Vivienne, 40.* |
à Leipsig, chez Breitkopf & Haertel | *à Londres, chez Wessel & Cie*

11 leaves (350 x 270 mm): pp. [i] engr title page. [ii] blank, 1–19 engr music, [20] blank.

CAPTION TITLE: p. 1, 'SONATE. | » *CHOPIN*. Op: 35.'.

FOOTLINE: p. 1, 'T. 891. » B. et Cie 6475. *F. Benoit, Grav.–Impr.*'; pp. 2–19, 'T. 891.'.

WRAPPER (pale brown): pp. [1] same as title page, [2–3] blank, [4] advt.

ADVT: wrapper p. 4, 'CHEZ G. BRANDUS, DUFOUR ET Ce, ÉDITEURS, , RUE RICHELIEU.'. Lists works of Ch. Voss, Ed. Wolff, Emile Prudent.

STAMPS: publisher, style Bra/A (see Appendix 8).

CONDITION: This copy is opened but untrimmed and, although some of the plates show signs of wear, it is in unusually fine condition.

---

1. *Date:* based on the Brandus plate number (Table 5A). (From the publisher name in the advt, the wrapper is later, probably 1854–57.)
2. This score is an impression taken from the Troupenas plates acquired by Brandus in 1850 (Table 5A, and Grabowski, 1994, p. 34).
3. For further comments see 35-Bra-1, note 3.

Paris: **Brandus (6482) [*ca* 1851]** **35-Bra-2** **M23.C54 S691**

MARCHE FUNÈBRE | Exécutée aux Funérailles | *DE* | L'AUTEUR | FRED. CHOPIN. |
Extraite de sa Sonate. | *Op. 35 « » Prix: 5 f* | *A. Lafont.* | *Paris, chez E. Troupenas & Cie Rue Nve Vivienne, 40.*

6 leaves (300 x 241 mm): pp. [i] engr title page, [ii, 1] blank, 2–9 engr music, [10] blank.

CAPTION TITLE: p. 2, 'MARCHE FUNÈBRE | Extraite de la Sonate de | FRED. CHOPIN. | Op: 35.'.

FOOTLINE: p. 2, 'E.T. et Cie 891. » B. et Cie 6482.'; pp. 3–9, 'E.T. et Cie 891.'.

TEXT: The Marche takes up 4 pages of music (pp. 2–5) in this extract, whereas in the complete sonata 35-Bra-1 (which has the same Troupenas plate number), it is set in only 3 pages.

STAMPS: Könyvtera Szerv. Kozponti Fov. Zeneiskola (Library of the National Conservatory, Budapest).

---

1. *Date:* based on the Brandus plate number (Table 5A).
2. This extract edition includes the finale (presto) on pp. 6–9.
3. According to Grabowski (1994, p. 23), the extract edition by Troupenas (from which the present score is derived) is based on the final ("O'Meara") impression of the sonata.

Leipzig: Breitkopf & Härtel (6329) [= 1840] **35-BH-5** **M23.C54 S712**

SONATE | pour le Piano | composée | par | FRÉD. CHOPIN. | *Oeuv. 35.* « Propriété des Editeurs. » *Pr. 1 Thlr. 4 Gr.* | *Leipzig, chez Breitkopf & Härtel.* | *Paris, chez Troupenas & C.º* « » *Londres, chez Wessel & C.º* | *6329.* | *Enrégistré aux Archiv de l'Union.*

12 leaves (338 x 270 mm): pp. [1] lith title page, [2] blank, 3–23 engr music, [24] blank.

CAPTION TITLE: p. 3, ' » F. Chopin. Op. 35.'.

SUB-CAPTION: p. 3, 'SONATE.'; p. 10, 'SCHERZO.'; p. 17, 'MARCHE | FUNEBRE.'; p. 20, 'FINALE.'.

FOOTLINE: pp. 3–23, '6329'.

WRAPPER (buff): pp. [1] same as title page, [2–3] blank, [4] advt.

ADVT: wrapper p. [4], 'Publications Nouvelles pour le Pianoforte | DE | Breitkopf & Härtel à Leipzig.'. Chopin works listed are Opp. 25–31, 33, 34, and four-hand arrangements of all except Op. 25.

TEXT: On p. 3 the double bar between bars 4 and 5 is erroneously dotted for repeat (see Rosen, p. 275).

STAMPS: none.

CONDITION: This copy is in original condition — a clear impression and untrimmed, unblemished leaves.

1. *Date:* first-edition inference (date code fe, p. 17).

Leipzig: Breitkopf & Härtel (6329) [1841–50] **35-BH-1** **M23.C54 S7**

The transcription of this title page is the same as that of 35-BH-5, except here the price is *"1 Thlr. 5 Ngr."*.

12 leaves (325 x 263 mm): pp. [1] lith title page, [2] blank, 3–23 engr music, [24] blank.

CAPTION TITLE: p. 3, ' » F. Chopin. Op. 35.'.

SUB-CAPTION: p. 3, 'SONATE.'; p. 10, 'SCHERZO.'; p. 17, 'MARCHE | FUNEBRE.'; p. 20, 'FINALE.'.

FOOTLINE: pp. 3–23, '6329'.

TEXT: On p. 3 the double bar between bars 4 and 5 is erroneously dotted for repeat (see Rosen, p. 275).

STAMPS: publisher, style BH/K (see Appendix 8).

1. *Date:* currency inference (date code c1, p. 17) and name of Paris publisher (Table 5A).

Leipzig: Breitkopf & Härtel (8728) [*ca* 1853] **35-BH-3** **M23.C54 S7161**

MARCHE FUNÈBRE | pour le Piano | tirée DE LA SONATE Oeuvr. 35. | *de* | Frédéric Chopin. | *N.º 8728.* « Propriété des Editeurs. » *Pr. 10 Ngr.* | Leipzig, chez Breitkopf & Härtel. | Paris, chez Troupenas & C.º « » Londres, chez Wessel & C.º | *Enrégistré aux Archive de l'Union.*

3 leaves (333 x 258 mm): pp. [1] lith title page, [2] blank, 3–5 engr music, [6] blank.

CAPTION TITLE: p. 3, 'MARCHE FUNÈBRE. | » F. Chopin.'.

FOOTLINE: pp. 3–5, '8728'.

35-BH-3 *(continued)*

35-BH-3 *(concluded)*

STAMPS: publisher, style BH/C (see Appendix 8).

1. *Date:* based on the plate number (Table 5C), assumed to take precedence over the title-page reference to Troupenas, acquired by Brandus in 1850.
2. This score corresponds to Hob-336.

Leipzig: **Breitkopf & Härtel (8728) [after 1853]** **35-BH-4** **M23.C54 S7162**

The transcription of this title page is the same as that of 35-BH-3, except here the fourth line is *"DE"* (instead of *"de"*).

3 leaves (326 x 254 mm): pp. [1] lith title page, [2] blank, 3–5 lith music, [6] blank.

CAPTION TITLE: p. 3, 'MARCHE FUNÈBRE. | » Fr. Chopin.'.

FOOTLINE: p. 3, 'Stich und Druck von Breitkopf & Härtel in Leipzig. « 8728'; pp. 4–5, '8728'.

PLATES: The music plates differ from those of 35-BH-3. The layout and music notation are the same, but the positions of the pedal and other performance marks differ slightly. There are also more substantial differences. For example, in bar 18 there is an accent on the last beat in 35-BH-3 but not in 35-BH-4. The same is true for the next-to-last beat in bar 20. In the first beat of the first bar of the last system of the Marche there is a C in the right hand in 35-BH-3 but not in 35-BH-4.

STAMPS: publisher, style BH/G (see Appendix 8).

1. *Date:* The plate number dates from 1853 (Table 5C), but as this score is lithographed, it is probably a later issue of the originally engraved edition (35-BH-3).

Leipzig: **Breitkopf & Härtel (6329) [1872–73]** **35-BH-2** **M23.C54 S716**

The transcription of this title page is the same as that of 35-BH-5, except here the price is *"1 Thlr. 5 Ngr. – Mk. 3.50."*.

12 leaves (340 x 270 mm): pp. [1] lith title page, [2] blank, 3–23 lith music, [24] blank.

CAPTION TITLE: p. 3, '» F. Chopin. Op. 35.'.

SUB-CAPTION: p. 3, 'SONATE.'; p. 10, 'SCHERZO.'; p. 17, 'MARCHE | FUNÈBRE.'; p. 20, 'FINALE.'.

FOOTLINE: pp. 3–23, '6329'.

PLATES: Although the layout of the music is the same, the state of these plates differs from that of 35-BH-5 and 35-BH-1. For example, in 35-BH-2 the last bar on p. 7 has a pedal-off mark and a long diminuendo, both of which are absent in 35-BH-5. Apparently, 35-BH-1 was reprinted from the plates of 35-BH-5 without correction, while 35-BH-2 is a transfer from corrected plates (or perhaps was printed from new, directly lithographed plates). However, the erroneous repeat in the first system is still present (see "TEXT" in 35-BH-5).

STAMPS: publisher, styles BH/B and BH/I (see Appendix 8); dealer, Maartens Brothers, New York.

1. *Date:* currency inference (date code c3, p. 17).

IMPROMPTU IN F SHARP MAJOR
Opus 36

Paris: Troupenas (892) 1840	*Composed* 1839
Leipzig: Breitkopf & Härtel (6333) 1840	Brown 129
London: Wessel (3550) 1840	Chominski & Turlo 44

***Paris:* Brandus (6477) [*ca* 1851]** **36-Bra-1** **M25.C54 I345**

ÉDITION ORIGINALE | OEUVRES COMPLÈTES POUR LE PIANO | DE | FRÉDÉRIC CHOPIN | SEULE ÉDITION AUTHENTIQUE | SANS CHANGEMENTS NI ADDITIONS, PUBLIÉE D'APRÈS LES ÉPREUVES CORRIGÉES PAR L'AUTEUR LUI-MÊME. | [list of works Opp. 1–35] | Op. 36. Deuxième impromptu en *fa* dièse majeur 5 " | [list of works Opp. 37–65 and three additional works] | Paris, BRANDUS ET Cie, Éditeurs | 103, rue de Richelieu, 103. | [below the decorated border:] IMPRIMERIE CENTRALE DES CHEMINS DE FER. « »
A. CHAIX ET C[o], RUE BERGÈRE, 20, A PARIS | 10970-3

5 leaves (348 x 268 mm): pp. [i] lith (or letterpress?) title page, [ii, 1] blank, 2–7 engr music, [8] blank.

CAPTION TITLE: p. 2, '*IMPROMPTU.* « » F. CHOPIN, Op: 36.'.

FOOTLINE: p. 2, '(T. 892.) » B. et Cie 6477.'; pp. 3–7, '(T. 892.)'. The Troupenas plate numbers are almost illegible.

STAMPS: publisher, style Bra/E (see Appendix 8).

1. *Date:* based on the Brandus plate number (Table 5A).
2. In the list of works on the title page, "Trois [nouvelles] études" (B130) is assigned opus number 66.

***Leipzig:* Breitkopf & Härtel (6333) [= 1840]** **36-BH-1** **M25.C54 I35**

2 [ème] | *IMPROMPTU* | pour le Piano | composé | PAR | FRÉD. CHOPIN. |
Oeuvr. 36. « Propriété des Editeurs. » *Pr. 12 Gr.* | *Leipzig, chez Breitkopf & Härtel.* |
Paris, chez Troupenas & Co « » *Londres, chez Wessel & Co* | *6333.* | *Enrégistré aux Archives de l'Union.*

4 leaves (322 x 257 mm): pp. [1] lith title page, [2] blank, 3–7 engr music, [8] blank.

CAPTION TITLE: p. 3, '» F. Chopin. Op. 36.'.

SUB-CAPTION: p. 3, 'IMPROMPTU.'.

FOOTLINE: pp. 3–7, '6333'.

STAMPS: publisher, style BH/C (see Appendix 8).

1. *Date:* first-edition inference (date code fe, p. 17).
2. The tempo here is "Allegretto", whereas in the Brandus (Troupenas) and Wessel editions it is "Andantino".

London: Wessel (3550) [= 1840] **36-W-1** **M25.C54 I36**

LES AGRÉMENS AU SALON. | Nº 40. | 2E | IMPROMPTU. | *pour le* | Piano Forte, | Composé | par | FREDERIC CHOPIN. | *Copyright of the Publishers.* | OP. 36. « *Ent. Sta. Hall.* » *Price 2/6* | *Paris, Troupenas.* « » *Leipzig, Breitkopff* [*sic*] *& Härtel.* | *LONDON,* | WESSEL & Cº *Importers of Foreign Music. Publishers of the Works, by* | CHOPIN, LISZT, HENSELT, KUHLAU, HILLER, HUMMEL, WEBER, THALBERG, &c. | Nº 67, Frith Street, Corner of Soho Square.

5 leaves (341 x 250 mm): pp. [i] engr title page, [ii] blank, [1] advt, 2–7 engr music, [8] blank.

CAPTION TITLE: p. 2, '*LES AGRÉMENS AU SALON. Nº 40.* | *DEUXIÈME IMPROMPTU. (OP: 36.)* | *Composé par F. CHOPIN.*'.

FOOTLINE: p. 2, ' * Copyright of Wessel & Cº « » (W & Cº Nº 3550.)'; pp. 3–6, 'CHOPIN. 2de Impromptu. Op: 36. « (W & Cº Nº 3550.)'; p. 7, 'CHOPIN. 2me Impromptu. Op: 36. « | WESSEL & Cº Nº 67, FRITH St CORNER OF SOHO SQUARE. (Nº 3550.)'.

ADVT: p. [1], 'PAGE A. | CATALOGUE OF WESSEL AND CO.'S CHOICE PUBLICATIONS OF MODERN PIANO-FORTE MUSIC. | Nº 6, FRITH STREET, SOHO SQUARE, LONDON.'. The lists have Chopin works through Op. 27.

STAMPS: publisher, W/C? and W/B?.

1. *Date:* first-edition inference (date code fe, p. 17).
2. The title page is shown by Chominski & Turlo (plate 18).
3. For comments about Wessel's 1840 editions see Appendix 7.

NOCTURNES IN G MINOR AND G MAJOR
Opus 37

Paris: Troupenas (893) 1840	*Composed* 1838–39
Leipzig: Breitkopf & Härtel (6334) 1840	Brown 119
London: Wessel (3554) 1840	Chominski & Turlo 118

Paris: **Troupenas (893) [= 1840]** 37-T-2 **M25.C54 N85 c.2**

DEUX NOCTURNES | *Pour* | Le Piano | Composés | PAR | FRED. CHOPIN | Op: 37. « » Prix: 6f. | *A. Lafont.* | *à PARIS, chez E. TROUPENAS & Cie. Rue Neuve Vivienne, 40.* | *à Londres, chez Wessel & Cie.* « » *à Leipzig, chez Breitkopf & Haertel.*

6 leaves (326 x 257 mm): pp. [i] engr title page, [ii, 1] blank, 2–9 engr music, [10] blank.

CAPTION TITLE: p. 2, '*DEUX NOCTURNES* ÷ pour le piano forte. « Ier. NOCTURNE. » F. CHOPIN Op: 37.'; p. 5, 'IIme. NOCTURNE.'.

FOOTLINE: pp. 2–8, 'T. 893.'; p. 9, 'T. 893. » Paris, E. TROUPENAS et Cie., 40, rue neuve Vivienne.'.

STAMPS: publisher, style T/B (see Appendix 8).

1. *Date:* first-edition inference (date code fe, p. 17).
2. From copies in the Bibliothèque Nationale, Kallberg (1983, pp. 545–47; see also Kallberg 1996, pp. 169–71) identified two early impressions of the Troupenas edition of Op. 37, one (call it imp-0) that lacks opus number and price on the title page and appears to be a proof copy, and one (call it imp-1) with complete title page and numerous corrections.
3. The matter has also been discussed by Grabowski (1994, pp. 23–24), who called attention to another impression (call it imp-2), in the O'Meara collection, with additional corrections and thus later than imp-1). The O'Meara copy also differs from imp-1 in having a price of 5 f, rather than the original price 6 f.
4. Where do this collection's 37-T-1 and 37-T-2 fit into this sequence? The first point to note is that 37-T-2 has the original price 6 f, and 37-T-1 the later price 5 f. Jeffrey Kallberg (personal communication, April 1999) confirmed that the music of 37-T-1 and 37-T-2 is identical to that of imp-1. Considering also the price, it follows that 37-T-2 is identical to imp-1 (the first published impression), while 37-T-1 is an issue chronologically between imp-1 and imp-2, with only the change in price and no change in music.

Paris: **Troupenas (893) [*ca* 1840]** 37-T-1 **M25.C54 N85 c.1**

The transcription of this title page is the same as that of 37-T-2, except here the price is "5f.".

6 leaves (329 x 259 mm): pp. [i] engr title page, [ii, 1] blank, 2–9 engr music, [10] blank.

CAPTION TITLE: p. 2, '*DEUX NOCTURNES* ÷ pour le piano forte. « Ier. NOCTURNE. » F. CHOPIN Op: 37.'; p. 5, 'IIme. NOCTURNE.'.

FOOTLINE: pp. 2–8, 'T. 893.'; p. 9, 'T. 893. » Paris, E. TROUPENAS et Cie., 40, rue neuve Vivienne.'.

STAMPS: publisher, style T/B (see Appendix 8); dealer, Scharfenberg & Luis, New York.

37-T-1 *(continued)*

37-T-1 *(concluded)*

1. *Date:* first-edition inference (date code fe, p. 17); also see note 2.
2. Grabowski (1994, p. 24) refers to a copy in the O'Meara collection with price 5 francs (as in 37-T-1) as a second impression, the first having price 6 francs (37-T-2).
3. For further comments see 37-T-2, note 4.

Leipzig: **Breitkopf & Härtel (6334)** [= 1840] **37-BH-1** **M25.C54 N86**

DEUX NOCTURNES | pour le Piano | composés | par | FRÉD. CHOPIN. |
Oeuvr. 37. « Propriété des Editeurs » *Pr. 16 Gr.* | *Leipzig, chez Breitkopf & Härtel.* |
Paris, chez Troupenas & Co. « » *Londres, chez Wessel & Co* | *6334.* | *Enrégistré aux Archives de l'Union.*

6 leaves (310 x 243 mm): pp. [1] lith title page, 2–11 engr music, [12] blank.

CAPTION TITLE: p. 2, '» F. Chopin Op. 37.'.

SUB-CAPTION: p. 2, 'NOCTURNE I.'; p. 6, 'NOCTURNE II.'.

FOOTLINE: pp. 2–11, '6334'.

STAMPS: publisher, style BH/D (see Appendix 8).

BINDING: library cloth.

1. *Date:* first-edition inference (date code fe, p. 17).

Leipzig: **Breitkopf & Härtel (6334)** [after 1845] **37-BH-2** **M25.C54 N862**

DEUX NOCTURNES | POUR LE PIANO | composés | par | FRÉD. CHOPIN. |
Op. 37. | Propriété des Editeurs. | Leipzig, chez Breitkopf & Härtel. |
Paris, chez Brandus & Co « » Londres, chez Wessel & Co |
Pr. 20 Ngr. | *6334.* | *Enrégistré aux Archives de l'Union.*

6 leaves (340 x 265 mm): pp. [1] lith title page, 2–11 lith music, [12] blank.

CAPTION TITLE: p. 2, '» F. Chopin Op. 37'.

SUB-CAPTION: p. 2, 'NOCTURNE I.'; p. 6, 'NOCTURNE II.'.

FOOTLINE: pp. 2–11, '6334'.

STAMPS: publisher, styles BH/I and BH/J (see Appendix 8); dealer, Schirmer, New York.

1. *Date:* based on the name of the Paris publisher (Table 5A).

Mendrisio: **Pozzi (327)** [after 1840] **37-Po-1** **M25.C54 N853**

DEUX NOCTURNES | *Pour* | Le Piano | COMPOSÉS | PAR | *FRED. CHOPIN* |
N. 327. « *Op. 37.* » *Fr. 2. ___.* | *Mendrisio, chez C. Pozzi*

5 leaves (323 x 249 mm): pp. [1] engr title page, 2–9 engr music, [10] blank.

CAPTION TITLE: p. 2, 'DEUX NOCTURNES ÷ pour le piano forte. « 1er NOCTURNE. » F. CHOPIN OP. 37'; p. 5, '11me NOCTURNE.'.

37-Po-1 *(continued)*

37-Po-1 *(concluded)*

FOOTLINE: pp. 2–9, '327'.

STAMPS: none.

---

1. *Date:* No evidence was found, but it is likely the Italian edition is derived from the German.

BALLADE IN F MAJOR
Opus 38

Paris: Troupenas (925) 1840 — *Composed* 1839
Leipzig: Breitkopf & Härtel (6330) 1840 — Brown 102
London: Wessel (3555) 1840 — Chominski & Turlo 3

Paris: **Troupenas (925) [= 1840]** 38-T-1 **M25.C54 B22**

2me | BALLADE | *Pour LE Piano* | Dédiée | à Robert Schumann | *Par* | F. CHOPIN. | Op: 38 « » Prix: 5 ^{f} | A. L. | *PARIS, chez E. TROUPENAS & Cie Rue Neuve Vivienne, 40.* | *Londres, chez Wessel & Cie* « » *Leipzig, chez Breitkopff* [*sic*] *& Haertel.*

5 leaves (345 x 270 mm): pp. [i] engr title page, [ii, 1] blank, 2–7 engr music, [8] blank.

CAPTION TITLE: p. 2, '2me *BALLADE* ÷ par F. CHOPIN. ÷ Op: 38.«'.

FOOTLINE: pp. 2–7, 'T. 925'.

WRAPPER (blue): pp. [1] same as title page, [2–4] blank.

STAMPS: publisher, style T/B (see Appendix 8).

1. *Date:* first-edition inference (date code fe, p. 17).

Leipzig: **Breitkopf & Härtel (6330) [= 1840]** 38-BH-2 **M25.C54 B21**

BALLADE | pour le Piano | dediée | A Monsieur Robert Schumann | PAR | FRÉD. CHOPIN. | *Oeuvr. 38.* « Propriété des Editeurs. » *Pr. 16. Gr.* | *Leipzig, chez Breitkopf & Härtel.* | *Paris, chez Troupenas & Co* « » *Londres, chez Wessel & Co* | *6330.* | *Enrégistré aux Archives de l'Union.*

6 leaves (337 x 270 mm): pp. [1] lith title page, [2] blank, 3–11 engr music, [12] blank.

CAPTION TITLE: p. 3, '» F. Chopin. Op. 38.'.

SUB-CAPTION: p. 3, 'BALLADE.'.

FOOTLINE: pp. 3–11, '6330'.

WRAPPER (light blue): pp. [1] same as title page, [2–3] blank, [4] advt.

ADVT: wrapper p. [4], 'Publications Nouvelles pour le Pianoforte | DE | BREITKOPF & HÄRTEL à LEIPZIG.'. The following Chopin works are listed: Opp. 25–31, 33–37, 42 (including four-hand arrangements for Opp. 26, 33 and 34).

STAMPS: publisher, style BH/D (see Appendix 8).

CONDITION: This copy is in original condition — a clear impression and untrimmed, unblemished leaves.

1. *Date:* first-edition inference (date code fe, p. 17).

Leipzig: **Breitkopf & Härtel (6330) [1841–50]** **38-BH-1** **M25.C54 B2**

BALLADE | POUR LE PIANO | dédiée | A MONSIEUR ROBERT SCHUMANN | par | FRÉD. CHOPIN. | Op. 38. | Propriété des Editeurs. | Leipzig, chez Breitkopf & Härtel. | Paris, chez Troupenas & C$^{\underline{o}}$. « » Londres, chez Wessel & C$^{\underline{o}}$. | *Pr. 20 Ngr.* | *6330.* | *Enrégistré aux Archives de l'Union.*

6 leaves (336 x 265 mm): pp. [1] lith title page, [2] blank, 3–11 lith music, [12] blank.

CAPTION TITLE: p. 3, 'BALLADE. | » F. Chopin, Op. 38.'.

FOOTLINE: p. 3, 'Stich, Druck und Verlag von Breitkopf & Härtel in Leipzig. « 6330'; pp. 4–11, '6330'.

STAMPS: publisher, style BH/J (see Appendix 8).

1. *Date:* currency inference (date code C1, p. 17) and name of Paris publisher (Table 5A). The first edition is priced in Groschen (Hob-346).
2. This score corresponds to Hob-347.

SCHERZO IN C SHARP MINOR
Opus 39

Paris: Troupenas (926) 1840 — *Composed* 1839
Leipzig: Breitkopf & Härtel (6332) 1840 — Brown 125
London: Wessel (3556) 1840 — Chominski & Turlo 199

Leipzig: **Breitkopf & Härtel (6332) [= 1840]** **39-BH-1** **M25.C54 S6 c.1**

3ème | *SCHERZO* | pour le Piano | dédié | *A Monsieur Adolphe Gutmann* | par | FRÉD. CHOPIN. | *Oeuvr. 39.* « Propriété des Editeurs. » *Pr. 20 Gr.* | *Leipzig, chez Breitkopf & Härtel.* | *Paris, chez Troupenas & Cº* « » *Londres, chez Wessel & Cº* | *6332.* | *Enrégistré aux Archives de l'Union.*

8 leaves (330 x 257 mm): pp. [1] engr title page, [2] blank, 3–15 engr music, [16] blank.

CAPTION TITLE: p. 3, '» F. Chopin. Op. 39.'.

SUB-CAPTION: p. 3, 'SCHERZO.'.

FOOTLINE: pp. 3–14, '6332'; p. 15, '6332.'.

STAMPS: none.

ANNOTATIONS: handwritten "5" on each recto page.

1. *Date:* first-edition inference (date code fe, p. 17).

Leipzig: **Breitkopf & Härtel (6332) [= 1840]** **39-BH-3** **M25.C54 S6 c.2**

The transcription of this title page is the same as that of 39-BH-1.

8 leaves (335 x 270 mm): pp. [1] lith title page, [2] blank, 3–15 engr music, [16] blank.

CAPTION TITLE: p. 3, '» F. Chopin. Op. 39.'.

SUB-CAPTION: p. 3, 'SCHERZO.'.

FOOTLINE: pp. 3–14, '6332'; p. 15, '6332.'.

WRAPPER (tan): pp. [1] same as title page, [2–3] blank, [4] advt.

ADVT: wrapper p. [4], 'Publications Nouvelles pour le Pianoforte | DE | BREITKOPF & HÄRTEL à LEIPZIG.'. The following Chopin works are listed: Opp. 25–41, 33–37, 42 (including four-hand arrangements for Opp. 26, 33 and 34).

STAMPS: publisher, style BH/D (see Appendix 8).

CONDITION: This copy is in original condition — a clear impression with untrimmed, unblemished leaves.

1. *Date:* first-edition inference (date code fe, p. 17).

Leipzig: **Breitkopf & Härtel (6332) [1872–73]** **39-BH-2** **M25.C54 S62**

The transcription of this title page is the same as that of 39-BH-1, except here the price is "*25 Ngr. = Mk. 2.50.*".

39-BH-2 *(continued)*

39-BH-2 *(concluded)*

8 leaves (317 x 262 mm): pp. [1] lith title page, [2] blank, 3–15 lith music, [16] blank.

CAPTION TITLE: p. 3, '» F. Chopin. Op. 39.'.

SUB-CAPTION: p. 3, 'SCHERZO.'.

FOOTLINE: p. 3, 'Stich und Druck von Breitkopf & Härtel in Leipzig. « 6332'; pp. 4–15, '6332'.

STAMPS: none.

---

1. *Date:* currency inference (date code c3, p. 17).

POLONAISES IN A MAJOR AND C MINOR
Opus 40

Paris: Troupenas (977) 1840	*Composed* 1838–39
Leipzig: Breitkopf & Härtel (6331) 1840	Brown 120
London: Wessel (3557) 1840	Chominski & Turlo 152

Paris: **Troupenas (977) [= 1840]** **40-T-1** **M32.C54 P809**

DEUX POLONAISES | *Pour* | Le Piano | Dédiées à | à [*sic*] M.r Jules Fontana | *PAR* | FRED. CHOPIN. | *A. L.* | *Op: 40.* « » *Prix: 6.f* | *à PARIS, chez E. TROUPENAS & C.ie Rue Neuve Vivienne, 40.* | *Londres, chez Wessel.* « » *Leipzig, chez Breitkopff* [*sic*] *& Haertel.*

6 leaves (328 x 259 mm): pp. [i] engr title page, [ii, 1] blank, 2–9 engr music, [10] blank.

CAPTION TITLE: p. 2, '*DEUX POLONAISES* ÷ pour le Piano ÷ par CHOPIN. « POLONAISE N.o 1.'; p. 6, 'POLONAISE N.o 2.'.

FOOTLINE: p. 2, 'T 977'; p. 3, 'T 977 » *F. Benoit, Grave.-Impr.*'; pp. 4–9, 'T 977'.

STAMPS: publisher, style T/A (see Appendix 8).

1. *Date:* first-edition inference (date code fe, p. 17).

Leipzig: **Breitkopf & Härtel (6331) [1841–50]** **40-BH-1** **M32.C54 P81**

Deux | POLONOISES | POUR LE PIANO | dédiées | à son ami | *Jules Fontana* | PAR | FRÉD. CHOPIN. | *Oeuvr. 40.* « Propriété des Editeurs. » *Pr. 20 Ngr.* | *Leipzig, chez Breitkopf & Härtel.* | *Paris, chez Troupenas & C.o.* « » *Londres, chez Wessel & C.o* | *6331.* | *Enrégistré aux Archives de l'Union.*

6 leaves (326 x 256 mm): pp. [1] lith title page, [2] blank, 3–11 engr music, [12] blank.

CAPTION TITLE: p. 3, '» F.Chopin. Op. 40.'.

SUB-CAPTION: p. 3, 'POLONAISE. | N.o 1.'; p. 7, 'POLONAISE. | N.o 2.'.

FOOTLINE: pp. 3–11, '6331'.

STAMPS: none.

INSCRIPTIONS: handwritten "6" on recto of every leaf.

BINDING: library cloth.

1. *Date:* currency inference (date code c1, p. 17) and name of Paris publisher (Table 5A); also see note 2.
2. The price of the first issue is 16 Gr. (Chominski & Turleo, p. 168).
3. This score corresponds to Hob-355.

Leipzig: **Breitkopf & Härtel (6587) [*ca* 1841]** **40-BH-2** **M211.C54 P762**

DEUX POLONOISES | *arrangées* | pour le Piano à quatre mains | composées | par | FRÉD. CHOPIN. | *Op. 40.* « Propriété des Editeurs. » *Pr. 20 Ngr.* | *Leipzig, chez Breitkopf & Härtel.* | *Paris, chez Troupenas & Co. Londres, chez Wessel & Co* | *6587.* | *Enrégistré aux Archives de l'Union.*

8 leaves (232 x 318 mm, oblong): pp. [1] lith title page, 2–15 engr music, [16] blank.

CAPTION TITLE: p. 2, '» Fr. Chopin. Op. 40.'; p. 3, the same.

SUB-CAPTION: p. 2, 'N° 1. | POLONOISE.'; p. 3, the same; p. 8, system 3, 'N° 2. | POLONOISE.'; p. 9, the same.

HEADLINE: versos, 'SECONDO.'; rectos, 'PRIMO.'.

FOOTLINE: pp. 2–15, '6587'.

STAMPS: none.

1. *Date:* based on the plate number (Table 5C).

Leipzig: **Breitkopf & Härtel (6331) [after 1841]** **40-BH-3** **M32.C54 P8102**

The transcription of this title page is the same as that of 40-BH-1.

6 leaves (329 x 263 mm): pp. [1] lith title page, [2] blank, 3–11 lith music, [12] blank.

CAPTION TITLE: p. 3, '» F. Chopin, Op. 40.'.

SUB-CAPTION: p. 3, 'POLONAISE. | N° 1.'; p. 7, 'POLONAISE. | N° 2.'.

FOOTLINE: pp. 3–11, '6331'.

STAMPS: publisher, styles BH/I and BH/J (see Appendix 8).

1. *Date:* currency inference (date code C1, p. 17); also see note 2.
2. This lithographed score is presumably later than the engraved 40-BH-1.

London: **Wessel (3557) [1848–56]** **40-W-1** **M32.C54 P808**

N^{o} [handwritten "43"] OF | WESSEL & Co.'s COMPLETE COLLECTION | OF | *the Compositions* | OF | FREDERIC CHOPIN | FOR THE | Piano Forte. | Solo & Duet | [list of works, Wessel 1–42] | 43 "LES FAVORITES" *Deux Polonoises. (Set 2). Op. 40. 4/* | [list of works, Wessel 44–71] | *Ent. Sta. Hall.* « *Copyrights.* » *Price . Solo* [handwritten "4/ "] ÷ " *Duet* [blank] | *LONDON,* | WESSEL & Co *Importers and Publishers of* FOREIGN MUSIC, | *(by special Appointment) to H.R.H. the Duchess of Kent.* | N° 229, Regent Street, Corner of Hanover Street.

8 leaves (334 x 251 mm): pp. [i] engr title page, [ii] blank, 1–13 engr music, [14] advt.

CAPTION TITLE: p. 1, ' *"LES FAVORITES" DEUX POLONOISES, COMPOSÉES PAR FREDERIC CHOPIN, OP. 40.* | DÉDIÉES À SON AMI JULES FONTANA.'.

SUB-CAPTION: p. 1, '*N° 1.*'; p. 6, '*N° 2.*'.

40-W-1 *(continued)*

40-W-1 *(concluded)*

FOOTLINE: p. 1, 'Copyright of WESSEL & C°. « (N°. 3557) » This work forms the 2d. Set of two Polonoises.'; pp. 2–12, 'CHOPIN, Les Favorites, 2 Polonaises. Op: *40.* « (W & C°. N°. 3557)'; p. 13, 'CHOPIN, Les Favorites, 2 Polonaises. Op. *40.* « (N°. 3557) WESSEL & C°. '.

ADVT: p. [14], '[clipped to] A CATALOGUE OF EASY PIANO-FORTE MUSIC, WALTZES, & QUADRILLES, PUBLISHED BY WESSEL & Co.'. There are no Chopin works in the lists.

STAMPS: publisher, style W/D (see Appendix 8).

---

1. *Date:* Wessel inference (date code W1, p. 17).

MAZURKAS IN E MINOR, B MAJOR, A FLAT MAJOR, C SHARP MINOR
Opus 41

Paris: Troupenas (978) 1840 — *Composed* 1838–39
Leipzig: Breitkopf & Härtel (6335) 1840 — Brown 122
London: Wessel (3558) 1840 — Chominski & Turlo 76

***Paris:* Troupenas (978) [= 1840]** **41-T-1** **M32.C54 M511**

QUATRE | Mazurkas | *Pour* | LE PIANO | Dédiées à son Ami | Etienne Witwicki | *Par* | FRED. CHOPIN. | Op. 41. Prix: 6f. | *A. L.* | *PARIS, chez E. TROUPENAS & Cie. Rue Neuve Vivienne, 40.* | *Londres, chez Wessel & Cie.* « » *Leipzig, Breitkopff* [*sic*] *& Haertel.*

7 leaves (349 x 270 mm): pp. [i] engr title page, [ii, 1] blank, 2–11 engr music, [12] blank.

CAPTION TITLE: p. 2, '*F. CHOPIN* Op: 41. «'.

SUB-CAPTION: p. 2, 'No. 1.'; and so on through p. 8, 'No. 4.'.

FOOTLINE: p. 2, 'T. 978.'; p. 3, 'T. 978. » *F. Benoit. Grav. Impr.*'; pp. 4–11, 'T. 978.'.

STAMPS: publisher, style T/B (see Appendix 8); dealer, Denizot, Tours.

1. *Date:* first-edition inference (date code fe, p. 17).

***Leipzig:* Breitkopf & Härtel (6335) [= 1840]** **41-BH-2** **M32.C54 M512**

QUATRE MAZOURKAS | pour le Piano | dédiées | *A Monsieur Etienne Witwicki* | par | FRÉD. CHOPIN. | *Oeuvr. 41.* « Propriété des Editeurs » *Pr. 18 Gr.* | *Leipzig, chez Breitkopf & Härtel.* | *Paris, chez Troupenas & Co.* « » *Londres, chez Wessel & Co.* | *6335.* | *Enrégistré aux Achives de l'Union.*

7 leaves (306 x 234 mm): pp. [1] lith title page, [2] blank, 3–13 engr music, [14] blank.

CAPTION TITLE: p. 3, '» F. Chopin. Op. 41.'.

SUB-CAPTION: p. 3, 'No. 1.'; and so on through p. 12, 'No. 4.'.

FOOTLINE: pp. 3–13, '6335'.

STAMPS: publisher, style BH/D (see Appendix 8); dealer, Lucca, Milan.

1. *Date:* first-edition inference (date code fe, p. 17).
2. Leaves 2, 7 are hinged together and likewise leaves 3, 6 and 4, 5 thus making the title leaf a singleton.

***Leipzig:* Breitkopf & Härtel (6335) [1841–50]** **41-BH-1** **M32.C54 M5**

The transcription of this title page is the same as that of 41-BH-2, except here the price is "*22 1/2 Ngr.*".

7 leaves (318 x 262 mm): pp. [1] lith title page, [2] blank, 3–13 engr music, [14] blank.

CAPTION TITLE: p. 3, '» F. Chopin. Op. 41.'.

41-BH-1 *(continued)*

41-BH-1 *(concluded)*

SUB-CAPTION: p. 3, 'N° 1.'; and so on through p. 12, 'N° 4.'.

FOOTLINE: pp. 3–13, '6335'.

STAMPS: publisher, style BH/G? (see Appendix 8); dealer, Tinter, Vienna.

---

1. *Date:* currency inference (date code c1, p. 17) and name of Paris publisher (Table 5A).

Leipzig: **Breitkopf & Härtel (6335) [1872–73]** **41-BH-3** **M32.C54 M513**

The transcription of this title page is the same as that of 41-BH-2, except here the price is *"22 1/2 Ngr. = Mk. 2.25."*.

7 leaves (325 x 258 mm): pp. [1] lith title page, [2] blank, 3–13 lith music, [14] blank.

CAPTION TITLE: p. 3, 'QUATRE MAZURKAS. | » F. Chopin, Op. 41.'.

SUB-CAPTION: p. 3, 'N° 1.'; and so on through p. 12, 'N° 4.'.

FOOTLINE: p. 3, '6335 | Stich und Druck von Breitkopf & Härtel in Leipzig «'; pp. 4–13, '6335'.

STAMPS: none.

---

1. *Date:* currency inference (date code c3, p. 17).

London: **Wessel (3558) [= 1840]** **41-W-1** **M32.C54 M52**

N° [handwritten "44"] OF | WESSEL & C°.'s COMPLETE COLLECTION | OF | *the Compositions* | OF | FREDERIC CHOPIN | FOR THE | Piano Forte. | Solo & Duet | [list of works, Wessel 1–43] | 44 "SOUVENIR *de* LA POLOGNE" *7th Set of Mazurkas. Op. 41. 3/6 [Duet] 6/-* | [list of works, Wessel 45] | *Ent. Sta. Hall. « Copyrights. » Price . Solo* [handwritten "3/6"] ÷ " *Duet* [blank] | *LONDON,* | WESSEL & C° *Importers and Publishers of,* FOREIGN MUSIC, | *(by special Appointment) to, H.R.H. the Duchess of Kent.* | N° 67, Frith Street, Corner of Soho Square.

7 leaves (332 x 251 mm): pp. [i] engr title page, [ii] blank, [1] advt, 2–11 engr music, [12] blank.

CAPTION TITLE: p. 2, '*LES AGRÉMENS au SALON, N° 47.* | "SOUVENIR de la POLOGNE", 7th Set of MAZURKAS, | Composed by | FREDERIC CHOPIN. Op: 41.'; pp. 4, 6, 8, 'SOUVENIR de la POLOGNE, 7th Set of MAZURKAS, CHOPIN.'.

SUB-CAPTION: p. 2, 'N° 1.'; and so on through p. 8, 'N° 4.'.

FOOTLINE: p. 2, 'Copyright of Wessel & C° « » (W & C° N° 3558)'; pp. 3–10, 'CHOPIN, 7th Set of Mazurkas, Op: 41. « » (W & C° N° 3558)'; p. 11, 'CHOPIN, 7th Set of Mazurkas, Op: 41. « | (N° 3558) WESSEL & C° N° 67, FRITH STREET, Corner of SOHO SQUARE.'.

ADVT: p. [1], '[clipped to] No. 67, FRITH STREET, CORNER OF SOHO SQUARE.'. This is Wessel's "PAGE E", with Chopin works listed through op. 42 (as on the title page).

STAMPS: publisher, style W/C? (see Appendix 8).

---

1. *Date:* first-edition inference (date code fe, p. 17); also see notes 2 and 3.
2. Chominski & Turlo mention a later issue in which *"LES AGRÉMENS au SALON, N° 47"* does not appear in the caption title.

WALTZ IN A FLAT MAJOR
Opus 42

Paris: Pacini (3708) 1840	*Composed* 1840
Leipzig: Breitkopf & Härtel (6419) 1840	Brown 131
London: Wessel (3559) 1840	Chominski & Turlo 211

***Paris:* Pacini (3708) [= 1840]** **42-Pa-1** **M32.C54 W469**

GRANDE | VALSE NOUVELLE | Pour *LE* Piano | Composée par | F. CHOPIN |
Œuv. 42. « » *Prix: 6 f.* | *Prop. de l'Editeur.* | *PARIS, au Magasin de Musique de PACINI, Boulevart Italien, 11.* |
Londres, chez Wessel et Cie. « » *Leipsic, chez Breitkopf et Haertel.*

6 leaves (335 x 253 mm): pp. [i] engr title page, [ii, 407] blank, 408–415 engr music, [416] blank.

CAPTION TITLE: p. 408, 'VALSE » Par CHOPIN Op: 42. | No. 68. ÷ Des Cent-et-Un. «'.

FOOTLINE: p. 408, 'à Paris Chez PACINI « 3708. » Boulevard des Italiens 11.'; pp. 409–415, '3708.'.

STAMPS: none.

1. *Date:* first-edition inference (date code fe, p. 17).
2. The pagination comes from Pacini's album *Cent-et-un,* in which this waltz is no. 68 (Brown, p. 135).
2. Grabowski (1994, p. 26) notes two impressions, of which this — with address *"Boulevart Italien, 11"* — is the first.

***Paris:* Brandus & Dufour (10195) [*ca* 1860]** **42-BD-1** **M32.C54 W471**

GRANDE | VALSE | nouvelle | POUR | PIANO | PAR | F. CHOPIN. | *A.V.* | *Op: 42.* « » *Prix: 6 f.* |
PARIS, G. BRANDUS et S. DUFOUR, éditeurs, | *103, rue Richelieu, au 1er.*

6 leaves (343–349 x 271 mm): pp. [i] engr title page, [ii, 1] blank, 2–9 engr music, [10] blank.

CAPTION TITLE: p. 2, 'VALSE | » *F. CHOPIN.* ÷ Op: 42.'.

FOOTLINE: p. 2, 'G. BRANDUS et S. DUFOUR 103 Rue Richelieu. « B. et D. 10195.'; pp. 3–8, 'B. et D. 10195.'; p. 9, 'B. et D. 10195. Imp. THIERRY Fres. 1 Cité Bergère.'.

WRAPPER (yellow): pp. [1] same as title page, [2, 3] blank, [4] advt.

ADVT: wrapper p. [4], 'Extrait du Catalogue de G. Brandus et S. Dufour, éditeurs, | *Rue de Richelieu,* 103, *au* 1er, *à Paris.* | MUSIQUE DE PIANO.'. There are no Chopin works in the list.

IMPOSITION: Leaves 3 and 4 are singletons.

STAMPS: publisher, style BD/D (see Appendix 8).

1. *Date:* based on the plate number (Table 5A).

Leipzig: **Breitkopf & Härtel (6419) [=1840]** **42-BH-3** **M32.C54 W473**

VALSE | pour le Pianoforte | *composée* | PAR | FRÉD. CHOPIN. |
Oeuv. 42. « Propriété des Editeurs. » *Pr. 16. Gr.* | *Leipzig, chez Breitkopf & Härtel.* |
Paris, chez Pacini. « » *Londres, chez Wessel & C°.* | *6419.* | *Enrégistré aux Achives de l'Union.*

6 leaves (342 x 272 mm): pp. [1] lith title page, [2] blank, 3–11 engr music, [12] blank.

CAPTION TITLE: p. 3, 'VALSE. | » F. Chopin, Oeuvr. 42.'.

FOOTLINE: pp. 3–11, '6419'.

WRAPPER (faded pink): pp. [1] same as title page, [2–3] blank, [4] advt.

ADVT: wrapper p. [4], 'Publications Nouvelles pour le Pianoforte | DE | BREITKOPF & HÄRTEL à LEIPZIG.'. Chopin works are listed from Opp. 25 through 34 (including four-hand arrangements for Opp. 26, 33 and 34.

STAMPS: publisher, style BH/D (see Appendix 8).

CONDITION: This copy is in original condition — a clear impression and untrimmed, unblemished leaves.

1. *Date:* first-edition inference (date code fe, p. 17).

Leipzig: **Breitkopf & Härtel (6419) [after 1840]** **42-BH-1** **M32.C54 W47**

The transcription of this title page is the same as that of 42-BH-3, except here the price is *"20 Ngr."*.

6 leaves (320 x 254 mm): pp. [1] lith title page, [2] blank, 3–11 engr music, [12] blank.

CAPTION TITLE: p. 3, 'VALSE. | » F. Chopin, Oeuvr. 42.'.

FOOTLINE: pp. 3–11, '6419'.

STAMPS: publisher, style BH/F (see Appendix 8).

1. *Date:* currency inference (date code c1, p. 17).

Leipzig: **Breitkopf & Härtel (6419) [1872–73]** **42-BH-2** **M32.C54 W439**

VALSE | pour le Pianoforte | composée | *par* | FRÉD. CHOPIN. |
Oeuv. 42. « Propriété des Editeurs. » *Pr. 20 Ngr. = Mk. 2. __* | *Leipzig, chez Breitkopf & Härtel.* |
Paris, chez Pacini. « » *Londres, chez Wessel & C°.* | *6419.* | *Enrégistré aux Achives de l'Union.*

6 leaves (318 x 262 mm): pp. [1] lith title page, [2] blank, 3–11 lith music, [12] blank.

CAPTION TITLE: p. 3, 'VALSE. | » F. Chopin, Op. 42.'.

FOOTLINE: p. 3, 'Stich und Druck von Breitkopf & Härtel in Leipzig. « 6419'; pp. 4–11, '6419'.

STAMPS: none.

1. *Date:* currency inference (date code c3, p. 17).

London: Wessel (3559) [= 1840] 42-W-1 M32.C54 W472

N° [handwritten "45"] OF | WESSEL & C°.'s COMPLETE COLLECTION | OF | *the Compositions* | OF | FREDERIC CHOPIN | FOR THE | Piano Forte. | Solo & Duet | [list of works, Wessel 1–44] | 45 CENT-*et*-UN, *Grande* VALSE *in A* [flat] *Op. 42. 3/-* [*Duet*] *3/6* | *Ent. Sta. Hall.* « *Copyrights.* » *Price . Solo* [handwritten "3/-"] ÷ " *Duet* [blank] | *LONDON,* | WESSEL & C° *Importers and Publishers of* FOREIGN MUSIC, | *(by special Appointment) to, H.R.H. the Duchess of Kent.* | N° 67, Frith Street, Corner of Soho Square.

6 leaves (331 x 251 mm): pp. [i] engr title page, [ii] blank, [1] advt, 2–9 engr music, [10] blank.

CAPTION TITLE: p. 2, ' *"CENT __ ET __ UN."* | *GRANDE VALSE, Composée par FREDERIC CHOPIN.*'.

FOOTLINE: p. 2, '*Copyright of WESSEL & C° « (W & C° N° 3559.)'; pp. 3–8, 'CHOPIN, Cent _ et _ Un. Valse. Op: 42. « (W & C° N° 3559.)'; p. 9, 'CHOPIN, Cent _ et _ Un. Valse. Op: 42. « | WESSEL & C° N° 67, FRITH St CORNER OF SOHO SQUARE. (N° 3559.)'.

ADVT: p. [1], '[clipped to] THE WORKS OF BEETHOVEN, CHOPIN, LISZT, &c. PIANO SOLO AND ORGAN MUSIC. | No. 67, FRITH STREET, CORNER OF SOHO SQUARE.'. This is Wessel's "PAGE E", with Chopin works listed through op. 42 (as on the title page).

STAMPS: publisher, style W/C (see Appendix 8).

1. *Date:* first-edition inference (date code fe, p. 17).
2. Note that Wessel 45 (Op. 42) is the last work listed on the title page.
3. The title transcription given by Chominski & Turlo (p. 214) is for the caption title, not the title proper.
4. For comments about Wessel's 1840 editions see Appendix 7.

Mendrisio: **Pozzi (448) [after 1840]** **42-Po-1** **M32.C54 W468**

VALSE | pour le Pianoforte | *composée* | PAR | FRED. CHOPIN. | *Op: 42.* | *N. 448.* « » *Fr. 2.50.* | *Mendrisio, chez C. Pozzi*

6 leaves (323 x 249 mm): pp. [i] engr title page, [ii] blank, 1–9 engr music, [10] blank.

CAPTION TITLE: p. 1, 'VALSE. | » F. Chopin Oeuvr. 42.'.

FOOTLINE: pp. 1–9, '448.

STAMPS: none.

1. *Date:* No evidence was found, but it is likely the Italian edition is derived from the German.

TARANTELLE IN A FLAT MAJOR
Opus 43

Paris: Troupenas (1073) 1841	*Composed* 1841
Leipzig: Schuberth (449) 1841	Brown 139
London: Wessel (5295) 1841	Chominski & Turlo 205

***Leipzig:* Schuberth (449) [= 1841]** **43-Schu-1** **M31.C54 T19**

TARANTELLE | pour Le Pianoforte | *PAR* | FR. CHOPIN. | Op. 43. |
à 2 mains: ÷ 14 gGr: « » *à 4 mains: ÷ 1 Thlr.* | Propriété des Editeurs | *449. 455.* |
Schuberth & Comp. — Hambourg et Leipsic. | *Paris, chez Troupenas et Comp.*
St. Petersbourg à l'Odeon. Londres, chez Wessel & Comp. | Enregistré aux Archives de l'Union.

7 leaves (329 x 258 mm): pp. [1] engr title page, [2] blank, 3–13 engr music, [14] blank.

CAPTION TITLE: none.

FOOTLINE: pp. 3–12, '449'; p. 13, '» Stich u. Druck v. J. Schulze Hambg: | 449'.

PLATES: The music plates have decorative borders.

STAMPS: dealer, Scharfenberg, New York.

1. *Date:* first-edition inference (date code fe, p. 17).
2. Plate number 455 on the title page is that of the four-hand edition (see British Library, *CPM*, p. 56).

***Leipzig:* Schuberth (449) [after 1850]** **43-Schu-2** **M31.C54 T192**

a | mon ami Auguste Gathy. | Tarantelle | *pour le* | Pianoforte | PAR | FR. CHOPIN. |
à 2 mains: ÷ 2/3 Thlr. « » *à 4 mains: ÷* 1 Thlr. | Op. 43. | Propriété des Editeurs. | Schuberth & Co. |
HAMBOURG, LEIPZIC & NEW-YORK. | Enregistré aux Archives de l'Union. |
NOUVELLE EDITION. [slanted backward]

7 leaves (346 x 270 mm): pp. [1] engr title page, [2] blank, 3–13 engr music, [14] blank.

CAPTION TITLE: none.

FOOTLINE: pp. 3–12, '449'; p. 13, '» Stich u. Druck v. J. Schulze Hambg. | 449'.

WRAPPER (pale yellow): pp. [1] same as title page, [2–3] blank, [4] advt.

ADVT: wrapper p. 4, 'DIED. KRUG'S | PIANOFORTE-WERKE | erscheinen im Verlage von | SCHUBERTH & Co. Hamburg, Leipzig & New-York.'.

PLATES: The music plates have decorative borders, as in 43-Schu-1.

STAMPS: publisher, style Schu/A (on wrapper) (see Appendix 8); dealer, Plenge, Copenhagen (on wrapper).

1. *Date:* The New York branch of the firm was established in 1850 (Krummel & Sadie, 1990, p. 419).
2. Brown (p. 142) refers to a spurious dedication to Gathy in connection with a London (Augener) republication. Chominski & Turlo (p. 207) refer to this Schuberth edition as a Titelauflage, and to the dedication as inauthentic. Niecks (1888, II, p. 77) notes the dedication without comment; in the index he describes Gathy as a "writer on music and teacher" (p. 362). Bronarski (vol. 2, pp. 11–40) is silent about Gathy.

London: Wessel (5295) [*ca* 1847] 43-W-1 M31.C54 T17

N° [handwritten "46"] OF | WESSEL & C°.'s COMPLETE COLLECTION | OF | *the Compositions* | OF | FREDERIC CHOPIN | FOR THE | Piano Forte. | Solo & Duet | [list of works, Wessel 1–45] | 46 TARANTELLE *in A* [flat]. *Op. 43. 3/6* | [list of works, Wessel 47–68] | *Ent. Sta. Hall.* « *Copyrights.* » *Price. Solo* [handwritten "3/6 "] ÷ " *Duet* [blank] | *LONDON,* | WESSEL & C° *Importers and Publishers of* FOREIGN MUSIC, | *(by special Appointment) to H.R.H. the Duchess of Kent.* | N° 229, Regent Street, Corner of Hanover Street.

7 leaves (340 x 252 mm): pp. [i] engr title page, [ii] blank, 1–11 engr music, [12] advt.

CAPTION TITLE: p. 1. 'TARANTELLE, | OP: 43. | *Composed by FREDERIC CHOPIN.*'.

FOOTLINE: p. 1, '(W. & S. N° 5295.)'; pp. 2–10, 'CHOPIN. Tarantelle. Op: 43. « » (W. & S. N° 5295.)'; p. 11, 'CHOPIN. Tarantelle. Op: 43. « » (N° 5295.) | Wessel & C° '.

ADVT: p. [12], 'PAGE B. | CATALOGUE OF WESSEL & Co.'s CHOICE PUBLICATIONS OF MODERN-PIANO FORTE MUSIC.'. The lists include Chopin Opp. 5, 10, 25.

IMPOSITION: Binding and rebinding obscure the position of the singleton.

STAMPS: publisher, style W/C? (see Appendix 8).

1. *Date:* based on the list of works on the title page. It ends with Op. 63, published by Wessel in 1847, and lacks Op. 64, published in 1848.

Milan: Ricordi (13042) [*ca* 1841] 43-Rico-1 M31.C54 T18

TARANTELLE | Pour Piano | PAR | F. CHOPIN. | *Op. 43.* | *Enr. dans l'Arch de l'Union ÷ 13042.* « » *Propriété des Édit*[rs] ÷ *Fr 2.25.* | *MILAN* | *I. R. ÉTABLISSEMENT NATIONAL PRIVIL*[é] | DE JEAN RICORDI | RUE DES OMENONI N° 1720. | *Florence, J. Ricordi et Jouhaud.* « *Mendrisio, C. Pozzi* » *Paris, E. Troupenas et C*[e] | Londres, Wessel et Ce « » Hambourg, Schubert [*sic*] et Ce

5 leaves (323 x 249 mm): pp. [1] engr title page, 2–9 engr music, [10] blank.

CAPTION TITLE: p. 2, '» F. CHOPIN Op: 43.'.

FOOTLINE: pp. 2–9, 'P 13042 Q'.

STAMPS: successor, embossed and partly cropped, but "TITO RICORDI" is at the top.

1. *Date:* Chominski & Turlo, p. 325.
2. As indicated in the title, Ricordi was a member of the German/Austrian publishers Union. Since Schuberth was also a member (see 43-Schu-1), presumably Ricordi was prohibited from publishing the Tarantelle in Germany or Austria, but evidently was free to publish in Italy.

POLONAISE IN F SHARP MINOR
Opus 44

Paris: M. Schlesinger (3477) 1841	*Composed* 1841
Vienna: Mechetti (3577) 1841	Brown 135
London: Wessel (5226) 1842	Chominski & Turlo 154

Paris: M. Schlesinger (3477) [= 1841] — **44-mS-1** — **M32.C54 P812**

Polonaise | POUR | PIANO | *dédiée à Madame* | *la Princesse* Charles de Beauvau *née de Komar* | *PAR* | *F. CHOPIN.* | A.V. | *Op: 44.* « » *Prix 7.f 50* | *A PARIS, chez* MAURICE SCHLESINGER, *Rue Richelieu, 97.* | *Vienne, chez P. Mechetti.* « *3477. M.S.* » *Propriété des Editeurs.* | *Londres, Wessel et Stapleton.*

7 leaves (337 x 259 mm): pp. [i] engr title page, [ii] blank, 1–11 engr music, [12] blank.

CAPTION TITLE: p. 1, 'F. CHOPIN Op: 44. « » *POLONAISE.*'.

SUB-CAPTION: p. 1, 'POLONAISE.'.

FOOTLINE: p. 1, 'F. Chopin Op: 44. Polonaise. M.S. 3477. Maurice Schlesinger 97 rue Richelieu.'; pp. 2–11, 'M.S. 3477.'.

STAMPS: none.

1. *Date:* first-edition inference (date code fe, p. 17).

Vienna: Mechetti (3577) [= 1841] — **44-Mec-3** — **M32.C54 P813**

Polonaise | pour le | PIANO | dédiée | à Madame la Princesse | CHARLES DE BEAUVAU | née de Komar | par | F. Chopin. | Oeuvre 44. « » Prix fl. 1.30. A.de.C. | Propriété des Editeurs. — Enregistré dans l'Archive de l'Union. | VIENNE, | CHEZ PIETRO MECHETTI Qm CARLO, | Marchand de Musique et de beaux Arts de la Cour J[I]mp. et Roye | Place St Michel No 1153. | Paris chez E. Troupenas & Cie | [below the floral design:] *Lithogr. de J. Rauh* « » *Berndt lith.*

10 leaves (325 x 254 mm): pp. [1] title page, [2] blank, 3–19 engr music, [20] blank.

CAPTION TITLE: p. 3, 'POLONAISE | par | F CHOPIN. | Oeuvre 44.'.

SUB-CAPTION: p. 3, 'Polonaise.'.

FOOTLINE: p. 3, 'Pietro Mechetti. No 3577.; pp. 4–19, 'P.M. No 3577.'.

STAMPS: none.

1. *Date:* first-edition inference (date code fe, p. 17); also see note 2.
2. This issue, with Troupenas as the Paris publisher, presumably precedes those with Schlesinger (44-Mec-2 and 44-Mec-1).
3. The title page is printed in blue.

Vienna: **Mechetti (3577) [*ca* 1841]** **44-Mec-2** **M32.C54 P815**

The transcription of this title page is the same as that of 44-Mec-3, except here the Paris publisher is "M. Schlesinger." and below the floral design there is no indication of the lithographers.

10 leaves (325 x 250 mm): pp. [1] engr title page, [2] blank, 3–19 engr music, [20] blank.

CAPTION TITLE: p. 3, 'POLONAISE | par | F. CHOPIN. | Oeuvre 44.'.

SUB-CAPTION: p. 3, 'Polonaise.'.

FOOTLINE: p. 3, 'Pietro Mechetti. N° 3577.'; pp. 4–19, 'P.M. N° 3577.'.

STAMPS: none.

1. *Date:* first-edition inference (date code fe, p. 17), but the date is questioned because 44-Mec-3, which cites Troupenas, is probably earlier.
2. This score corresponds to Hob-370, shown in his plate 25 (p. 161).

Vienna: **Mechetti (3577) [after 1841]** **44-Mec-1** **M32.C54 P82**

The transcription of this title page is the same as that of 44-Mec-2, except here at the end there is "| [below the floral design:] » *Berndt lith.* | Art. Anst. v. Reiffenstein & Resch in Wien.".

8 leaves (332 x 260 mm): pp. [1] lith title page, 2–15 engr music, [16] blank.

CAPTION TITLE: p. 2, 'POLONAISE | par | F. CHOPIN. | Op. 44.'.

FOOTLINE: p. 2, 'P.M. 3577. | Druck von A. Eckel in Wien. «'; pp. 3–15, 'P.M. 3577.'.

STAMPS: none.

1. *Date:* The music layout is in 14 pages here, whereas it is in 17 pages in the first edition 44-Mec-3.
2. The plate for p. 3 is tilted slightly.
3. This score corresponds to Hob-371.

London: **Wessel (5296) [1848–56]** **44-W-1** **M32.C54 P822**

N° [handwritten "47"] OF | WESSEL & C°.'s COMPLETE COLLECTION | OF | *the Compositions* | OF | FREDERIC CHOPIN | FOR THE | Piano Forte. | Solo & Duet | [list of works, Wessel 1–46] | 47 GRAND POLONOISE *in F* [sharp] *min. Op. 44. 4/-* | [list of works, Wessel 48–71] | *Ent. Sta. Hall.* « *Copyrights.* » *Price. Solo* [handwritten "4/– "] ÷ " *Duet* [blank] | *LONDON,* | WESSEL & C° *Importers and Publishers of* FOREIGN MUSIC, | *(by special Appointment) to H.R.H. the Duchess of Kent.* | N° 229, Regent Street, Corner of Hanover Street.

8 leaves (334 x 250 mm): pp. [i] engr title page, [ii] blank, [1] advt, 2–13 engr music, [14] blank.

CAPTION TITLE: p. 2. 'SECOND GRAND POLONAISE, | *Composed by* | *FREDERIC CHOPIN.* | » OP: 44.'.

44-W-1 *(continued)*

44-W-1 *(concluded)*

FOOTLINE: p. 2, 'Copyright of Wessel & C° « (W.&S. N° 5296.)'; pp. 3–12, 'CHOPIN, Grand Polonaise Op. 44. « (W.&S. N° 5296.)'; p. 13, 'CHOPIN, Grand Polonaise Op. 44. « (W & S N° 5296.) » WESSEL & C° N° 229, Regent Street.'.

ADVT: p. [1], '[clipped to] CATALOGUE OF WESSEL & Co.'s PUBLICATIONS OF MODERN PIANO DUETS,'. This is Wessel's advertisement "PAGE D". The lists include duets, arranged, of Chopin Opp. 1, 3, 6, 7, 9, 15, 16, 17, 18, 19, 22, 24, 29, 32, 33, 34.

STAMPS: publisher, style W/D (see Appendix 8).

---

1. *Date:* Wessel inference (date code W1, p. 17).

PRELUDE IN C SHARP MINOR
Opus 45

Paris: M. Schlesinger (3518) 1841 — *Composed* 1841
Vienna: Mechetti (3594) 1841 — Brown 141
London: Wessel (5297) 1842 — Chominski & Turlo 190

***Paris:* M. Schlesinger (3518) [= 1841]** **45-mS-1** **M25.C54 P91**

Prélude | pour | LE PIANO | *dédie à Mademoiselle* | *La Princesse Elisabeth Tchernischeff* | *ET* COMPOSÉ *PAR* | F. CHOPIN | *Op. 45.* « » *Prix. 6.f* | *Paris,* MAURICE SCHLESINGER, *Editeur* | *Rue Richelieu, 97.* | *Vienne, chez Mechetti.* « *M.S. 3518* » *Londres, chez Wessel et C.ie* | » *Propriété des Editeurs.*

5 leaves (318 x 258 mm): pp. [i] engr title page, [ii] blank, 1–7 engr music, [8] blank.

CAPTION TITLE: 1, 'PRÉLUDE | *PAR* | F. Chopin | OP: 45.'.

FOOTLINE: p. 1, 'F. Chopin. op. 45. « M.S. 3518. » Maurice Schlesinger. 97. rue Richelieu.'; pp. 2–6, 'M.S. 3518.'; p. 7, 'M.S. 3518. » Maurice Schlesinger. 97. rue Richelieu.'.

STAMPS: publisher, style mS/A (see Appendix 8).

CONDITION: The plate impressions are uniformly clear — uncommon for Schlesinger editions in this collection.

1. *Date:* first-edition inference (date code fe, p. 17).
2. Grabowski (1994, p. 15) mentions a first printing by Schlesinger in *Keepsake des Pianistes* (*Revue et Gazette Musicale,* 12 December 1841), with numerous errors that were corrected in this edition (45-mS-1).

***Paris:* Brandus & Dufour (M.S. 3518) [after 1857]** **45-BD-1** **M25.C54 P912**

ÉDITION ORIGINALE | OEUVRES COMPLÈTES POUR LE PIANO | DE | FRÉDÉRIC CHOPIN | SEULE EDITION AUTHENTIQUE | SANS CHANGEMENTS NI ADDITIONS, PUBLIÉE D'APRÈS LES ÉPREUVES CORRIGÉES PAR L'AUTEUR LUI-MÊME. | [list of works Opp. 1–44] |
Op. 45. Prélude en *ut* dièse mineur (dédié à la princesse Tchernischeff). 6 " |
[list of works Opp. 46–65 and three works without opus number] |
Paris, G. BRANDUS ET S. DUFOUR, Éditeurs | 103, rue de Richelieu, 103. |
[below the decorated border:] IMPRIMERIE CENTRALE DES CHEMINS DE FER. « »
A. CHAIX ET C°, RUE BERGÈRE, 20, A PARIS | 10304

5 leaves (348 x 268 mm): pp. [i] lith title page, [ii] blank, 1–7 engr music, [8] blank.

CAPTION TITLE: p. 1, 'PRÉLUDE | *PAR* | F. Chopin | OP: 45.'.

FOOTLINE: p. 1, 'F. Chopin. op 45 « M.S. 3518. » Maurice Schlesinger. 97. rue Richelieu.'; pp. 2–6, 'M.S. 3518.'; p. 7, 'M.S. 3518. » Maurice Schlesinger. 97. rue Richelieu.'.

STAMPS: publisher, style BD/C (see Appendix 8).

45-BD-1 *(continued)*

45-BD-1 *(concluded)*

1. *Date:* based on the publisher's name (Table 5A); see notes 2 and 3.
2. The Brandus & Dufour partnership ended with the death of Dufour in 1872.
3. Chominski & Turlo (p. 255) assign 1859–78 for the Brandus collected edition.
4. Brown (p. 145) states that editorial corrections were made by Liszt for the *Gesamtausgabe* of Breitkopf & Härtel (1878–80). Hob-377 and plate 26 (Hoboken, p. 163) support this statement. Eigeldinger (1997, p. 233, note 3) assigns the Liszt corrections to the Brandus & Dufour collective edition issue (45-BD-1). Perhaps both statements are correct.
5. This score corresponds to Hob-377.

Vienna: **Mechetti (3594) [= 1841]** | **45-Mec-1** | **M25.C54 P9 c.1**

PRÉLUDE | pour le | PIANO | *dédié à Mademoiselle la Princesse* | Elisabeth Czernicheff | par | F. Chopin. | Oeuvre 45. « » Prix 45 kr. A. de. C. | Propriété des Editeurs. « » Enrégistré dans l'Archive de l'Union. | VIENNE | chez Pietro Mechetti q^m Carlo, | Marchand de Musique et de beaux Arts de la Cour J.[I.] et R^e | *PARIS, chez Maurice Schlesinger.* | [below the decorated border:] Art. Anst. [?] v. Reiffenstein & [...?] « » Federz. von Berndt

4 leaves (336 x 261 mm): pp. [1] lith title page, [2] blank, 3–7 engr music, [8] blank.

CAPTION TITLE: p. 3, 'PRÉLUDE | *par* | F. Chopin. | *Oeuvre 45.*'.

FOOTLINE: p. 3, 'Pietro Mechetti. N° 3594.'; pp. 4–7, 'P.M. N° 3594.'.

WRAPPER (light purple): pp. [1] same as title page, [2–4] blank.

STAMPS: none.

1. *Date:* first-edition inference (date code fe, p. 17).
2. Mechetti first issued Op. 45 in "Album-Beethoven. Dix Morceaux brillants pour le piano ..." (Eigeldinger, 1997, p. 233, note 1). Eigeldinger (*loc. cit.,* note 3) also mentions textual differences between the German and French separate editions (45-Mec-1, 45-mS-1).
3. Brown (p. 145) asserts that Mechetti's title page cites Ewer as the English publisher, but that citation does not appear in 45-Mec-1, or in Hob-374 or Chominski & Turlo (p. 186).

Vienna: **Mechetti (3594) [= 1841]** | **45-Mec-2** | **M25.C54 P9 c.2**

The transcription of this title page is the same as that of 45-Mec-1.

4 leaves (340 x 262 mm): pp. [1] lith title page, [2] blank, 3–7 engr music, [8] blank.

CAPTION TITLE: p. 3, 'PRÉLUDE | *par* | F. Chopin. | *Oeuvre 45.*'.

FOOTLINE: p. 3, 'Pietro Mechetti. N° 3594.'; pp. 4–7, 'P.M. N° 3594.'.

WRAPPER (blue): pp. [1] same as title page, [2–3] blank, [4] advt.

ADVT: wrapper p. [4], 'Franz Schubert's Original-Werke und Arrangements dieser Werke für Pianoforte im Verlage von C. A. Spina.'.

STAMPS: dealer, Hansen, no place; on wrapper, the same, and with sticker of Schultz, Aalborg.

45-Mec 2 *(continued)*

45-Mec 2 *(concluded)*

CONDITION: Compared with 45-Mec-1, this copy has somewhat better plate impressions.

---

1. *Date:* first-edition inference (date code fe, p. 17).
2. For additional comments, see 45-Mec-1, notes 2 and 3.

ALLEGRO DE CONCERT IN A MAJOR
Opus 46

Paris: M. Schlesinger (3481) 1841	*Composed* 1834–41
Leipzig: Breitkopf & Härtel (6651) 1841	Brown 72
London: Wessel (5298) 1842	Chominski & Turlo 1

Paris: **M. Schlesinger (3481) [= 1841]** **46-mS-1** **M25.C54 A39**

ALLEGRO | DE | Concert, POUR le Piano, | dédié à | *Mademlle* F. MULLER, *de Vienne* | *PAR* | F. CHOPIN | *A.V.* | *Op: 46.* « » *Prix 7 f 50* | *A PARIS, chez* MAURICE SCHLESINGER, *Rue Richelieu, 97.* | *Leipzig, chez Breitkopf et Haertel.* « *3481. M.S.* » *Propriété des Editeurs.* | *Londres, Wessel et Stapleton.*

9 leaves (348 x 268 mm): pp. [i] engr title page, [ii, 1] blank, 2–15 engr music, [16] blank.

CAPTION TITLE: p. 2, 'F. CHOPIN Op: 46. « » *ALLEGRO de CONCERT.*'.

FOOTLINE: pp. 2–13, 'M.S. 3481.'; p. 14, 'F. Chopin Op: 46. « M.S. 3481.'; p. 15, 'Maurice Schlesinger « M.S. 3481. » rue Richelieu 97.'.

WRAPPER (green): pp. [1] half-title page, [2–4] blank.

HALF TITLE: wrapper p. [1], 'Allegro DE Concert | F. CHOPIN | Op: 46.'.

STAMPS: successor, style Bra/A (see Appendix 8).

1. *Date:* first-edition inference (date code fe, p. 17).

Leipzig: **Breitkopf & Härtel (6651) [= 1841]** **46-BH-1** **M25.C54 A4**

ALLEGRO DE CONCERT | pour le Piano | composé et dédié | *A Mademoiselle F. Müller* | PAR | FRÉD. CHOPIN. | *Op. 46.* « Propriété des Editeurs. » *Pr. 1 Thlr. 6 Ngr.* | *Leipzig, chez Breitkopf & Härtel.* | *Paris, chez M. Schlesinger.* | *6651.* | *Enrégistré aux Archives de l'Union*

12 leaves (340 x 268 mm): pp. [1] engr title page, [2, 3] blank, 4–23 engr music, [24] blank.

CAPTION TITLE: p. 4, ' » Fr. Chopin Op. 46.'.

SUB-CAPTION: p. 4, 'ALLEGRO | de | CONCERT.'.

FOOTLINE: pp. 4–23, '6651'.

STAMPS: publisher, style BH/G? (see Appendix 8); dealer, Theune, Amsterdam (see Appendix 8).

ANNOTATIONS: owner's signature.

1. *Date:* first-edition inference (date code fe, p. 17).

Leipzig: **Breitkopf & Härtel (6651) [1872–73]** **46-BH-2** **M25.C54 A41**

The transcription of this title page is the same as that of 46-BH-1, except here the price is "*1 Thlr. 6 Ngr. = Mk. 3.60*".

11 leaves (326 x 258 mm): pp. [1] lith title page, 2–21 lith music, [22] blank.

46-BH-2 *(continued)*

46-BH-2 *(concluded)*

CAPTION TITLE: p. 2, ' » Fr. Chopin Op. 46.'.

SUB-CAPTION: p. 4, 'ALLEGRO | de | CONCERT.'.

FOOTLINE: pp. 4–23, '6651'.

STAMPS: publisher, style BH/I (see Appendix 8).

---

1. *Date:* currency inference (date code c3, p. 17).

BALLADE IN A FLAT MAJOR
Opus 47

Paris: M. Schlesinger (3486) 1841	*Composed* 1841
Leipzig: Breitkopf & Härtel (6652) 1842	Brown 136
London: Wessel (5299) 1842	Chominski & Turlo 4

Paris: **M. Schlesinger (3486) [= 1841]** **47-mS-1** **M25.C54 B32 c.1**

3.E | *BALLADE* | POUR | le Piano, | dédiée | à Mademoiselle Pauline de Noailles | *PAR* | *F. CHOPIN.* | *A.V.* | *Op: 47.* « » *Prix 7:f 50* | *A PARIS, chez* MAURICE SCHLESINGER, *Rue Richelieu, 97.* | *Leipzig, chez Breitkopf et Haertel.* « *M.S. 3486.* » *Propriété des Editeurs.* | *Londres, Wessel et Stapelton* [*sic*].

9 leaves (333 x 263 mm): pp. [i] engr title page, [ii, 1] blank, 2–15 engr music, [16] blank.

CAPTION TITLE: p. 2, 'F. CHOPIN. Op: 47. « » 3.e Ballade.'.

FOOTLINE: p. 2, 'M.S. 3486. » Maurice Schlesinger, rue de Richelieu 97.'; pp. 3–14, 'M.S. 3486.'; p. 15, same as p. 2.

STAMPS: successor, style Bra/A (see Appendix 8).

ANNOTATIONS: stamped page numbers 139–156.

1. *Date:* first-edition inference (date code fe, p. 17).

Paris: **M. Schlesinger (3486) [= 1841]** **47-mS-2** **M25.C54 B32 c.2**

The transcription of this title page is the same as that of 47-mS-1.

9 leaves (352 x 275 mm): pp. [i] engr title page, [ii, 1] blank, 2–15 engr music, [16] blank.

CAPTION TITLE: p. 2, 'F. CHOPIN. Op: 47. « » 3.e Ballade.'.

FOOTLINE: p. 2, 'M.S. 3486. » Maurice Schlesinger, rue de Richelieu 97.'; pp. 3–14, 'M.S. 3486.'; p. 15, same as p. 2.

WRAPPER (faded pink): pp. [1] half title '3.E | BALLADE | F. CHOPIN | OP: 47. | AV', [2–4] blank.

STAMPS: publisher, style mS/B (see Appendix 8).

CONDITION: This copy is in original condition — a clear impression with untrimmed, unblemished leaves.

1. *Date:* first-edition inference (date code fe, p. 17).

Leipzig: **Breitkopf & Härtel (6652) [= 1842]** **47-BH-1** **M25.C54 B3**

BALLADE | pour le Piano | dédiée | À Mademoiselle Pauline de Noailles | par | FRÉD. CHOPIN. | *Op. 47.* « Propriété des Editeurs. » *Pr. 24 Ngr.* | *Leipzig, chez Breitkopf & Härtel.* | *Paris, chez M. Schlesinger.* | *6652.* | *Enrégistré aux Archives de l'Union.*

8 leaves (327 x 256 mm): pp. [1] lith title page, [2, 3] blank, 4–14 engr music, [15, 16] blank.

47-BH-1 *(continued)*

47-BH-1 *(concluded)*

CAPTION TITLE: p. 4, '3$^{\underline{me}}$ BALLADE. | » F. Chopin Oeuv. 47.'.

FOOTLINE: pp. 4–14, '6652'.

STAMPS: publisher, style BH/F (see Appendix 8).

ANNOTATIONS: handwritten "13" on all recto pages.

BINDING: library cloth.

---

1. *Date:* first-edition inference (date code fe, p. 17).

Leipzig: **Breitkopf & Härtel (6652) [after 1842]** **47-BH-3** **M25.C54 B31**

The transcription of this title page is the same as that of 47-BH-1.

8 leaves (333 x 257 mm): pp. [1] lith title page, [2, 3] blank, 4–14 lith music, [15, 16] blank.

CAPTION TITLE: p. 4, '3$^{\underline{me}}$ BALLADE. | » F. Chopin Oeuv. 47.'.

FOOTLINE: pp. 4–14, '6652'.

STAMPS: publisher, style BH/I (see Appendix 8).

---

1. *Date:* This score is a lithographed issue of the engraved 47-BH-1.

Leipzig: **Breitkopf & Härtel (6652) [1872–73]** **47-BH-2** **M25.C54 B33**

The transcription of this title page is the same as that of 47-BH-1, except here the price is *"24 Ngr. = Mk. 2.40."*.

7 leaves (340 x 270 mm): pp. [1] lith title page, 2–12 lith music, [13, 14] blank.

CAPTION TITLE: p. 2, '3$^{\underline{me}}$ BALLADE. | » F. Chopin Oeuv. 47.'.

FOOTLINE: pp. 2–12, '6652'.

WRAPPER (faded purple): pp. [1] collective title page, [2, 3] blank, [4] advt.

COLLECTIVE TITLE: wrapper p. [1], 'OEUVRES DE PIANO | DE | FRÉD. CHOPIN.' The list of works is classified in eleven genres: Valses, Notturnos, Ballades, Sonates, Etudes, Mazurkas, Polonaises, Scherzos, Impromptus, Preludes, and Concertos, Variations etc. The last opus number listed is 65.

ADVT: wrapper p. [4], 'JOSEPH HAYDN'S WERKE | im Verlage von | BREITKOPF & HÄRTEL IN LEIPZIG.'.

STAMPS: publisher, style BH/I (see Appendix 8).

---

1. *Date:* currency inference (date code c3, p. 17).

NOCTURNES IN C MINOR AND F SHARP MINOR
Opus 48

Paris: M. Schlesinger (3487) (3488) 1841	*Composed* 1841
Leipzig: Breitkopf & Härtel (6653) 1842	Brown 142
London: Wessel (5300) (5301) 1842	Chominski & Turlo 120

Paris: **M. Schlesinger (3487) [= 1841]** **48#1-mS-1** **M25.C54 N9021 c.1**

13^{E} et 14^{E} | *NOCTURNE* | POUR | PIANO | *dédiés* | à Mademoiselle Laure Duperré, | *PAR* | F. CHOPIN. | *A.V.* | *Op: 48.* « » *Chaque 6*^{f} | N^{o} [blank] | *En deux Livres* | *À PARIS, chez* MAURICE SCHLESINGER, *Rue Richelieu, 97.* | *Leipzig, chez Breitkopf et Haertel.* « *3487. M.S.* » *Propriété des Editeurs.* | *Londres, Wessel et Stapelton* [*sic*].

6 leaves (333 x 262 mm): pp. [i] engr title page, [ii, 1] blank, 2–9 engr score, [10] blank.

CAPTION TITLE: p. 2, 'F. CHOPIN. Op: 48. « » 13e et 14e Nocturnes.'.

SUB-CAPTION: p. 2, '13^{e} | NOCTURNE'.

FOOTLINE: p. 2, 'M.S. 3487. » Maurice Schlesinger rue de Richelieu 97.'; pp. 3–8, 'M.S. 3487.'; p. 9, same as p. 2.

STAMPS: successor, style Bra/A (see Appendix 8).

ANNOTATIONS: stamped page numbers 147–158.

1. *Date:* first-edition inference (date code fe, p. 17).
2. Although no number is entered on the title page, this score is Op. 48#1.

Paris: **M. Schlesinger (3487) [= 1841]** **48#1-mS-2** **M25.C54 N9021 c.2**

The transcription of this title page is the same as that of **48#1-mS-1.**

6 leaves (350 x 275 mm): pp. [i] engr title page, [ii, 1] blank, 2–9 engr score, [10] blank.

CAPTION TITLE: p. 2, 'F. CHOPIN. Op: 48. « » Deux Nocturnes.'.

SUB-CAPTION: p. 2, '13^{e} | NOCTURNE'.

FOOTLINE: p. 2, 'M.S. 3487. » Maurice Schlesinger rue de Richelieu 97.'; pp. 3–8, 'M.S. 3487.'; p. 9, same as p. 2.

WRAPPER (faded rose): pp. [1] half title, [2–4] blank.

HALF TITLE: wrapper p. [1], '13^{E} et 14^{E} | NOCTURNE | F. Chopin | OP: 48. | *N° 1. 13^{e} Nocturne.* « » *N° 2. 14^{e} Nocturne.* | N^{o} [handwritten "13"]| AV'

STAMPS: publisher, style mS/B (see Appendix 8).

CONDITION: This copy is in original condition — a clear impression with untrimmed, unblemished leaves.

1. *Date:* first-edition inference (date code fe, p. 17).
2. Although no number is entered on the title page, this score is Op. 48#1.
3. The caption title differs slightly from that of 48#1-mS-1.

Paris: **M. Schlesinger (3488) [= 1841]** **48#2-mS-1** M25.C54 N9022

The transcription of this title page is the same as that of **48#1-mS-1**, including plate number 3487.

6 leaves (333 x 262 mm): pp. [i] engr title page, [ii, 1] blank, 2–9 engr music, [10] blank.

CAPTION TITLE: p. 2, 'F. CHOPIN. Op: 48. « » 13$^{e.}$ et 14$^{e.}$ Nocturnes.'.

SUB-CAPTION: p. 2, '14^{e} | NOCTURNE.'.

FOOTLINE: p. 2, 'M.S. 3488. » Maurice Schlesinger rue de Richelieu 97.'; pp. 3–8, 'M.S. 3488.'; p. 9, same as p. 2.

STAMPS: publisher, style mS/A (see Appendix 8).

ANNOTATIONS: stamped page numbers 159–170.

1. *Date:* first-edition inference (date code fe, p. 17).
2. Although no number is entered on the title page, this score is Op. 48#2.

Leipzig: **Breitkopf & Härtel (6653) [= 1842]** **48-BH-1** M25.C54 N9 c.1

DEUX NOCTURNES | pour le Piano | composées et dédiées | À MADEMOISELLE LAURE DUPERRÉ | PAR | *FRÉD. CHOPIN.* | *Op. 48.* « Propriété des Editeurs. » *Pr. 27 Ngr.* | *Leipzig, chez Breitkopf & Härtel.* | *Paris, chez M. Schlesinger.* | *6653.* | *Enrégistré aux Archives de l'Union.*

9 leaves (329 x 258 mm): pp. [1] lith title page, [2] blank, 3–16 engr music, [17, 18] blank.

CAPTION TITLE: p. 3, '13me NOCTURNE. | » Fr. Chopin. Oeuv. 48.'; p. 10, '14me NOCTURNE.'.

FOOTLINE: pp. 3–16, '6653'.

STAMPS: none.

ANNOTATIONS: handwritten "14" on each recto page.

1. *Date:* first-edition inference (date code fe, p. 17).

Leipzig: **Breitkopf & Härtel (6653) [= 1842]** **48-BH-3** M25.C54 N9 c.2

The transcription of this title page is the same as that of 48-BH-1.

8 leaves (324 x 260 mm): pp. [1] lith title page, [2] blank, 3–16 engr music.

CAPTION TITLE: p. 3, '13me NOCTURNE. | » Fr. Chopin. Oeuv. 48.'; p. 10, '14me NOCTURNE.'.

FOOTLINE: pp. 3–16, '6653'.

IMPOSITION: Leaf 5 is a singleton (see note 2).

STAMPS: publisher, style BH/F (see Appendix 8).

1. *Date:* first-edition inference (date code fe, p. 17).
2. This copy differs from 48-BH-1 only in lacking the final blank leaf, pp. [17, 18], which probably was removed when the score was bound with others. The conjugate of the missing leaf is the title leaf, which is tipped to leaf 2. The singleton, leaf 5, is tipped to leaf 6.

Leipzig: **Breitkopf & Härtel (6653) [after 1842]** 48-BH-2 M25.C54 N9023

The transcription of this title page is the same as that of 48-BH-1.

9 leaves (342 x 268 mm): pp. [1] lith title page, [2] blank, 3–16 lith music, [17, 18] blank.

CAPTION TITLE: p. 3, '13me NOCTURNE. | » Fr. Chopin. Oeuv. 48.'; p. 10, '14me NOCTURNE.'.

FOOTLINE: pp. 3–16, '6653'.

WRAPPER (green): pp. [1] collective title page, [2, 3] blank, [4] advt.

COLLECTIVE TITLE: wrapper p. [1], 'NOTTURNOS | FÜR DAS PIANOFORTE | VON | FR. CHOPIN. | [list of nocturnes Opp. 15, 27, 37] | " [Op.] 48. in C moll u. Fis moll 27 " [Ngr.] | [list of nocturnes Opp. 55, 62] | Eigenthum der Verleger. | LEIPZIG, BREITKOPF & HÄRTEL. | Eingetragen in das Vereins-Archiv. | (Diese Notturnos sind in demselben Verlege im Arrangement zu 4 Händen erscheinen.)'.

ADVT: wrapper p. [4], 'CHOPIN'S PIANOFORTE-WERKE, | welche mit Eigenthumsrecht im Verlage von | BREITKOPF & HÄRTEL in Leipzig | erscheinen sind.'. The list includes Opp. 12–65, followed by two additional entries: a thematic catalogue of Chopin's published compositions, and a portrait of Chopin after the medallion by Bovy.

STAMPS: publisher, style BH/J (see Appendix 8); dealer, Scharfenberg & Luis, New York.

1. *Date:* This score is a lithographed printing of the engraved 48-BH-1.
2. The wrapper is designed for the Breitkopf & Härtel collected edition of 1852–67 (Chominski & Turlo, p. 256). There are eleven volumes in that edition, of which the "Notturnos" is the second.

FANTAISIE IN F MINOR
Opus 49

Paris: M. Schlesinger (3489) 1841 | *Composed* 1841
Leipzig: Breitkopf & Härtel (6654) 1842 | Brown 137
London: Wessel (5301) 1842 | Chominski & Turlo 42

Paris: M. Schlesinger (3489) [= 1841] **49-mS-1** **M25.C54 F215**

Fantaisie | POUR | *PIANO,* | *dédiée à Madame* | La Princesse Catherine de Sonzzo | *PAR* | *F. CHOPIN.* | *A.V.* | *Op: 49.* « » *Prix 7 ! f 50* | *A PARIS, chez* MAURICE SCHLESINGER, *Rue Richelieu, 97.* | *Leipzig, chez Breitkopf et Haertel.* « *3489 M.S.* » *Propriété des Editeurs.* | *Londres, Wessel et Stapelton* [*sic*].

10 leaves (324 x 251 mm): pp. [i] engr title page, [ii, 1] blank, 2–16 engr music, [17, 18] blank.

CAPTION TITLE: p. 2, 'FANTAISIE | PAR | *F. CHOPIN,* OP. 49.'.

FOOTLINE: p. 2, 'F. CHOPIN, op 49. « M.S. 3489. » Maurice Schlesinger, rue de Richelieu, 97.'; pp. 3–15, 'M.S. 3489.'; p. 16, 'F. CHOPIN, op. 49. « M.S. 3489. » Maurice Schlesinger, rue de Richelieu, 97.'.

STAMPS: dealer, Frey-Popp, Geneva.

1. *Date:* first-edition inference (date code fe, p. 17).
2. The dedicatee's name — Souzzo — is misspelled here. The same misspelling appears in the transcription of the French-edition title by Chominski & Turlo (p. 95). On the other hand, 49-BH-1 as well as Hob-393 and Chominski & Turlo (p. 95) has the correct spelling in the German edition. Strangely, Brown (p. 140) ascribes the incorrect spelling to the German edition, while making no comment about the French edition.
3. The title page of 49-mS-1 corresponds to the second of two impressions shown by Grabowski (1992, vol. 3, plate 85); the first impression (*loc. cit.*, plate 84) does not cite the London publisher.

Leipzig: Breitkopf & Härtel (6654) [after 1842] **49-BH-1** **M25.C54 F216**

FANTAISIE | POUR LE PIANO | composée et dédiée | À Madame la Princesse « | » Catherine de Souzzo | par | FRÉD. CHOPIN. | *Op. 49.* « Propriété des Editeurs. » *Pr. 1 Thlr. 6 Ngr.* | *Leipzig, chez Breitkopf & Härtel* | *Paris, chez M. Schlesinger.* | *6654.* | *Enregistré aux Archives de l'Union.*

12 leaves (319 x 251 mm): pp. [1] lith title page, 2–22 lith music, [23, 24] blank.

CAPTION TITLE: p. 2, 'FANTAISIE. | » Fr. Chopin. Oeuv. 49. | Marcia. «'.

FOOTLINE: pp. 2–22, '6654'.

STAMPS: dealer, Roothaan, Amsterdam.

1. *Date:* based on the fact that the music is lithographed.

49-BH-1 *(continued)*

49-BH-1 *(concluded)*

2. The music occupies 21 pages in 49-BH-1 but only 15 pages in 49-mS-1. This difference is mainly the result of layouts with an average of 4.2 systems per page in the Breitkopf edition and 5.1 in the Schlesinger edition. The Breitkopf layout is less compact horizontally as well as vertically, with an average 3.7 bars per system compared with 4.3 in the Schlesinger edition. According to the pagination in Chominski & Turlo (p. 96), the English edition has 18 pages of music (assuming page 2 is the first), midway between the French and German editions.

MAZURKAS IN G MAJOR, A FLAT MAJOR, C SHARP MINOR
Opus 50

Paris: M. Schlesinger (3692) 1842	*Composed* 1842
Vienna: Mechetti (3682) 1842	Brown 145
London: Wessel (5303) 1842	Chominski & Turlo 80

***Paris:* M. Schlesinger (3692) [= 1842]** 50-mS-1 M32.C54 M549

3 | MAZURKAS | POUR | *PIANO* | dédiées à | Monsieur Léon Szmitkowski, | PAR | F. CHOPIN. | *AV | Op: 50. « » Prix 7.f 50. | A PARIS, chez MAURICE SCHLESINGER, Rue Richelieu, 97. | Londres, Wessel et Stapleton. « Propé des Editeurs. » Vienne, P. Mechetti | M.S. 3692.*

9 leaves (348 x 268 mm): pp. [i] engr title page, [ii, 1] blank, 2–15 engr music, [16] blank.

CAPTION TITLE: p. 2, '» F. Chopin Op: 50. | TROIS MAZURKAS | POUR LE PIANO.'.

SUB-CAPTION: p. 2, 'No. 1.'; p. 6, 'No. 2.'; p. 10, 'No. 3.'.

FOOTLINE: p. 2, 'M.S. 3692. » Maurice Schlesinger 97 Rue Richelieu.'; pp. 3–15, 'M.S. 3692.'.

WRAPPER (buff): pp. [1] same as title page, [2, 3] blank, [4] advt.

ADVT: wrapper p. [4], 'BRANDUS ET Ce, EDITEURS, 103, RUE RICHELIEU. | MUSIQUE DE PIANO'. No Chopin works are listed.

STAMPS: successor, style BD/C (see Appendix 8).

1. *Date:* first-edition inference (date code fe, p. 17).

***Paris:* Brandus (M.S. 3692) [1851–54]** 50-Bra-1 M32.C54 M552

ÉDITION ORIGINALE | OEUVRES COMPLÈTES POUR LE PIANO | DE | FRÉDÉRIC CHOPIN | SEULE ÉDITION AUTHENTIQUE | SANS CHANGEMENTS NI ADDITIONS, PUBLIÉE D'APRÈS LES ÉPREUVES CORRIGÉES PAR L'AUTEUR LUI-MÊME. | [list of works Opp. 1–49] | Op. 50. Trois mazurkas (dédiées à Léon Szmitkowski) 7 50 | [list of works Opp. 51–65, followed by Trois études (B130, listed as Op. 66) and Grand duo (B70)] | Paris, BRANDUS ET Cie, Éditeurs | 103, rue de Richelieu, 103. | [below the decorated border:] IMPRIMERIE CENTRALE DES CHEMINS DE FER. « » A. CHAIX ET CO, RUE BERGÈRE, 20, A PARIS. — 6138-7.

9 leaves (330 x 263 mm): pp. [i] letterpress title page, [ii, 1] blank, 2–15 engr music, [16] blank.

CAPTION TITLE: p. 2, 'TROIS MAZURKAS ÷ POUR LE PIANO » F. Chopin Op: 50.'.

SUB-CAPTION: p. 2, 'No. 1.'; p. 6, 'No. 2.'; p. 10, 'No. 3.'.

FOOTLINE: pp. 2–14, 'M.S. 3692.'; p. 15, 'M.S. 3692. » Imp. BUTTNER-THIERRY, 1, cité Bergère, Paris'.

STAMPS: publisher, style Bra/E (see Appendix 8); dealer, Bouchot, Paris.

1. *Date:* based on publisher name and address (Table 5A).

Vienna: **Mechetti (3682) [= 1842]** 50-Mec-1 M32.C54 M55

Trois | MAZOURKAS | pour le | *PIANO* | dédiées à | Monsieur Léon Szmitkowski | par | F. CHOPIN. | *Propriété des Editeurs.* | *Enrégistré dans l'Archive de l'Union.* | *Oeuvre 50.* « » *Prix f. 1.—. A.de.C.* | VIENNE | chez Pietro Mechetti q$^{\underline{m}}$ Carlo, | *Marchand-Editeur de Musique et de beauz* [*sic*] *Arts de la Cour I. et R.* | *Place St Michel N° 1153.* | *Paris chez M. Schlesinger.* « » *Londres chez Wessel et Stapleton.*

6 leaves (337 x 261 mm): pp. [1] engr title page, [2] blank, 3–11 engr music, [12] blank.

CAPTION TITLE: p. 3, 'TROIS ÷ *MAZOURKAS* ÷ par ÷ F. CHOPIN. ÷ I. » Oeuvre 50.'; p. 6, 'II.'; p. 8, 'III.'.

FOOTLINE: pp. 3–11, 'P.M. N° 3682.'.

WRAPPER (blue): pp. [1] same as title page, [2–4] blank.

STAMPS: none.

BINDING: library cloth.

1. *Date:* first-edition inference (date code fe, p. 17).

Vienna: **Mechetti (3682) [= 1842]** 50-Mec-2 M32.C54 M5501

The transcription of this title page is the same as that of 50-Mec-1.

6 leaves (325 x 259 mm): pp. [1] engr title page, [2] blank, 3–11 engr music, [12] blank.

CAPTION TITLE: p. 3, 'TROIS ÷ *MAZOURKAS* ÷ par ÷ F. CHOPIN. » Oeuvre 50.'.

SUB-CAPTION: p. 3, '*N$^{\underline{o}}$* 1.'; p. 6, '*N$^{\underline{o}}$* 2.'; p. 8, '*N$^{\underline{o}}$* 3.'.

FOOTLINE: p. 3, 'Pietro Mechetti. N$^{\underline{o}}$ 3682.'; pp. 4–11, 'P.M. N$^{\underline{o}}$ 3682.'.

STAMPS: none.

1. *Date:* first-edition inference (date code fe, p. 17).
2. The caption title, sub-caption and footline (on p. 3) differ slightly from those in 50-Mec-1.
3. This score corresponds to Hob-398.

London: **Wessel (5303) [= 1842]** 50-W-1 M32.C54 M551

N^{o} [handwritten "54"] OF | WESSEL & Co.'s COMPLETE COLLECTION | OF | *the Compositions* | OF | FREDERIC CHOPIN | FOR THE | Piano Forte. | Solo & Duet | [list of works, Wessel 1–53] | 54 "SOUVENIR *de* LA POLOGNE" *8th Set of Mazurkas,* | *ded. to Mr Henry Field of Bath.* *Op. 50.* *4/6* | *Ent. Sta. Hall.* « *Copyrights.* » *Price.* *Solo* [handwritten "4/6"] ÷ " *Duet* [blank] | *LONDON,* | WESSEL & Co *Importers and Publishers of,* FOREIGN MUSIC, | *(by special Appointment) to, H.R.H. the Duchess of Kent.* | N° 67, Frith Street, Corner of Soho Square.

9 leaves (331 x 251 mm): pp. [i] engr title page, [ii] blank, [1] advt, 2–15 engr music, [16] blank.

50-W-1 *(continued)*

50-W-1 *(concluded)*

CAPTION TITLE: p. 2, 'SOUVENIRS DE LA POLOGNE. | *EIGHTH SET OF MAZURKAS,* | Dedicated to Mr HENRY FIELD, of BATH, | *Composed by* | *F. CHOPIN. OP: 50.*'.

SUB-CAPTION: p. 2, '*Nº 1.*'; p. 6, '*Nº 2.*'; p. 10, '*Nº 3.*'.

FOOTLINE: p. 2, 'Copyright. « » (W & S. Nº 5303.)'; pp. 3–14, 'CHOPIN. 8th Set of Mazurkas. Op: 50. « » (W & S. Nº 5303.)'; p. 15, 'CHOPIN. 8th Set of Mazurkas. Op: 50. « » (Nº 5303.) | LONDON, WESSEL & STAPLETON, Music Sellers to Her Majesty, H.R.H. The Duchess of Kent, The Court | & The Army, Nº 67, Frith Street, Corner of Soho Square'.

ADVT: p. [1], '[cut down to] THE WORKS OF BEETHOVEN, CHOPIN, LISZT, &c. PIANO SOLO AND ORGAN MUSIC. | No. 67, FRITH STREET, CORNER OF SOHO SQUARE.'. This is Wessel's "PAGE E", with Chopin works listed through op. 42.

STAMPS: publisher, style W/C (see Appendix 8).

---

1. *Date:* first-edition inference (date code fe, p. 17).

IMPROMPTU IN G FLAT MAJOR
Opus 51

Paris: M. Schlesinger (3847) 1843	*Composed* 1842
Leipzig: Hofmeister (2900) 1843	Brown 149
London: Wessel (5304) 1843	Chominski & Turlo 45

***Paris:* M. Schlesinger (3847) 1843** **51-mS-2** **M25.C54 I41 c.2**

Gazette Musicale du 9 Juillet 1843. « | 3^{E} | IMPROMPTU | POUR | Piano | *dédié à Madame* |
La Comtesse Esterhazy | *née Comtesse Balthyany,* | PAR | F. CHOPIN | A.V. | *Op: 51.* « » *Prix 6 ^{f}* |
A PARIS, chez MAURICE SCHLESINGER, Rue Richelieu, 97 |
Londres, Wessel et Stapleton. « » *Leipzig, F. Hofmeister.*

6 leaves (320 x 245 mm): pp. [i] lith title page, [ii] blank, 1–9 lith music, [10] blank.

CAPTION TITLE: p. 1, '*Troisième* ÷ IMPROMPTU ÷ par ÷ F. CHOPIN. » Op: 51.'.

FOOTLINE: p. 1, 'M.S. 3847. » Maurice Schlesinger rue de Richelieu 97.'; pp. 2–8, 'M.S. 3847.'; p. 9, none.

STAMPS: successor, style BD/A (see Appendix 8).

1. *Date:* given explicitly on the title page.
2. The date of registration of Op. 51 at the Dépôt Légal is 8 May 1843, and the date of notice in the *Bibliographie de la France* is 10 June 1843 (Kallberg, 1983, p. 538). The former date is adopted by Chominski & Turlo (p. 99) as the formal date of publication, while Brown (p. 153) evidently uses the date of issue in the *Gazette Musicale* (July 1843). As to whether the *Gazette* issue preceded the independent engraved publication (51-mS-1), it is not possible to say with certainty, but the fact that the imposition error (note 3) was corrected in the engraved issue suggests that the *Gazette* was first. However, Grabowski (1994, p. 17) points out that "In the earlier impression registered on 8 May 1843 whose format and paper quality are the same as the other compositions for sale, the sequence of pages is correct. It is hard to explain why, two months later the correct pagination was altered.".
3. This issue of the Impromptu — as a supplement to *Gazette Musicale* (of which Schlesinger was publisher) — contains an error in imposition, about which Chopin wrote to Schlesinger as follows (July 22): "Dear friend, — In the Impromptu which you have issued with the paper of July 9, there is a confusion in the paging, which makes my composition unintelligible. Though I cannot at all pretend to take the pains which our friend Moscheles bestows on his works, I consider myself, however, with regard to your subscribers, in duty bound to ask you on this occasion to insert in your next number an *erratum:* — | Page 3 — read page 5. | Page 5 — read page 3. | If you are too busy or too lazy to write to me, answer me through the *erratum* in your paper, and that shall signify to me that you, Madame Schlesinger, and your children are all well. — Yours very truly, F. Chopin." (Niecks, II, pp. 272–273).

***Paris:* M. Schlesinger (3847) [= 1843]** **51-mS-1** **M25.C54 I41 c.1**

The transcription of this title page is the same as that of 51-mS-2, except here the first line of 51-mS-2 is absent.

6 leaves (327 x 258 mm): pp. [i] engr title page, [ii] blank, 1–9 engr music, [10] blank.

CAPTION TITLE: p. 1, '*Troisième* | IMPROMPTU | par | F. CHOPIN. » Op: 51.'.

51-mS-1 *(continued)*

51-mS-1 *(concluded)*

FOOTLINE: p. 1, 'M.S. 3847. » Maurice Schlesinger rue de Richelieu 97.'; pp. 2–8, 'M.S. 3847.'; p. 9, none.

STAMPS: successor, style BD/A; dealer, Clo[...?], Lyon.

DATE: first-edition inference (date code fe, p. 17).

Paris: **Brandus & Dufour (M.S. 3847) [after 1857]** **51-BD-1** **M25.C54 I412**

ÉDITION ORIGINALE | OEUVRES COMPLÈTES POUR LE PIANO | DE | FRÉDÉRIC CHOPIN | SEULE ÉDITION AUTHENTIQUE | SANS CHANGEMENTS NI ADDITIONS, PUBLIÉE D'APRÈS LES ÉPREUVES CORRIGÉES PAR L'AUTEUR LUI-MÊME. | [list of works Opp. 1–50] | Op. 51. Troisième impromptu en *sol* bémol (dédié à la comtesse | Esterhazy) 6 " | [list of works Opp. 52–65 and three works without opus number] | Paris, G. BRANDUS ET S. DUFOUR, Éditeurs | 103, rue de Richelieu, 103. | [below the decorated border:] IMPRIMERIE CENTRALE DES CHEMINS DE FER. « » A. CHAIX ET CO, RUE BERGÈRE, 20, A PARIS | 238-0

6 leaves (348 x 270 mm): pp. [i] lith title page, [ii] blank, 1–9 engr music, [10] blank.

CAPTION TITLE: p. 1, '*Troisième* ÷ IMPROMPTU ÷ par ÷ F. CHOPIN. » Op: 51.'.

FOOTLINE: p. 1, 'M.S. 3847. » Maurice Schlesinger rue de Richelieu 97'; pp. 2–8, 'M.S. 3847.'; p. 9, none.

STAMPS: successor, style Bra/D (see Appendix 8).

1. *Date:* based on the publisher's name on the title page (Table 5A).
2. The partnership ended with the death of Dufour in 1872.
3. Chominski & Turlo (p. 255) give 1859–78 for the Brandus collected edition.
4. This score corresponds to Hob-405.

Leipzig: **Hofmeister (2900) [= 1843]** **51-Ho-1** **M25.C54 I4**

ALLEGRO VIVACE | POUR LE | PIANOFORTE | DEDIÉ | À MADAME | LA COMTESSE ESTERHÁZY, | NEÉ COMTESSE BATHYANY | PAR | FRÉDERIC CHOPIN. | OP. 51. « » PR. 20 NGR. | Propriété des Editeurs. | Enregistré aux Archives de l'Union. | LEIPZIG, CHEZ FREDÉRIC HOFMEISTER. | LONDON, CHEZ WESSEL & Cie PARIS, CHEZ M. SCHLESINGER. | St PETERSBOURG, CHEZ E. E. HOLTZ. | VARSOVIE, CHEZ G. SENNEWALD. | *2900*.

6 leaves (320 x 245 mm): pp. [1] lith title page, [2] blank, 3–11 engr music, [12] blank.

CAPTION TITLE: p. 3, 'Allegro vivace. | IMPROMPTU. | » F. Chopin. Op. 51.'.

FOOTLINE: pp. 3–11, '2900'.

STAMPS: none.

BINDING: library cloth.

1. *Date:* first-edition inference (date code fe, p. 17).
2. From Deaville's data (see 1-Ho-2, note 3), the first print run of 51-Ho-1 was 50 copies, in 1843. Through 1878 a total of 3,000 copies was printed, on average about 83 copies annually.

BALLADE IN F MINOR
Opus 52

Paris: M. Schlesinger (3957) 1843	*Composed* 1842–43
Leipzig: Breitkopf & Härtel (7001) 1843	Brown 146
London: Wessel (5305) 1844	Chominski & Turlo 5

Paris: **M. Schlesinger (3957) [= 1843]** **52-mS-2** **M25.C54 B42 c.2**

à Madame Nathaniel | de Rothschild | 4^{E}. | BALLADE | POUR | *PIANO* | PAR | F. CHOPIN | *AV* | *Op: 52.* « » *Pr: 7.^{f} 50.* | *A PARIS, chez* M^{CE}. SCHLESINGER, *Rue Richelieu, 97* | *Londres, Wessel et Stapleton.* « *Prop^{é}. des Editeurs.* » *Leipzig, Breitkopf et Hartel.* | *M.S. 3957.*

8 leaves (328 x 257 mm): pp. [i] engr title page, [ii] blank, 1–13 engr music, [14] blank.

CAPTION TITLE: p. 1, 'F. CHOPIN Op: 52. « » 4me. *BALLADE.*'.

FOOTLINE: p. 1, 'Maurice Schlesinger « M.S. 3957. » rue Richelieu 97.'; pp. 2–13, 'M.S. 3957.'.

STAMPS: publisher, style mS/A (see Appendix 8).

---

1. *Date:* first-edition inference (date code fe, p. 17).
2. The above title page, with dedication at the top, agrees with Chominski & Turlo (p. 74). Grabowski (1994, p. 20) refers to this placement as that of the first edition.

Paris: **M. Schlesinger (3957) [*ca* 1843]** **52-mS-1** **M25.C54 B42 c.1**

4^{E}. | BALLADE | POUR | PIANO | dédiée | *à Mme. Nathaniel de Rothschild* | PAR | F. CHOPIN | *AV* | *Op: 52.* « » *Pr: 7.^{f} 50.* | *A PARIS, chez* M^{CE}. SCHLESINGER, *Rue Richelieu, 97* | *Londres, Wessel et Stapleton.* « *Prop^{é}. des Editeurs.* » *Leipzig, Breitkopf et Hartel.* | *M.S. 3957.*

8 leaves (332 x 262 mm): pp. [i] engr title page, [ii] blank, 1–13 engr music, [14] blank. An extra blank leaf of later vintage is tipped to the verso of the last leaf of the score.

CAPTION TITLE: p. 1, 'F. CHOPIN Op: 52. « » 4me. *BALLADE.*'.

FOOTLINE: p. 1, 'Maurice Schlesinger « M.S. 3957. » rue Richelieu 97.'; pp. 2–13, 'M.S. 3957.'.

STAMPS: successor, style Bra/B (see Appendix 8).

ANNOTATIONS: stamped page numbers 157–172.

---

1. *Date:* The above title page agrees with Hob-407, stated there to be a first edition; see note 2.
2. Grabowski (1994, p. 20) regards this as a second edition, but does not hazard a date. He refers to the title page of the first as having a different layout, with dedication at the top, as in 52-mS-2.

Leipzig: **Breitkopf & Härtel (7001) [= 1843]** **52-BH-1** **M25.C54 B4**

BALLADE | pour le Piano | *dédiée* | à Madame la Baronne C. de Rothschild | par | F. CHOPIN. | Op. 52 « Propriété des Editeurs. » Pr. 1 Thlr. | *Leipzig, chez Breitkopf & Härtel.* | *Paris, chez M. Schlesinger.* « » *Londres, chez Wessel & Stapleton.* | *7001.* | *Enrégistré aux Archives de l'Union.*

10 leaves (329 x 257 mm): pp. [1] lith title page, [2] blank, 3–18 engr music, [19, 20] blank.

CAPTION TITLE: p. 3, ' » F. Chopin. Op. 52.'.

SUB-CAPTION: p. 3, 'BALLADE.'.

FOOTLINE: pp. 3–18, '7001'.

STAMPS: none.

ANNOTATIONS: handwritten "18" on all recto pages.

1. *Date:* first-edition inference (date code fe, p. 17).
2. See 53-BH-3, notes 2 and 3.

POLONAISE IN A FLAT MAJOR
Opus 53

Paris: M. Schlesinger (3958) 1843	*Composed* 1842–43
Leipzig: Breitkopf & Härtel (7002) 1843	Brown 147
London: Wessel (5306) 1844	Chominski & Turlo 155

Leipzig: **M. Schlesinger (3958) [= 1843]** **53-mS-1** **M32.C54 P833**

à M.r AUGUSTE LÉO. | GRANDE | POLONAISE | *brillante* | POUR | Piano, | PAR | F. CHOPIN | *AV* | *Op: 53.* | *Pr: 7.f 50.* | *A PARIS, chez* M.CE SCHLESINGER, *Rue Richelieu, 97.* | *Londres, Wessel et Stapleton.* « *Prop*e *des Editeurs.* » *Leipzig, Breitkopf et Hartel.* | *M.S. 3958.*

7 leaves (328 x 257 mm): pp. [i] engr title page, [ii, 1] blank, 2–11 engr music, [12] blank.

CAPTION TITLE: p. 2, 'F. CHOPIN Op: 53. « » *POLONAISE.*'.

FOOTLINE: p. 2, 'M.S. 3958. « » Maurice Schlesinger rue Richelieu 97'; pp. 3–11, 'M.S. 3958.'.

STAMPS: publisher, style mS/A (see Appendix 8).

INSCRIPTIONS: owners signature.

1. *Date:* first-edition inference (date code fe, p. 17).

Leipzig: **Breitkopf & Härtel (7002) [= 1843]** **53-BH-3** **M32.C54 P8302**

POLONOISE | POUR LE PIANO | *dédiée* | à Monsieur Auguste Leo | PAR | F. CHOPIN. | Op. 53. « Propriété des Editeurs. » Pr. 1 Thlr. | *Leipzig, chez Breitkopf & Härtel.* | *Paris, chez M. Schlesinger.* « » *Londres, chez Wessel & Stapleton.* | *7002.* | *Enrégistré aux Archives de l'Union.*

10 leaves (320 x 254 mm): pp. [1] lith title page, [2] blank, 3–19 engr music, [20] blank.

CAPTION TITLE: p. 3, '» F. Chopin, Op. 53.'.

SUB-CAPTION: p. 3, 'POLONAISE.'.

FOOTLINE: pp. 3–19, '7002'.

STAMPS: publisher, style BH/G (see Appendix 8); dealer, Theune, Amsterdam.

1. *Date:* first-edition inference (date code fe, p. 17). Also see notes that follow.
2. Chopin conveyed copyright of Opp. 52, 53, 54 to Breitkopf & Härtel in a note dated 31 October 1843 (Kallberg, 1983, p. 823). The publisher registered the three works in November (see Table 4B) and gave them successive plate numbers 7001, 7002, 7003.
3. Since they were published virtually simultaneously, it is of interest to compare the title pages of these three works. The following discussion concerns only the placement of words and the use of capitalization and italicization. It does not concern calligraphy or artwork, which vary considerably in these scores. In particular, apart from genre, dedicatee and plate number, the transcriptions of 52^{I} (meaning 52-BH-1) and 54^{I} differ only in line 3, where 52^{I} has *"dédiée"* and 54^{I} has "dédié". The correspondimg transcriptions by Hoboken (respectively Hob-406 and Hob-411, both stated to be first editions) are the same as those of 52^{I} and 54^{I}. Chominski & Turlo (pp. 74 and 197) also give the same transcriptions.

53-BH-3 *(continued)*

53-BH-3 *(concluded)*

In contrast, the transcriptions of 53^3 and 53^1 differ from those of 52^1 and 54^1, and from each other. The transcriptions of Op. 53 in Hob-408 and in Chominski & Turlo (p. 170) are the same as that of 53^3 (apart from italicization, which is not indicated by either of these sources). However, neither Hoboken nor Chominski & Turlo has a transcription that corresponds to 53^1. On camparing the transcription of 53^3 with that of 52^1 we can see only two differences (apart from genre, dedicatee and plate number): lines 2 and 5 are in upper case in 53^3 and in lower case in 52^1. On the other hand there are many differences betweeen the transcriptions of 53^1 and 52^1.

To establish the chronology of 53^3 and 53^1 we must know (i) which is the earlier one, and (ii) whether the earlier one is a first or later issue. In the following comments I assume that scores 52^1 and 54^1 are in fact first issues of these editions. Regarding (i), note that in 53^3 the genre name is spelled "POLONOISE" (as in the score described by Fuld, p. 435), while in 53^1 it is "POLONAISE". The 'o' spelling, which also appears in the Wessel edition (53-W-1), is probably the earlier one. This inference is consistent with the fact that the transcription of 53^3 is much closer to that of 52^1 than it is to 53^1. Regarding (ii), I found no evidence that a score of Op. 53 exists with the same layout as that of Opp. 52 and 54, and this leads to the inference that 53^3 is in fact a first issue.

Leipzig: **Breitkopf & Härtel (7002) [after 1843]** **53-BH-1** **M32.C54 P83**

POLONAISE | pour le | PIANO | dédiée | *à Monsieur Auguste Leo* | par | F. Chopin. | Op. 53. | Propriété des Editeurs. | *Leipzig, Breitkopf & Härtel.* | *Paris, M. Schlesinger.* « » *Londres, Wessel & Stapleton.* | Pr. 1 Thlr. | *Enrégistré aux Archives de l'Union.* | *7002.*

10 leaves (326 x 258 mm): pp. [1] lith title page, [2] blank, 3–19 engr music, [20] blank.

CAPTION TITLE: p. 3, '» F. Chopin, Op. 53.'.

SUB-CAPTION: p. 3, 'POLONAISE.'.

FOOTLINE: pp. 3–19, '7002'.

STAMPS: publisher, style BH/G (see Appendix 8).

1. *Date:* see 53-BH-3, notes 2 and 3.

Leipzig: **Breitkopf & Härtel (10141) [1872–73]** **53-BH-2** **M211.C54 P77**

POLONAISE | pour le | PIANO | dédiée | *à Monsieur Auguste Leo* | par | F. Chopin. | Op. 53. | Arrangement pour deux Pianos par L. Röhr. | Propriété des Editeurs. | *Leipzig, Breitkopf & Härtel.* | *Pr. 1 Thlr. 5 Ngr. = Mk. 3.50.* | *Enrégistré aux Archives de l'Union.* | *10141.*

Pianoforte I. 6 leaves (337 x 267 mm): pp. [1] lith title page, [2] blank, 3–11 engr music, [12] blank.

CAPTION TITLE: p. 3, 'POLONAISE. | » F. Chopin, Op. 53 arr.'.

HEADLINE: pp. 3–11, 'Pianoforte I.'.

FOOTLINE: p. 3, 'Stich und Druck von Breitkopf & Härtel in Leipzig. « | 10141'; pp. 4–11, '10141'.

Pianoforte II. 5 leaves (338 x 266 mm): pp. 1–10 engr music.

CAPTION TITLE: p. 3, 'POLONAISE. | » F. Chopin, Op. 53 arr.'.

HEADLINE: pp. 1–10, 'Pianoforte II.'.

FOOTLINE: pp. 1–10, '10141'.

53-BH-2 *(continued)*

53-BH-2 *(concluded)*

WRAPPER (light brown): pp. [1] same as title page, [2, 3] blank, [4] advt.

ADVT: wrapper p. [4], 'MUSIKWERKE | für 2 Pianoforte zu 4 oder zu 8 Händen | im Verlage von | BREITKOPF & HÄRTEL in Leipzig.'. Two Chopin works are listed in addition to the present work: the Marche funèbre from Op. 35 arranged for two pianos and 8 hands, and the Concerto Op. 21 arranged for two pianos and four hands. Prices are in thaler and neugroschen.

IMPOSITION: The first and last leaves of Pianoforte II are conjugate; leaf 3 is a singleton.

STAMPS: publisher, style BH/B (see Appendix 8); dealer, Hug, Basel (embossed).

---

1. *Date:* currency inference (date code c3, p. 17).
2. The plate number indicates a date *ca* 1861 for the first edition of this arrangement.

London: Wessel (5306) [1848–56] 53-W-1 M32.C54 P832

N^o^ [handwritten "57"] OF | WESSEL & Co.'s COMPLETE COLLECTION | OF | *the Compositions* | OF | FREDERIC CHOPIN | FOR THE | Piano Forte. | Solo & Duet | [list of works, Wessel 1–56] | 57 "EIGHTH POLONOISE" *in A* [flat] . *Op. 53, 3/6* | [list of works, Wessel 58–71] | *Ent. Sta. Hall.* « *Copyrights.* » *Price, Solo* [handwritten "3/6"] | *LONDON,* | WESSEL & Co *Importers and Publishers of* FOREIGN MUSIC, | *(by special Appointment) to H.R.H. the Duchess of Kent.* | N° 229, Regent Street, Corner of Hanover Street.

7 leaves (334 x 250 mm): pp. [i] engr title page, [ii] blank, 1–11 engr music, [12] advt.

CAPTION TITLE: p. 1, '8ME POLONOISE | Composée par | FREDERIC CHOPIN. | Op: 53.'.

FOOTLINE: p. 1, 'Copyright of WESSEL & Co « » (W & Co N° 5306.)'; pp. 2–10, 'CHOPIN, 8me Polonoise, Op: 53. « » (W & Co N° 5306.)'; p. 11, 'CHOPIN, 8me Polonoise, Op: 53. « | (N° 5306) WESSEL & Co N° 67, Frith Street, Corner of Soho Square.'.

ADVT: p. [12], 'PAGE S. | WESSEL & Co.'s EDITIONS OF THE PIANOFORTE WORKS (SOLO) BY CHOPIN, | HELLER, SCHULHOFF, KULLAK, AND AGUILAR.'; at the foot, 'WESSEL & Co., 229, REGENT STREET, CORNER OF HANOVER STREET, (FIRST FLOOR.)'. Chopin works are listed through Op. 64, and the Marche Funèbre extracted from the Sonata Op. 35.

STAMPS: publisher, style W/D (see Appendix 8).

---

1. *Date:* Wessel inference (date code W1, p. 17).

SCHERZO IN E MAJOR
Opus 54

Paris: M. Schlesinger (3959) 1843 | *Composed* 1842–43
Leipzig: Breitkopf & Härtel (7003) 1843 | Brown 148
London: Wessel (5307) 1844 | Chominski & Turlo 200

***Paris:* M. Schlesinger (3959) [= 1843]** **54-mS-2** **M25.C54 S53 c.2**

à Mlle Clotilde de Caraman. | 4^{E} | SCHERZO | POUR | Piano, | PAR | *F. CHOPIN* | A.V. | *Op: 54.* « » *Pr: 9* ^{f} | *A PARIS, chez* M^{CE} SCHLESINGER, *Rue Richelieu, 97.* | *Londres, Wessel et Stopleton.* [*sic*] « *Prop*^{é} *des Editeurs.* » *Leipzig, Breitkopf et Hartel.* | *M.S. 3959.*

10 leaves (330 x 260 mm): pp. [i] engr title page, [ii] blank, 1–17 engr music, [18] blank.

CAPTION TITLE: p. 1, 'F. CHOPIN Op. 54 « » 4me SCHERZO.'.

FOOTLINE: p. 1, 'M. Schelsinger. [*sic*] rue Richelieu 97. « M.S. 3959.'; pp. 2–16, 'M.S. 3959.'; p. 17, same as p. 1.

STAMPS: publisher, style mS/A (see Appendix 8).

1. *Date:* first-edition inference (date code fe, p. 17).
2. Grabowski (1994, p. 20) refers to the above title, with dedication at the top, as that of the first edition, in agreement with Chominski & Turlo (p. 197). For further remarks, see 54-mS-1, note 2.

***Paris:* M. Schlesinger (3959) [*ca* 1843]** **54-mS-1** **M25.C54 S53 c.1**

4^{E} | SCHERZO | POUR | Piano, | *dédié à Mlle CLOTILDE de Caraman* | PAR | *F. CHOPIN* | A.V. | *Op: 54.* « » *Pr: 9* ^{f} | *A PARIS, chez* M^{CE} SCHLESINGER, *Rue Richelieu, 97.* | *Londres, Wessel et Stopleton.* [*sic*] « *Prop*^{é} *des Editeurs.* » *Leipzig, Breitkopf et Hartel.* | *M.S. 3959.*

10 leaves (332 x 264 mm): pp. [i] engr title page, [ii] blank, 1–17 engr music, [18] blank.

CAPTION TITLE: p. 1, 'F. CHOPIN Op. 54 « » 4me SCHERZO.'.

FOOTLINE: p. 1, 'M. Schelsinger. [*sic*] rue Richelieu 97. « M.S. 3959.'; pp. 2–16, 'M.S. 3959.'; p. 17, same as p. 1.

STAMPS: successor, style Bra/B (see Appendix 8).

ANNOTATIONS: stamped page numbers 91–110.

1. *Date:* first-edition inference (date code fe, p. 17); also see note 2.
2. The title above agrees with Hob-414, stated there to be a first edition. In Hob-415 (stated there to be a Titelauflage), and in Chominski & Turlo (p. 197), the dedication is at the top (as in 54-mS-2). These two sources disagree as to which of these issues is the original one. Grabowski (1994, p. 20) refers to the above title as that of the second edition, in agreement with Chominski & Turlo, but does not hazard a date.

Leipzig: **Breitkopf & Härtel** (7003) [= 1843] **54-BH-1** **M25.C54 S7**

SCHERZO | pour le Piano | dédié | *à Mademoiselle Jeanne de Caraman* | par | F. CHOPIN. | Op. 54. « Propriété des Editeurs. » Pr. 1 Thlr. 5 Ngr. | *Leipzig, chez Breitkopf & Härtel.* | *Paris, chez M. Schlesinger.* « » *Londres, chez Wessel & Stapleton.* | *7003.* | *Enrégistré aux Archives de l'Union.*

12 leaves (314 x 250 mm): pp. [1] lith title page, [2] blank, 3–23 engr music, [24] blank.

CAPTION TITLE: p. 3, 'SCHERZO | *par* | F. CHOPIN. | Op. 54.'.

FOOTLINE: pp. 3–23, '7003'.

STAMPS: publisher, style BH/G (see Appendix 8).

BINDING: library cloth.

1. *Date:* first-edition inference (date code fe, p. 17).
2. See 53-BH-3, notes 2 and 3.

NOCTURNES IN F MINOR AND E FLAT MAJOR
Opus 55

Paris: M. Schlesinger (4084) 1844 — *Composed* 1842–44
Leipzig: Breitkopf & Härtel (7142) 1844 — Brown 152
London: Wessel (5308) 1845 — Chominski & Turlo 122

***Paris:* M. Schlesinger (4084) [= 1844]** **55-mS-1** **M25.C54 N912**

2 | NOCTURNES | POUR LE | PIANO | dédiés à | Mademoiselle J. W. Stirling | *PAR* | F. CHOPIN | *AV* | *Op: 55.* « » *Prix 7.f 50* | *A PARIS, chez* M.CE SCHLESINGER, *Rue Richelieu, 97* | *Londres, Wessel et Stapleton.* « *Propé des Editeurs.* » *Leipzig, Breitkopf et Hartel.*

7 leaves (332 x 255 mm): pp. [i] engr title page, [ii, 1] blank, 2–11 engr music, [12] blank.

CAPTION TITLE: p. 2, 'DEUX | NOCTURNES. | par | F. CHOPIN. | No. 1.'; p. 7, 'No. 2.'.

FOOTLINE: p. 2, 'F. CHOPIN. Op: 55. « M.S. 4084. » Maurice Schlesinger rue Richelieu 97.'; pp. 3–11, 'M.S. 4084.'.

STAMPS: successor, style BD/C (see Appendix 8); dealer, Flaxland, Paris.

1. *Date:* first-edition inference (date code fe, p. 17).

***Leipzig:* Breitkopf & Härtel (7142) [= 1844]** **55-BH-1** **M25.C54 N91**

DEUX | NOCTURNES | pour le Pianoforte | dédiés | *à Mademoiselle J. W. Stirling* | par | F. CHOPIN. | *Op. 55.* « Propriété des Editeurs. » *Pr. 20 Ngr.* | *Leipzig, chez Breitkopf & Härtel.* | *Paris, chez Schlesinger.* « » *Londres, chez Wessel & Stapleton.* | *7142.* | *Enrégistré aux Archives de l'Union.*

6 leaves (313 x 255 mm): pp. [1] lith title page, [2] blank, 3–11 engr music, [12] blank.

CAPTION TITLE: p. 3, 'No 1. | » F. Chopin. Op. 55.'; p. 8, 'No 2.'.

FOOTLINE: pp. 3–11, '7142'.

WRAPPER (green): pp. [1] same as title page, [2, 3] blank, [4] advt.

ADVT: wrapper p. [4], 'FRIEDRICH KALKBRENNER'S | PIANOFORTE-WERKE | welche im Verlag von | BREITKOPF & HÄRTEL in LEIPZIG | erscheinen sind.'.

STAMPS: publisher, style BH/F (see Appendix 8).

CONDITION: excellent plate impressions throughout.

BINDING: library cloth.

1. *Date:* first-edition inference (date code fe, p. 17).

London: Wessel (5308) [1848–56] 55-W-1 M25.C54 N914

N° [handwritten "59"] OF | WESSEL & C°.'s COMPLETE COLLECTION | OF | *the Compositions* | OF | FREDERIC CHOPIN | FOR THE | Piano Forte. | Solo & Duet | [list of works, Wessel 1–58] | 59 15ME & 16ME NOCTURNO, *ded. to Miss J. W. Stirling. in F min. E* [flat] *Op. 55. 3/6* | [list of works, Wessel 60–71] | *Ent. Sta. Hall.* « *Copyrights.* » *Price.* [handwritten "3/6"] | *LONDON,* | WESSEL & C° *Importers and Publishers of* FOREIGN MUSIC, | *(by special Appointment) to H.R.H. the Duchess of Kent.* | N° 229, Regent Street, Corner of Hanover Street.

6 leaves (330 x 255 mm): pp. [i] engr title page, [ii] blank, 1–10 engr music.

CAPTION TITLE: p. 1, '15*me* *NOCTURNO Composé par FREDERIC CHOPIN. Op: 55.* | *Dédié à Mademoiselle I.W. STIRLING.*'; p. 6, '16*me* *NOCTURNO Composé par FREDERIC CHOPIN. Op: 55.* | *Dédié à Mademoiselle I.W. STIRLING.*'.

FOOTLINE: p. 1, 'Copyright of Wessel & Co. « (W & C° N° 5308)'; pp. 2–4, 'CHOPIN 15me Nocturno Op. 55. « (W & C° N° 5308)'; p. 5, 'CHOPIN 15me Nocturno Op. 55. « Wessel & Co. » (N° 5308)'; pp. 6–9, 'CHOPIN 16me Nocturno Op. 55. « (W & C° N° 5308)'; p. 10, 'CHOPIN 16me Nocturno Op. 55. « Wessel & Co. » (N° 5308)'.

IMPOSITION: Leaf 4 is a singleton.

STAMPS: publisher, style W/D (see Appendix 8).

CONDITION: A blank leaf conjugate to the title leaf is missing.

1. *Date:* Wessel inference (date code W1, p. 17).

MAZURKAS IN B MAJOR, C MAJOR, C MINOR
Opus 56

Paris: M. Schlesinger (4085) 1844	*Composed* 1843–44
Leipzig: Breitkopf & Härtel (7143) 1844	Brown 153
London: Wessel (5309) 1845	Chominski & Turlo 83

***Paris:* M. Schlesinger (4085) [= 1844]** **56-mS-1** **M32.C54 M571**

3 | MAZURKAS | POUR | Piano, | dédiées à Madem.^{lle} | C. MABERLY | PAR | *F. CHOPIN* | *AV* | *Op: 56.* « » *Prix: 9 fr.* | *A PARIS, chez* M.^{CE} SCHLESINGER, *Rue Richelieu, 97.* | *Londres, Wessel et Stapleton.* « *Prop.^{é} des Editeurs.* » *Leipzig, Breitkopf et Hartel.*

10 leaves (349 x 272 mm): pp. [i] engr title page, [ii] blank, 1–17 engr music, [18] blank.

CAPTION TITLE: p. 1, 'TROIS | MAZURKAS. | par | F. CHOPIN. | N.º 1.'; p. 8, 'N.º 2.'; p. 11, 'N.º 3.'.

FOOTLINE: p. 1, 'F. CHOPIN. Op: 56. « M.S. 4085. » Maurice Schlesinger rue Richelieu 97.'; pp. 2–17, 'M.S. 4085.'.

WRAPPER (yellow): pp. [1] half-title page, [2–4] blank.

HALF TITLE: wrapper p. [1], '3 | MAZURKAS | F. CHOPIN | *Op: 56.* | *A.V.* | *Paris* M.^{CE} *SCHLESINGER Editeur*'.

STAMPS: successor, style BD/B (see Appendix 8).

1. *Date:* first-edition inference (date code fe, p. 17).
2. Grabowski (1994, p. 20) found that "The price indicated on the title-page of the copy registered in August 1844 is 7^{50}. All subsequent editions of this Opus cost 9 francs."

***Leipzig:* Breitkopf & Härtel (7143) [= 1844]** **56-BH-1** **M32.C54 M57**

3 | MAZOURKAS | pour le | PIANOFORTE | dédiées | à Mademoiselle C. Maberly | par | F. CHOPIN. | *Op. 56.* « Propriété des Editeurs. » *Pr. 25 Ngr.* | *Leipzig, chez Breitkopf & Härtel.* | *Paris, chez Schlesinger.* « » *Londres, chez Wessel & Stapleton.* | *7143.* | *Enrégistré aux Archives de l'Union.*

8 leaves (336 x 269 mm): pp. [1] lith title page, [2] blank, 3–15 engr music, [16] blank.

CAPTION TITLE: p. 3, 'N° 1. | » F. Chopin. Op. 56.'; p. 8, 'N.º 2.'; p. 10, 'N.º 3.'.

FOOTLINE: pp. 3–15, '7143'.

STAMPS: publisher, style BH/J (see Appendix 8).

1. *Date:* first-edition inference (date code fe, p. 17).

London: Wessel (5309) [1848–56] 56-W-1 M32.C54 M572

Nº [handwritten "60"] OF | WESSEL & Cº.'s COMPLETE COLLECTION | OF | *the Compositions* | OF | FREDERIC CHOPIN | FOR THE | Piano Forte. | Solo & Duet | [list of works, Wessel 1–59] | 60 "SOUVENIRS *de* LA POLOGNE" *9 th Set of Mazurkas.* | *ded. to Miss C. Maberly. Op. 56. 4/6* | [list of works, Wessel 61–71] | *Ent. Sta. Hall.* « *Copyrights.* » *Price. Solo* [handwritten "4/6"] ÷ " *Duet* [blank] | *LONDON,* | WESSEL & Cº *Importers and Publishers of,* FOREIGN MUSIC, | *(by special Appointment) to H.R.H. the Duchess of Kent.* | Nº 229, Regent Street, Corner of Hanover Street.

9 leaves (334 x 252 mm): pp. [i] engr title page, [ii] blank, 1–15 engr music, [16] advt.

CAPTION TITLE: p. 1, ' "SOUVENIRS DE LA POLOGNE." | 9th SET OF MAZURKAS composed by FREDERIC CHOPIN, Op: *56.* | *DEDICATED TO MISS C. MABERLY.*'.

FOOTLINE: p. 1, 'Copyright of Wessel & Cº « » (W & Cº Nº 5309)'; pp. 2–14, 'CHOPIN, 9th Set of Mazurkas. Op: 56. « » (W & Cº Nº 5309)'; p. 15, 'CHOPIN, 9th Set of Mazurkas. Op: 56. « | (Nº 5309) WESSEL & Cº '.

ADVT: p. [16], heading cut off; there are no Chopin works in the lists.

STAMPS: publisher, style W/D (see Appendix 8).

1. *Date:* Wessel inference (date code W1, p. 17).
2. The three mazurkas are identified (in the sub-caption) by tempo, not by number.

BERCEUSE IN D FLAT MAJOR
Opus 57

Paris: Meissonnier (2186) 1845	*Composed* 1844
Leipzig: Breitkopf & Härtel (7259) 1845	Brown 154
London: Wessel (6313) 1845	Chominski & Turlo 7

Paris: **Meissonnier (2186) [= 1845]** **57-Mei-1** **M25.C54 B5**

BERCEUSE | POUR LE | PIANO | dédiée à | *Mademoiselle Elise Gavard* | PAR | F. CHOPIN | A. Vialon. | Op: 57. « » Prix 5f | *A PARIS, chez* J. MEISSONNIER, *Rue Dauphine, 22.* | *Londres, Wessel et CIE* « *J.M. 2186.* » *Leipzig, Breitkopf et Hartel.*

4 leaves (330 x 257 mm): pp. [i] engr title page, [ii] blank, 1–5 engr music, [6] blank.

CAPTION TITLE: p. 1, 'BERCEUSE | par F. CHOPIN op: 57'.

FOOTLINE: pp. 1–5, 'J.M. 2186.'.

STAMPS: publisher, style Mei/A (see Appendix 8).

ANNOTATIONS: handwritten "23" on all recto pages.

1. *Date:* first-edition inference (date code fe, p. 17).
2. An image of the title page is reproduced on this catalogue's cover.

Leipzig: **Breitkopf & Härtel (7259) [= 1845]** **57-BH-1** **M25.C54 B49**

BERCEUSE | POUR LE PIANO | dédiée | *à Mademoiselle Elise Gavard* | par | FRÉD. CHOPIN. | Op. 57. | Propriété des Editeurs. | Leipzig, chez Breitkopf & Härtel. | *Paris, chez J. Meissonnier.* « » *Londres, chez Wessel & Stapleton.* | Pr. 15 Ngr. | *7259.* | *Enrégistré aux Archives de l'Union.*

4 leaves (325 x 263 mm): pp. [1] lith title page, [2] blank, 3–7 engr music, [8] blank.

CAPTION TITLE: p. 3, 'BERCEUSE | pour le PIANOFORTE, composée | PAR | F. CHOPIN. | Op. 57.'.

FOOTLINE: pp. 3–7, '7259'.

STAMPS: publisher, style BH/K (see Appendix 8).

1. *Date:* first-edition inference (date code fe, p. 17).
2. Evidence that this is the first edition includes: presence of "Fine" at the end (p. 7) and absence of an imprint in the footline on p. 3, as well as various missing pedal-off marks (Richard Macnutt, personal communication, 1995). Doubtless 57-BH-3 is a later edition, with "PIANO" instead of "PIANOFORTE" in the caption title, and with the imprint on p. 3.

Leipzig: **Breitkopf & Härtel (7259) [after 1845]** **57-BH-3** **M25.C54 B514**

BERCEUSE | POUR LE PIANO | dédiée | à Mademoiselle Elise Gavard | par | FRÉD. CHOPIN. | Op. 57. | Propriété des Editeurs. | Leipzig, chez Breitkopf & Härtel. | Paris, chez J. Meissonnier. « » Londres, chez Wessel & Stapleton. | Pr. 15 Ngr. | 7259 | *Enrégistré aux Archives de l'Union.*

57-BH-3 *(continued)*

57-BH-3 *(concluded)*

4 leaves (340 x 269 mm): pp. [1] engr title page, [2] blank, 3–7 engr music, [8] blank.

CAPTION TITLE: p. 3, 'BERCEUSE | pour le PIANO composée | PAR | F. CHOPIN. | *OP. 57.*'.

FOOTLINE: p. 3, 'Stich und Druck von Breitkopf & Härtel in Leipzig. « | 7259'; pp. 4–7, '7259'.

TEXT: The music plates differ from those of 57-BH-1. The music layout is different, and some pedal-off marks are present that are absent in 57-BH-1, for example on p. 5 in system 3, bar 1.

STAMPS: publisher, style BH/G (see Appendix 8); dealer, Roothaan, Amsterdam.

1. *Date:* see notes.
2. Although the design of this title page differs from that of 57-BH-1, the lettering is identical except for the use of italics. However, the music plates are different; see TEXT above.
3. This score probably corresponds to Hob-425.

***Leipzig:* Breitkopf & Härtel (7259) [after 1845]** **57-BH-4** **M25.C54 B515**

BERCEUSE | POUR LE | PIANO | dédiée | *à Mademoiselle Elise Gavard* | par | Fréd. Chopin. | Op. 57. | Propriété des Editeurs. | Leipzig, Breitkopf & Härtel. | Paris, J. Meissonnier. « » Londres, Wessel & Stapleton. | *Pr. 15 Ngr.* | *Enrégistré aux Archives de l'Union* | *7259.*

4 leaves (328 x 259 mm): pp. [1] lith title page, [2] blank, 3–7 lith music, [8] blank.

CAPTION TITLE: p. 3, 'BERCEUSE | pour le PIANO composée | PAR | F. CHOPIN. | *OP. 57.*'.

FOOTLINE: p. 3, 'Stich und Druck von Breitkopf & Härtel in Leipzig. « | 7259'; pp. 4–7, '7259'.

STAMPS: publisher, style BH/J (see Appendix 8).

1. *Date:* see note 2.
2. The design of this title page differs from those of 57-BH-3 and 57-BH-1. It lacks *"chez"* with the publishers' names, and has the plate number as the last line. It probably is the third and final design in the chronology of Breitkopf & Härtel's various reissues of Op. 57.
3. This score corresponds to Hob-426.

***Leipzig:* Breitkopf & Härtel (7259) [1872–73]** **57-BH-4** **M25.C54 B52**

The transcription of this title page is the same as that of 57-BH-2, except here the price is *"15 Ngr. = Mk. 1.50."*.

4 leaves (335 x 258 mm): pp. [1] lith title page, [2] blank, 3–7 lith music, [8] blank.

CAPTION TITLE: p. 3, 'BERCEUSE | pour le PIANO composée | PAR | F. CHOPIN. | *OP. 57.*'.

FOOTLINE: p. 3, 'Stich und Druck von Breitkopf & Härtel in Leipzig « | 7259'; pp. 4–7, '7259'.

STAMPS: publisher, styles BH/B and BH/I (see Appendix 8); dealer, Schirmer, New York.

1. *Date:* currency inference (date code c3, p. 17).
2. This score corresponds to Hob-427.

London: Wessel (6313) [1848–56] 57-W-1 **M25.C54 B521**

Nº [handwritten "61"] OF | WESSEL & Cº.'s COMPLETE COLLECTION | OF | *the Compositions* | OF | FREDERIC CHOPIN | FOR THE | Piano Forte. | Solo & Duet | [list of works, Wessel 1–60] | 61 "LA BERCEUSE" *Andante, in D* [flat] *Op. 57. 2/6* | [list of works, Wessel 62–71] | *Ent. Sta. Hall. « Copyrights. » Price, Solo* [handwritten "2/6"] ÷ " *Duet* [blank] | *LONDON,* | WESSEL & Cº *Importers and Publishers of,* FOREIGN MUSIC, | *(by special Appointment) to, H.R.H. the Duchess of Kent.* | Nº 229, Regent Street, Corner of Hanover Street.

9 leaves (326 x 251 mm): pp. [i] engr title page, [ii] blank, 1–7 engr music, [8] advt.

CAPTION TITLE: p. 1, ' "LA BERCEUSE." | *ANDANTE, Composée par FREDERIC CHOPIN. Op: 57.* | *Dédiée à Mademoiselle ELISE GAVARD.*'.

FOOTLINE: p. 1, '* Copyright of WESSEL & Cº London ÷ BREITKOPFF [*sic*] & HARTEL, Leipzig. ÷ J. MEISSONIER [*sic*], Paris « (W & Cº Nº 6313.)'; pp. 2–6, 'CHOPIN, Op. 57, La Berceuse. « » (W & Cº Nº 6313.)'; p. 7, 'CHOPIN, Op. 57, La Berceuse. « | (Nº 6313.) WESSEL & Cº '.

ADVT: p. [8], 'PAGE C. | A CATALOGUE OF EASY PIANO-FORTE MUSIC, WALTZES, & QUADRILLES, PUBLISHED BY WESSEL & Co.'. There are no Chopin works in the lists.

STAMPS: Cropping of the lower margin removed all but the tops of two stamps, one blind, the other inked.

1. *Date:* Wessel inference (date code W1, p. 17).

Philadelphia: North (1074) [*ca* 1872] 57-No-1 **M25.C54 B523**

COMPOSITIONS POUR PIANOFORTE | PAR | FRÉD. CHOPIN. |

NOCTURNE, in E*b*. OP. 9. *Nº 2.*	3	☆
FIVE MAZURKAS, OP. 7.	6	"
POLONAISE, in C# *minor* OP. 26. *Nº 1.*	4	"
FOUR PRELUDES, *selected from* OP. 28.	4	"
IMPROMPTU, OP. 29.	5	"
2nd SCHERZO, in B *minor* OP. 31.	15	"
NOCTURNE CÉLÈBRE, in B. OP. 32. *Nº 1.*	3 1/2	"
NOCTURNE LAMENTO, in A*b*. OP. 32. *Nº 2.*	4	"
MARCHE FUNÈBRE, *from* OP. 35.	3 1/2	"
POLONAISE, in A. *(Militaire)* OP. 40. *Nº 1.*	4	"
3d BALLADE, in A*b*. OP. 47.	10	"
BERCEUSE, OP. 57.	4	"
FANTAISIE IMPROMPTU, in C# *min.* OP. 66.	7 1/2	"

PHILADELPHIA. F. A. NORTH & CO. 1026 CHESTNUT ST. | *Washington.* ÷ W. G. METZEROTT & Cº « *San Francisco.* ÷ M. GRAY. » *St. Louis.* ÷ BALMER & WEBER. | *Chicago.* ÷ MOLTER & WURLITZER. « » *Detroit.* ÷ WEISS & VAN LAER. | *Stackpole N-Y.*

4 leaves (329 x 263 mm): pp. [1] engr title page, [2] blank, 3–7 engr music, [8] advt.

CAPTION TITLE: p. 3, 'BERCEUSE. | Op: 57 « » F. CHOPIN.'.

FOOTLINE: pp. 3–7, 'F.A.N. & Co. 1074. 5.'.

57-No-1 *(continued)*

57-No-1 *(concluded)*

ADVT: p. [8], '*Mr. G. ANDRÉ had no connection with the late firm bearing his name for several years.* | F. A. NORTH & CO. | (LATE OF G. ANDRÉ & CO.) | No. 1026 Chestnut Street, Philadelphia, | IMPORTERS, PUBLISHERS AND DEALERS IN | FOREIGN AND AMERICAN MUSIC, | KEEP CONSTANTLY ON HAND | VOCAL MUSIC, CONSISTING OF | [list] | INSTRUMENTAL MUSIC. | [list] | THEORETICAL AND BIOGRAPHICAL WORKS, in English, French and German. | MUSIC PAPER, BLANK BOOKS, STRINGS, etc. | *Catalogues furnished gratis on application, and mailed free of postage.*'. No works by Chopin are in the lists.

STAMPS: dealer, Ellis, (Washington ?).

---

1. *Date:* based on publisher's address (see Dichter and Shapiro, 1941, p. 217).

SONATA IN B MINOR
Opus 58

Paris: Meissonnier (2187) 1845	*Composed* 1844
Leipzig: Breitkopf & Härtel (7260) 1845	Brown 155
London: Wessel (6314) 1845	Chominski & Turlo 203

Paris: **Meissonnier (2187) [= 1845]** **58-Mei-1** **M23.C54 S718**

SONATE | POUR LE | PIANO | *Dédiée à* Madame *la Comtesse* | E. de Perthius, | PAR | F. CHOPIN. | A. Vialon. | Op: 58. « » Prix 15^{f} | *A PARIS, chez* J. MEISSONNIER, *Rue Dauphine, 22.* | *Londres, Wessel et CIE « J.M. 2187. » Leipzig, Breitkopf et Hartel.*

17 leaves (346 x 270 mm): pp. [i] engr title page, [ii, 1] blank, 2–30 engr music, [31, 32] blank.

CAPTION TITLE: 'SONATE | par F. CHOPIN op: 58'.

FOOTLINE: pp. 2–30, 'J.M. 2187.'.

STAMPS: publisher, style Mei/A (see Appendix 8).

1. *Date:* first-edition inference (date code fe, p. 17).

Paris: **Meissonnier (2187) [= 1845]** **58-Mei-2** **M23.B41 S6992**

The transcription of this title page is the same as that of 58-Mei-1.

16 leaves (328 x 259 mm): pp. [i] engr title page, [ii, 1] blank, 2–30 engr music.

CAPTION TITLE: 'SONATE | par F. CHOPIN op: 58'.

SUB-CAPTION: '*PIANO*'.

FOOTLINE: pp. 2–30, 'J.M. 2187.'.

IMPOSITION: Leaf 9 is a singleton.

STAMPS: publisher, style Mei/B (see Appendix 8).

CONDITION: The final blank leaf was removed for binding. The title leaf is tipped to leaf 2.

BOUND WITH: 35-T-1; for details, see Appendix 2.

BINDING: red morocco prize binding; see Appendix 2.

1. *Date:* first-edition inference (date code fe, p. 17).
2. If this score were not bound with other scores, it would be c.2 of 58-Mei-1 (which would be c.1).

Leipzig: **Breitkopf & Härtel (7260) [= 1845]** **58-BH-1** **M23.C54 S719**

SONATE | pour le Piano | dédiée | à Madame la Comtesse E. de Perthius | par | FRÉD. CHOPIN. | Op. 58. | Propriété des Editeurs. | Leipzig, chez Breitkopf & Härtel. | *Paris, chez J. Meissonnier.* « » *Londres, chez Wessel & Stapleton.* | Pr. 1 Thlr. 15 Ngr. | *7260.* | *Enrégistré aux Archive de l'Union.*

16 leaves (323 x 262 mm): pp. [1] lith title page, 2–31 engr music, [32] blank.

58-BH-1 *(continued)*

58-BH-1 *(concluded)*

CAPTION TITLE: p. 2, 'SONATE. | » Fr. Chopin, Op. 58.'.

FOOTLINE: pp. 2–31, '7260'.

STAMPS: none.

1. *Date:* first-edition inference (date code fe, p. 17).
2. This score corresponds to Hob-429 without the wrapper. See note 2 in 58-BH-3 for further comment.

Leipzig: **Breitkopf & Härtel** (7260) [after 1845] **58-BH-3** **M23.C54 S721**

SONATE | POUR LE | PIANO | dédiée | à Madame la Comtesse E. de Perthius | par | Fréd. Chopin. | Op. 58. | Propriété des Editeurs. | Leipzig, Breitkopf & Härtel. | Paris, J. Meissonnier. « » Londres, Wessel & Stapleton. | Pr. 1 Thlr. 15 Ngr. | *Enrégistré aux Archive de l'Union.* | *7260.*

16 leaves (328 x 255 mm): pp. [1] lith title page, [2] blank, 3–31 engr music, [32] blank.

CAPTION TITLE: p. 3, 'SONATE. | » Fr. Chopin, Op. 58.'.

FOOTLINE: pp. 3–31, '7260'.

STAMPS: publisher, style BH/B (see Appendix 8).

1. *Date:* see note 2.
2. The design of the title page differs from that of 58-BH-1, although the syntax is almost the same (the only differences are the absence of "chez" with the publishers' names, and the position of the plate number). Further, the two scores have the same music plates, except that 58-BH-3 has numerous pedal-off signs not present in 58-BH-1, for example the one above the plate number in the last system on p. 12 (Richard Macnutt, personal communication, 1995). For this reason, 58-BH-3 (which corresponds to Hob-430), although engraved, is dated as a non-first issue. Probably it is the first reissue.

Leipzig: **Breitkopf & Härtel** (7260) [after 1845] **58-BH-2** **M23.C54 S722**

SCHERZO | pour le Piano | tiré DE LA SONATE Oeuvr. 58. | par | Fréd. Chopin. | Propriété des Editeurs. | Leipzig, Breitkopf & Härtel. | Paris, J. Meissonnier. « » Londres, Wessel & Stapleton. | *Pr. 10 Ngr.* | *Enrégistré aux Archive de l'Union.* | *7260.*

4 leaves (325 x 254 mm): pp. [11] lith title page, 12–15 engr music, [16–18] blank.

CAPTION TITLE: none.

SUB-CAPTION: p. 12, 'SCHERZO.'.

FOOTLINE: pp. 12–15, '7260'.

STAMPS: publisher, style BH/J (see Appendix 8); dealer, Schirmer, New York.

1. *Date:* Probably this score is the first issue of the extract edition.
2. Starting from "par", the design of the title page is similar to that of 58-BH-3, rather than to 58-BH-1.

Leipzig: Breitkopf & Härtel (C.VIII.2) 1878 **58-BH-4** **M23.C54 S724**

Friedr. Chopin's | Werke. | Band VIII. | Sonaten für das Pianoforte |

No.		*M*	*Pf*	
1. Sonate. Op. 35. B moll	Pr.	1	35	netto
2. Sonate. Op. 58. H moll	"	2	10	–

Band VIII. Sonaten. Broch. Pr. *M* 3.60. n. geb. Pr. *M* 5.60. n. | Verlag von Breitkopf & Härtel in Leipzig.

14 leaves (338 x 270 mm): pp. [1] lith title page [series title in red], 2–27 lith music, [28] advt.

CAPTION TITLE: p. 2, 'Chopin's Werke. « SONATE ÷ für das Pianoforte ÷ von ÷ FRIEDRICH CHOPIN. ÷ Op. 58. ÷ Gräfin E. von Perthius gewidmet. » Band VIII. Nº 2.'.

FOOTLINE: p. 2, 'Stich und Druck von Breitkopf & Härtel in Leipzig. « C.VIII.2. » Ausgegeben 1878.'; pp. 3–27, 'C.VIII.2.'.

ADVT: p. [28], 'KLAVIER-SONATEN | im Verlage von BREITKOPF & HÄRTEL in Leipzig.'. Chopin sonatas Opp. 35 and 58 are listed.

STAMPS: publisher, style BH/L (see Appendix 8).

1. *Date:* Note the explicit publication date in the footline.
2. This score is from Breitkopf & Härtel's collected edition of 1878–80, edited by Bargiel, Brahms, Franchomme, Liszt, Reinecke, and Rudorff (Chominski & Turlo, pp. 257–58).

MAZURKAS IN A MINOR, A FLAT MAJOR, F SHARP MINOR
Opus 59

Paris: Brandus (4292) 1846	*Composed* 1845
Berlin: Stern (71) 1845	Brown 157
London: Wessel (6315) 1845	Chominski & Turlo 86

Paris: Brandus (M.S. 4292) [= 1846] 59-Bra-1 M32.C54 M574

3 | MAZURKAS | POUR | PIANO | PAR | F. CHOPIN | *A.V.* | *Op: 59.* « » *Pr: 7.f 50* |
PARIS, | *Maison M.CE SCHLESINGER, BRANDUS et C.IE Successeurs,* | *Rue Richelieu, N.o 97.* |
Berlin, Stern et C.IE « *B. et C.IE 4292.* » *Londres, Wessel et C.IE*

9 leaves (347 x 269 mm): pp. [i] engr title page, [ii] blank, 1–15 engr music, [16] blank.

CAPTION TITLE: p. 1, 'TROIS | MAZURKAS. | par | F. CHOPIN. | N.o 1.'; p. 6, 'N.o 2.'; p. 10, 'N.o 3.'.

FOOTLINE: p. 1, 'F. CHOPIN. Op: 59. « M.S. 4292. » Maurice Schlesinger rue Richelieu 97.'; pp. 2–15, 'M.S. 4292.'.

WRAPPER (blue): pp. [1] same as title page, [2–4] blank.

STAMPS: successor, style BD/C (see Appendix 8).

1. *Date:* first-edition inference (date code fe, p. 17).

Berlin: Stern (71) [= 1845] 59-St-1 M32.C54 M575

TROIS MAZOURKAS | pour Le Piano | par | FRÉD. CHOPIN | Op. 59. « Propriété des Editeurs »
Pr. 5/6 Thlr. | Enrégistré aux Archives de l'Union | *Berlin chez Stern & C.o , Werd. Markt 6.* |
Paris chez M. Schlesinger. « Londres chez Wessel. » St. Petersbourg chez M. Bernard. |
Varsovie chez Spiess & C.o | St & C.o 71. | *Hof Lthgr. F. Silber, Berlin.*

8 leaves (326 x 254 mm): pp. [1] lith title page, [2] blank, 3–15 engr music, [16] blank.

CAPTION TITLE: p. 3, 'MAZURKA. | » F. Chopin. Op. 59. | N.o 1. «'; p. 8, 'MAZURKA. | N.o 2. «'; p. 11, 'MAZURKA. | N.o 3. «'.

FOOTLINE: p. 3, 'Propriété des Editeurs. « S. et C.o 71 » Berlin chez Stern et C.o '; pp. 4–15, 'S. et C.o 71'.

STAMPS: publisher, style St/A (see Appendix 8); agent, Spiess, Warsaw.

1. *Date:* first-edition inference (date code fe, p. 17).
2. The title transcribed by Chominski & Turlo (p. 128) has the name of the lithographer, as above, but Hob-432 does not. The latter is considered a later issue by Chominski & Turlo (p. 445).

London: **Wessel (6315) [1848–56]** 59-W-1 M32.C54 M576

Nº [handwritten "63"] OF | WESSEL & Cº.ˢ COMPLETE COLLECTION | OF | *the Compositions* | OF | FREDERIC CHOPIN | FOR THE | Piano Forte. | Solo & Duet | [list of works, Wessel 1–62] | 63 "SOUVENIRS *de* LA POLOGNE" *10 th Set of Mazurkas. Op. 59.* 4/- | [list of works, Wessel 64–71] | *Ent. Sta. Hall.* « *Copyrights.* » *Price. Solo* [handwritten "4/-"] ÷ " *Duet* [blank] | *LONDON,* | WESSEL & Cº *Importers and Publishers of,* FOREIGN MUSIC, | *(by special Appointment) to H.R.H. the Duchess of Kent.* | Nº 229, Regent Street, Corner of Hanover Street.

8 leaves (334 x 250 mm): pp. [i] engr title page, [ii] blank, 1–13 engr music, [14] advt.

CAPTION TITLE: p. 1, 'WESSEL & Cºˢ COMPLETE COLLECTION OF THE WORKS OF FREDERIC CHOPIN. | *Nº 63. TENTH SET OF MAZURKAS Op: 59.*'.

SUB-CAPTION: p. 1, '*Nº 1.*'; p. 6, '*Nº 2.*'; p. 9, '*Nº 3.*'.

FOOTLINE: p. 1, 'Copyright of Wessel & Cº « (W & Cº Nº 6315)'; pp. 2–12, 'CHOPIN, Op. 59. Mazurkas, Set 10. « (W & Cº Nº 6315)'; p. 13, 'CHOPIN, Op. 59. Mazurkas, Set 10. « WESSEL & Cº » (Nº 6315)'.

ADVT: p. [14], 'PAGE Q. | A CATALOGUE OF NEW MUSIC FOR THE HARP. GUITAR. SONGS WITH GUITAR, AND BASS SONGS, | PUBLISHED BY WESSEL «'.

STAMPS: publisher, style W/D (see Appendix 8).

---

1. *Date:* Wessel inference (date code W1, p. 17).
2. The heading of the advertisement indicates deletion of text after "WESSEL", probably to remove reference to Stapleton.

BARCAROLLE IN F SHARP MAJOR
Opus 60

Paris: Brandus (4609) 1846 — *Composed* 1845–46
Leipzig: Breitkopf & Härtel (7545) 1846 — Brown 158
London: Wessel (6317) 1846 — Chominski & Turlo 6

Leipzig: **Breitkopf & Härtel (7545) [= 1846]** — **60-BH-2** — **M25.C54 B449**

BARCAROLLE | pour le Piano | dédiée | *A Madame la Baronne de Stockhausen* | par | FRÉD. CHOPIN. | Op. 60. « Propriété des Editeurs. » Pr. 20 Ngr. | Leipzig, chez Breitkopf & Härtel. | *Paris, chez Brandus & C$^{\underline{o}}$. « » Londres, chez Wessel. | 7545. | Enrégistré aux Archives de l'Union.*

6 leaves (317 x 245 mm): pp. [1] lith title page, [2] blank, 3–11 engr music, [12] blank.

CAPTION TITLE: p. 3, 'BARCAROLLE. | » F. Chopin. Op. 60.'.

FOOTLINE: pp. 3–11, '7545'.

STAMPS: publisher, style BH/G (see Appendix 8).

1. *Date:* first-edition inference (date code fe, p. 17).

Leipzig: **Breitkopf & Härtel (7545) [after 1846]** — **60-BH-1** — **M25.C54 B45**

The transcription of this title page is the same as that of 60-BH-2.

6 leaves (337 x 267 mm): pp. [1] lith title page, [2] blank, 3–11 lith music, [12] blank.

CAPTION TITLE: p. 3, 'BARCAROLLE. | » F. Chopin. Op. 60.'.

FOOTLINE: pp. 3–11, '7545'.

STAMPS: publisher, styles BH/I and BH/J (see Appendix 8); dealer, Seyffardt's, Amsterdam.

1. *Date:* The title page is identical to that of 60-BH-2, but the music is lithographed.

POLONAISE-FANTAISIE IN A FLAT MAJOR
Opus 61

Paris: Brandus (4610) 1846	*Composed* 1846
Leipzig: Breitkopf & Härtel (7546) 1846	Brown 159
London: Wessel (6318) 1846	Chominski & Turlo 156

Paris: **Brandus (4610) [= 1846]** **61-Bra-1** **M32.C54 P853**

Polonaise-Fantaisie | POUR | *PIANO* | *dédiée à Madame A. Veyret* | PAR | F. CHOPIN. | *A. Vialon.* | *OP: 61.* « » *PR. 7 f 50* | *PARIS,* | *MAISON M^CE SCHLESINGER,* | BRANDUS et CIE | *Successeurs, Rue Richelieu, 97.* | *Leipzig, Breitkopf et Hartel* « *B. et CIE 4610.* » *Londres, Wessel et Compagnie.*

8 leaves (336 x 261 mm): pp. [i] engr title page, [ii] blank, 1–13 engr music, [14] blank.

CAPTION TITLE: p. 1, 'POLONAISE FANTAISIE. | par | F. CHOPIN. | Op: 61.'.

FOOTLINE: p. 1, 'B. et Cie 4610. » Brandus et Cie rue Richelieu 97.'; pp. 2–6, 8–12, 'B. et Cie 4610.'; p. 13, same as p. 1. There is no footline on p. 7.

STAMPS: publisher, styles Bra/B and Bra/C (see Appendix 8).

1. *Date:* first-edition inference (date code fe, p. 17).

Leipzig: **Breitkopf & Härtel (7546) [= 1846]** **61-BH-1** **M32.C54 P85**

POLONAISE FANTAISIE | POUR LE | PIANO | dédiée | À Madame A. Veyret | par | FRÉD. CHOPIN. | Op. 61. « Propriété des Editeurs. » Pr. 27 1/2 Ngr. | Leipzig, chez Breitkopf & Härtel. | *Paris, chez Brandus & Co* « » *Londres, chez Wessel.* | *7546.* | *Enrégistré aux Archives de l'Union.*

9 leaves (333 x 262 mm): pp. [1] lith title page, [2] blank, 3–17 engr music, [18] blank.

CAPTION TITLE: p. 3, 'POLONAISE FANTAISIE. | » F. Chopin. Op. 61.'.

FOOTLINE: pp. 3–17, '7546'.

WRAPPER (buff): pp. [1] half-title page, [2, 3] blank, [4] advt.

HALF TITLE: wrapper p. [1], 'POLONAISE FANTAISIE | par | F. CHOPIN. | Op. 61. | Leipzig, chez Breitkopf & Härtel. | Pr. 27 1/2 Ngr.'.

ADVT: wrapper p. [4], 'FRANÇOIS HÜNTEN'S | PIANOFORTE-WERKE | welche mit Eigenthumsrecht im Verlage von | BREITKOPF & HÄRTEL IN LEIPZIG | erscheinen sind.'.

STAMPS: publisher, style BH/K? (see Appendix 8); dealer, Schott, Mainz (see Appendix 8).

1. *Date:* first-edition inference (date code fe, p. 17).

London: Wessel (6318) [1848–56] 61-W-1 M32.C54 P852

N° [handwritten "66"] OF | WESSEL & C°.'s COMPLETE COLLECTION | OF | *the Compositions* | OF | FREDERIC CHOPIN | FOR THE | Piano Forte. | Solo & Duet | [list of works, Wessel 1–65] | 66 "POLONAISE FANTAISIE" *in A* [flat] *Op. 61. 4/6* | [list of works, Wessel 67–71] | *Ent. Sta. Hall.* « *Copyrights.* » *Price. Solo* [handwritten "4/6"] ÷ " *Duet* [blank] | *LONDON,* | WESSEL & C° *Importers and Publishers of* FOREIGN MUSIC, | *(by special Appointment) to H.R.H. the Duchess of Kent.* | N° 229, Regent Street, Corner of Hanover Street.

9 leaves (334 x 252 mm): pp. [i] engr title page, [ii] blank, 1–15 engr music, [16] advt.

CAPTION TITLE: p. 1, 'WESSEL & C°s COMPLETE COLLECTION OF THE WORKS OF FREDERIC CHOPIN. | *N° 66.* POLONAISE FANTASIE [*sic*]. *Op. 61.*'.

FOOTLINE: p. 1, '» (W & C° N° 6318)'; pp. 2–14, 'CHOPIN. Op. 61. POLONAISE FANTASIE [*sic*]. « (W & C° N° 6318)'; p. 15, 'CHOPIN. Op. 61. POLONAISE FANTASIE [*sic*]. « (N° 6318) » WESSEL & C° N° 229. Regent St Corner of Hanover S^t '.

ADVT: p. [16], '[clipped to] A CATALOGUE OF EASY PIANO-FORTE MUSIC, WALTZES, & QUADRILLES, PUBLISHED BY WESSEL & Co'. There are no Chopin works in the lists.

STAMPS: publisher, style W/D (see Appendix 8).

1. *Date:* Wessel inference (date code W1, p. 17).

NOCTURNES IN B MAJOR AND E MAJOR
Opus 62

Paris: Brandus (4611) 1846	*Composed* 1846
Leipzig: Breitkopf & Härtel (7547) 1846	Brown 161
London: Wessel (6319) 1846	Chominski & Turlo 124

***Paris:* Brandus (4611) [= 1846]** **62-Bra-1** **M25.C54 N919**

2 | NOCTURNES | *POUR* | *PIANO* | dédiés | *à Mlle R. de Könneritz* | PAR | F. CHOPIN. | *A. Vialon.* | *OP: 62.* « » *PR: 7^{f} 50* | *PARIS,* | *MAISON M^{CE} SCHLESINGER,* | BRANDUS et CIE | *Successeurs, Rue Richelieu, 97.* | *Leipzig, Breitkopf et Hartel.* | *Londres, Wessel et CIE* | *B. et CIE 4611*

8 leaves (350 x 268 mm): pp. [i] engr title page, [ii, 1] blank, 2–13 engr music, [14] blank.

CAPTION TITLE: p. 2, 'N°. 1. « DEUX NOCTURNES ÷ PAR ÷ F. CHOPIN. ÷ *Op*: 62.'; p. 8, 'N° 2.'.

FOOTLINE: p. 2, 'B. et Cie 4611. » Brandus et Cie 97. rue Richelieu.'; pp. 3–12, 'B. et Cie 4611.'; p. 13, same as p. 2.

WRAPPER (pink): pp. [1] same as title page, [2, 3] blank, [4] advt.

ADVT: wrapper p. [4], 'Chez brandus et Ce, éditeurs, 103, rue Richelieu, | OEUVRES DE | BEETHOVEN | NOUVELLE ÉDITION DE LA | COLLECTION COMPLÈTE | … | [and at the foot:] PARIS. — IMPRIMERIE CENTRALE DE NAPOLÉON CHAIX ET C^{E}, RUE BERGÈRE, 20.'.

STAMPS: publisher, style Bra/A (see Appendix 8).

1. *Date:* first-edition inference (date code fe, p. 17).

***Leipzig:* Breitkopf & Härtel (7547) [= 1846]** **62-BH-1** **M25.C54 N92**

DEUX | NOCTURNES | pour le Piano | dédiés | À MADEMOISELLE R. DE KÖNNERITZ | par | FRÉD. CHOPIN. | Op. 62. « Propriété des Editeurs. » Pr. 22 1/2 Ngr. | Leipzig, chez Breitkopf & Härtel. | *Paris, chez Brandus & Co.* « » *Londres, chez Wessel.* | *7547.* | *Enrégistré aux Archives de l'Union.*

7 leaves (312 x 255 mm): pp. [1] lith title page, [2] blank, 3–13 engr music, [14] blank.

CAPTION TITLE: p. 3, 'N^{o} I. | » F. Chopin. Op. 62.'; p. 8, 'N° II.'.

FOOTLINE: pp. 3–13, '7547'.

STAMPS: publisher, style BH/H (see Appendix 8).

1. *Date:* first-edition inference (date code fe, p. 17).

MAZURKAS IN B MAJOR, F MINOR, C SHARP MINOR
Opus 63

Paris: Brandus (4742) 1847	*Composed* 1846
Leipzig: Breitkopf & Härtel (7714) 1847	Brown 162
London: Wessel (6319) 1846	Chominski & Turlo 89

Paris: **Brandus (4742) [*ca* 1847]** **63-Bra-1** **M32.C54 M581**

3 | MAZURKAS | POUR | PIANO | *dédiées à Madame la Comtesse* | *Laure Czosnowska* | PAR | *F. CHOPIN.* | *A. V.* | *Op: 63.* « » *Prix 6 f.* | *PARIS,* | *Maison M^CE. SCHLESINGER,* BRANDUS et CIE. *Successeurs, Rue Richelieu, N°. 97.* | *Leipzig, Breitkopf et Hartel « B. et CIE. 4742. » Londres, Jullien et CIE.*

6 leaves (333 x 263 mm): pp. [i] engr title page, [ii, 1] blank, 2–10 engr music.

CAPTION TITLE: p. 2, 'F. CHOPIN. « » Op: 63. | TROIS MAZURKAS. | N°. 1.'; p. 6, 'N°. 2.'; p. 8, 'N°. 3.'.

FOOTLINE: p. 2, 'B. et Cie. 4742. » Brandus et Cie. rue Richelieu 97.'; pp. 3–9, 'B. et Cie. 4742.'; p. 10, 'Brandus et Cie. rue Richelieu 97. « B. et Cie. 4742.'.

STAMPS: publisher, style Bra/B (see Appendix 8).

ANNOTATIONS: stamped page numbers 163–174.

1. *Date:* first-edition inference (date code fe, p. 17), but also see note 2.
2. Grabowski (1994, p. 31) refers to this issue — with Jullien (mistakenly) as London publisher — as a third impression. He does not give a date.

Leipzig: **Breitkopf & Härtel (7714) [= 1847]** **63-BH-2** **M32.C54 M58 c.2**

À MADAME LA COMTESSE LAURE CZOSNOWSKA. | TROIS | MAZOURKAS | pour le Piano | composées | par | FRÉD. CHOPIN. | Op. 63. | Propriété des Editeurs. | Leipzig, chez Breitkopf & Härtel. | *Paris, chez Brandus & Co.* | Pr. 20 Ngr. | *7714.* | *Enrégistré aux Archives de l'Union.*

6 leaves (315 x 256 mm): pp. [1] lith title page, [2] blank, 3–10 engr music, [11, 12] blank.

CAPTION TITLE: p. 3, 'TROIS MAZURKAS. | » F. Chopin, Op. 63.'.

SUB-CAPTION: p. 3, 'N°. 1.'; p. 6, 'N°. 2.'; p. 8, 'N°. 3.'.

FOOTLINE: pp. 3–10, '7714'.

STAMPS: publisher, style BH/K (see Appendix 8).

1. *Date:* first-edition inference (date code fe, p. 17).
2. This score corresponds to Hob-447.

Leipzig: **Breitkopf & Härtel (7714) [*ca* 1847]** **63-BH-1** **M32.C54 M58 c.1**

The transcription of this title page is the same as that of 63-BH-2.

6 leaves (340 x 268 mm): pp. [1] lith title page, [2] blank, 3–10 engr music, [11, 12] blank.

63-BH-1 *(continued)*

63-BH-1 *(concluded)*

CAPTION TITLE: p. 3, 'TROIS MAZURKAS. | » F. Chopin, Op. 63.'.

SUB-CAPTION: p. 3, 'N° 1.'; p. 6, 'N° 2.'; p. 8, 'N° 3.'.

FOOTLINE: p. 3, 'Stich und Druck von Breitkopf & Härtel in Leipzig. « 7714'; pp. 4–10, '7714'.

STAMPS: publisher, style BH/J (see Appendix 8).

---

1. *Date:* see note 2.
2. This score is probably somewhat later than Hob-447, which does not have "Stich und Druck ..." in the footline. It is earlier than Hob-448, which does have "Stich und Druck ..." and is priced in Marks.
3. In the sub-caption we see "N° " here but, curiously, "N°·" in 63-BH-2.

London: **Wessel (6320) [1848–56]** **63-W-1** **M32.C54 M582**

N° [handwritten "68"] OF | WESSEL & C°.'s COMPLETE COLLECTION | OF | *the Compositions* | OF | FREDERIC CHOPIN | FOR THE | Piano Forte. | Solo & Duet | [list of works, Wessel 1–67] | 68 "SOUVENIRS *de* LA POLOGNE" *11th Set of Mazurkas. Op. 63, 3/-* | [list of works, Wessel 69–71] | *Ent. Sta. Hall.* « *Copyrights.* » *Price. Solo* [handwritten "3/-"] ÷ " *Duet* [blank] | *LONDON,* | WESSEL & C° *Importers and Publishers of,* FOREIGN MUSIC, | *(by special Appointment) to H.R.H. the Duchess of Kent.* | N° 229, Regent Street, Corner of Hanover Street.

6 leaves (333 x 249 mm): pp. [1] engr title page, 2–10 engr music, [11, 12] blank.

CAPTION TITLE: p. 2, 'À MADAME LA COMTESSE LAURE CZOSNOWSKA. | ELEVENTH SET OF MAZURKAS | COMPOSED BY | F. CHOPIN. OP: 63.'.

SUB-CAPTION: p. 2, '*N° 1.*'; p. 6, '*N° 2.*'; p. 8, '*N° 3.*'.

FOOTLINE: p. 2, '(W & C° N° 6320.)'; pp. 3–9, 'CHOPIN. 11th Set of Mazurkas. Op: 63. « » (W & C° N° 6320.)'; p. 10, 'CHOPIN. 11th Set of Mazurkas. Op: 63. « (N° 6320.) » WESSEL & C° N° 229, REGENT STREET, CORNER OF HANOVER ST:'.

STAMPS: publisher, style W/D (see Appendix 8).

---

1. *Date:* Wessel inference (date code W1, p. 17).
2. Pagination with [1] (rather than [i]) for the title page is unusual in Wessel's Chopin editions.

WALTZES IN D FLAT MAJOR, C SHARP MINOR, A FLAT MAJOR
Opus 64

Paris: Brandus (4743.(1)) (4743.(2)) (4743.(3)) 1847	*Composed* 1847
Leipzig: Breitkopf & Härtel (7715) (7716) (7717) (7721) 1847	Brown 164
London: Wessel (6321) (6322) (6323) 1848	Chominski & Turlo 212

Opus 64, Waltzes 1, 2, 3

Leipzig: **Breitkopf & Härtel (7721) [= 1847]** **64-BH-1** **M32.C54 W6**

Trois | VALSES | pour le Piano | composées | par | FRÉD. CHOPIN. | Op. 64. | Propriété des Editeurs. | Leipzig, chez Breitkopf & Härtel. | *Paris, chez Brandus & C°.* | Pr. 1 Thlr. | *7721.* | *Enrégistré aux Archives de l'Union.*

10 leaves (338 x 265 mm): pp. [1] lith title page, [2] blank, [3] lith half-title page, 4–19 engr music, [20] blank.

HALF TITLE: p. [3], 'TROIS VALSES | composées | PAR | F. CHOPIN. | Op. 64.'.

CAPTION TITLE: p. 4, 'TROIS VALSES | composées | PAR | F. CHOPIN. | Op. 64.'.

SUB-CAPTION: p. 4, 'N°. 1.'; p. 8, 'N°. 2.'; p. 14, 'N°. 3.'.

FOOTLINE: pp. 4–19, '7721'.

STAMPS: none.

BINDING: library cloth.

1. *Date:* first-edition inference (date code fe, p. 17).
2. Fuld (p. 613) notes two variants (see notes that follow), but was unable to establish priority.
3. The design of the title page does not match that of any of the other Breitkopf editions of Op. 64 in the collection.
4. Hoboken has two copies, Hob-453 and 454, the former dated 1847 and the latter classified as a Titelauflage. The title pages are the same, except that in Hob-454 the last two lines are interchanged. Fuld (p. 613) refers to differences in the music as well. His copies, both dated 1847, are now Fuld C53 and C54 in the Pierpont Morgan Library; they correspond respectively to Hob-453 and 454. This collection's score, 64-BH-1, corresponds to Hob-454.
5. A Breitkopf & Härtel half title is unusual in this collection. It is described in Hob-453, but there the first line (Trois Valses) is in lower case, whereas in 64-BH-1 it is upper case. This raises the possibility of an error in the Hoboken transcription.
6. Of the three publishers of the first editions, only Breitkopf & Härtel issued Op. 64 with all three waltzes.

Opus 64, Waltz 1

Paris: **Brandus (4743(1)) [= 1847]** **64#1-Bra-1** **M32.C54 W621**

à Madame la Comtesse | Delphine Potocka. | 3 | *VALSES* | POUR | le Piano, | PAR | F. CHOPIN. | AV | *Op: 64.* « » *Prix 5.f* | N° 1. | *PARIS,* | *Maison M.CE SCHLESINGER,* BRANDUS et C.IE *Successeurs, Rue Richelieu, N° 97.* | *Leipzig, Breitkopf et Hartel* « *B. et C.IE 4743.* » *Londres, Jullien et C.IE*

4 leaves (347 x 270 mm): pp. [i] engr title page, [ii, 1] blank, 2–5 engr music, [6] blank.

CAPTION TITLE: p. 2, 'F. CHOPIN. « » Op: 64. 3 VALSES. | VALSE.'.

FOOTLINE: p. 2, 'B. et C.ie 4743.(1) » Brandus et C.ie rue Richelieu 97.'; pp. 3–5, 'B. et C.ie 4743.(1)'.

WRAPPER (pink): pp. [1] same as title page, [2–4] blank.

STAMPS: publisher, style Bra/B (see Appendix 8).

1. *Date:* first-edition inference (date code fe, p. 17).

Paris: **Brandus & Dufour (B. et C.ie 4743(1)) [after 1853]** **64#1-BD-1** **M32.C54 W6211**

The transcription of this title page is the same as that of **64#1-Bra-1.**

4 leaves (349 x 273 mm): pp. [i] engr title page, [ii, 1] blank, 2–5 engr music, [6] blank.

CAPTION TITLE: p. 2, 'F. CHOPIN. « » Op: 64. 3 VALSE. ÷ N° 1. | VALSE.'.

FOOTLINE: p. 2, 'B. et C.ie 4743.(1.) » G. Brandus, Dufour et C.ie 103 rue Richelieu.'; pp. 3–4, 'B. et C.ie 4743.(1)'; p. 5, 'Imp. Thierry Fs 1 Cité Bergère. « B. et C.ie 4743.(1)'.

WRAPPER (green): pp. [1] same as title page, [2–3] blank, [4] advt.

ADVT: wrapper p. [4], 'MUSIQUE NOUVELLE DE PIANO | Publiée par G. BRANDUS et S. DUFOUR, éditeurs, 103, rue de Richelieu.'. The list includes three Chopin works: *"2e nocturne", "6e valse", and "Marche funèbre".*

TEXT: The state of this score differs from that of 64#1-Bra-1, although the layout of the music is the same. For example: there are differences in the notations for pedal marks and in the fonts for performance marks; there is no "FINE" at the end of the first system on p. 3; on pp. 4, 5 the page numbers are misplaced into the recto, verso positions, respectively; on p. 5 the footline has the name of the printer.

STAMPS: publisher, style BD/C (see Appendix 8).

CONDITION: The plates are rather worn.

1. *Date:* based on the name of the publisher in the footline (Table 5A).

Paris: **Richault (4353) [*ca* 1860]** **64#1-Rich-1** **M32.C54 W62**

3 | VALSES | *POUR* | LE PIANO | *dédiées* | *N? 1* ÷ à Madame la Ctesse Delphine Potocka « » *N? 2* ÷ à Mme la Bonne Nathaniel de Rothschild | *N? 3* ÷ à Melle la Ctesse Catherine Branicka. | *et Composées* | *PAR* | FR. CHOPIN | *6e 7e 8e Livre* « » *Prix 6 f chaque* | ŒUV: 64 | *N?* [blank] | *PARIS,* S. RICHAULT, *EDITr,* | *Boulevart Poissonière, 26 au 1er.* | Æ | *4353. R.*

4 leaves (330 x 250 mm): pp. [i] lith title page, [ii, 79] blank, 80–83 lith music, [84] blank.

CAPTION TITLE: p. 80, '6me VALSE | F. CHOPIN Op: 64. « | 4me LIVRE de trois Valses. « » à Madame la Comtesse Delphine POTOCKA.'.

FOOTLINE: pp. 80–83, '4353.R.'.

STAMPS: publisher, style Rich/B (see Appendix 8); dealer, Maho, Paris.

ANNOTATIONS: handwritten page numbers 76–83.

1. *Date:* This score is from volume 3 of the 12 volumes of Chopin's collected works edited by Tellefsen and published by Richault *ca* 1860, with plate numbers 4351 to 4362 (Chominski & Turlo, p. 279; Brown, p. 185). The title-page address, 26 Boulevard Poissonniére, was occupied from 1841 until the firm moved to 4 Boulevard des Italiens in October 1862 (Devriès & Lesure, p. 365).

Leipzig: **Breitkopf & Härtel (7715) [= 1847]** **64#1-BH-1** **M32.C54 W6201**

Trois | VALSES | pour le Piano | composées | par | FRÉD. CHOPIN. | Op. 64. | *No I.* « » *Pr. 15 Ngr.* | Propriété des Editeurs. | Leipzig, chez Breitkopf & Härtel. | Paris, chez Brandus & Co | *7715. 16. & 17.* | *Enrégistré aux Archives de l'Union.*

4 leaves (319 x 249 mm): pp. [1] lith title page, [2, 3] blank, 4–7 engr music, [8] blank.

CAPTION TITLE: p. 4, 'VALSE.'.

SUB-CAPTION: p. 4, 'No. 1.'.

FOOTLINE: pp. 4–7, '7715'.

STAMPS: publisher, style BH/C (see Appendix 8); dealer, Höpfert, Osnabrück (see Appendix 8).

1. *Date:* first-edition inference (date code fe, p. 17); also see note 2.
2. Fuld (p. 613) assigns to the first edition the date 1849, on the basis of a published announcement.
3. The layout of the title page differs slightly from that described in Hob-451: instead of what is shown above, the third and fourth lines in Hob-451 are 'pour le PIANO composées | par FRÉD. CHOPIN.'. This may not be a correct transcription, because "composées" is unlikely to be on the same line as "pour le PIANO", and "par" is unlikely to be on the same line as "FRÉD. CHOPIN".
4. Concerning various title-page designs for the Breitkopf editions of Op. 64, see Appendix 3.

Leipzig: **Breitkopf & Härtel (9619) [*ca* 1858]** 64#1-BH-2 M32.C54 W6202

Trois | VALSES | pour le | PIANO | composées | PAR | FREDERIC CHOPIN. |
Op. 64. | *N° I.* « Propriété des Editeurs. » *Pr. 15 Ngr.* | Leipzig, chez Breitkopf & Härtel. |
Paris, chez Brandus & C° | *9619. 7716. 17.* | *Enrégistré aux Archives de l'Union.*

4 leaves (343 x 270 mm): pp. [1] lith title page, [2] blank, 3–7 lith music, [8] blank.

CAPTION TITLE: p. 3, 'VALSE. | » Fr. Chopin, Op. 64. N° 1.'.

SUB-CAPTION: There is space for a sub-caption but it is blank.

FOOTLINE: p. 3, 'Stich und Druck von Breitkopf & Härtel in Leipzig. | 9619'; pp. 4–7, '9619'.

STAMPS: publisher, style BH/E (see Appendix 8); dealer, ?, New York.

1. *Date:* based on plate number 9619 (Table 5C).
2. Concerning various title-page designs for the Breitkopf editions of Op. 64, see Appendix 3.

Leipzig: **Breitkopf & Härtel (9619) [*ca* 1861]** 64#1-BH-3 M32.C54 W6203

Trois | VALSES | pour le Piano | composées | par | FRÉD. CHOPIN. | Op. 64. | *N° I.* «
Propriété des Editeurs. » *Pr. 15 Ngr.* | Leipzig, chez Breitkopf & Härtel. |
Paris, chez Brandus & C° | *Enrégistré aux Archives de l'Union.* | *9619. 10097. 98.*

4 leaves (325 x 255 mm): pp. [1] lith title page, [2] blank, 3–7 lith music, [8] blank.

CAPTION TITLE: p. 3, 'VALSE. | » Fr. Chopin, Op. 64. N° 1.'.

SUB-CAPTION: There is space for a sub-caption but it is blank.

FOOTLINE: p. 3, 'Stich und Druck von Breitkopf & Härtel in Leipzig. | 9619'; pp. 4–7, '9619'.

TEXT: The music plates appear to be the same as those of 64#1-BH-2, except for corrections, one of which is dotting of the half-notes in the last three bars on p. 4. However, the design of the title page does not match that of any of the other editions of Op. 64 in the collection (see Appendix 3).

STAMPS: none.

1. *Date:* based on plate number 10097 on the title page (Table 5C).
2. Concerning various title-page designs for the Breitkopf editions of Op. 64, see Appendix 3.

Brussels: **Schott (I 6) [*ca* 1880]** 64#1-Schott-1 M32.C54 W6206

OEUVRES POUR LE PIANO | composées par | F. CHOPIN | 1^R VOLUME | VALSES, BERCEUSE, MARCHE FUNEBRE. | [thematic list of Opp. 18, 34(#1, 2, 3), 42, 64(#1, 2, 3), 57, 35] |
2^E VOLUME ÷ NOCTURNES | 3^E VOLUME ÷ MAZURKAS | CHAQUE VOLUME net. Fr 7. — |
En volumes, en édition in 8°. Separément en édition in 4°. | Paris, Maison Schott ÷
1 Rue Auber, (Maison du Grand Hôtel.) « » Bruxelles, Schott frères, ÷ 82 Montagne de la Cour. |
Londres, Schott & C° ÷ 159 Regent Street.

3 leaves (323 x 256 mm): pp. [1] lith title page, 2–5 engr music (serial 44–47), [6] blank.

CAPTION TITLE: p. 2, 'VALSE. | » F. Chopin, Op. 64. N° 1.'.

64#1-Schott-1 *(continued)*

64#1-Schott-1 *(concluded)*

FOOTLINE: pp. 2–5, 'I 6'. See note 3.

STAMPS: dealer, Roothaan, Amsterdam.

1. *Date:* See note 2.
2. This score is from Schott's collected edition of 1880 (Chominski & Turlo, p. 320). It has a passe-partout title page with decorated border.
3. The separate-issue page numbers 2–5 are in the footline; serial page numbers 44–47 are in the headline.

London: Wessel (6321) [= 1848] 64#1-W-1 M32.C54 W6204

Nº [handwritten "69"] OF | WESSEL & Cº.s COMPLETE COLLECTION | OF | *the Compositions* | OF | FREDERIC CHOPIN | FOR THE | Piano Forte. | Solo & Duet | [list of works, Wessel 1–68] | 69 DEUX VALSES. *Nº 1, in D* [flat] | *Op. 64, ea. 2/-* | [list of works, Wessel 70–71] | *Ent. Sta. Hall. « Copyrights. » Price. Solo* [handwritten "2/-"] | *LONDON,* | WESSEL & Cº *Importers and Publishers of* FOREIGN MUSIC, | *(by special Appointment) to H.R.H. the Duchess of Kent.* | Nº 229, Regent Street, Corner of Hanover Street.

4 leaves (334 x 250 mm): pp. [i] engr title page, [ii] blank, [1] advt, 2–5 engr music, [6] blank.

CAPTION TITLE: p. 2, 'WESSEL & CO'S EDITION OF FREDERIC CHOPIN'S WORKS. Nº 69. | VALSE. | DEDIÉE À MADAME LA COMTESSE DELPHINE POTOCKA, BY | FREDERIC CHOPIN.'.

SUB-CAPTION: p. 2, 'OP: 64. | (1RE)'.

FOOTLINE: p. 2, '(W & Cº Nº 6321)'; pp. 3–4, 'CHOPIN, Op: 64. Valse. (1re) « » (W & Cº Nº 6321)'; p. 5, 'CHOPIN, Op: 64. Valse. (1re) « (Nº 6321) » WESSEL & Cº Nº 229, REGENT STREET, CORNER OF HANOVER STREET.'.

ADVT: p. [1], '[clipped? to] WESSEL & CO.S CATALOGUE OF MODERN PIANOFORTE WORKS, CONTINUED FROM PAGES A. B. C. E. & S.'. There are no Chopin works.

STAMPS: publisher, style W/D (see Appendix 8).

1. *Date:* first-edition inference (date code fe, p. 17).

London: Wessel (6321) [1856–60] 64#1-W-2 M32.C54 W62041

This score lacks the title page.

3 leaves (334 x 250 mm): pp. [i, ii] missing, [1] advt, 2–5 engr music, [6] blank.

CAPTION TITLE: p. 2, 'WESSEL & CO'S EDITION OF FREDERIC CHOPIN'S WORKS. Nº 69. | VALSE. | DEDIÉE À MADAME LA COMTESSE DELPHINE POTOCKA, BY | FREDERIC CHOPIN.'.

SUB-CAPTION: p. 2, 'OP: 64. | (1RE)'.

FOOTLINE: p. 2, '(W & Cº Nº 6321)'; pp. 3–4, 'CHOPIN, Op: 64. Valse. (1re) « » (W & Cº Nº 6321)'; p. 5, 'CHOPIN, Op: 64. Valse. (1re) « (Nº 6321) WESSEL & Cº '.

64#1-W-2 *(continued)*

64#1-W-2 *(concluded)*

ADVT: p. [1], 'PIANOFORTE COMPOSITIONS, | OF | IGNACE TEDESCO.'; at the foot, 'WESSEL & CO., 18, HANOVER SQUARE.'.

STAMPS: This score lacks the title page.

---

1. *Date:* based on the address in the advt (Table 5D).

***London:* Cramer, Beale (4368) [= 1848]** **64#1-CB-1** **M32.C54 W6205**

Nº [blank] | DEUX VALSES | *pour le* | PIANO | *par* | F. CHOPIN. | *ENT. STA. HALL.* « OP. 64. » *Pr. 2/* | *LONDRES:* | CRAMER, BEALE & CIE 201, REGENT ST. | *& 67, CONDUIT ST.*

4 leaves (344 x 248 mm): pp. [i] engr title page, [ii, 1] blank, 2–5 engr music, [6] blank.

CAPTION TITLE: p. 2, 'VALSE. Nº *1.* | » F. CHOPIN. OP: 64.'.

FOOTLINE: pp. 2–5, '4368'.

STAMPS: publisher, style CB/A (see Appendix 8).

---

1. *Date:* first-edition inference (date code fe, p. 17).
2. Brown (p. 171): "Cramer & Beale's edition was pirated. They published the third waltz later as 'Op. 64: no. 3'.".

Opus 64, Waltz 2

***Paris:* Brandus (4743(2)) [= 1847]** **64#2-Bra-1** **M32.C54 W622 c.1**

à Madame la Baronne | Nathaniel de Rothschild. | TROIS | VALSES | POUR | PIANO | PAR | *F. CHOPIN.* | AV | *Op: 64.* « » *Prix 5.^{f}* | Nº 2. | *PARIS,* | *Maison M^{CE} SCHLESINGER,* BRANDUS et CIE *Successeurs, Rue Richelieu, 97.* | *Leipzig, Breitkopf et Hartel* « *B. et CIE 4743.* » *Londres, Jullien et CIE*

5 leaves (350 x 270 mm): pp. [i] engr title page, [ii, 1] blank, 2–7 engr music, [8] blank.

CAPTION TITLE: p. 2, 'F. CHOPIN « » Op: 64. 3 VALSES. | VALSE.'.

SUB-CAPTION: p. 2, 'Nº 2.'.

FOOTLINE: pp. 2–7, 'B. et Cie 4743.(2)'.

WRAPPER (yellow): pp. [1] same as title page, [2, 3] blank, [4] advt.

ADVT: wrapper p. [4], 'BRANDUS et Cie, éditeurs de musique, 87, rue Richelieu. | MUSIQUE FACILE DE PIANO.'. No Chopin works are listed. See note 2.

STAMPS: publisher, style Bra/A (see Appendix 8).

---

1. *Date:* first-edition inference (date code fe, p. 17).
2. Brandus occupied the premises at 87 rue Richelieu in 1849–50 (Table 5A).

Paris: **Brandus** (4743(2)) [= 1847] **64#2-Bra-2** **M32.C54 W622 c.2**

The transcription of this title page is the same as that of **64#2-Bra-1.**

5 leaves (336 x 260 mm): pp. [i] engr title page, [ii, 1] blank, 2–7 engr music, [8] blank.

CAPTION TITLE: p. 2, 'F. CHOPIN. « » Op: 64. 3 VALSES. | VALSE.'.

SUB-CAPTION: p. 2, 'N° 2.'.

FOOTLINE: pp. 2–7, 'B. et Cie 4743.(2)'.

STAMPS: publisher, style Bra/B (see Appendix 8).

1. *Date:* first-edition inference (date code fe, p. 17).

Leipzig: **Breitkopf & Härtel** (7716) [= 1847] **64#2-BH-1** **M32.C54 W6235**

Trois | VALSES | pour le | PIANO | composées | PAR | FREDERIC CHOPIN. | Op. 64. | *N^{o} I.* [*sic*] « Propriété des Editeurs. » *Pr. 15 Ngr.* | Leipzig, chez Breitkopf & Härtel. | Paris, chez Brandus & Co | *7715. 16. 17.* | *Enrégistré aux Archives de l'Union.*

4 leaves (323 x 256 mm): pp. [1] lith title page, [2] blank, 3–7 engr music, [8] blank.

CAPTION TITLE: p. 3, 'VALSE.'.

SUB-CAPTION: p. 3, 'N$^{o.}$ 2.'.

FOOTLINE: pp. 3–7, '7716'.

STAMPS: publisher, style BH/G (see Appendix 8).

1. *Date:* first-edition inference (date code fe, p. 17).
2. The music plates of 64#2-BH-1 differ from those of #2 in 64-BH-1.
3. Concerning various title-page designs for the Breitkopf editions of Op. 64, see Appendix 3.

Brussels: **Schott** (I 7) [*ca* 1880] **64#2-Schott-1** **M32.C54 W6237**

OEUVRES POUR LE PIANO | composées par | F. CHOPIN | 1^{R} VOLUME | VALSES, BERCEUSE, MARCHE FUNEBRE. | [thematic list of Opp. 18, 34(#1, 2, 3), 42, 64(#1, 2, 3), 57, 35] | 2^{E} VOLUME ÷ NOCTURNES | 3^{E} VOLUME ÷ MAZURKAS | CHAQUE VOLUME net. Fr 7. — | En volumes, en édition in 8°. Separément en édition in 4°. | Paris, Maison Schott ÷ 1 Rue Auber, (Maison du Grand Hôtel.) « » Bruxelles, Schott frères, ÷ 82 Montagne de la Cour. | Londres, Schott & Co ÷ 159 Regent Street.

4 leaves (323 x 256 mm): pp. [1] lith title page, 2–7 engr music (serial 48–53), [8] blank.

CAPTION TITLE: p. 2, 'VALSE. | » F. Chopin, Op. 64. N° 2.'.

FOOTLINE: pp. 2–7, 'I 7'. See note 3.

64#2-Schott-1 *(continued)*

64#2-Schott-1 *(concluded)*

STAMPS: dealer, Roothaan, Amsterdam.

1. *Date:* See note 2.
2. This score is from Schott's collected edition of 1880 (Chominski & Turlo, p. 320). It has a passe-partout title page with decorated border.
3. The separate-issue page numbers 2–7 are in the footline; serial page numbers 48–53 are in the headline.

London: **Wessel (6322) [= 1848]** **64#2-W-1** **M32.C54 W625**

N° [handwritten "70"] OF | WESSEL & C°.'s COMPLETE COLLECTION | OF | *the Compositions* | OF | FREDERIC CHOPIN | FOR THE | Piano Forte. | Solo & Duet | [list of works, Wessel 1–69] | 70 D° [DEUX VALSES.] *N° 2, in C* [sharp] *min.* | *Op. 64, ea. 2/-* | [list of works, Wessel 71] | *Ent. Sta. Hall.* « *Copyrights.* » *Price, Solo* [handwritten "2/-" ÷ " *Duet* [blank]] | *LONDON,* | WESSEL & C° *Importers and Publishers of* FOREIGN MUSIC, | *(by special Appointment) to H.R.H. the Duchess of Kent.* | N° 229, Regent Street, Corner of Hanover Street.

4 leaves (334 x 249 mm): pp. [1] engr title page, 2–7 engr music, [8] advt.

CAPTION TITLE: p. 2, 'WESSEL & CO'S EDITION OF FREDERIC CHOPIN'S WORKS. N° 70. | VALSE. | DÉDIÉE A MADAME LA BARONNE NATHANIEL DE ROTHSCHILD, PAR | FREDERIC CHOPIN.'.

SUB-CAPTION: p. 2, 'OP: 64. | 2ME'.

FOOTLINE: p. 2, '(W & C° N° 6322)'; pp. 3–6, 'CHOPIN, Op: 64. Valse. (2me) « (W & C° N° 6322)'; p. 7, 'CHOPIN, Op: 64. Valse. (2me) « (N° 6322) » WESSEL & C° N° 229, REGENT STREET, CORNER OF HANOVER STREET.'.

ADVT: p. [8], 'PAGE T. | WESSEL & Co.'s SERIES OF GERMAN SONGS, (THIRD LIST. No. 274 to 500.) | 229, REGENT STREET, CORNER OF HANOVER STREET.'.

STAMPS: publisher, style W/D (see Appendix 8).

1. *Date:* first-edition inference (date code fe, p. 17).
2. Pagination with [1] (rather than [i]) for the title page is unusual in Wessel's Chopin editions.

London: **Cramer, Beale (4369) [= 1848]** **64#2-CB-1** **M32.C54 W6236**

N° [blank] | DEUX VALSES | *pour le* | PIANO | *par* | F. CHOPIN. | *ENT. STA. HALL.* « OP. 64. » *Pr. 2/* | *LONDRES:* | CRAMER, BEALE & CIE 201, REGENT ST. | *& 67, CONDUIT ST.*

5 leaves (330 x 259 mm): pp. [i] engr title page, [ii, 1] blank, 2–7 engr music, [8] blank.

CAPTION TITLE: p. 2, 'VALSE. N° 2. | » F. CHOPIN. OP: 64.'.

FOOTLINE: pp. 2–7, '4369'.

STAMPS: none.

INSCRIPTIONS: "Mr [?] Crompton".

64#2-CB-1 *(continued)*

64#2-CB-1 *(concluded)*

1. *Date:* first-edition inference (date code fe, p. 17).
2. Brown (p. 171): "Cramer & Beale's edition was pirated. They published the third waltz later as 'Op. 64: no. 3'.".

Opus 64, Waltz 3

Paris: **Brandus (4743(3)) [= 1847]** **64#3-Bra-1** **M32.C54 W623**

à Mademoiselle Comtesse | Catherine Branicka. | TROIS VALSES | POUR | *PIANO* | PAR | F. CHOPIN. | AV | *Op: 64.* « » *Prix 5.f* | N° 3. | *PARIS,* | *Maison M.CE SCHLESINGER,* BRANDUS et C.IE *Successeurs, Rue Richelieu, N° 97.* | *Leipzig, Breitkopf et Hartel « B. et C.IE 4743. » Londres, Jullien et C.IE*

5 leaves (336 x 260 mm): pp. [i] engr title page, [ii, 1] blank, 2–7 engr music, [8] blank.

CAPTION TITLE: p. 2, 'F. CHOPIN « » Op: 64. 3 VALSES, | VALSE.'.

SUB-CAPTION: p. 2, 'N° 3.'.

FOOTLINE: pp. 2–6, 'B. et C.ie 4743.(3)'; p. 7, 'B. et C.ie 4743.(3) » Brandus et C.ie rue Richelieu 97.'.

STAMPS: publisher, style Bra/B (see Appendix 8).

1. *Date:* first-edition inference (date code fe, p. 17).

Paris: **H. Lemoine (5368) [*ca* 1859]** **64#3-hL-1** **M32.C54 W624**

à Mademoiselle la Comtesse | Catherine Branicka. | 3 | VALSES | *POUR* | PIANO | PAR | FR. CHOPIN | Op. 64. N° 3. | *Prix net 55 Centimes.* | P. | *à Paris, H. LEMOINE, Editeur.* | *Rue S.t Honoré, N° 256.* | *COMMISSION (HL. 5368.) EXPORTATION.* | [handwritten:] *Lith. Boisgontier Boul.d S.t Jacques 16.*

4 leaves (301 x 224 mm): pp. [1] lith title page, 2–7 lith music, [8] blank.

CAPTION TITLE: p. 2, 'VALSE | FR. CHOPIN Op. 64. « » *à M.elle la C.esse Catherine BRANICKA* | N° 3.'.

FOOTLINE: p. 2, '12.e [?] Degré des Tablette du Pianiste de Hry LEMOINE. « 5368. HL. » *M.me V.e RIS graveur.*'; pp. 3–7, '5368. HL.'.

STAMPS: successor, style aL/C (see Appendix 8); dealer, Emery, Geneva.

1. *Date:* based on Chominski & Turlo (p. 270), and in agreement with Devriès & Lesure (p. 280) for plate number 5368.
2. This score is part of the Lemoine collected edition of 1859–94 (Chominski & Turlo, p. 270).

Leipzig: **Breitkopf & Härtel (7717) [= 1847]** **64#3-BH-1** **M32.C54 W6258**

Trois | VALSES | pour le Piano | composées | par | FRÉD. CHOPIN. | Op. 64. | *N° I. [sic]* « » *Pr. 15 Ngr.* | Propriété des Editeurs. | Leipzig, chez Breitkopf & Härtel. | Paris, chez Brandus & C.° | *7715. 16. & 17.* | *Enrégistré aux Archives de l'Union.*

4 leaves (317 x 255 mm): pp. [1] lith title page, [2] blank, 3–7 engr music, [8] blank.

CAPTION TITLE: p. 3, 'VALSE.'.

64#3-BH-1 *(continued)*

64#3-BH-1 *(concluded)*

SUB-CAPTION: p. 3, 'No. 3.'.

FOOTLINE: pp. 3–7, '7717'.

STAMPS: publisher, style BH/C (see Appendix 8); dealer, Bekker, Utrecht.

1. *Date:* first-edition inference (date code fe, p. 17).
2. The music plates of 64#3-BH-1 differ from those of 64-BH-1.
3. Concerning various title-page designs for the Breitkopf editions of Op. 64, see Appendix 3.

***Brussels:* Schott (I 8) [*ca* 1880]** **64#3-Schott-1** **M32.C54 W6256**

OEUVRES POUR LE PIANO | composées par | F. CHOPIN | 1R VOLUME | VALSES, BERCEUSE, MARCHE FUNEBRE. | [thematic list of Opp. 18, 34(#1, 2, 3), 42, 64(#1, 2, 3), 57, 35] | 2E VOLUME ÷ NOCTURNES | 3E VOLUME ÷ MAZURKAS | CHAQUE VOLUME net. Fr 7. — | En volumes, en édition in 8o. Separément en édition in 4o. | Paris, Maison Schott ÷ 1 Rue Auber, (Maison du Grand Hôtel.) « » Bruxelles, Schott frères, ÷ 82 Montagne de la Cour. | Londres, Schott & Co ÷ 159 Regent Street.

4 leaves (323 x 256 mm): pp. [1] lith title page, 2–7 engr music (serial 54–59), [8] blank.

CAPTION TITLE: p. 2, 'VALSE. | » F. Chopin, Op. 64. No 3.'.

FOOTLINE: pp. 2–7, 'I 8'. See note 3.
STAMPS: dealer, Roothaan, Amsterdam.

1. *Date:* See note 2.
2. This score is from Schott's collected edition of 1880 (Chominski & Turlo, p. 320). It has a passe-partout title page with decorated border.
3. The separate-issue page numbers 2–7 are in the footline; serial page numbers 54–59 are in the headline.

***London:* Wessel (6323) [= 1848]** **64#3-W-1** **M32.C54 W626**

No [handwritten "71"] OF | WESSEL & Co.'s COMPLETE COLLECTION | OF | *the Compositions* | OF | FREDERIC CHOPIN | FOR THE | Piano Forte. | Solo & Duet | [list of works, Wessel 1–70] | 71 VALSE. *No 3, in A* [flat] | *Op. 64, ea. 2/-* | *Ent. Sta. Hall. « Copyrights. » Price.* [handwritten "2/"] | *LONDON,* | WESSEL & Co *Importers and Publishers of* FOREIGN MUSIC, | *(by special Appointment) to H.R.H. the Duchess of Kent.* | No 229, Regent Street, Corner of Hanover Street.

4 leaves (334 x 250 mm): pp. [1] engr title page, 2–7 engr music, [8] advt.

CAPTION TITLE: p. 2, 'WESSEL & CO'S EDITION OF FREDERIC CHOPIN'S WORKS. No 71. | VALSE, | DÉDIÉE À MADAME LA COMTESSE CATHERINE BRANICKA. | PAR | FREDERIC CHOPIN.'.

SUB-CAPTION: p. 2, 'OP: 64. | (3ME)'.

FOOTLINE: p. 2, '(W & Co No 6323.)'; pp. 3–6, 'CHOPIN, Op: 64. Valse. (3me) « » (W & Co No 6323.)'; p. 7, 'CHOPIN, Op: 64. Valse. (3me) « (No 6323.) » WESSEL & Co No 229, REGENT STREET, CORNER OF HANOVER STREET.'.

64#3-W-1 *(continued)*

64#3-W-1 *(concluded)*

ADVT: p. [8], 'PAGE S. | WESSEL & Co.'s EDITIONS OF THE PIANOFORTE WORKS (SOLO) BY CHOPIN, | HELLER, SCHULHOFF, KULLAK, AND AGUILAR.'. Chopin works are listed through Op. 64, and the Marche Funèbre extracted from the Sonata Op. 35.

STAMPS: publisher, style W/D (see Appendix 8).

1. *Date:* first-edition inference (date code fe, p. 17).

SONATA IN G MINOR FOR PIANO AND CELLO
Opus 65

Paris: Brandus (4744) 1847	*Composed* 1845–46
Leipzig: Breitkopf & Härtel (7718) 1848	Brown 160
	Chominski & Turlo 204

Paris: **Brandus (4744) [= 1847]** — **65-Bra-1** — **M231.C54 S612**

SONATE | POUR | Piano et Violoncelle, | *dédiée à son ami* | *A. Franchomme,* |
Professeur au Conservatoire de Paris, | PAR | F. CHOPIN. | *A.V.* | *Op: 65.* « » *Prix 15* ^{f} |
PARIS, | *Maison M*^{CE} *SCHLESINGER,* BRANDUS et CIE *Successeurs, Rue Richelieu, N°. 97.* |
Leipzig, Breitkopf et Hartel « *B. et C*^{IE} *4744.* » *Londres, Jullien et C*^{IE}

Piano: 17 leaves (350 x 267 mm): pp. [i] engr title page, [ii] blank, 1–31 engr music, [32] blank.

CAPTION TITLE: p. 1, 'F. CHOPIN. « » Op. 65. | SONATE.'.

FOOTLINE: p. 1, 'B. et Cie 4744. » Brandus et Cie rue Richelieu 97.'; pp. 2–31, 'B. et Cie 4744.'.

Violoncelle: The cello part is not present in this copy.

TEXT: The piano part includes the cello staff throughout.

STAMPS: successor, style BD/D (see Appendix 8).

1. *Date:* first-edition inference (date code fe, p. 17).

Paris: **Brandus & Dufour (4744) [after 1857]** — **65-BD-1** — **M231.C54 S6**

ÉDITION ORIGINALE | OEUVRES COMPLÈTES POUR LE PIANO | DE | FRÉDÉRIC CHOPIN | SEULE ÉDITION AUTHENTIQUE | SANS CHANGEMENTS NI ADDITIONS, PUBLIÉE D'APRÈS LES ÉPREUVES CORRIGÉES PAR L'AUTEUR LUI-MÊME. | [list of works Opp. 1–64] | Op. 65. Sonate, piano et violoncelle (dédiée à Franchomme) 15 " [f] | [list of three works without opus number] | Paris, G. BRANDUS ET S. DUFOUR, Éditeurs | 103, rue de Richelieu, 103. |
[below the decorated border:] IMPRIMERIE CENTRALE DES CHEMINS DE FER. « »
A. CHAIX ET Ce, RUE BERGÈRE, 20, A PARIS. | 238-0

Piano: 17 leaves (344 x 275 mm): pp. [i] lith title page, [ii] blank, 1–31 engr music, [32] blank.

CAPTION TITLE: p. 1, 'F. CHOPIN. « » Op. 65. | SONATE.'.

FOOTLINE: p. 1, 'B. et Cie 4744. » Brandus et Cie rue Richelieu 97.'; pp. 2–31, 'B. et Cie 4744.'.

Violoncelle: 5 leaves (344 x 275 mm): pp. 1–10 engr music.

CAPTION TITLE: p. 1, 'F. CHOPIN. « » Op: 65. | SONATE.'.

HEADLINE: pp. 2–10, 'VIOLONCELLE.'.

FOOTLINE: pp. 1–10, 'B. et Cie 4744.'.

TEXT: The piano part includes the cello staff throughout.

65-BD-1 *(continued)*

65-BD-1 *(concluded)*

STAMPS: successor, style Bra/E (see Appendix 8); dealer, Maho, Paris.

1. *Date:* based on the publisher's name (Table 5A).

Paris: **Richault (4360) [*ca* 1860]** **65-Rich-1** **M231.C54 S61**

dédiée à son Ami | A. Franchomme. | SONATE | POUR | PIANO et VIOLONCELLE | OU VIOLON | PAR | F. CHOPIN | Æ | *Op: 65.* « » *Prix: 20.f* | *La Partie de Violon par David* | *PARIS,* S. RICHAULT, *EDITr* | *Boulev.t Poissonière, 26 au 1er* | Æ | *4360 R.*

Piano: 21 leaves (350 x 270 mm): pp. [i] engr title page, [ii, 71] blank, 72–109 engr music, [110] blank.

CAPTION TITLE: p. 72, 'a son Ami A: FRANCHOMME. | SONATE. | Pour PIANO et VIOLONCELLE. « » *F. CHOPIN, Oeuvre* 65.'.

FOOTLINE: pp. 72–109, '4360. R.'.

Violoncelle: 5 leaves (350 x 270 mm): pp. 1–10 engr music.

CAPTION TITLE: p. 1, same as piano, p. 72.

HEADLINE: pp. 1–10, 'VIOLONCELLE.'.

FOOTLINE: pp. 1–10, '4360. R. (3)'.

Violon: 4 leaves (350 x 270 mm): pp. 1–8 engr music.

CAPTION TITLE: p. 1, '» F. CHOPIN, Op: 65.'.

HEADLINE: pp. 1–8, 'VIOLON.'.

FOOTLINE: pp. 1–8, '4360. R.'.

STAMPS: publisher, style Rich/A (see Appendix 8); dealer, Flaxland, Paris.

1. *Date:* This score is from volume 10 of the 12 volumes of Chopin's collected works edited by Tellefsen and published by Richault *ca* 1860, with plate numbers 4351 to 4362 (Chominski & Turlo, p. 279; Brown, p. 185). The title-page address, 26 Boulevard Poissonniére, was occupied from 1841 until the firm moved to 4 Boulevard des Italiens in October 1862 (Devriès & Lesure, p. 365).
2. The pagination indicates that Op. 65 follows Op. 3 in volume 10 (see 3-Rich-1).

Leipzig: **Breitkopf & Härtel (7718) [1872–73]** **65-BH-1** **M231.C54 S613**

SONATE | pour Piano et Violoncelle | dédiée | à son ami Aug. Franchomme | Prof. du Conservatoire de musique à Paris | par | FRÉD. CHOPIN. | Op. 65. | Propriété des Editeurs. | Leipzig, chez Breitkopf & Härtel. | *Paris, chez Brandus & Co.* | Pr. 2 Thlr. | Mk. 6. __ | *Enrégistré aux Archive de l'Union.* | *7718.*

Piano: 18 leaves (305 x 244 mm): pp. [1] lith title page, [2] blank, 3–35 engr music, [36] blank.

CAPTION TITLE: p. 3, 'SONATE. | » F. Chopin, Op. 65.'.

FOOTLINE: pp. 3–35, '7718'.

Violoncelle: 4 leaves (305 x 244 mm): pp. 1–8 engr music.

CAPTION TITLE: p. 1, '» F. Chopin, Op. 65.'.

SUB-CAPTION: p. 1, 'SONATE.'.

65-BH-1 *(continued)*

65-BH-1 *(concluded)*

HEADLINE: pp. 1–8, 'VIOLONCELLE.'.

FOOTLINE: pp. 1–8, '7718'.

TEXT: The piano part includes the cello staff throughout.

STAMPS: publisher, style BH/I (see Appendix 8); dealer (agent?), Stanley, Lucas, Weber; London.

---

1. *Date:* currency inference (date code c3, p. 17).
2. This score corresponds to Hob-459.

POSTHUMOUS WORKS EDITED BY FONTANA
Opus 66 – Opus 73

Paris: Meissonnier Fils (3523)–(3532) 1855
Berlin: A. Schlesinger (4392)–(4401) 1855

Composed 1827–49
Brown: see individual works
Chominski & Turlo: see individual works

Paris: Meissonnier Fils (3523)–(3532) [= 1855] 66/73-MeiF-1 M22.C54 P577

ŒUVRES | POSTHUMES | POUR | PIANO | DE | FRÉD. CHOPIN | PUBLIÉS SUR MANUSCRITS ORIGINAUX AVEC AUTORISATION | DE SA FAMILLE | PAR | JULES FONTANA. |

1re Livraison.	FANTAISIE-IMPROMPTU.	Prix 6 "
2e —	QUATRE MAZURKAS. No 1 à 4	6 "
3e —	QUATRE MAZURKAS. No 5 à 8	6 "
4e —	DEUX VALSES. No 1 et 2	6 "
5e —	TROIS VALSES. No 3 à 5	6 "
6e —	TROIS POLONAISES. No 1, 2 et 3	Chaque 6 "
7e —	NOCTURNE, MARCHE FUNÈBRE et 3 ÉCOSSAISES	6 "
8e —	RONDO A DEUX PIANOS	15 "

LA COLLECTION COMPLÈTE | PRÉCÉDÉE D'UNE PRÉFACE PAR J. Fontana, ET ornée d'un Portrait LITHOGRAPHIÉ PAR RAUNHEIM. | *Brochée,* 20 *fr. net.* — *Reliée,* 30 *fr. net.* | Paris, J. MEISSONNIER FILS, éditeur-commissionnaire, 18, rue Dauphine, | PROPRIÉTAIRE POUR LA FRANCE ET LA BELGIQUE. | Berlin, A. M. Schlesinger. « » Londres, Stationner's [*sic*] Hall. | Paris — Impr. de L. Martinet, rue Mignon, 2.

3 leaves of preliminaries (336 x 258 mm): pp. [i] colored lith collective title page, [ii] blank, [iii] colored lith portraits of Chopin, [iv] blank, 1–2 preface by Fontana ("Paris, Mai 1855").

FOOTLINE: pp. 1–2 'J.M. 3523 à 3532.'.

TEXT: The portraits of Chopin (p. [iii]) are: a full face, dated 1830; a bust in profile, dated 1839; and a profile, dated 1847. At the foot: "Imp. Lemercier, Paris" and "Raunheim 1855.".

STAMPS: publisher, style Mei/B (see Appendix 8).

INSCRIPTIONS: presentation "Hommage à Mme. P. Viardot | J. Fontana | 1857." on title page.

BINDING: contemporary mottled boards, modern half calf.

1. *Date:* first-edition inference (date code fe, p. 17).
2. This bound *(reliée)* volume contains the French edition of the complete set of eight posthumous works edited by Fontana. After the preliminaries, paginated above, are the individual works, each paginated individually, and each with an abbreviated title similar to a half title. The above entry describes the volume as a whole. Separate entries that follow, by opus number, describe the individual works.
3. The Meissonnier and the Gérard editions have no Opus numbers. These were presumably assigned by Schlesinger (see the footline in 66-aS-1). For other comments on Opp. 66–73, see Appendix 4.

FANTAISIE-IMPROMPTU IN C SHARP MINOR
Opus 66

Paris: Meissonnier Fils (3523) 1855	*Composed* 1834
Berlin: A. Schlesinger (4392) 1855	Brown 87
London: Ewer (—) ?	Chominski & Turlo 46

Paris: **Meissonnier Fils (3523) [= 1855]** **66-MeiF-1** **M22.C54 P577**

Fantaisie-Impromptu | 1re Livraison | *des œuvres posthumes* | DE | F. CHOPIN | *A.V.* | *(J. M. 3523.)*

6 leaves (336 x 258 mm): pp. [i] engr half-title page, [ii] blank, 1–9 engr music, [10] blank.

CAPTION TITLE: p. 1, 'FANTAISIE - IMPROMPTU | par | FRÉDÉRIC CHOPIN. | OEuvres posthumes. « » 1ère Livraison.'.

SUB-CAPTION: p. 1, '(vers 1834) | *PIANO.*'.

FOOTLINE: p. 1, 'Paris, imp. Bauve, 14 rue St Marc. « J.M. 3523.'; pp. 2–9, 'J.M. 3523.'.

STAMPS: none.

BOUND WITH: See 66/73-MeiF-1, note 2.

1. *Date:* first-edition inference (date code fe, p. 17).
2. For the collective title, see 66/73-MeiF-1 (preceding this entry).

Paris: **Gérard (J.M. 3523) [after 1866]** **66-Gér-1** **M25.C54 F211**

ŒUVRES | POSTHUMES | POUR | PIANO | DE | FRÉD. CHOPIN | PUBLIÉES SUR MANUSCRITS ORIGINAUX AVEC AUTORISATION | DE SA FAMILLE | PAR | JULES FONTANA |

1re LIVRAISON.	FANTAISIE-IMPROMPTU.	Prix	6 "
2e —	QUATRE MAZURKAS. Nos 1 à 4		6 "
3e —	QUATRE MAZURKAS. Nos 5 à 8		6 "
4e —	DEUX VALSES. Nos 1 à 2		6 "
5e —	TROIS VALSES. Nos 3 à 5		6 "
6e —	TROIS POLONAISES. Nos 1, 2 et 3	Chaque	6 "
7e —	NOCTURNE, MARCHE FUNÈBRE et TROIS ÉCOSSAISES		6 "
8e —	RONDO A DEUX PIANOS		15 "

LA COLLECTION COMPLÈTE | PRÉCÉDÉE D'UNE PRÉFACE PAR J. Fontana, et ornée d'un portrait LITHOGRAPHIÉ PAR RAUNHEIM | *Brochée,* 20 *fr. net.* *Reliée,* 30 *fr. net.* | PARIS | *ANCIENNE MAISON MEISSONNIER* | CI-DEVANT RUE DAUPHINE | E, GÉRARD et Cie , boulevard des CAPUCINES, 12, et rue SCRIBE, 2 | Maison du Grand-Hôtel | Berlin, A. M. Schlesinger. « » Londres, Stationner's Pall. [*sic*] | PARIS. — IMPRIMERIE DE E. MARTINET, RUE MIGNON, 2.

6 leaves (340 x 253 mm): pp. [i] lith collective title page, [ii] blank, 1–9 lith music, [10] advt.

CAPTION TITLE: p, 1, 'FANTAISIE-IMPROMPTU | par | FRÉDÉRIC CHOPIN. | OEuvres posthumes. « » 1ère Livraison.'.

66-Gér-1 *(continued)*

66-Gér-1 *(concluded)*

SUB-CAPTION: p. 1, '(vers 1834) | *PIANO.*'.

FOOTLINE: p. 1, 'Paris. Imp. Bauve [?], 14 rue St Marc. « J.M. 3523.'; pp. 2–9, 'J.M. 3523.'.

ADVT: p. [10], '*ANCIENNE MAISON MEISSONNIER, ci-devant rue Dauphine,* | EXTRAIT DU CATALOGUE DE MUSIQUE DE PIANO | DE E. GERARD et Cie, éditeurs-commissionnaires, boulevard des CAPUCINES , 12, et rue SCRIBE, 2. | MAISON DU GRAND HOTEL.'. Chopin works listed are Opp. 57, 58, and the œuvres posthumes.

STAMPS: publisher, style Gér/B (see Appendix 8); dealer, Maison Beethoven, Brussels.

---

1. *Date:* based on the address (Table 5B).
2. The title page is not colored. Its layout is the same as that of 73-Gér-1.

Berlin: **A. Schlesinger (4392) [= 1855]** **66-aS-1** **M25.C54 F21 c.1**

ŒUVRES POSTHUMES | POUR LE | PIANO | DE | FRÉD. CHOPIN | PUBLIÉS SUR MANUSCRITS ORIGINAUX AVEC AUTORISATION | DE SA FAMILLE, | PAR JULES FONTANA. |

1re LIVRAISON		FANTAISIE-IMPROMPTU. Op. 66.	2/3	THLR
2^e	—	QUATRE MAZURKAS No. 1–4. Op. 67.	2/3	"
3^e	—	QUATRE MAZURKAS No. 5–8. Op. 68.	2/3	"
4^e	—	DEUX VALSES No. 1–2. Op. 69.	2/3	"
5^e	—	TROIS VALSES No. 3–5. Op. 70.	2/3	"
6^e	—	TROIS POLONAISES No. 1. 2. 3. Op. 71.	à 2/3	"
7^e	—	NOCTURNE, MARCHE FUNÈBRE, 3 ECOSSAISES. Op. 72.	2/3	"
8^e	—	RONDO à DEUX PIANOS. Op. 73.	1 3/4	"

LA COLLECTION COMPLÈTE | PRÉCÉDÉE D'UNE PRÉFACE PAR J. FONTANA ET ORNEE D'UN PORTRAIT LITHOGR. PAR WALDOW, D'APRÈS ARY SCHEFFER. | PR. NET. 5 THLR. | PROPRIÉTÉ DES ÉDITEURS ENREGISTRÉE AUX ARCHIVES DE L'UNION. | BERLIN, CHEZ AD. MT. SCHLESINGER, 34 LINDEN. | PARIS & BRUXELLES, J. MEISSONNIER FILS. « » LONDRES, COPY-RIGHT, ENTERED AT STATIONERS HALL. | FIRENZE, G. G. GUIDI. « | S. 4392–4401. | DRUCK VON L. BURKHARDT IN BERLIN.

7 leaves (325 x 260 mm): pp. [1] lith (or letterpress?) collective title page, [2] blank, 3–11 engr music, [12] blank, [13, 14] preface.

CAPTION TITLE: p. 3, 'FANTAISIE – INPROMPTU [*sic*] | par | FRÉDÉRIC CHOPIN. | Oeuvres posthumes. Livr. I. « » Op. 66.'.

SUB-CAPTION: p. 3, '(vers 1834.) | PIANO.'.

FOOTLINE: p. 3, 'S. 4392. | Op. 66. indique l'ordre chronologique de la publication. l'Éditeur. « » Berlin, Propriété de Ad. Mt. Schlesinger'; pp. 4–11, 'S. 4392.'.

STAMPS: publisher, style aS/B (see Appendix 8).

---

1. *Date:* first-edition inference (date code fe, p. 17).
2. The misspelling of Impromptu in the caption title is corrected in 66-aS-2.

66-aS-1 *(continued)*

66-aS-1 *(concluded)*

3. The "Nietack" version of the title page is shown by Hoboken (plate 28, p. 189).
4. For other comments, see Appendix 4.

***Berlin:* A. Schlesinger (4392) [= 1855]** **66-aS-2** **M25.C54 F21 c.2**

The transcription of this title page is the same as that of 66-aS-1.

7 leaves (333 x 265 mm): pp. [i] lith (or letterpress?) collective title page, [ii] blank, [1, 2] preface, 3–11 engr music, [12] blank.

CAPTION TITLE: p. 3, 'FANTAISIE – IMPROMPTU | par | FRÉDÉRIC CHOPIN. | Oeuvres posthumes. Livr. I. « » Op. 66.'.

SUB-CAPTION: p. 3, '(vers 1834.) | PIANO.'.

FOOTLINE: p. 3, 'S. 4392. | Op. 66. indique l'ordre chronologique de la publication. l'Éditeur. « » Berlin, Propriété de Ad. Mt. Schlesinger'; pp. 4–11, 'S. 4392.'.

WRAPPER (blue): pp. [1] individual title page, [2, 3] advt, [4] blank.

INDIVIDUAL TITLE: wrapper p. [1], 'FANTAISIE–IMPROMPTU | Op. 66. | FR. CHOPIN. | Berlin, Propriété de A.d M.t Schlesinger. | PARIS, MEISSONNIER. FLORENCE, GUIDI. PETERSBOURG, [BLANK] LONDRES, COPY-RIGHT. | S. 4392.'.

ADVT: wrapper pp. [2, 3], 'Neue Musikalien | erscheinen 1858—1859 im Verlage der | Schlesinger'schen Buch- und Musikhandlung in BERLIN. | Durch alle solide Musikhandlungen zu haben.'. The list on p. 2 includes "Chopin. Oeuvres posthumes p. Piano. Op. 66–73. 9 Livr. à — 20 [Sgr.]" and "Dernière pensée musicale. Op. 68 VIII. — 5 [Sgr.]", as well as Op. 66 and Op. 69 arranged for piano four hands. The list on p. 3 has Chopin's songs Op. 74 in both the German- and Polish-language editions. At the end is a book on harmony dated 1860.

STAMPS: publisher, style aS/B (see Appendix 8).

BINDING: library cloth.

1. *Date:* first-edition inference (date code fe, p. 17). Although the wrapper advertisement has an 1860 date, there is no evidence this score is not a first edition.
2. For other comments, see Appendix 4.

***Milan:* Lucca (13614) [1856–62]** **66-Lu-1** **M25.C54 F208**

Fantaisie–Impromptu | *POUR* | PIANO | *1.re Livraison* | des œuvres posthumes | DE [slanted backward] | F. CHOPIN | *Propr. de l'Editeur* | » *13614 — Fr. 3.50* | MILAN F. LUCCA |
Florence, Dacci — Chiasso, Euterpe Ticinese — Naples, Girard et C — Turin, Blanchi

6 leaves (330 x 260 mm): p. [i] engr title page, [ii] blank, 1–9 engr music, [10] blank.

CAPTION TITLE: p. 1, 'FANTAISIE=IMPROMPTU | Œuvres posthumes « 1.ére LIVRAISON. » F. CHOPIN.'.

FOOTLINE: p. 1, *'Presso F. Lucca: Milano « v* 13614 *v'*; pp. 2–9, *'v* 13614 *v'*. The footline has series page numbers 5–13.

66-Lu-1 *(continued)*

66-Lu-1 *(concluded)*

STAMPS: none.

---

1. *Date:* The terminal date is from Chominski & Turlo, p. 272.
2. "Prop. de l'Editeur" on the title page appears to have been struck through.

MAZURKAS IN G MAJOR, G MINOR, C MAJOR, A MINOR
Opus 67

Paris: Meissonnier Fils (3524) 1855
Berlin: A. Schlesinger (4393) 1855

Composed 1835–49
Brown 93
Chominski & Turlo 92

***Paris:* Meissonnier Fils (3524) [= 1855]** **67-MeiF-1** **M22.C54 P577**

4 | MAZURKAS | *Nº 1 à 4.* | 2e Livraison | *des œuvres posthumes* | DE | F. CHOPIN | *A.V.* | *(J. M. 3524.)*

6 leaves (336 x 258 mm): pp. [i] engr half-title page, [ii, 1] blank, 2–10 engr music.

CAPTION TITLE: p. 2, 'QUATRE MAZURKAS | Nº 1 à 4 | par | FRÉDÉRIC CHOPIN. | OEuvres posthumes. « » 2e Livraison.'.

SUB-CAPTION: p. 2, '(1835) | Nº 1.'; p. 4, '(1849) | Nº 2.'; p. 6, '(1835) | Nº 3.'; p. 8, '(1846) | Nº 4.'.

FOOTLINE: p. 2, 'Paris, Imp: Bauve, 14 rue St Marc. « J.M. 3524.'; pp. 3–10, 'J.M. 3524.'.

STAMPS: none.

BOUND WITH: See 66/73-MeiF-1, note 2.

1. *Date:* first-edition inference (date code fe, p. 17).
2. For the collective title, see 66/73-MeiF-1 (preceding 66-MeiF-1).

***Paris:* Gérard (J.M. 3524) [after 1859]** **67-Gér-1** **M32.C54 M5852**

ŒUVRES | POSTHUMES | POUR | PIANO | DE | FRÉD. CHOPIN | PUBLIÉS SUR MANUSCRITS ORIGINAUX AVEC AUTORISATION | DE SA FAMILLE | PAR | JULES FONTANA |

1re Livraison.	FANTAISIE-IMPROMPTU.	Prix	6 "
2e —	QUATRE MAZURKAS. Nos 1 à 4		6 "
3e —	QUATRE MAZURKAS. Nos 5 à 8		6 "
4e —	DEUX VALSES. Nos 1 et 2		6 "
5e —	TROIS VALSES. Nos 3 à 5		6 "
6e —	TROIS POLONAISES. Nos 1, 2 et 3	Chaque	6 "
7e —	NOCTURNE, MARCHE FUNÈBRE et TROIS ÉCOSSAISES		6 "
8e —	RONDO A DEUX PIANOS		15 "

LA COLLECTION COMPLETE | PRÉCÉDÉE D'UNE PRÉFACE PAR J. Fontana, ET ornée d'un Portrait LITHOGRAPHIÉ PAR RAUNHEIM | *Brochée:* 20 *fr. net.* — *Reliée:* 30 *fr. net.* | ANCIENNE MAISON J. MEISSONNIER. | É. GÉRARD et Cie, éditeurs-commissionnaires, 18, RUE DAUPHINE, A PARIS | Berlin, A. M. Schlesinger. « » Londres, Stationner's Hall. | Paris. — Imp. de E. Martinet, rue Mignon. 2.

7 leaves (349 x 270 mm): pp. [i] colored lith title page, [ii, 1] blank, 2–10 engr music, [11] blank, [12] advt.

CAPTION TITLE: p. 2, 'QUATRE MAZURKAS | Nº 1 à 4 | par | FRÉDÉRIC CHOPIN. | OEuvres posthumes. « » 2e Livraison.'.

67-Gér-1 *(continued)*

67-Gér-1 *(concluded)*

SUB-CAPTION: p. 2, '(1835) | Nº 1.'; p. 4, '(1849) | Nº 2.'; p. 6, '(1835) | Nº 3.'; p. 8, '(1846) | Nº 4.'.

FOOTLINE: p. 2, 'Paris, Imp: Bauve, 14 rue St. Marc. « J.M. 3524.'; pp. 3–10, 'J.M. 3524.'.

ADVT: p. [12], 'ANCIENNE MAISON MEISSONNIER | EXTRAIT DU CATALOGUE DE MUSIQUE DE PIANO | DE E. GÉRARD ET CIE, Éditeurs-Commissionnaires, 18, RUE DAUPHINE'. The list includes Chopin's Berceuse Op. 57, Sonate Op. 58, and the posthumous works Opp. 66–73.

WRAPPER (faded yellow): pp. [1] half title, [2] blank, [3, 4] advt.

HALF TITLE: wrapper p. [1], '4 | MAZURKAS | *Nº 1 à 4.* | 2e. Livraison | *des œuvres posthumes* | DE | F. CHOPIN | *A. V.* | *(J. M. 3524.)*'.

ADVT: wrapper p. [3], 'ANCIENNE MAISON J. MEISSONNIER. | OUVRAGES DE FRANÇOIS HUNTEN ÉDITÉS PAR | E. GÉRARD ET CIE, Éditeurs-Commissionnaires, 18, RUE DAUPHINE. | PIANOS DE BOISSELOT ET FILS.'; p. [4], 'Ancienne maison Meissonnier. « EXTRAIT DU CATALOGUE DE MUSIQUE DE PIANO » Ancienne maison Meissonnier. | DE E. GÉRARD ET CIE, Éditeurs-Commissionnaires, 18, RUE DAUPHINE.'. There are no Chopin works in these lists.

STAMPS: publisher, style Gér/A (see Appendix 8).

---

1. *Date:* based on the publisher's address (Table 5B).
2. Except for the publisher's imprint, the layout of the title page is the same as that of 66/73-MeiF-1. The wording and spelling are also the same, except for the word "COMPLETE", which here has no accent on the first "E".

***Berlin:* A. Schlesinger (4393) [= 1855]** **67-aS-1** **M32.C54 M585**

ŒUVRES POSTHUMES | POUR LE | PIANO | DE | FRÉD. CHOPIN | PUBLIÉS SUR MANUSCRITS ORIGINAUX AVEC AUTORISATION | DE SA FAMILLE, | PAR JULES FONTANA. |

1re LIVRAISON.	FANTAISIE-IMPROMPTU	2/3	THLR
2e —	QUATRE MAZURKAS No. 1–4	2/3	"
3e —	QUATRE MAZURKAS No. 5–8	2/3	"
4e —	DEUX VALSES No. 1–2	2/3	"
5e —	TROIS VALSES No. 3–5	2/3	"
6e —	TROIS POLONAISES No. 1. 2. 3	à 2/3	"
7e —	NOCTURNE, MARCHE FUNÈBRE, TROIS ÉCOSSAISES	2/3	"
8e —	RONDO à DEUX PIANOS	1 3/4	"

LA COLLECTION COMPLÈTE | PRÉCÉDÉE D'UNE PRÉFACE PAR J. FONTANA, ET ORNÉE D'UN PORTRAIT LITHOGR. PAR WALDOW, D'APRÈS ARY SCHEFFER. | PR. NET. 5 THLR. | PROPRIÉTE DES ÉDITEURS. ENREGISTRÉE AUX ARCHIVES DE L'UNION. | BERLIN, CHEZ AD. MT. SCHLESINGER, 34 LINDEN. | PARIS & BRUXELLES, J. MEISSONNIER FILS. « » LONDRES, COPY-RIGHT, ENTERED AT STATIONERS HALL. | FIRENZE, G. G. GUIDI. « » PETERSBOURG, DUFOUR & CO. | S. 4392–4401. | DRUCK VON F. NIETACK IN BERLIN.

7 leaves (315 x 252 mm): pp. [1] lith title page, [2, 3] blank, 4–12 engr music, [13, 14] preface.

CAPTION TITLE: p. 4, 'QUATRE MAZURKAS | Nº 1 à 4 | par | FRÉDÉRIC CHOPIN. | Œuvres posthumes. Livr. II. « » Op. 67.'.

SUB-CAPTION: p. 4, '(1835.) | Nº 1.'; p. 6, '(1849.) | Nº 2.'; p. 8, '(1835.) | Nº 3.'; p. 10, '(1846.) | Nº 4.'.

67-aS-1 *(continued)*

67-aS-1 *(concluded)*

SUB-CAPTION: p. 4, '(1835.) | Nº 1.'; p. 6, '(1849.) | Nº 2.'; p. 8, '(1835.) | Nº 3.'; p. 10, '(1846.) | Nº 4.'.

FOOTLINE: p. 4, 'Op. 67. indique l'ordre chronologique de la publication. l'Editeur. « » Berlin. Propriété de Ad. Mt. Schlesinger. | S. 4393.'; pp. 5–12, 'S. 4393.'.

STAMPS: publisher, style aS/B (see Appendix 8).

---

1. *Date:* first-edition inference (date code fe, p. 17).
2. Each page of music has the complete-edition pagination (pp. 12–20) centered at the top.
3. For other comments, see Appendix 4.

MAZURKAS IN C MAJOR, A MINOR, F MAJOR, F MINOR
Opus 68

Paris: Meissonnier Fils (3525) 1855	*Composed* 1827–49
Berlin: A. Schlesinger (4394) 1855	Brown 18
	Chominski & Turlo 96

***Paris:* Meissonnier Fils (3525) [= 1855]** **68-MeiF-1** **M22.C54 P577**

QUATRE | Mazurkas | *N.º 5 à 8.* | 3.ᵉ Livraison | *des œuvres posthumes* | DE | F. CHOPIN | *A.V.* | *(J. M. 3525.)*

6 leaves (336 x 258 mm): pp. [i] engr half-title page, [ii, 1] blank, 2–9 engr music, [10] blank.

CAPTION TITLE: p. 2, 'QUATRE MAZURKAS | Nº 5 à 8 | par | FRÉDÉRIC CHOPIN. | OEuvres posthumes. « » 3.ᵉ Livraison.'.

SUB-CAPTION: p. 2, '(1830) | N.º 5.'; p. 4, '(1827) | N.º 6.'; p. 6, '(1830) | N.º 7.'; p. 8, '(1849) | N.º 8.'.

FOOTLINE: p. 2, 'Paris, Imp: Bauve, 14 rue S.ᵗ Marc. « J.M. 3525.'; pp. 3–9, 'J.M. 3525.'.

STAMPS: none.

BOUND WITH: See 66/73-MeiF-1, note 2.

1. *Date:* first-edition inference (date code fe, p. 17).
2. For the collective title, see 66/73-MeiF-1 (preceding 66-MeiF-1).

***Berlin:* A. Schlesinger (4394) [= 1855]** **68-aS-1** **M32.C54 M59**

The transcription of this title page is the same as that of 67-aS-1.

7 leaves (315 x 252 mm): pp. [1] lith title page, [2, 3] blank, 4–11 engr music, [12] blank, [13, 14] preface.

CAPTION TITLE: p. 4, 'QUATRE MAZURKAS | N.º 5 à 8 | par | FRÉDÉRIC CHOPIN. | Œuvres posthumes. Livr. III. « » Op. 68.'.

SUB-CAPTION: p. 4, '(1830.) | N.º 5.'; p. 6, '(1827.) | N.º 6.'; p. 8, '(1830.) | N.º 7.'; p. 10, '(1849.)* | N.º 8.'. On p. 10 the sub-caption has the following footnote, "Cette Mazurka est la dernière inspiration que Chopin ait jetée sur le papier, peu de temps avant sa mort; il était déjà trop malade pour l'essayer au piano.". Following this is a German translation.

FOOTLINE: p. 4, 'Op. 68. indique l'ordre chronologique de la publication. l'Editeur. « » Berlin. Propriété de Ad. Mt. Schlesinger. | S. 4394.'; pp. 5–11, 'S. 4394.'.

STAMPS: publisher, style aS/B (see Appendix 8).

1. *Date:* first-edition inference (date code fe, p. 17).
2. Each page of music has the complete-edition pagination (pp. 22–29) centered at the top.
3. For other comments, see Appendix 4.

WALTZES IN A FLAT MAJOR AND B MINOR
Opus 69

Paris: Meissonnier Fils (3526) 1855	*Composed* 1829–35
Berlin: A. Schlesinger (4395) 1855	Brown 95
	Chominski & Turlo 215

***Paris:* Meissonnier Fils (3526) [= 1855]** **69-MeiF-1** **M22.C54 P577**

[half title:] 2 | VALSES | *N° 1 à 2* | 4e Livraison | *des œuvres posthumes* | DE | F. CHOPIN | *A.V.* | *J. M. 3526.*

6 leaves (336 x 258 mm): pp. [i] engr half-title page, [ii, 1] blank, 2–10 engr music.

CAPTION TITLE: p. 2, 'DEUX VALSES | N°s 1 et 2 | par | FRÉDÉRIC CHOPIN. | OEuvres posthumes. « » 4e Livraison.'.

SUB-CAPTION: p. 2, '(1836) | 1re | VALSE'; p. 6, '(1829) | 2^e | VALSE'.

FOOTLINE: p. 2, 'Paris, Imp: Bauve, 14 rue St Marc. « J.M. 3526.'; pp. 3–10, 'J.M. 3526.'.

STAMPS: none.

BOUND WITH: See 66/73-MeiF-1, note 2.

1. *Date:* first-edition inference (date code fe, p. 17).
2. For the collective title, see 66/73-MeiF-1 (preceding 66-MeiF-1).
3. For earlier editions of Op. 69#2 see B35-Ew-1, note 2.

WALTZES IN G FLAT MAJOR, F MINOR, D FLAT MAJOR
Opus 70

Paris: Meissonnier Fils (3527) 1855 — *Composed* 1829–42
Berlin: A. Schlesinger (4396) 1855 — Brown 40
Chominski & Turlo 217

Paris: Meissonnier Fils (3527) [= 1855] — **70-MeiF-1** — **M22.C54 P577**

Trois Valses | *N 3 à 5* | 5e Livraison | *des œuvres posthumes* | DE | F. CHOPIN | *A.V.* | *(J. M. 3527.)*

6 leaves (336 x 258 mm): pp. [i] engr half-title page, [ii, 1] blank, 2–9 engr music, [10] blank.

CAPTION TITLE: p. 2, 'TROIS VALSES | N°s 3 4 et 5 | par | FRÉDÉRIC CHOPIN. | OEuvres posthumes. « » 5e Livraison.'.

SUB-CAPTION: p. 2, '(1835) | 3^{e} | VALSE'; p. 5, '(1845) | 4^{e} | VALSE'; p. 8, '(1830) | 5^{e} | VALSE'.

FOOTLINE: p. 2, 'Paris, Imp: Bauve, 14 rue St Marc. « J.M. 3527.'; pp. 3–9, 'J.M. 3527.'.

STAMPS: none.

BOUND WITH: See 66/73-MeiF-1, note 2.

1. *Date:* first-edition inference (date code fe, p. 17).
2. For the collective title, see 66/73-MeiF-1 (preceding 66-MeiF-1).
3. For earlier editions of Op. 70#2 see B35-Ew-1, note 2.

Berlin: A. Schlesinger (4396) [= 1855] — **70-aS-1** — **M32.C54 W7**

The transcription of this title page is the same as that of 67-aS-1.

7 leaves (315 x 252 mm): pp. [1] lith title page, [2, 3] blank, 4–11 engr music, [12] blank, [13, 14] preface.

CAPTION TITLE: p. 4, 'TROIS VALSES | N°s 3, 4 et 5. | par | FRÉDÉRIC CHOPIN. | Oeuvres posthumes. Livr. V. « » Op. 70.'.

SUB-CAPTION: p. 4, '(1835.) | 3^{e} | VALSE.'; p. 7, '(1843.) | 4^{e} | VALSE.'; p. 10, '(1830.) | 5^{e} | VALSE.'.

FOOTLINE: p. 4, 'S. 4396. | Op. 70. indique l'ordre chronologique de la publication. l'Editeur. « » Berlin. Propriété de Ad. Mt. Schlesinger.'; pp. 5–11, 'S. 4396.'.

STAMPS: publisher, style aS/B (see Appendix 8).

1. *Date:* first-edition inference (date code fe, p. 17).
2. Each page of music has the complete-edition pagination (pp. 40–47) centered at the top.
3. For other comments, see Appendix 4.

POLONAISES IN D MINOR, B FLAT MAJOR, F MINOR
Opus 71

Paris: Meissonnier Fils (3528) (3529) (3530) 1855
Berlin: A. Schlesinger (4397) (4398) (4399) 1855

Composed 1827, 1828, 1829
Brown 11, 24, 30
Chominski & Turlo 157

Opus 71, Polonaise 1

***Paris:* Meissonnier Fils (3528) [= 1855]** **71#1-MeiF-1** **M22.C54 P577**

3 | Polonaises | 6e Livraison | *des œuvres posthumes* | DE | F. CHOPIN |
A.V. | *(N°* [blank]*)* « » *Chaque: 6 f.* | *J. M. 3528. 29. 30*

6 leaves (336 x 258 mm): pp. [i] engr half-title page, [ii, 1] blank, 2–9 engr music, [10] blank.

CAPTION TITLE: p. 2, '1re POLONAISE | par | FRÉDÉRIC CHOPIN. | OEuvres posthumes. « » 6ème Livraison N° 1.'.

SUB-CAPTION: p. 2, '(1827) | *PIANO.*'.

FOOTLINE: p. 2, 'Paris, Imp: Bauve, 14 rue St Marc. « J.M. 3528.'; pp. 3–9, 'J.M. 3528.'.

STAMPS: none.

BOUND WITH: See 66/73-MeiF-1, note 2.

1. *Date:* first-edition inference (date code fe, p. 17).
2. For the collective title, see 66/73-MeiF-1 (preceding 66-MeiF-1).

***Berlin:* A. Schlesinger (4397) [= 1855]** **71#1-aS-1** **M32.C54 P856**

ŒUVRES POSTHUMES | POUR LE | PIANO | DE | FRÉD. CHOPIN | PUBLIÉS SUR MANUSCRITS ORIGINAUX AVEC AUTORISATION | DE SA FAMILLE, | PAR JULES FONTANA. |

1re LIVRAISON.		FANTAISIE-IMPROMPTU. Op. 66	2/3	THLR
2e	—	QUATRE MAZURKAS No. 1–4. Op. 67	2/3	"
3e	—	QUATRE MAZURKAS No. 5–8. Op. 68	2/3	"
4e	—	DEUX VALSES No. 1–2. Op. 69	2/3	"
5e	—	TROIS VALSES No. 3–5. Op. 70	2/3	"
6e	—	TROIS POLONAISES No. 1. 2. 3. Op. 71	à 2/3	"
7e	—	NOCTURNE, MARCHE FUNÈBRE, 3 ÉCOSSAISES. Op. 72	2/3	"
8e	—	RONDO à DEUX PIANOS. Op. 73	1 3/4	"

LA COLLECTION COMPLÈTE | PRÉCÉDÉE D'UNE PRÉFACE PAR J. FONTANA, ET ORNÉE D'UN PORTRAIT LITHOGR. PAR WALDOW, D'APRÈS ARY SCHEFFER. | PR. NET 5 THLR. | PROPRIÉTÉ DES ÉDITEURS. ENREGISTRÉE AUX ARCHIVES DE L'UNION. | BERLIN, CHEZ AD. MT. SCHLESINGER, 34 LINDEN. | PARIS & BRUXELLES, J. MEISSONNIER FILS. « » LONDRES, COPY-RIGHT, ENTERED AT STATIONERS HALL. | FIRENZE, G. G. GUIDI. « » PETERSBOURG, DUFOUR & Co. | LONDRES, EN COMMISSION CHEZ G. SCHEURMANN ET Co., 86. NEWGATE-STREET. | S. 4392–4401. | DRUCK VON L. BURKHARDT IN BERLIN.

71#1-aS-1 *(continued)*

71#1-aS-1 *(concluded)*

6 leaves (331 x 259 mm): pp. [3] lith title page, 4–11 engr music, [12] blank, [13, 14] preface.

CAPTION TITLE: p. 4, 'Ire POLONAISE | PAR | FRÉDÉRIC CHOPIN. | Oeuvres posthumes Livr. VI. N^o^ I. « » Op. 71. N° 1.'.

SUB-CAPTION: p. 4, '(1827) | PIANO.'.

FOOTLINE: p. 4, 'Op. 71. indique l'ordre chronologique de la publication. l'Editeur. « S. 4397. » Berlin. Propriété de Ad. Mt. Schlesinger.'; pp. 5–11, 'S. 4397.'.

STAMPS: publisher, style aS/B (see Appendix 8).

---

1. *Date:* first-edition inference (date code fe, p. 17).
2. Each page of music has the complete-edition pagination (pp. 48–55) centered at the top.
3. For other comments, see Appendix 4.

Opus 71, Polonaise 2

Paris: **Meissonnier Fils (3529) [= 1855]** **71#2-MeiF-1** **M22.C54 P577**

A half title is not present; see 71#1-MeiF-1.

6 leaves (336 x 258 mm): pp. 2–9 engr music (see imposition).

CAPTION TITLE: p. 2, '2e POLONAISE | par | FRÉDÉRIC CHOPIN. | OEuvres posthumes. « » 6ème Livraison N° 2.'.

SUB-CAPTION: p. 2, '(1828) | *PIANO.*'.

FOOTLINE: p. 2, 'Paris, Imp. Bauve, 14 rue St Marc. « J.M. 3529.'; pp. 3–9, 'J.M. 3529.'.

IMPOSITION: The first page of music is on the verso of the last leaf of Op. 71#1.

STAMPS: none.

BOUND WITH: See 66/73-MeiF-1, note 2.

---

1. *Date:* first-edition inference (date code fe, p. 17).
2. For the collective title, see 66/73-MeiF-1 (preceding 66-MeiF-1).

Berlin: **A. Schlesinger (4398) [= 1855]** **71#2-aS-1** **M32.C54 P858**

The transcription of this title page is the same as that of **71#1-aS-1.**

6 leaves (334 x 256 mm): pp. [3] lith title page, 4–11 engr music, [12] blank, [13, 14] preface.

CAPTION TITLE: p. 4, 'IIe POLONAISE | PAR | FRÉDÉRIC CHOPIN. | Oeuvres posthumes. Livr. VI. N° II. « » Op. 71. N° II.'.

SUB-CAPTION: p. 4, '(1828.) | PIANO.'.

FOOTLINE: p. 4, 'Op. 71. indique l'ordre chronologique de la publication. l'Editeur. « S. 4398. » Berlin. Propriété de Ad. Mt. Schlesinger.'; pp. 5–11, 'S. 4398.'.

71#2-aS-1 *(continued)*

71#2-aS-1 *(concluded)*

STAMPS: publisher, style aS/B (see Appendix 8); dealer, Rahr, Utrecht (see Appendix 8).

---

1. *Date:* first-edition inference (date code fe, p. 17).
2. Each page of music has the complete-edition pagination (pp. 56–63) centered at the top.
3. For other comments, see Appendix 4.

Opus 71, Polonaise 3

Paris: **Meissonnier Fils** (3530) [= 1855] **71#3-MeiF-1** **M22.C54 P577**

A half title is not present; see 71#1-MeiF-1.

6 leaves (336 x 258 mm): pp. 2–9 engr music, [10] blank (see imposition).

CAPTION TITLE: p. 2, ' 3e POLONAISE | par | FRÉDÉRIC CHOPIN. | OEuvres posthumes « » 6ème Livraison N° 3.'.

SUB-CAPTION: p. 2, '(1829) | *PIANO.*'.

FOOTLINE: p. 2, 'Paris, Imp: Bauve, 14 rue St Marc. « J.M. 3530.'; pp. 3–9, 'J.M. 3530.'.

IMPOSITION: The first page of music is on the verso of the last leaf of Op. 71#2.

STAMPS: none.

BOUND WITH: See 66/73-MeiF-1, note 2.

---

1. *Date:* first-edition inference (date code fe, p. 17).
2. For the collective title, see 66/73-MeiF-1 (preceding 66-MeiF-1).]

NOCTURNE IN E MINOR
MARCHE FUNÈBRE IN C MINOR
ÉCOSSAISES IN D MAJOR, G MAJOR, D FLAT MAJOR
Opus 72

Paris: Meissonnier Fils (3531) 1855
Berlin: A. Schlesinger (4400) 1855

Composed 1826–27
Brown 19, 20, 12
Chominski & Turlo 126, 50, 11

Paris: Meissonnier Fils (3531) [= 1855] **72-MeiF-1** **M22.C54 P577**

NOCTURNE, | Marche funèbre | ET | 3 | ÉCOSSAISES. | *7.e Livraison des œuvres posthumes* | DE | F. CHOPIN | *A.V.* | *J. M. 3531.*

6 leaves (336 x 258 mm): pp. [i] engr half-title page, [ii, 1] blank, 2–10 engr music.

CAPTION TITLE: p. 2, 'NOCTURNE, MARCHE FUNÈBRE | et Trois Écossaises. | par | FRÉDÉRIC CHOPIN. | OEuvres posthumes. « » 7.e Livraison. | NOCTURNE.'; p. 5, 'MARCHE FUNÈBRE.'; p. 8, 'TROIS ÉCOSSAISES.'.

SUB-CAPTION: p. 2, '(1827) | *PIANO.*'; p. 5, '(1829) | Tempo di marcia.'; p. 8, '(1830) | N.o 1.'; p. 9 system 2, 'N.o 2.'; p. 10, 'N.o 3.'.

FOOTLINE: p. 2, 'Paris, Imp. Bauve, 14 rue S.t Marc. « J.M. 3531.'; pp. 3–10, 'J.M. 3531.'.

STAMPS: none.

BOUND WITH: See 66/73-MeiF-1, note 2.

1. *Date:* first-edition inference (date code fe, p. 17).
2. The three works appear respectively on pp. 2–4, 5–7, 8–10.
3. For the collective title, see 66/73-MeiF-1 (preceding 66-MeiF-1).

Berlin: A. Schlesinger (4400) [*ca* 1855] **72-aS-1** **M25.C54 N93**

The transcription of this title page is the same as that of 66-aS-1.

6 leaves (330 x 253 mm): pp. [3] lith title page, 4–12 lith music, [13, 14] preface.

CAPTION TITLE: p. 4, 'NOCTURNE, MARCHE FUNÈBRE | ET TROIS ÉCOSSAISES | par | FRÉDÉRIC CHOPIN | NOCTURNE. | Oeuvres posthumes. Livr. VII. « » Op. 72.'; p. 7, 'MARCHE FUNÈBRE. | par | FRÉDÉRIC CHOPIN. (1829).'; p. 10, 'TROIS ECOSSAISES | par | FRÉDÉRIC CHOPIN. (1830).'.

SUB-CAPTION: p. 4, '(1827.) | PIANO.'; p. 7, '(1829.) | PIANO.'; p. 10, 'N° 1.'; p. 11 system 2, 'N° 2.'; p. 12, 'N° 3.'.

FOOTLINE: p. 4, 'S. 4400. | Op. 72. indique l'ordre chronologique de la publication. l'Editeur. « » Berlin. Propriété de Ad. Mt. Schlesinger. ÷ Schnell-pressen-Druck der Röder'schen Officin in Leipzig.'; pp. 5–12, 'S. 4400.'.

72-aS-1 *(continued)*

72-aS-1 *(concluded)*

STAMPS: dealer (agent?), Ewer, London (see Appendix 8).

---

1. *Date:* first-edition inference (date code fe, p. 17), but the date is questioned because the music is lithographed.
2. Each page of music has the complete-edition pagination (pp. 72–80) centered at the top.
3. For other comments, see Appendix 4.

RONDO IN C MAJOR FOR TWO PIANOS
Opus 73

Paris: Meissonnier Fils (3532) 1855 — *Composed* 1828
Berlin: A. Schlesinger (4401) 1855 — Brown 27
Chominski & Turlo 196

***Paris:* Meissonnier Fils (3532) [= 1855]** — **73-MeiF-1** — **M22.C54 P577**

RONDO | à | Deux Pianos | *8e Livraison des œuvres posthumes* | DE | F. CHOPIN |
A.V. | *J. M. 3532*

Piano primo: 10 leaves (336 x 258 mm): pp. [i] engr half-title page, [ii, 1] blank, 2–17 engr music, [18] blank.

CAPTION TITLE: p. 2, 'RONDO | Pour deux Pianos | par | FRÉDÉRIC CHOPIN. | OEuvres posthumes. « » 8ème Livraison. '.

SUB-CAPTION: p. 2, '(1828) | *PIANO.*'.

HEADLINE: pp. 2–17, 'PIANO PRIMO.'.

FOOTLINE: p. 2, 'Paris, Imp. Bauve, 14 rue St Marc. « J.M. 3532.'; pp. 3–17, 'J.M. 3532.'.

Piano secondo: 8 leaves (336 x 258 mm): pp. [1] blank (but see note 2), 2–15 engr music, [16] blank.

CAPTION TITLE: p. 2, same as in Piano primo.

SUB-CAPTION: p. 2, same as in Piano primo.

HEADLINE: pp. 2–15, 'PIANO SECONDO.'.

FOOTLINE: p. 2, 'Paris, imp. Bauve, 14 rue St Marc. « J.M. 3532.'; pp. 3–15, 'J.M. 3532.'.

STAMPS: publisher, style Mei/B (see Appendix 8).

BOUND WITH: For piano primo, see 66/73-MeiF-1, note 2). Piano secondo is not bound with piano primo or with the 66/73-MeiF-1 volume.

1. *Date:* first-edition inference (date code fe, p. 17).
2. Piano secondo has a handwritten half title on p. [1].
3. For the collective title, see 66/73-MeiF-1 (preceding 66-MeiF-1).

Paris: **Gérard (J.M. 3532) [after 1866]** **73-Gér-1** **M214.C54 R77**

Œuvres | POSTHUMES | POUR | PIANO | DE | FRÉD. CHOPIN | PUBLIÉS SUR MANUSCRITS ORIGINAUX AVEC AUTORISATION | DE SA FAMILLE | PAR | JULES FONTANA |

1re Livraison.	FANTAISIE-IMPROMPTU	Prix	6 "
2e —	QUATRE MAZURKAS. Nos 1 à 4		6 "
3e —	QUATRE MAZURKAS. Nos 5 à 8		6 "
4e —	DEUX VALSES. Nos 1 à 2		6 "
5e —	TROIS VALSES. Nos 3 à 5		6 "
6e —	TROIS POLONAISES. Nos 1, 2 et 3	Chaque	6 "
7e —	NOCTURNE, MARCHE FUNÈBRE et TROIS ÉCOSSAISES		6 "
8e —	RONDO A DEUX PIANOS		15 "

LA COLLECTION COMPLÈTE | PRÉCÉDÉE D'UNE PRÉFACE PAR J. Fontana, et ornée d'un Portrait LITHOGRAPHIÉ PAR RAUNHEIM | *Brochée:* 20 *fr. net. Reliée:* 30 *fr. net.* | PARIS | *ANCIENNE MAISON MEISSONNIER* | CI-DEVANT RUE DAUPHINE | É. GÉRARD et Cie , boulevard des CAPUCINES, 12, et rue SCRIBE, 2, | Maison du Grand Hôtel. | Berlin, A. M. Schlesinger. « » Londres, Stationner's Pall. [*sic*] | PARIS. – IMPRIMERIE DE E. MARTINET, RUE MIGNON, 2.

Piano primo: 9 leaves (327 x 257 mm): pp. [1] lith title page, 2–17 engr music, [18] advt.

CAPTION TITLE: p, 2, 'RONDO | Pour deux Pianos | par | FRÉDÉRIC CHOPIN. | OEuvres posthumes. « » 8ème Livraison.'.

SUB-CAPTION: p. 2, '(1828) | *PIANO.*'.

HEADLINE: pp. 2–17, 'PIANO PRIMO.'.

FOOTLINE: p. 2, 'Paris. Imp. Bauve [?] 14 rue St. Marc. « J.M. 3532.'; pp. 3–17, 'J.M. 3532.'.

ADVT: p. [18], '*ANCIENNE MAISON MEISSONNIER, ci-devant rue Dauphine,* | EXTRAIT DU CATALOGUE DE MUSIQUE DE PIANO | DE E. GÉRARD et Cie, éditeurs-commissionnaires, boulevard des CAPUCINES, 12, et rue SCRIBE, 2, | MAISON DU GRAND HOTEL'. Chopin works listed are Opp. 57, 58, and the œuvres posthumes.

Piano secondo: not present in this copy.

STAMPS: publisher, style Gér/B (see Appendix 8).

1. *Date:* based on the publisher's address (Table 5B).
2. The title page is not colored. Its wording and spelling are the same as that of 66-Gér-1, except that here "PUBLIÉS" has only one "E", and "P" in "Portrait" is capitalized.

Berlin: **A. Schlesinger (4401) [= 1855]** **73-aS-1** **M214.C54 R772**

The transcription of this title page is the same as that of 67-aS-1.

Piano primo: 11 leaves (343 x 265 mm): pp. [i] lith title page, [ii, 1] blank, 2–17 engr music, [18] blank, [19, 20] preface.

CAPTION TITLE: p. 2, 'RONDO | POUR DEUX PIANOS | PAR | FRÉDÉRIC CHOPIN. | OEuvres posthumes. Livr. VIII. « » Op. 73.'.

73-aS-1 *(continued)*

73-aS-1 *(concluded)*

SUB-CAPTION: p. 2, '(1828) | PIANO.'.

HEADLINE: pp. 2–17, 'Piano Primo.'.

FOOTLINE: p. 2, 'Op. 73. indique l'ordre chronologique de la publication. l'Editeur. « S. 4401. » Berlin, Propriété de Ad. Mt. Schlesinger.'; pp. 3–17, 'S. 4401.'.

Piano secondo: 8 leaves (345 x 263 mm): pp. [1] blank, 2–15 engr music, [16] blank.

CAPTION TITLE: p. 2, same as in Piano primo.

SUB-CAPTION: p. 2, same as in Piano primo.

HEADLINE: pp. 2–15, 'Piano Secondo.'.

FOOTLINE: p. 2, same as in Piano Primo; pp. 3–15, 'S. 4401.'.

IMPOSITION: The first [i, ii] and last [19, 20] leaves of Piano primo are conjugate; leaf 6 is a singleton.

STAMPS: publisher, style aS/C (see Appendix 8); dealer, ?, Rotterdam.

---

1. *Date:* first-edition inference (date code fe, p. 17).
2. Each page of music in the Piano Primo score has the complete-edition pagination (pp. 82–97) centered at the top.
3. For other comments, see Appendix 4.

SONGS FOR VOICE WITH PIANO ACCOMPANIMENT
Opus 74

Berlin: A. Schlesinger (4638–4653) 1857 (Polish text)	*Composed* 1827–47
Berlin: A. Schlesinger (4797–4812) 1859 (German text)	Brown 32
Warsaw: Gebethner (84–99) 1859 (Polish text)	Chominski & Turlo 129

***Berlin:* A. Schlesinger (4797) [1864–71]** **74#1-aS-1** **M1621.C54 S76 no.1**

[The following transcription shows the text of Op. 74 title-page design C.]

Polnische Lieder | von Witwicki, Zaleski, Mickiewicz etc. [slanted backward] |
für eine Singstimme | mit Begleitung des Pianoforte [slanted backward] | componirt von | FR. CHOPIN. |
In deutscher Bearbeitung von Ferd. Gumbert. | Op. 74. « » Pr. 2 1/2 Thlr.

Nº 1.	Mädchens Wunsch.	7 1/2 Sgr.	Nº 9.	Eine Melodie.	5 Sgr.
„ 2.	Frühling.	7 1/2 „	„ 10.	Reitersmann vor der Schlacht.	7 1/2 „
„ 3.	Trübe Wellen.	7 1/2 „	„ 11.	Zwei Leichen.	7 1/2 „
„ 4.	Bacchanal.	5 „	„ 12.	Meine Freuden.	7 1/2 „
„ 5.	Was ein junges Mädchen liebt.	5 „	„ 13.	Melancholie.	7 1/2 „
„ 6.	Mir aus den Augen.	7 1/2 „	„ 14.	Das Ringlein.	7 1/2 „
„ 7.	Der Bote.	7 1/2 „	„ 15.	Die Heimkehr.	7 1/2 „
„ 8.	Mein Geliebter.	5 „	„ 16.	Lithauisches Lied.	7 1/2 „

Nº 17. Grabgesang [blank] Sgr.

Berlin, Eigenthum u. Verlag der SCHLESINGER'schen Buch- und Musikhandlung. (R. LIENAU) |
London, Ent[ed] at Stat. Hall [slanted backward] | S. 4797–4812

3 leaves (324 x 261 mm): pp. [1] engr title page, [2] blank, 3–5 engr music (serial 3–5), [6] blank.

CAPTION TITLE: p. 3, 'Nº 1. MÄDCHEN'S WUNSCH, polnisches Lied von FR. CHOPIN. | (ZYCZENIE PIOSNKA SIELSKA STEF. WITWICKIEGO.) Op. 74. | *In deutscher Bearbeitung von FERD. GUMBERT.*'.

FOOTLINE: p. 3, 'S. 4797. » Berlin, Verlag und Eigenthum der Schlesinger'schen Buch–u. Musikhandlung.'; pp. 4–5, 'S. 4797.'.

STAMPS: publisher, style aS/D (see Appendix 8).

BOUND WITH: See Appendix 5, paragraph 1.

---

1. *Date:* see Appendix 5.
2. For further details about Op. 74, see Appendix 5.

Berlin: **A. Schlesinger (6670) [after 1873]** 74#1-aS-2 M1621.C54 S735

[The following transcription shows the text of Op. 74 title-page design F.]

Polnische Lieder | von WITWICKI, ZALESKI, MICKIEWICZ etc. |
für eine Singstimme | mit Begleitung « » des Pianoforte | componirt von | FR. CHOPIN. |
In deutscher Bearbeitung von Ferd. Gumbert. | Op. 74. « complet 8º » Pr. M. 1. __

Nº 1. Mädchens Wunsch.
" 2. Frühling.
" 3. Trübe Wellen.
" 4. Bacchanal.
" 5. Was ein junges Mädchen liebt.
" 6. Mir aus den Augen.
" 7. Der Bote.
" 8. Mein Geliebter.
Nº 9. Eine Melodie.
" 10. Reitersmann vor der Schlacht.
" 11. Zwei Leichen.
" 12. Meine Freuden.
" 13. Melancholie.
" 14. Das Ringlein.
" 15. Die Heimkehr.
" 16. Lithauisches Lied.

Nº 17. Grabgesang.

Ausg. f. Sopran od. Tenor. « » Ausg. f. Alt od. Baryton.

Berlin, Eigenthum u. Verlag der SCHLESINGER'schen Buch- und Musikhandlung. (R. LIENAU) |
London, Ent[ed] at Stat. Hall. | s. 6669 / 70. | WIEN, bei CARL HASLINGER q[dm] TOBIAS.

2 leaves (326 x 259 mm): pp. [1] lith title page, 2–3 lith music, [4] blank.

CAPTION TITLE: p. 2, 'Original-Tonart. ÷ Ausgabe für Alt od: Baryton. « 1. ÷ Mädchens Wunsch. | » Fr. Chopin, Op. 74.'.

SUB-CAPTION: p. 2, 'PIANO | 1829.'.

FOOTLINE: pp. 2–3, 'S. 6670'.

STAMPS: dealer, Waanders, Rotterdam.

1. *Date:* see Appendix 5.
2. For further details about Op. 74, see Appendix 5.

***Berlin:* A. Schlesinger (4798) [= 1859]** **74#2-aS-1** **M1621.C54 S76 no.2**

[The following transcription shows the text of Op. 74 title-page design A.]

16 | Polnische Lieder | von Witwicki, Zaleski, Mickiewicz etc.[slanted backward] | für eine Singstimme | mit Begleitung des Pianoforte [slanted backward] | componirt von | FR. CHOPIN. | In deutscher Bearbeitung von Ferd. Gumbert. | Op. 74.

1. Mädchens Wunsch.
2. Frühling.
3. Trübe Wellen.
4. Bacchanal.
5. Was ein junges Mädchen liebt.
6. Mir aus den Augen.
7. Der Bote.
8. Mein Geliebter.
9. Eine Melodie.
10. Reitersmann vor der Schlacht.
11. Zwei Leichen.
12. Meine Freuden.
13. Melancholie.
14. Das Ringlein.
15. Die Heimkehr.
16. Lithauisches Lied.

Complet Pr. 2 1/2 Thlr. Einzeln à [handwritten 7 1/2] Sgr.

Eigenthum der Verlagshandlung. [slanted backward] | Berlin, in der SCHLESINGER'schen Buch- und Musikhandlung. | Paris und Leipzig, Fr. Volkmar. [slanted backward] « London, Ent^ed at Stat. Hall. [slanted backward] » Warschau, Gebethner et Cie [slanted backward] | S. 4797–4812. | Chopin, Zbiór ś piewów Polskich, ulozeny z manuskruptów oryginalnych i widany prezez J. Fontane. Pr. 2 5/6 Thlr.

3 leaves (324 x 261 mm): pp. [1] engr title page, [2] blank, 3–5 engr music (serial 6–8), [6] blank.

CAPTION TITLE: p. 3, 'N° 2. FRÜHLING, polnisches Lied von FR. CHOPIN. | WIOSNA PIONSKA SIELSKA STEF. WITWICKIEGO. Op. 74. | *In deutscher Bearbeitung von FERD. GUMBERT.*'.

FOOTLINE: p. 3, 'S. 4798. » Berlin, Verlag und Eigenthum der Schlesinger'schen Buch–u. Musikhandlung.'; pp. 4–5, 'S. 4798.'.

STAMPS: publisher, style aS/B (see Appendix 8).

BOUND WITH: See Appendix 5, paragraph 1.

1. *Date:* see Appendix 5.
2. For further details about Op. 74, see Appendix 5.

***Berlin:* A. Schlesinger (4799) [= 1859]** **74#3-aS-1** **M1621.C54 S76 no.3**

The title page is identical to that of 74#2-aS-1 (design A).

3 leaves (324 x 261 mm): pp. [1] engr title page, 2–5 engr music (serial 9–12), [6] blank.

CAPTION TITLE: p. 2, 'N° 3. TRÜBE WELLEN, polnisches Lied von FR. CHOPIN. | (SMUTNA RZEKA PIOSNKA SIELSKA STEF. WITWICKIEGO.) Op. 74. | *In deutscher Bearbeitung von FERD. GUMBERT.*'.

FOOTLINE: p. 2, 'S. 4799. » Berlin, Verlag und Eigenthum der Schlesinger'schen Buch–u. Musikhandlung.'; pp. 3–5, 'S. 4799.'.

STAMPS: publisher, style aS/B (see Appendix 8).

74#3-aS-1 *(continued)*

74#3-aS-1 *(concluded)*

BOUND WITH: See Appendix 5, paragraph 1.

1. *Date:* see Appendix 5.
2. For further details about Op. 74, see Appendix 5.

Berlin: A. Schlesinger (4800) [1860–63] 74#4-aS-1 M1621.C54 S76 no.4

[The following transcription shows the text of Op. 74 title-page design B.]

16 | Polnische Lieder | von Witwicki, Zaleski, Mickiewicz etc. [slanted backward] |
für eine Singstimme | mit Begleitung des Pianoforte [slanted backward] | componirt von | FR. CHOPIN. |
In deutscher Bearbeitung von Ferd. Gumbert. | Op. 74.

Nº		Sgr.	Nº		Sgr.
1.	Mädchens Wunsch.	7 1/2	9.	Eine Melodie.	5
2.	Frühling.	7 1/2	10.	Reitersmann vor der Schlacht.	7 1/2
3.	Trübe Wellen.	7 1/2	11.	Zwei Leichen.	7 1/2
4.	Bacchanal.	5	12.	Meine Freuden.	7 1/2
5.	Was ein junges Mädchen liebt.	5	13.	Melancholie.	7 1/2
6.	Mir aus den Augen.	7 1/2	14.	Das Ringlein.	7 1/2
7.	Der Bote.	7 1/2	15.	Die Heimkehr.	7 1/2
8.	Mein Geliebter.	5	16.	Lithauisches Lied.	7 1/2
		Complet Pr. 2 1/2 Thlr.	Einzeln à [blank] Sgr.		

Eigenthum der Verlagshandlung. [slanted backward] | Berlin, in der SCHLESINGER'schen Buch- und Musikhandlung. | Paris und Leipzig, Fr. Volkmar. [slanted backward] « London, Ent$^{\underline{ed}}$ at Stat. Hall. [slanted backward] » Warschau, Gebethner et C$^{\underline{ie}}$ [slanted backward] | S. 4797–4812. | Chopin, Zbiór ś piewów Polskich, ulozeny z manuskruptów oryginalnych i widany prezez J. Fontane. Pr. 2 5/6 Thlr.

2 leaves (324 x 261 mm): pp. [1] engr title page, 2–3 engr music (serial 13–14), [4] blank.

CAPTION TITLE: p. 2, 'Nº 4. BACCHANAL, polnisches Lied von FR. CHOPIN. | (HULANKA PIOSNKA SIELSKA STEF. WITWICKIEGO.) Op. 74. | *In deutscher Bearbeitung von FERD. GUMBERT.*'.

FOOTLINE: p. 2, 'S. 4800. » Berlin, Verlag und Eigenthum der Schlesinger'schen Buch–u. Musikhandlung.'; p. 3, 'S. 4800.'.

STAMPS: publisher, style aS/B (see Appendix 8).

BOUND WITH: See Appendix 5, paragraph 1.

1. *Date:* see Appendix 5.
2. For further details about Op. 74, see Appendix 5.

Berlin: A. Schlesinger (4801) [1860–63] 74#5-aS-1 M1621.C54 S76 no.5

The title page is identical to that of 74#4-aS-1 (design B).

2 leaves (324 x 261 mm): pp. [1] engr title page, 2–3 engr music (serial 15–16), [4] blank.

74#5-aS-1 *(continued)*

74#5-aS-1 *(concluded)*

CAPTION TITLE: p. 2, 'N° 5. WAS EIN JUNGES MÄDCHEN LIEBT, polnisches Lied von FR. CHOPIN. | (GDZIE. :LUBI PIOSKA SIELSKA STEF. WITWICKIEGO.) Op. 74. | *In deutscher Bearbeitung von FERD. GUMBERT.*'.

FOOTLINE: p. 2, 'S. 4801. » Berlin, Verlag und Eigenthum der Schlesinger'schen Buch–u. Musikhandlung.'; p. 3, 'S. 4801.'.

STAMPS: publisher, style aS/B (see Appendix 8).

BOUND WITH: See Appendix 5, paragraph 1.

---

1. *Date:* see Appendix 5.
2. For further details about Op. 74, see Appendix 5.

***Berlin:* A. Schlesinger (4801) [1860–63]** **74#5-aS-3** **M1621.C54 S74**

The title page is identical to that of 74#4-aS-1 (design B).

2 leaves (333 x 261 mm): pp. [1] engr title page, 2–3 engr music (serial 15–16), [4] blank.

CAPTION TITLE: p. 2, 'N° 5. WAS EIN JUNGES MÄDCHEN LIEBT, polnisches Lied von FR. CHOPIN. | (GDZIE.:LUBI PIOSKA SIELSKA STEF. WITWICKIEGO.) Op. 74. | *In deutscher Bearbeitung von FERD. GUMBERT.*'.

FOOTLINE: p. 2, 'S. 4801. » Berlin, Verlag und Eigenthum der Schlesinger'schen Buch–u. Musikhandlung.'; p. 3, 'S. 4801.'.

STAMPS: publisher, style aS/B (see Appendix 8).

ANNOTATIONS: handwritten page numbers 225–228 (see 74#6-aS-2).

---

1. *Date:* see Appendix 5.
2. For further details about Op. 74, see Appendix 5.

Berlin: **A. Schlesinger (6670) [1864–71]** 74#5-aS-2 **M1621.C54 S739**

[The following transcription shows the text of Op. 74 title-page design D.]

Polnische Lieder | von Witwicki, Zaleski, Mickiewicz etc. [slanted backward] | für eine Singstimme | mit Begleitung des Pianoforte [slanted backward] | componirt von | FR. CHOPIN. | In deutscher Bearbeitung von Ferd. Gumbert. | Op. 74. « » Pr. 2 1/2 Thlr.

Nº 1.	Mädchens Wunsch.	7 1/2 Sgr.	Nº 9.	Eine Melodie.	5 Sgr.
„ 2.	Frühling.	7 1/2 „	„ 10.	Reitersmann vor der Schlacht.	7 1/2 „
„ 3.	Trübe Wellen.	7 1/2 „	„ 11.	Zwei Leichen.	7 1/2 „
„ 4.	Bacchanal.	5 „	„ 12.	Meine Freuden.	7 1/2 „
„ 5.	Was ein junges Mädchen liebt.	5 „	„ 13.	Melancholie.	7 1/2 „
„ 6.	Mir aus den Augen.	7 1/2 „	„ 14.	Das Ringlein.	7 1/2 „
„ 7.	Der Bote.	7 1/2 „	„ 15.	Die Heimkehr.	7 1/2 „
„ 8.	Mein Geliebter.	5 „	„ 16.	Lithauisches Lied.	7 1/2 „

Nº 17. Grabgesang. 10 Sgr.

Ausg. f. Sopran od. Tenor. « » Ausg. f. Alt od. Baryton.

Berlin, Eigenthum u. Verlag der SCHLESINGER'schen Buch- und Musikhandlung. (R. LIENAU) | London Ent^{ed} at Stat Hall [slanted backward] | S. 4797_4812

2 leaves (328 x 260 mm): pp. [i] lith title page, 11–12 lith music, verso blank.

CAPTION TITLE: p. 11, 'Ausgabe für Alt ÷ od: Baryton. « 5. ÷ Was ein junges Mädchen liebt. | » Fr. Chopin, Op. 74.'.

SUB-CAPTION: p. 11, 'PIANO.'.

FOOTLINE: pp. 11–12, 'S. 6670'.

IMPOSITION: Page 11 is imposed as a verso, p. 12 as a recto.

STAMPS: none.

1. *Date:* see Appendix 5.
2. The editions with title-page design D, E, or F have only serial pagination.
3. For further details about Op. 74, see Appendix 5.

Berlin: **A. Schlesinger (4802) [1860–63]** 74#6-aS-2 **M1621.C54 S741**

The title page is identical to that of 74#4-aS-1 (design B).

3 leaves (333 x 259 mm): pp. [1] engr title page, [2] blank, 3–5 engr music (serial 17–19), [6] blank.

CAPTION TITLE: p. 3, 'Nº 6. MIR AUS DEN AUGEN, polnisches Lied von FR. CHOPIN. | (PRECZ Z MOICH OCZU SLOWA A. WICKIEWICZA.) Op. 74. | *In deutscher Bearbeitung von FERD. GUMBERT.*'.

FOOTLINE: p. 3, 'S. 4802. » Berlin, Verlag und Eigenthum der Schlesinger'schen Buch–u. Musikhandlung.'; pp. 4–5, 'S. 4802.'.

STAMPS: publisher, style aS/B (see Appendix 8).

74#6-aS-2 *(continued)*

74#6-aS-2 *(concluded)*

ANNOTATIONS: handwritten page numbers 229–234 (see 74#5-aS-3).

1. *Date:* see Appendix 5.
2. For further details about Op. 74, see Appendix 5.

Berlin: **A. Schlesinger (4802) [1864–71]** **74#6-aS-1**

The title page is identical to that of 74#1-aS-1 (design C).

3 leaves (324 x 261 mm): pp. [1] lith title page, [2] blank, 3–5 engr music (serial 17–19), [6] blank.

CAPTION TITLE: p. 3, 'N° 6. MIR AUS DEN AUGEN, polnisches Lied von FR. CHOPIN. | (PRECZ Z MOICH OCZU SLOWA A. WICKIEWICZA.) Op. 74. | *In deutscher Bearbeitung von FERD. GUMBERT.*'.

FOOTLINE: p. 3, 'S. 4802. » Berlin, Verlag und Eigenthum der Schlesinger'schen Buch–u. Musikhandlung.'; pp. 4–5, 'S. 4802.'.

STAMPS: publisher, style aS/E (see Appendix 8).

BOUND WITH: See Appendix 5, paragraph 1.

1. *Date:* see Appendix 5.
2. For further details about Op. 74, see Appendix 5.

Berlin: **A. Schlesinger (4803) [1860–63]** **74#7-aS-1**

The title page is identical to that of 74#4-aS-1 (design B).

3 leaves (324 x 261 mm): pp. [1] engr title page, [2] blank, 3–5 engr music (serial 20–22), [6] blank.

CAPTION TITLE: p. 3, 'N° 7. DER BOTE, polnisches Lied von FR. CHOPIN. | (POSEL PIOSNKA SIELSKA STEF. WITWICKIEGO.) Op. 74. | *In deutscher Bearbeitung von FERD. GUMBERT.*'.

FOOTLINE: p. 3, 'S. 4803. » Berlin, Verlag und Eigenthum der Schlesinger'schen Buch–u. Musikhandlung.'; pp. 4–5, 'S. 4803.'.

STAMPS: publisher, style aS/B (see Appendix 8).

BOUND WITH: See Appendix 5, paragraph 1.

1. *Date:* see Appendix 5.
2. For further details about Op. 74, see Appendix 5.

Berlin: **A. Schlesinger (4804) [1860–63]** **74#8-aS-1**

The title page is identical to that of 74#4-aS-1 (design B).

2 leaves (324 x 261 mm): pp. [1] engr title page, 2–3 engr music (serial 23–24), [4] blank.

74#8-aS-1 *(continued)*

74#8-aS-1 *(concluded)*

CAPTION TITLE: p. 2, 'Nº 8. MEIN GELIEBTER, polnisches Lied von FR. CHOPIN. | (SLICZNY CHLOPIEC SLOWA BOGDANA ZALESKIEGO.) Op. 74. | *In deutscher Bearbeitung von FERD. GUMBERT.*'.

FOOTLINE: p. 2, 'S. 4804. » Berlin, Verlag und Eigenthum der Schlesinger'schen Buch–u. Musikhandlung.'; p. 3, 'S. 4804.'.

STAMPS: publisher, style aS/B (see Appendix 8).

BOUND WITH: See Appendix 5, paragraph 1.

1. *Date:* see Appendix 5.
2. For further details about Op. 74, see Appendix 5.

***Berlin:* A. Schlesinger (4805) [1860–63]** **74#9-aS-1** **M1621.C54 S76 no.9**

The title page is identical to that of 74#4-aS-1 (design B).

2 leaves (324 x 261 mm): pp. [1] engr title page, 2–3 engr music (serial 25–26), [4] blank.

CAPTION TITLE: p. 2, 'Nº 9. EINE MELODIE, polnisches Lied von FR. CHOPIN. | (MELODIA SLOWA ANONYMA.) Op. 74. | *In deutscher Bearbeitung von FERD. GUMBERT.*'.

FOOTLINE: p. 2, 'S. 4805. » Berlin, Verlag und Eigenthum der Schlesinger'schen Buch–u. Musikhandlung.'; p. 3, 'S. 4805.'.

STAMPS: publisher, style aS/D (see Appendix 8).

BOUND WITH: See Appendix 5, paragraph 1.

1. *Date:* see Appendix 5.
2. For further details about Op. 74, see Appendix 5.

***Berlin:* A. Schlesinger (4806) [1860–63]** **74#10-aS-1** **M1621.C54 S76 no.10**

The title page is identical to that of 74#4-aS-1 (design B).

3 leaves (324 x 261 mm): pp. [1] engr title page, [2] blank, 3–5 engr music (serial 27–29), [6] blank.

CAPTION TITLE: p. 3, 'Nº 10. DER REITERSMANN VOR DER SCHLACHT, polnisches Lied von FR. CHOPIN. | (WOJAK PIOSNKA SIELSKA STEF. WITWICKIEGO.) Op. 74. | *In deutscher Bearbeitung von FERD. GUMBERT.*'.

FOOTLINE: p. 3, 'S. 4806. » Berlin, Verlag und Eigenthum der Schlesinger'schen Buch–u. Musikhandlung.'; pp. 4–5, 'S. 4806.'.

STAMPS: publisher, style aS/B (see Appendix 8).

BOUND WITH: See Appendix 5, paragraph 1.

1. *Date:* see Appendix 5.
2. For further details about Op. 74, see Appendix 5.

***Berlin:* A. Schlesinger (4807) [1860–63]** **74#11-aS-1** **M1621.C54 S76 no.11**

The title page is identical to that of 74#4-aS-1 (design B).

3 leaves (324 x 261 mm): pp. [1] engr title page, [2] blank, 3–5 engr music (serial 30–32), [6] blank.

CAPTION TITLE: p. 3, 'Nº 11. ZWEI LEICHEN, polnisches Lied von FR. CHOPIN. | (DWOJAKI KONIEG DUMKA BAGDUNA ZALESKIEGO.) Op. 74. | *In deutscher Bearbeitung von FERD. GUMBERT.*'.

FOOTLINE: p. 3, 'S. 4807. » Berlin, Verlag und Eigenthum der Schlesinger'schen Buch–u. Musikhandlung.'; pp. 4–5, 'S. 4807.'.

STAMPS: publisher, style aS/B (see Appendix 8).

BOUND WITH: See Appendix 5, paragraph 1.

1. *Date:* see Appendix 5.
2. For further details about Op. 74, see Appendix 5.

***Berlin:* A. Schlesinger (4808) [1860–63]** **74#12-aS-1** **M1621.C54 S76 no.12**

The title page is identical to that of 74#4-aS-1 (design B).

3 leaves (324 x 261 mm): pp. [1] engr title page, [2] blank, 3–5 engr music (serial 33–35), [6] blank.

CAPTION TITLE: p. 3, 'Nº 12. MEINE FREUDEN, polnisches Lied von FR. CHOPIN. | (MOJA PIESCZOTKA SLOWA A MICKIEWICZA.) Op. 74. | *In deutscher Bearbeitung von FERD. GUMBERT.*'.

FOOTLINE: p. 3, 'S. 4808. » Berlin, Verlag und Eigenthum der Schlesinger'schen Buch–u. Musikhandlung.'; pp. 4–5, 'S. 4808.'.

STAMPS: publisher, style aS/B (see Appendix 8).

BOUND WITH: See Appendix 5, paragraph 1.

1. *Date:* see Appendix 5.
2. For further details about Op. 74, see Appendix 5.

***Berlin:* A. Schlesinger (4809) [1860–63]** **74#13-aS-1** **M1621.C54 S76 no.13**

The title page is identical to that of 74#4-aS-1 (design B).

3 leaves (324 x 261 mm): pp. [1] engr title page, [2] blank, 3–5 engr music (serial 36–38), [6] blank.

CAPTION TITLE: p. 3, 'Nº 13. MELANCHOLIE, polnisches Lied von FR. CHOPIN. | (NIEMA CZEGO TRZEBA, SLOWA BOGDANA ZALESKIEGO.) Op. 74. | *In deutscher Bearbeitung von FERD. GUMBERT.*'.

FOOTLINE: p. 3, 'S. 4809. » Berlin, Verlag und Eigenthum der Schlesinger'schen Buch–u. Musikhandlung.'; pp. 4–5, 'S. 4809.'.

STAMPS: publisher, style aS/D? (see Appendix 8).

74#13-aS-1 *(continued)*

74#13-aS-1 *(concluded)*

BOUND WITH: See Appendix 5, paragraph 1.

---

1. *Date:* see Appendix 5.
2. For further details about Op. 74, see Appendix 5.

Berlin: A. Schlesinger (4810) [1860–63] **74#14-aS-1** **M1621.C54 S76 no.14**

The title page is identical to that of 74#4-aS-1 (design B).

3 leaves (324 x 261 mm): pp. [1] engr title page, [2] blank, 3–5 engr music (serial 39–41), [6] advt.

CAPTION TITLE: p. 3, 'Nº 14. DAS RINGLEIN, polnisches Lied von FR. CHOPIN. | (PIERSCIEN, PIOSNKA SIELSKA STEF. WITWICKIEGO.) Op. 74. | *In deutscher Bearbeitung von FERD. GUMBERT.*'.

FOOTLINE: p. 3, 'S. 4810. » Berlin, Verlag und Eigenthum der Schlesinger'schen Buch–u. Musikhandlung.'; pp. 4–5, 'S. 4810.'.

ADVT: p. [4], 'Aus dem Verlage der Schlesinger'schen Buch- und Musikhandlung in Berlin.'. There are no Chopin works in the list.

STAMPS: publisher, style aS/D (see Appendix 8).

BOUND WITH: See Appendix 5, paragraph 1.

---

1. *Date:* see Appendix 5.
2. For further details about Op. 74, see Appendix 5.

Berlin: A. Schlesinger (6670) [after 1873] **74#14-aS-2** **M1621.C54 S748**

The title page is identical to that of 74#1-aS-2 (design F).

2 leaves (327 x 261 mm): pp. [i] lith title page, [ii] blank, 31 lith music, [32] blank.

CAPTION TITLE: p. 31, 'Ausgabe für Alt od: Baryton. « 14. ÷ Das Ringlein. | » Fr. Chopin, Op. 74.'.

SUB-CAPTION: p. 31, voice: 'GESANG. | 1841.', piano: 'PIANO.'.

FOOTLINE: pp. 31, 'S. 6670'.

STAMPS: none.

---

1. *Date:* see Appendix 5.
2. The editions with title-page design D, E, or F have only serial pagination.
3. For further details about Op. 74, see Appendix 5.

Berlin: A. Schlesinger (4811) [1860–63] **74#15-aS-1** **M1621.C54 S76 no.15**

The title page is identical to that of 74#1-aS-2 (design B).

74#15-aS-1 *(continued)*

74#15-aS-1 *(concluded)*

3 leaves (324 x 261 mm): pp. [1] engr title page, [2] blank, 3–5 engr music (serial 42–44), [6] blank.

CAPTION TITLE: p. 3, 'Nº 15. DIE HEIMKEHR, polnisches Lied von FR. CHOPIN. | (NARZECZONY, PIOSNKA SIELSKA STEF. WITWICKIEGO.) Op. 74. | *In deutscher Bearbeitung von FERD. GUMBERT.*'.

FOOTLINE: p. 3, 'S. 4810 [*sic*]. » Berlin, Verlag und Eigenthum der Schlesinger'schen Buch–u. Musikhandlung.'; pp. 4–5, 'S. 4811.'.

STAMPS: publisher, style aS/B (see Appendix 8).

BOUND WITH: See Appendix 5, paragraph 1.

---

1. *Date:* see Appendix 5.
2. For further details about Op. 74, see Appendix 5.

Berlin: **A. Schlesinger (6670) [after 1873]** | **74#16-aS-2** | **M1621.C54 S751**

[The following transcription shows the text of Op. 74 title-page design E.]

Polnische Lieder | von Witwicki, Zaleski, Mickiewicz etc. [slanted backward] |
für eine Singstimme | mit Begleitung des Pianoforte [slanted backward] | componirt von | FR. CHOPIN. | In deutscher Bearbeitung von Ferd. Gumbert. | Op. 74. « » Pr. M. 7,50.

		M.			M.
Nº 1.	Mädchens Wunsch.	0,80	Nº 9.	Eine Melodie.	0,50
„ 2.	Frühling.	0,80	„ 10.	Reitersmann vor der Schlacht.	0,80
„ 3.	Trübe Wellen.	0,80	„ 11.	Zwei Leichen.	0,80
„ 4.	Bacchanal.	0,50	„ 12.	Meine Freuden.	0,80
„ 5.	Was ein junges Mädchen liebt.	0,50	„ 13.	Melancholie.	0,80
„ 6.	Mir aus den Augen.	0,80	„ 14.	Das Ringlein.	0,80
„ 7.	Der Bote.	0,80	„ 15.	Die Heimkehr.	0,80
„ 8.	Mein Geliebter.	0,50	„ 16.	Lithauisches Lied.	0,80

Nº 17. Grabgesang. M. 1.

Ausg. f. Sopran od. Tenor. « » Ausg. f. Alt od. Baryton.

Berlin, Eigenthum u. Verlag der SCHLESINGER'schen Buch- und Musikhandlung. (R. LIENAU) | London Ent^{ed} at Stat Hall [slanted backward] | S. 4797–4812 | Wien, bei CARL HASLINGER q$^{\underline{dm}}$ TOBIAS.

3 leaves (328 x 260 mm): pp. [i] lith title page, [ii] blank, 35–37 lith music, [38] blank.

CAPTION TITLE: p. 35, '16. | Lithuanisches Lied. | Ausgabe für Alt od: Baryton. « | » Fr. Chopin, Op. 74.'.

SUB-CAPTION: p. 35, 'PIANO.'.

FOOTLINE: pp. 35–37, 'S. 6670'.

STAMPS: dealer, Waanders, [Amsterdam?].

---

1. *Date:* see note 3.
2. The editions with title-page design D, E, or F have only serial pagination.
3. For further details about Op. 74, see Appendix 5.

Berlin: A. Schlesinger (6670) [ca 1874] **74#16-aS-1** **M1621.C54 S75**

The title page is identical to that of 74#1-aS-2 (design F).

3 leaves (320 x 260 mm): pp. [i] lith title page, [ii] blank, 35–37 lith music, [38] blank.

CAPTION TITLE: p. 35, '16. | Lithauisches Lied. | Ausgabe für Alt. od: Baryton. « | » Fr. Chopin, Op. 74.'.

SUB-CAPTION: p. 35, 'PIANO | 1831.'.

FOOTLINE: pp. 35–37, 'S. 6670'.

STAMPS: dealer, Gebrüder Zug, Zürich.

1. *Date:* see note 3.
2. The editions with title-page design D, E, or F have only serial pagination.
3. For further details about Op. 74, see Appendix 5.

POLONAISE IN G SHARP MINOR
Brown 6

Mainz: Schott (17943) 1864 | *Composed* 1822–24
Warsaw: Kaufmann (20) 1864 | Brown 6
Chominski & Turlo 163

***Mainz:* Schott (17943) [1864–71]** **B6-Schott-1** **M32.C54 P839**

à Madame Du-Pont. | POLONAISE | pour | PIANO | par | FR. CHOPIN. | OEUVRE POSTHUME. | N°. 17943. « Propriété pour tous pays. » Pr. 54 kr. | MAYENCE | chez les fils de B. Schott. | Bruxelles, Schott frères. ÷ 82 Montagne de la Cour. « » Londres Schott & Cie. ÷ 159 Regent Street. | Paris, Maison Schott, 30 rue neuve S^t^. Augustin. | Dépôt général de notre fonds de Musique: | LEIPZIG ÷ C.F. Leede. « » ROTTERDAM ÷ W.F. Lichtenauer. | Enregistré aux Archives de l'Union, | au Mininstère de l'Intérieur de France et à Stationers Hall. | *Varsovie, chez J. Kauffmann.*

5 leaves (333 x 262 mm): pp. [i] lith title page, [ii] blank, 1–7 lith music, [8] blank.

CAPTION TITLE: p. 1, 'POLONAISE | PAR | F. CHOPIN | Oeuvre Posthume.'.

FOOTLINE: pp. 1–7, '17943.'.

WRAPPER (brown): pp. [1] half-title page, [2, 3] blank, [4] advt.

HALF TITLE: wrapper p. [1], 'Polonaise | PAR | Fr. Chopin. | OEUVRE POSTHUME.'.

ADVT: wrapper p. [4], '*Catalogue des Ouvrages pour le Piano de* | F. Godefroid, J. Gregoir, J. Herz, F. Kalkbrenner, J. Leybach, L. de Meyer, E. Pauer & J. Rosenhain, | Bruxelles, chez Schott Frères. « *publiés par LES FILS DE B. SCHOTT à MAYENCE.* » Londres, chez Schott & Comp.'.

STAMPS: none.

1. *Date:* based on the assumption the first edition was engraved, and on the absence of reference to the four-hand edition (see B6-Schott-2).

***Mainz:* Schott (17943) [*ca* 1871]** **B6-Schott-2** **M32.C54 P8391**

à Madame Du-Pont. | POLONAISE | pour | PIANO | par | FR. CHOPIN. | OEUVRE POSTHUME. | Propriété pour tous pays. | MAYENCE | chez les fils de B. Schott. | Bruxelles, Schott frères. ÷ 82 Montagne de la Cour. « » Londres Schott & Cie. ÷ 159 Regent Street. | Paris, Maison Schott, 30 rue neuve S^t^. Augustin. | Dépôt général de notre fonds de Musique: | LEIPZIG ÷ C.F. Leede. « » ROTTERDAM ÷ W.F. Lichtenauer. | Enrégistré aux Archives de l'Union, | au Mininstère de l'Intérieur de France et à Stationers Hall. | *Varsovie, chez J. Kauffmann.* | *17943. 20525.*

5 leaves (342 x 273 mm): pp. [i] lith title page, [ii] blank, 1–7 engr music, [8] blank.

CAPTION TITLE: p. 1, 'POLONAISE | PAR | F. CHOPIN | Oeuvre posthume.'.

FOOTLINE: pp. 1–7, '17943.'.

B6-Schott-2 *(continued)*

B6-Schott-2 *(concluded)*

WRAPPER (pale yellow): pp. [1] half-title page, [2, 3] blank, [4] advt.

HALF TITLE: wrapper p. [1], 'Polonaise | PAR | Fr. Chopin. | OEUVRE POSTHUME. | à 2 mains ÷ Pr. 54 kr. « » à 4 mains ÷ Pr. 1 Fl. 12 kr.'.

ADVT: wrapper p. [4], '*Catalogue des Ouvrages pour le Piano de* | F. Godefroid, J. Gregoir, J. Herz, F. Kalkbrenner, J. Leybach, L. de Meyer, E. Pauer & J. Rosenhain, | Bruxelles, chez Schott Frères. « *publiés par LES FILS DE B. SCHOTT à MAYENCE.* » Londres, chez Schott & Comp.'.

STAMPS: none.

1. *Date:* based on the plate number 20525 of the four-hand edition (Deutsch, 1961, p. 23).
2. This score corresponds to Hob-513, stated there to be a first edition, in conflict with plate number 20525 of the four-hand edition.

Warsaw: **Kaufmann (20) [*ca* 1864]** **B6-Ka-1** **M32.C54 P84**

POLONAISE | pour le Piano-Forte | composée et dediée | à M$^{\underline{e}}$ Du-Pont | par | FR. CHOPIN. | OEUVRE POSTHUME. | Propriété de l'Editeur | VARSOVIE JOSEF KAUFMANN. | 20

4 leaves (293 x 235 mm): pp. [1] lith title page, [2] blank, 3–7 lith music, [8] blank.

CAPTION TITLE: p. 3, 'POLONEZ.'.

FOOTLINE: p. 3, [footnote in Polish and in French] 'Autant que l'on puisse juger d'après le manuscript et sa dédication, cette composition musicale a été écrite par Frédéric Chopin à l'âge de 14 ans, et n'était nulle part publiée jusqu'à présent. — | 20 | Stich und Schnellpressen-Druck der Röder'schen Officin in Leipzig. «'; pp. 4–7, '20'.

WRAPPER: lacks front leaf; pp. [3] blank, [4] advt.

ADVT: wrapper p. [4], 'KOMPOZYCYE MUZYCZNE | WYDANE NAKLADEM | KSIEGARNI I SKLADU NUT MUZYCZNYCH | JÓZEFA KAUFMANN. | Krakowski Przedmieście No. 442, (71).'. The footline is "Drukiem Breitkopfa i Härtela w Lipsku.". The Chopin works listed are, for piano, this polonaise, and for voice, 10 songs.

STAMPS: none.

1. *Date:* The date is questioned because the music is lithographed.
2. The title page is a color lithograph with a bust of Chopin on a pedestal.

VARIATIONS IN E MAJOR
('Der Schweitzerbub')
Brown 14

Paris: Richault (10869) 1851	*Composed* 1824
Vienna: Haslinger (8148) 1851	Brown 14
London: Cocks (9728) 1852	Chominski & Turlo 117

***Vienna:* Haslinger (8148) [= 1851]** **B14-Ha-1** **M27.C54 V3**

VARIATIONS | sur | un Air national allemand | pour le | Pianoforte |
composées | par | FRÉDÉRIC CHOPIN. | Oeuvre posthume. | *Propriété des Editeurs.* |
N.º 8148. « Enrégistré dans l'Archive de l'Union. » Prix 45 x C.M. |
VIENNE, | *chez Charles Haslinger quondam Tobie,* | *Marchand de Musique etc. de la Cour Imp. et Royale.* |
Leipsic, chez B. Hermann. | Londres, chez R. Cocks & C.º « Milan, chez Jean Ricordi. »
Paris, chez Simon Richault.

6 leaves (340 x 265 mm): pp. [1] engr title page, [2, 3] blank, 4–11 engr music, [12] blank.

CAPTION TITLE: p. 4, 'Chopin Fr. Oeuvre posthume. «'.

FOOTLINE: p. 4, '(8148.) | Eigenthum und Verlag der k.k. Hof- Kunst- und Musikalienhandlung des Tobias Haslinger in Wien.'; pp. 5–11, 'T.H. 8148.'.

STAMPS: none.

1. *Date:* first-edition inference (date code fe, p. 17).

WALTZES IN B MINOR AND F MINOR
('Deux valses mélancoliques')
Brown 35

Cracow: Wildt (—) 1852 | *Composed* 1829–41
London: Wessel (8015) 1853 | Brown 35
London: Ewer (—) 1854 | Chominski & Turlo 216

***London:* Ewer (—) [= 1854]** B35-Ew-1 M32.C54 W678

DEUX VALSES | Mélancoliques, | COMPOSÉES POUR LE | PIANO FORTE, | *et écrites sur l'album* | de Mme la Comtesse P^{XXX} | EN 1844. | Par | FRÉDÉRIC CHOPIN. | OEUVRE POSTHUME. | ENT. STA. HALL « » PRICE 1^{s}/6 | London, | J. J. EWER & Co | *390, Oxford Street.*

3 leaves (336 x 246 mm): pp. [1] engr title page, [2] blank, [3]–6 engr music.

CAPTION TITLE: p. [3], 'DEUX VALSES MÉLANCOLIQUES. | » FRÉDÉRIC CHOPIN.'.

SUB-CAPTION: p. [3], '*N*^{o} 1.'; p. 4, system 4, '*N*^{o} 2.'.

FOOTLINE: p. [3], none; pp. 4–6, 'CHOPIN. DEUX VALSES. «'.

STAMPS: none.

INSCRIPTIONS: "W.S. Bennett Esq. | With the Pubs. compl." on title page.

1. *Date:* first-edition inference (date code fe, p. 17).
2. This publication, and those by Wildt (Hob-475) and by Wessel, preceded the Fontana edition of posthumous works (1855), in which the two waltzes of the Ewer edition are numbered, respectively, Op. 70#2 and Op. 69#2. There are numerous textual differences between this and the Fontana edition.
3. The publisher's presentation is to the composer William Sterndale Bennett (1816–1875).

POLONAISE IN G FLAT MAJOR
Brown 36

Mainz: Schott (20029) 1870
Warsaw: Kaufmann (136) 1870

Composed 1829
Brown 36
Chominski & Turlo 165

Mainz: **Schott (20029) [= 1870]** **B36-Schott-1** **M32.C54 P87**

POLONAISE | {en Sol-b majeur} | POUR [slanted backwards] | PIANO | *PAR* | FR. CHOPIN. | Oeuvre posthume. | N? 20029. « » Pr. 54 kr. | Propriété pour tous pays. | MAYENCE CHEZ LES FILS DE B. SCHOTT. | Bruxelles, Schott fréres. ÷ 82 Montagne de la Cour. « Paris, Maison Schott. ÷ 1 Rue Auber (M?n du G?d Hôtel) » Londres, Schott & C?ie ÷ 159 Regent Street | Dépôt général de notre fonds de Musique: | LEIPZIG, C. F. LEEDE. | Enregistré aux Archives de l'Union | au Ministère de l'Intérieur de France et à Stationers Hall. | Varsovie chez J. Kauffmann.

5 leaves (348 x 280 mm): pp. [1] lith title page, 2–8 lith music, [9, 10] blank.

CAPTION TITLE: p. 2, 'POLONAISE. | OEUVRE POSTHUME. « » F. CHOPIN.'.

FOOTLINE: p. 2, 'Stich und Druck von B. SCHOTT'S SÖHNEN in MAINZ. « 20029.'; pp. 3–8, '20029.'.

WRAPPER (blue): pp. [1] half-title, [2, 3] blank, [4] advt.

HALF TITLE: wrapper p. [1], 'POLONAISE | (en Sol-[bémol] majeur.) | PAR | FR. CHOPIN. | Oeuvre Posthume.'.

ADVT: wrapper p. [4], '*Catalogue des Ouvrages pour le Piano de* | F. Godefroid, J. Gregoir, J. Herz, F. Kalkbrenner, J. Leybach, L. de Meyer, E. Pauer & J. Rosenhain, | Bruxelles, chez Schott Frères. « *publiés par LES FILS DE B. SCHOTT à MAYENCE.* » Londres, chez Schott & Comp.'.

STAMPS: none.

1. *Date:* first-edition inference (date code fe, p. 17).
2. The authenticity of this work has often been questioned (Niecks, II, p. 354; Brown, p. 40; Chominski & Turlo, p. 178). Niecks says "Nothing but the composer's autograph [not extant] could convince one of the genuineness of this piece. There are here and there passages which have the Chopin ring, indeed, seem to be almost bodily taken from some other of his works, but there is also a great deal which it is impossible to imagine to have come at any time from his pen — the very opening bars may be instanced.". However, Weinstock (p.434) asserts, without explanation, "The hint that the G-flat major Polonaise might be a pastiche has proved to be unjustified, for there is no longer any doubt of the genuineness of the work, which appears to date from 1829, thus being contemporary with the F-minor Concerto. There is no reason, however, to revise Niecks's judgement of the music as music."

WALTZ IN E MINOR
Brown 56

Warsaw: Kaufmann (159) 1868 | *Composed* 1830
Mainz: Schott (19551) 1868 | Brown 56
Chominski & Turlo 222

Mainz: **Schott (19551) [= 1868]** — **B56-Schott-1** — **M32.C54 W73**

VALSE | (Mi - min.) | POUR LE | PIANO | PAR | F. CHOPIN | Oeuvre posthume. |
N° 19551. « » Pr. 45 Kr. | Propriété pour tous pays. | MAYENCE CHEZ LES FILS DE B. SCHOTT. |
Bruxelles Schott frères. ÷ 82 Montague de la Cour. « Londres, Schott & Cie ÷ 159 Regent Street. »
Paris, Maison Schott. ÷ 1 Rue Auber. (M^{on} du G^{d} Hôtel.). | Dépôt général de notre fonds de Musique: |
LEIPZIG, C.F. LEEDE. | Enregistré aux Archives de l'Union, |
au Ministère de l'Intérieur de France et à Stationers Hall. | Varsovie, J. Kaufmann.

4 leaves (320 x 245 mm): pp. [1] lith title page, 2–7 lith music, [8] blank.

CAPTION TITLE: p. 2, 'VALSE. | OEUVRE POSTHUME. « » F. CHOPIN.'.

FOOTLINE: p. 2, 'Stich und Druck von B. SCHOTT'S SÖHNEN in Mainz. « | 19551.'; pp. 3–7, '19551.'.

STAMPS: none.

1. *Date:* first-edition inference (date code fe, p. 17).

Mainz: **Schott (19551) [*ca* 1871]** — **B56-Schott-2** — **M32.C54 W731**

VALSE | (Mi - min.) | POUR LE | PIANO | PAR | F. CHOPIN | Oeuvre posthume. |
Propriété pour tous pays. | MAYENCE CHEZ LES FILS DE B. SCHOTT. | Bruxelles Schott frères. ÷
82 Montague de la Cour. « Londres, Schott & Cie ÷ 159 Regent Street. » Paris, Maison Schott. ÷
1 Rue Auber. (M^{on} du G^{d} Hôtel.). | Dépôt général de notre fonds de Musique: | LEIPZIG, C.F. LEEDE. |
Enregistré aux Archives de l'Union, | au Ministère de l'Intérieur de France et à Stationers Hall. |
19551. 20526.

4 leaves (345 x 274 mm): pp. [1] lith title page, 2–7 lith music, [8] blank.

CAPTION TITLE: p. 2, 'VALSE. | OEUVRE POSTHUME. « » F. CHOPIN.'.

FOOTLINE: p. 2, 'Stich und Druck von B. SCHOTT'S SÖHNEN in Mainz. « | 19551.'; pp. 3–7, '19551.'.

STAMPS: none.

1. *Date:* based on the plate number 20526 of the four-hand edition (Deutsch, 1961, p. 23).
2. This title page, with no price, corresponds to Hob-519, stated there to be a first edition. However, that is in conflict with the added plate number 20526. The same is true of the description by Chominski & Turlo (p. 222).

DUO CONCERTANT IN E MAJOR FOR PIANO AND CELLO
Brown 70

Paris: M. Schlesinger (1376) 1833	*Composed* 1831
Berlin: A. Schlesinger (1777) 1833	Brown 70
London: Wessel (1076) (1077) 1833	Chominski & Turlo 10

Paris: **M. Schlesinger (1376) [= 1833]** **B70-mS-1** **M233.C54 D9**

Grand Duo | Concertant | pour Piano *ET* Violoncelle | *sur des Thémes de* | ROBERT LE DIABLE | *dedié* à *Mad*^{lle} | Adèle Forest | par | FRÉDÉRIC CHOPIN | de Varsovie | ET | AUGUSTE FRANCHOMME | *Violoncelle solo de l'Opera Royal Italien, et 1*^{er} *Violoncelle* | de la Chambre du Roi | *MV* | *Prix: 9*^{f} | *Propriété des Editeurs* | *A PARIS, Chez* MAURICE SCHLESINGER *Rue Richelieu, 97.* | *à BERLIN, Chez A. M. Schlesinger*

Piano: 11 leaves (342 x 273 mm): pp. [i] engr title page, [ii, 1] blank, 2–18 engr music, [19, 20] blank.

CAPTION TITLE: p. 2, 'F. CHOPIN. et A. FRANCHOMME. « | Grand Duo Concertant sur des themes de Robert le Diable. «'.

FOOTLINE: pp. 2–18, 'M.S. 1376'.

Violoncelle: 3 leaves (342 x 273 mm): pp. [1] blank, 2–5 engr music, [6] blank.

CAPTION TITLE: p. 2, 'F. CHOPIN et A. FRANCHOMME. ÷ Grand Duo Concertant sur des thêmes de Robert le Diable. « » Tiré Λ Poussé V.'.

HEADLINE: pp. 2–5, 'VIOLONCELLE.'.

FOOTLINE: pp. 2–5, 'M.S. 1376'.

TEXT: The piano part includes a cello staff throughout.

STAMPS: successor, style BD/D (see Appendix 8).

CONDITION: The title-page plate impression is weak and partly illegible.

1. *Date:* first-edition inference (date code fe, p. 17).

Berlin: **A. Schlesinger (1777) [= 1833]** **B70-aS-1** **M233.C54 D91**

GRAND DUO | concertant | *pour* | *Piano et Violoncelle* | *sur des Thèmes de* | Robert le diable | composé | *par* | FRÉDÉRIC CHOPIN | *ET* | AUGUSTE FRANCHOMME. | *Propriété des Editeurs ÷ Enrégistré dans l'Archive de l'Union » Pr. 1 1/6 Rthl.* | BERLIN, | *chez Ad. Mt. Schlesinger, libraire et éditeur de musique.* | *Paris, chez Maurice Schlesinger.* | *1777.*

Piano: 10 leaves (325 x 257 mm): pp. [1] title page, [2, 3] blank, 4–20 engr music.

CAPTION: p. 4, 'F. CHOPIN. et A. FRANCHOMME « | Grand Duo concertant sur des thêmes de Robert le diable. «'.

FOOTLINE: p. 4, 'S. 1777. » Berlin chez Ad. Mt. Schlesinger.'; pp. 5–20, 'S. 1777.'.

Violoncelle: not present in this copy.

TEXT: The piano part includes a cello staff throughout.

B70-aS-1 *(continued)*

B70-aS-1 *(concluded)*

IMPOSITION: Leaf 6 is a singleton.

STAMPS: publisher, style aS/A (see Appendix 8).

CONDITION: The piano part lacks the final blank leaf (Hob-503 has it), as indicated by an even number of leaves, a central singleton (leaf 6), and a title leaf tipped to leaf 2.

---

1. *Date:* first-edition inference (date code fe, p. 17).

MAZURKA IN C MAJOR
Brown 82

Mainz: Schott (20030) 1870
Warsaw: Kaufmann (171) 1869

Composed 1833
Brown 82
Chominski & Turlo 246

***Mainz:* Schott (20030) [= 1870]** **B82-Schott-1** **M32.C54 M612**

MAZURKA | (en Ut majeur.) | *pour* | Piano | par | FR. CHOPIN. | Oeuvre posthume. |
N° 20030. « » Pr. 36 kr. | Propriété pour tous pays. | MAYENCE CHEZ LES FILS DE B. SCHOTT. |
Bruxelles, Schott frères. ÷ 82 Montagne de la Cour. « Paris, Maison Schott. ÷
1 Rue Auber (M^{on} du G^{d} Hôtel) » Londres, Schott & Cie ÷ 159 Regent Street |
Dépôt général de notre fonds de Musique: | LEIPZIG, C. F. LEEDE. |
Enregistré aux Archives de l'Union | au Ministère de l'Intérieur de France et à Stationers Hall. |
Varsovie chez J. Kauffmann.

3 leaves (346 x 277 mm): pp. [1] lith title page, 2–5 lith music, [6] blank.

CAPTION TITLE: p. 2, 'MAZURKA. | OEUVRE POSTHUME. « » F. CHOPIN.'.

FOOTLINE: p. 2, 'Stich und Druck von B. SCHOTT'S SÖHNEN in MAINZ. « 20030.'; pp. 3–5, '20030.'.

WRAPPER (yellow): pp. [1] same as title page, [2] blank, [3, 4] advt.

ADVT: wrapper pp. [3, 4], 'CATALOGUE | de Morceaux instructifs et récréatifs pour le Piano | Bruxelles, chez Schott Freres. « *publiés par LES FILS DE B. SCHOTT à Mayence.* » Londres, chez SCHOTT & Comp'.

STAMPS: none.

1. *Date:* first-edition inference (date code fe, p. 17).
2. Chominski & Turlo (p. 246) classify this mazurka as a work of doubtful authenticity; it is not included in their main list of Chopin's works. Brown includes it without comment as to authenticity. Niecks (II, p. 236) is non-committal.

VARIATION IN E MAJOR
('Hexameron')
Brown 113

Paris: Troupenas (1066) 1841 — *Composed* 1837
Vienna: Haslinger (7700) 1839 — Brown 113
London: Cramer (406) 1840 — Chominski & Turlo 230

Vienna: **Haslinger (7700) [= 1839]** — **B113-Ha-1** — **M27.L77 H61**

HEXAMERON. | MORCEAU DE CONCERT. | Grandes | VARIATIONS DE BRAVOURE | pour Piano | *sur la* | *Marche des* PURITAINS *de Bellini.* | Composées | *pour le Concert de Mme la Princesse Belgiojoso au Bénéfice des pauvres* | par M.M. | LISZT, THALBERG, | PIXIS, HENRI HERZ, CZERNY et CHOPIN. | *Propriété des Editeurs.* | *N° 7700.* « *Enrégistré dans l'Archive de l'Union.* » *Prix f 3.* _ *C.M.* ÷ ß [Rthlr.] *2.* _ | Vienne, chez Tob. Haslinger, | *Marchand de Musique etc. de la Cour I. et Roy^le.* | *Graben N° 618.* | *Paris, chez B. Latte.* « » *Londres, chez M. Mori.*

18 leaves (340 x 265 mm): pp. [i] engr title page, [ii] blank, [1] engr dedication, 2–31 engr music, [32–34] blank.

DEDICATION (in red): p. [1], 'Dédiées | à Madame la Princesse | CHRISTINE DE BELGIOJOSO.'.

CAPTION TITLE: p. 2, '*HEXAMERON.*'.

FOOTLINE: p. 2, '*(7700)* | *Eigenthum und Verlag der k.k. Hof- Kunst- und Musikalienhandlung des Tobias Haslinger in Wien.*'; pp. 3–31, '*T.H. 7700.*'.

WRAPPER (yellow): pp. [1] engr half-title page, [2–4] blank.

HALF TITLE (in red and black): wrapper p. [1], 'HEXAMÉRON | Morceau de Concert | pour | PIANO. | Vienne, chez Tob. Haslinger, | *Marchand de Musique etc. de la Cour I. et Roy^le.* | *Graben N° 618.* | *Paris, chez B. Latte.* « » *Londres, chez M. Mori.*'.

STAMPS: dealer, Theune, Amsterdam (see Appendix 8).

CONDITION: a superb copy in its original state, untrimmed and unbound.

1. *Date:* first-edition inference (date code fe, p. 17).
2. Title page in blue and black.
3. The theme of these variations is taken from Bellini's opera *I Puritani di Scorzia.* The various composers contributed as follows: pp. 2–7, Introduction and Theme, Liszt; pp. 8–9, Variation 1, Thalberg; pp. 10–11, Variation 2, Liszt; p. 12 and first 11 bars of p. 13, Variation 3, Pixis; p. 13, bridge, Liszt; pp. 14–15, Variation 4, Herz; pp. 16–18 and first 5 bars of p. 19, Variation 5, Czerny; pp. 19–21, bridge, Liszt; p. 22 and first 2 bars of p. 23, Variation 6, Chopin; p. 23, bridge, Liszt; pp. 24–31, Finale, Liszt.
4. Brown (p. 118) lists Latte as the Paris publisher, as does the above Haslinger title page. However, Chominski & Turlo (p. 236) show Troupenas, and comment that they were unable to confirm the Latte publication. They also give an early edition by Ricordi (1838).
5. The London publisher was Cramer, not Mori.

ETUDES IN F MINOR, A FLAT MAJOR, D FLAT MAJOR
('Trois Nouvelles Etudes')
Brown 130

Paris: M. Schlesinger (2345) 1840	*Composed* 1839–40
Berlin: A. Schlesinger (2207.(3)) 1840	Brown 130
London: Chappell (6084) 1841	Chominski & Turlo 38

***Berlin:* A. Schlesinger (2207.(3)) [= 1840]** **B130-aS-1** **M21.E85**

ETUDES DE PERFECTIOÑEMENT | (Etüden für Spieler höherer Ausbilding) | *composées* | pour le Pianoforte | *PAR* | F. Chopin, Th. Döhler, Heller, Ad. Henselt, F. Liszt, | F. Mendelssohn-Bartholdy, Moscheles, Rosenhain, | Taubert, S. Thalberg, Ed. Wolff etc. | *fesant Suite aux Exercises élémetaires et Etudes progressives* | et composées expressement pour la | Méthode des Méthodes | de Moscheles et Fétis | *PROPRIÉTÉ DES EDITEURS.* « » *ENREGISTRÉ AUX ARCHIVES DE L'UNION.* | *Berlin, chez* AD. MT. SCHLESINGER, *Unter den Linden N°. 34.* | *Paris, M. Schlesinger.* « *Moscou, Lehnhold.* » *Londres, Chappel.* | *S. 2207.*

31 leaves (321 x 256 mm): pp. [1] engr title page, 2–61 engr music, [62] blank.

CAPTION TITLE: p. 2, '*) 20 ETUDES de perfectioñement. « L'ENJOUEMENT, ETUDE. (I) | » 2 ETUDES par J. MOSCHELES.'; p. 6, ' L'AMBITION, ETUDE. (I) | » J. MOSCHELES.'; p. 10, '3 ETUDES composées par F. CHOPIN. (I)'; p. 11 system 4, 'ETUDE.'; p. 13 system 4, 'ETUDE.'. After Chopin's etudes, caption titles continue in a similar manner.

SUB-CAPTION: p. 10, 'N° 1. | PIANO.'; p. 11, system 4, 'N° 2. | PIANO.'; p. 13, system 4, 'N° 3. | PIANO.'. Other sub-captions are similar.

FOOTLINE: p. [2], '(*) Eigends für diese Schule geschrieben. ÷ Expressement écrites pour cette Méthode. « S. 2207.(3) » Berlin, Propriété de Ad. Mt. Schlesinger.'; pp. 3–5, 'S. 2207.(3)'; p. 6, '(I) Eigends für diese Schule componirt. ÷ Expressement écrites pour cette Méthode. « S. 2207.(3)'; pp. 7–9, 'S. 2207.(3)'; p. 10, 'Eigends für diese Schule geschrieben. ÷ (I) Expressement écrites pour cette Méthode. « S. 2207.(3) » Berlin, Propriété de Ad. Mt. Schlesinger.'; pp. 11–14, 'S. 2207.(3)'. After Chopin's etudes, footlines continue in a similar manner.

STAMPS: publisher, style aS/D (see Appendix 8).

1. *Date:* first-edition inference (date code fe, p. 17).
2. The three etudes by Chopin are on pp. 10–14.
3. The title page is shown by Chominski & Turlo (plate 7).

MAZURKA IN A MINOR
('Notre Temps')
Brown 134

Paris: *France Musicale* (7–12) 1841	*Composed* 1841
Mainz: Schott (6493.2) 1842	Brown 134
London: Wessel (6316) 1846	Chominski & Turlo 106

***Paris:* *France Musicale* ([9]) [= 1841]** **B134-FM-1** **M21.S62**

SIX | MORCEAUX DE SALON | POUR LE PIANO, | *Spécialement composé* | pour la | FRANCE MUSICALE | [list, numbers 1, 2] | N° 3 Mazourke F. CHOPIN | [list, numbers 4–6] | PARIS | Bureaux de la FRANCE MUSICALE, 6 Rue N^ve St Marc. [this line slanted backward] | MAYENCE | Chez les fils B. SCHOTT. |
[at the foot of the floral design:] J. Galouzeau, Fecit. « » Lith. de Guillas.

15 leaves (350 x 267 mm): pp. [i] lith collective title page, [ii, 1] blank, 2–6 engr music (Kalkbrenner), 1–4 engr music (Bertini), 1–3 engr music (Chopin), 2–4 engr music (Wolff), 2–7 engr music (Osborne), 2–6 engr music (de Kontski), [28] blank.

CAPTION TITLE: Chopin p. 1, 'MAZOURKE, | POUR PIANO | Par F. CHOPIN.'. Each of the six works has a caption title.

SUB-CAPTION: Chopin p. 1, 'N° 3.'. The other sub-captions are similar.

FOOTLINE: Chopin p. 1, '» Mayence chez les fils B. SCHOTT.'; pp. 2–3, none. Each of the other works has a first-footline imprint "à Mayence chez les fils B. SCHOTT. «", and — except Chopin — a plate number ("7." for the first work, "12." for the last).

STAMPS: none.

1. *Date:* first-edition inference (date code fe, p. 17).
2. The plate number of the Chopin mazurka should be 9, but is not present.
3. Each of the six works is individually but not serially paginated.
4. Chominski & Turlo show the title page (plate 3).
5. Grabowski (1994, p. 27) finds evidence for a second impression of this edition in 1845, and suggests (p. 28), as a title more appropriate on the basis of chronology, "Mazurka from the Album La France Musicale". He also speculates that the imprint in the footlines may indicate that Schott financed the French publication in exchange for the German rights (p. 28, footnote 51).

***Paris:* *France Musicale* ([9]) 1841** **B134-FM-2** **M2.3.F8 F73**

[album title page:] ALBUM | DE LA | FRANCE MUSICALE, | POUR LE PIANO. | 1841. | Prix: 20 Francs. | Paris. | *Bureaux de la France Musicale, N° 6, rue Neuve-Saint-Marc* | Mayence, chez les fils B. Schott.

2 leaves (332 x 260 mm): pp. [i] letterpress album title page, [ii, iii] blank, [iv] advt.

B134-FM-2 *(continued)*

B134-FM-2 *(concluded)*

ADVT: p. [iv of the album], LA FRANCE MUSICALE | JOURNAL DES ARTISTES ET DES GENS DU MONDE. ¶ Chaque numéro contient seize à vingt quatre collonnes de text. | Les abonnés reçoivent gratuitement deux Albums par an: un de Chant, au 1er Janvier; l'autre, pour le Piano, au 1er Juillet. En outre, la FRANCE MUSICALE publie tous les mois des morceaux de chant de nos plus *célébres Compositeurs,* avec les belles Lithographies, des Valses et Quadrilles, et des Portraits d'artistes par GRÉVEDON, ALOPHE, CÉLESTIN NANTEUIL, DEVERIA, JULLIEN, etc. ¶ Les nouveaux Souscripteurs qui d'abonneront pour une année auront non-seulement à l'Album des Pianistes mais encore à l'Album de Chant qui a paru le 1er janvier 1841. Ce magnifique Album est composé des Mélodies 1° *L'hirondelle et le Prisonnier,* par Mme VIARDO-GARCIA; 2° *Amour et Folie,* par AUBER; 3° *Sisca l'Albanaise,* par HALÉVY; 4° *Ah! Par pitié,* par Ad. ADAM; 5° *Viens!* par A. THOMAS; 6° Le *Voile blanc,* par H. MONPOU. | Conditions de l'abonnement: | PARIS. ÷ Six mois, 12 fr. — Un an, 24 fr. « DÉPARTEMENTS. ÷ Six mois, 14 fr. — Un an, 28 fr. » Six mois, 16 fr. — Un an, 32 fr. | ON S'ABONNE: | A Paris, au Bureaux de Musique de la FRANCE MUSICALE, 6, *rue Neuve-St-Marc.* | EN PROVINCE, chez tous les Marchands de Musique, chez les Libraires et aux bureaux de poste et des Messageries. | A L'ÉTRANGER, chez les principaux Marchands de Musique et les principaux Libraires.

[internal title page:] SIX | MORCEAUX DE SALON | POUR LE PIANO, | *Spécialement composé* | pour la | FRANCE MUSICALE | [numbers 1, 2] | N° 3 Mazourke F. CHOPIN | [numbers 4–6] | PARIS | Bureaux de la FRANCE MUSICALE, 6 Rue Nve St Marc. [this line slanted backward] | MAYENCE | Chez les fils B. SCHOTT. | [at the foot of the floral design:] J. Galouzeau, Fecit. « » Lith. de Guillas.

15 leaves (332 x 260 mm): pp. [i] lith internal title page, [ii, 1] blank, 2–6 engr music (Kalkbrenner), 1–4 engr music (Bertini), 1–3 engr music (Chopin), 2–4 engr music (Wolff), 2–7 engr music (Osborne), 2–6 engr music (de Kontski), verso blank.

CAPTION TITLE: Chopin p. 1, 'MAZOURKE, | POUR PIANO | Par F. CHOPIN.'.

SUB-CAPTION: Chopin p. 1, 'N° 3.'.

FOOTLINE: Chopin p. 1, '» Mayence chez les fils B. SCHOTT.'; pp. 2–3, none. There is no plate number; however, number 9 had evidently been assigned, as indicated by the other plate numbers.

STAMPS: none.

BOUND WITH: numerous *France Musicale* publications; for details see Appendix 6.

BINDING: collector's binding; for details see Appendix 6.

---

1. *Date:* first-edition inference (date code fe, p. 17).
2. The caption title, sub-caption and footline above refer to the Chopin mazurka. The other five works in the album have similar features, except that each has a plate number in the footline ("7." for the first work, "12." for the last). See B134-FM-1 for other comments.

Paris: **Brandus (4840) [*ca* 1848]** **B134-Bra-1** **M32.C54 M617**

MAZURKA | POUR | le Piano, | *PAR* | *F. CHOPIN* | *AV* | Prix 4f. 50c. | *PARIS,* | BRANDUS et CIE. | *Successeurs de Mce. SCHLESINGER, Rue Richelieu, No. 97.* | *Mayence chez les Fils de B. Schotte* [*sic*]

4 leaves (349 x 270 mm): pp. [i] engr title page, [ii] blank, 1–5 engr music, [6] blank.

CAPTION TITLE: p. 7, 'MAZURKA. | *ELEGANTE* | Pour le Piano « » Par F. CHOPIN.'.

FOOTLINE: p. 1, 'B. et Cie. 4840. » Brandus. et Cie. 97. rue Richelieu'; pp. 2–4, 'B. et Cie. 4840.'; p. 5, same as p. 1.

WRAPPER (dull yellow): pp. [1] engr half-title page, [2–4] blank.

HALF TITLE: wrapper p. [1], 'MAZURKA | *ÉLÉGANTE* | F. Chopin.'.

STAMPS: publisher, style Bra/A (see Appendix 8).

1. *Date:* based on the plate number and address (Table 5A).
2. On the basis of an advertisement, Grabowski (1994, p. 30) gives 1848 as the date of the first Brandus edition. He discusses the source for this edition, and in particular considers the possibility Brandus acquired the mazurka directly from the Escudier brothers, proprietors of *La France Musicale.* He does not discuss Troupenas as a possible source, apparently because he found no evidence a Troupenas edition ever existed (see B134-Schott-1, note 2).

Mainz: **Schott (6493.2) [= 1842]** **B134-Schott-1** **M32.C54 M616**

MAZOURKA | POUR LE | PIANO | PAR | F. CHOPIN | NOTRE TEMPS No. 2. | No. 6493. « Propriété des Editeurs. – Enregistré aux Archives de l'Union. » Pr. 36 kr. | *MAYENCE,* | *ANVERS ET BRUXELLES* | chez les fils de B. SCHOTT. | Dépôt général de notre fonds Musique: à Leipzig chez Gme. Haertel. à Vienne chez H. F. Müller. | *Paris chez Troupenas.*

3 leaves (325 x 252 mm): pp. [i] lith title page, [ii] blank, 1–3 engr music, [4] blank.

CAPTION TITLE: p. 1, 'MAZOURKE | *par* | F. CHOPIN.'.

SUB-CAPTION: p. 1, 'No. 2.'.

FOOTLINE: pp. 1–3, '6493.2.'.

STAMPS: none.

1. *Date:* first-edition inference (date code fe, p. 17).
2. The citation of Troupenas as the Paris publisher is puzzling. Brown (p. 138) asserts "The French republication was advertised in the journal *La France Musicale,* 5 January 1845, as on sale at the 'Bureau Central de Musique'.", and implies that the publisher was Troupenas, whom he cites on p. 137 for an edition of January 1845 with plate number 978. As pointed out by Grabowski (1994, pp. 27–28, footnote 50), this plate number is incorrect, as it belongs to Chopin's Mazurkas Op. 41, published by Troupenas in 1841. (Likewise, the Wessel plate number given by Brown is also wrong: see B134-W-1, note 3.) Grabowski further states that he found no evidence there was any edition by Troupenas, and points out that the 'Bureau Central de Musique' mentioned by Brown was actually an agency for *La France Musicale.* However, according to Chominski & Turlo (p. 136), the A-minor mazurka was distributed by Troupenas (no evi-

B134-Schott-1 *(continued)*

B134-Schott-1 *(concluded)*

dence is given), as well as by the Escudier brothers, proprietors of *La France Musicale.* If this arrangement began with the original publication in 1841, it is conceivable there was a Troupenas issue at that time with plate number close to 978. Although Grabowski states that he found no mention of the Mazurka in A minor in any Troupenas catalogue, some involvement by Troupenas is implied by the citation of that publisher in the Schott editions. Such citations are not always reliable, and in this case it could have been made simply as an inference by Schott from the fact that Troupenas did in fact publish a succession of Chopin's works in 1840 and 1841. Nevertheless, until more information is available, the existence and characterization of the Troupenas edition should be considered uncertain.

***Mainz:* Schott (7118) [*ca* 1843]** **B134-Schott-2** **M211.C54 M617**

MAZOURKA | POUR | le Piano, | composé par | F. CHOPIN | arrangé à quatre mains. |
N° 7118 « » Pr 45 kr. | Propriété des Editeurs. Enregistré aux Archives de l'Union. | MAYENCE |
ANVERS ET BRUXELLES | chez les fils de B. Schott. | Dépôt général de notre fonds de Musique:
à Leipzig chez C.F. Leede. à Vienne chez H. F. Müller. | *Paris, chez Troupenas.*

3 leaves (345 x 275 mm): pp. [1] lith title page, 2–5 engr music, [6] blank.

CAPTION TITLE: p. 1, 'F. CHOPIN MAZURKE. « » arr: à 4 mains par G.M. SCHMIDT.'; p. 2, the same.

HEADLINE: pp. 2, 4, 'SECONDA.'; pp. 3, 5, 'PRIMA.'.

FOOTLINE: pp. 2–5, '7118.'.

WRAPPER (yellow): pp. [1] same as title page, [2, 3] blank, [4] advt.

ADVT: wrapper p. [4]. 'Catalogue de Morceaux à 4 Mains | *pour le Piano* | de H. Bertini, Fréd. Burgmüller, Th. Döhler, Fr. Hünten & S. Thalberg. | Publiées par LES FILS DE B. SCHOTT à Mayence. | Bruxelles, chez SCHOTT FRERES. « » Londres, schez SCHOTT & Comp.'.

STAMPS: none.

1. *Date:* based on the plate number (Deutsch, p. 23).

***Mainz:* Schott (6493.2) [after 1873]** **B134-Schott-3** **M32.C54 M6162**

The transcription of this title page is the same as that of **B134-Schott-1**, except here the price is "1. M.".

3 leaves (342 x 270 mm): pp. [i] lith title page, [ii] blank, 1–3 engr music, [4] blank.

CAPTION TITLE: p. 1, 'MAZOURKE | *par* | F. CHOPIN.'.

SUB-CAPTION: p. 1, 'N° 2.'.

FOOTLINE: pp. 1–3, '6493.2.'.

WRAPPER (yellow): pp. [1] same as title page, [2, 3] blank, [4] advt.

ADVT: wrapper p. [4], '*Catalogue des Ouvrages pour le Piano de* | F. Godefroid, J. Gregoir, J. Herz, F. Kalkbrenner, J. Leybach, L. de Meyer, E. Pauer & J. Rosenhain, | Bruxelles, chez Schott Frères. « *publiés par LES FILS DE B. SCHOTT à MAYENCE.* » Londres, chez Schott & Comp.'.

STAMPS: none.

1. *Date:* currency inference; see date code c3, p. 17, also note 2.

B134-Schott-3 *(continued)*

B134-Schott-3 *(concluded)*

2. This score, priced in Marks, corresponds to Hob-510 (stated to be a first edition, 1842), while B134-Schott-1, priced in kroner, corresponds to Chominski & Turlo p. 136 (also stated to be a first edition).
3. See B134-Schott-1, note 2 for comments about the Troupenas attribution.

***London:* Wessel (6316) [1848–56]** **B134-W-1** **M32.C54 M619**

Nº [handwritten "64"] OF | WESSEL & Cº.'s COMPLETE COLLECTION | OF | *the Compositions* | OF | FREDERIC CHOPIN | FOR THE | Piano Forte. | Solo & Duet | [list of works, Wessel 1–63] | 64 "CRACOW" *Mazurka. in A min. Op. 59 bis. 2/-* | [list of works, Wessel 65–71] | *Ent. Sta. Hall. « Copyrights. » Price. Solo* [handwritten "2/-"] ÷ " *Duet* [blank] | *LONDON,* | WESSEL & Cº *Importers and Publishers of* FOREIGN MUSIC, | *(by special Appointment) to, H.R.H. the Duchess of Kent.* | Nº 229, Regent Street, Corner of Hanover Street.

4 leaves (334 x 250 mm): pp. [i] engr title page, [ii] blank, 1–5 engr music, [6] advt.

CAPTION TITLE: p. 1, 'WESSEL & CO'S. COMPLETE COLLECTION OF THE WORKS OF FREDERIC CHOPIN. | CRACOW. | *Nº 64.* | MAZOURKE. | » *OP: 59. bis.*'.

FOOTLINE: p. 1, '(W & Cº Nº 6316.)'; pp. 2–4, 'CHOPIN. Op: 59. bis. "Cracow." « » (W & Cº Nº 6316.)'; p. 5, 'CHOPIN. Op: 59. bis. "Cracow." « | (Nº 6316.) WESSEL & Cº '.

ADVT: p. [6], '[clipped to] CONTINUATION OF WESSEL [long blank space] CATALOGUE OF THEIR PIANOFORTE PUBLICATIONS, | COMPRISING THE SOLO WORKS OF BEETHOVEN, CHOPIN, LISZT, HENSELT, &c. ORGAN MUSIC, | PIANOFORTE STUDIES, TRIOS, QUARTETTS, QUINTETTS, &c. &c. &c.'. This is advt "Page E", with Chopin works listed through Op. 42.

STAMPS: publisher, style W/C? (see Appendix 8).

1. *Date:* Wessel inference (date code W1, p. 17).
2. The blank space after "WESSEL" in the heading of the advertisement indicates a deletion, probably of reference to Stapleton.
3. Brown (p. 137) gives an incorrect plate number, 6313, which is the plate number for Wessel's edition of the Berceuse Op. 57.

MAZURKA IN A MINOR
('Emile Gaillard')
Brown 140

Paris: M. Schlesinger (—) 1841	*Composed* 1840
Paris: Chabal (—) 1841	Brown 140
Berlin: Bote & Bock (3359) 1855	Chominski & Turlo 105

Berlin: Bote & Bock (3359) [= 1855] **B140-BB-1** **M32.C54 M631**

MAZOURKA | pour le | PIANO | composée par | FR. CHOPIN. | Pr. 12 1/2 Sgr. | Propriété des Editeurs. Ent. Sta. Hall. « » Enrégistré aux Archives de l'Union | Wien, *Gustav Lewi.* ÷ Dresden, *Friedel.* ÷ Leipzig, *Leede.* « BERLIN ÷ CHEZ ED. BOTE & G. BOCK. ÷ (G. Bock.) ÷ Marchand Editeur de Musique de S.M. le Roi ÷ et de S.A.R. le Prince Albert de Prusse. ÷ Posen au Marché N° 6. » Hamburg, *Cranz.* ÷ Breslau, *Saha.* ÷ Stettin, *Simon.*

4 leaves (325 x 253 mm): pp. [1] lith title page with portrait, [2] blank, 3–7 lith music, [8] blank.

CAPTION TITLE: p. 3, 'MAZOURKA | DEDIÉE | A SON AMI EMILE GAILLARD | PAR | FR: CHOPIN.'.

FOOTLINE: p. 3, 'Propriété des Editeurs. « B.&B. 3359. » Berlin chez Ed. Bote u. G. Bock'; pp. 4–6, 'B.&B. 3359.'; p. 7, 'B.&B. 3359. » Stich und Druck von Ed. Bote & G. Bock. Berlin.'.

STAMPS: dealer, Veit, Prague.

1. *Date:* first-edition inference (date code fe, p. 17).

Appendix

Appendix 1
VARIETIES OF TITLE PAGES OF OPUS 34

Each of the publishers — M. Schlesinger, Breitkopf & Härtel, and Wessel — issued the three waltzes of Op. 34 separately. The Schlesinger edition has a different title-page design for each waltz, as shown by Grabowski (1992, vol. 3, figs. 45, 46, 47). The three waltzes of the Wessel edition have the same title-page design, shown by Chominski & Turlo (plate 20). (This collection has the Wessel score only for #1, in Wessel's later, collective form of title page.)

The situation with the Breitkopf editions is more complicated, at least four title-page designs having been used. The following table summarizes the evidence available from scores in this collection and in Hoboken. In chronological order, the four designs are denoted D1, D2, D3, D4. The entries in the table are catalogue or

Title-page designs in Breitkopf & Härtel editions of Opus 34

	Hoboken collection				*This collection*			
Opus	D1	D2	D3	D4	D1	D2	D3	D4
34#1	325^{a}	328^{a}	—	—	—	1^{a}	—	$2^{e}, 3^{e}$
34#2	326^{b}	330^{b}	—	—	$2^{b}, 3^{b}$	4^{b}	1^{c}	—
34#3	327^{d}	—	—	—	$3^{d}, 4^{d}$	—	1^{d}	2^{d}

score numbers that identify the particular scores in question. For example, Hob-325 is Op. 34#1 in design D1, while in this collection the entry in the 34#3 row and D4 column identifies 34#3-BH-2, abbreviated #3–2 in this discussion. All scores in the table have lithographed title pages, and all have engraved music except this collection's #1–2 (in the D4 column).

Design D1, used in the first editions, has a "sunburst" background (Hoboken, plate 23, p. 145). All D1 scores in the table are priced in Groschen except #2–3, which is in Neugroschen. All other scores in the table are priced in Neugroschen, and one, #1–2, is also in Marks. In the transcriptions of the Hoboken D1 scores, the name of the title-page lithographer appears in Hob-325 and 326 but not in 327. (Possibly this is an oversight.) The lithographer's name does appear in #3–3 and #3–4.

Designs D2, D3, D4 of the later editions are different from each other and from D1. The differences involve all of the main attributes of title-page design: art work, syntax, font style, and layout. Some of these differences can be detected by comparing the title-page transcriptions, as indicated in the following transcriptions of the first six words of each of the four designs. However, artwork and certain aspects of layout escape

D1: *TROIS* | VALSES | Brillantes | *POUR LE* | PIANO

D2: Trois | VALSES | Brillantes | *POUR LE* | PIANO

D3: Trois | VALSES | Brillantes | pour le | PIANO

D4: Trois | VALSES | BRILLANTES | pour le Piano

notice except by facsimile reproduction. For example, it is common to see a line of text set in an arc, with the middle of the line lower than the ends. This is the case with the composer's name in D2, and with "Propriété des Editeurs" in D4. In the latter design, two other lines are in an arc raised, rather than lowered, in the middle. Such design features usually are not mentioned in quasi-facsimile transcription.

Another way to compare the different issues is by means of the caption title. Remarkably, five slightly different styles of caption title are associated with the four title-page designs listed above. They are indicated in the table by superscripts a, b, c, d, e. The differences are minor, as can be seen from the caption-title transcriptions, but any difference is significant from the standpoint of identification. (For example, the word 'par' is engraved as "par" in caption-title styles a and e; as *"PAR"* in b and d; and as "PAR" in c.)

Appendix 2
THE VOLUME WITH OPUS 35 AND OPUS 58

Scores of Chopin's sonatas Opp. 35 and 58 are included in an elegant collector's volume awarded as a prize by the Paris Conservatoire. In addition to the two Chopin works, the volume contains thirteen other early-to-mid-nineteenth-century piano compositions; all are sonatas for piano solo.

The fifteen pieces are arranged in the volume alphabetically by composer, and are listed in that order in the following brief descriptions.

- **Beethoven**, Sonata Op. 2#1. *Paris:* Farrenc (A.F. 238) [*ca* 1831–36]
  9 leaves: [i] engr title page, [ii, 1] blank, 2–15 (serial 2–15) engr music, [16] blank.
- **Beethoven**, Sonata Op. 7. *Paris:* Farrenc (A.F. 169) [*ca* 1829–31]
  11 leaves: [i] engr title page, [ii, 1] blank, 2–19 (serial 52–69) engr music, [20] blank.
- **Beethoven**, Sonata Op. 13. *Paris:* Farrenc (A.F. 180) [*ca* 1831–36]
  9 leaves: [i] engr title page, [ii] blank, 1–15 (serial 1–15) engr music, [16] blank.
- **Beethoven**, Sonata Op. 22. *Paris:* Farrenc (A.F. 174) [*ca* 1831–36]
  12 leaves: [i] engr title page, [ii] blank, 1–21 (serial 40–60) engr music, [22] blank.
- **Beethoven**, Sonata Op. 26. *Paris:* Farrenc (A.F. 232) [*ca* 1831–36]
  10 leaves: [i] engr title page, [ii, 1] blank, 2–17 (serial 61–76) engr music, [18] blank.
- **Beethoven**, Sonata Op. 31#1. *Paris:* Farrenc (A.F. 176) [*ca* 1831–36]
  13 leaves: [i] engr title page, [ii] blank, 1–23 (serial 22–44) engr music, [24] blank.
- **Chopin**, Sonata Op. 35. *Paris:* Troupenas (T. 891) [1840]
  11 leaves: [i] engr title page, [ii] blank, 1–19 engr music, [20] blank.
- **Chopin**, Sonata Op. 58. *Paris:* Meissonnier (J.M. 2187) [1845]
  11 leaves: [i] engr title page, [ii] blank, 1–19 engr music, [20] blank.
- **Dussek**, Sonatas Op. 35##1–3. *Paris:* Joly (1454) [*ca* 1837–48]
  26 leaves: [i] engr title page, [ii, 1] blank, 2–49 engr music, [50] blank.
- **Hummel**, Sonata Op. 13. *Paris:* Legouix (O.L. 85) [*ca* 1845–48]
  11 leaves: [i] engr title page, [ii] blank, 1–19 engr music, [20] blank.
- **Hummel**, Sonata Op. 55. *Paris:* Leduc (2017) [184748]
  9 leaves: [i] engr title page, [ii] blank, 1–16 engr music.
- **Hummel**, Sonata Op. 81. *Paris:* Brandus (B. et Cie 345) [*ca* 1846]
  20 leaves: [i] engr title page, [ii] blank, 1–37 engr music, [38] blank.
- **Marmontel**, Sonata (no opus number). *Paris:* Prilipp (no plate number) [*ca* 1841–48]
  13 leaves: [i] engr title page, [ii, 1] blank, 2–23 engr music, [24] blank.
- **Moscheles**, Sonata Op. 49. *Paris:* Aulagnier (1?) [*ca* 1832–44]
  8 leaves: [i] engr title page, [ii, 227] blank, 228–240 engr music.
- **Weber**, Sonata Op. 24. *Paris:* Legouix (O.L. 112) [*ca* 1845–48]
  15 leaves: [i] engr title page, [ii, 1] blank, 2–27 engr music, [28] blank.

Except for Chopin, dates are based on plate numbers and addresses from Devriès & Lesure (1988), but are quite uncertain in most cases.

The binding is decorated elaborately in gilt on the upper and lower boards and on the spine; all edges are gilt. The upper board reads 'Conservatoire de Musique | & de Déclamation | *Concours de* 1849 | 1ER PRIX DE SOLFÈGE | DÉCERNÉ A M^{ELLE} E. CASSELIN.'. The lower board is monogrammed 'E.C.'. The spine reads 'MUSIQUE | DE | PIANO'. The size of the volume is 34 x 26 x 4 cm.

Appendix 3
VARIETIES OF TITLE PAGES OF OPUS 64

Each of the publishers — Brandus, Breitkopf & Härtel, and Wessel — issued the three waltzes of Op. 64 separately. In addition, Breitkopf & Härtel issued an edition with all three waltzes. The Brandus edition has a different title-page design for each waltz, as shown in facsimile by Grabowski (1992, vol. 3, figs. 109, 110, 111). All of the Wessel editions of Op. 64 have the collective title-page design.

As with the waltzes Op. 34, the situation with the Breitkopf & Härtel editions of Op. 64 is more complicated than that of the other publishers, at least three title-page designs having been used. The following table summarizes the evidence available from scores in this collection and in Hoboken. The three designs are denoted D1, D2, D3. Only the separately issued waltzes are included in the table. (The design of Breitkopf & Härtel's title page for the edition with all three waltzes differs from those of the separate waltzes.) The entries

Title-page designs of Breitkopf & Härtel editions of Opus 64

	Hoboken collection			*This collection*		
Opus	D1	D2	D3	D1	D2	D3
64#1	—	450[b]	—	1[a]	2[b]	3[b]
64#2	451[a]	—	—	—	1[a]	—
64#3	—	452[a]	—	1[a]	—	—

in the table identify the particular scores in question. For example, Hob-450 is Op. 64#1 in design D2, while in this collection the entry in the 64#2 row and D2 column identifies 64#2-BH-1, abbreviated #2–1 in this discussion. All scores in the table have lithographed title pages and engraved music, except for this collection's #1–2 and #1–3, which have lithographed music. The latter two scores have plate number 9619; all others have the original 7715. All scores are priced at 15 Ngr.

Another way to compare the different issues is by means of the caption title. Only two styles of caption title are associated with the three title-page designs listed above. They are indicated in the table by superscripts a, b. The differences can be seen by comparing the transcriptions given in the descriptions of 64#1-BH-1 and 64#1-BH-2.

Appendix 4
PRINTINGS OF OPUS 66 TO OPUS 73

The collection's scores of the Meissonnier Fils edition of the posthumous works edited by Fontana are those issued in a complete set. The main title page for this bound volume is in collective form, as described under score number 66/73-MeiF-1. A frontispiece and the two-page preface by Fontana follow the title page. The eight works in the volume are described in proper sequence in the catalogue. Each has a half title. The French publisher also issued them separately, each with a series title page. The collection's Gérard reprints of Opp. 66, 67 and 73 are examples of the separate issues. The Meissonnier and the Gérard editions have no Opus numbers, which presumably were assigned by Schlesinger (see the footline in 66-aS-1).

The collection's scores of the A. Schlesinger editions of the posthumous works edited by Fontana are those issued separately, rather than in a complete set. Each has a collective title page. Entries in the table that follows describe pagination of these individual works. Fuld (p. 223) notes three variant printings of the Schlesinger editions: two are by Burkhardt, the other by Nietack. In this collection, Opp. 66, 71, 72 are from the two Burkhardt printings, while Opp. 67, 68, 70, 73 are from the Nietack printing. (The collection lacks the A. Schlesinger editions of Op. 69 and Op. 71#3.) The variants differ in details of the title page and possibly in some internal details. I have no information about their chronology. The music is engraved in all scores except 72-aS-1.

Variant printings of A. Schlesinger editions of Opera 66–73

score number	*printing variant*	*individual pagination*	*serial pagination*
66-aS-1	B1	[1] t, [2] b, 3–11 m, [12] b, [13, 14] p	none
66-aS-2	B1	[i] t, [ii] b, [1, 2] p, 3–11 m, [12] b	none
67-aS-1	N	[1] t, [2, 3] b, 4–12 m, [13, 14] p	12–20 m
68-aS-1	N	[1] t, [2, 3] b, 4–11 m, [12] b, [13, 14] p	22–29 m
70-aS-1	N	[1] t, [2, 3] b, 4–11 m, [12] b, [13, 14] p	40–47 m
71#1-aS-1	B2	[3] t, 4-11 m, [12] b, [13, 14] p	48–55 m
71#2-aS-1	B2	[3] t, 4-11 m, [12] b, [13, 14] p	56–63 m
72-aS-1	B1	[3] t, 4-12 m, [13, 14] p	72–80 m
73-aS-1	N	[i] t, [ii, 1] b, 2–17 m, [18] b, [19, 20] p	82–97 m
		piano secondo: [1] b, 2–15 m, [16] b	none

In the second column of the table, B1, B2, N signify the Burkhardt and Nietack variants. In the pagination the abbreviations are: "t" for title page, "b" for blank, "p" for preface, and "m" for music. Fontana's preface ("Paris, Mai 1855.") is in German and French; it is appended in all scores except for 66-aS-2, where it is in the preliminaries. The serial pagination indicated above is consistent with pagination of the complete edition, which from Fuld's comments, is [i] t, [ii] b, [1, 2] p, 3–97 m, [98] b.

In design B1 the title page does not identify the London agent; in B2 it does (Scheurmann). In B1 the title page does not have a Petersbourg agent; in B2 it does (Dufour). In N the title page does not identify the London agent, but it does have the Petersbourg agent.

Appendix 5
VARIETIES OF TITLE PAGES OF OPUS 74

All of the collection's scores of the songs Op. 74 are separate issues, each with a title page. Fifteen scores numbered 74#n-aS-1 where n = 1 to 15 are in a bound collector's volume. Each of the others is in a separate enclosure. The collection does not have a score for #17 or a copy of the "complete" (collective) edition, which has a preface by Fontana.

Six title-page designs are found in the collection's scores of Op. 74, of which only two can be inferred to correspond to the first edition. The others are more difficult to date. In the following table the designs are

Title-page designs of A. Schlesinger editions of Opus 74

title-page design	*found in score number*	*inferred publication date*	*title-page plate numbers*	*footline plate number*	*title-page price, complete*	*lines slanted backward*	*Lienau imprint?*	*Haslinger agency?*
A	2^1, 3^1	1859	S. 4797–4812	†	2.5 Th.	2, 4, –5, –3	no	no
B	4^1, 5^1, 5^3, 6^2, 7^1–15^1	1860–63	S. 4797–4812	†	2.5 Th.	2, 4, –5, –3	no	no
C	1^1, 6^1	1864–71	S. 4797–4812	†	2.5 Th.	2, 4, –2	yes	no
D	5^2	1864–71	S. 4797–4812	S. 6670	2.5 Th.	2, 4, –2	yes	no
E	16^2	after 1873	S. 4797–4812	S. 6670	7.5 Mk.	2, 4, –3	yes	yes
F	1^2, 14^2, 16^1	after 1873	s. 6669/70	S. 6670	1.0 Mk.	none	yes	yes

labeled A, B, C, D, E, F and are listed in probable chronological order. The numbers in the second column identify individual scores. For example, 2^1 means score number 74#2-aS-1, and 16^2 means 74#16-aS-2. In the column *"footline plate number"* the † symbol means the appropriate plate number in the sequence 4797–4812. Note that "S. 6670" apparently was used as a publisher number (rather than plate number) for the five scores of designs D, E, F.

It was a practice of some German title-page engravers occasionally to use lettering slanted backward, rather then forward as with italics. All designs except F exhibit this style. The column headed *"lines slanted backward"* indicates on which lines of text this type of lettering occurs. Positive line numbers start from the title "Polnische Lieder" as line 1. Negative numbers are counted from the bottom of the page, –1 being the bottom line, –2 the second from the bottom, and so on.

Inferred publication dates in the table are based on various pieces of evidence. The inferences were made in the following way.

- *Song 17.* Designs A and B have the number "16" at the head of the title page. This number was of course removed when song 17 was included, as in designs C, D, E, F. The clear implication is that C, D, E, F are later than A and B.
- *Lienau.* Lienau acquired Schlesinger's firm in 1864 (Krummel & Sadie, p. 410). It follows from the next-to-last column in the table that A and B probably were issued before 1864, and C, D, E, F after 1863. This is consistent with the preceding inference.
- *Thaler.* In discussing the collective edition, Brown (p. 34) asserts that song 17 was added to the original set of 16 in *ca* 1868, but on p. 104 (in connection with the separate publication of #17) he gives 1872 for that date. Chominski & Turlo (pp. 161–62) give a range 1864–73 for the first issue of #17. Since C and D are priced only in thaler, they should have a date before 1872 (see Introduction, "Dating notation"). The table accordingly shows C and D in the range 1864–71. This is consistent with the two preceding inferences.
- *Individual prices.* All designs have a price for the complete set of songs, as indicated in the table. In addition B, C, D, E have printed prices for individual songs. However, no individual printed prices are given in A or F. Close visual comparison of title pages A and B shows that the same plates were used. The spacing

between some characters makes clear that B is a modification of A. There were three modifications: (i) the floral decoration below "Op. 74" in A was removed, (ii) in its place a price column for songs 1–8 was inserted, and (iii) a price column was added for songs 9–16. From this we can infer that B follows A, but since it lacks the Lienau imprint, it precedes C. The result is the range 1860–63 for B, as indicated.

- *Haslinger.* Carl Haslinger is listed (on the last line) in E and F, but is not listed in A, B, C, D. Since Lienau acquired Haslinger in 1874 (Krummel & Sadie, p. 279), E and F should have a date later than 1873, as indicated in the table. This is consistent with the fact that they are priced only in marks. Note also that at the time of the currency transition in 1872–73 from Thaler to Marks, the equivalence was 1 Th. = 3 Mk., which corresponds to the change from 2.5 Th. in D to 7.5 Mk. in E for the price of the collective edition.
- *Plate number.* According to Deutsch (p. 22) number 6670 appeared in 1874, but that is not consistent with design D, which has 6670 internally and is priced in thaler. Although score 16^2, representing design E, has number 6670 internally, it has the original plate numbers on the title page, whereas F has 6669/70 on the title page (and 6670 internally). This leads to the inference that F is later than E. Moreover, unlike the price in E, the 1.0-Mk. price in F does not correspond to the 2.5-Th. price in D, so presumably it represents a later revaluation of currency. Without knowing when this revaluation took place, there appears to be no basis for making a better estimate of the date for F.
- *Decorations.* Art work on the title pages consists mainly of decorations of the title "Polnische Lieder". Two styles are evident. One, which appears in A, B, C, D, E consists of lightly drawn, somewhat abstract flourishes that surround the two words of the title. The other style is seen in the three F scores. Here the flourishes are sharply defined and have a more floral character, with stems that rise vertically through the leading letters "P" and "L". These flourishes do not surround the title.
- *Publisher stamps.* Three types of A. Schlesinger stamps are found here. All are circular and in blue ink. In the catalogue descriptions they are identified as S1, which has "SCHLESINGER | SCHE" in the middle and "BUCH U. MUSIKHANDLUNG" along the circular border; S2, with "BERLIN" in the middle and "SCHLESINGERSCHE BUCH U. MUSIKHANDL." on the border; and S3, a smaller circle with only "S'SCHE | B. u. M." in the middle. Stamp S1 appears in the two A scores and in B scores 4^I, 5^I, 7^I, 8^I, 10^I, 11^I, 12^I, 15^I. Stamp S2 appears in B scores 9^I, 13^I, 14^I, and in C score 1^I. Stamp S3 appears only in C score 6^I. In D score 5^2 and the four scores of E and F there is no publisher stamp. From these data it seems likely that the chronological order of the stamps is S1, S2, S3.

All of the above title-page (and footline) information, including the contents of the table, is derived from the scores in this collection, and from no other source. It is of course possible other title-page designs exist that are not in the collection. Hoboken has only one title page (Hob-499), which has design A and is stated to be a first edition, 1859. The same is apparently the case for the copy described by Chominski & Turlo (p. 161).

Pagination can provide some insight into chronology. Separate-issue page numbers for the collection's scores of 1^I –15^I appear in the normal verso/recto positions. In addition, the music plates in these scores have serial page numbers (centered at the head) for the collective issue. Collectively these numbers fall continuously in the range 3–44, leaving three music pages 45–47 for song 16. This is consistent with Hoboken's description of the collective first edition of the original 16 songs (Hob-499), which in the present catalogue's style is [i] title page, [ii] blank, [1] preface, [2] blank, 3–47 text, [48] blank.

The five scores of designs D, E, F have only serial page numbers. However, these numbers are not the same as in the corresponding scores of A, B, C; in particular, the last page number for song 16^I is 37 instead of 47. The scores in D, E, F are evidently part of an edition in which the music is laid out with repeats, in all songs for which that is possible, as in scores 1^2 and 14^2. The first edition, however, is formatted without the use of repeats. This change in the layout of the music is probably what accounts for publisher number 6670 indicated in the footlines of D, E, F. The collection does not have a score with the number 6669 indicated on the title page of design F.

Designs C and D are assigned the same range of dates, because it is not known when the 6669/70 edition appeared. Nevertheless, since D belongs to that edition, score 5^2 must be later than the two scores of design C (see table), which are paginated in the original sequence.

Appendix 6
THE VOLUME WITH BROWN 134

The B134-FM-2 score of Chopin's *"Notre Temps"* mazurka is included in a collector's volume of songs and piano pieces. The binding is contemporary half leather (34 x 27 cm) with gilt decoration. All of these pieces were issued by *France Musicale*, the weekly journal of musical news and commentary ("Journal des artistes et des gens du monde") published in Paris from 1837 by Escudier frères. In 1841, the journal began to issue music scores. According to the advertisement on p. [iv], annual subscribers to *France Musicale* received complimentary monthly songs and semi-annual albums, one in January with songs, the other in July with piano pieces. The present volume consists mainly of selections of these publications for the years 1841 and 1842, presumably collected and bound by a subscriber. Following are details of its principal features.

- *Contents:* The volume does not have a comprehensive title page. It contains three "albums" — two from 1841, one from 1842 — and an assortment of separate songs, as well as a few piano pieces. For convenience of discussion, the contents are arranged here in five groups A, B, C, D, E, which are approximately chronological in that order. (In the bound volume the groups appear in the non-chronological order B, D, A, C, E.) Group A is the first of the semi-annual albums for 1841, consisting of six songs. Group B is the second semi-annual album for 1841, with six piano pieces including the Chopin mazurka. Group C consists of 10 'monthly' songs of 1842, and has a laid-down album title page presumably supplied by the publisher at the end of the year. Group D is a potpourri of 19 songs, perhaps including some 'monthly' songs of 1842. The last group, E, has three piano pieces, probably from 1842.
- *Plate numbers:* These reflect the early publishing history of *France Musicale*. Following are the plate numbers of the five groups of scores. The Chopin mazurka is the third piece in group B, with plate number ab-

A	six songs, January 1841	1, 2, 3, 4, 5, —.
B	six piano pieces, July 1841	7, 8, —, 10, 11, 12.
C	10 songs, 1842	none.
D	19 songs, [1842]	F.M. 97, F.M. 108, F.M. 109, F.M. 116, F.M. 127(6); the other 14, none.
E	three piano pieces, [1842]	F.M. 103, F.M. 104, F.M. 121.

  sent but implicitly 9. In group A, implicit plate number 6 is for a song by Halévy.
- *Dates:* Devriès & Lesure (p. 165) give 1842 as the year corresponding to plate numbers in the range F.M. 79–174, which is the basis used above for dating groups D and E. The dates for groups A, B, C appear explicitly on the respective title pages. Prefix "F.M." was used beginning in May 1842 to indicate that the works in question were primary publications under the *France Musicale* imprint, whereas before that, the scores were taken on assignment from other publishers (*op. cit.*, p. 163).
- *Imprints:* The phrase "Mayence et Anvers chez les fils B. SCHOTT" appears in the footline on the first page of music in each of the 10 scores of group C, and also on the paste-down title page. It is not clear whether this implies that Schott was an agent or a primary publisher (with copyright). The same is the case for group B, except for a slight change of wording ("à Mayence" instead of "Mayence et Anvers"), but in group A there is no reference to Schott. In groups D and E some scores refer to Schott, some do not.
- *Title-page design:* In group D each title page (except those of songs 16–19) has a fanciful scene that depicts the subject matter in nineteenth-century manner. In C there are no scenes, and in A there are scenes (in miniature) on the album title page but not on the individual title pages.

The outline below has only summary descriptions that lack most of these details, but a detailed description of group B is given in the main catalogue under B134-FM-2.

In the summary descriptions, the first name in parentheses after "lith title page" identifies the design artist, the second name the lithographer. The name after "engr title page" identifies the engraver. The first name in parentheses after "engr music" identifies the composer, and for songs, the second name identifies the lyricist. The abbreviation "pn" means 'plate number'. Within each of the five groups the scores are listed in the order of their appearance in the volume.

A. Album of six popular songs, 1841.

- [i] album lith title page (Sorrieu/Guillet, ALBUM DE LA FRANCE MUSICALE, 1841), [ii] blank.

1. pp. 1–5 engr music (Auber/—, AMOUR ET FOLIE, pn 1), [6] blank.
2. pp. 1–5 engr music (Thomas/Lesguillon, VIENS, pn 2), [6] blank.
3. pp. 1–3 engr music (Viardot-Garcia/—, L'HIRONDELLE ET LE PRISONNIER, pn 3).
4. pp. [4–5] engr music (Monpou/Lécluse, LE VOILE BLANC, pn 4).
5. pp. [6–7] engr music (Adam/Eichomme, OH! PAR PITIÉ NE M'AIMEZ PLUS, pn 5), [8] blank.
6. pp. [9–11] engr music (Halévy/Escudier, SISCA L'ALBANAISE, no pn), [12] blank.

B. Album of six piano pieces, 1841.

- [i] album letterpress title page (ALBUM DE LA FRANCE MUSICALE POUR LE PIANO, 1841), [ii, iii] blank [iv] advt. (This album title page is not present in B134-*FM*-1.)
- [i] internal lith title page (Galouzeau/Guillet, SIX MORCEAUX DE SALON POUR LE PIANO), [ii, 1] blank. (For details see B134-*FM*-2.)

1. pp. 2–6 engr music (Adam, MARCHE FUNEBRE, arr by Kalkbrenner, pn 7).
2. pp. 1–4 engr music (Bertini, MELODIE DRAMATIQUE, pn 8).
3. pp. 1–3 engr music (Chopin, MAZOURKE, no pn).
4. pp. 2–4 engr music (Wolff, NOCTURNE, pn 10).
5. pp. 2–7 engr music (Osborne, MARIE, pn 11).
6. pp. 2–6 engr music (Kontski, APPARITION AU BAL, pn 12), [7] blank.

C. Album of 10 popular songs, 1842.

- pp. [1] album lith title page (Nanteuil/Bertauts, ALBUM de CHANT, 1842), blue paper laid down.

1. pp. 2–10 engr music (Niedermeyer/Deschamps, UNE VOIX DANS L'ORAGE), [11] blank.
2. pp. [12–13] engr music (Monpou/Gourdin, PAUVRE HELENE), [14] blank.
3. pp. [15–17] engr music (Monpou/Plouvier, MON FILS CHARMANT).
4. pp. [18–19] engr music (Adam/Richomme, PLUS HEUREUX QU'UN ROI).
5. pp. [20–21] engr music (Clapisson/Courcy, DE LOIN JE N'AI PLUS PEUR DE VOUS).
6. pp. [22–23] engr music (Labarre/Gourdin, MERCI MONSEIGNEUR).
7. pp. [24–25] engr music (Mazel/—, LE LAI DU CHASSEUR PRISONNIER), [26] blank.
8. pp. [27–29] engr music (Vogel/Lagache, SATAN).
9. pp. [30–31] engr music (Barroilhet/Escudier, OH! VOUS SAVEZ POURQUOI). [32] blank.
10. pp. [33–35] engr music (Beauplan/Beauplan, J'AI PEUR), [36] blank.

D. Nineteen popular songs (18 title pages), [1842]

- no album title page.

1. pp. [1] lith title page (Meuilleron/Bertauts),
   [2–3] engr music (Puget/Lemoline, NINA LA BRUNE, pn F.M. 108), [4] blank.

2. pp. [1] lith title page (Nanteuil/Bertauts),
[2–3] engr music (Vogel/Masson, PETITE SOEUR ET MOI, pn F.M. 116), [4] blank.

3. pp. [1] lith title page (Nanteuil/Bertauts),
[2–3] engr music (Boieldieu/Gourdin, TU NE SAIS PAS ENFANT CE QUE C'EST QUE L'AMOUR!, no pn), [4] blank.

4. pp. [1] lith title page (Nanteuil/Bertauts),
[2–3] engr music (Roger/—, LE FOU D'AMOUR, pn F.M. 109), [4] blank.

5. pp. [1] lith title page (Nanteuil/Bertauts),
[2–3] engr music (Adam/Richomme), JE N'Y PENSE PLUS, no pn), [4] blank.

6. pp. [1] lith title page (Sorrieu/Bertauts),
[2–3] engr music (Flotow/Plouvier, MARIA, no pn), [4] blank.

7. pp. [1] lith title page (Sorrieu/Bertauts),
2–5 engr music (Labarre, SYLVIA, Romance sans Paroles, no pn), [6] blank.

8. pp. [1] lith title page (Sorrieu/Bertauts),
[2–3] engr music (Heinefetter/Porte, PAUVRE MARIE, no pn), [4] blank.

9. pp. [1] lith title page (Sorrieu/Bertauts),
[2–3] engr music (Adam/Escudier, FLORIDA, no pn), [4] blank.

10. pp. [1] lith title page (Nanteuil/Bertauts),
[2–4] lith music (Vieuxtemps/Lamartine, LE PAPILLON, no pn).

11. pp. [1] lith title page (Sorrieu/Bertauts),
[2–3] engr music (Dancla/Huard, LA REINE DE L'ONDE, no pn), [4] blank.

12. pp. [1] lith title page (Nanteuil/Bertauts),
[2–3] lith music (Barriolhet/—, LA PETITE SAVOYARDE, no pn), [4] blank.

13. pp. [1] lith title page (Nanteuil/Bertauts),
[2–3] lith music (Puget/Musset, LE RHIN ALLEMAND, no pn), [4] blank.

14. pp. [1] lith title page (Nanteuil/Bertauts),
[2–3] lith music (Adam/Richomme, LA WILI, no pn), [4] blank.

15. pp. [i] lith title page (Leroux/Bertauts), [ii] blank,
1–3 lith music (Gretry/—, UNE FIÈVRE BRULANTE, no pn), [4] blank.

16, 17. pp. [1] engr title page (Vialon),
[2–3] engr music (Monpou/Pluvier, MAL D'AMOUR, no pn),
2–3, [4] engr music (Monpou/Pluvier, L'HEURE OU LE JOUR S'ENDORT, no pn).

18. pp. [1] engr title page ([Vialon]),
2–3 engr music (Clapisson/Humbert, JE NE SUIS QU'UNE FEMME!, pn F.M. 97), [4] blank.

19. pp. [1] engr title page,
2–3 engr music (Girard/de Leuven & Brunswick, LES DIX, ROMANCE, pn F.M. 127(6)), [4] blank.

E. Two piano pieces and one fragment, [1842].

- no album title page.

1. no title page, pp. 1–5 engr music (Prudent, ANDANTE, pn F.M. 121), [6] blank.
2. no title page, pp. 3 engr music (fragment, pn F.M. 103, probably Cramer waltz Op. 20/1), [4] blank.
3. pp. [1] engr title page ([Vialon]) (Cramer Op. 20, LES PERLES, TROIS VALSES),
2–3 engr music (VALSE No. 2, pn F.M. 104), [4] blank.

Appendix 7
VARIETIES OF WESSEL TITLE PAGES

Wessel classified many of his publications in various series with names that characterize the style, genre, or technical difficulty of the works included. With only a few exceptions each of his Chopin editions published in 1833–40 (through Op. 41) was classified in one of five such series. A two-letter abbreviation for each series

AP: *L'Amateur Pianiste* PF: *Album des Pianistes de Première Force*
PM: *Le Pianiste Moderne* AS: *Les Agrémens au Salon* MT: *Modern Trios*

name is used in the following table, based on data from Chominski & Turlo, Brown, the British Library, the New York Public Library, and this collection. The third column lists the serial number of the work within the

Opus	*Series*	*Number*	*Notes*
1	AP	1	
2	PF	17	
3	PM	50	ps
4	—	—	np
5	PM	11	†
6	AP	8	†
7	AP	9	†
8	MT	1	†
9	AP	66, 67	†
10	—	—	ns
11	PF	24	
12	—	—	np
13	PF	21	
14	PF	22	
15	AP	68	†
16	AP	24	†
17	AP	27	†
18	AP	28	†
19	AP	54	
20	AP	56	†
21	PF	33	
22	PF	34	
23	AP	69	†
24	AP	80	†
25	—	—	ns
26	AP	83	†
27	AP	84	†
28	—	—	ns
29	PM	57	
30	PM	61	
31	PM	59	
32	PM	60	
33	PM	94	
34	PM	95, 96, 97	
35	AS	39	
36	AS	40	
37	—	—	ns
38	AS	30	
39	AS	45	
40	—	—	ns
41	AS	47	
B-70	—	—	ns

Notes: np: not published by Wessel; ps: piano-solo arrangement; ns: not known to be in any of these series; † first issued without a series designation

series. In addition to multi-composer series such as those above, Wessel devised special series for Chopin's works. For these he used names that caused the composer much aggravation, such as "Souvenir de la Pologne" for the mazurkas, "Murmeres de la Seine" or "Les Zephyrs" for the nocturnes, and "La Gaité" or "Les Favorites" for the polonaises.

Wessel acquired Opp. 35–42 by means of three contracts in 1839–40 (Kallberg, 1996, p. 205), and published all of these works in 1840. The first three he issued with individual title pages (for Op. 36 see 36-W-1; for Opp. 35 and 37 see Chominski & Turlo), but all works with opus number equal to or greater than 38 have collective title pages, as far as is known to the writer. (The last three series designations indicated above are included in the caption titles; for Opp. 38 and 39 see Chominski & Turlo; for Op. 41 see 41-W-1.)

Wessel's collective title pages can be dated by means of the last work listed. Many copies have complete lists, through Op. 64, the latest published by Wessel, while many others have incomplete lists and thus correspond to earlier issue dates. However, the writer knows no incomplete list that ends with a work earlier than

Op. 42. This is consistent with the inference that, after issuing Opp. 35–37 with individual titles, Wessel adopted the collective-title format for Opp. 38–42 — the other 1840 editions — and for all subsequent first editions. He also used the same collective format for many reissues of earlier editions. The only exception known to the writer is 3-W-1 (dated 1856–60), which is described as a "New edition", edited by Fontana. A collective format designed for piano-duet arrangements also exists (Op. 29, PN 5358, British Library shelfmark h.473.(9.)).

Grabowski (2001) has lately analyzed the collective title pages and found an evolution from 1840 to 1860 that includes 14 versions and various sub-versions. Eleven of the 14 versions involved expansions of the number of works listed, as more were published, starting from 45 in 1840 and ending with 71 in 1848. Sub-versions involve changes in prices, titles, dedications and other details.

Appendix 8
TITLE PAGE STAMPS

SURVEY OF STAMPS

Among the collection's roughly 420 Chopin scores, there are approximately 330 title pages with stamps. The aim of this appendix is to give first a brief survey of the stamp population, then quantitative data and photographic reproductions of some of the stamps. Quantitative data are given in a table that lists the 53 distinct designs found among the publisher stamps. Photographic images of the tabulated stamps are reproduced in the "gallery" that follows the table. Also included in the table and gallery is a selection of eight of the approximately 95 dealer stamps.

Title-page stamps applied by a publisher (or publisher's successor) are noted in the STAMPS field in the score's description. Dealer (or publisher's agent) stamps are also noted, but if none of these four types of stamp is present, "none" is entered. Other stamps, such as by a library or private owner, are not considered.

Title-page stamps applied by a publisher (or publisher's successor) are noted in the STAMPS field in the score's description. Dealer (or publisher's agent) stamps are also noted, but if none of these four types of stamp is present, "none" is entered. Other stamps, such as by a library or private owner, are not considered.

About 70 per cent of the scores have publisher stamps, and about one-fifth of these also have dealer stamps. The accompanying chart gives a more detailed census of the scores with publisher (p) and/or dealer (d) stamps. Of particular interest is the relatively large number of scores (124, about 30 per cent) without

number of scores	p yes	p no	sum
d yes	60	35	95
d no	235	89	324
sum	295	124	419

publisher stamps, which suggests that at least for some publishers the stamps did not serve a useful purpose. Most of the scores without publisher stamps also have no dealer stamps, as shown in the table.

The primary Chopin publishers for whom there are no publisher stamps are two Leipzig publishers Kistner (23 scores) and Hofmeister (four scores), and the Vienna publishers Haslinger (six scores) and Mechetti (eight scores). It is also noteworthy that two publishers who did use stamps, namely M. Schlesinger and Breitkopf & Härtel, did not use them on all their scores. The accompanying census charts are similar to the one above, but instead of referring to all publishers, they refer only to M. Schlesinger (mS) and Breitkopf & Härtel (BH). Of the collection's 58 Schlesinger scores, for example, 34 have no publisher stamp, and of 130 Breitkopf & Härtel

number of scores	mS yes	mS no	sum
d yes	9	1	10
d no	15	33	48
sum	24	34	58

number of scores	BH yes	BH no	sum
d yes	28	2	30
d no	77	23	100
sum	105	25	130

scores, 25 have no publisher stamp.

For ease of reference each publisher-stamp design is assigned a code, called the stamp's "style". The style is expressed in terms of the publisher identity code (as in Table 2B) and a style letter A, B, C, … . A style in italics indicates an embossed ("blind") stamp — for example, *Bra/C.* In the STAMPS field of the score's description the style is used to identify the stamp and as a cross-reference to the table and gallery.

Most of the collection's publishers who applied stamps used more than one stamp design. Generally, the design is either a cursive representation of the publisher's signature (apparently favored by the French publishers represented in the collection), or a lettered indication of the publisher's name and, in some cases, address. There are a few stamps with both cursive and lettered elements, such as the Pleyel publisher stamp Pl/A on score 16-Pl-1, and the Theune dealer stamp on Haslinger score B113-Ha-1, both of which are among the images displayed in the gallery.

The impressions of the majority of the stamps were made with either black or blue ink. The device used to make the impression was presumably a metal plate for intaglio impressions, a rubber stamp for relief impressions, or an embossing tool for blind impressions. There is wide variation in the stamps' legibility, depending on the quality of the device in hand and on the care used in making the impression. In many cases portions of the stamp were cropped when the leaves of the score were trimmed.

Blind stamps are less common than inked stamps. Although they are inconspicuous and therefore generally do not detract from the aesthetic appearance of the title page, for the same reason it is often visually difficult to detect them. Regrettably, in many cases their text is almost illegible.

In this collection there are 13 different designs of Breitkopf & Härtel stamps, more than twice the variety found for any of the other publishers. Nine of the Breitkopf designs are based on the "lyre" motif; differences between some of these are barely detectable. Other publishers or dealers also used this motif. There are no cursive stamps among the Breitkopf & Härtel designs, and only one blind stamp *(BH/A)*. All stamps in the gallery are contemporary (19th century) with exception of BH/M, which has the acronym "VEB" (Wolkseigener Betrieb) used in East Germany following World War II.

The collection's A. Schlesinger group, with six designs, has one cursive stamp (aS/A) and one blind stamp *(aS/C)*. In contrast, of five Wessel designs, all but one are for blind stamps.

Of the 27 designs by various French publishers in the collection, only one — by Brandus — is for a blind stamp (of which there is only one copy). This appears on a score published in 1846 (61-Bra-1), the year of Brandus's formal succession to the M. Schlesinger firm. After that, Brandus, as well as Brandus & Dufour, used only inked, cursive stamps.

One of the most unusual stamps encountered is BH/I, which occurs on 14 of the 130 B&H scores. This stamp has an especially finely executed lyre design, and its carefully aligned position creates the appearance that it is part of the lithographic plate. No other stamp in the collection has these attributes. Although I recorded it in the copy-specific STAMPS field, I believe it is probably a print-specific element.

In some cases the publisher in the stamp style is not the same as the original publisher of the score. For example, the third entry in the table is for the stamp with style Bra/A, the source of which is score 17-mS-1, published by M. Schlesinger *ca* 1834. When Brandus acquired the Schlesinger firm, in 1846, he probably acquired the plates of this score, or at least some un-stamped copies of the original printing. Thus Bra/A on 17-mS-1 is an example of what in the STAMPS field is described as a "successor" stamp rather than a publisher stamp. This situation is illustrated by the accompanying census chart, which gives the number of scores published by M. Schlesinger that have either the publisher stamp (mS) or that of his successor (Bra). (There are of

number of scores	**mS yes**	**mS no**	**sum**
Bra yes	0	19	19
Bra no	24	15	39
sum	24	34	58

course Brandus stamps on scores for which Brandus is the publisher, such as Bra/C (61-Bra-1).) Note that according to the census, no M. Schlesinger score has both a Schlesinger and a Brandus stamp.

The foregoing survey pertains only to the scores that are described in this catalogue. It is not intended to imply generalizations as to the purpose, application or design of title-page stamps.

In the table of stamp designs on the next three pages, the first column identifies the stamp's style, as defined above. The second column gives the number of title pages on which the design appears. The third and fourth columns show the approximate dimensions of the stamp, included because the images in the gallery are enlarged by various unstated factors. The next column identifies the score that served as the source for the photographic image, and the last column has this score's estimated publication date (taken from the score's imprint data in the Description part of the catalogue).

For each design the most legible example was selected for reproduction in the gallery. Thus the date of the source's score is not necessarily the date of the collection's earliest score on which the stamp appears. All that can be inferred from the source date is that the stamp in question was first used on or before that date.

In the gallery that follows the table, stamp images are presented in the same order as in the table (except aL/A and aL/B, which are transposed in the gallery). Each is identified in its legend by the stamp's style (as defined above) and, in parentheses, by the score number of its source. In the brief list of dealer stamps tabulated and displayed after the publisher stamps, the dealer's name is used instead of a style.

TABLE OF STAMP DESIGNS

French publishers

stamp design style	number of title pages	stamp height (mm)	stamp width (mm)	source score number	source score date
		M. Schlesinger (Paris)			
mS/A	9	29	76	9-mS-1	1833
mS/B	15	15	49	11-mS-3	1833
		Brandus (Paris)			
Bra/A	16	10	55	17-mS-1	*ca* 1834
Bra/B	14	15	65	23-mS-1	1836
Bra/C	1	24	35	61-Bra-1	1846
Bra/D	1	12	47	51-BD-1	after 1857
Bra/E	3	12	40	65-BD-1	after 1857
		Brandus & Dufour (Paris)			
BD/A	1	16	54	51-mS-1	1843
BD/B	4	18	54	56-mS-1	1844
BD/C	7	10	45	7-mS-1	1846–48
BD/D	7	9	47	42-BD-1	*ca* 1860
		Pleyel, Prilipp, Catelin, and Troupenas (Paris)			
Pl/A	1	46	90	16-Pl-1	1834
Pr/A	1	20	64	19-Pr-1	1834
Ca/A	1	22	43	28-Ca-1	1839
T/A	2	20	*ca* 52	35-T-1	1840
T/B	3	20	50	37-T-2	1840
		Meissonnier and Gérard (Paris)			
Mei/A	2	15	55	58-Mei-1	1845
Mei/B	2	20	43	58-Mei-2	1845
Gér/A	1	20	45	67-Gér-1	after 1859
Gér/B	2	21	49	66-Gér-1	after 1866
		H. Lemoine and A. Lemoine (Paris)			
hL/A	1	22	55	18-hL-2	*ca* 1842
aL/A	2	30	44	10-hL-1	*ca* 1842
aL/B	1	25	63	18-hL-1	*ca* 1859
aL/C	3	25	44	34#3-hL-1	*ca* 1861
		Richault, Heugel, and Leduc (Paris)			
Rich/A	1	*ca* 17	*ca* 45	3-Rich-1	*ca* 1860
Rich/B	3	36	30	64#1-Rich-1	*ca* 1860
Led/A	1	17	41	34#1-Led-1	1859–60
Heu/A	1	15	31	22-Heu-1	after 1867

German publishers

stamp design style	number of title pages	stamp height (mm)	stamp width (mm)	source score number	source score date
Breitkopf & Härtel (Leipzig)					
BH/A	1	11	16	17-BH-4	1834
BH/B	7	8	10	20-BH-2	after 1835
BH/C	13	18	16	21-BH-5	1836
BH/D	17	17	16	22-BH-1	1836
BH/E	3	16	15	17-BH-2	after 1840
BH/F	10	16	15	29-BH-1	after 1840
BH/G	13	18	15	29-BH-2	after 1840
BH/H	2	15	14	34#3-BH-1	after 1840
BH/I	15	15	11	37-BH-2	after 1845
BH/J	22	18	15	37-BH-2	after 1845
BH/K	6	16	14	63-BH-2	1847
BH/L	3	21	41	58-BH-4	1878
BH/M	4	20	39	4-BH-1	1880
A. Schlesinger (Berlin)					
aS/A	1	13	59	B70-aS-1	1833
aS/B	21	16	16	66-aS-1	1855
aS/C	1	11	27	73-aS-1	1855
aS/D	6	19	19	74#9-aS-1	1860–63
aS/E	1	?	12	74#6-aS-1	1864–71
Peters (Leipzig)					
Pe/A	1	13	14	19-Pe-1	after 1840

English publishers

stamp design style	number of title pages	stamp height (mm)	stamp width (mm)	source score number	source score date
Wessel (London)					
W/A	4	19	19	9#3-W-1	1833
W/B	6	5	5	24-W-1	1836–39
W/C	15	19	19	50-W-1	1842
W/D	18	28	38	64#1-W-1	1848
W/E	2	29	29	6-W-2	1856–60
Cramer & Beale (London)					
CB/A	1	13	22	64#1-CB-1	1848

Selected dealers or agents

dealer name	**dealer place**	**number of title pages**	**stamp height (mm)**	**stamp width (mm)**	**source score number**	**source score date**
Retté	Paris	1	24	45	16-mS-1	*ca* 1834
Sennewald	Warsaw	1	19	44	11-Ki-4	after 1833
Ewer	London	1	*ca* 25	*ca* 45	72-aS-1	*ca* 1855
Scheurmann	London	3	28	?	7-W-3	1856–60
Schott	Mainz	1	22	36	61-BH-1	1846
Theune	Amsterdam	2	34	29	B113-Ha-1	1839
Höpfert	Osnabrück	1	16	16	64#1-BH-1	1847
Rahr	Utrecht	1	24	22	71#2-aS-1	1855

GALLERY OF STAMPS

French publishers

mS/A (9-mS-1)

mS/B (11-mS-3)

Bra/A (17-ms-1)

Bra/B (23-mS-1)

Bra/C (61-Bra-1)

Bra/D (51-BD-1)

Bra/E (65-BD-1)

BD/A (51-mS-1)

BD/B (56-mS-1)

BD/C (7-mS-1)

BD/D (42-BD-1)

French publishers *(continued)*

Pl/A (16-PL-1)

Pr/A (19-Pr-1)

Ca/A (28-Ca-1)

T/A (35-T-1)

T/B (37-T-2)

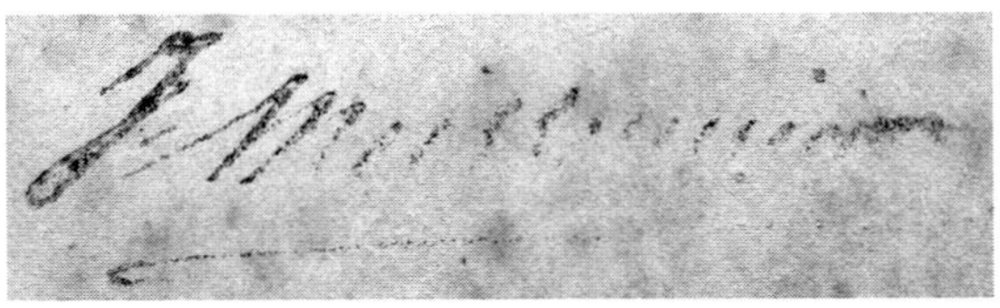

Mei/A (58-Mei-1)

Mei/B (58-Mei-2)

Gér/A (67-Gér-1)

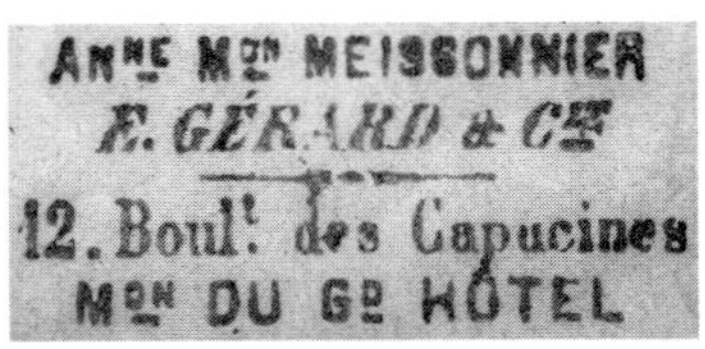

Gér/B (66-Gér-1)

French publishers *(concluded)*

hL/A (18-hL-2)

aL/B (18-hL-1)

aL/A (10-hL-1)

aL/C (34#3-hL-1)

Rich/A (3-Rich-1)

Rich/B (64#1-Rich-1)

Heu/A (22-Heu-1)

Led/A (34#1-Led-1)

German publishers

BH/A (17-BH-4)

BH/B (20-BH-2)

BH/C (21-BH-5)

BH/D (22-BH-1)

BH/E (17-BH-2)

BH/F (29-BH-1)

BH/G (29-BH-2)

BH/H (34#3-BH-1)

BH/I (37-BH-2)

BH/J (37-BH-2)

BH/K (63-BH-2)

German publishers *(concluded)*

BH/L (58-BH-4)

BH/M (4-BH-1)

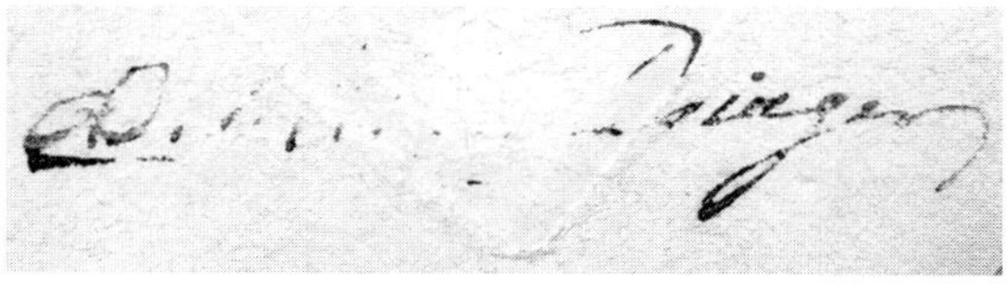

aS/A (B70-aS-1)

aS/B (66-aS-1)

aS/C (73-aS-1)

aS/D (74#9-aS-1)

aS/E (74#6-aS-1)

Pe/A (19-Pe-1)

English publishers

W/A (9#3-W-1)

W/B (24-W-1)

W/C (50-W-1)

W/D (64#1-W-1)

W/E (6-W-2)

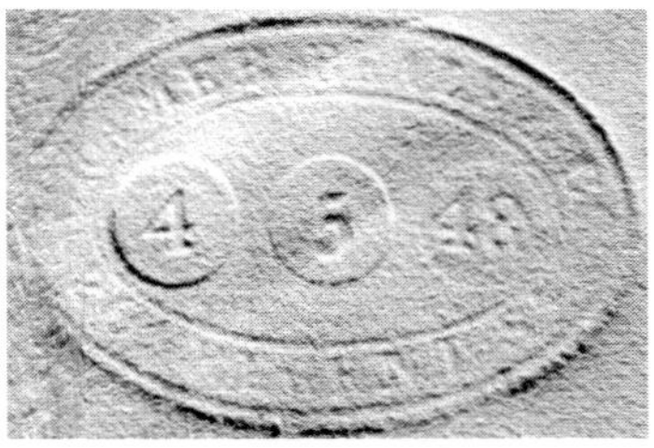

CB/A (64#1-CB-1)

Selected dealers or agents

Retté (16-mS-1)

Sennewald (11-Ki-4)

Ewer (72-aS-1)

Scheurmann (7-W-3)

Schott (61-BH-1)

Theune (B113-Ha-1)

Höpfert (64#1-BH-1)

Rahr (71#2-aS-1)

Tables

The tables deal with general aspects of Chopin's entire oeuvre and with related data for his publishers. In contrast to the other parts of the catalogue, they are not based on the Library's Chopin collection (with exception of Table 2B and Table 6).

Table 1A
Chopin's works listed by work number

The work number is the opus number or, for works without opus number, the Brown number. The table lists all 74 works with opus number, and 13 works without opus number. Publications after 1870 are not included. (For details, see "Chopin's works" in the Introduction, p. 3.) Explanations of column headings are as follows.

C&T This is the index number, from 1 through 230, for the 105 works listed as authentic in the thematic index by Chominski & Turlo (1990). Of these, the table below excludes works originally published after 1870. Since Chominski & Turlo assign an index number to each composition, works with more than one composition have more than one index number. For example, the four Mazurkas of Op. 41 have index numbers 76 through 79. In all such cases, the table shows only the first number (76 for Op. 41), which suffices for locating the Chominski & Turlo publication data. (The three compositions in Op. 72 are different genres, so are listed separately in the table, the only such case in the list.)

B This is the index number, from 1 through 168, for the works listed in the thematic index by Brown (1972). If two or more compositions are in the same work, Brown gave them the same index number if they were composed at about the same time; otherwise, some have different numbers. For example, the four Mazurkas Op. 41 have index numbers 122 (for Op. 41#2) and 126 (for the other three). In such cases, the table shows only the number where Brown gives publication data (122 for Op. 41).

Op This is the opus number, from 1 through 74. Works without opus number have "—" in this column.

Year This is the first-edition publication year according to Chominski & Turlo. Since first editions of almost all of Chopin's works were published in more than one place, there is often more than one year for each work. Here only the earliest year is given. For more detail refer to Table 2A.

Work title This is the title used in the present catalogue. For more detail refer to Table 1B. All works are for piano solo unless otherwise noted.

Notes Reference to notes at the end of the table is by work number.

C&T	*B*	*Op*	*Year*	*Work title*	*Notes*
192	10	1	1825	Rondo in C minor	
225	22	2	1830	Variations in B flat major for piano and orchestra ('Là ci darem la mano')	
148	41	3	1831	Polonaise in C major for piano and cello	3
201	23	4	1851	Sonata in C minor	
193	15	5	1828	Rondo in F major	
51	60	6	1832	Mazurkas in F sharp minor, C sharp minor, E major, E flat minor	6
56	61	7	1832	Mazurkas in B flat major, A minor, F minor, A flat major, C major	7
206	25	8	1832	Trio in G minor for piano, violin, and cello	
108	54	9	1832	Nocturnes in B flat minor, E flat major, B major	
14	42	10	1833	Etudes	
47	53	11	1833	Concerto in E minor for piano and orchestra	
226	80	12	1833	Variations in B flat major ('Hérold')	
41	28	13	1834	Fantaisie in A major for piano and orchestra	13
194	29	14	1834	Rondo in F major for piano and orchestra ('Krakowiak')	
111	55	15	1833	Nocturnes in F major, F sharp major, G minor	
195	76	16	1833	Rondo in E flat major	
60	77	17	1834	Mazurkas in B flat major, E minor, A flat major, A minor	
207	62	18	1834	Waltz in E flat major	

(continued)

C&T	B	Op	Year	Work title	Notes
8	81	19	1834	Bolero in C major	
197	65	20	1835	Scherzo in B minor	
48	43	21	1836	Concerto in F minor for piano and orchestra	
149	58	22	1836	Polonaise in E flat major for piano and orchestra	
2	66	23	1836	Ballade in G minor	
64	89	24	1836	Mazurkas in G minor, C major, A flat major, B flat minor	
26	78	25	1837	Etudes	
150	90	26	1836	Polonaises in C sharp minor, E flat minor	
114	91	27	1836	Nocturnes in C sharp minor, D flat major	
166	107	28	1839	Preludes	
43	110	29	1837	Impromptu in A flat major	
68	105	30	1837	Mazurkas in C minor, B minor, D flat major, C sharp minor	
198	111	31	1837	Scherzo in B flat minor	
116	106	32	1837	Nocturnes in B major, A flat major	
72	115	33	1838	Mazurkas in G sharp minor, C major, D major, B minor	
208	94	34	1838	Waltzes in A flat major, A minor, F major	
202	128	35	1840	Sonata in B flat minor	
44	129	36	1840	Impromptu in F sharp major	
118	119	37	1840	Nocturnes in G minor, G major	
3	102	38	1840	Ballade in F major	
199	125	39	1840	Scherzo in C sharp minor	
152	120	40	1840	Polonaises in A major, C minor	
76	122	41	1840	Mazurkas in E minor, B major, A flat major, C sharp minor	
211	131	42	1840	Waltz in A flat major	
205	139	43	1841	Tarantelle in A flat major	
154	135	44	1841	Polonaise in F sharp minor	
190	141	45	1841	Prelude in C sharp minor	
1	72	46	1841	Allegro de concert in A major	
4	136	47	1841	Ballade in A flat major	
120	142	48	1841	Nocturnes in C minor, F sharp minor	
42	137	49	1841	Fantaisie in F minor	49
80	145	50	1842	Mazurkas in G major, A flat major, C sharp minor	
45	149	51	1843	Impromptu in G flat major	
5	146	52	1843	Ballade in F minor	
155	147	53	1843	Polonaise in A flat major	
200	148	54	1843	Scherzo in E major	
122	152	55	1844	Nocturnes in F minor, E flat major	
83	153	56	1844	Mazurkas in B major, C major, C minor	
7	154	57	1845	Berceuse in D flat major	
203	155	58	1845	Sonata in B minor	
86	157	59	1845	Mazurkas in A minor, A flat major, F sharp minor	
6	158	60	1846	Barcarolle in F sharp major	
156	159	61	1846	Polonaise-fantaisie in A flat major	
124	161	62	1846	Nocturnes in B major, E major	
89	162	63	1847	Mazurkas in B major, F minor, C sharp minor	
212	164	64	1847	Waltzes in D flat major, C sharp minor, A flat major	

(continued)

C&T	*B*	*Op*	*Year*	*Work title*	*Notes*
204	160	65	1847	Sonata in G minor for piano and cello	
46	87	66	1855	Fantaisie-impromptu in C sharp minor	66
92	93	67	1855	Mazurkas in G major, G minor, C major, A minor	
96	18	68	1855	Mazurkas in C major, A minor, F major, F minor	
215	95	69	1855	Waltzes in A flat major, B minor	
217	40	70	1855	Waltzes in G flat major, F minor, D flat major	
157	11	71	1855	Polonaises in D minor, B flat major, F minor	
126	19	72#1	1855	Nocturne in E minor	72
50	20	72#2	1855	Marche funèbre in C minor	72
11	12	72#3	1855	Ecossaises in D major, G major, D flat major	72
196	27	73	1855	Rondo in C major for two pianos	
129	32	74	1857	Songs for voice with piano accompaniment	74
163	6	—	1864	Polonaise in G sharp minor	
227	14	—	1851	Variations in E major ('Der Schweitzerbub')	
(216)	35	—	1852	Waltzes in B minor, F minor ('Deux valses mélancoliques')	
165	36	—	1870	Polonaise in G flat major	
222	56	—	1868	Waltz in E minor	
10	70	—	1833	Duo concertant in E major for piano and cello	
—	82	—	1870	Mazurka in C major	B82
230	113	—	1838	Variations in E major ('Hexameron')	
38	130	—	1840	Etudes in F minor, A flat major, D flat major ('Trois Nouvelles Etudes')	B130
106	134	—	1841	Mazurka in A minor ('*Notre Temps*')	B134
105	140	—	1841	Mazurka in A minor ('Emile Gaillard')	

Notes
(by work number)

3 Various titles of Op. 3 are: uniform, "Introduction et polonaise brillante"; Richault, "Polonaise Brillante Précédée d'une Introduction"; Mechetti, "Introduction et Polonaise Brillante"; Wessel, the same; Chominski & Turlo, "Polonez"; Brown, "Introduction" (B52) and "Polonaise" (B41).

6, 7 The Mazurka in C major appears as Op. 6#5 in the Paris (M. Schlesinger) edition, and as Op. 7#5 in the Leipzig (Kistner) edition. The London publisher (Wessel) did not include it in early editions of Op. 6 or Op. 7, but it does appear as the last mazurka in a late edition of Op. 7 (see 7-W-3).

13 Various titles of Op. 13 are: uniform, "Grande fantaisie"; Kistner, the same; M. Schlesinger, "Fantaisie"; Wessel, "Fantaisie brillante"; Chominski & Turlo, "Fantazja"; Brown, "Grand Fantasia".

49 Various titles of Op. 49 are: uniform, "Fantasia"; all publishers, "Fantaisie"; Chominski & Turlo, "Fantazja"; Brown, "Fantasia".

66 Various titles of Op. 66 are: uniform, "Fantaisie-Impromptu"; all publishers, the same; Brown, the same; Chominski & Turlo, "Impromptu-fantaisie".

72 Op. 72 has the single, uniform title "Nocturne, marche funèbre, et 3 écossaises.". The publishers give it a similar title, but its three parts are indexed separately by Chominski & Turlo (and by Brown).

74 The uniform title of Op. 74 is "Polish songs". Gebethner's and Schlesinger's title for the Polish-language edition is "Zbiór spiewów Polskich", and Schlesinger's title for the German edition is "Polnische Lieder". Chominski & Turlo's title is "Piesni"; Bown's is "Songs for voice and PF."

(continued)

B82 The authenticity of this work was questioned by Chominski & Turlo (p. 246).

B130 The uniform title of B130 is "Etudes de perfectionement.". The work is also known as "Trois Nouvelles Etudes" (Brown) and "Etudes de la Méthode des Méthodes" (Chominski & Turlo).

B134 The uniform title is "Mazurkas, piano, B. 134, A minor". Other titles are "Mazurek A-Moll" (Chominski & Turlo), "Mazurka in A minor *(Notre Temps)"* (Brown). The *"Notre Temps"* designation is often used. It is explained by Brown (p. 137): "This mazurka was first published in 'Six Morceaux de Salon' (no. 1) by the Bureau de la *France Musicale* on 4 July 1841. Chopin's mazurka and four other pieces from this collection were then published by Schott's Sons, Mainz, in an album entitled 'Notre Temps' (6493/no. 2), in February 1842." Grabowski (1994, p. 28) suggests *"Mazurka from the album La France Musicale"*.

Table 1B

Chopin's works listed alphabetically

The individual lines are the same as those of Table 1A but they are listed alphabetically by "work title", which appears at the head of the first page of the work's catalogue entry. This title is based on English-language conventions, and is similar to the University of Chicago Library's "uniform title" (see Glossary). In almost all cases the first word of the work title is the same as that of the uniform title. The lexical order of work titles is therefore almost the same as that of the uniform titles. Exceptions are described in notes. For an explanation of other column headings and for *Notes*, refer to Table 1A.

C&T	*B*	*Op*	*Year*	*Work title*	*Notes*
1	72	46	1841	Allegro de concert in A major	
2	66	23	1836	Ballade in G minor	
3	102	38	1840	Ballade in F major	
4	136	47	1841	Ballade in A flat major	
5	146	52	1843	Ballade in F minor	
6	158	60	1846	Barcarolle in F sharp major	
7	154	57	1845	Berceuse in D flat major	
8	81	19	1834	Bolero in C major	
47	53	11	1833	Concerto in E minor for piano and orchestra	
48	43	21	1836	Concerto in F minor for piano and orchestra	
10	70	—	1833	Duo concertant in E major for piano and cello	
11	12	72#3	1855	Ecossaises in D major, G major, D flat major	72
14	42	10	1833	Etudes	
26	78	25	1837	Etudes	
38	130	—	1840	Etudes in F minor, A flat major, D flat major ('Trois Nouvelles Etudes')	B130
41	28	13	1834	Fantaisie in A major for piano and orchestra	13
42	137	49	1841	Fantaisie in F minor	49
46	87	66	1855	Fantaisie-impromptu in C sharp minor	66
43	110	29	1837	Impromptu in A flat major	
44	129	36	1840	Impromptu in F sharp major	
45	149	51	1843	Impromptu in G flat major	
50	20	72#2	1855	Marche funèbre in C minor	72
51	60	6	1832	Mazurkas in F sharp minor, C sharp minor, E major, E flat minor	
56	61	7	1832	Mazurkas in B flat major, A minor, F minor, A flat major, C major	
60	77	17	1834	Mazurkas in B flat major, E minor, A flat major, A minor	
64	89	24	1836	Mazurkas in G minor, C major, A flat major, B flat minor	
68	105	30	1837	Mazurkas in C minor, B minor, D flat major, C sharp minor	
72	115	33	1838	Mazurkas in G sharp minor, C major, D major, B minor	
76	122	41	1840	Mazurkas in E minor, B major, A flat major, C sharp minor	
80	145	50	1842	Mazurkas in G major, A flat major, C sharp minor	
83	153	56	1844	Mazurkas in B major, C major, C minor	
86	157	59	1845	Mazurkas in A minor, A flat major, F sharp minor	
89	162	63	1847	Mazurkas in B major, F minor, C sharp minor	
92	93	67	1855	Mazurkas in G major, G minor, C major, A minor	
96	18	68	1855	Mazurkas in C major, A minor, F major, F minor	
—	82	—	1870	Mazurka in C major	B82
106	134	—	1841	Mazurka in A minor ('*Notre Temps*')	

(continued)

C&T	B	Op	Year	Work title	Notes
105	140	—	1841	Mazurka in A minor ('Emile Gaillard')	
108	54	9	1832	Nocturnes in B flat minor, E flat major, B major	
111	55	15	1833	Nocturnes in F major, F sharp major, G minor	
114	91	27	1836	Nocturnes in C sharp minor, D flat major	
116	106	32	1837	Nocturnes in B major, A flat major	
118	119	37	1840	Nocturnes in G minor, G major	
120	142	48	1841	Nocturnes in C minor, F sharp minor	
122	152	55	1844	Nocturnes in F minor, E flat major	
124	161	62	1846	Nocturnes in B major, E major	
126	19	72#1	1855	Nocturne in E minor	72
148	41	3	1831	Polonaise in C major for piano and cello	3
149	58	22	1836	Polonaise in E flat major for piano and orchestra	
150	90	26	1836	Polonaises in C sharp minor, E flat minor	
152	120	40	1840	Polonaises in A major, C minor	
154	135	44	1841	Polonaise in F sharp minor	
155	147	53	1843	Polonaise in A flat major	
156	159	61	1846	Polonaise-fantaisie in A flat major	
157	11	71	1855	Polonaises in D minor, B flat major, F minor	
163	6	—	1864	Polonaise in G sharp minor	
165	36	—	1870	Polonaise in G flat major	
166	107	28	1839	Preludes	
190	141	45	1841	Prelude in C sharp minor	
192	10	1	1825	Rondo in C minor	
193	15	5	1828	Rondo in F major	
194	29	14	1834	Rondo in F major for piano and orchestra ('Krakowiak')	
195	76	16	1833	Rondo in E flat major	
196	27	73	1855	Rondo in C major for two pianos	
197	65	20	1835	Scherzo in B minor	
198	111	31	1837	Scherzo in B flat minor	
199	125	39	1840	Scherzo in C sharp minor	
200	148	54	1843	Scherzo in E major	
201	23	4	1851	Sonata in C minor	
202	128	35	1840	Sonata in B flat minor	
203	155	58	1845	Sonata in B minor	
204	160	65	1847	Sonata in G minor for piano and cello	
129	32	74	1857	Songs for voice with piano accompaniment	74
205	139	43	1841	Tarantelle in A flat major	
206	25	8	1832	Trio in G minor for piano, violin, and cello	
225	22	2	1830	Variations in B flat major for piano and orchestra ('Là ci darem la mano')	
226	80	12	1833	Variations in B flat major ('Hérold')	
227	14	—	1851	Variations in E major ('Der Schweitzerbub')	
230	113	—	1838	Variations in E major ('Hexameron')	
207	62	18	1834	Waltz in E flat major	
208	94	34	1838	Waltzes in A flat major, A minor, F major	
211	131	42	1840	Waltz in A flat major	
212	164	64	1847	Waltzes in D flat major, C sharp minor, A flat major	

(continued)

C&T	*B*	*Op*	*Year*	*Work title*	*Notes*
215	95	69	1855	Waltzes in A flat major, B minor	
217	40	70	1855	Waltzes in G flat major, F minor, D flat major	
(216)	35	—	1852	Waltzes in B minor, F minor ('Deux valses mélancoliques')	
222	56	—	1868	Waltz in E minor	

Notes

See notes in Table 1A.

Table 2A

Chopin's publishers listed by work number

The listing order is by work number, as in Table 1A. Each entry has a publisher code (see Table 2B), a plate number in parentheses, and a year of publication (Chominski & Turlo). Separate parentheses are used for multiple plate numbers when there are separate title pages. Publications after 1870 are not included.

C&T	*B*	*Op*	*Short title*	*Publisher code, plate number, publication year*	*Notes*
192	10	1	Rondo	mS (1986) 1836, aS (2019) 1835, W (1423) 1836	1
225	22	2	Variations (p/o)	mS (1312) 1833, Ha (5489) 1830, W (820) 1833	
148	41	3	Polonaise (p/c)	Rich (3301) 1835, Mec (2178) 1831, W (1662, 1663) 1836	3
201	23	4	Sonata	Rich (10868) 1851, Ha (8147) 1851, Co (9727) 1852	
193	15	5	Rondo	Schon (608, 606, 602) 1840, Ho (2121) 1836, W (1552) 1837	5
51	60	6	Mazurkas	mS (1341) 1833, Ki (996) 1832, W (958) 1833	
56	61	7	Mazurkas	mS (1342) 1833, Ki (997) 1832, W (959) 1833	
206	25	8	Trio (p/v/c)	mS (1344) 1833, Ki (999) 1832, W (924) 1833	
108	54	9	Nocturnes	mS (1287) 1833, Ki (995) 1832, W (916) (917) 1833	
14	42	10	Etudes	mS (1399) 1833, Ki (1018) (1019) 1833, W (960) (961) 1833	10
47	53	11	Concerto (p/o)	mS (1409) 1833, Ki (1020–22) 1833, W (1086) 1834	11
226	80	12	Variations	mS (1499) 1834, BH (5495) 1833	
41	28	13	Fantaisie (p/o)	mS (1574) 1834, Ki (1033, 1034) 1834, W (1083) 1834	
194	29	14	Rondo (p/o)	mS (1586) 1834, Ki (1038, 1039) 1834, W (1084) 1834	
111	55	15	Nocturnes	mS (1529) 1833, BH (5502) 1833, W (1093) 1834	
195	76	16	Rondo	Pl (16) 1833, BH (5525) 1834, W (1143) 1834	16
60	77	17	Mazurkas	Pl (2912) 1833, BH (5527) 1834, W (1144) 1834	17
207	62	18	Waltz	mS (1599) 1834, BH (5545) 1834, W (1157) 1834	18
8	81	19	Bolero	Pr (237) 1834, Pe (2505) 1834, W (1491) 1835	19
197	65	20	Scherzo	mS (1832) 1835, BH (5599) 1835, W (1492) 1835	
48	43	21	Concerto (p/o)	mS (1940) 1836, BH (5654) 1836, W (1642) 1836	
149	58	22	Polonaise (p/o)	mS (1926) 1836, BH (5709) 1836, W (1643) 1836	
2	66	23	Ballade	mS (1928) 1836, BH (5706) 1836, W (1644) 1836	
64	89	24	Mazurkas	mS (1870) 1835, BH (5647) 1836, W (1645) 1836	24
26	78	25	Etudes	mS (2427) 1837, BH (5832) (5833) 1837, W (1832) (1833) 1837	25
150	90	26	Polonaises	mS (1929) 1836, BH (5707) 1836, W (1647) 1836	
114	91	27	Nocturnes	mS (1935) 1836, BH (5666) 1836, W (1648) 1836	
166	107	28	Preludes	Ca (560) 1839, BH (6088) 1839, W (3098) (3099) 1839	
43	110	29	Impromptu	mS (2467) 1837, BH (5850) 1838, W (2166) 1837	
68	105	30	Mazurkas	mS (2489) 1837, BH (5851) 1838, W (2170) 1837	
198	111	31	Scherzo	mS (2494) 1837, BH (5852) 1838, W (2168) 1837	
116	106	32	Nocturnes	mS (2500) 1837, aS (2180(1)) (2180(2)) 1837, W (2169) 1837	
72	115	33	Mazurkas	mS (2714) 1838, BH (5985) 1838, W (2279) 1838	
208	94	34	Waltzes	mS (2715.1) (2716.2) (2717.3) 1838, BH (6032) (6033) (6034) 1838, W (2280) (2281) (2282) 1838	
202	128	35	Sonata	T (891) 1840, BH (6329) 1840, W (3549) 1840	
44	129	36	Impromptu	T (892) 1840, BH (6333) 1840, W (3550) 1840	
118	119	37	Nocturnes	T (893) 1840, BH (6334) 1840, W (3554) 1840	
3	102	38	Ballade	T (925) 1840, BH (6330) 1840, W (3555) 1840	38
199	125	39	Scherzo	T (926) 1840, BH (6332) 1840, W (3556) 1840	

(continued)

C&T	B	Op	Short title	Publisher code, plate number, publication year	Notes
152	120	40	Polonaises	T (977) 1840, BH (6331) 1840, W (3557) 1840	
76	122	41	Mazurkas	T (978) 1840, BH (6335) 1840, W (3558) 1840	
211	131	42	Waltz	Pa (3708) 1840, BH (6419) 1840, W (3559) 1840	
205	139	43	Tarantelle	T (1073) 1841, Schu (449) 1841, W (5295) 1841	43
154	135	44	Polonaise	mS (3477) 1841, Mec (3577) 1841, W (5226) 1842	44
190	141	45	Prelude	mS (3518) 1841, Mec (3594) 1841, W (5297) 1842	
1	72	46	Allegro de Concert	mS (3481) 1841, BH (6651) 1841, W (5298) 1842	
4	136	47	Ballade	mS (3486) 1841, BH (6652) 1842, W (5299) 1842	
120	142	48	Nocturnes	mS (3487) (3488) 1841, BH (6653) 1842, W (5300) (5301) 1842	
42	137	49	Fantaisie	mS (3489) 1841, BH (6654) 1842, W (5301) 1842	49
80	145	50	Mazurkas	mS (3692) 1842, Mec (3682) 1842, W (5303) 1842	
45	149	51	Impromptu	mS (3847) 1843, Ho (2900) 1843, W (5304) 1843	
5	146	52	Ballade	mS (3957) 1843, BH (7001) 1843, W (5305) 1844	
155	147	53	Polonaise	mS (3958) 1843, BH (7002) 1843, W (5306) 1844	
200	148	54	Scherzo	mS (3959) 1843, BH (7003) 1843, W (5307) 1844	
122	152	55	Nocturnes	mS (4084) 1844, BH (7142) 1844, W (5308) 1845	
83	153	56	Mazurkas	mS (4085) 1844, BH (7143) 1844, W (5309) 1845	
7	154	57	Berceuse	Mei (2186) 1845, BH (7259) 1845, W (6313) 1845	
203	155	58	Sonata	Mei (2187) 1845, BH (7260) 1845, W (6314) 1845	
86	157	59	Mazurkas	Bra (4292) 1846, St (71) 1845, W (6315) 1845	
6	158	60	Barcarolle	Bra (4609) 1846, BH (7545) 1846, W (6317) 1846	
156	159	61	Polonaise-fantaisie	Bra (4610) 1846, BH (7546) 1846, W (6318) 1846	
124	161	62	Nocturnes	Bra (4611) 1846, BH (7547) 1846, W (6319) 1846	
89	162	63	Mazurkas	Bra (4742) 1847, BH (7714) 1847, W (6320) 1847	63
212	164	64	Waltzes	Bra (4743(1)) (4743(2)) (4743(3)) 1847, BH (7721) 1847, BH (7715) (7716) (7717) 1847, W (6321) (6322) (6323) 1848	
204	160	65	Sonata (p/c)	Bra (4744) 1847, BH (7718) 1848	
46	87	66	Fantaisie-impromptu	MeiF (3523) 1855, aS (4392) 1855	66
92	93	67	Mazurkas	MeiF (3524) 1855, aS (4393) 1855	
96	18	68	Mazurkas	MeiF (3525) 1855, aS (4394) 1855	
215	35	69	Waltzes	MeiF (3526) 1855, aS (4395) 1855	
217	40	70	Waltzes	MeiF (3527) 1855, aS (4396) 1855	
157	11	71	Polonaises	MeiF (3528) (3529) (3530) 1855, aS (4397) (4398) (4399) 1855	
126	19	72#1	Nocturne	MeiF (3531) 1855, aS (4400) 1855	
50	20	72#2	Marche funèbre	MeiF (3531) 1855, aS (4400) 1855	
11	12	72#3	Ecossaises	MeiF (3531) 1855, aS (4400) 1855	
196	27	73	Rondo (2 ps)	MeiF (3532) 1855, aS (4401) 1855	
129	32	74	Songs (voice/p)	aS (4638–4653) 1857, aS (4797–4812) 1859, Geb (84–99) 1859	
163	6	—	Polonaise	Schott (17943) 1864, Ka (20) 1864	
227	14	—	Variations	Rich (10869) 1851, Ha (8148) 1851, Co (9728) 1852	
(216)	35	—	Waltzes	Wildt (—) 1852, W (8015) 1853, Ew (—) 1854	
165	36	—	Polonaise	Schott (20029) 1870, Ka (136) 1870	B36
222	56	—	Waltz	Schott (19551) 1868, Ka (159) 1868	
10	70	—	Duo concertant (p/c)	mS (1376) 1833, aS (1777) 1833, W (1076, 1077) 1833	B70
—	82	—	Mazurka	Schott (20030) 1870, Ka (171) 1869	B82
230	113	—	Variations	T (1066) 1841, Ha (7700) 1839, Cr (406) 1840	

(continued)

C&T	*B*	*Op*	*Short title*	*Publisher code, plate number, publication year*	*Notes*
38	130	—	Etudes	mS (2345) 1840, aS (2207(3)) 1840, Chap (6084) 1841	B130
106	134	—	Mazurka	*FM* (9) 1841, Schott (6493.2) 1842, W (6316) 1846	B134
105	140	—	Mazurka	mS (—) 1841, Chab (—) 1841, BB (3359) 1855	

Notes
(by work number)
("B" refers to Brown, "C&T" to Chominski & Turlo,
"*CPM*" to the British Library's *Catalogue of Printed Music.*)

1 The first publication is Brz (—) 1825. This and the others for Op. 1 in the table are for piano two hands. Chopin's four-hand version was published as Ho (1977) 1834, aS (1955) 1835, W (1424) 1836 (see B p. 9 and C&T p. 188). A slightly later two-hand edition is Ho (2375) 1838.

3 B p. 41 notes a republication aS (—) 1832, and various editions for piano solo: W (1860) 1837, mS (3729) 1842, and others.

5 The first publication is Brz (—) 1828.

10 The early publication Lu (1378) (1379) 1836 should be noted (C&T p. 272).

11 B p. 57 has Schlesinger PN "1343", apparently an error.

16 B p. 80 and C&T p. 192 note a publication mS (1703) 1834. Chominski & Turlo have Wessel PN "1094".

17 B p. 81 notes a publication mS (1704) 1834.

18 *CPM* p. 58 has Bre (—) *ca* 1870, not in Chominski & Turlo or Brown.

19 B p. 87: "Prillip's [*sic*] first edition has no publisher's number; it was added to later editions."

24 C&T p. 117 have Schlesinger PN "1070", apparently an error.

25 The early publication Lu (1721) (1722) 1837 should be noted (C&T p. 272).

38 C&T p. 72 have Wessel PN "3182", apparently an error.

43 The C&T p. 207 title transcription shows a Schuberth four-hand version with PN 455.

44 B p. 139 notes that Wessel's plate number should have been 5296.

49 B p. 140 notes that Wessel's plate number should have been 5302, as 5301 was used for Opus 48#2.

63 B p. 168 notes that Wessel's plate number should have been 6320.

66 B p. 91 notes a publication by Ewer, date unknown.

B36 B p. 40 has Kaufmann PN "170".

B70 The title transcription by C&T p. 80 shows a Wessel piano/violin version. B p. 75 has Wessel PN "1085", which conflicts with 1076, 1077 given by Chominski & Turlo; perhaps it is for the piano/violin version. Brown notes piano four-hand arrangements aS (2238) 1838 and mS (2799) 1839.

B82 The authenticity of this work was questioned by Chominski & Turlo (p. 246).

B130 C&T pp. 91, 92 note republications aS (2423) 1841 and mS (4102) 1845.

Table 2B

Chopin's publishers listed alphabetically

The first part of Table 2B lists all primary publishers (see Glossary) represented in the collection, and all works that each published. Works are identified by work number (Table 1A).

Code	*Primary publishers represented in the collection*	*Year founded*	*Years of publication of Chopin works*	*Work numbers of Chopin works published*
BB	Bote & Bock (Berlin)	1838	1855	B140
BH	Breitkopf & Härtel (Leipzig)	1719	1833–48	12, 15–18, 20–31, 33–42, 46–49, 52–58, 60–65
Bra	Brandus (Paris)	1846	1846–47	59–65
Ca	Catelin (Paris)	1839	1839	28
FM	*La France Musicale* (Escudier, Paris)	1837	1841	B134
Ha	Haslinger (Vienna)	1826	1830–51	2, 4, B14, B113
Ho	Hofmeister (Leipzig)	1807	1834–43	1, 5, 51
Ka	Kaufmann (Warsaw)	?	1864–70	B6, B36, B56, B82
Ki	Kistner (Leipzig)	1831	1832–34	6–11, 13, 14
Mec	Mechetti (Vienna)	1811	1831–42	3, 44, 45, 50
Mei	Meissonnier (Paris)	1821	1845	57, 58
MeiF	Meissonnier Fils (Paris)	1845	1855	66–73
Pa	Pacini (Paris)	1810	1840	42
Pe	Peters (Leipzig)	1814	1834	19
Pl	Pleyel (Paris)	(1832)	1833	16, 17
Pr	Prilipp (Paris)	1834	1834	19
Rich	Richault (Paris)	1816	1835–51	3, 4, B14
aS	A. Schlesinger (Berlin)	1810	1833–59	1, 32, 66–74, B70, B130
mS	M. Schlesinger (Paris)	1821	183544	1, 2, 6–18, 20–27, 29–34, 44–56, B70, B130, B140
Schott	Schott (Mainz)	1780	1842–70	B6, B36, B56, B82, B134
Schu	Schuberth (Hamburg)	1826	1841	43
St	Stern (Berlin)	?	1845	59
T	Troupenas (Paris)	1825	1840–41	35–41, 43, B113
W	Wessel (London)	1823	1833–53	1–3, 5–11, 13–64, B35, B70, B134

The second part of Table 2B lists all primary publishers who are not represented in the collection, and all works that each published.

Code	*Primary publishers represented in the collection*	*Year founded*	*Years of publication of Chopin works*	*Work numbers of Chopin works published*
Brz	Brzezina (Warsaw)	(1822)	1825–28	1, 5
Chab	Chabal (Paris)	1840	1841	B140
Chap	Chappell (London)	1810	1841	B130
Co	Cocks (London)	1823	1852	4, B14
Cr	Cramer (London)	1824	1840	B113

(continued)

TABLE 2B

Code	Primary publishers represented in the collection	Year founded	Years of publication of Chopin works	Work numbers of Chopin works published
Geb	Gebethner (Warsaw)	1857	1859	74
Schon	Schonenberger (Paris)	1830	1840	5

The third part of Table 2B lists the collection's holdings of editions issued by secondary publishers. Publications after 1875 are not included.

Code	Primary publishers represented in the collection	Year founded	Years of publication of Chopin works	Work numbers of Chopin works published
BD	Brandus & Dufour (Paris)	1854	1854–60	2, 42, 45, 51, 64#1, 65
Bre	Brewer (London)	*ca* 1849	*ca* 1870	18
CB	Cramer & Beale (London)	1844	1848	64#1, 64#2
Ew	Ewer (London)	*ca* 1823	1854	B35
Gér	Gérard (Paris)	1859	1860–67?	66, 67, 73
Heu	Heugel (Paris)	1842	after 1867	22
hL	H. Lemoine (Paris)	1817	*ca* 1843–59	18, 23, 34#3, 64#3
Jur	Jurgenson (Moscow)	1861	1875	28
Led	Leduc (Paris)	*ca* 1842	*ca* 1859–60	34#1
Lu	Lucca (Milan)	1825	*ca* 1836–62	9, 10, 16, 18, 25, 27, 28(II), 66
No	North (Philadelphia)	?	*ca* 1872	57
Po	Pozzi (Mendrisio)	?	*ca* 1834–41	15, 30, 34, 37, 42
Rico	Ricordi (Milan)	1808	*ca* 1841	43

Table 3A
Chopin's French publishers listed by year of publication

Publication data are from Table 2A. Publisher data are from Hopkinson (1954) and Devriès & Lesure (1988).

Year	*Work number*	*Publisher*
1833	2, 6–11, 15, B70	Maurice Schlesinger, 97 Rue Richelieu (copyright of Opus 10 sold to Lemoine in 1842)
	16, 17	Ignàce Pleyel et Cie, 18 Boulevard Montmartre (firm acquired by Prilipp in 1834; some stock acquired by Schlesinger)
1834	12–14, 18	Maurice Schlesinger, 97 Rue Richelieu (copyright of Opus 18 sold to Lemoine in 1844)
	19	Prilipp et Cie, 18 Boulevard Montmarte
1835	3	Simon Richault, 16 Boulevard Poissonière
	20, 24	Maurice Schlesinger, 97 Rue Richelieu
1836	1, 21–23, 26, 27	Maurice Schlesinger, 97 Rue Richelieu
1837	25, 29–32	Maurice Schlesinger, 97 Rue Richelieu (copyright of Opus 25 sold to Lemoine in 1842)
1838	33, 34	Maurice Schlesinger, 97 Rue Richelieu
1839	28	Adolphe Catelin et Cie., 26 Rue Grange-Batelière (copyright of Op. 28 sold to Brandus in 1846)
1840	5	Schonenberger, 10 Boulevard Poissonière
	35–41	E. Troupenas & Cie, 40 Rue Neuve-Vivienne
	42	Pacini, 11 Boulevard des Italiens
	B130	Maurice Schlesinger, 97 Rue Richelieu
1841	43, B113	E. Troupenas & Cie, 40 Rue Neuve-Vivienne (firm acquired by Brandus in 1850)
	44–49	Maurice Schlesinger, 97 Rue Richelieu
	B134	*La France Musicale* (Escudier Frères)
	B140	Chabal, 10 Boulevard des Italiens
1842	50	Maurice Schlesinger, 97 Rue Richelieu
1843	51–54	Maurice Schlesinger, 97 Rue Richelieu
1844	55, 56	Maurice Schlesinger, 97 Rue Richelieu (firm acquired by Brandus in 1846)
1845	57, 58	J. Meissonnier, 22 Rue Dauphine
1846	59–62	Brandus et Cie, 97 Rue Richelieu
1847	63–65	Brandus et Cie, 97 Rue Richelieu
1851	4, B14	Simon Richault, 26 Boulevard Poissonière
	[35–41, 43, B113]	[Brandus et Cie, 103 Rue Richelieu (republication of Troupenas plates, acquired by Brandus in 1850)]
1855	66–73	J. Meissonnier Fils, 22 Rue Dauphine

Table 3B

Chopin's German and Austrian Publishers Listed by Year of Publication

The publication data are from Table 2A. Publisher data are from Krummel & Sadie (1990).

Year	*Work number*	*Publisher*	*Place*
1830	2	Tobias Haslinger	Vienna
1831	3	Pietro Mechetti quondam Carlo	Vienna
1832	6–9	[Carl] Friedrich Kistner	Leipzig
1833	10, 11	[Carl] Friedrich Kistner	Leipzig
	12, 15	Breitkopf & Härtel	Leipzig
	B70	Ad. Mt. [Adolph Martin] Schlesinger	Berlin
1834	1	Friedrich Hofmeister	Leipzig
	13, 14	[Carl] Friedrich Kistner	Leipzig
	16–18	Breitkopf & Härtel	Leipzig
	19	C. F. Peters	Leipzig
1835	1	Ad. Mt. [Adolph Martin] Schlesinger	Berlin
	20	Breitkopf & Härtel	Leipzig
1836	5	Friedrich Hofmeister	Leipzig
	21–24, 26, 27	Breitkopf & Härtel	Leipzig
1837	25	Breitkopf & Härtel	Leipzig
	32	Ad. Mt. [Adolph Martin] Schlesinger	Berlin
1838	29–31, 33, 34	Breitkopf & Härtel	Leipzig
1839	28	Breitkopf & Härtel	Leipzig
	B113	Tobias Haslinger	Vienna
1840	35–42	Breitkopf & Härtel	Leipzig
	B130	Ad. Mt. [Adolph Martin] Schlesinger	Berlin
1841	43	J. [Julius] Schuberth & Co.	Hamburg
	44, 45	Pietro Mechetti quondam Carlo	Vienna
	46	Breitkopf & Härtel	Leipzig
1842	47–49	Breitkopf & Härtel	Leipzig
	50	Pietro Mechetti quondam Carlo	Vienna
	B134	B. Schott's Söhne	Mainz
1843	51	Friedrich Hofmeister	Leipzig
	52–54	Breitkopf & Härtel	Leipzig
1844	55, 56	Breitkopf & Härtel	Leipzig
1845	57, 58	Breitkopf & Härtel	Leipzig
	59	Stern & Co.	Berlin
1846	60–62	Breitkopf & Härtel	Leipzig

(continued)

Year	*Work number*	*Publisher*	*Place*
1847	63, 64	Breitkopf & Härtel	Leipzig
1848	65	Breitkopf & Härtel	Leipzig
1851	4, B14	Charles [Carl] Haslinger quondam Tobie [Tobias]	Vienna
1855	66–73	Ad. Mt. [Adolph Martin] Schlesinger	Berlin
	B140	Bote & Bock	Berlin
1857	74 (Polish)	Ad. Mt. [Adolph Martin] Schlesinger	Berlin
1859	74 (German)	Ad. Mt. [Adolph Martin] Schlesinger	Berlin
1864	B6	B. Schott's Söhne	Mainz
1868	B56	B. Schott's Söhne	Mainz
1870	B36	B. Schott's Söhne	Mainz
	B82	B. Schott's Söhne	Mainz

Table 4A

Chopin's M. Schlesinger, Brandus, and Troupenas editions listed by plate number

The registration date (year-month) is taken from Chominski & Turlo (1990, pp. 42–44).

M. Schlesinger editions listed by plate number

C&T	*B*	*Op*	*Short title*	*Plate number*	*Registration date*	*Notes and comments*
108	54	9	Nocturnes	1287	1833-??	
225	22	2	Variations (p/o)	1312	1833-??	
51	60	6	Mazurkas	1341	1833-06	
56	61	7	Mazurkas	1342	1833-06	
206	25	8	Trio (p/v/c)	1344	1833-??	
10	70	—	Duo concertant (p/c)	1376	1833-07	
14	42	10	Etudes	1399	1833-06	issued in one book
47	53	11	Concerto (p/o)	1409	1833-06	see note 11
226	80	12	Variations	1499	1834-01	
111	55	15	Noctures	1529	1833-12	
41	28	13	Fantaisie (p/o)	1574	1834-04	
194	29	14	Rondo (p/o)	1586	1834-06	
207	62	18	Waltz	1599	1834-06	
195	76	16	Rondo	1703	1834-06	see B p. 80
60	77	17	Mazurkas	1704	1834-??	see B p. 81
197	65	20	Scherzo	1832	1835-02	
64	89	24	Mazurkas	1870	1835-12	see note 24
149	58	22	Polonaise (p/o)	1926	1836-07	
2	66	23	Ballade	1928	1836-07	
150	90	26	Polonaises	1929	1836-07	
114	91	27	Nocturnes	1935	1836-07	
48	43	21	Concerto (p/o)	1940	1836-07	
192	10	1	Rondo	1986	1836-??	
38	130	—	Etudes	2345	1840-11	see note B130
26	78	25	Etudes	2427	1837-10	issued in one book
43	110	29	Impromptu	2467	1837-10	
68	105	30	Mazurkas	2489	1837-12	
198	111	31	Schrzo	2494	1837-12	
116	106	32	Nocturnes	2500	1837-12	
72	115	33	Mazurkas	2714	1838-10	
208	94	34	Waltzes	2715, 2716, 2717	1838-12	issued separately
10	70	—	Duo concertant (p/c)	2799	1839-??	piano duet (B p. 76)
105	140	—	Mazurka	—	1841-07	
154	135	44	Polonaise	3477	1841-11	
1	72	46	Allegro de Concert	3481	1841-11	
4	136	47	Ballade	3486	1841-11	
120	142	48	Nocturnes	3487, 3488	1841-11	issued separately
42	137	49	Fantaisie	3489	1841-11	
190	141	45	Prelude	3518	1841-11	

(continued)

C&T	B	Op	Short title	Plate number	Registration date	Notes and comments
80	145	50	Mazurkas	3692	1842-09	
148	41	3	Polonaise (p/c)	3729	1842-??	piano solo (B p. 44)
45	149	51	Impromptu	3847	1843-05	
5	146	52	Ballade	3957	1843-12	
155	147	53	Polonaise	3958	1843-12	
200	148	54	Scherzo	3959	1843-12	
122	152	55	Nocturnes	4084	1844-08	
83	153	56	Mazurkas	4085	1844-08	
38	130	—	Etudes	4102	1845-04	see note B130

Notes
(by work number)
("B" refers to Brown, "C&T" to Chominski & Turlo)

11 B p. 57 has PN 1343, but C&T p. 103 and this collection's copy of the piano-only edition have 1409.

24 B p. 93 has PN 1870, while C&T p. 117 and Hob-274 p. 123 have 1070, probably an engraver's error.

B130 B p. 133 says the first of the three parts of *Méthode des Méthodes de Moscheles et Fétis* was published in 1837. The third part, *Etudes de Perfectionement*, published in 1840, contains, among other contributions, the three etudes of Chopin. C&T p. 91 (and B p. 134) note the later, separate publication of the Chopin etudes as *Trois Nouvelles Etudes*, mS (4102) 1845 and aS (2423) 1841. Brown gives 1841 for both dates, and Hob-507 p. 210 has 1847 for the aS date.

Brandus editions listed by plate number

C&T	B	Op	Short title	Plate number	Registration date	Notes and comments
86	157	59	Mazurkas	4292	1846-03	
6	158	60	Barcarolle	4609	1846-11	
156	159	61	Polonaise-fantaisie	4610	1846-11	
124	161	62	Nocturnes	4611	1846-11	
89	162	63	Mazurkas	4742	1847-10	
212	164	64	Waltzes	4743	1847-10	
204	160	65	Sonata (p/c)	4744	1847-10	

E. Troupenas editions listed by plate number

C&T	B	Op	Short title	Plate number	Registration date	Notes and comments
202	128	35	Sonata	891	1840-05	
44	129	36	Impromptu	892	1840-05	
118	119	37	Nocturnes	893	1840-06	
3	102	38	Ballade	925	1840-10	
199	125	39	Scherzo	926	1840-12	
152	120	40	Polonaises	977	1840-12	
76	122	41	Mazurkas	978	1840-12	
230	113	—	Variations	1066	1841-??	
205	139	43	Tarantelle	1073	1841-10	

Table 4B

Chopin's Kistner, Breitkopf & Härtel, and A. Schlesinger editions listed by plate number

The registration date (year-month) is taken from Chominski & Turlo (1990, pp. 42–44).

Kistner editions listed by plate number

C&T	*B*	*Op*	*Short title*	*Plate number*	*Registration date*	*Comments*
108	54	9	Nocturnes	995	1832-12	
51	60	6	Mazurkas	996	1832-12	
56	61	7	Mazurkas	997	1832-12	
206	25	8	Trio	999	1832-12	
14	42	10	Etudes	1018, 1019	1833-08	issued in two books
47	53	11	Concerto	1020–1022	1833-09	
41	28	13	Fantaisie	1033. 1034	1834-05	
194	29	14	Rondo	1038, 1039	1834-07	

Breitkopf & Härtel editions listed by plate number

C&T	*B*	*Op*	*Short title*	*Plate number*	*Registration date*	*Comments*
226	80	12	Variations	5495	1833-11	
111	55	15	Nocturnes	5502	1833-12	
195	76	16	Rondo	5525	1834-03	
60	77	17	Mazurkas	5527	1834-03	
207	62	18	Waltz	5545	1834-07	
197	65	20	Scherzo	5599	1835-03	
64	89	24	Mazurkas	5647	1836-01	
48	43	21	Concerto (p/o)	5654	1836-04	
114	91	27	Nocturnes	5666	1836-05	
2	66	23	Ballade	5706	1836-06	
150	90	26	Polonaises	5707	1836-07	
149	58	22	Polonaise (p/o)	5709	1836-08	
26	78	25	Etudes	5832, 5833	1837-10	issued in two books
43	110	29	Impromptu	5850	1838-01	
68	105	30	Mazurkas	5851	1838-01	
198	111	31	Scherzo	5852	1838-02	
72	115	33	Mazurkas	5985	1838-11	
208	94	34	Waltzes	6032, 6033, 6034	1838-12	issued separately
166	107	28	Preludes	6088	1839-09	
202	128	35	Sonata	6329	1840-05	
3	102	38	Ballade	6330	1840-10	
152	120	40	Polonaises	6331	1840-12	
199	125	39	Scherzo	6332	1840-11	
44	129	36	Impromptu	6333	1840-05	
118	119	37	Nocturnes	6334	1840-06	

(continued)

C&T	B	Op	Short title	Plate number	Registration date	Notes and comments
76	122	41	Mazurkas	6335	1840-12	
211	131	42	Waltz	6419	1840-07	
1	72	46	Allegro de Concert	6651	1841-12	
4	136	47	Ballade	6652	1842-01	
120	142	48	Nocturnes	6653	1842-01	
42	137	49	Fantaisie	6654	1842-01	
5	146	52	Ballade	7001	1843-11	
155	147	53	Polonaise	7002	1843-11	
200	148	54	Scherzo	7003	1843-11	
122	152	55	Nocturnes	7142	1844-12	
83	153	56	Mazurkas	7143	1844-12	
7	154	57	Berceuse	7259	1845-07	
203	155	58	Sonata	7260	1845-07	
6	158	60	Barcarolle	7545	1846-11	
156	159	61	Polonaise-fantaisie	7546	1846-11	
124	161	62	Nocturnes	7547	1846-11	
89	162	63	Mazurkas	7714	1847-11	
212	164	64	Waltzes	7715, 7716, 7717	1847-11	issued separately
204	160	65	Sonata (p/c)	7718	1848-01	
212	164	64	Waltzes	7721	1847-11	issued in one book

A. SCHLESINGER EDITIONS LISTED BY PLATE NUMBER

C&T	B	Op	Short title	Plate number	Registration date	Comments
10	70	—	Duo concertant (p/c)	1777	1833-07	
192	10	1	Rondo (4 hands)	1955	1835-12	
192	10	1	Rondo (p solo)	2019	1835-12	
116	106	32	Nocturnes	2180	1837-12	
38	130	—	Etudes	2207.3	1840-08	
10	70	—	Duo concertant (p/c)	2238	1838-??	piano duet (B p. 76)
38	130	—	Etudes	2423	1841-??	see Table 4A, note B130
46	87	66	Fantaisie-impromptu	4392	1855-05	
92	93	67	Mazurkas	4393	1855-05	
96	18	68	Mazurkas	4394	1855-05	
215	95	69	Waltzes	4395	1855-05	
217	40	70	Waltzes	4396	1855-05	
157	11	71	Polonaises	4397, 4398, 4399	1855-05	issued separately
126	19	72#1	Nocturne	4400	1855-05	
50	20	72#2	Marche funèbre	4400	1855-05	
11	12	72#3	Ecossaises	4400	1855-05	
196	27	73	Rondo (2 ps)	4401	1855-05	
129	32	74	Songs (in Polish)	4638–4653	1857-??	see B p. 34
129	32	74	Songs (in German)	4797–4712	1859-01	see B p. 34

Table 4C

Chopin's Wessel editions listed by plate number

Registration date (year–month-day) is taken from Kallberg (1983, pp. 537–538). Where a day is not given, the date is from Chominski & Turlo (1990, pp. 42–44). The "*W*" column gives Wessel's sequence numbers in his collected edition.

C&T	*B*	*Op*	*Short title*	*Plate number*	*Registration date*	*W*	*Notes and comments*
225	22	2	Variations (p/o)	820	1833-??	2	
108	54	9	Nocturnes	916, 917	1833-06	7, 8	issued in two books
206	25	8	Trio (p/v/c)	924	1833-07	—	see note 8
51	60	6	Mazurkas	958	1833-08	5	
56	61	7	Mazurkas	959	1833-08	6	
14	42	10	Etudes	960, 961	1833-08	9, 10	issued in two books
10	70	—	Duo concertant (p/c)	1076, 1077	1833-12	—	see note B70
41	28	13	Fantaisie (p/o)	1083	1834-04-15	12	
194	29	14	Rondo (p/o)	1084	1834-05	13	
10	70	—	Duo concertant (p/v?)	1085?	1833-12?	—	see note B70
47	53	11	Concerto (p/o)	1086	1834-05	11	
111	55	15	Nocturnes	1093	1834-05	14	
195	76	16	Rondo	1094	1834-08-30	15	see note 16
60	77	17	Mazurkas	1144	1834-08-26	16	see note B
207	62	18	Waltz	1157	1834-08-30	17	
192	10	1	Rondo (p solo)	1423	1836-03	1	
192	10	1	Rondo (p duet)	1424	1836-??	(1)	
8	81	19	Bolero	1491	1835-04-21	18	
197	65	20	Scherzo	1492	1835-08	19	
193	15	5	Rondo	1552	1837-10	4	
48	43	21	Concerto (p/o)	1642	1836-05-25	20	see note B
149	58	22	Polonaise (p/o)	1643	1836-05-30	21	
2	66	23	Ballade	1644	1836-05-30	22	
64	89	24	Mazurkas	1645	1836-04-20	23	
150	90	26	Polonaises	1647	1836-05-30	26	
114	91	27	Nocturnes	1648	1836-05-30	27	
148	41	3	Polonaise (p/c)	1662, 1663	1836-04	3	
26	78	25	Etudes	1832, 1833	1837-10-14	24, 25	issued in two books
148	41	3	Polonaise (p solo)	1860	1837-10	(3)	B p. 44, C&T p. 164
43	110	29	Impromptu	2166	1837-10-14	30	
198	111	31	Scherzo	2168	1837-11-21	32	
116	106	32	Nocturnes	2169	1837-11-21	33	
68	105	30	Mazurkas	2170	1837-11-21	31	
72	115	33	Mazurkas	2279	1838-11-02	34	
208	94	34	Waltzes	2280, 2281, 2282	1838-12-01	35, 36, 37	issued separately
166	107	28	Preludes	3098, 3099	1839-08-30	28, 29	issued in two books
202	128	35	Sonata	3549	1840-06-10	38	see note B
44	129	36	Impromptu	3550	1840-06-01	39	see note B
118	119	37	Nocturnes	3554	1840-06-19	40	
3	102	38	Ballade	3555	1840-10-01	41	see note 38

(continued)

C&T	B	Op	Short title	Plate number	Registration date	W	Notes and comments
199	125	39	Scherzo	3556	1840-10-01	42	
152	120	40	Polonaises	3557	1840-10-31	43	
76	122	41	Mazurkas	3558	1840-12-01	44	see note B
211	131	42	Waltz	3559	1840-06-30	45	see note B
205	139	43	Tarantelle	5295	1841-10-22	46	
154	135	44	Polonaise	5226	1842-01-20	47	see note 44
190	141	45	Prelude	5297	1842-01-20	48	
1	72	46	Allegro de concert	5298	1842-01-20	49	
4	136	47	Ballade	5299	1842-01-20	50	
120	142	48	Nocturnes	5300, 5301	1842-01-20	51, 52	issued in two books
42	137	49	Fantaisie	5301	1842-01-20	53	see note 49
80	145	50	Mazurkas	5303	1842-07-21	54	see note B
45	149	51	Impromptu	5304	1843-04-07	55	see note B
5	146	52	Ballade	5305	1844-03-01	56	
155	147	53	Polonaise	5306	1844-03-01	57	
200	148	54	Scherzo	5307	1844-03-01	58	
122	152	55	Nocturnes	5308	1845-04-22	59	
83	153	56	Mazurkas	5309	1845-04-22	60	
7	154	57	Berceuse	6313	1845-04-22	61	see notes 57 and B
203	155	58	Sonata	6314	1845-04-22	62	
86	157	59	Mazurkas	6315	1845-04-22	63	see note B
106	134	—	Mazurka	6316	1846-01	64	
6	158	60	Barcarolle	6317	1846-10-07	65	see note B
156	159	61	Polonaise-fantaisie	6318	1846-10-07	66	
124	161	62	Nocturnes	6319	1846-10-07	67	
89	162	63	Mazurkas	6320	1847-12	68	
212	164	64	Waltzes	6321, 6322, 6323	1848-09	69, 70, 71	issued separately
216	35	—	Waltzes	8015	1853-07	—	see note B35

Notes

(by work number)

("B" refers to Brown, "C&T" to Chominski & Turlo)

8 Wessel issued the Trio Op. 8 as the first in his "Series of Modern Trios" (B p. 27, C&T p. 210), but did not include it in his collected edition.

16 B p. 80 has PN 1143, but the title transcribed by C&T (p. 192) has PN 1094. The latter agrees with the New York Public Library copy (*National Union Catalog*, **107**, 692).

38 C&T p. 72 have PN 3182.

44 B p. 139 notes that the plate number should have been 5296 — perhaps an engraver's error.

49 B p. 240 notes that the plate number should have been 5302, as 5301 was used for Op. 48#2 (Wessel's 48 bis).

57 Brown asserts "Wessel's edition of the Berceuse is the only one in his complete series on which he printed the names of both continental publishers.". They appear at the foot of the first page of music.

B35 B p. 38: The "Deux valses mélancoliques" (Fontana's Opp. 69#2 and 70#2) was published in 1852 by Wildt (Cracow), in 1853 by Wessel, and in 1854 by Ewer.

(continued)

B70 The Duo Concertant for piano and cello was is included in Wessel's collected edition. The title transcribed by Chominski & Turlo (p. 80, and reproduced in plate 14) does not have a plate number, but they give PN 1076, 1077 for the piano/cello edition. The existence of a piano/violin version is noted on the title. B pp. 75–76 does not mention the latter version but gives PN 1085 for the first edition. Perhaps this is in fact for the violin part?

B Brown's dates differ from those tabulated above in the following cases:

Op	*B's page*	*B's date*
17	81	1834-08-30
21	47	1836-11
35	131	1840-07
36	131	1840-07
41	126	1840-12-09
42	131	1840-07

Op	*B's page*	*B's date*
50	149	1842-10
51	153	1843-06
57	158	1845-06
59	161	1845-12
60	163	1846-09

Chominski & Turlo agree with Brown in two of these cases: Op. 41 (C&T p. 123) and Op. 59 (C&T p. 128).

Table 5A

M. Schlesinger, Brandus, and E. Troupenas plate numbers and addresses

The data are from Devriès & Lesure (1988, pp. 78–79, 389–390). A gap between the last plate number of a year and the first number of the next year indicates a range of numbers whose dates are uncertain.

M. Schlesinger and Brandus plate numbers and addresses

Year	*Range of plate numbers*	*Name of publisher*	*Address of publisher*
		Maurice Schlesinger (from 1824)	97, rue de Richelieu (from 1824)
1830	M. S. 920–1064		
1831	1074–1109		
1832	1135–1180		
1833	1287–1530		
1834	1553–1599		
1835	1832–1884		
1836	1926–2294		
1837	2350–2538		
1838	2537–2714		
1839	2724–2983		
1840	3035–3166		
1841	3218–3486		
1842	3506–3772		
1843	3847–3959		
1844	4018–4105		
1845	4140–4309		
1846	B. & Cie 4293–4661	Brandus et Cie (from January)	(97, rue de Richelieu)
1847	4628		
1848	4744		
1849	4906		87, rue de Richelieu (from January)
1850	4965–5087		
1851	5288–5301, 8730–8867		103, rue de Richelieu (from January)
1852	8911–9112		
1853	9220–9274		
1854	9265–9474	G. Brandus, Dufour et Cie (from September)	
1855	9509–9628		
1856	9630–9748		
1857	9829		
1858	B. & D. 10000–10029	G. Brandus et S. Dufour (from February)	
1859	10082–10145		
1860	10199–10300		
1872	B. & Cie 11759	Brandus et Cie (from August)	

(continued)

E. TROUPENAS PLATE NUMBERS AND ADDRESSES

Year	*Range of plate numbers*	*Name of publisher*	*Address of publisher*
		E. Troupenas (from 1825)	23, rue Saint-Marc Feydeau (from 1829)
1830	334–432		
1831	463–521		
1832	610		
1833	630		
1834	768–845		
1835	T. 134	E. Troupenas & Cie (from July)	40, rue Neuve-Vivienne (from July)
1836	176–267		
1837	317–419		
1838	576		
1839	701–797		
1840	969		
1841	1073		
1842	1148–1193		
1843	1352		
1844	T. M. 1356–1632		
1845	E. T. & Cie 1720–1774		
1846	1822–1971		
1847	1986–2134		
1848	2178–2228		
1849	2259–2293		
1850	2401	acquired by Brandus et Cie (October)	

Table 5B

Meissonnier and Gérard plate numbers and addresses

The data are from Devriès & Lesure (1988, pp. 187–188, 316–317). A gap between the last plate number of a year and the first number of the next year indicates a range of numbers whose dates are uncertain.

Year	*Range of plate numbers*	*Name of publisher*	*Address of publisher*
		J. Meissonnier (from 1825)	22, rue Dauphine (from 1829)
1840	J. M. 1184–1186		
1841	1228–1376		
1842	1434–1608		
1843	1643, 1720, 1768–1861		
1844	2043–2046		
1845	2129–2185		
1846	2258–2335	J. Meissonnier et fils (from January)	
1847	2404–2528		
1848	2530	J. Meissonnier fils (from October)	
1849	2753		
1850	2755–2813		18, rue Dauphine (from August)
1851	3047–3059		
1852	3107		
1853	3248–3287		
1854	3334–3451		
1855	3523–3601		
1856	3669–3673	J. Meissonnier – Xavier Boisselot (from May)	
1857	—		
1858	—		
1859	—	E. Gérard & Cie (from December)	(18, rue Dauphine)
1860	C. M. 9327–9387		
1861	9416–9618		
1862	9654–9801		
1863	9830–9983		
1864	9967–10173		1, rue de la Chaussée-d'Antin (from October)
1865	10229–10320		
1866	10380–10616		
1867	10503–10616		12, boulevard des Capucines *et* 2, rue Scribe (from January)
1868	10680–10960		
1869	10828–11093		
1870	11116		

Table 5C
Kistner and Breitkopf & Härtel plate numbers

The data are from Deutsch (1961, pp. 9–10). A gap between the last plate number of a year and the first number of the next year indicates a range of numbers whose dates are uncertain.

Kistner plate numbers

Year	*Range of plate numbers*	*Year*	*Range of plate numbers*
1830	540	1860	2486–2487
1831	974	1861	—
1832	979–999	1862	2659
1833	1018–1032	1863	—
1834	1033–1039	1864	2778–2809
1835	—	1865	2482–2973
1836	—	1866	—
1837	—	1867	—
1838	—	1868	3551–3555
1839	1215	1869	—
1840	1290–1294	1870	—
1841	1300	1871	3724–3760
1842	1316–1362	1872	3802–3805
1843	1395	1873	3880–4001
1844	1400–1442	1874	—
1845	—	1875	4314–4561
1846	1489	1876	4729
1847	1559–1561	1877	—
1848	1639–1644	1878	3884–5064
1849	1645–1707	1879	5129–5450
1850	1743–1755		
1851	1760–1840		
1852	1900–1901		
1853	1967–1970		
1854	2015–2021		
1855	—		
1856	—		
1857	2230–2267		
1858	2306		
1859	—		

(continued)

Breitkopf & Härtel plate numbers

Year	Range of plate numbers	Year	Range of plate numbers
1830	4980–5051	1860	10000
1831	5140–5195	1861	10062–10160
1832	5243–5284	1862	10188–10448
1833	5469–5502	1863	10544
1834	5525–5595	1864	10613–10642
1835	—	1865	10659
1836	5647–5709	1866	10897–11026
1837	5783–5833	1867	11327–11370
1838	5835–6034	1868	11504
1839	6053–6177	1869	11578
1840	6203–6419	1870	—
1841	6167–6651	1871	11685–12442
1842	6654–6719	1872	—
1843	6821–7003	1873	13000
1844	7014–7143	1874	13483
1845	7204–7263	1875	13598–14000
1846	7327–7547	1876	14260–14309
1847	7714–7721	1877	14492–14652
1848	7774–7899	1878	14762–14959
1849	7914–8062	1879	14999–15291
1850	8089–8300		
1851	8347–8411		
1852	8417–8497		
1853	8600–8742		
1854	8795–9001		
1855	9138		
1856	9262–9305		
1857	9318–9467		
1858	9690–9793		
1859	9942		

Table 5D

Wessel plate numbers and addresses

The data are from Neighbour & Tyson (1965, pp. 41–42) and Humphries & Smith (1970, p. 328). A gap between the last plate number of a year and the first number of the next year indicates a range of numbers whose dates are uncertain. Plate numbers in brackets are for Chopin's works (Table 4C). With minor exceptions, these are in agreement with Neighbour & Tyson, but they provide more information after 1840.

Year	*Range of plate numbers*	*[Chopin]*	*Name of publisher*	*Address of publisher*
			Wessel & Stodart (from *ca* 1823)	6 Frith Street, Soho Square (from 1828)
1830	—	—		
1831	—	—		
1832	W. & S. 604–628	—		
1833	718–957	[820–1077]		
1834	936–1428	[1083–1157]		
1835	1454–1536	[1491–1492]		
1836	1587–1645	[1423–1663]		
1837	1915–2170	[1832–2170]		
1838	W. & Co. 2343–2282	[2279–2282]	Wessel & Co.	(6 Frith Street, Soho Square)
1839	2699–3099	[3098–3099]	Wessel & Stapleton	67 Frith Street, corner of Soho Square
1840	3141–3558	[3549–3559]		
1841	4000	[5295]		
1842	—	[5226–5303]		
1843	5000	[5304]		
1844	—	[5305–5307]		
1845	—	[5308–6315]	Wessel & Co.	(67 Frith Street, corner of Soho Square)
1846	—	[6316–6319]		229 Regent Street, corner of Hanover Square
1847	7000	[6320]		
1848	—	[6321–6323]		
1849	—	—		
1850	—	—		
1851	—	—		
1852	—	—		
1853	—	[8015]		
1854	—	—		
1855	—	—		
1856	—	—		18 Hanover Square
1857	—	—		
1858	—	—		
1859	—	—		
1860	—	—	acquired by Ashdown & Parry	

Table 6

PUBLISHED IMAGES OF CHOPIN TITLE PAGES

The listing order is by opus number, then Brown number for works without opus number. For publisher codes, see Table 2B. Footnotes are numbered separately for each source. The number after the hyphen is the page number, except for Grabowski and Chominski & Turlo, where it is the figure number. Grabowski's reproductions — for French publishers only — are the most extensive, but are partly illegible. Chominski & Turlo's reproductions include some for secondary publishers (plates 26, 27, 28, 30, 31, 39, 40); these are not listed here. Duleba (1975, pp. 158, 159) reproduces 24 title pages but the images are illegibly small. (See further comments at the end of the table.) This table lists only printed images. Digital images of the entire University of Chicago Chopin collection can be viewed online (http://chopin.lib.uchicago.edu).

C&T	*B*	*Op*	*Short title*	*Grabowski (1992)*	*C&T (1990)*	*Hoboken (1986)*	*Bory (1951)*	*Burger (1990)*	*Platzman (1997)*
192	10	1	Rondo	mS-36		Ho-79[1]	Brz-51	Brz-29	Ho-18
225	22	2	Variations (p/o)	mS-2		Ha-81[2]	Ha-56[1]		W-24
148	41	3	Polonaise (p/c)	Rich-29; mS-39		Mec-84[3]	Mec-67		Rich-26[1]
201	23	4	Sonata	Rich-113					Ha-30
193	15	5	Rondo	Schon-54	Schon-5		Brz-51	Brz-33	W-34
51	60	6	Mazurkas	mS-3, 4[1]	mS-4[1]	W-91[4]	Ki-72	Ki-106	mS-36[2]
56	61	7	Mazurkas	mS-5; Bra-6[2]	Ki-12[2]		mS-72	mS-62	
206	25	8	Trio (p/v/c)	mS-7			Ki-57	Ki-106	
108	54	9	Nocturnes	mS-1			Ki-96	Ki-105	W-48
14	42	10	Etudes	mS-9, 10, 11[3]; Lem-12		mS-97[5]	mS-96[2]	mS-101[1]	Ki-52[3]
47	53	11	Concerto (p/o)	mS-13; Bra-14[4]	W-15		mS-95	Ki-57; mS-57	Ki-cover
226	80	12	Variations	mS-15			BH-95	BH-107	
41	28	13	Fantaisie (p/o)	mS-22, 23[5]			Ki-69	Ki-45	
194	29	14	Rondo (p/o)	mS-24			Ki-57	Ki-125	
111	55	15	Nocturnes	mS-16, 17[6]		mS-111	mS-95	mS-125	
195	76	16	Rondo	Pl-18; mS-19	Pl-6		mS-96	mS-125	BH-70
60	77	17	Mazurkas	Pl-20; mS-21				BH-125	
207	62	18	Waltz	mS-25; Lem-26			mS-104		Lu-80
8	81	19	Bolero	Pr-27		Pe-115[6]		Pe-105[2]	Pr-82
197	65	20	Scherzo	mS-28					
48	43	21	Concerto (p/o)	mS-35			mS-69	mS-54	
149	58	22	Polonaise (p/o)	mS-31					
2	66	23	Ballade	mS-32					W-96
64	89	24	Mazurkas	mS-30			mS-149		
26	78	25	Etudes	mS-37; Lem-38		W-127[7]		BH-101	mS-100
150	90	26	Polonaises	mS-33	BH-24, 25				
114	91	27	Nocturnes	mS-34			W-211[3]		
166	107	28	Preludes	Ca-48; Bra-49		Ca-133	Ca-133	Ca-201	
43	110	29	Impromptu	mS-40	BH-22, 23; W-16				
68	105	30	Mazurkas	mS-41					
198	111	31	Scherzo	mS-42					
116	106	32	Nocturnes	mS-43	aS-9[3]				

(continued)

C&T	*B*	*Op*	*Short title*	*Grabowski (1992)*	*C&T (1990)*	*Hoboken (1986)*	*Bory (1951)*	*Burger (1990)*	*Platzman (1997)*
72	115	33	Mazurkas	mS-44		BH-141[8]			
208	94	34	Waltzes	mS-45, 46, 47[7]	W-20	BH-145[9]			mS-124
202	128	35	Sonata	T-55, 56[8]	T-37[4]; W-17		BH-146		
44	129	36	Impromptu	T-57, 58[8]	W-18		T-147		
118	119	37	Nocturnes	T-59, 60, 61[9]	W-19				T-136
3	102	38	Ballade	T-63			BH-113	BH-143	
199	125	39	Scherzo	T-64			T-133		
152	120	40	Polonaises	T-65			T-147		
76	122	41	Mazurkas	T-66			T-147		
211	131	42	Waltz	Pa-62					Pa-146
205	139	43	Tarantelle	T-74, 75[10]	T-38[4]	T-159			Schu-150
154	135	44	Polonaise	mS-76, 77[8]		Mec-161		Mec-227	Mec-152
190	141	45	Prelude	mS-86, 87[11]	Mec-11[5]				
1	72	46	Allegro de Concert	mS-78, 79[8]					
4	136	47	Ballade	mS-80, 81[8]					
120	142	48	Nocturnes	mS-82, 83[8]					
42	137	49	Fantaisie	mS-84, 85[8]			BH-154		
80	145	50	Mazurkas	mS-88, 89[12]				mS-249	Mec-164
45	149	51	Impromptu	mS-90, 91[13]					mS-168[4]
5	146	52	Ballade	mS-92, 93[14]			mS-154	mS-249	
155	147	53	Polonaise	mS-94, 95[15]			BH-154	BH-249	
200	148	54	Scherzo	mS-96, 97			mS-154	mS-249	
122	152	55	Nocturnes	mS-98			BH-187	BH-313	BH-178
83	153	56	Mazurkas	mS-99, 100					
7	154	57	Berceuse	Mei-101			Mei-164		
203	155	58	Sonata	Mei-102				Mei-265	
86	157	59	Mazurkas	Bra-103					St-188
6	158	60	Barcarolle	Bra-104		Bra-183	Bra-167	Bra-272	
156	159	61	Polonaise-fantaisie	Bra-105			Bra-164	Bra-272	
124	161	62	Nocturnes	Bra-106					Bra-194
89	162	63	Mazurkas	Bra-107, 108[16]					
212	164	64	Waltzes	Bra-109, 110, 111				BH-284[3]	CB-202
204	160	65	Sonata (p/c)	Bra-112			Bra-173	BH-272	
46	87	66/73	Posthumous works	MeiF-115; Gér-116					MeiF-210[5]
46	87	66	Fantaisie-impromptu			aS-189[10]			aS-214[6]
92	93	67	Mazurkas						
96	18	68	Mazurkas						
215	35	69	Waltzes						
217	40	70	Waltzes						
157	11	71	Polonaises						
126	19	72#1	Nocturne						
50	20	72#2	Marche funèbre						
11	12	72#3	Ecossaises						
196	27	73	Rondo (2 ps)						
129	32	74	Songs (voice/p)	Ham-117		Geb-205	Geb-211		

(continued)

C&T	*B*	*Op*	*Short title*	*Grabowski (1992)*	*C&T (1990)*	*Hoboken (1986)*	*Bory (1951)*	*Burger (1990)*	*Platzman (1997)*
163	6	—	Polonaise						Ka-238[7]
227	14	—	Variations	Rich-114					
—	35	—	Waltes			Wildt-197			E-242
165	36	—	Polonaise			Geb-215[11]			
222	56	—	Waltz						
10	70	—	Duo concertant (p/c)	mS-8	aS-13[6]; W-14		aS-92	aS-107	
—	82	—	Mazurka in C major		Ka-39				
230	113	—	Variations	T-71			Ha-117	Ha-156	
38	130	—	Etudes	mS-50, 51, 52, 53[17]	aS-7			aS-222[4]	
106	134	—	Mazurka	Esc-72; *FM*-73	FM-3				Schott-252
105	140	—	Mazurka	Chab-67, 68, 69, 70					BB-256[8]

Footnotes for Grabowski

(Numbers in parentheses are figure numbers.)

1 The "quatre" Mazurkas (3) and "Cinq" Mazurkas" (4) issues.

2 A new edition, but with the Schlesinger title page.

3 Three issues: "J." Liszt (9), "F." Liszt (10), "F." Liszt and "1er Livre" (11).

4 With "1ER" as the first line (14).

5 Without and with citations of Breitkopf & Härtel and Wessel.

6 In the "PRIX" area: "quatuor" (22), "quintette" (23).

7 Three different title-page designs: Op. 34#1 (45), Op. 34#2 (46), Op. 34#3 (47).

8 Without and with citation of Wessel.

9 Price: none (59), "6f." (60), "5f." (61).

10 Without and with citation of Ricordi.

11 *Gazette Musicale* issue of Op. 50#1 (86).

12 Price: "6f." (88), "7f. 50" (89).

13 *Gazette Musicale* issue (91).

14 Two different title pages. This collection's 52-mS-1 corresponds to (93).

15 Price: "7f. 50" (94), "9 fr." (95).

16 Citation of English publisher: none (107), "Jullien et Cie" (108).

17 Four editions: three in 1840, one in 1845.

Footnotes for Chominski & Turlo

1 The "quatre" Mazurkas issue.

2 The "QUATRE" Mazurkas issue.

3 "Album du Pianiste" issue, with compositions by ten composers.

4 A four-hand arrangement by Fontana.

(continued)

5 "ALBUM-BEETHOVEN" issue, with contributions from ten composers.

6 The "pour Piano et Violon" edition, designated Op. 15.

Footnotes for Hoboken

1 Four-hand edition, with portrait.

2 "ODEON" series title, with lithographed scene of an odeum portal.

3 The "ou Violon" edition.

4 With top line "L'AMATEUR PIANISTE, N° 8 et 9.".

5 The "J." Liszt issue.

6 Sunburst design, price in Gr.

7 Collective format with complete list, and address 18 Hanover Square.

8 First edition, with unusual decorated border.

9 First edition of Op. 34#1, with sunburst design.

10 Collective format, Nietack printing.

11 Collective format, with misprint "Ges moll" instead of Ges dur.

Footnotes for Bory

1 Series title and individual title.

2 The "J." Liszt issue.

3 Collective title through Op. 50.

Footnotes for Burger

1 The "J." Liszt issue.

2 Sunburst design, price in Gr.

3 The edition with three waltzes.

4 "Album du Pianiste" issue, with compositions by 17 composers.

Footnotes for Platzman

1 Decorated border.

2 The "Cinq" Mazurkas issue.

3 The "J." Liszt issue of Livre I.

4 The *Gazette Musicale* issue.

5 Collective format.

6 Collective format, Burkhardt printing.

7 Color lithograph, with bust of Chopin.

8 With portrait.

(continued)

Comments on Duleba

Duleba's reproductions are not listed in Table 6, because they are nearly illegible. They include the following title pages not among those cited in the table.

Opus	*Publisher*	*Comments*
7	Kistner	The "CINQ" mazurkas issue.
10	Kistner	The "F." Liszt issue.
15	Breitkopf	
18	Wessel	The first issue, not in a series.
20, 24, 30, 31	Breitkopf	
33	Breitkopf	Without the decorated border.
34	Breitkopf	Without the sunburst background.

Index

INDEX

The index lists the collection's scores in the order they appear in the Descriptons part of the catalogue. The columns contain respectively imprint data, score number, call number, and the description page number. (The first three columns are explained in "Score-identification group", p. 6.) A bullet (•) at the beginning of a line identifies a score added to the collection after publication of the first edition of the catalogue.

WORKS WITH OPUS NUMBER

(continued)

(continued)

(continued)

(continued)

(continued)

WORKS WITHOUT OPUS NUMBER